PUBLICATIONS DE LA SECTION HISTORIQUE DU MAROC

LES
SOURCES INÉDITES
DE
L'HISTOIRE DU MAROC

PAR

Le L*-Colonel H. DE CASTRIES

PREMIÈRE SÉRIE — DYNASTIE SAADIENNE

ARCHIVES ET BIBLIOTHÈQUES D'ANGLETERRE

TOME II

History cannot be written from manuscripts
Mark Pattison.

PARIS
PAUL GEUTHNER
13, rue jacob, 13

LONDRES
LUZAC ET Cⁱᵉ
46, great russell street, 46

1925

LES
SOURCES INÉDITES
DE
L'HISTOIRE DU MAROC

PREMIÈRE SÉRIE — DYNASTIE SAADIENNE

COLLECTION DE LETTRES, DOCUMENTS ET MÉMOIRES

ANGLETERRE

ANTONIVS SHERLEYVS ANGLVS EQVES AVRATVS

cum priuil. S.Cæ.M.tis

Magni Sophi Persarum Legatus inuictissimo
Cæsari Ceterisque Principibus Christianis:
huiusce Amicitie et Auctor et ductor
EX ORE, AD OS.
S. Cæ. M.tis sculptor Ægidius Sadeler. D D:

Marco Sadeler excudit.

ANTHONY SHERLEY
AMBASSADEUR AU MAROC. 1605-1606

PUBLICATIONS DE LA SECTION HISTORIQUE DU MAROC

LES
SOURCES INÉDITES
DE
L'HISTOIRE DU MAROC

PAR

Le Lt-Colonel H. DE CASTRIES

PREMIÈRE SÉRIE — DYNASTIE SAADIENNE

ARCHIVES ET BIBLIOTHÈQUES D'ANGLETERRE

TOME II

History cannot be written from manuscripts.
Mark Pattison.

PARIS
PAUL GEUTHNER
13, RUE JACOB, 13

LONDRES
LUZAC ET Cie
46, GREAT RUSSELL STREET, 46

1925

ONT COLLABORÉ A CE VOLUME

MM. Léon Bogaert.
    André Dreux, archiviste paléographe.
    Gilbert Jacqueton,   —
    René Planchenault,   —

I

LETTRE D'ÉLISABETH A MOULAY AHMED EL-MANSOUR[1]

D. Antonio a fait connaître à la Reine les offres que lui a transmises son ambassadeur de la part du Chérif. — Élisabeth remercie Moulay Ahmed de son intention de contribuer à la restauration de D. Antonio, restauration qu'elle a particulièrement à cœur. — Répondant au désir exprimé par le Chérif, elle s'engage à fournir au prétendant des troupes et des ressources, dès que l'argent promis aura été reçu. — Elle envoie Edward Prynne pour traiter de cette affaire avec Moulay Ahmed.

Greenwich, février 1589 [n. st. 1590].

Au dos, alia manu: Copia da segunda carta que la Serenissima Reina escrivio por Duarte Perin ao emperador de Marrocos.

Muy alto y muy poderoso Señor,

Aviendonos estos dias pasados dado parte el rey Don Antonio de como le aveis de nuevo hecho muy reales offrescimientos por su embaxador que ay reside[2], prometiendo de cumplir con el dinero de qual ya le aveis dado esperança para la empresa de Portugal, y que para tal effecto embeareys por aca recaudo com hombre espresso[3], nos a parescido bien de agradesceroslo muy de coraçon por nuestras proprias cartas, como quien toma tan a pechos y tiene

1. La présente lettre fut écrite sous l'inspiration et la dictée de D. Antonio. V. *infra*, p. 4.
2. Mathias Becudo: V. 1ʳᵉ *Série, Angleterre*, t. I, p. 533, note 1. Los offres dont il est ici question avaient, sans doute, été rapportées par Cardenas.
3. On a vu (*ibidem*, p. 527) l'espoir qu'avaient fondé D. Antonio et les Anglais sur l'assistance de Moulay Ahmed pour leur expédition en Portugal et la déconvenue qu'il avaient éprouvée. Malgré les avertissements de Cardenas (V. *ibidem*, pp. 535-537), ils continuèrent de prêter l'oreille aux promesses du Chérif, encouragés, d'ailleurs, par Mathias Becudo, à qui ce même Cardenas reprochait son optimisme. V. *ibidem*, p. 536, note 1.

DE CASTRIES.

los negocios del dicho rey por tan encomendados que necesariamente no podemos dexar de ser con mucha obligacion a quien se offeresce de concurrir com nos em socorer y ayudarle; queriendoos tãobien, por el mesmo medio, asegurar para mayor satisfacion vuestra y certidumbre de nuestro buen animo y voluntad y desseo em lo que toca a los negocios y restitucion del dicho rey en su estado. Y cumpliendo vos de vuestra parte con embiar aquy hombre espresso con recaudo del dinero, como lo aveys prometido, *no fallaremos tanbien de la nuestra de darle fuerças y medios bastantes para cobrar y deffender su Estado como conviene;* y, pues desseavades tener desto certedumbre por nuestras proprias cartas, esperamos que, aviendo em ello cumplido con vuestro desseo, sera parte que os resolvays agora realmente y con la mayor brevedad que pudierdes a embiar el ayuda que prometeys, para que, sin perder mas tiempo, se hagan luego los aparejos necessarios para la dicha empresa.

Y, porque avemos mandado a nuestro criado, el capitan Prin[1], al qual embiamos espressamente sobre este negocio, que lo trate con vos mas particularmente de boca, no os diremos mas, sino rogaros que le deis en ello credito como a nos mesma.

Hecha en nuestro palacio real de Grenwich, a ... del mes de Febrero 1589.

Public Record Office. — State Papers, Foreign, Portugal, vol. II. — Minute.

1. Edward Prynne. Ce personnage était originaire des îles portugaises, mais né d'un père anglais. V. lettre de Francisco da Costa, 8 mars 1589, *1re Série, Espagne*. Il était donc de nationalité mixte. Les documents espagnols le nomment Duarte Perin ou Duarte Perin Correa. Il était un des fidèles de D. Antonio et lui servait d'interprète en Angleterre (V. *infra*, p. 12). En mars 1588, ce prince avait tenté de s'évader avec lui de ce pays sous un déguisement (*Archives Nationales, K 1567, n° 39*). Les fugitifs avaient été arrêtés à Douvres et Edward Prynne emprisonné (*Ibid., n° 54*). Il avait fait un premier voyage au Maroc comme capitaine des navires qui y menèrent D. Christophe. Il débarquait le jeune prince à Safi le 7 janvier 1589 et il était de retour en Angleterre avant le 13 mai. V. *1re Série, France*, t. II, pp. 168, 177, 181, 184, 186. Il partit dans les premiers jours de mars 1590 pour sa nouvelle mission (V. *ibid.*, p. 187 et *infra*, pp. 4 et 11) et arriva à Safi le 2 (n. st. 12) avril. Moulay Ahmed le retint contre son gré au Maroc, où il était encore en avril 1591. V. *infra*, pp. 12, 25 et 48. Edward Prynne, en 1600, est chargé d'assurer le retour au Maroc de l'ambassadeur Abd el-Ouahed. V. *infra*, p. 190. Le 20 avril 1625, il porte à Charles Ier une lettre de condoléances de D. Christophe pour la mort de Jacques Ier. *Public Record Office, State Papers, Foreign, Portugal, vol. III.*

II

LETTRE DE BEAUVOIR-LA-NOCLE[1] ET DE FRESNE[2] A HENRI IV

(Extrait)

Le roi du Maroc a promis d'envoyer à D. Antonio un subside en argent, à la condition que la reine d'Angleterre s'engageât de son côté à soutenir ce prince. — La Reine a écrit à Moulay Ahmed, vers qui se rend Edward Prynne pour négocier l'affaire. — D. Antonio désire que le roi de France intervienne également en sa faveur auprès du Chérif, que cette démarche encouragera à tenir sa promesse. — Le Roi décidera s'il veut envoyer quelqu'un au Maroc ou écrire à Moulay Ahmed.

Londres, 3 mars 1590.

Adresse : Au Roy.
Au dos, alia manu : M. de Fresne, du 3 mars 1590.

Sire,

Il n'y a que douze jours que nous avons depesché le sieur de Captot vers V. M.

. . . .

Post-scriptum : Sire, le roy de Portugal nous a voulu voyr, ces jours passés, et, après nous avoyr amplement declaré la confiance qu'il avoyt de l'amitié de V. M. et l'esperance qui le nourrit d'en recevoyr plus certain tesmoignage, quand Dieu luy aura fait la grace de vous pouvoir informer que les malheurs survenus cy-devant en ses affaires[3] ne lui doibvent estre imputés et qu'il a encore des

---

1. Jean de La Fin, sieur de Beauvoir-la-Nocle, Lurcy, Los Angères, etc., conseiller d'État, ambassadeur en Angleterre (1589-1595) ; il mourut en 1599.

2. Philippe Canaye, sieur de Fresne (1551-1610), conseiller d'État sous Henri III, adjoint à Beauvoir-La-Nocle dans son ambassade en Angleterre, fut nommé lui-même ambassadeur auprès des princes protestants de l'Empire (1591-1593). Ambassadeur à Venise de 1601 à 1607.

3. Allusion aux deux échecs de D. An

moyens en main pour maintenir son bon droit, il nous a communiqué des lettres que le roy de Maroco luy escrit[1], par lesquelles il l'asseure d'une bonne somme de deniers, pourveu que la royne d'Angleterre luy promette de le favoriser aussi de sa part. Dont laditte dame ayant esté advertie a escrit audit roy de Maroco une lettre telle que ledit roy Don Antonio l'a voulu dicter, et mesme a donné un sien navire pour la conduitte d'un gentilhomme portugais nommé Eduard Perino, qui s'en va audit Maroco pour advancer cet affaire. Nous avons promis audit roy Don Antonio de faire entendre à V. M. le desir qu'il a d'estre accompagné du tesmoignage de vostre amitié, pour la ferme asseurance qu'on luy a donné que, si V. M. envoye vers ledit roy de Maroco et luy promet de vouloyr ayder ledit roy Don Antonio, il en sera beaucoup plus hardi et affectionné à l'acquit de ses promesses.

Si donc V. M. pense qu'il soyt expedient, pour le bien de cet affaire, d'octroyer cette faveur à ce pauvre prince, elle advisera ou d'envoyer homme exprès audit Maroco, ou nous faire tenir icy sa lettre pour la mettre entre les mains dudit roy de Portugal, lequel espere avoir encore quelques moyens de fatiguer son ennemy.

. . . .

Sire,

Nous prions Dieu qu'Il vous preserve de tous dangers et augmente vostre prosperité à vostre plein contentement.

De Londres, ce 3 de mars 1590.

Vos très-humbles et très-obéissants subjects et serviteurs,

Signé : Beauvoir-la-Nocle.
De Fresne.

British Museum. — Egerton Mss., 6, f. 48. — Original[2].

tonio, l'un en 1582, aux Açores, l'autre, en 1589, en Portugal. V. t. I, p. 323, n. 4.

1. La lettre d'Élisabeth au Chérif (V. le document précédent) parle seulement de nouvelles offres transmises à D. Antonio par son ambassadeur à Merrakech. La lettre que ce prince aurait communiquée à Beauvoir-la-Nocle n'a pas été conservée.

2. Publié par [Francis-Henry EGERTON], dans *The Life of Thomas Egerton, Chancellor of England*, 3e édition, in-4°, s. l. n. d., p. 325.

III

LETTRE DE FRESNE A REVOL[1]

(Extrait)

D. Antonio désire que Henri IV envoie un ambassadeur au Chérif pour agir en sa faveur. — Moulay Abd el-Malek avait autrefois recherché l'amitié de Henri III et D. Antonio affirme que Moulay Ahmed serait très disposé à reprendre ces projets d'alliance, malgré les avances de Philippe II, qui vient de lui céder la place d'Arzila et une autre frontera. — L'ambassadeur envoyé par Henri IV au Maroc devrait être un homme de qualité; Fresne propose M. de Buzenval. — Protocole épistolaire employé par D. Antonio dans sa correspondance avec le Chérif. — M. de Buzenval pourrait, après son ambassade au Maroc, revenir par la Turquie, où il susciterait des embarras au roi d'Espagne. — Le navire qui porte les lettres de la Reine et de D. Antonio au Chérif doit passer à Dieppe; il pourrait y prendre celles de Henri IV.

Londres, 3 mars 1590.

Adresse : A Monsieur, M. de Revol, conseiller et secretaire d'Estat.

Au dos, alia manu : M. de Fresne, du 3ᵉ mars 1590.

Monsieur,

Vous verrés par celle que monsieur de Beauvoyr et moy escrivons au Roy ce que le roy de Portugal desire de Sa Majesté. L'affaire meritoyt bien un homme exprès; mais pour ce que ce courrier s'est presenté tout à propos et que nous sommes asseurés

---

1. Louis de Revol (1531-1594), président à la Chambre des Comptes de Dauphiné, commissaire des guerres, secrétaire d'État aux Affaires Étrangères et à la Guerre du 15 septembre 1588 au 24 septembre 1594.

de sa fidelité, nous avons espargné la despence, car aussi n'avons-nous aucune particularité à vous dire, sinon que ce pauvre prince desire que le Roy escrive en sa faveur au roy de Maroco et luy promette de le favoriser de tout ce qui luy sera possible : vray est qu'il desireroyt bien que le Roy y voulust envoyer quelque homme d'entendement tout exprès, pour ce qu'il esperoyt que la presence d'un ambassadeur du Roy rendroit ce barbare plus prompt à desbourcer ce qu'il luy a promis et à ne craindre pas tant l'Hespagnol comme il fait.

Nous luy avons respondu là-dessus que Sa Majesté, n'ayant encore nulle amitié avec le More, avoyt peu de subject d'y envoyer un ambassadeur[1]. Il nous a repliqué que le predecesseur dudict More[2] avoyt longuement recherché l'amitié du feu roy, congnoissant qu'elle luy serait utile contre l'Hespagnol, mais les mauvais conseillers furent cause que Sa Majesté mesprisa les occasions que ledict More[3] luy presentoyt de travailler l'Hespagnol[4] ; et partant, le roy Antonio

---

1. L'avènement de Henri IV était trop récent pour qu'il eût pu entrer en relations personnelles avec Moulay Ahmed ; mais la France était alors représentée au Maroc par Arnoult de Lisle, qui avait remplacé, en 1588, Guillaume Bérard. Ce dernier avait résidé au Maroc, avec le titre officiel de consul, depuis 1578. En 1599, Étienne Hubert succédait à Arnoult de Lisle et restait un an à Merrakech. Arnoult de Lisle y retourna en 1606 et y séjourna jusqu'en juin 1607. Avant 1578, des négociations diplomatiques, dont les plus anciennes remontent à 1533, avaient déjà eu lieu entre la France et le Maroc, mais sans aboutir à des relations suivies. Sur tous ces faits, V. 1re Série, France, t. III, Introduction, pp. xiii-xxi.

2. Le predecesseur dudict More : Moulay Abd el-Malek.

3. Ledict More : Moulay Abd el-Malek.

4. C'est à la demande de Moulay Abd el-Malek que Guillaume Bérard, qui avait déjà séjourné au Maroc, y était revenu comme consul en 1578. Moulay Abd el-Malek recherche l'amitié de Henri III, comme il recherchait celle des princes chrétiens en général. On connaît (V. 1re Série, Angleterre, t. I, pp. 206-210, 239-249) ses négociations avec l'Espagne et ses bons procédés pour Edmund Hogan. Il est possible, comme l'affirmait D. Antonio à Fresne, qu'il ait incité Henri III à « travailler l'Hespagnol », quoique cela ne soit pas démontré par les documents. Les instructions pour Guillaume Bérard et une lettre de ce dernier datée de Merrakech, 28 août 1583 (V. 1re Série, France, t. II, pp. 22 et 105) signalent seulement, comme objets de ses négociations avec Moulay Abd el-Malek, puis avec Moulay Ahmed, le libre accès des ports marocains pour les navires français, la délivrance des captifs, des conventions commerciales touchant le cuivre et le salpêtre. G. Bérard se plaint, d'ailleurs, dans sa lettre, de la négligence que montre Henri III dans ses rapports avec Moulay Ahmed : « Car, en trois ans, il [le Chérif] n'a receu que les premières lettres que je aportiz et celles qu'aporta l'homme que j'avois envoyé vers Sa Magesté. Pour ce, il semble que Sa Magesté en face

se promet que le More sera très aise de reno[ver] et conclurre l'alliance, encore que l'Hespagnol le flatte autant [qu'il] peut, et, pour le destourner de l'amitié dudict roy Dom Antonio, luy [donne] Arzilla[1] et encore une autre place que le roy Sebastien avoit co[nquise en] la Barbarie[2]. Voylà comment ce grand protecteur de la religion cath[olique satisfaict] son ambition aux despens de la Chrestienté.

Si Sa Majesté trouve à propos d'[envoyer] à Maroco, elle le pourroyt faire, soubz umbre de prier ce roy de ne fav[oriser] rebelles et remettre entre ses mains ce qui se pourroyt trouver de..... et personnes en ses terres et pays, comme c'est chose seure que les marcha[nds de] Rouen y font grand traffic[3].

Le roy d'Hespagne a un ambassadeur ord[inaire auprès] du roy de Maroco[4], tellement que, si Sa Majesté y vouloyt envoyer de sa part, le [roy] Dom Antonio dit qu'il seroyt besoing que ce fût quelqu'homme de qualité. Peut-estre que monsieur de Buzanval ne refuseroit pas cette charge, car il a esté fort diligent à s'informer icy des affaires de ce pays-là.

Et, pour ce que ces barbares sont fort curieux de lettres, nous nous sommes enquis comment ledict roy de Portugal luy escrit. Il nous a monstré sa lettre au-dessus de laquelle il y a aussi en portugais[5] : *Al muy alto y muy poderoso señor Muley Hamet, empe-*

peu de compte. » *Ibid.*, p. 108. Ce passage, rapproché des allégations de D. Antonio, indiquerait que Henri III n'avait pas vu ni utilisé les avantages que lui offrait une politique d'entente avec le Maroc contre Philippe II.

1. Sur la cession d'Arzila à Moulay Ahmed (13 septembre 1589), V. *1re Série*, France, t. II, p. 286, note 5.

2. On ignore à quelle autre place de Barbarie Fresne fait allusion.

3. Comme prétexte à l'envoi d'un ambassadeur au Chérif, Henri IV, suggérait Fresne, prierait ce prince de lui livrer les biens et les personnes des rebelles, c'est-à-dire des partisans de la Ligue, trafiquant au Maroc. Fresne ajoute, à l'appui de sa proposition, que les marchands de Rouen, une des villes les plus importantes tenues par la Ligue, font un grand commerce avec ce pays. La remarque était exacte. V. *1re Série*, Angleterre, pp. 51, 555, et France, t. I, p. 303, t. II, pp. 133, 143. Au XVIIe siècle, deux membres d'une des grandes maisons de commerce de Rouen, les frères Thomas et Jean-Baptiste Le Gendre, eurent avec le Maroc des relations très actives. V. France, t. III, Introduction, pp. LIX-LXIV.

4. Francisco da Costa, ambassadeur du Portugal auprès de Moulay Ahmed *el Mansour* en 1579, demeura au Maroc comme agent de l'Espagne, après la réunion des deux couronnes. Il mourut à Merrakech en avril 1591. V. *infra*, p. 54.

5. La suscription reproduite par Fresne est en langue espagnole.

rador *de Maruecos, rey de Fez y de Sus,* etc. Et commence sa lettre par ces motz: *Muy allo y muy poderoso Señor.*

Et peut-estre que, si de là monsieur de Buzanval[1] alloyt vers le Turc, il trouveroyt moyen, par son industrie, de donner tant d'affaires aux Castillans chez eux qu'ils seroyent constraintz de laisser les autres en pays.

Le navire qui porte les lettres de la Royne et du roy Dom Antonio à Maroco doibt aller à Dieppe et charger là quelques marchandises, de manière que les lettres du Roy pourroyent arriver à temps pour estre envoyées par mesme moyen. Ledict navire s'appelle « Weit-Hand » et le maistre du navire se nomme Mattheo Coqueres.

Ledict roy Dom Antonio nous a aussy donné advis qu'ung certain Portugais, qui est parti, puis peu de jours, pour aller trouver le Roy, et se faict nommer Francesco-Antonio Sose, est juif de religion, espion du roy d'Hespagne et homme duquel il ne se faut aucunement fier.

. . . .

Je vous bayse bien humblement les mains, et prie Dieu, Monsieur, qu'il vous donne très-heureuse et longue vie.

De Londres, ce 3ᵉ de mars 1590.

Vostre humble et plus affectionné serviteur et amy.

De Fresne[2].

British Museum. — *Egerton Mss., 6, f. 50.* — *Original*[3].

1. Paul Choart, seigneur de Buzenval, gentilhomme de la Chambre du roi de Navarre et son agent en Angleterre (1586-1589), ambassadeur de France dans les Pays-Bas (1592-1607), mort à La Haye le 31 août 1607.

2. Suivent quelques lignes de Beauvoir-la-Nocle et un post-scriptum de Fresne.

3. Publié dans *The Life of Thomas Egerton*, etc., pp. 326-327.

IV

LETTRE DE D. CHRISTOPHE[1] A BURGHLEY

Il compte sur les bons offices de Burghley pour recouvrer sa liberté.

Merrakech, 25 mai 1590.

Au dos : A Monsieur, Monsieur l'grand tresourier d'Angleterre. — *Alia manu :* Don Christovão, younger sonne to the King of Portingal, from Marrocos.

Monsieur,

La souvenance que j'ay de la bonne volonté et amour que me avés monstré, quan je party de ce royaume vers estuy-cy, me faict croir que le remede de ma liberté sera tousjours sertain ; car, tandis que je le seray de vostre faveur, ne me peut la fortune aprocher à cy miserable estat, que je desespoire de la avoir. Et je vous puis aseurer en verité que je nella desire moins pour employer la vie au recouvrement de Portugal que au service de la serenissime Royne, à qui je la doit, et le comfeseray tousjours. Et pour que je say que tous les necessités sentent en eus-mesmes l'effect de vostre bonté et virtu, il est impossible que manqués avec elle aus captifs, et principallement à un que non moins vous respeite et ayme que à père.

Priant Dieu, Monsieur, vous donner heureuse vie, avec la santé que vous desirés et le accomplissiment de vos desirs.

De Marrocos, le 25ᵐᵉ de may.

Vostre très-humble serviteur,

Signé : Don Christovão.

British Museum. — *Lansdowne Mss., 63, f. 138.* — *Original.*

---

1. Sur ce personnage et sur son séjour au Maroc, V. 1ʳᵉ *Série, Angleterre,* t. I, p. 527 et note 3, et France, t. II, Doc. LXXXI, pp. 198-201.

30 MAI 1590

V

LETTRE D'EDWARD PRYNNE[1] A WALSINGHAM

Il a été envoyé au Maroc avec une lettre d'Élisabeth en faveur de D. Antonio. — Il débarque à Safi le 12 avril. — A son arrivée à Merrakech, le Chérif envoie le Juif Cheikh Rutty pour le saluer et le loger ; il lui accorde une pension de six onces par jour. — Prynne se rend à la Cour, accompagné de tous les marchands et des gentilshommes de la suite de D. Christophe. — Il est introduit, seul avec l'ambassadeur de D. Antonio, auprès du Chérif et lui remet la lettre d'Élisabeth. — Moulay Ahmed proteste de son amitié pour la Reine et promet à Edward Prynne de le dépêcher promptement. — Mais, depuis plus d'un mois, Prynne attend vainement une nouvelle audience. — Il doute fort qu'il obtienne bientôt son congé ; il aspire à quitter le Maroc. — Trois marchands anglais ont été assassinés par un Espagnol, sans que justice soit faite. — Trois autres, Dicanson, Robert Lions et Augustine Lane ont été emprisonnés ; les deux premiers sont morts; le troisième, très malade, est toujours détenu, malgré les instances de Prynne. — Prynne demande que la Reine écrive pour lui faire obtenir son congé ou qu'elle l'autorise à réclamer au Chérif une réponse aux lettres écrites par elle en faveur de ses sujets.

Merrakech, 20 [n. st. 30] mai 1590.

Au dos : To the righte honnerable Sir Francis Walsingham, Knighte, Principall Secretary to her Mag^{tie}, and one of her moste honerable Privie Cownsell, geve this. — *Alia manu :* May 20, 1590. Edward Prin, at Marruecos, to Mr Secretary decessed[2].

Righte Honerable,

My humble dewty considered, etc. — Finding myselfe so many

---

1. Sur ce personnage, V. *supra*, p. 2, note 1.

2. Walsingham était mort le 6 avril 1590.

and sondrye wayes bownd to your Honore, I thoughte in dewtie, notwithstanding my owne unworthines, to write unto your Honnor; for the which I crave that acostomed favor I have many times fownd and receaved at your Honnors handes.

Yt is not unknowne unto your Honnor the cawse of my coming into this contrye and in what sorte : the which was as it hathe pleased her Mag^{tie}, of her bowntyfull goodnes, in geving me the name of her servant, in a letter from her to the Kinge of Barbery. I truste your Honnor shall not heare otherwise of me but that I have caried myselfe with that respecte that apertains to a servant of so greate a prince. The effecte of my message was alltogether to the fortherance and good of that power and destressed Kinge Donne Antonio ; the which I have used according to the dereccion I had.

Yt maye please your Honnor to knowe that, the second daye of Aprill[1], I arived at Saphia, wheare I stayed thre dayes, and after, by the dereccion of the Alcaid there, I tooke my jornye towardes Morocos, being guided with xii horsemen. And being entred into the cittye, the Kinge sente to me a Jewe, whoese name is Checke Rutty[2], to bid me wellcome, together with orther to lodge me, and with alowance of sixe ounces a daye ; the which I did excepte, being forced with yt, giving the Kinge thanckes for his liberallitye towardes me.

I had audience within sixe dayes after, being one a Wednesdaye : at which time the Kinge had all his alcaides and elches[3] in a place neare unto him, he sitting all alone in a very great rome upon a hie seate, with as great magestie as mighte bee acoording to theire manners. I was acompanied with all the marchantes here and the gentllemen of Don Christopher[4], to the nomber of fowerty horse.

1. Le prochain départ d'Edward Prynne pour le Maroc était annoncé, le 3 mars, par Beauvoir-la-Nocle et Fresne. Le navire qui l'emportait devait passer à Dieppe. V. *supra*, pp. 4 et 8.

2. En espagnole : Jeque Rute. Ce Juif est mentionné, dans un document espagnol, comme un personnage influent, « par qui le Chérif se gouverne ». V. *1re Série*, Espagne, 4 août 1589. Il appartenait à une famille israélite de Fez, dont les représentants, après avoir été agents et interprètes des Mérinides, avaient passé au service des Chérifs. Le nommé Jaco Rute, interprète du sultan Ahmed *el-Ouattassi*, est souvent mentionné dans les documents portugais. Cf. *1re Série*, Portugal, t. II, *passim*.

3. *Elches*, renégats.

4. D. Christophe avait été envoyé au Maroc avec une suite nombreuse. V. *1re*

The Kinge Donne Antonios imbaseter[1] wente with me : only wee two entered where the Kinge was, with one of his greate, with a greate bunche of fethers, beating of the flies from his face. As sonne as I came before him, having done my dewty, he comanded me to cover before I had spoken[2]; the which being done, I delivered my message and letter. The which he received, makinge a showe of joye, answered me, after that he did aske howe her Mage[tie] ded, that he was one that loved and honered Her Mag[tie], greatly desiring God to awgmente her Mag[ties] state with the victory of all her enemies, and that I was wellcome to him, willing me to be merry, and that, God willing, very shortly, I sholde come againe unto him, and have my despatche to my content. The which, to this daye, being the xx[th] of Maye, above a monthe sence I had the firste awdience, I colde not gette another daye, but allwayes referred with fayre wordes, sainge that he hathe a greate care to despatche me, and that it shalbe to my content. Thus his fayre wordes want not; but I doe greatly dowbte that I shall not onely misse of that good despatche, but rather be kepte here longer time then I wishe.

I hard a winckelinge that I sholde scarce gette out of the contrie when I wolde, notwithstanding I am her Mag[ties] servant: an ode Spanierd did not sticke to saye, as it hathe come to my hearing, that Donne Antonio sholde misse of his interpreter in England[3], and that my bede was very well made for gettinge awaye so sone againe. In truthe yt hathe made me mistruste greatly the honnye this King hathe putte in my lips of his sixe ounnces a daye, that he dothe allowe me (the which I scorne) in respecte to be kepte here : for I wolde rather be in Englande in that pore state I was before, then here amongest thes doges with fower times more allowance then now I have.

The smale acompte this doge makes of our Inglishe nation[4] (as

Série, France, t. II, pp. 167, 168; Espagne, 8 mars 1589.

1. Mathias Becudo. V. supra, p. 1 et note 2.

2. Sur tout le cérémonial ici décrit, cf. t. I, p. 226, et 1re Série, France, t. II, pp. 50, 51.

3. Edward Prynne était en Angleterre l'interprète de D. Antonio.

4. Les plaintes d'Edward Prynne sur les mauvais traitements dont sont victimes les Anglais sont à rapprocher de celles du mar-

by example firste of thoes three honeste marchantes that were killed here by a base preaste, ille begotten sonne of a Spanierd[1]; and no justice done upon this mallyfactor and his companions, notwithstanding her Mag[ties] moste honorable letter in that behalfe, but rather some of them at liberty; and the Spanyerdes not sticke to saye that, if the holle compainy had bine killed, that never a Spanierd sholde lease a drope of bloude for it) yt dothe apere very well by this Kinges delinges, that not onely hathe not used justice, but rather geveth entertainement unto the malyfactor : and her Mag[ties] letter unto this daye hathe not bine answered[2].

Likewise of late, he hathe very unjustly putt thre of our natione in a moste myserable prison, where two of them, whoes names were one Dicansone and the other Robert Lions[3], died in a very shorte time, bothe in one daye, moste mysserable. The other, whoes name is Awsten Lane[4], a jentleman borne, remains in that mysserable place stille, notwithstandinge I broughte with me her Mag[ties] letter to this Kinge[5] towardes the favore of thes her power subjectes, and notwithstanding I fownde two of them dead, and the other in litle better case. And in fowerty and five dayes I have bine here, offringe my heade for the apperance of Awsten Lane, I cane not gette him out of this moste misserable holle, where I doe expecte howerly that he hathe taken that waye which his

chand emprisonné à Taroudant et de celles de Cardenas. V. t. I, pp. 479, 537.

1. Lorsque parvint à Merrakech, à la fin de 1588, la nouvelle de la défaite complète de l'Invincible Armada, des marchands anglais, néerlandais et français organisèrent avec des cavaliers indigènes une promenade par la ville pour célébrer la destruction de la flotte espagnole. Au cours de cette manifestation, ils se portèrent devant la maison de l'agent espagnol Diego Marin. Celui-ci irrité sortit avec un serviteur et dispersa les cavaliers, dont il tua plusieurs à coups de poignard. Le Chérif dut le faire arrêter et mettre en prison. GUADALAJARA, Prodicion y destierro de los Moriscos, f. 83 v°. Il ne fut remis en liberté qu'en décembre 1606 par Moulay Abdallah ben ech-Cheikh, quand il s'empara de Merrakech. V. *1re Série*, Dépôts divers, Florence, à la date du 14 février 1607.

2. Cette lettre d'Élisabeth à Moulay Ahmed el-Mansour n'a pas été retrouvée. Elle fut apportée de Merrakech à Fez en mars 1589 par un compagnon des victimes anglaises. V. *1re Série*, Espagne, à la date du 20 mars 1589.

3. Sur ce personnage, V. *1re Série*, Angleterre, t. I, p. 470, note 13.

4. Sur ce personnage, V. *ibidem*, p. 356, note 1.

5. Cette lettre, apportée par Edward Prynne, était différente de celle qui a été publiée ci-dessus, Doc. I, p. 1. Elle n'a pas été retrouvée.

fellowes hathe : a moste greavous case that thus her Mag^ties subjectes shalle be so unjustly used.

A nomber of sutche other like matters I colde write your Honnor, the which goethe to the very harte of me to thinke of them ; with the which I wille not troble your Honnor.

This is to requeste your Honnors accostomed favor that I maye have her Mag^ties favorable letter to this Kinge for my departure out of this lande, for that I stand in great dowbte ; elce, yf it please her Mag^tie, of her goodnes, to doe me that favor and honnor to awthorise me that I maye demand the answere of her Mag^ties letters written in the behalfe of her subjectes, that I maye in that showe my dewty to her Mag^tie and love to her subjectes.

In hope of thes favors at your Honnors handes, I reste praing the Allmightie God longe to continew your Honnor with increase of state.

At Morocus, the xx^th of Maye ann° 1590.

Your Honnors assured servant,
Signé : Edward Prynne.

Public Record Office. — State Papers, Foreign, Barbary States, vol. XII. — Original.

VI

LETTRE D'EDWARD PRYNNE A JOHN STANHOPE[1]

Prynne a été reçu le 7 juin par le Chérif, qui lui a déclaré qu'il ne pouvait le laisser partir avant d'avoir écrit lui-même à la Reine et d'en avoir reçu réponse. — Prynne compte sur l'aide de Stanhope. — Moulay Ahmed serait disposé à secourir D. Antonio, mais la peur de l'Espagne le retient. — Certains lui font même entrevoir un rapprochement entre l'Espagne et l'Angleterre. — Il suffirait d'une lettre énergique d'Élisabeth pour l'amener soit à rendre la liberté à D. Christophe, soit à tenir ses promesses, et elle contribuerait à assurer aux Anglais un meilleur traitement. — Le Chérif redoute d'autant plus la Reine qu'il la croit capable de déterminer les Turcs à l'attaquer. — Cette lettre l'effraierait et redonnerait du crédit à Prynne. — Prynne recommande D. Christophe, prince digne d'intérêt. — Il croit que Moulay Ahmed se décidera à agir, si l'on apprend l'entrée du roi de France à Paris.

Merrakech, 12 [n. st. 22] juin 1590.

Au dos : To the righte worshippfull Mr John Stanhope[2], Skoer, geave thes, att the Cowrt. — *Alia manu :* 12 Junii 1590. Edward Prin, from Morocos, to Mr John Stanhoppe.

Reight Worshippfull,

Affter my humble deutie considered, etc. — I have writine unto your Worshipe at large by a chipe of Londone in May last. Thes ffewe lynes now are only too leat your Worshipe too understand that thes King of Barbarie hathe not, acorthinge too his owne promes, keapt tooche, notwithstanding a geavethe verye good wordes.

---

1. Cette lettre fut reçue entre le 3 et le 28 août. V. *infra*, p. 30, note 2.
2. John Stanhope (1545?-1621), maître des postes (20 juin 1590), trésorier de la Chambre (1596), baron Stanhope of Harrington (1605).

The 7 of June, I had audiense ; at which tyme I dead thinke too have had my despache and too acome home in thes shipe. Bot yt hathe fallen owt, contrarye too my expectacione : ffor thes Kinge ansered me that it was verye neseserye that I showd stay hear untell he wrot and had his anser ffrome her Mag^tie ; too the which I dead what I cowld too have leave and too be the mesenger ; boot I cowld not prevayle. The which hathe pot me in a verye greatt dowt ; and am asewred that, withowt her Mag^ties leter, I shall not geatt leave too depert. Notwithstandinge that he alowes me 6 onces a day, yet I owld rather be in Ingland in the stat I was beffor I came hether.

Your Worshipes acostomed ffavores hathe inbowlded me to troble you, the rather ffor that I have no other unto home to pott my trost. And notwithstandinge I doe cknow myseallffe alltoogether onwordye, yet, in hope of your Worshipes goodnes, I rest with some conffort. The trewthe is the dooge desciares to have some confferance with her Mag^tie and too heallpe the Kinge Done Antonyo ; boot he ys the verest coward, that leaves and ffeares the Kinge of Spayne so muche that he dares not too enter in anye mater against him withowt some teackle. And hear wantes not them thatt potts him in the head that her Mag^tie and the Kinge of Spayne will come to agreamentt ; the which mackethe him afferd, and cknowes not whatt too doe. Boot thes muche.

If I wer wordie too adveyse, I doe asewer myseallffe thatt, yf her Mag^tie wold writt a leter too thes Kinge in some coler, thatt yt showld tacke effectt too geatt thes power genttleman Dom Crystover owt of his handes, or elles with thanckes he owld ckeape his promes ; and this may be an ocasione too have her subjettes beter used at thes Kinges handes. Ffear wordes will not geatt anye thinge of a cowards handes ; boot a sharpe leter wyll macke him luck abowt.

For the trewthe ys, thowffe her Mag^tie be ffar ffrome him, that he ffeares her and soposes that she may doo him hert by meanes of the Turcke, besides her owne meanes ; ffor by exeanple hear ys news thatt the Turcke comes done ; he dothe soo muche ffear his cominge as the Kinge of Spayne may ffear [1]. And I hard by one of

---

1. Sur les rapports du Chérif et du Grand Seigneur, V. 1re Série, Angleterre, t. I, p. 368, note 1. Sur les faits qui pouvaient plus particulièrement inquiéter

his howse, a Portingall genttleman, that serves him in the plase of a carver, thatt the Kinge showld see thatt her Mag^{tie} is the only cawser of the Turckes cominge downe.

Too conclud, thes pagane ys a verye coward, and nothinge will bowe him beter then a charpe leter ffrome her Mag^{tie}, as she hathe greatt cawse too writt him in thatt sort, as ffyrst, in the behallffe of her subjettes that wher kylld hear[1], she wrot a leter, and, too thes day, ther ys no justes doone, nether her Mag^{ties} leter ansered.

Deivers others I cowld mensione hear, thatt her Mag^{tie} hathe writine, and thes Kinge never maid anye requon to doo justes. Boot yf he showld see her Mag^{tie} with a hevye ffrowne, I doe asewre myseallffe he will rune in too a mouse howld. I wold I myt deserve the delivery of thatt leter. I doo not dowt, if I had thatt good ffortione, boot I showld geatt creaditt and doo her Mag^{tie} good serves therin ; as I have, notwithstandinge I had not anye orther, yet I have doone somewhatt for the merchantes and will allways doo as longe as I ame hear.

Y pray your Worshipe too pardone my tedeus leter and too remember me, boot ffyrst thes power prince, the which I doo asewer myseallffe dothe and will deserve so muche ffavor att her Mag^{ties} handes. I ame in some hope thatt, if we have ones newes that the Kinge of Franse ys in Paris, thatt thes Kinge will doo some good thinge. I will advertis your Worshipe by everye shipe thatt shall hapen to goo ffrome thes.

In the meane tyme, I comit myseallffe holy unto your Worshipe, hoes lyffe the Allmightie God preserve with the increase of statt.

Att Marocos, the XII of June, anno 1590.

Your Worshipes asewred too his power,

Signé : Edwarde Prynne.

Public Record Office. — *State Papers, Foreign, Barbary States, vol. XII.* — *Original.*

Moulay Ahmed en 1590, cf. *infra*, Doc. VIII, p. 26.

1. Sur cette affaire, V. *supra*, p. 13 et notes 1 et 2.

VII

LETTRE DE MOULAY AHMED EL-MANSOUR A ÉLISABETH[1]

Il a reçu par Edward Prynne la lettre d'Élisabeth. — La promesse de subsides qu'il a faite à D. Antonio est subordonnée aux secours que la Reine fournira elle-même à ce prince. — Il retient l'envoyé d'Élisabeth jusqu'au départ des troupes qu'il envoie à la conquête du Soudan, afin de s'entretenir ensuite à loisir avec lui. — Il prie Élisabeth de le tenir au courant de ses intentions en ce qui touche D. Antonio.

Merrakech, 19 Chabân 998 [23 juin 1590].

Adresse extérieure[2] : الا صالة الراسخة القدم السامية المنار والعَلَم
اصالة السلطانة الجليلة الاصيلة الشهيرة الاثيرة الخطيرة السلطانة ايزبيل صاحبة
مملكة نكلطيرة

Invocation : بسم الله الرَّحمن الرَّحيم ۞ صلى الله على سيدنا ومولانا
محمد وعلى آله وصحبه وسَلَّم تسليمًا

SIGNE DE VALIDATION[3].

من عبد الله تعالى المجاهد في سبيله الامام المنصور بالله امير المومنين بن

---

1. V. un fac-similé de cette lettre, p. 18, Pl. I.
2. Cette adresse est écrite sur la feuille de papier qui devait envelopper à la fois la missive arabe et sa traduction originale en espagnol (V. *infra*, p. 24, note 2). Elle forme, dans le manuscrit *Royal Letters, II*, un document à part, classé sous le n° 12.
3. La présente lettre, sans doute à cause de ses grandes dimensions, a été coupée en

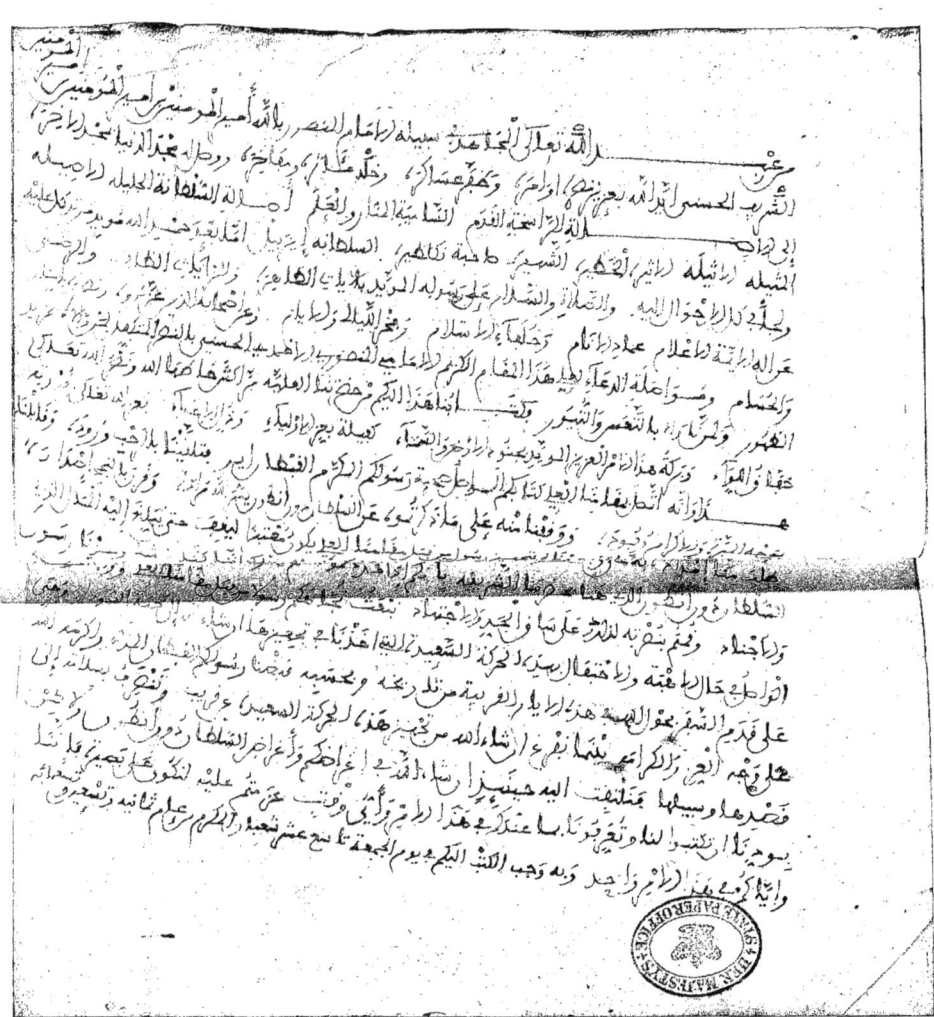

LETTRE DE MOULAY AHMED EL-MANSOUR A LA REINE ÉLISABETH
19 CHABAN 998 (23 Juin 1590).
D'après l'original conservé au Public Record Office.

أمير المومنين بن أمير المومنين الشريف الحسنى ايد الله بعزيز نصره اوامره
وظهر عساكره وخلد مآثره ومباخره و وصل له مجد الدنيا بمجد الاخره
الى الاصالة الراسخة القدم السامية المنار والعلم اصالة السلطانة الجليله
الاصيله المثيله الاثيله الاثيره الخطيره الشهيره صاحبة نكلطيره السلطانة إِيزِيبِل
اما بعد حمد الله مؤيّد من توكل عليه ولجأ فى كل الاحوال اليه والصلاة
والسلام على رسوله المؤيد بالايات الظاهره والرايات الظاهره والرضى عن اله
الائمة الاعلام عماد الانام وخلفاء الاسلام وفخر الليالى والايام وعن اصحابه
الذين عزّزوه ونصروه بالسنان والحسام ومواصلة الدعاء لعلى هذا المقام الكريم
الامامى المنصورى الاحمدى الحسنى بالنصر المتكفل لمن والاه بمزيد الظهور
ولمن ناواه بالتعس والتبور * فكتابنا هذا اليكم من حضرتنا العليه بمراكش
حاطها الله ونصر الله تعالى خفّاق اللواء، وبركة هذا الامر العزيز المويّد يجنود
الارض والسماء كفيلة بعز الاولياء، وذل الاعداء، بعز الله تعلى وفدرته
هذا وانه اتصل بمقامنا العلى كتابكم الواصل صحبة رسولكم المكرم القبطان
اير فتلفينا بالرحب وروده وقابلنا بوجه المبرة والاكرام وجوده ووفينا منه على ما
ذكرتموه عن السلطان دون انطون يسر الله مراده وفرن بالنجح اصداره وايراده
من انه ذكر لكم اننا قد وعدناه بتجهيز رسول من قبل مقامنا العلى يكون معتبرا

deux parties et forme, dans le manuscrit *Royal Letters*, II, deux documents distincts, mais sous la même cote 21 : l'un contient l'invocation et le signe de validation, l'autre, le corps de la lettre. V. un fac- similé du signe de validation, p. 20, Pl. II. Sur le déchiffrement de ce signe, cf. H. DE CASTRIES, *La diplomatique des princes de la dynastie saadienne*, au chapitre: *Signes de validation*.

ليقب حتى يبلغ اليه المال الذى طلب منّا امداده به على وجه السلف والى هذا وصل الله اكرامكم يحيط بعلمكم اننا لا شك وعدنا رسول السلطان دون انطون الذى هنا بحضرتنا الشريفة بانكم اذا مددتموه لهذا العام بما يطلب منكم من العساكر والاجناد وقمتم بنصرته لذلك على ساق الجد والاجتهاد نبعث تجاهكم رسولا من قبل مقامنا العلى ووافانا رسولكم الواصل فى حال الاهبة والاحتفال بهذه الحركة السعيدة التى اخذنا فى تجهيزها ان شاء الله الى جهة السودان وهى على قدم السفر بحول الله فى هذه الايام القريبة من تاريخه وبحسبه فبعثنا رسولكم القبطان المذكور اكرمه الله على وجه العز والكرامة بثنا نبرغ ان شاء الله من تجهيز هذه الحركة السعيدة عن قريب وتنصرف بسلامة الى قصدها وسبيلها فنلتفت اليه حينئذ ان شاء الله فى اغراضكم واغراض السلطان دون انطون ولاكن بودنا ان تكتبوا لنا وتعرفونا بما عندكم فى هذا الامر واىّ وقت عزمتم عليه لنكون على بصيرة فانا وايَّاكم فى هذا الامر واحد

وبه وجب الكتب اليكم فى يوم الجمعة تاسع عشر شعبان المكرم من عام ثمانية وتسعين وتسعمايه

Public Record Office. — State Papers, Royal Letters, vol. II, n° 21. — Original[1].

---

[1]. Il existe de cette lettre : 1° une traduction espagnole originale, émanant de la chancellerie chérifienne ; elle est publiée ci-après ; 2° trois exemplaires d'une traduction contemporaine anglaise faite d'après l'espagnol, conservés dans le même volume (*Royal Letters II*) sous les n°s 10, 13 et 14 ; 3° une traduction portugaise, faite également d'après l'espagnol, dans *State Pap., Foreign, Portugal*, vol. II.

PL. II.

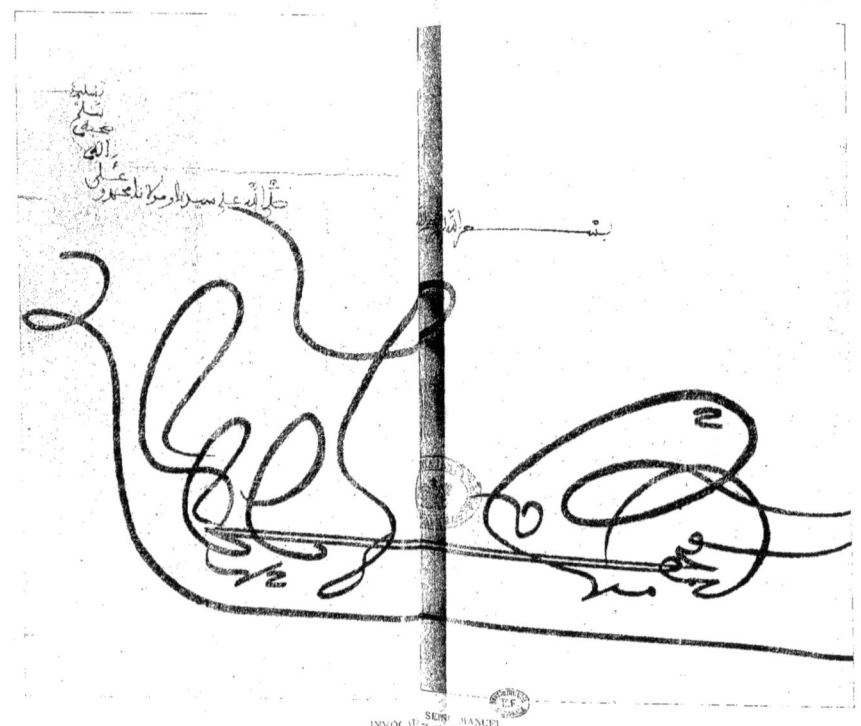

SCEAU MANUEL,
INVOCATION EL-MANSOUR
DE LA LETTRE DE MOULAY EL-MANSOUR A LA REINE ÉLISABETH
D'après l'original au Public Record Office.

VIIbis

LETTRE DE MOULAY AHMED EL-MANSOUR A ÉLISABETH

(Traduction)

Merrakech, 19 Chabân 998 [23 juin 1590].

Adresse: A l'auguste Majesté dont le flambeau et l'étendard sont élevés, la souveraine imposante et de haute lignée, la célèbre, la distinguée, la magnanime reine Élisabeth, qui gouverne le royaume d'Angleterre.

Au nom de Dieu le Clément, le Miséricordieux ! — Que Dieu bénisse notre seigneur et maître Mohammed, sa famille et ses compagnons ! Qu'Il leur accorde la plénitude du salut !

Signe de validation.

De la part du serviteur de Dieu Très-Haut, du combattant dans la voie de Dieu, l'imam victorieux par la grâce de Dieu, le Commandeur des Croyants, fils du Commandeur des Croyants, fils du Commandeur des Croyants, le chérif hassénien. Dieu, par sa puissance victorieuse, affermisse son autorité, fasse triompher ses armées, perpétue sa trace illustre et joigne sa gloire en ce monde à sa gloire dans l'autre !

A l'auguste Majesté dont le flambeau et l'étendard sont élevés, la souveraine imposante et de haute lignée, la célèbre, la distinguée, la magnanime reine Élisabeth, qui gouverne le royaume d'Angleterre.

Louange à Dieu qui assiste quiconque se confie en Lui et s'abandonne à Lui du soin de ses affaires ! Que la bénédiction et le salut de Dieu soient répandus sur son Envoyé, dont la mission a été attestée par des miracles éclatants et par la victoire de ses étendards ! Que les membres de sa famille, imams illustres, soutiens de l'humanité, vicaires de l'Islam, gloire des nuits et des jours, soient agréés de Dieu, ainsi que ses compagnons qui accroissaient sa puissance et ses victoires par la lance et le tranchant des sabres ! Invoquons Dieu afin qu'Il accorde à cette seigneurie généreuse, imamienne, mansourienne, ahmédienne, hassénienne[1], une victoire éclatante qui garantira ses fidèles et qui sera un malheur et une perdition pour ses ennemis !

Notre présente lettre vous est adressée de notre capitale illustre Merrakech — Dieu l'enveloppe de sa protection ! Que Dieu Très-Haut accorde la victoire à l'étendard flottant, à cette providentielle autorité, dont la puissance est raffermie par les armées de la terre et du ciel, assurant la suprématie des fidèles et l'humiliation des ennemis, grâce à la puissance et au pouvoir de Dieu Très-Haut.

Votre lettre[2], envoyée par votre ambassadeur, le généreux capitaine Aïr[3], est parvenue à Notre Haute Seigneurie. Nous l'avons reçue avec plaisir et des sentiments de généreuse bienveillance. Nous avons pris connaissance de ce que vous dites du roi D. Antonio — que Dieu réalise ses désirs et le fasse réussir dans tous ses actes ! — Ce prince vous a annoncé que nous lui avions promis d'envoyer auprès de vous un ambassadeur de Notre Seigneurie, homme de crédit, qui serait chargé de lui remettre les subsides qu'il nous avait demandés à titre de prêt.

Voici ce qu'il en est de cette affaire — Dieu vous comble de ses faveurs ! — Il est tout à fait exact que nous avions promis à l'ambassadeur[4] du prince D. Antonio qui se trouve actuellement dans notre capitale d'envoyer auprès de vous un ambassadeur de Notre Haute Seigneurie, mais cette promesse était subordonnée à la

---

1. Ces qualificatifs désignent l'imâm Ahmed el-Mansour, de la race de Hassen. Cf. H. DE CASTRIES, La diplomatique des princes de la dynastie saadienne, au chapitre : Suscription.

2. C'est la lettre de février 1590. V. supra, Doc. I, p. 1.

3. Le texte arabe porte sans aucun doute possible خ) Aïr. Il est difficile d'expliquer comment le nom du capitaine Prynne, car c'est de lui qu'il s'agit manifestement, a pu être ainsi déformé. L'interprète espagnol a lu : Here. Le traducteur anglais et le traducteur portugais (V. supra, p. 20, note 1) ont restitué dans leurs versions le nom de Prynne.

4. Mathias Becudo. Sur ce personnage, V. supra, p. 1, note 2.

condition que vous auriez vous-même secouru ce prince cette année, en lui envoyant des troupes et en faisant vos efforts pour le faire triompher.

Votre ambassadeur qui vient d'arriver ici nous a trouvé occupé aux préparatifs d'une expédition fortunée que nous nous proposons de diriger sur le Soudan[1], s'il plaît à Dieu; elle est prête à partir et se mettra en route, sous peu de jours, grâce à la puissance de Dieu. C'est dans ces circonstances que nous retenons ici votre ambassadeur le susdit capitaine — Dieu l'honore! — Il restera à notre Cour, honoré et bien traité jusqu'à ce que nous ayons, s'il plaît à Dieu, complètement achevé les préparatifs de cette expédition fortunée, ce qui ne saurait tarder. Dès qu'elle sera partie pour sa destination, nous consacrerons notre attention, s'il plaît à Dieu, aux questions qui vous intéressent ainsi que le roi D. Antonio. Mais nous désirerions recevoir de vous une lettre nous éclairant sur vos intentions à ce sujet et nous indiquant le moment que vous jugerez opportun pour agir, afin que nous nous tenions sur nos gardes, car, dans cette affaire, nous et vous ne faisons qu'un[2].

Tels sont les motifs qui nous ont fait vous écrire cette lettre ce jourd'hui, vendredi dix-neuf[3] du mois béni de Chabân de l'année neuf cent quatre-vingt-dix-huit[4].

1. Sur cette expédition, V. infra, p. 66, et 1re Série, France, t. II, p. 193, note 2. Cf. H. de CASTRIES, La conquête du Soudan par El-Mansour, dans Hespéris, 1923.

2. On peut rapprocher cette réponse dilatoire de la lettre qu'écrivit, à la même date, Moulay Ahmed à D. Antonio sur le même sujet, le 19 octobre 1590. V. 1re Série, France, t. II, p. 191.

3. Le vendredi tombait le 18 et non le 19 Chabân 998.

4. Cette lettre fut reçue en Angleterre entre le 3 et le 28 août. V. infra, p. 30, n. 2 et p. 37. — On lit au dos de la version portugaise cette phrase enchevêtrée : « Copie de la lettre que l'empereur du Maroc écrivit à la Reine en réponse à celle qu'apporta Duarte Perin, qui vint après Francisco Caldeira, par le [retour du] navire dans lequel il était parti. »

VII[ter]

LETTRE DE MOULAY AHMED EL-MANSOUR A ÉLISABETH[1]

(Traduction espagnole[2])

Merrakech, 19 Chabân 998 [23 juin 1590].

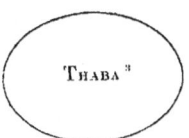
Thaba[3]

Esta carta va deqlaramdo lo que dyze em la del Rey em lemgua morysqua para la reyna Yzabel, reyna de Ynglatera. E lo que comyemsa em la carta de dytados no se puede poner em lemgua castelana; el emtemto delha es : carta del Rey para la Reyna, com dyzer en e[l]ha los dytados que se am de dyzer, aquerda uno, por el Rey e por la Reyna[4].

Vuesa carta com vueso embyado capytam Here resebymos e la resebymos com mumcho comtemto e plazer. E emtemdymos delha lo que dyzeys por el rey Dom Amtonho : que el le dyxo que nos le aprometymos de mamdarle hum embaxador de nuesa caza real, que fuese de manera para que le ayegase alha el dynero que pydyo de nos le ayudasemos com elho prestado.

---

1. V. un fac-similé de cette lettre, p. 26, Pl. III.

2. Cette traduction a été faite à la cour du Chérif pour accompagner l'original arabe. L'interprète explique, dans le premier paragraphe, qu'il s'est abstenu de traduire le préambule. Les versions anglaise et portugaise faites en Angleterre reproduisent cette explication.

3. Sur ce thaba de petites dimensions est reproduit le grand signe de validation qui se voit sur le document arabe.

4. Entendez : Les titres donnés à la Reine et au Chérif sont équivalents.

Lo que em elho pasa es que nos avyamos aprometydo al embaxador del rey Dom Amtonho[1], el que agora esta aquy em nuesa corte, que, sy vos hotros le ayudasedes para este anho com todo lo que pydyere, amsy de juemte como de molysyom, estomces le mamdaryamos nueso embaxador de nuesa caza real, como pydyo e vos dyxo.

E, por halharnos aguora vueso embaxador[2] aparejamdo syerta juemte que mamdo a la Guyneha para la tomar, porque la razom e la justysa nos lo mamda hazer amsy e somos hoblygados a amsy lo hazer, la qual juemte esta ya de partyda, e por este cauza detuvymos aquy este ducho embyado, el dycho capytam, com muncha [honrra], em tamto que comqluymos de despachar esta juemte, que sera muy presto, e emtemderemos luego con el em vueso neguosyo, a vuesa voluntad e del rey Dom Amtonho.

E queremos que nos esqryvays e nos haguay[s] saber lo que teneyse em este neguosyo e quando hazer, para que nos tambyem estemos sobre el avyzo, porque nos e vos hotros em este negosyo somos hunos.

Esqryta em nuesa corte real em Maruecos, dia de vyernes 19 del mes de Xababam, amho de 998.

Public Record Office. — State Papers, Foreign, Royal Letters, vol. II, n° 11. — Traduction.

1. Mathias Becudo.   2. Edward Prynne.

VIII

LETTRE D'EDWARD BARTON[1] A ROBERT CECIL

(Extrait)

Ancienne inimitié existant entre le roi de Fez et Hassan, le capitan-pacha, qui a épousé une femme de Moulay Ahmed et qui élève un fils qu'elle a eu de celui-ci. — Le Grand Seigneur, à la demande de Hassan-Pacha, a donné l'ordre, il y a trois ans, à Moulay Ahmed de doter cet enfant d'un revenu. — Hassan-Pacha n'a pas envoyé cet ordre à Moulay Ahmed, dont la désobéissance apparente indispose le Grand Seigneur. — Il a obtenu l'envoi d'un chaouch pour réclamer les trois années d'arriéré de ce revenu, et espère qu'un refus du Chérif amènera la guerre. — Il est à craindre que Moulay Ahmed ne remette D. Christophe à Philippe II, afin de s'assurer l'aide de l'Espagne contre les Turcs. — Hassan-Pacha intrigue pour que le prince portugais soit réclamé par le Sultan, qui pourrait s'en servir, en cas de conflit avec l'Espagne. — Barton suggère à la Reine d'envoyer un vaisseau pour ramener D. Christophe ; on informerait le Chérif des intentions du Grand Seigneur qui, sous couleur d'une intervention en Portugal, préparerait, en réalité, une expédition contre le Maroc. — Pour parer à ce danger et éviter un refus qui lui ferait encourir la disgrâce du Grand Seigneur, Moulay Ahmed devrait renvoyer D. Christophe en Angleterre. — Barton estime qu'il n'y a pas lieu de dévoiler au Chérif les autres intrigues de Hassan-Pacha, car cela pourrait l'inciter à remettre D. Christophe au roi d'Espagne.

Péra, 24 juin [n. st. 4 juillet] 1590.

Au dos, alia manu : 24 Junii 1590. M. Barton.

Right Honorable,

As ten dayes past I sent unto your Honnour Thomas Wilcock, one of my house, with the Grand Signors[2] letters.

. . . .

---

1. Edward Barton, ambassadeur à Constantinople, venait d'arriver dans cette ville, où il mourut de la peste en 1597.
2. Amurat III (1574-1595).

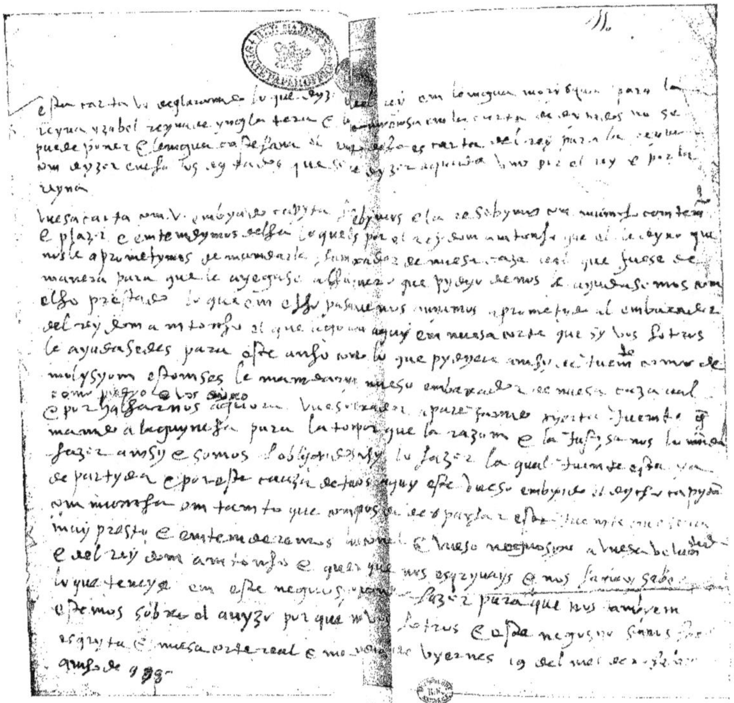

Touching the affaires of these partes [1], your Honour shall understand that here hath been an aunciend ennimity between the King of Fesse and Hassan Bassa, admirall [2], who, being a craftie foxe and hoping for a daie to worke this King a mischief, did marie with Muli Hamets wife [3], and who since hath nourished a childe of hers [4] begotten by Muli Hamet. For which childe, three yeeres since, he hath obteyned letters and commandement of the Grand Seignour [5] to the King of Fesse that he should have the revenues of a certain province in the kingdome of Fesse, which was his fathers patrimony [6], for his maintennance. Which letters of the Grand Seigniours of malice he sent not to Fesse, thoughe he dissembled with the Grand Seigniour to have sent them, onelie to bring the King in the Grand Seigniours disgrace for disobedience.

And now, a moneth since, procured the Grand Seignour to sende two Chiausses to him, the one to advise him of his prosperous succes in Persia [7], the other to admonishe him to send the whole three yeeres revenues of the said province, at 30 000 duckets [8] by

---

1. Cf. 1re Série, France, t. II, pp. 188-190, une lettre de John Stanhope à D. Antonio, dans laquelle sont données, presque dans les mêmes termes, ces nouvelles de Constantinople. C'est sans doute par Barton que Stanhope aura été renseigné.

2. Hassan-Pacha, renégat vénitien, deux fois pacha d'Alger (1577-1580 et 1582-1588), capitan-pacha de 1588 à 1591, date de sa mort.

3. Barton commet une erreur : il s'agit ici, non d'une femme et d'un fils de Moulay Ahmed el-Mansour, mais de la femme et du fils de Moulay Abd el-Malek, son frère aîné. Ces deux chérifs avaient vécu, réfugiés à Constantinople, pendant le règne de leur frère aîné Moulay Abdallah el-Ghâlib. A la mort de ce dernier (1574), Moulay Abd el-Malek partit pour le Maroc, où, avec l'appui des Turcs, il voulait faire valoir ses droits. Il laissa à Alger sa femme, fille du renégat dalmate Hadji Mourad, et son fils Moulay Ismaïl, né en mars 1575 (V. 1re Série, Angleterre, t. I, p. 154 et note 2). Cette femme et son enfant demeurèrent à Alger jusqu'à la mort de Moulay Abd el-Malek (4 août 1578). Postérieurement, Hassan-Pacha l'épousa et l'emmena avec le jeune Moulay Ismaïl à Constantinople. Cf. 1re Série, Dépôts divers, Venise, aux dates 25 janvier 1588 et 28 juin 1589.

4. Moulay Ismaïl. V. note précédente.

5. Ce « commandement » ne pouvait être qu'une invitation bénévole, car les sultans saadiens ne reconnaissaient nullement la suprématie du Grand Seigneur. V. Torrès, cap. 64. Sur les relations des sultans de Constantinople avec les chérifs, cf. lettre d'Amurat III à Moulay Ahmed el-Mansour (12-21 août 1580) dans 1re Série, Espagne, à la date précitée.

6. L'expression même employée par Barton aurait dû lui faire comprendre qu'il ne pouvait s'agir d'un fils de Moulay Ahmed el-Mansour, le chérif régnant.

7. La paix avec la Perse venait d'être signée le 21 mars 1590.

8. Si cette nouvelle n'est pas entièrement

yeere, thincking by the greatnes of the summe to make the King disobedient to the Grand Seignours letters and so incensing to make warres uppon that kingdome, which Hassan Bassa hath long since desired[1] and now hath found this dyvelislish meanes, which I doubt wille cause of great tumult in those parts.

And the greater for that, as it is heere reported, Don Antonio hath his second sonne[2] there with the King, whome, not without good reason, Hassan Bassa doth suspect that, uppon theis rumors, he will send to the king of Spaine to curre favour with him and to have his aid, yf need be. Which Hassan Bassa desyring to prevent[3], doth dissemble his practisie against the King as much as he maie and is procuring with the Grand Seignour to send to the King for the said sonne of Don Antonio, to keepe him here as an eyesoore to Spaine, least he shoulde ryse in the King of Fesses favour.

This is a matter of great consideration and herefore I desire your Honour to sende me your often speedie advice whether at all or how farre her Majestie will have me to deale in this cause, yf the said sonne of Don Antonio chaunce to come hither; for, without your Honours order, I shalbe afraide to deale to or fro therein.

Yf I might be so bolde to councell your Honour or to give advice herein, I should not thinck it amisse that of purpose her Majestie did sende a shipp to Barbary for him, enforming the King that, at Hassan Bassas percurement, the Grand Signour will send to demand him, to the intent that, under that coloure of his fynding in his behalf to make a vyage for Portugale, they might, with helpe of the soldiors of Argiers and Tunis, unawares sett uppon him and deprive him of his kingdome; and, denying him, take occasion of displeasure against him. Which danger he maie shunne in sending beforehand at her Majesty the saide youth unto her Highnes.

---

erronée, les faits sont certainement très mal présentés : le sultan de Constantinople n'ayant en aucune façon le pouvoir d'attribuer à un prince, fût-il chérif, les revenus d'une province marocaine.

1. Hassan-Pacha avait le secret espoir de voir son beau-fils Moulay Ismaïl remplacer Moulay Ahmed el-Mansour comme souverain du Maroc.

2. D. Christophe.

3. Hassan-Pacha était opposé à la remise de D. Christophe à Philippe II; celle-ci, qui pouvait procurer à Moulay Ahmed el-Mansour l'appui de l'Espagne et le consolider au Maroc, était contraire à ses visées pour Moulay Ismaïl.

But I thinck not convenient to advise him of Hassan Bassas other proceedings of Muli Hamets sonne, for then I thinck he would soone resolve to sende Don Antonios sonne to the King of Spaine. Your Honour is wise enough to consider of the matter; and for me, it is sufficient to have advised your Honor, as futurely I will, what soon shall succeed, because Hassan Bassa, for the good affection he beareth me, doth keepe nothing secret from me.

. . . .

For the present, I have not but commend your Honour with the desire of all prosperitie to the same.

From Pera, the 24 of June 1590[1].

Public Record Office. — State Papers, Foreign, Turkey, vol. II. — Original.

1. Ce document n'est pas signé, bien qu'il soit un original, annoté par Burghley.

IX

MÉMOIRE SUR LES AFFAIRES DE PORTUGAL[1]

On lit dans les lettres d'Edward Prynne qu'après avoir été bien accueilli par le Chérif à son arrivée, en avril, il dut attendre jusqu'au 7 juin pour une nouvelle audience. — Le Chérif écrivit alors à Élisabeth et à D. Antonio, et il retient Prynne au Maroc jusqu'à ce qu'il ait reçu leurs réponses. — Ses lettres ne renferment rien de plus que le renouvellement de ses promesses. — Pour s'excuser de n'avoir fourni ni argent ni hommes à la flotte anglaise envoyée à Lisbonne, il prétend, au dire de Prynne, que son ambassadeur, n'ayant pas été renvoyé à temps au Maroc, n'a pu le prévenir des préparatifs. — Il convient que la Reine lui écrive, pour lui rappeler qu'elle avait compté sur son aide en Portugal, lui montrer qu'il ne pouvait pas ignorer l'expédition qui se préparait, et l'inviter à envoyer l'argent promis à D. Antonio, moyennant quoi elle assistera elle-même ce prince. — Pour rendre cette lettre plus efficace, la Reine devrait écrire au Grand Seigneur, en le priant d'agir dans le même sens auprès du Chérif.

[Avant le 28 août 1590][2].

Au dos, alia manu: For King Antonio. Extract of certaine letters. Morocco.

---

1. Le présent Mémoire se divise en deux parties. La première est un résumé des lettres écrites du Maroc par Edward Prynne. D'après les indications fournies dans le texte et dans les notes marginales, ce sont quatre lettres, respectivement datées des 1ᵉʳ mai, 20 mai, 7 juin et 12 juin. Celle du 20 [n. st. 30] mai à Walsingham et celle du 12 [n. st. 22] juin à John Stanhope ont été publiées ci-dessus; celles du 1ᵉʳ et du 7 juin, qui paraissent avoir été adressées à la Reine, manquent. V. *infra*, p. 37, note 1. La deuxième partie du Mémoire est une ébauche des lettres que son auteur conseillait d'écrire au Chérif et au Grand Seigneur. V. *infra*, p. 32 et n. 3, 33 et n. 2.

2. Le présent Mémoire est postérieur au 24 juillet [n. st. 3 août] 1590, date d'un projet de lettre d'Élisabeth au Chérif, dans lequel la Reine, après avoir réclamé justice pour ses sujets assassinés ou emprisonnés, demandait le renvoi d'Ed-

It appeareth, by letters from Prym of the first of May[1], that upon his first arrival he was wel used of the King of Morocco, of whome he had present audience, and, after the deliverie of hir Maties letters, had promise that, within vi daies, he should have answer, and hir Matie should be satisffied. After which time he had no more audience nor any other ordre, though he used all the means he could to procure it, til the vii^{th} of June ; at which time the King resolved to write his letters to hir Matie and to the King Antonio[2], and so did ; with the which letters he would not suffer Prym to returne, who was ernest therein, but said it were necessarie he should staie til answer of those letters were returned. Those letters import no more but a reitering of his former promises, that, if hir Matie will conclude on any thing for the aide of the King Antonio, he wil then be ready to performe all that he hath promised either by letter, or by his owne embassador, or by word of mowth to the King Antonio his embassador[3].

By a letter to Mr Secretary[4] (of the xx of May)[5], it seems the King of Morocco excuseth himself that his embassador[6] was not suffered to returne in tyme to give him notice of hir Maties preparacion ; which was the only let he sent not his money nor men to assist the Queens forces that went to Lisbon.

As wel by Pryms first letter of May as by his second of the vii^{th}

---

ward Prynne et de D. Christophe (*British Museum, Lansdowne Mss., 94. f. 98*). Ce projet fut abandonné et remplacé par le document suivant, dont la minute primitive était du 18 [n. st. 28] août. V. *infra*, p. 34 et note 1.

1. En marge, de la main de Robert Cecil : « 1° Maii ».

2. Il résulte de ce passage que Moulay Ahmed écrivit en même temps à Elisabeth et à D. Antonio. On a vu ci-dessus (p. 1) la lettre à la Reine, datée du 19 Chabán 998 [23 juin 1590]. La lettre à D. Antonio est évidemment celle dont la traduction latine a été publiée dans *1re Série*, France, t. II, p. 191. La date du vendredi 19 octobre 998 lui a été faussement attribuée par le traducteur, Gabriel Sionita. Les dates des deux documents étaient certainement identiques, car le jour de la semaine, le quantième et l'année sont les mêmes. C'est sur le mois que porte l'erreur de Sionita.

3. Mathias Becudo.

4. En marge, de la main de Robert Cecil « To Mr Secretary, xx May. »

5. Les mots : *of the xx of May* ont été insérés par Robert Cecil. La lettre de Prynne du 20 mai ne parle pas des excuses du Chérif qui sont rapportées ici. Ce détail a dû être emprunté à l'une des lettres qui n'ont pas été conservées et attribué par erreur à celle du 20 mai.

6. Merzouk Raïs. V. *1re Série*, Angleterre, t. I, p. 512 et note 3.

of June[1], it seems he finds that the King of Morocco doth but seek shifts and delaies, as the excuse of not coming of his embassador in time, and now a new offer to draw the Queen to a new charge to the which he would contribute, further that he deferred his answer thus long by reason of his preparing a voiage to Guinne, as he writeth in his owne letter to hir Ma[tie].

Wherfore it is required[2] that hir Ma[tie] would write to him[3], remembring him how, upon his first offer and promise of assistance with men and money to the King Antonio, she had made a great army, transported in a nombre of her owne roial ships, in the which the King Antonio himself went, attended on with some of hir nobility and divers great captains, to hir very great charge, with assurance that some should have met hir generals in Portugall from him, at least with such money as was promised, synce it could not be but he must needs have some worde therof either from his owne embassador, who saw the preparacion here long afore it went out, as also by such merchants ships as trade his dominions[4].

Now therfore, since neither the King Antonio thincketh the tyme as yet fit for him to attempt Portugal ageaine, nor hir Ma[tie] can, upon any such soden, prepare hir forces to that ende, she requiereth that he wil send the King Antonio the money was promised, bicawse the said King hath some other journey in hand, which may prejudice the King of Spaine greatly and inrich himself. The which money she thincketh both he is bound partly by his word to send, and the rather for that he hath the security of his sonnes Don Christophers person in his owne hands til he be satisfied; in which action likewise he shall not want hir aide and furtherance, as is best knowne to the King Antonio himself. The which some of money, if she shall find that he doth send with expedicion by any embassador of his owne in returne with hir servaunt Prym, or otherwise as he shall thinck good, for whome she looketh presently

---

1. En marge, de la main de Robert Cecil : « 7 Junii. »
2. En marge, de la main de Robert Cecil : « K. Ant. req. — A letter to J° Stanhop, 12 Junii. » On se rappelle que, dans cette lettre, Prynne insistait pour que la Reine écrivît une lettre énergique au Chérif.
3. V. infra, Doc. X, p. 34.
4. Sur l'expédition de Drake et de Norris en Portugal en 1589, V. 1re Série, Angleterre, t. I, pp. 527-529.

upon the receipt of these letters, then she shall take it thanckfully, and thinck this great charge she hath bene at the better bestowed, and be reddy hereafter to joyne with him further in assisting the King Antonio to his right, and procuring him to performe such promises betwixt the two Kings as he hath past betwene them.

To make this letter have the better succes, it is thought requisite that hir Matie be pleased to write to the Great Signeur of Constantinople, requiring him to stand frendly to the pore banished King Antonio, and especially to write his letters to the Sherif of Morocco, requiring him to satisfy the King Antonio with such somes of money as he heretofore promised the King to send to him, and wherwith he made hir acquainted by his embassador, and for the which he hath a sonne of the King in pledge til he shalbe satisfied, and wherof the King Antonio hath speciall need now towards the performance of a voiage which he hath in hand ageainst the King of Spaine[1], which may be very commodious to himself[2].

Public Record Office. — State Papers, Foreign, Barbary States, vol. XII. — Original.

1. Si l'on s'en rapporte à ce que dit Mathias Becudo (V. *infra*, p. 52), le projet de D. Antonio aurait été de se faire rétablir sur le trône de Portugal avec l'aide des Turcs.

2. La lettre d'Élisabeth au Grand Seigneur est conçue dans les termes indiqués au présent Mémoire. La minute, conservée au British Museum (*Cotton Mss.*, Nero B. VIII, f. 54), n'est pas datée, non plus que la lettre d'envoi de la Reine à Edward Barton, son ambassadeur à Constantinople. *State Papers, Turkey*, vol. II, n° 17. Peu après leur envoi, Élisabeth écrivit de nouveau à Barton, le 3 septembre [n. st.] 1590, pour lui dire que Don Antonio lui avait demandé d'écrire une seconde lettre au Grand Seigneur au sujet de son affaire et de la faire porter par un agent nommé Francisco Caldeira de Brito. *British Museum, Cotton Mss., Nero B. VIII, f. 59 v°*. La lettre spéciale de la Reine, demandée par D. Antonio, fut envoyée. C'est le document XI, p. 40.

X

LETTRE D'ÉLISABETH A MOULAY AHMED EL-MANSOUR[1]

La conduite antérieure de Moulay Ahmed avait fait croire à Élisabeth qu'elle pouvait compter sur son amitié. — Mais le Chérif, après avoir promis, l'année dernière, d'aider D. Antonio à reconquérir son royaume, a manqué de parole et fait échouer l'expédition en Portugal. — Maintenant, il laisse sans réponse et retient au Maroc l'envoyé de la Reine, Edward Prynne. — En outre, il emprisonne des marchands anglais, dont deux sont morts. — A la requête de Prynne, Élisabeth avait écrit au Chérif pour réclamer le congé de cet agent et de D. Christophe, ainsi que la libération des marchands. — La lettre allait partir quand Élisabeth en a reçu une nouvelle de Prynne et une du Chérif, dans laquelle celui-ci promet d'aider D. Antonio, si l'Angleterre lui fournit elle-même des secours, mais ajoute que, pour l'instant, ses troupes vont être employées au Soudan. — Malgré sa défiance trop justifiée, Élisabeth consent à attendre l'effet de la dernière proposition du Chérif. — Considérant l'énormité de ses propres dépenses, elle prie Moulay Ahmed de s'acquitter de cette promesse en envoyant à D. Antonio la somme d'argent qu'il réclamera pour l'exécution d'une entreprise qu'il médite actuellement. — Elle demande que Prynne reçoive son congé et que justice soit faite dans l'affaire des marchands. — S'il n'est pas fait droit aux justes demandes de la Reine, elle a la certitude que le Grand Turc, qui favorise les sujets anglais, ne permettra pas que le Chérif les maltraite, pour faire plaisir aux Espagnols.

20 [n. st. 30] août 1590.

Au dos, alia manu: 20 August 1590. — Copie of the Queen's lettre to the King of Moroccos

1. Le texte de cette lettre est, à quelques variantes près, la traduction d'une minute en anglais, datée du 18 [n. st. 28] août 1590, qui est conservée au British Museum, *Lansdowne Mss., 94, ff. 100-103.* Une autre minute en anglais, de la main de Burghley, se trouve au Public Record Office, *St. Pap., For., Royal Letters, vol. II, n° 17.*

Muy alto y muy poderoso Señor,

Como, en las cosas naturales, se vee que los tiempos hazen variar sus operaciones, de manera que unas vezes seran de mayor y otras de menor efeto, ni mas ni menos acontesce qu'en negocios de principes y de las amistades qu'entr'ellos se tratan, la diversidad de los tiempos y de las occasiones que se offrescen son causa que a vezes se confirman las tales amistades, a vezes se resfrian, y en fin tambien se pueden renovar. Exemplo nos paresce que de poco aca tenemos d'ello, en vuestra manera de proceder para con nos, pues, aviendonos, al principio de vuestro reynado, hecho tales offrescimientos de amistad y tratado a nuestros vassallos que ay passan con tanta dulçura y humanidad, que teniamos por cierto que no nos negariades cosa que os pudieszemos con razon pedir para nos mesma o en favor de nuestros vassallos o amigos, vemos todavia que, de poco aca, se han offrescido occasiones que nos pueden hazer mudar de parescer, o a lo menos poner en duda que no teneys agora la mesma intencion.

Porque, desque os uvimos el año passado rogado, por cartas y otros recaudos, que diessedes socorro al rey Don Antonio para cobrar su estado de Portugal, qual prometistes de cumplir por cartas, y por dicho del qu'embiastes por Embaxador[1], de manera qu'el dicho rey Don Antonio os embio a su hijo Don Christoval por peño de que cumpliria los conciertos que con vos uviese assentado, aviendo nos (con la opinion que teniamos de que, conforme a vuestra promessa, embiariades socorro de gente y de dinero a Portugal) hecho, por lo que a nos tocava, un armada de muchos navios y embiado en ella para la dicha empresa de Portugal un exercito que juntamos con mucha costa, sucedio que no acudistes a tiempo con el dicho socorro que de vos s'esperava, por donde se vino a perder la occasion y comodidad que se offrescia de poner al dicho Rey en su estado[2].

Lo qual nos a dado harta materia de sospechar que no perseverays en vuestra primera intencion d'entretener con nos una buena y syncera amistad, aviendonos aun de nuevo aumentado esta sospecha

---

1. Merzouk Raïs. V. *supra*, p. 31, n. 6.   2. V. *supra*, p. 32, note 4.

con la manera de proceder que aveys tenido con nuestro criado Eduard Pryn. El qual llevandoos cartas de nuestra parte, aunque al principio hiziestes muestra de recibirlo con mucha honra y humanidad, todavia, en harto tiempo despues, ni le quisistes dar respuesta ni audiencia, nonostante las diligencias que sobr'ello hizo, antes usastes con el de muchas dilaciones, o, como a el mesmo le paresce, lo burlastes, sin concederle ni aun que se oyessen las causas de algunos mercaderes nuestros vassallos, los quales, sin porque, estavan en carceles tan miserables, que, de tres, dos murieron subitamente, achacados de las dichas carceles [1], o quiça por violencia de sus enemigos, los quales deven de aver tomado alas y favor de algunos Españoles [2], para usar de semejantes crueldades con nuestros vassallos.

De manera que nuestro dicho criado Pryn, no sabiendo lo que le podria acontescer en su propria persona, se nos a quexado por sus cartas [3] del mal tratamiento que a el y a los otros nuestros vassallos se haze por alla, suplicandonos que os rogassemos que lo dexeys bolver en salvo, y tambien que pusiessedes a los dichos mercaderes en libertad, dando fianças que responderan a todo lo que se les pudiere demandar. En conformidad de lo qual, os escrevimos una carta con mucha instancia, trayendoos a la memoria como no aviades cumplido con vuestra promessa de dar socorro al rey Don Antonio, aunque le deteneys ay a su hijo, con infinito dolor de su coraçon. El qual todavia nos dize que se lo tratays con mucha honor y liberalidad; pero, con todo esso, visto que no teniades intencion de ayudarle, conforme a vuestra promessa, os rogamos por la dicha carta que le torneys a embiar a su hijo, y tambien que despidays a nuestro criado Prin y pongays a nuestros vassallos los mercaderes en libertad.

Todas estas particularidades son contenidas en las dichas cartas, las quales todavia por suerte no os fueron embiadas [4] hasta que, muy a proposito, llegaron otras mas frescas que las primeras para nos y para el dicho rey Don Antonio, de parte de nuestro criado Prin y

---

1. Sur cette affaire, V. *supra*, pp. 13-14.
2. Entre autres Diego Marin. V. *supra*, p. 13 et note 1.
3. V. *supra*, Doc. V, p. 10.
4. Cette lettre d'Élisabeth au Chérif, qui n'avait pas encore été envoyée, était celle du 24 juillet [n. st. 3 août] 1590. V. *supra*, p. 30, note 2.

de parte de Don Christoval para el dicho Rey[1], por las quales hemos visto que aviades despues dado audiencia al dicho Prin y cartas que nos embiasse, con las quales le aviades assegurado que recibiriamos contento y satisfacion, mandandole que no partiesse hasta que uviessemos embiado respuesta sobre lo contenido en las dichas cartas. Las quales hemos tambien recebido, y por ellas visto lo que dezis, aunque muy tarde, es a saber mas de un año despues del tiempo que s'esperava, que, si quisiessemos agora ayudar al dicho rey Don Antonio, vos tambien de vuestra parte, teniendo sobr'ello respuesta nuestra, embiariades el socorro de gente y de dinero que aviades antes prometido ; añadiendo todavia, nonostante este offrescimiento, que os convenia emplear vuestros soldados para cobrar ciertas provincias de Guinea, sin declararos particularmente en las dichas cartas sobr'el tiempo quando las podriades embiar en servicio del dicho rey Don Antonio.

Sobr'esto querriamos saber que conjetura os paresce que devamos de hazer de lo qu'escrevis d'esta manera y tan tarde, ya que la sazon del año es casi passada y despues de aver tambien corrido mas de un año entero desde que embiamos nuestro socorro, gastamos nuestros dineros y pusimos en riesgo las vidas de nuestros vassallos, lo qual no hizieramos sino fundada en la esperança que nos aviades dado de que de vuestra parte acudiriades tambien a tiempo. Demas d'esto, las ultimas cartas de nuestro dicho criado no hazen mencion ninguna de que nuestros vassallos que ay estan sean mejor tratados. Pero, nonostante todo lo sucedido d'esta manera contra nuestra opinion, somos de natural que no podemos assolutamente achacaros estos sinsabores o falta de amistad o de promessa, hasta que ayamos tambien provado lo que podra suceder de alguna parte d'estos vuestros ultimos offrescimientos.

Por lo qual, visto que ya es muy tarde para formar aqui exercito que pueda servir este año, y que allende desso hemos ya gastado mucho el año passado en la empresa de Portugal, y, sin las costas qu'hemos ya hecho este año, nos conviene gastar mucho mas, no

---

1. Il résulte de ce passage que Prynne avait écrit, par le même courrier, des lettres à la reine Élisabeth (le 7 [n. st. 17] juin, V. supra, p. 32 et note 1), à D. Antonio et à D. Christophe. Ces lettres n'ont pas été retrouvées.

solamente para defender nuestros proprios reynos de Yngalaterra y de Yrlanda, sino tambien para ayudar a nuestros vezinos, como el rey de Francia, nuestro muy querido hermano [1], y otros, contra el rey d'España, el qual tiene hartos reynos y estados con que se podria contentar, si no fuesse su demasiada cudicia de abarcar tambien los de los otros que no le pertenescen, seriamos de mucha satisfacion y os tendriamos por ello mucha obligacion, si quisiessedes cumplir lo que de nuevo prometeys, con prestar al dicho Rey, teniendo a su hijo por peño, la suma de dineros que os pedira, para poner por efeto una empresa d'importancia [2] que se le offresce, mediante la qual espera cobrar su estado, o por lo menos alcançar medio de poderse entretener muy aventajadamente, hasta que Dios sea servido de tomar vengança del rey d'España, el qual tan injusta y tyrannicamente le usurpa su estado. Y con esto, no solamente cobrareys la buena opinion que soliamos tener de vuestr'amistad, pero tambien hareys señalado servicio a Dios, socorriendo, con los medios que os a dado, a los que se hallan opprimidos.

Demas d'esso, os tornamos tambien a reyterar lo que os escreviamos por las otras, las quales no os avemos aun embiado, que despidays a nuestro criado Eduard Pryn, y seays contento de oyrlo humanamente sobre los negocios de nuestros vassallos qu'estan ay encarcelados y cruelmente tratados, por medio de los Españoles sus enemigos, a los quales se haze ay mas favor de lo que quiça de aqui adelante hallareys que conviene a vuestro servicio.

Pero tambien por otra parte, si no quisierdes conceder lo que con tanta razon os pedimos, allende que nos tendremos occasion de hazer tanto menos caso de vuestr'amistad, sabemos tambien de cierto qu'el Gran Turco, el qual usa de mucho favor y humanidad con nuestros vassallos, no tendra a bien que los maltrateys por dar contento a los Españoles.

Con esto pondremos fin a esta carta, la qual va escrita mas a la larga de lo que solemos, porque las circunstancias de lo qu'en ella

---

1. Henri IV avait reçu d'Élisabeth en février précédent un subside de 50000 écus ; il allait en recevoir un autre de 28000 en octobre. *Lettres missives de Henri IV*, t. III, p. 286.

2. Il s'agissait probablement de restaurer, avec l'aide des Turcs, D. Antonio sur le trône de Portugal. V. *infra*, p. 52.

se contiene lo requieren, rogando al sumo Dios, qu'es Rey de los Reyes y Señor de lo Señores, qu'encamine los coraçones de todos los reyes a bivir en paz los unos con los otros, sin usurpar lo que no pertenesce, de que sucederia muy gran bien, quietud y reposo a todo el mundo [1].

Signé : Francisco Caldeira de Brito [2].

Public Record Office. — *State Papers, Foreign, Royal Letters, vol. II, n° 18.* — *Minute.*

1. Le présent texte ne parut sans doute pas suffisant, car, le 24 août [n. st. 3 septembre], il en fut rédigé un autre (*Public Record Office, State Papers, Foreign, Royal Letters, vol. II, n° 19*). Le 19 octobre, on fit de cette lettre une nouvelle rédaction, en espagnol, dans laquelle on supprima ce qui ne concernait pas D. Antonio. Le subside demandé au Chérif était de 100000 mitqals, et s'il ne pouvait être fourni, on priait le Chérif de renvoyer D. Christophe à son père. Ce dernier texte a été publié dans *Briefve et sommaire description de la vie et mort de Dom Antoine*, pp. 91-96.

2. Cette signature est celle du traducteur de la lettre. V. *infra*, p. 41, note 1.

XI

LETTRE D'ÉLISABETH AU GRAND SEIGNEUR

Dans une lettre antérieure, elle recommandait au Grand Seigneur la cause de D. Antonio. — Ce prince a décidé d'envoyer à Constantinople son serviteur Francisco Caldeira de Brito. — Élisabeth prie le Grand Seigneur d'accorder à cet agent une lettre pour le Chérif, qui décide celui-ci à exécuter les promesses qu'il a faites à D. Antonio. — Elle lui saura gré de l'aide apportée par lui à ce prince contre le roi d'Espagne, qui aspire à la monarchie universelle.

Londres, 24 août [n. st. 3 septembre] 1590[1].

Copie of her Maties letter to the Grand Seignor for Don Antonio. August 24, 1590.

Elizabetha, Dei optimi maximi, mundi conditoris et rectoris unici, clementia, Angliæ, Franciæ et Hiberniæ regina, veræ fidei contra omnes idolatras falso christianum nomen profitentes invictissima et potentissima propugnatrix, augustissimo, invictissimo imperatori, Sultan Murad Cham[2], ottomanici regni dominatori potentissimo imperiique Orientis monarchiæ supra omnes soli et supremo, salutem et multos, cum summa rerum omnium optimarum affluentia, lætos et felices annos.

Augustissime et invictissime Imperator,

Ante paucos jam dies, ad Imperatoriam Vestram Majestatem litteras dedimus, quibus de variis vestris in nos beneficiis, tam versus regem Francorum, fratrem nostrum charissimum, injuste

---

1. Sur les circonstances dans lesquelles fut écrite la présente lettre, V. *supra*, p. 33, note 2.
2. Amurat III.

regis Hispani armis oppugnatum, in gratiam nostram ostensis, quam erga serenissimum Poloniæ regem de pacis conditionibus nostro respectu illi oblatis, gratias maxime singulares egimus. Eisdem etiam serenissimi Lusitani regis Antonii causam crudeliter ab hispano regno exuti Sublimi Vestræ Majestati de meliore nota serio commendavimus. Quas litteras, duplici via, tam per Venetorum civitatem quam per Londinensis civitatis portum, ut tanto certius in manus vestras traderentur, mitti jussimus.

Hoc vero tempore, cum idem serenissimus rex Antonius subditum ac famulum suum fidelem Franciscum Caldera de Brito ad Sublimem Vestram Majestatem mittat, iterum ejus precibus adducta eandem summopere rogamus ut prioribus vestris meritis in predictos duos reges, amicos et confœderatores nostros, hoc etiam velit adjungere, ut minister iste, regis sui nomine, litteras Sublimitatis Vestræ ad regem Morocci Muley Hamet obtineat, quibus rex ille ad ea quæ regi Antonio promisit perficienda pertrahatur[1].

Ita omnipotentis Dei altissimi summam in nos benignitatem pio et grato animo semper recolemus, non solum quod nos ab iniquis regis Hispani conatibus multos jam annos liberarit, sed quod nobilissimos duos reges, alterum Franciæ qui primarius christiani orbis princeps semper est habitus, alterum Portugalliæ verum heredem, per Majestatis Vestræ authoritatem nostra causa præstitam, sublevarit contra regis Hispani potentiam, qui, cum plura regna, quam regere rite queat, possideat, aliorum tamen ita ambitiose armis invadit, ut orbis universi imperium affectare videatur. Quicquid igitur Majestas Vestra in serenissimi regis Antonii gratiam nostro rogatu præstiterit, erit id non illi solum, sed nobis etiam illius respectu longe gratissimum[2].

---

1. Francisco Caldeira de Brito avait déjà été envoyé par D. Antonio au Maroc, après l'arrivée de D. Christophe en ce pays (janvier 1589) et avant qu'Edward Prynne s'y rendît en mission (avril 1590). Au dire de Mathias Becudo, il s'y était très maladroitement comporté. Il avait ordre, après avoir remis la présente lettre au Grand Seigneur, de revenir par le Maroc. V. infra, p. 53.

2. La présente lettre n'arriva à Constantinople qu'en février 1591, portée par Thomas Wilcox, secrétaire d'Edward Barton; car Francisco Caldeira de Brito, faute d'argent, ne put dépasser Dantzig. Le 27 février 1591 [n. st.], Barton envoya à la Reine la réponse du Grand Seigneur et une lettre du grand vizir à D. Antonio, en date du 2 février 1591, annonçant au prétendant qu'Amurat III avait envoyé l'ordre au

42   3 SEPTEMBRE 1590

Deus optimus maximus, cœli et terræ conditor, Majestatem Vestram quam diutissime salvam servet et incolumem.

Datæ in regia nostra civitate Londini, die ..... mensis Augusti, anno Servatoris nostri Jhesu Christi 1590, regni vero nostri xxxii^{do}.

British Museum. — Cotton Mss., Nero B. VIII, f. 60. — Copie [1].

Chérif de faire partir immédiatement D. Christophe pour Constantinople. Le Grand Seigneur, de qui D. Antonio sollicitait l'assistance, eût voulu, comme Moulay Ahmed et pour les mêmes raisons politiques, posséder D. Christophe à sa cour en otage. Il comptait se servir de lui comme d'une menace à l'adresse de Philippe II. Le 30 janvier 1592, il écrivait encore à Élisabeth que, conformément aux désirs de cette princesse, il avait fait enjoindre à Moulay Ahmed d'envoyer D. Christophe à la Sublime Porte et de mettre en liberté les Anglais trafiquant dans son royaume. V. lettre de Barton à Burghley du 20 avril 1591 [n. st.], *State Papers. Foreign, Turkey, vol. II*; cf. 1re Série, France, t. II, pp. 200, 201; Dépôts divers, Venise, lettres de l'ambassadeur vénitien au Doge du 5 janvier 1591, du 14 janvier (avec annexe), du 2 mars 1591 (avec annexe du 2 février), du 7 février 1592 (avec annexe du 30 janvier).

1. Cette lettre a été publiée dans l'ouvrage intitulé : *Briefve et sommaire description de la vie et mort de Dom Anthoine...* p. 82. Cf. *supra*, p. 39, note 1.

XII

LETTRE ENVOYÉE D'ANDALOUSIE A BURGHLEY

(Extrait)

L'un des endroits les plus sûrs pour les navires destinés à attaquer les galions espagnols revenant des Indes est la côte du Maroc, près de Mazagan.

Andalousie, 13 [n. st. 23] décembre 1590.

Au dos : To the right honorable the Lorde High Treasorer of England. — *De la main de Burghley :* 13 December 1590. From Andalozia.

Ther ys gone owt of the ryver of Sivill, since the first of this monethe, seaven small shipps of advice to the Indias.

. . . .

Those that ar to wayte ther comminge[1] must be dellycate shipps of sayle, and must rowe lykewise, if neede requyer, 15 or 16 hores[2] in a syde. One of the surest places to meete with them wilbe uppon the cost of Barbarye, neere Masagan; for which ther may be apointed 6 or 8 small shipps of the qualyties afforsaid, and other 2 good shipps well apointed with them, and another company to ly 10 or 12 leages of the yland of Calles, and so to range towardes the cost of Barbarye.

. . . .

The aucthor hereof hopithe to receave for his travell a ffrindlye rewarde, when he shall bringe the other half of the token that goithe herewith inclosed.

Wrytten in Andalozia, the 13th of December, anno 1590.

By a wellwiller of her Maties.

Public Record Office. — *State Papers, Foreign, Spain, vol. III.* — *Original.*

1. L'arrivée de la flotte des Indes.   2. *Hores,* pour oars, rames.

XIII

LETTRE DE MELCHIOR PETONEY A MIGUEL DE MOURA[1]

Il expose à Miguel de Moura que l'hinterland d'Arguin est un pays très riche en blé, en orge, en bétail, en fruits, et particulièrement en mines d'or. — Mais comme il n'y a pas de commerce à Arguin, les indigènes portent cet or très loin, au Maroc ou à Tombouctou. — Il serait donc très désirable que Philippe II envoyât chaque année à Arguin deux ou trois navires chargés de verroteries, couteaux, cloches, toiles, miroirs et autres produits, contre lesquels les indigènes échangent leur or au Maroc. — Ainsi refluerait vers Arguin l'immense quantité d'or qui passe aux mains du Chérif.

Arguin, 20 janvier 1591.

A relation sent by Melchior Petoney to Migil de Moura at Lisbon, from the iland and castle of Arguin[2], standing a little to the southward of Cape Blanco, in the northerly latitude of 19 degrees, concerning the rich and secret trade from the inland of Africa thither. Anno 1591.

As concerning the trade to this castle and iland of Arguin, your Worship is to understand, that, if it would please the Kings Majesty to send hither two or three caravels once in a yeere with Flanders and Spanish commodities, as bracelets of glasse, knives, belles, linnen-cloth, looking-glasses, with other kinds of small wares, his Highnesse might do great good here. For 50 leagues up into the land the Moores have many exceeding rich golde mines; insomuch that they bring downe their golde to this castle to traffique with us; and for a small trifle they will give us a great wedge of gold. And because here is no trade, the sayd Moores cary their golde to Fez[3], being 250 leagues distant from hence, and there doe exchange the same for the foresayd kindes of commodities. By this

---

1. Sur ce personnage, V. 1re Série, Angleterre, t. I, p. 305, note 2.
2. Sur Arguin, cf. 1re Série, France, t. II, p. 271 et note 7.
3. Sur l'importation de l'or du Soudan au Maroc, V. *infra*, pp. 84, 146 et 224, n. 1.

meanes also his Majesty might stop that passage, and keepe the King of Fez from so huge a masse of golde. Scarlet-clothes and fine purples are greatly accepted of in these parts.

It is a most fertile countrey within the land, and yeeldeth great store of wheat, flesh of all kindes and abundance of fruits. Therefore if it were possible, you should do well to deale with his Majesty, either himselfe to send a couple of caravels, or to give your Worship leave to traffique here; for here is a very good harbour, where ships may ride at ancre hard by the castle.

The countrey where all the golde mines are is called the kingdome of Darha[1]. In this kingdome are great store of cities and townes; and in every city and towne a captaine with certaine souldiers; which captaines are lords and owners of the sayd townes. One city there is called Couton[2], another Xanigeton[3], as also the cities of Tubguer, Azegue, Amader, Quaherque and the town of Faroo[4]. The which townes and cities are very great and fairely built, being inhabited by rich Moores, and abounding with all kinde of cattell, barley and dates. And here is such plenty of golde found upon the sands by the rivers side that the sayd Moores usually carry the same northward to Marocco, and southward to the city of Tombuto in the land of Negros, which city standeth about 300 leagues from the kingdome of Darha; and this kingdome is but 60 leagues from this iland and castle of Arguin.

Wherefore I beseech your Worship to put his Majesty in remembrance hereof; for the sayd cities and townes are but ten dayes journey from hence. I heartily wish that his Majesty would send two or three marchants to see the state of the countrey, who might travell to the aforesayd cities, to understand of their rich trade. For any man may go safe from those places. And thus, without troubling of your Worship any further, I humbly take my leave.

From the iland and castle of Arguin, the 20 of January 1591.

Your Worships servant,   Melchior Petoney.

Hakluyt. — The Principal Navigations... of the English Nation. — Édition 1598-1600, tome II, 2ᵉ partie, p. 188.

1. L'Adrar.
2. *Couton*, sans doute Ouadan.
3. *Xanigeton*, Chingueti.
4. Localités non identifiées.

XIV

LETTRE DE MATHIAS BECUDO [1] A D. ANTONIO

Moulay Ahmed a reçu des mains d'Edward Prynne une lettre de la Reine; quelques jours après, Becudo, admis en audience, lui a remis celle de D. Antonio, et lui a rappelé ses promesses. — Réponses dilatoires du Chérif, qui veut abréger l'audience. — Becudo insiste pour que D. Christophe puisse quitter le Maroc, ainsi que le demande D. Antonio dans sa lettre. — Moulay Ahmed, troublé par cette demande, ajourne sa décision. — Becudo, qui l'attend encore, a vainement tenté d'avoir une nouvelle audience. — Moulay Abd el-Malek avait promis autrefois au Grand Seigneur, qui devait l'aider à conquérir le Maroc, de donner le royaume de Fez à un fils qu'il laissait en Turquie; Moulay Ahmed aurait lui-même souscrit à cette promesse. — Moulay Abd el-Malek aurait, en outre, institué par testament son fils comme héritier du royaume de Fez, et laissé à Moulay Ahmed les royaumes de Merrakech et de Sous. — Devenu maître du Maroc, Moulay Abd el-Malek se retourna contre les Turcs et rechercha l'alliance du Portugal et de l'Espagne. — D. Sébastien repoussa inconsidérément les offres d'amitié de Moulay Abd el-Malek. — Mais ce dernier et Philippe II firent alliance et convinrent d'attaquer les Turcs d'Alger par mer et par terre, les places maritimes devant revenir à l'Espagne et les places de l'intérieur au Chérif. — La mort d'Abd el-Malek renversa ces desseins. — Le Grand Seigneur a demandé à Moulay Ahmed d'exécuter les promesses faites par son frère et lui, mais le Chérif traîne les choses en longueur, objectant que ses sujets ne lui permettront jamais de remettre son pays entre les mains d'officiers turcs. — Moulay Ahmed n'ose, par crainte des Turcs, rompre ses engagements avec le roi d'Espagne, mais il ne veut pas lui livrer Larache. — D. Antonio devra être très circonspect en négociant avec Hassan-Pacha pour les services qu'il attend de ce dernier auprès du Grand Seigneur, car il a des intelligences avec le Chérif. — Becudo ne peut pénétrer les desseins de Moulay Ahmed sur D. Christophe. — Hassan-Pacha craint qu'il se joigne à Philippe II contre les Turcs. — Becudo approuve l'idée d'une lettre

---

1. Sur ce personnage, V. *supra*, p. 1, note 2.

qu'écrirait le Grand Seigneur à Moulay Ahmed en faveur de D. Antonio ; mais il n'est pas d'avis qu'il réclame l'envoi de D. Christophe à sa cour. — Cette demande, à laquelle Moulay Ahmed pourrait bien ne pas accéder, brouillerait D. Antonio avec ce prince et le compromettrait auprès des Chrétiens, sans que les promesses d'assistance des Turcs pour recouvrer le Portugal en soient plus solides. — Apprenant que l'envoyé de D. Antonio à Constantinople, Francisco Caldeira, doit revenir par le Maroc, Becudo rappelle les maladresses antérieures de cet agent, qui, à peine arrivé à Safi, annonça qu'il apportait des lettres de D. Antonio et d'Élisabeth pour le Chérif. — Ce prince les réclama à Becudo, qui, n'ayant pas jugé opportun de les lui remettre alors, s'est attiré son antipathie. — Becudo conseille à D. Antonio d'envoyer ses lettres au Maroc par l'entremise des marchands, plutôt que par des courriers spéciaux, dont l'arrivée provoque des commentaires et qui coûtent fort cher à D. Christophe. — Il ne compte pas communiquer au Chérif les nouvelles que D. Antonio a reçues de Constantinople. — D. Francisco da Costa, l'ambassadeur de Philippe II, vient de mourir. — Il a voulu être enterré dans la maison du Juif qui le logeait.

Merrakech, 18 avril 1591.

Au dos, alia manu : 18 Aprill 1591. — Lettres from Mathias Boquido to the King of Portyngall Don Antonio.

Señor,

By the last ship that came from London to Safia, I receved three letters of your M^{ties}, which rejoyced me greatlie ; for that havinge receaved manye from Diego Botello[1], and seinge none of yours, I feared some sicknes was the cause ; but nowe, God be praised, I am freed of that feare and care ; whoe graunt your Matie lyfe for his service and welfare of the afflicted kingdome of Portingall.

The copies of the lettres which your Matie and the most excellent Quene wrote unto this Emperour I have senne. That of your Matie lyked me verie well. That of the Quenes[2] was a litle coulde, and not

---

[1]. Sur ce personnage, confident de D. Antonio, V. *1re Série*, France, t. II, p. 136, note 1.

[2]. C'est la lettre du 20 [n. st. 30] août 1590. V. *supra*, Doc. X, p. 34. Cf. cependant p. 39, note 1.

soe urgent and effectuall as was requisit. Edward Prynne presented the Quenes lettre. And some dayes after, I presented the lettre of your Matie, in privat audience, and declared at large all that I had donne in the service of your Matie in the court of this Emperour, since my beinge here, puttinge him in memorie what he had spoken and had promised to your Matie and the Quene. All which he harkened unto with pacience, and affirmed yt to be trewe, as yt ys ; for I dreamed not that which I writ one his behalfe ; neyther cann he denye that which he hath written soe many tymes to your Matie and to the Quene.

He answered me that he would take order in all thinges, and soe dispatched me awaye. I requested him to heare me foure woordes. He answeared I should delyver them to Ruti[1]. And importunatinge him further to heare me, he was contented yet a litle ; and soe I proceeded, charginge him with his former promises. But, seinge yt not possible to entreat of all I had to saye, I resolved to leave of the rest of my causes, and asked lycence of him for Don Cristopher to departe, in such sorte as your Matie required in your lettre.

He was verie greatlie moved therat, and sayed unto me that yt was not tyme to demaunde such licence, and that he must staye untill yt was senne what he would doe.

I answeared that some yeares were passed, in which yt was hoped to see the resolucion that his Majestie would take in the thinges which he had promised, and that, seinge hitherto noe effect, I demaunded the said licence, accordinge as your Matie required in the said lettre which yow writt unto him ; putting the lettre into the handes of the alcayde Azux[2], who was present when I made this demaunde.

He answeared he would bethinke himselfe of all thinges, and then would send for me, and geve me an answeare.

Untill this daye, he hath not called for me. Yet have I sought verie much, bye meanes of Xec Ruti, to have accesse ageine ; with

---

1. Sur ce personnage, V. *supra*, p. 11, note 2.

2. Le caïd Abd el-Aziz ben Saïd el-Mezouar, el-Ouzguithi, el-Ouerzazati, dit le caïd Azzouz, l'un des premiers personnages de la cour de Moulay Ahmed el-Mansour. V. *1re Série*, France, t. II, p. 199, note 5, et *infra*, p. 380, et *passim*.

whome I dare not imparte anye causes, fearinge that which your Ma*tie* also feareth.

He¹ sent his sonne-in-lawe, Moyses Levi², unto Fez; and I am of opinion yt was not withowt cause; and commaunded another to come, whoe ys better receaved, and of more sufficiencie to helpe him, for that he ys verie slowe, and in a manner unapt to handle any affaires.

These be the termes wherein I stande, this present daye, the 15 of Aprill, with this Emperour, not withowt grete greife of mynde, seinge the hurt that, bye his dilatorie dealinge and irresolucion, may come to the kingdome of Portugall.

They saye here that the Kinge of Castilla ys dead, and that the Kinge of Fraunce ys entered Parris; albeit the Castellins, whoe know the matter best, doe seme to conceall and cover yt, as well the one as the other.

At what tyme Muley Abd el-Melec, brother to this Emperour, came with the ayde of the Great Turke³ to surpreise these kingdoms, he promised the said Turcke, bye woorde and bye writinge under his hande, that, God gyvinge him victorie, he would gyve the kingdome of Fez unto a sonne⁴ wich he left in Turkie; and they say likewise that this Emperour did promise and underwrite the lyke. They saye further that Abd el-Melec proceadinge in the journey (whereon would to God he had never gonne!), he left that sonne for heyre of the kingdome of Fez by his will, which your Ma*tie* affirmeth to be maried with the daughter of Hassam Baixa⁵, and left this Emperour kinge of this kingdome and of Sus.

---

1. *Ile*. Cheikh Ruti. V. *supra*, p. 48 et n. 1.

2. Le personnage mentionné ici est sans doute le même Moïse Lévi qui se trouvait à La Haye en 1617 et présentait aux États-Généraux une requête dans laquelle il se qualifie de trésorier du Chérif. V. *1re Série*, Pays-Bas. t. III, année 1617, *passim*.

3. Sur l'aide apportée par le sultan Amurat III à Moulay Abd el-Malek pour la conquête du Maroc, V. *1re Série*, France, t. I, p. 346, Sommaire, et pp. 449-463; Espagne, aux années 1574-1576, *passim*.

4. Moulay Ismaïl. V. *supra*, p. 27 et

notes 3 et 4. Le Sultan chercha, plus tard, à opposer ce personnage à Moulay Ahmed el-Mansour. — Sur les conditions du concours prêté par Amurat III à Moulay Abd el-Malek, V. *1re Série*, France, t. I, p. 512, note 1.

5. Sur ce personnage, V. *supra*, p. 27 et note 2. Il mourut cette année même (1591). Moulay Ismaïl n'était pas son gendre, comme le supposait D. Antonio, mais son beau-fils. Hassan-Pacha avait, en effet, épousé la veuve de Moulay Abd el-Malek. V. *ibidem*, notes 3 et 4.

After that Abd el-Melec was possessed of his kingdome, in liewe of the frendships that the Turke had donn him, he sowght meanes to make warre ageinst him in Argier ; and the better to effect this, he travailed much to kepe himselfe in league with the Christian kinges, especiallie with the Kinge of Portugall and Castill.

The Lorde had determined to chasten our sinnes, and permitted that our uncircumspect Kinge Don Sebastian should not accept of the honorable frendship which the More Kinge (and not barbarous) did present and make offer unto him. He remayned freinde and allied himselfe with the Kinge Don Philippe, with such condicions as your Matie well knoweth and the Portugall nacion doth alredie bewayle.

These two frendes purposed to make warre uppon the Turke bye sea and bye land at Argiere, with condicion that the fortes uppon the sea coast should remayne to the King of Castill, and the places one the lande unto the Moore[1].

The death of Abd el-Melec overthrewe all these intencions, and the Turke sought by all meanes that this Emperour should performe all that he and his brother had promised him. Which this Emperour hath allwais promised to doe uppon a good and saffe occasion, certificeinge the Turke that he feared that the Moares his subjectes would arise ageinst him, and would not consent that he should delyver his lande into the handes of Turkishe capteyns, enemies of the Moares[2]. And in this sort doth he entertaine the Turke untill this daye, and with money, kepinge almost continuallie his embassador in the Turkes court, to answeare in all causes that shalbe nedefull.

The grevous sinnes of Portugall put this Emperour into the estate wherin he ys at this instant; and pretendinge to benefit himselfe with that which our synnes hath brought him unto, he seketh to be reputed of the world for mightie and puissant, as in treuth he ys.

He hath an[3] intencion to delyver Fez unto his nephew[4], and hath commaunded hit to be verie much fortified with three bullwerkes,

---

1. Sur les rapports de Moulay Abd el-Malek avec Philippe II, V. *1re Série*, Angleterre, t. I, pp. 197, 198 et 206-210.
2. Sur l'hostilité des Maures contre les Turcs, V. *ibidem*, p. 183 et note 2.
3. *Sic*. Le sens demanderait plutôt *no*.
4. Il ne peut s'agir que de Moulay Ismaïl, fils de Moulay Abd el-Malek. V. p. 49, n. 5.

which, accordinge as men tell me, are in such sorte as, yf those within hit be loyall, they wilbe verie harde to be gotten.

Those agrementes which Abd el-Melec had made with the King of Castilla, this Emperour doth still embrace and kepe; and beinge in feare of the Turke, dareth not to breake with him, and yet will not delyver over Larache unto him[1]; but after yt ys made stronge, as men say yt ys alredie, he pretendeth to entertaine by much wisdome and circumspection, in despite of Achitoca[2].

Hassan Baxa, bye meanes of his sonne-in-lawe, will doe those offices which your Matie wisheth with the Turke; yet likewize, as God knoweth, he hath intelligence with this Emperor. But, with the sonne-in-lawe[3], I have attempted to doe (with many ownces) that which I did once move your Matie of bye writinge. He[4] would that your Matie should sende to worke the Xarifez that be in Portingall[5]; and the Baxa to this purpose keepeth one of his men in this Court, which was here when I came hither. Therefore, yf your Matie exspect any service from the said Baxa, yt behoveth yow that yow be pleased to deall with him with cunninge and circumspection.

It falleth not within the compasse of my understandinge what this Emperour will doe with Don Christopher. And soe saieth this Baxa that he will committ some villanye, or will helpe King Phillip ageinst the Turke, when yt shalbe nedefull, for *in eadem navigant nave*. And yf the Turke once put fote in Barbaria (which God forbidd!), all Spaine shall finde an evill cominge of him into hit.

The lettre of the Turke unto this Emperour[6], wherein he may incite him to accomplishe that which he promised to your Matie and the Quene (kepinge yt for his securitie as a juell of greete estimacion), I suppose and beleve yt may be of much profit, especiallie

---

1. V. 1re Série, Angleterre, t. I, p. 164, note 1, et page 536.
2. Nom impossible à identifier. Le traducteur de cette lettre, dont l'original était en portugais, l'a sans doute mal transcrit.
3. Moulay Ismaïl. — Avant de se rendre au Maroc en 1586, Mathias Becudo avait résidé à Constantinople pour D. Antonio.
4. V. 1re Série, France, t. II, p. 124 et n. 2.
4. *He*, Hassan-Pacha.
5. Sur ces chérifs, V. 1re Série, Angleterre, t. I, p. 534, note 2.
6. V. *supra*, Doc. XI, p. 40, la lettre d'Élisabeth au Grand Seigneur sollicitant ce dernier d'écrire au Chérif en faveur du prétendant D. Antonio.

yf yt come written in such forme as ys requisit. One the other side, yf he require Don Christopher[1], that cannot at any tyme lyke me, except that your Matie be verie well assured that the Turke will putt yow in Portugall; a thinge wherein your Matie most premeditat many tymes, and verie effectuallie consult with your freendes. For besides that this Emperour happelie will not doe that which the Turke shall require of him (as I am of opinion he will not), your Matie shall be in such sorte discovered, as yow shall not easelie defende that which men will saye, that your Matie, to atchieve your enterprise, was of consent and agrement with the Turke; for yt may be beleved that the Turke would not enter into soe difficult affaires without licence and privitie of your Matie.

And when the Turke should require this, and that this Emperour alone will not deall therein for his honor and reputacion, he must doe more then two thinges therein; that when yt shall be for the benefitt and honor of your Matie, yt shalbe well; but when the Turke should not imploye his meaninge for us, then shall your Matie be deprived of all benefitt one the Turkes behalfe, and with this Emperour he will dissolve the frendship which he, accordinge to his speches, desireth to conserve with your Matie. For the Turke ys also a Mahumetaine, and for that cause your Matie owght to deall with him verie circomspectlie and cautelouslie.

Don Christopher shall not be soe well in the court of the Great Turke as he ys in this. And therein let your Matie beleve me: the Turke ys farre of, this Emperour ys a neyghbour. It will cost your Matie much to have Don Cristopher ageine, yf the Great Turke had him once in his power. And yf your Matie have any thinge to doe with him, let yt be passed bye apparaunt and cleere contractes; and God graunt that may suffice and serve the tourne, and that one daye yt cost yow not Ormus[2], yf yow will have your sonne, *meliore fortuna dignus*.

Commannde that I may write your Matie my opinion concerninge this matter; this which I doe, and that litle which I write ys that which I understand, and wherof your Matie, with your

---

1. V. *supra*, p. 28, note 3.
2. *Ormus*, l'île d'Ormuz, à l'entrée du golfe Persique. Les Portugais l'occupaient depuis 1515.

clere and singuler judgment, maye drawe foorth matter that concerneth your service, proffit and honor.

Your Matie saieth in the lettre which yow wrote me, that yow were dispatchinge of Francisco Caldeyra[1] for Constantinoble, and I hard say yesterday that Manoell de Brito[2] should report that he should come hither bye the waye of Levante.

Yf he come, I praye God he enter with a better foate then he did when he came from the westwarde; for, straythwaies as he arrived at Safia, with his banners displayed, he said he brought lettres of your Maties and of the Quenes to the Emperour; and yt had sufficed for him to have said he was your Maties servant, and that he came bye your commaundement to visit Don Christopher your sonne. The Alcayde sent advise hereof to the Emperour. And soe sone as he[3] was come, he[4] commaunded one to come aske for the lettres. And because as then I was not resolved to delyver them, I sent him worde that Francisco Caldeyra came to noe other purpose then to see howe Don Christopher fared; which he woold not beleve. And for this cause, and two other matters I did ageinst his lykinge, he cannot loke plesantlie one me. I have also amended other matters that Caldeyra did speake at Tweltyee[5] in Safia, which may doe some hurt unto your Maties service.

This ys for no other purpose but that your Matie might have regard that, yf happelie yow send hither any man, which by nature ys of light behaviour and open mouthed, he may be sent better bridled.

I take yt for a great deall surer that the lettres which your Matie sendeth hither may be sent by meanes of some merchantes which have theire factors here, then bye a man of purpose. For, besides the avoydinge of the bruites that arise when they come into Safia (because all are accompted embassadors), your Matie shall excuse the alcayde of that place from writinge, which ys a miserable

---

1. Sur ce personnage, V. *supra*, p. 41, notes 1 et 2.
2. Ce personnage faisait partie de la suite de D. Christophe au Maroc et remplissait auprès de ce jeune prince les fonctions de grand chambellan. V. *1re Série*, France, t. II, p. 168.
3. *He*, Francisco Caldeira.
4. *He*, Moulay Ahmed.
5. *Tweltyee*, Toletoli, caïd de Safi. V. *1re Série*, Pays-Bas, t. III, p. 274 et n. 5, et *passim*.

captive of his Kinge; and further, yow shall not oppresse the howse of Don Christover with these cariers of letters. For he which came last, whoe as they saye came to doe this service to your Matie of his owne purse, came to Safia indebted, which Don Christopher caused to be paid; and notwithstandinge all the honor and reward that he gave him, he retourned discontented.

I thanke your Matie for the good hope yow putt me in, that yow may doe much, althoughe all should fayll that this Emperour hath promised. As yet he hath not called for me, I doe not meane to impart any of those advises unto him, which your Matie sent me of Constantinoble, bycause he shall not thinke yt to be your invencion[1]. Neyther yet will I speake of the enterprise here, yf he speake not to me therof[2]; for as your Matie sayeth, there ys noe cause to dispaire of our cause of Portugall.

The newes of Fraunce were here much rejoysed at bye the Frenchmen, which had receyved the lyke bye another way. They certified Don Francisco da Costa[3] of the same newes[4].

The said da Costa died iij dayes past; nowe shall he be neyther Earle nor Vicerey, as he exspected, in this lyfe. The Kinge of Castilla lost a good servaunt in this Court, and we have one grete enemye lesse in the same. He died, as I saye, sodenlye, and left not his thinges soe well disposed of as was exspected in an ould man, discreet and grave, as they saye he was. He willed himselfe to be

1. Il faut entendre que Becudo s'abstiendra de communiquer au Chérif les nouvelles que D. Antonio a reçues de Constantinople, parce que Moulay Ahmed les croirait inventées par le prétendant, ce que Becudo veut éviter.

2. L'entreprise à laquelle Becudo fait ici allusion est sans doute la même dont il est question ci-dessus (p. 33) dans le *Mémoire sur les affaires de Portugal*. On a vu supra, p. 52, qu'elle consistait à faire restaurer D. Antonio en Portugal avec l'aide des Turcs. Ce passage de la lettre de Becudo fait supposer que le prétendant avait obtenu du Grand Seigneur des assurances encourageantes. Ces assurances auraient pu impressionner Moulay Ahmed et le disposer

à tenir ses engagements, s'il n'y avait pas eu lieu de craindre, pensait Becudo, qu'il ne les crût imaginées à dessein pour vaincre ses hésitations.

3. Sur ce personnage, V. *supra*, p. 7, note 4.

4. Au moment où Paris, menacé par la famine, allait être contraint de se rendre à Henri IV, le duc de Parme avait réussi à s'emparer de Lagny et à ravitailler la capitale (septembre 1590); mais des dissentiments s'élevèrent entre lui et les chefs de la Ligue, et, au mois de novembre, il se retirait en Flandre, harcelé par les troupes du roi de France. C'est, sans doute, la nouvelle de cette retraite qui était parvenue au Maroc.

buried in the house of a Jewe, where he lodged, havinge bye Godes goodnes a hallowed churchyarde in this lande. The Lorde have memorie of his soule, for death ys noe revenge.

I beseach your Matie of your greatnes and royall humanitie to tolleratt and perdon the necligences and faultes of my lettres that yow may finde in them, and call to remembraunce that I have not had one onlye daye of helth since I came into this contrie.

Our Lorde have your royall person, etc.

From Morocas, the 18th of Aprill 1591.

Matias Biquudo.

Public Record Office. — State Papers, Foreign, Portugal, vol. II. — Traduction officielle[1].

---

[1]. L'original de cette lettre, écrite en portugais par Becudo, a dû rester entre les mains de D. Antonio, le gouvernement anglais ne gardant qu'une traduction.

XV

AFFAIRE ABRAHAM REYNOLDS CONTRE WILLIAM RESOULD

(Extrait)

21-27 avril [n. st. 1er-7 mai] 1591.

Au dos, alia manu: xxi° die Aprilis, anno regni regine Elizabethe, etc., xxxiii°. — Defendens vocetur per nuntium camere. — Abraham Raynold, Esquire, complainant; William Resolde, defendant.

Conclusions d'Abraham Reynolds.

Le demandeur, qui a été employé pendant quatre ans au Maroc comme facteur de William Resould, réclame à ce dernier une somme de cent quarante-quatre livres, montant de diverses provisions à lui dues et de taxes par lui acquittées, qu'il a omis de porter en compte. — Il demande que William Resould soit cité devant la Cour des Requêtes.

To the Queenes most excellent Matie,

Humbly sheweth unto your Matie your humble, true and obeydient subject Abraham Reynoldes, of the cyttie of London, that:

Wheras your said subject, having ben employed by the space of eight yeares now past or therabouts, in trade and trafficke of marchandize in the kingdom of Barbery, in the parties beyond seas, for and on the behalf of certayne your Highnes subjects, being marchantts of your Maties cittye of London, and having carefully allwayes for the most parte attended the same trade in the said realme and domynions of Barbery, during which tyme of your subjects aboade thear, in those partes, that is to saye about fower yeares now last past, your subject, being earnestlie solycyted, prayed and entreated by and on the beehalf of one William Resould, cittyzen and grocer of London and a marchant trading into those parties, that the same your subject would (amonge other his buysines for other marchantts) deale as factor and agent for him, the same William Resould, in trade of marchandize for those parts, promising and protesting most faythfullie and assuredlye that your subjects paynes and travell therin to bee taken should be fullye by him, the said William Resould, satysfied, recompenced and allowed, according to the course of the place, and to the order and allowance which other marchants trafficking ther and elcewhere doe observe and hold towardes their factors and dealers.

Upon the assured hope of the true and unfayned accomplyshmentt of which sayd fayre wourdes and promises, your said subject, taking upon him the burthen, care and chardge of the buysynes and dealings of the said William Resould in marchandize, in the said partes of Barbery, did deale as factor and agent for him, the same William Resould, by and during the space of fower yeares or therabouts now past, and, as occasion served, did, to the best of his skyll and knowledge, not onlye utter and putt awaye to the use of William Resould such commodities and wares as were sent thither by the said William Resould, but also did from thence retorne and send unto the said William Resould, into your Highnes said realme of England, divers other comodyties and other marchandize out of those partes, such as either by the direccon of the said William Resould weare appoynted to be conveyed, or wear lykely to bee then most vendable and saleable in England.

During the tyme of which your subjects dealings for him, the said William Resould, as aforesaid, your said subject, at dyvers and sondrie tymes, by oversighte (happening chieflie through the multytude of your subjects affayres and buysynes), did send over to England, unto the said William Resould, dyvers parcells of wares and marchandize, without taking any allowance or defalcacon, either of any chardges for shipping and otherwyse, or of provizion for himself, a matter there and elcewheare usuall amonge marchants, and consysting of an allowance after the rate of v^{li} in the c^{li}, termed by the name of provizion, growing dewe for all suche goodes and wares as are either uttered or sold beyond sea by factor, or by any factor sent or transported; the most parte of which said chardges your subject was forced to disburse out of his owne monye, in customs and duties arysing in those regions and payable for the same goodes so sent unto the said William Resould or uttered for him by factor, as aforesaid.

By meanes wherof, and other just true and playne reckonings, it appeareth that the said William Resould is indebtted unto your subjecte, *de claro*, by waye of surplusage of accompt, more then ever your subjecte receaved or is accompttable for unto the said William Resould, in the some of one hundreth forty fower poundes and od monie of lawfull Englishe monye.

Now so it is, most gracious Soveraigne, that your said poore subjecte, having now retorned into England from Barbery, and having made up and fynished his said accomptt..... and having reduced the same into writing; wich reckoning he, your said subjecte, hath tendred and offred unto the said William Resould; ... yett that to paye, hee the same William Resould, hitherto hath refused and doth yet refuse and denye, somtymes denying ther is not dewe unto your subjecte so muche as bee requireth, otherwhiles offering to make paymentt unto your subject, in some comodytie not now vendable, of the greatest parte of the said debtt and surplusage of accomptt.....

In tender consyderacion whereof..... and for that also, by course of common lawe, your subject hath not any dewe remedye either for the said overplus and surplusage by him dysbursed, or of the residue of suche reasonable allowances as of right are answerable unto your said subject, in respect of his said factorshipp, but remaynelh chieflie to be releyved by your most gracious favor and clemencye, usually extended in cases of lyke extremitie.

Maye it therefore please your Highnes, the premises tenderly consydered, to geve order that one of your Highnes messengers, attending your Highnes honorable Courte of Requests, at Westminster, bee sent unto the said William Resould, commanding him forthwith to appeare before your Highnes, in the same honorable Courte of Requests, at Westminster, to answer to the premisses and to stand to suche order and dyreccion therein as to your Highnes honorable Counsell of that Courte shalbee thought in equytie and good conscyence most fytt and convenient.

And your said subject shall, according to his most bounden dutye, daylie pray to God for your Highnes longe lyffe in health, most prosperouslie and longe to raigne over us.

Signé : Wil. Wynter.

Réplique de William Resould.

William Resould, défendeur, expose qu'il a fait au demandeur et à son frère, lesquels étaient alors au Maroc comme facteurs des marchands Henry Colthirst et Simon Lawrence, des envois de draps, soieries et safran pour une valeur de sept cent quatre-vingt-six livres environ. — Les frères Reynolds, en échange, lui ont retourné, après un fort long temps, de l'indigo, produit peu recherché, et, plus tard encore, des marchandises dont la plupart lui ont été comptées à des prix si élevés qu'il ne peut les vendre sans de très fortes pertes. — Le défendeur ajoute qu'il n'est perçu au profit du Chérif qu'un droit d'un dixième sur les marchandises importées ; ce droit est acquitté en nature. — Quant aux taxes à l'exportation, elles sont insignifiantes. — William Resould demande une indemnité pour le préjudice qui lui a été causé.

The answere of William Resold, deffendant, to the bill of complaynt of Abraham Raynoldes, complaynant, xxvii° die Aprilis, anno regni regine Elizabethe xxxiii^{tio}.

The said deffendant sayethe that the saide bill of complaynte ..... is altogether untrew.....

The said deffendant, for trew and playne declaration of the trughte, sayethe that, aboute the tyme specified in the saide bill of complaynte, the saide complaynant beinge beyonde the seas in the kingdome of Barberye, as servaunte and apprentize unto one Mr Henry Colthurste[1], of London, merchaunte, whoese servaunte and apprentize the saide complaynant, as this deffendant thinkes, steell is, which said Colthurste the saide deffendant had also served as

---

1. V. 1re Série, Angleterre, t. I, p. 469, note 11.

any apprentize; and the saide deffendant, after his yeares of apprentesshippe or service expired, and then remayninge in the house of the saide Mr Colthurste, did, withe the previtie, good allowance, lysence and leave of the saide Mr Colthurste, firste sende over, unto the countrie of Barbery menconed in the bill, certen goodes or merchandize to this complaynant and his brother Richard Raynoldes, who also, at that tyme, served one Symon Lawrence[1], whoe was partner with the saide Colthurste and others in that trade of merchaundize.

And afterwardes, this deffendant, beinge departed owt of his saide masters service, did, for a smale tyme after, send over and transporte other lyke merchaundize to the saide complaynant and his saide brother, or one of them; which said merchaundize, by the order of his the complaynants said brother, as this deffendant hath harde, did come altogeather, or the moste parte thereof, to the order, government and disposicion of the complaynant, for that, as the deffendant hathe harde, the complainants saide brother did fully leave the same with the complainant, at his cominge from the said place; the totall of all which merchaundize, so by the said deffendant sent over unto the complaynant and his saide brother, was, to the remembraunce of this deffendant, the some of 786^li or thereaboutes; all which said wares and merchandize, amountinge to the saide some of 786^li or thereaboutes, weare by this deffendant sent over in forme aforesaid, parte to the complaynant, and parte to his sayde brother, about the tyme sett downe in the complaynants bill, but within a great deale lease tyme then fower yeares.

And this deffendant further sayethe that hee, this deffendant, having trusted the saide complaynant and his saide brother with the said wares and merchandize amountinge to the some of 786^li as aforesaide, being all Englishe cloathes, and some smale quantytie of saffarne and silkes, the said complaynant, nor his sayde brother, made noe retorne therof by a longe space, and then made retorn but for a smale parte therof, in aneale[2], being a badde and unvendeable comoditie.

---

1. V. 1re Série, Angleterre, t. I, p. 469 et note 15.

2. Aneale, anil, nom arabe de l'indigo, V. ibidem, p. 187.

And the said deffendant further sayethe that he had not a full retorne of his wares and comodities untell midsommer last past or theraboutes; which this deffendant sayethe hathe bine all in bad commodities, and that the moste parte thereof are at suche unreasonable rates and highe prices, suche as, for the moost parte of them, the saide deffendant cannot make any sale thereof to this present daye; the complaynant having rated the aneal sent over betwine xii^{li} and xv^{li} the hunderedweighte, wheras of the best therof the said deffendant cannott make salle for vi^{li} the hunderedwheighte, to the great hinderaunce, lose and almoste the utter undouinge of the deffendant.....

And as towchinge any payment of costomes for the said wares so sent over by the deffendant, as aforesaide, into the said cuntrye of Barbery, this deffendant sayethe that ther is no other costome ther deu unto the Kinge but the xth parte of suche comoditie as so is sent over, which the King takethe of the same wares, and not in mony; and this deffendant saiethe that, for the wares which are sent owt of the saide cuntrye of Barbery, that very littell or smale customes or duities are aunswered for the same, and that the said complaynant had allwayes monye in his hand of the wares he sent him to aunsweare all customes and dewties.....

From whiche matters this defendant is reddy to be averr and to prove, as this honorable Courte shall awarde, and prayethe to be dismissed with his reasonable costes and charges in that behaulfe wrongfully susteyned, etc.

Signé: Rudhale.

Public Record Office. — Court of Requests, Proceedings, Bundle 75, n° 30. — Original.

XVI

REQUÊTE DE O. STYLE, N. STYLE ET S. LAWRENCE

(Extrait)

Ils demandent qu'on les admette parmi les membres de la Compagnie du Levant. — Leurs trois principaux commerces étaient avec l'Espagne, la France et le Maroc. — Ils sont écartés par les guerres des deux premiers pays et le commerce au Maroc est en telle décadence qu'il ne vaut pas la peine d'être continué.

18 [n. st. 28] juin 1591.

Au dos : 18 Junii 1591. — Reasons whye Olyver Style, Nicolas Style and Symon Lawrence[1], marchantes adventurers of London, maye be admitted into the fredome of trafyke to the Levante seas[2].

Reasons whye (yf yt soe seme good unto your Lordship) Olyver Style, Nycolas Style and Symon Lawrence, theyr partener, maye be admitted into the fredome of trafyke to the Levante seas.

. . . .

Forthlye, for that, theyre chyefe trade heretofore havinge bynne into France, Spayne, and Barberye, the two firste are nowe by reason of trobles cut of, and the thirde growne soe badde (as they saye) that yt is not worthe the foloinge.

. . . .

Public Record Office. — State Papers, Domestic, Elizabeth, vol. CCXXXIX, n° 41. — Original.

---

1. Ces trois marchands étaient membres de la *Barbary Company*. Sur le présent Document, V. *1re Série*, Angleterre, t. I, p. 453, Introduction critique.

2. Il était alors question de reconstituer, en les fusionnant, la Compagnie de Venise et la Compagnie du Levant, dont les privilèges étaient venus à expiration. C'est ce qui explique la requête d'Oliver Style et de ses associés.

XVII

REQUÊTE DES MARCHANDS TRAFIQUANT DANS LE LEVANT

(Extrait)

Ils s'élèvent contre toute admission de nouveaux marchands dans leur Compagnie. — Un trop grand nombre d'adhérents ruinerait leur commerce, comme il a ruiné récemment celui du Maroc, où l'affluence des draps anglais en a causé la dépréciation, tandis que les sucres de qualité inférieure y atteignaient des prix élevés.

[Juillet 1591][1].

Au dos, alia manu: The Turquie and Venice merchantes[2]. — That in consideration of the great charges they have been at in the maintenance of the sayd trade with their agent etc., theire maie not anie other be inserted into the newe patentes[3].

To the right honorable the Lord High Treasorer of Englonde.

Right Honorable,

The marchantes tradinge Turkey and Venice do most humble beseech the same to have consideracion of the grete charge they have susteyned in discoveringe and upholdinge the said trades.

. . . .

Wherefore if your suppliantes (who allredie are far to many for those trades) shold receve the discoragement offred through the

---

1. La présente requête dut suivre de près le mémoire d'Oliver Style et consorts, contre lequel elle constitue une protestation.
2. V. *supra*, p. 62, note 2.
3. Entendez : les nouvelles lettres patentes qui devaient rétablir la Compagnie du Levant et qui furent, en effet, expédiées à la date du 7 janvier 1592 [n. st. 17 janvier 1593] (*ap.* Hakluyt, éd. 1598-1600, t. II, 2ᵉ partie, pp. 295-303).

sutes of some persones[1] whose strange humors are never satisfied, havinge no regard howe weightie a matter it is not to overchardge a trade, it muste nedes followe in those trades and with your suppliantes as of late it hath don with the trade of Barbary and those marchauntes, which some persons of like disposition to theise, enforcinge into that trade and so overleyinge the same, have broughte our Inglish cloth there into contempte, and advanced their drosse and base sugers to hie price, and so not onlie spoyled and overthrowen that trade, but undon theymselves and many an honest marchant olde traders, whose livinge before it was[2].

. . . .

And accordinge to our bounden dueties wee will daiely pray for the prosperous estate of your Honor longe to continew.

Signé : Edward Osborne. — George Barne. — John Harte. — William Mashur. — J^{no} Spencer. — Nicholas Mosley[3]. — Thomas Cordell. — Henry Andersey. — Henrye Farrington[4]. — Leonard Pointz. — Richard Martyn. — William Garway. — Edward Holmden[5]. — Henry Hewett. — Roger Clarke. — Pawll Bayninge. — Andrew Bayninge. — Richard Staper[6]. — Robart Sadlar.

Public Record Office. — State Papers, Domestic, Elizabeth, vol. CCXXXIX, n° 44. — Original.

1. Allusion au mémoire d'Oliver Style.
2. Malgré l'opposition qui était faite à leur demande, Oliver Style, Nicholas Style et Simon Lawrence eurent gain de cause, comme le prouve l'insertion de leurs noms dans les lettres patentes du 17 janvier 1593.

V. *supra*, p. 63, note 3.
3. V. *infra*, p. 201 et note 1.
4. V. *1re Série*, Angleterre, t. I, p. 467 et note 2 ; p. 469 et note 19.
5. V. *ibidem*, p. 469, note 12.
6. V. *ibidem*, p. 469, note 5.

XVIII

NOTE DE RICHARD TOMSON[1]

Nouvelles extraites par Richard Tomson de diverses lettres du Maroc. — Mathias Becudo, dans une lettre du 18 avril adressée à D. Antonio, disculpe Edward Prynne d'une faute qui lui était imputée. — D. Christophe écrit, le 24 avril, que le caïd Djouder, commandant les troupes du Chérif au Soudan, a battu et tué trente mille indigènes, qu'il a pris Gago et envoyé au Maroc la tête de leur roi, qui fut montrée à l'ambassadeur turc. — D. Christophe ajoute que beaucoup supposent que cette nouvelle a été mise en circulation pour en imposer au dit ambassadeur, qui est parti le lendemain pour la Turquie. — Edward Prynne, dans sa lettre du 24 avril à Diego Botelho, annonce également cette défaite des noirs et la mort de D. Francisco da Costa. — Il écrit qu'on lui a remis une lettre du Lord Trésorier et prétend que cette lettre a été forgée par un certain Monox. Il attend le consentement de Botelho avant de dévoiler ce faux, attendu que Monox se fait passer pour un ambassadeur de D. Antonio.

1591.

In Mathias Biquudo's lettre of the 18th of Aprill 1591 to the Kinge[2], he seameth to entreat the Kinge to perdon the displeasure his Majestie had taken ageinst Edward Prin for a letter he wrote, addinge part of the faulte to Docter Lopes[3], that delyvered the same.

Don Cristoval, in his lettre of the 24 Aprill to Don Antonio, doth

---

1. Sur ce personnage, V. *infra*, p. 101, note 2.

2. Cette lettre n'a pas été retrouvée, de même que les autres qui sont analysées dans le présent document. Elle est différente de la lettre de Mathias Becudo à D. Antonio, qui a été publiée ci-dessus, Doc. XLV, p. 46.

3. Rodrigo Lopes, médecin juif originaire du Portugal. Installé en Angleterre depuis 1559, il devint, en 1586, premier médecin de la Reine. Impliqué dans un complot qui avait pour but d'empoisonner Élisabeth et D. Antonio, il fut exécuté le 7 juin 1594. Sur ce personnage, V. Hume, *Treason and Plot...*, 1901, pp. 115-152.

write of an overthrowe gyven by the alcayde Saudar[1], who had the leadinge of the Kinges forces into Ginea, ageinst 30 thowsand Alarves, which had joyned themselves together, under cooler to come serve the Kinge, but pretended treason unto him; which cominge to the knowlege of the alcayde, he sett uppon them and slewe them all[2]. And the Kinge of these Alarbes, beinge in a citie called Gago, yt was yelded, and the Kinges hed sent into Barberie, and shewed unto the Turkes embassador[3]. Yet in the ende of the

1. Le pacha Djouder, l'un des principaux personnages de la cour de Moulay Ahmed el-Mansour et chef, pour un temps, du corps des Andalous. Sur son passé, El-Oufrâni dit simplement qu'il était un affranchi de Moulay Ahmed, mais Es-Sadi raconte qu'à son avènement, Moulay Ahmed, voulant se venger des caïds de son frère, les fit mettre à mort, que seuls furent épargnés les caïds Djouder et Mohammed Tâba, que le premier fut interné dans une maison de campagne, où il resta douze ans et dont il fut tiré pour prendre le commandement de l'expédition du Soudan. Il partit de Merrakech au mois d'octobre 1590, battit les troupes du prince soudanais Askia-Ishâq ben Askia-Daoud et s'empara de Gago (Gao), puis de Tombouctou (V. notes suivantes). Moulay Ahmed, indigné qu'il eût accueilli et transmis à Merrakech les ouvertures de paix d'Askia-Ishâq, lui retira le haut commandement de ses troupes et le confia au caïd Mahmoud ben Zergoun, qui arriva à Tombouctou, selon Es-Sadi, au mois d'août 1591. Djouder demeura au Soudan sous les ordres de ce caïd. Lorsque Mahmoud ben Zergoun, qui, tombé en disgrâce, avait péri dans une rencontre avec des Soudanais, fut remplacé par le caïd El-Mansour ben Abd er-Rahman (mars 1595), Moulay Ahmed partagea l'autorité entre ce dernier, qui reçut le commandement des troupes, et Djouder, à qui fut laissée l'administration du pays. El-Mansour ben Abd er-Rahman, mort le 9 novembre 1596, eut pour successeur le caïd Mohammed Tâba, qui mourut, à son tour, le 11 mai 1598. On prétendit que l'un et l'autre avaient été empoisonnés par Djouder. Rappelé à Merrakech par Moulay Ahmed, Djouder quitta le Soudan le 27 Ramadan 1007 [23 avril 1599]. Lorsque Moulay Ahmed, ayant marché sur Fez contre son fils révolté Moulay ech-Cheikh, se fut emparé de lui, il chargea Djouder de le conduire à Meknès et de l'y mettre en prison. Moulay Ahmed étant mort peu après (août 1603), Djouder amena Moulay ech-Cheikh à Merrakech et le remit dans les mains de Moulay Abou Farès, dont il prit le parti dans les luttes qui éclatèrent entre les fils de Moulay Ahmed. Il fut mis à mort (décembre 1606) par Moulay Abdallah, fils de Moulay ech-Cheikh. V. infra, pp. 340, 341 et 363 (Relation de Ro. C.); 1re Série, Pays-Bas, t. I, pp. 82-84, 212; Es-Sadi, passim; El-Oufrâni, pp. 163-168, 196, 198, 292, 296, 310; H. de Castries, La conquête du Soudan par El-Mansour, dans Hespéris. 1923.

2. Cette bataille eut lieu à Toundibi le 17 Djoumada I 999 (13 mars 1591). Es-Sadi, trad. Houdas, p. 219. Celui-ci, qui a lu par erreur Djoumada II, donne l'équivalence du 12 avril. Un événement ayant eu lieu au Soudan à cette dernière date, n'aurait pu être connu à Merrakech le 24 avril.

3. Ce dernier fait est erroné. Après la perte de sa capitale, Askia-Ishâq se retira sur la rive droite du Niger, et ce ne fut qu'en Djoumada II 1000 (15 mars-12 avril 1592) qu'il fut tué par les gens du Gourma. Es-Sadi, p. 231.

lettre, he saieth that many doe ymagin yt to be but a fame spredd abroade, to advaunce the Kinges might and successe in the warres to the Turkes embassadour, who departed for Turkye the day followinge; hopinge, yf yt be trewe, the Kinge will the better procede in the ayde of Don Antonio.

Edward Prin, in his lettre of the 24 Aprill 1591 to Diego Botello[1], doth write the lyke newes of the overthrowe of the Alarves, with the lyke conclusion that Don Cristovall doth. He writeth of the death of Don Francisco de Costa, embassadour for Kinge Phillip.

He writeth that one Robert gave him a lettre of the Lord Tresourer, which he affirmeth to be counterfeyted by Monox[2]; and writeth to Botello howe yt ys as daungerous a matter to conceall hit, as to doe yt; and yet deferreth the manefestacion therof, untill he hath Bottellos consent, bycause Monox taketh uppon him the name of Don Antonio servaunt, and to be his embassador.

He writeth also that he understandeth that John Rale ys a partaker in the counterfeytinge of the lettres and pasportes.

All the rest of the lettres that I have read conteyne noe matter of moment, but ordenarie congratulacions from frende to frende.

Signé: Per Ric. Tomson.

Public Record Office. — *State Papers, Foreign, Portugal, vol. II.* — *Original.*

1. Sur ce personnage, V. *supra*, p. 47, note 1.
2. On ignore qui étaient ce Monox et son complice John Rale mentionné quelques lignes plus bas. On trouve un Duarte Monox, riche marchand anglais, arrêté aux Canaries, en vertu d'une décision du tribunal de l'Inquisition du 11 septembre 1604. *British Museum, Egerton Mss., vol. 1512, ff. 52-62.*

XIX

LETTRE DE MOULAY AHMED EL-MANSOUR A ÉLISABETH

La Reine lui a demandé de renvoyer D. Christophe en Angleterre et lui a reproché d'avoir tardé à lui écrire. — Moulay Ahmed allègue comme excuse qu'il était absorbé par les préparatifs de l'expédition du Soudan ; ce retard était, d'ailleurs, sans inconvénient, puisque l'ambassadeur anglais qui devait emporter la lettre prolongeait son séjour au Maroc. — Celui-ci va partir avec la réponse du Chérif. — Moulay Ahmed n'oublie pas les promesses qu'il a faites à D. Antonio et se déclare prêt à les tenir, si la Reine vient elle-même en aide à ce prince. — Il compte en conférer avec son fils, Moulay ech-Cheikh, et dépêcher ensuite un serviteur à la cour d'Angleterre.

12 mars 1591 [n. st. 22 mars 1592].

En tête: The King of Moroccos letter englished. — 12 Martii 1591.

In the name of God the gever of all godlines.

The forme of this letter in the beginning, in the title or direction of the Emperor Mullay Hamed, Xarife, and that of the Queen of England, wee doo not put here, bycause we cannot pronounce them in the Portugall tongue[1], remitting to our letter, which goeth with this[2].

---

1. L'original arabe des lettres chérifiennes aux princes chrétiens était souvent, sinon même régulièrement, accompagné d'une traduction officielle en espagnol ou en portugais, faite par un interprète de la Cour. Cf. t. I, Doc. XLI, CLXXXII, pp. 101 et note 1, et 498. On a vu ci-dessus (p. 24) cet interprète s'abstenir de traduire la suscription, à cause des difficultés qu'il éprouvait à la mettre en espagnol. Le cas est le même ici pour la version portugaise sur laquelle a été faite la présente traduction anglaise.

2. L'interprète, qui parle au nom du Chérif, déclare s'en rapporter pour la suscription de la lettre au texte arabe. Celui-ci n'a pas été retrouvé.

From this our royall courte of Morocos, we write you that we remayne in prosperitie, and very much exalted — praise be geven to God!

Your loving and estemed letter[1] to us was geven by your servant the Captaine[2], the which was receaved of us with much honor and frendship. Werein we see what you write concerning the cause of Don Antonio, King of Portugall; in the which you demaunde that, seing we will not send the money that was promised to be lente, ther is noe cause whie his sonne should be detayned, requiring his delivery as sent hither by you unto this our royall courte. And also we understand by your letter you fynde yourselfe greeved for that you were not answered presentlie. Assure yourself that all your thynges, as well smalle as great, we receave them with much pleasure and contentment; take this for most certaine.

And if you will knowe the cause whie we did not answer the said letter, at that instant, it was bycause of theis kingdoms of Gyney and Tureg, which we invaded[3] — God be praized! — for as they are both great and far of, we have the more need to look unto them; and also those kingdoms wille be a great helpe to the other cause. Therefore you cannot thinck much that your letter was not answered presently. And the other cause was because he that brought it staid here[4], wherefore you have the lesse to be greeved. Now he goeth, he carrieth his answere; for we had it allwaies in memorie, and we stand allwaies in that which we have promised. If you give the ayde that is convenient and doe content us, then we knowe we shall goe through with it. For if we should joyne and not be accomplished withall, it will not agree well.

Wherupon we determyn to meete with our sonne, the prince Mullay Xeque, and others, to confer therupon; and at the retorning back, we intend to send a servant of ours with the ambassador to your courte. And if it chance that, at that tyme, you cannot

---

1. La lettre d'Élisabeth à Moulay Ahmed du 20 [n. st. 30] août 1590. V. supra, Doc. X, p. 34, et cf. p. 39, note 1. Cette lettre n'avait été remise au Chérif qu'en avril 1591. V. supra, p. 48.

2. Edward Prynne.

3. Sur l'expédition du Soudan, V. supra, p. 66 et notes 1, 2 et 3.

4. Ce fut Edward Prynne, qualifié plus loin « the Ambassador », qui remit au Chérif la lettre de la Reine. Prynne était au Maroc depuis le 2 [n. st. 12] avril 1590.

give the ayde, then send us wourde; the which we commend unto you, as we put our trust in you[1].

Dated at our royall courte, the end of the monthe.

Public Record Office. — State Papers, Foreign, Royal Letters, vol. II, n° 20. — Traduction

British Museum. — Cotton Mss., Nero B. VIII, f. 66[2]. *— Traduction.*

1. Dans la présente lettre du 22 mars 1592, le retour de D. Christophe en Angleterre, bien que demandé par la Reine, n'est pas encore envisagé comme prochain. Cependant il est probable qu'il quitta le Maroc en 1592, avant l'arrivée d'un chaouch envoyé par le Grand Seigneur pour exiger que le jeune prince fût conduit à Constantinople. V. *1re Série*, France, t. II, pp. 200-201. Le 31 mars 1593, D. Christophe est à Londres, où il a une maison. *Calendar of State Papers, Domestic, 1591-1594*. Il y a lieu de croire que ce fut en vue de négocier le départ de D. Christophe et pour le ramener en Angleterre qu'un vaisseau anglais, le « Saint-Gabriel », se rendit, dans la seconde quinzaine de juillet 1592, à Santa-Cruz-du-Cap-de-Guir, y resta douze jours et y débarqua un « ambassadeur » anglais, nommé « maestre Harbas ». Ce navire étant passé au retour par les Canaries, une chaloupe, à bord de laquelle se trouvaient plusieurs matelots et soldats, fut séparée par la tempête et obligée de se rendre prisonnière à Ténériffe. Le principal des Anglais, un soldat nommé Hugh Wingfield, fut dénoncé à l'Inquisition et arrêté. Il parvint à s'échapper. C'est par les pièces de son procès que nous connaissons cette ambassade. *Archives of the Spanish Inquisition in the Canaries, vol. VII, 2nd Series, ff. 167. 175, 218 v°*. Extrait publié, d'après les originaux, appartenant à la collection du marquis de Bute, par L. DE ALBERTI et A. B. WALLIS CHAPMAN, *English Merchants and the Spanish Inquisition in the Canaries*, Londres (Royal Historical Society), 1912, 8°, pp. 109-110, 114 et 116-117. Il n'a pas été possible d'identifier « maestre Harbas », et il n'a été trouvé aucun document dans les archives d'Angleterre sur le retour de D. Christophe.

2. Cette lettre est publiée dans RYMER's *Fœdera*, XVI, 155, d'après ce dernier texte.

XX

REQUÊTE DE ROBERT ZINZAN A ÉLISABETH

Robert Zinzan constate que les sucres raffinés en Angleterre proviennent presque tous du Brésil, de San-Thomé et du Maroc, qu'ils sont en poudre et, pour la plupart, très gâtés, qu'ils sont importés principalement par des étrangers, au grand préjudice des marchands anglais trafiquant au Maroc. — Les raffineurs les achètent à bas prix, les raffinent avec des substances malsaines et les vendent à gros bénéfices. — Ces mêmes raffineurs et divers autres marchands exportent d'Angleterre en pays étrangers de grandes quantités de sucre, raffiné et brut, ce qui produit une forte hausse de cette denrée dans le royaume. — Pour remédier à ces abus, Robert Zinzan propose que le raffinage, la vente et l'exportation du sucre ne puissent se faire sans l'autorisation d'un contrôleur et il prie la Reine de lui concéder par lettres patentes cet emploi.

3 [n. st. 13] juillet 1593 [1].

The reasons why the refyners of sugars shold be serveyed, that by meanes thereof the abuses myght be reformed.

Fyrst, of late yeres, the refynyng howses are increased from two to seaven, and the sugars which for the most parte they do refyne are Brazilia sugars, and St Tome sugars, and Barbary panneles [2], being all in powder and for the most parte very corrupte; which are brought in more by strangers and in strangers vessells then by Englyshe men, to the greate enrycheng of them and maynte-

---

1. Le présent Document est annexé à une lettre de même date, que Robert Zinzan adresse à Burghley pour le prier d'appuyer sa requête. *St. Pap., Dom., Eliz.,* vol. CCXLV, n° 48.

2. *Panneles,* terme vieilli (en français : pannelle) : sucre brun non purifié, inférieur à la moscouade.

naunce of their shippyng, and to the greate hyndrance of the Englyshe Barbary marchauntes¹ and decaye of the navygacion of thys realme.

Item, in refynyng of the sayd sugars, they do use dyvers compoundes, as egges greate store (whereby the pryses of them are raysed dearer in London more then of late yeres have ben), and also lyme, and other unwholsom compoundes; by meanes whereof they do reduce the sayd course and corrupte sugars, being in powder, which they do buy at lowe prises, into lose sugar, and do sell the same at hygh pryses, to their greate pryvate gaynes; which are not so wholsom for mans bodye as the same oughte to be, nor as Barbary sugars are, and therefore not fytt there shold be any other sugars refyned then such, as be whyte powder of sugar, which may well be refyned withoute any such compoundes.

For reformacion whereof may it please her Matie to prohybyt that no manner of whyte powder of sugar shalbe from henceforth refyned with any manner of compoundes, nor any of the sayd course corrupte sugars used or refyned, neyther yett after the refynyng thereof be putt to sale but such as to the surveyor thereof shalbe thoughte meet and wholsom for mans bodye, uppon such consyderacion for the surveyeng thereof, besydes the paynes and forfaytures as shalbe sett downe for the same.

Item, not only the sayd refyners, but also dyvers other marchauntes, do commenly transporte and carry oute of thys realme into forran contryes beyonde the seas greate quantyties, as well of the refyned sugars as of all sortes of other sugars, and with all the surropes of sugars called malasses, and other course sugars called panneles; by means whereof the pryses of sugar are greatly inhaunced, notwithstanding the greate quantytie that is brought in and refyned here, to the greate hyndrance of the commenweale, and her Matie receyving smale benefytt by the same.

For reformacion whereof, it may please her Matie to prohybytt that no sortes of sugar whatsoever, nor malasses, nor panneles shalbe from henceforth transported oute of any parte of her Maties domynyons, withoute specyall lycence of the sayd surveyor or

---

1. V. 1re Série, Angleterre, t. I, Introduction critique, p. 446.

hys offycers, uppon such paynes and forfaytures as shalbe thoughte meet for the same.

In consyderacion of all which premysses to be duly executed by the sayd surveyor, hys deputies, or assygnes, it may please her Matie to graunte the execucion thereof unto her servante Robert Zinzan, alias Alexander, by her Hyghnes letters patentz for the terme of .... [1] yeres, yelding and payeng yerely unto her Matie .... over and above all such dutyes and customes as have ben heretofore payed by waye of custome or otherwyse for the transportacion of sugars.

Public Record Office. — State Papers, Domestic, Elizabeth, vol. CCXLV, n° 48, 1. — Original.

1. En blanc dans le manuscrit.

XXI

MÉMOIRE DE RICHARD CARMERDEN

(Extrait)

Il formule ses raisons contre l'établissement d'une surveillance sur le raffinage du sucre. — On a faussement allégué la mauvaise qualité du sucre raffiné en Angleterre et les substances malsaines qui serviraient au raffinage. — Ce sucre est un produit pur, tel qu'il est extrait de la canne, et meilleur que celui qui est raffiné au Maroc. — Tout le sucre importé annuellement de San-Thomé et du Maroc en Angleterre, c'est-à-dire plus de mille tonnes, est destiné à y être raffiné.

12 [n. st. 22] juillet 1593.

Au dos, alia manu: 12 July 1593. — Reasons against the suite for survaie of sugar refined[1].

Reasons why the refining of sugers, paneles, malasses, etc., should be freely continued heere in London or elsewheere in her Maties realme of Englande without interruption or mollestacion.

Wheras it is imagined that refined suger is made of the refuse of suger brought from partes beyond the seas, and should be made with divers corrupte compoundes, as lyme, claye, egges, etc., and therfore should not be of the substance that Barbarye muthera, or other lose suger should be of, nether to be so holsome for mans bodye;

For answere wherof: refined suger is made of these compoundes,

---

1. Le présent Mémoire est une réplique à la précédente requête. — Sur la culture de la canne et sur le raffinage du sucre au Maroc, cf. 1re Série, Angleterre, t. I, Introduction, pp. v et vi; El-Oufrâni, Trad., p. 302.

viz. Brassil whit powder, Domingo suger, S¹ Thomas suger, Barberye broken suger, Brassil muskovathos, which hath all their substance as it came from the caine; as the best Barbery muthera, or any other suger hath very litle panneles, sometymes not all is used therein, and is mixte after the drose is taken from it.

It is certaine that no suger canne be made or his grocenes purged from hime without a lye, claye and eggs, though in very truth ther is not anye of these three remayneth therin, more then in the purest thinge that is made. True it is that Barberie suger is made with a lee made with ashes, and refined suger is made with a lee made with lyme, viz. a pecke of lyme is put into a cesterne of watter contayninge ii or iii tonnes, wher it setleth 12 houres till it be perfect cleare; then the saied watter is used with eges to drawe forth of the suger all his grocenes, beinge uppon a stronge fyre vii houres, the eges beinge turned to hardnes together with the granes of the suger; and strength of the watter are oftentymes scomed of in the tyme it boileth, so longe till it be turned from browne to whit as milke. Then is it strayned throughe a thicke brod clothe. Afterward, when it is could, whatsoever grocenes or heat might remain, it is purged forth by pure watter mixed with whit claye, which is put uppon the suger forme three tymes, whose nature is not to mixe with the suger, but to make hime perfecte whit and pure. It is thought by the learned phisition that a lye made with lyme is as wholsome as a lee made wich ashes, being so delayed with watter; without a lee no suger can be made.

Whereas it is thought all Brasill whit powder, or other broken suger maye be spent or eaten without being refined, here beinge brought into hir Maties portes about 1000 tonnes per yeare, whereof at leaste 2/3 partes is found so groce, with so stronge a sent, havinge sand, earth and other grocenes in it, that it is not fitt for any other use but to be refined. Also ther is brought in more than 1000 tonnes per yeare of S¹ Thomas suger, Brassill muskovathos and panneles, Barbery broken suger and panneles, which non of it doth serve for any other use but to be refined; which, if it should not be done here, it would be transported to Hambrow, Midelbrow and Amsterdame, where there is more thenn 30 refyninge houses.

Whereas in tymes past ther was 100 refyninge houses at one tyme in Andwerpe, England being furnished with refined suger from thence, now, thankes be to God, England doth furnishe the Lowe Contrye, Germanye and other contryes better cheape then they canne furnishe us.

If there should be no refyninge, but by the licence of one man, or by the handes of a fewe at his appoyntment, then no marchants or others would bringe ther powders in here, but rather carie it thither wher they maye have a better price. Howe inconvenient it would be to the comonwealth, that the buyer beinge compelled to take it att the handes of a fewe, and to paye 20^d for that which is sould for 12^d p. lb., as in tymes past it hath bine!

Refined suger is made nowe by some workemasters of our owne contrye, and many Inglishmen set on worke therbye, wheras in tymes past it was done altogether by strangers.

For all the grocest stuff which cometh from refined suger, called sirrop or mallases, with that which is brought from beyond the seas, beinge very neere 1 000 tonnes per yere, not anye of it is spent in England, but is transported into the Lowe Contryes, for the which hir Matie hath costome.

Howe inconvenient it would be for hir Maties costomes to have powders convayed for other partes which payeth costome inwardes, and refined suger good quantetye beinge passed forth payeth costome outwardes, it is to be considered of those that hath experience thereof.

Refined suger is not made with other compoundes here in England, then it hath bine from tyme to tyme in Andwerpe or elsewhere, nether cane be made more perfect there then it is here nor better cheape.

Signé : Richard Carmerden.

Public Record Office. — State Papers, Domestic, Elizabeth, vol. CCXLV, n° 52. — *Original.*

XXII

RELATION DU NAUFRAGE DU « TOBIE »

Naufrage du « Tobie » au sud du cap Spartel. — Douze hommes gagnent la terre à la nage. — Après avoir traversé un pays désert, ils rencontrent une troupe d'environ cinq mille Maures en armes, qui faisaient la fantasia. — Ils sont assaillis, frappés, traités d'Espagnols. — Le capitaine des Maures les interroge et les fait dépouiller de leur or et de leurs bijoux. — Le lendemain, traités en esclaves, menacés de coups, ils sont ramenés au navire, dont les Maures pillent la cargaison. — Emmenés sous escorte, ils arrivent à El-Ksar el-Kebir, où ils sont remis au caïd, qui les loge au mellah. — Ils partent pour Merrakech, avec d'autres captifs espagnols et français, escortés de neuf cents hommes. — Arrivée à l'oued Sebou, puis à Salé, puis en vue de Merrakech. — Ils font savoir leur présence aux marchands anglais. — Ils entrent dans Merrakech, la corde au cou, et sont amenés devant le Chérif. — Tenus en prison pendant quinze jours, ils sont rachetés pour sept cents onces par les marchands anglais et séjournent huit semaines avec eux au fondouk. — Conduits à Santa-Cruz, ils s'embarquent pour l'Angleterre. — Deux d'entre eux sont morts au Maroc.

1593-mars 1594.

The casting away of the « Tobie » neere cape Espartel, corruptly called cape Sprat, without the straight of Gibraltar on the coast of Barbarie, 1593.

The « Tobie » of London, a ship of 250 tunnes, manned with fiftie men, the owner whereof was the worshipfull M. Richard Staper[1], being bound for Livorno, Zante and Patras in Morea, being laden with marchandize to the value of 11 or 12 thousand pounds

---

1. Sur ce personnage, V. *1re Série*, Angleterre, t. I, p. 469, note 5.

sterling, set sayle from Blackwall[1], the 16 day of August 1593, and we went thence to Portesmouth, where we tooke in great quantitie of wheate, and set sayle foorth of Stokes bay in the Isle of Wight, the 6 day of October, the winde being faire; and the 16 of the same moneth we were in the heigth of cape S. Vincent, where, on the next morning, we descried a sayle, which lay in try right a head off us, to which we gave chase with very much winde, the sayle being a Spaniard, which wee found in fine so good of sayle that we were faine to leave her and give her over. Two days after this, we had sight of mount Chiego[2], which is the first highland which we descrie on the Spanish coast at the entrance of the straight of Gibraltar, where we had very foule weather and the winde scant two days together. Here we lay off to the sea.

That master, whose name was George Goodlay, being a young man, and one which never tooke charge before for those parts, was very proud of that charge which he was little able to discharge, neither would take any counsel of any of his company, but did as he thought best himselfe, and in the end of the two dayes of foule weather cast about, and the winde being faire, bare in with the Straights mouth. The 19 day at night, he thinking that he was farther off the land then he was, bare sayle all that night, and, an houre and an halfe before day, had ranne our shippe upon the ground on the coast of Barbarie, without the Straight, foure leagues to the south of cape Espartel. Whereupon, being all not a litle astonied, the master said unto us: « I pray you forgive me; for this is my fault and no mans else. » The company asked him whether they should cut off the maine maste : « No, sayd the master, we will hoyse out our boate. » But one of our men, comming speedily up, sayd : « Sir, the ship is full of water. » — « Well, sayd the master, then cut the mayne mast over boord. » Which thing we did with all speede. But the after-part suddenly split asunder, in such sort that no man was able to stand upon it, but all fled upon the foremast up into the shrouds thereof, and hung there for a time; but seeing nothing but present death approch (being so suddenly taken that

---

1. Faubourg à l'est de Londres.
2. Nom évidemment altéré. La montagne dont il s'agit devait être dans les environs de Tarifa.

we could not make a raft which we had determined), we committed ourselves unto the Lord, and beganne, with dolefull tune and heavy hearts, to sing the 12th psalme: « Helpe Lord for good and godley men, etc. » Howbeit, before we had finished four verses, the waves of the sea had stopped the breathes of most of our men. For the foremast, with the weight of our men and the force of the sea, fell downe into the water, and, upon the fall thereof, there were 38 drowned, and onely 12, by Gods providence, partly by swimming and other meanes of chests, got on shoare, which was about a quarter of a mile from the wracke of the ship. The master, called George Goodley, and William Palmer, his mate, both perished. M. Cæsar also, being captaine and owner, was likewise drowned; none of the officers were saved but the carpenter.

We twelve, which the Lord had delivered from extreme danger of the sea, at our comming ashore, fell in a maner into as great distresse. At our first comming on shore, we all fell downe on our knees, praying the Lord most humbly for his mercifull goodnesse. Our prayers being done, we consulted together what course to take, seeing we were fallen into a desert place, and we travelled all that day until night, sometimes one way and sometimes another, and could finde no kinde of inhabitants; only we saw where wilde beasts had bene, and places where there had bene houses, which after we perceived to have bene burnt by the Portugals. So at night falling into certaine groves of olive trees, we climed up and sate in them to avoid the danger of lions and other wilde beasts, whereof we saw many the next morning.

The next day, we travelled untill three of the clocke in the afternoone, without any food but water and wilde date roots; then, going over a mountaine, we had sight of cape Espartel; whereby we knew somewhat better which way to travell, and then we went forward untill we came to an hedgerow made with great long canes; we spied and looked over it, and beheld a number of men, as well horsemen as footmen, to the number of some five thousand, in skirmish together with small shot and other weapons. And after consultation what we were best to do, we concluded to yeeld ourselves unto them, being destitute of all meanes of resistance. So rising up, we marched toward them; who, espying us, foorthwith some hundred of them, with their javelings in their hands, came running towards us as though they would have run us thorow: howbeit they only strooke us flatling with their weapons and said that we were Spaniards; and we tolde them that we were Englishmen; which they would not beleeve yet.

By and by, the conflict being ended, and night approching, the captaine of the Moores, a man of some 56 yeres olde, came himselfe unto us, and, by his interpretor, which spake Italian, asked what we were, and from whence we came. One Thomas Henmer, of our company, which could speake Italian, declared unto him that we were marchants, and how, by great misfortune, our ship, marchandise and the greatest part of our company were pitifully cast away upon their coast. But he, void of humainity and all manhood, for all this, caused his men to strip us out of our apparell, even to our shirts, to see what money and jewels we had about us; which when they had found to the value of some 200 pounds in golde and pearles, they gave us some of our apparel againe, and bread and water onely to comfort us.

The next morning, they carried us downe to the shore, where our shippe was cast away, which was some sixteene miles from that place. In which journey they used us like their slaves, making us (being extreame weake) to carry their stuffe, and offering to beat us, if we went not so fast as they. We asked them why they used us so, and they replied that we were their captives. We sayd we were their friends, and that there was never Englishman captive to the King of Marocco. So we came downe to the ship, and lay there with them seven dayes, while they had gotten all the goods they could, and then they parted it amongst them.

After the end of these seven dayes, the captaine appointed twenty of his men wel armed, to bring us up into the countrey. And, the first night, we came to the side of a river called Alarach[1], where we lay on the grasse all that night; so, the next day, we went over the river, in a frigate of nine oares on a side, the river being in that place above a quarter of a mile broad, and, that day, we went to a towne of thirty houses called Totteon[2]. There we lay foure

---

1. L'oued Loukkos. 2. Dechera sur la route de Larache

dayes, having nothing to feed on but bread and water; and then we went to a towne called Cassuri[1], and there we were delivered by those twenty souldiers unto the Alcaide, which examined us what we were; and we tolde him. He gave us a goode answere, and sent us to the Jewes house, where we lay seven dayes.

In the meane while that we lay here, there were brought thither twenty Spaniards and twenty Frenchmen, which Spaniards were taken in a conflict on land, but the Frenchmen were by foule weather cast on land, within the Straights, about Cape de Gate[2], and so made captives. Thus, at the seven dayes end, we twelve Englishmen, the twelve French and the twenty Spaniards were all conducted toward Marocco, with nine hundred souldiers, horsemen and fotmen, and, in two dayes journey, we came to the river of Fez[3], where we lodged all night, being provided of tents. The next day, we went to a towne called Salle, and lay without the towne in tents. From thence, we travelled almost an hundred miles, without finding any towne[4], but, every night, we came to fresh water, which was partly running water and sometime raine water.

So we came at last within three miles of the city of Marocco, where we pitched our tents; and there we mette with a carrier, which did travell in the countrey for the English marchants; and by him we sent word unto them of our estate; and they returned the next day unto us a Moore, which brought us victuals, being at that instant very feeble and hungry; and withall sent us a letter with pene, inke and paper, willing us to write unto them what ship it was that was cast away, and how many and what men there were alive: « For, said they, we would knowe with speed, for to morow is the Kings court; and therefore we would know, for that you should come into the citie like captives. »

But, for all that, we were carried in as captives, and with ropes about our neckes, as well English as the French and Spaniards. And so we were carried before the King; and, when we came before

---

El-Ksar el-Kebir.

1. *Cassuri*: El-Ksar el-Kebir, la seule ville de la région où l'on trouve un caïd et un mellah.

2. Le cap de Gate est sur la côte d'Espagne et non sur la côte du Maroc.

3. L'oued Sebou.

4. La caravane suivit la route directe de Salé à Merrakech à travers le pays des Chaouïa.

him, he did commit us all to ward, where wee lay 15 dayes in close prison. And, in the end, we were cleared by the English marchants to their great charges; for our deliverance cost them 700 ounces, every ounce in that country contayning two shillings.

And, when we came out of prison, we went to the Alfandica[1], where we continued eight weekes with the English marchants; at the end of which time, being well apparelled by the bountie of our merchants, we were conveyed downe, by the space of eight dayes journey, to S. Cruz, where the English ships road; where we took shipping about the 20 of March, two in the « Anne Francis » of London, and five more of us, five dayes after, in the « Expedition » of London, and two more in a Flemish flieboat, and one in the « Mary Edward », also of London. Other two of our number died in the countrey of the bloodie-fluxe: the one at our first imprisonment at Marocco, whose name was George Hancock, and the other at S. Cruz, whose name was Robert Swancon; whose death was hastened by eating of rootes and other unnaturall things to slake their raging hunger in our travaile, and by our hard and cold lodging in the open fields without tents.

Thus, of fiftie persons, through the rashnesse of an unskilfull master, ten onely survived of us, and, after a thousand miseries, returned home poore, sicke and feeble into our country.

Richard Johnson. — William Williams, carpenter. — John Durham. — Abraham Rouse. — John Matthewes. — Thomas Henmore. — John Silvester. — Thomas Whiting. — William Church. — John Fox.

Hakluyt. — The Principal Navigations... of the English Nation. — Édition 1598-1600, tome II, 2ᵉ partie, pp. 201-203.

1. *Alfandica*, le fondouk.

XXIII

LETTRE DE LAWRENCE MADOC A ANTHONY DASSEL

Un kiahia des Andalous et un autre chef, envoyés par le Chérif avec le caïd Mahmoud ben Zergoun à Gago, en ont ramené trente mules chargées d'or. — Ils se sont eux-mêmes considérablement enrichis et sont revenus sans l'ordre du Chérif, qui ne leur payera pas leur solde. — Les caïds Mahmoud ben Zergoun, Djouder et Bou Ikhtyar restent à Gago. — Le caïd El-Mansour ben Abd er-Rahman est prêt à partir pour cette ville avec cinq mille hommes. — Nombreux otages ramenés du Soudan, parmi lesquels trois fils du Roi et le jurisconsulte Cheikh Ahmed Baba. — A l'arrivée du caïd El-Mansour, le caïd Mahmoud ben Zergoun reviendra à Merrakech avec le trésor.

Merrakech, 1er [n. st. 11] août 1594.

A briefe relation concerning the estate of the cities and provinces of Tombuto and Gago, written in Marocco the first of August 1594, and sent to M. Anthony Dassel, marchant of London[1].

My hearty commendations premised, — Your letter of late I received, and found that you would have me discover unto you the estate and quality of the countreyes of Tombuto and Gago. And that you may not thinke me to slumber in this action, wherein you would be truely and perfectly resolved, you shall understand, that not ten dayes past[2] here came a cahaia[3] of the Andoluzes home from

---

1. Anthony Dassel était membre de la Compagnie du Maroc. V. 1re Série, Angleterre, t. I, p. 470. Il figure également dans les lettres patentes instituant la *Guinea Company* en 1588. HAKLUYT, éd. 1598-1600, t. II, 2e partie, p. 123.

2. Sur cette caravane, cf. ES-SADI, *Tarikh es-Soudan*, p. 264, et 1re Série, Espagne, lettre de Baltasar Polo du 4 juin 1594. Il y a une légère divergence dans les dates données pour l'arrivée à Merrakech de la susdite caravane (ES-SADI: 21 mai ; Madoc : 1er août).

3. *Cahaia*, kiahia. Sur le sens de ce mot, qui appartient à la langue turque, V. 1re Série, Angleterre, t. I, p. 258, note 4. — Ce kiahia était le caïd Ahmed ben Yousef el-Euldji. Es-SADI, p. 264.

Gago, and another principall Moore, whom the King sent thither at the first with alcaide Hamode[1], and they brought with them thirty mules laden with gold. I saw the same come into the Alcasava with mine owne eies; and these men themselves came not poore, but with such wealth, that they came away without the Kings commandement, and for that cause the King will pay them no wages for the time they have beene there. On the other side, they dare not aske the King for any wages. And when alcaide Hamode saw that the cahaia of the Andoluzes would not stay in Gago with him, he thought good to send these thirty mules laden with golde by him, with letters of commendations, by which the King smelled their riches that they brought with them; and this was the cause of the Kings displeasure towards them.

So now there remaineth in Gago alcaide Hamode, and alcaide Jawdara[2], and alcaide Bucthare[3]. And here are in a readinesse to depart in the end of this next September alcaide Monsor ben Abd Rahaman, allies[4] Monsor Rico[5], with five thousand men most of the fettilase[6], that is to say of fier-mach and muskets. There is gone good store of reds and yellowes[7]; and this yere here was want

---

1. Il ne peut être question ici que de Mahmoud ben Zergoun, dont il a été parlé plus haut (p. 66, note 1). La confusion entre les noms d'Ahmed et de Mahmoud est souvent faite par les Européens.

2. Le pacha Djouder. Sur ce personnage, V. *ibidem*.

3. Le caïd Bou Ikhtyar. C'était, au dire d'Es-Sadi, un renégat. Fils d'un prince chrétien, en butte à des persécutions dans sa famille, il s'était réfugié près de Moulay Ahmed el-*Mansour*. Il fut envoyé par celui-ci à Tombouctou au mois de novembre 1593 et y mourut en 1594. On prétendit qu'il avait été empoisonné par le caïd Djouder. Es-SADI, pp. 262-264, 271, 324.

4. L'éditeur a pris ce mot pour un nom propre. Il faut entendre : *alias*.

5. Le caïd El-Mansour ben Abd er-Rahman, appelé aussi *Monsor Rico*, *Almanzorico*. V. *1re Série*, France, t. II, pp. 33-54.

Almanzorico est probablement le nom que lui donnaient les Chrétiens au Maroc et qu'ils avaient formé du nom arabe *El-Mansour*, en y joignant l'épithète : *rico*. Balthasar Polo, négociant de Valence établi à Merrakech et correspondant de Philippe II, dit, en effet : « C'est le plus grand caïd qui soit ici pour tout ce qui touche à la guerre, il est *riche* et puissant et le Chérif a beaucoup de confiance en lui ». Il fut nommé vice-roi du Soudan, en remplacement de Mahmoud ben Zergoun, et partit de Merrakech, à la tête de 3 000 hommes environ, le 27 octobre 1594. V. *supra*, p. 66, n. 1; *1re Série*, Espagne, aux dates des 28 juin, 23 septembre, 30 novembre 1594.

6. *Fettilase* فتيلة mèche d'arme à feu, et par extension arquebuse.

7. Il s'agit, sans doute, d'étoffes rayées jaune et rouge.

of the same commodity; but I trust the next yere will be no want.

But in fine the King doth prosper wel in those parts; and here are many pledges come hither, and namely three of the Kings sonnes of Gago and the Justice[1]. I saw them come in with the treasure. Now, when alcaide Monsor commeth to Gago, the which will be in January next, then returneth hither alcaide Hamode with all the treasure, and alcaide Monsor is to keepe Gago untill the King take further order. And thus much for Gago.

Thus not having any other thing to write at this present, I commend you to the mercifull tuition of the Almighty.

From Marocco, the first of August 1594.

Your assured friend,

Laurence Madoc.

Hakluyt. — The Principal Navigations..... of the English Nation. — Édition 1598-1600, tome II, 2ᵉ partie, p. 192.

1. Ce « Justice » amené en otage était le fameux jurisconsulte de Tombouctou Cheikh Ahmed Baba. Il fut arrêté par le caïd Mahmoud en octobre 1593, chargé de chaînes et conduit à Merrakech, où il arriva le 21 mai 1594 (V. *supra*, p. 79, note 2), d'après Es-Sadi, et non pas au mois de Ramadan 1003 [10 mai-9 juin 1595], comme le dit El.-Oufrâni, p. 170. Cheikh Ahmed Baba resta en prison à Merrakech usqu'au 20 mai 1596. « Devenu libre de sa personne, il se livra à l'enseignement de la théologie et vit aussitôt la foule accourir pour profiter de ses leçons. Il continua à demeurer à Merrakech jusqu'à la mort d'El-Mansour, qui ne l'avait fait sortir de prison qu'à la condition qu'il résiderait dans cette ville. Ce fut seulement à la mort de ce souverain qu'il obtint de son fils Zidân l'autorisation de retourner dans sa patrie. » Son attitude vis-à-vis d'El-Mansour fut toujours fière et indépendante et il embarrassa plusieurs fois le Chérif par sa morgue. Il est l'auteur d'ouvrages théologiques estimés. Cf. El.-Oufrâni, pp. 169-171; Es-Sadi, p. 264.

XXIV

LETTRE DE LAWRENCE MADOC A ANTHONY DASSEL

Le caïd Mahmoud ben Zergoun, parti pour le Soudan avec dix-sept cents hommes, dont un tiers est mort de soif, a pris Tombouctou et Gago, après une faible résistance des indigènes, incapables de soutenir la lutte. — Ceux-ci paieront un tribut annuel. — Le tribut de Tombouctou, qui est arrivé par caravane, est de soixante quintaux d'or ; le montant de celui de Gago sera connu, lors du retour du caïd Mahmoud au printemps prochain. — On dit que celui-ci apportera un trésor considérable. — Il conquiert sans coup férir tous les pays où il passe et descend vers la côte. — Le Chérif est en passe de devenir le plus riche souverain du monde. — Une mahalla est prête à partir avec un nouveau vice-roi, El-Mansour ben Abd er-Rahman. — On la dit forte de trois mille hommes ; mais Madoc la croit de deux mille, au plus, car les noirs ne peuvent opposer une résistance sérieuse. — Le caïd Mahmoud, qui n'attend plus que l'arrivée de son remplaçant, reviendra en janvier. — Un fils du Chérif, Moulay Bel-Hassen, a été massacré par ses hommes au Soudan.

Merrakech, 30 août[1] [n. st. 9 septembre] 1594.

Another briefe relation concerning the late conquest and the exceeding great riches of the cities and provinces of Tombuto and

---

1. La date finale de la présente lettre porte : 1ᵉʳ août. D'autre part, Hakluyt, dans la note qui précède le texte, la date du 30 août. Le premier quantième ne peut être qu'une erreur de transcription ou d'impression causée par le voisinage de la lettre précédente. En effet, si la teneur même des deux lettres établit bien que l'une et l'autre furent écrites en 1594, il n'est guère admissible que toutes deux l'aient été le même jour. Dans la précédente, Madoc accuse réception d'une lettre de Dassel ; dans celle-ci, de deux lettres du même Dassel arrivées par deux bateaux différents. Madoc répond une première fois; puis, quand la seconde lettre de Dassel arrive, comme elle contient les mêmes questions relatives au Soudan, il reprend le sujet. Il fait un récit rétrospectif de l'entrée à Tombouctou et à Gago des troupes marocaines, qui eut lieu en 1591. Il ajoute d'autres détails. Il confirme enfin le prochain retour du caïd Mahmoud, dont il parlait dans sa première lettre, ce qui prouve que, sans être

Gago, written from Marocco the 30 August 1594, to M. Anthony Dassel, marchant of London aforesayd.

Loving friend M. Dassel,

Two of your letters I have received, one by the shippe called « the Amity », the other by the « Concord » ; the chiefest matter therein was to be satisfied of the King of Marocco his proceedings in Guinea.

Therefore these are to let you understand that there went with alcaide Hamode[1] for those parts seventeene hundred men ; who passing over the sands, for want of water, perished one third part of them. And at their comming to the citie of Tombuto, the negros made some resistance ; but to small purpose, for that they had no defence but with their asagaies or javelings poisoned. So they tooke it, and proceeded to the city of Gago[2], where the negros were in number infinite, and meant to stand to the uttermost for their countrey ; but the Moores slew them so fast, that they were faine to yeeld, and do pay tribute by the yere.

The rent of Tombuto is 60 quintals of gold by the yeere ; the goodnesse whereof you know. What rent Gago will yeeld you shall know at the spring, for then alcaide Hamode commeth home. The rent of Tombuto is come by the cafelow or carovan, which is, as above is mentioned, 60 quintals.

The report is that Mahomed[3] bringeth with him such an infinite treasure as I never heard of ; it doth appeare that they have more golde then any other part of the world beside. The Alcaide winneth

---

du même jour, les deux documents furent écrits à peu d'intervalle l'un de l'autre.

1. V. supra, p. 66, note 1. Madoc raconte, dans les lignes qui suivent, la prise de Tombouctou et de Gago en 1591 et attribue, par erreur, au seul caïd Mahmoud des succès dont une part était l'œuvre de Djouder. Ce qu'il dit de l'infériorité des armes des noirs est également attesté par Es-Sadi et El-Oufrâni ; ils firent néanmoins une résistance héroïque. H. DE CASTRIES, La conquête du Soudan par El-Mansour, dans Hespéris, 1923, p. 451. Cf. ci-après, note 3.

2. En réalité, la prise de Tombouctou est postérieure à celle de Gago. Cette version de Laurence Madoc est la même que celle d'El-Oufrâni. L'erreur tient sans doute à la confusion que faisaient les Marocains entre Gago, la capitale, et Tombouctou, nœud essentiel des communications.

3. C'est le caïd Mahmoud ben Zergoun (V. ci-dessus, note 1), que Madoc appelle partout ailleurs Hamode, et à qui il donne ici son vrai nom.

all the countrey where he goeth without fighting, and is going downe towards the sea coast. This King of Marocco is like to be the greatest prince in the world for money[1], if he keepe this countrey. But I make account, as soone as the King of Spaine hath quietnesse in Christendome, he will thrust him out, for that the Kings force is not great as yet; but he meaneth to be stronger.

There is a campe ready to go now with a Viceroy[2]: the speech is with 3000 men, but I thinke they will be hardly 2000; for, by report, 3000 men are enough to conquer all the countrey, for they have no defence of importance against an enemy.

I think Hamode will be returned home in January or thereabout; for he stayeth but for the comming of the Viceroy.

Mulley Balasen, the Kings sonne of Marocco, was slain in Guinea[3] by his owne men, and they were presently killed, because they should tell no tales.

And thus leaving to trouble you, I commit you to God, who prosper you in all your proceedings.

From Marocco, the first[4] of August 1594.

Yours to command for ever,

Laurence Madoc.

Hakluyt. — The Principal Navigations..... of the English Nation. — Édition 1598-1600, tome II, 2ᵉ partie, pp. 192-193.

1. La réputation de riche souverain que valut à Moulay Ahmed la conquête du Soudan lui fit donner le surnom d'*ed-Dehebi* : le Doré.

2. Il s'agit des troupes que devait conduire au Soudan le caïd El-Mansour ben Abd er-Rahman, et que Madoc, dans sa précédente lettre, disait fortes de cinq mille hommes. V. *supra*, p. 84 et note 5.

3. Moulay Bel-Hassen, ou Moulay Ali, second fils de Moulay Ahmed *el-Mansour*, avait été massacré, le 18 mars 1594, non en Guinée, mais dans la province de Tadla, dont il était gouverneur. Il s'était attiré la haine des captifs chrétiens en les contraignant d'abjurer. V. *1ʳᵉ Série*, Angleterre, t. I, p. 256, Pl. III, le Tableau généalogique des princes de la dynastie saadienne, n° 23.

4. Sur cette date, V. *supra*, p. 86, n. 1.

XXV

EXTRAIT D'UNE LETTRE D'EDWARD HOLMDEN[1]

On dit qu'un personnage important va partir pour l'Angleterre comme ambassadeur du Chérif avec deux caïds et une suite de vingt-cinq ou trente personnes. — Moulay en-Nasser est venu d'Espagne à Melilla. — Il compte se joindre à des rebelles et marcher contre Moulay Ahmed. — Cette entreprise est téméraire, car Moulay ech-Cheikh est en campagne avec cinquante mille hommes. — L'émotion causée par l'arrivée de Moulay en-Nasser sera bientôt calmée.

Du Maroc, [après le 8 mai 1595[2]].

Au dos, alia manu: Extract of a letter of Ed. Holmdens, from Barbary.

Owt of a letter of Edward Holmdens, from Barbery.

It is still geven out that the Kinges ambassadowre shall goe for Englande, being a man of account, and two alkaydes with hym, and caryeth a retinue of twentye five or thirtye persones[3]. It is said he will goe in the « Swanne »; which if [he] doe, he

---

1. Edward Holmden, membre de la Compagnie du Maroc. V. *supra*, p. 64 et note 5, et *infra*, p. 103.
2. La lettre de Holmden mentionne l'arrivée et la présence à Melilla de Moulay en-Nasser, qui débarqua dans cette place le 8 mai 1595 et en repartit le 20 mai avec une mahalla de partisans.
3. D'après une lettre de Balthasar Polo, datée de Merrakech, 19 juin 1595, le bruit avait couru que le Chérif enverrait comme ambassadeur en Angleterre le caïd Ahmed ben Adel, personnage important. Depuis, on avait dit que l'ambassadeur serait un neveu du caïd Moussa ben Makhlouf, qui avait vécu en Portugal avec son oncle et qui était revenu au Maroc après la mort de ce dernier. Balthasar Polo, qui tenait ces renseignements de favoris du Chérif, les transmettait sous toutes réserves. Le 20 juillet, il écrivait qu'on parlait toujours de l'ambassade, mais qu'il ne croyait pas qu'elle dût avoir lieu. V. *1re Série*, Espagne, aux dates indiquées. Cf. France, t. II, p. 209 et note 1. Comme on ne trouve plus cette ambassade mentionnée dans les documents, il est probable que le projet, si tant est qu'il y en eut un, fut abandonné.

will be here[1] before Mechilmas[2]. The cause is not knowne[3].

The contry is somewhat disquieted by reasone Mully Nassar[4] is come owt of Spayne to a fort holde uppon this cost, called Mellilla, where he remayneth with store of treasure, as is reported; by meanes wherof he hoopes to joyne a company of the Kinges rebell subjectes and to come agaynst hym. But it is farre from all reason that he shold attempt aney suche matter uppon so weake groundes; and howsoever the people are inclyned to innovation, yet it is hard displacinge an established Kinge or rather Kinges, for that Mully Shecke[5] is abroad in campe with fiftye thowsande men.

This Mully[6] is second sonne to Mully Abdela[7], the right heyre to Mully Mahomet the Blacke Kinge[8], who had no issue[9]. By this meanes here is some rumowre, but likely to be soone pacefyed. God graunt quietnes, that we maye not be injured in owr trade!

Public Record Office. — State Papers, Foreign, Barbary States, vol. XII.

1. *Here*, en Angleterre.

2. *Mechilmas*, la Saint-Michel, c'est-à-dire le 29 septembre n. st.

3. La correspondance de Balthasar Polo nous apprend encore que le Grand Seigneur, à la requête de la reine d'Angleterre, aurait fait demander au Chérif, par son ambassadeur, de donner à celle-ci le libre accès du port de Santa-Cruz-du-Cap-de-Guir pour ses navires de guerre et de commerce et de l'y laisser établir un fort. Balthasar Polo n'avait pu connaître la réponse du Chérif; mais il ne croyait pas qu'elle pût être favorable. Le duc de Medina-Sidonia jugeait également Moulay Ahmed trop avisé pour accorder une pareille requête. V. *1re Série*, Espagne, lettres de Balthasar Polo et de Medina-Sidonia des 6 mai, 24 mai et 20 juillet 1595. On n'a trouvé aucune trace de cette affaire dans les documents anglais. Elle était, sans doute, en corrélation avec le projet d'ambassade en Angleterre un instant caressé par le Chérif.

4. Moulay en-Nasser, neveu de Moulay Ahmed *el-Mansour*. Il voulut détrôner celui-ci et fut vaincu en deux rencontres, à Er-Roken (3 août 1595) et à Taguate (12 mai 1596), où il fut pris et tué. V. *1re Série*, France, t. II, pp. 205-227; Espagne, aux années 1595, 1596.

5. Moulay ech-Cheikh, fils aîné de Moulay Ahmed *el-Mansour*. C'est lui qui commandait les troupes de ce prince à Er-Roken et à Taguate.

6. *This Mully*: entendez: Moulay en-Nasser.

7. Moulay Abdallah *el-Ghalib*, qui régna de 1557 à 1574.

8. Moulay Mohammed *el-Mesloukh*, détrôné en 1576 par son oncle Moulay Abd el-Malek et tué à la bataille d'El-Ksar el-Kebir (4 août 1578), où il combattait avec les Portugais. V. *infra*, p. 326.

9. C'est une erreur. Moulay Mohammed *el-Mesloukh* eut un fils, Moulay ech-Cheikh, réfugié, comme Moulay en-Nasser, en Espagne, où il se convertit au catholicisme et fut baptisé le 3 novembre 1593. V. *1re Série*, Pays-Bas, t. I, p. 42, note 1; France, t. II, pp. 204-205. — Sur les chérifs mentionnés dans cette note et dans celles qui précèdent. V. *1re Série*, Angleterre, t. I, Pl. III, p. 256, le Tableau généalogique des princes de la dynastie saadienne.

XXVI

MÉMOIRE SUR LE COMMERCE

(Extrait)

On importe d'Angleterre au Maroc des draps fins bleu foncé, des calottes rouges, des canons et des munitions, du bois de frêne pour faire des rames, des armures de toutes sortes ; si l'on est pris par les Espagnols, on est mis à mort. — On exporte de Santa-Cruz du sucre fin, du sucre brut, beaucoup de salpêtre, des dattes, des mélasses, des tapis, du coton ; il faut avoir un sauf-conduit pour les galères d'Espagne, autrement le trafic est dangereux.

[1595 ?]

Au dos, alia manu : A direction for trades of merchandize. — Trade. — 1595 ?

A speciall direction for divers trades of marchaundize to be used for sondrie placis, upon advertisements, as well for the chusinge of the time and wares for every of those placis, most beneficiall for those that use the trade of marchandize.

. . . .

En marge : All the yeare in greate shippes.

Item, for Barbary, very fyne clothes, sade blewes [1], of xxx[li] the clothe, and the redd cappes for marriners [2], and all kinde of greate

---

1. *Sade blewes :* bleu foncé. Ce drap était appelé au Maroc bernatha برناطة
V. 1re Série, Angleterre, t. 1, p. 113.

2. Il s'agit très probablement de la calotte rouge portée par les Maures et les Orientaux, connue sous les noms indigènes de chechia, fez, tarbouch, et appelée dans le langage commercial du temps : bonnet de Marseille, bonnet de Tunis. Si singulière que paraisse la chose, cette coiffure musulmane était fabriquée en Europe, d'où elle était importée dans le Levant et dans l'Afrique du Nord. Les principales manufactures se trouvaient en France, à Orléans, Marseille, Nay-en-Béarn, Aix et Prades. Les Français étaient

ordinaunce and other artellyrye, ashetimber for oares, armorr of all sortes. But yf the Spanyerdes take yowe trading with them, yow dye for it.

En marge: Comodities retorned from thence.

Item, owte of this contrye we lade from the porte of Santa-Cruse, Barbary sugers, bothe fyne and course¹, saltepeter, great aboundance and the best, also dates, melassos and cwte, Barbary carpettes, cotton. Yow must have safe-coundight for the gallyes, otherwyse the trade is dangerowse.

. . . .

Public Record Office. — *State Papers, Domestic, Elizabeth, vol. CCLV, n° 56*. — *Original*.

---

même appelés quelquefois à Smyrne « mercanti di barretti », à cause du grand commerce qu'ils faisaient de cet article. V. Savary, *Dict. universel du Commerce*, art. bonnets, commerce de Smyrne; Peyssonel, *Traité sur le commerce de la mer Noire*. Cf. *1re Série*, Espagne, t. I, p. 389 et note 1; p. 644, note 1. — L'expression *the redd capes for marriners*, employée par l'auteur du présent Mémoire, ne semble pas devoir être entendue *stricto sensu*. Il est évident que les marins du Chérif étaient trop peu nombreux pour que des bonnets à leur usage constituassent un objet d'importation au Maroc.

1. Sur la production du sucre de canne au Maroc, V. *supra*, Doc. XX, p. 71, et XXI, p. 74.

XXVII

RELATION DE ROGER MARBECK[1]

(Extrait)

Trente-huit esclaves marocains, échappés des galères espagnoles à la faveur du combat naval devant Cadix, se mettent à la merci du comte d'Essex, qui les renvoie au Maroc.

21 juin [n. st. 1er juillet] 1596[2].

En tête, alia manu: A breefe and a true discourse of the late honorable voyage unto Spaine and of the wynning, sacking and burning of the famous towne of Cadiz there,..... by Doctor Marbeck, attending upon the person of the right honorable the Lorde Highe Admirall of England, at the tyme of the saide action.

. . . .

While the Lordes Generalls[3] weare at Cadiz, there came to them certaine poor wretches, Turkes[4], to the number of 38, that had beene a longe tyme galley slaves and, ether at the very tyme of the fight by sea or ells immediatelie thereuppon, takeing their oportunitie, did then make their escape and swimme to land, yeelding themselves to the mercie of their honorable Lordshippes. It pleased them with all speede to apparrell them and to furnishe them with money and all other necessaries, and to bestowe on them a barke[5]

---

1. Roger Marbeck (1536-1605), médecin. Il accompagna Lord Howard dans l'expédition de Cadix.

2. C'est la date du combat naval devant Cadix. V. le récit de l'expédition dans Corbett, *The Successors of Drake*.

3. Le comte d'Essex et Lord Charles Howard, grand amiral d'Angleterre.

4. A cette époque, les Chrétiens confondaient tous les Musulmans sous le nom de Turcs. Il s'agit ici de Marocains.

5. Cette barque était une « caravelela »,

and pilott, and so to have them freelie conveyed into Barbery, willing them to lett the countrie to understand what was done and what they had seene¹. Whereby I doubt not but, as Her Matie is a most admirable prince alreadie over all Europe and all Affrike, Asie and Christendome, so the whole world hereafter shall have just cause to admire her infinite princelie vertues.

. . . .

British Museum. — *Sloane Mss.*, *226, f. 25 v°.* — *Original.*

que les Anglais avaient armée en course à Larache pour la côte d'Espagne ; ils la renvoyèrent à Larache avec les captifs maures libérés. V. *1re Série*, Espagne, aux dates des 8 août, 29 novembre et 10 décembre 1596. — L'arrivée à Cadix de la caravelle armée à Larache fit sans doute croire à une intervention des Marocains et la rumeur s'en répandit très amplifiée, comme en témoigne l'avis suivant : « En mesme temps que ladicte armée angloise est arrivée et pris port, est arrivé le second fils de Don Anthonie, assisté de six mille Barbares, subjetts du roy de Marroco, et ce, dedans un grand nombre de gallaires. » *Public Record Office, State Papers, Foreign, Spain, vol. V.*

1. A bord de la « caraveleta », s'embarqua un Portugais nommé Pedro Ferreira, porteur de lettres de D. Christophe et du comte d'Essex au Chérif. V. *infra*, Doc. XXXV, p. 109. — Dans un conseil de guerre tenu le 24 juin [n. st. 4 juillet] 1596, au logement du comte d'Essex, il fut décidé d'envoyer Sir Edward Hobby auprès du dit Chérif. *Lambeth Palace Library, vol. 250, ff. 330-363.* Il ne paraît pas avoir été donné suite à cette résolution.

XXVIII

LETTRE D'EDMUND WEDALL A ROBERT CECIL

Il envoie à Cecil un vol de faucons apportés à Middelbourg sur un navire venant du Maroc.

Flessingue, 1ᵉʳ [n. st. 11] septembre 1596.

Au dos : To the right honorable Sir Robert Cecill, Knight, Principall Secretarie to her Maᵗⁱᵉ.

Right Honorable,

The 28ᵗʰ of Auguste, ther came to Middleborow a ship fromp Barberie; she brought fowre or five Barberie faucons and tassells, of which I have sent your Honor a cast of the choycest faucons, the one an intermude hagarde, the other a sore haucke, both whole feathered. And thus desiering your Honor to accepte them from him that is whollie at your devotion, I humblie take my leave.

Vlishinge, the first of September 1596.
Your Honors in all service,

Signé : Edm. Wedall[1].

Hatfield House, Cecil Mss., 44, f. 44. — Original.

1. Par une lettre du 27 août [n. st. 6 septembre] 1597, Edmund Wedall annonce à Cecil un autre envoi de faucons, apportés également du Maroc à Middelbourg. *St. Pap., Domestic, Elizabeth, vol. CCLXIV, nº 93.*

XXIX

LETTRE DE MOULAY AHMED EL-MANSOUR A D. CHRISTOPHE[1]

Le Chérif offre à D. Christophe et à son frère un asile dans ses États et leur promet son appui.

Merrakech, 3ᵉ décade de Moharrem 1005 [14-23 septembre 1596[2]].

Au dos : Al principe mas engrandecido y poderoso he de alta fama he sangre y reyno, Don Christoval, hijo del rey Don Antonio, de mas alta fama, que Dios tenga.

Au dos, alia manu : Du roy de Moroccos au prince Don Emanuel.

Invocation : Con el nombre de Dios piadozo y miziricordioso, he la santificacion sea sobre su profeta!

Del siervo de Dios, el conquistador por su causa, el sucesor he ensalsado por Dios, el emperador de los Mouros y hijo del emperador de los Moros, nyeto[3] dell emperador de los Moros, xarifi de Dios, ell que prospere con el alsamiento su estado he su senhorio sobre los poderes de sus enemigos, he delante dell abatta su soberbia e su potestad, de cuyo valor en todo el mundo es grande, e nos em nostros reinos sublimamos como es razon he encumbramos como es razon con el debido acatamiento.

---

1. Cette lettre fut apportée par Pedro Ferreira. V. *infra*, p. 111 et n. 1. Elle parvint à D. Christophe le 16 novembre 1596. V. 1ʳᵉ *Série*, Pays-Bas, t. I, Doc. II, p. 4.
2. Cette date est celle d'une copie arabe conservée à la Bibliothèque de l'Université de Leyde, ms. 1365, fasc. A, n° 2.
3. Fils de l'empereur des Maures, petit-fils de l'empereur des Maures. Sur ces expressions, cf. H. DE CASTRIES, *La diplomatique des princes de la dynastie saadienne* (en préparation), au chapitre : *Suscription*.

El qual con el fabor de Dios avra contientamiento su protestacion y demanda, la potestade del principe engrandecido he poderoso he supremo valor, Dom Christoval, hijo del poderozo rey he de alta fama, ell rey Don Antonyo de Portugall, que Dios tienga, he legitimo heredero del reyno.

Y, despues de alavar a Dios, el qual ha sublimado el estado profetico he inpara a os que a el viene[n] con hexalsamiento y onra conplyda, la salvacion de Dios sea sobre su alto tezoro, el que livrara las criaturas del alboroto del supremo dia y sobre su familya allegara el eterno e alto estado profetico e engrandecydo, cuyo poder sera conplido exalçamiento a todos los que a el binieron.

Y si es que biniera a nuestras reales manos la carta que me abeis escrito[1], por la qual vos agardecemos mucho, amigo de nuestro coraçon y mas que amigo. Se quyzerdes benyr a mi estado, sereis muy bien venido, como uno de mis hijos. Mucho me emcomiendo a vostro hermano maior[2], e, se el quizere venir, venga con la gracia de Dios y sera muy bien venido, y todo lo que quizerdes alhares em my y biberes como quizerdes.

Yo tengo nuebas que queres tornar a pasar a Francya; y entiendo que la cauza he que teneis mucho trabajo por alla. En mi coraçon me peza, he, se hiceres licença de la reyna Elizabet, mas yncumbrada y engrandecyda, a todo tiempo sereis muy bien venidos, y, quando os la negare, enbiamelo a dezir.

Pezame mucho que no me aveis avertido despues que morio el Rey de mas alta fama, voestro padre, porque mas priesto os mandara vieredes a mi para remedio de vuestros trabajos he enparo de voestra fortuna. Y esto es me forçado hazerlo, porque ansi lo yzo ell rey de Portugal a nuestras cozas[3].

No mas, sino que me encomiendo ha entrambos dos; e viniendo alhares hun padre he todo lo que quizerdes, donde le sera deseada

---

1. La lettre que D. Christophe avait écrite au Chérif en juillet 1596, de Cadix, et qui avait été portée à Merrakech par Pedro Ferreira. V. supra, p. 94, note 1.

2. Le prince Emmanuel de Portugal, mort en 1638.

3. Le traducteur néerlandais avait écrit: « een coninck van Portugael », ce qui avait empêché de reconnaître D. Antonio. V. 1re Série, Pays-Bas, t. I, p. 6, la note 1, qui n'a plus de raison d'être. — D. Antonio, par sa lutte contre Philippe II, avait rendu un grand service à Moulay Ahmed.

De Castries.

toda onra, victoria he exsaltamiento de sus banderas reales, cuyo valor en todo el mundo sera conocido con el prospero çuseço. Con vuestra benyda sera anpleficada nuestra yntencion, con el favor de Dios supremo.

Hecha en nostra cuerte, em Marocos[1].

Lambeth Palace Library, vol. 653, n° 16. — Traduction officielle.

---

1. Malgré les offres de Moulay Ahmed el-*Mansour*, les princes portugais ne se rendirent pas au Maroc. Voyant qu'ils ne pouvaient plus espérer désormais l'assistance de l'Angleterre et de la France, ils résolurent de s'adresser aux Pays-Bas. Cf. 1re *Série*, Pays-Bas, t. I, Doc. VII et VIII, pp. 31 et 33.

XXX

LETTRE DE MOULAY AHMED EL-MANSOUR A ÉLISABETH

Il intercède, à la requête de son serviteur, le marchand Juan de Marchena, pour le neveu de ce dernier, Alonso Nuñez de Herrera, emmené de Cadix comme otage par les Anglais, et il offre de payer sa rançon. — Il demande un sauf-conduit pour les navires de Juan de Marchena, lesquels naviguent pour le compte chérifien.

Merrakech, 3e décade de Moharrem 1005 [14-23 septembre 1596[1]].

Au dos : De l'empereur de Moores à la reyne d'Angleterre, de mois de decembre 1596.

The Emperor of Morocco to Queen Elizabeth.

In the name of God powerfull and pitteful.

From the servant of the Soveraigne God, the honored by God, the Emperor of the Moores, son of the Emperor of Moores, son of the Emperor of Moores, Sariffe Hasani — God further his commandments and give victory unto his hoastes!

To her that hath, in the climes that followed the Messias, the great power whose foundations are firme, and all that know it, that followed the Messias, those that are nigh her, and those that dwell far from her, the Queen of high state, the ingreatened, the prosperous and famoused. And after praises to God the Great, the High to whose greatness the high heavens and the mightie mountaines doe bend;

---

1. La présente lettre fut apportée par Pedro Ferreira (V. *infra*, p. 111 et note 2), qui était aussi porteur de la lettre de Moulay Ahmed à D. Christophe (V. le Doc. précédent). Les deux lettres sont donc de la même date. La date de « December 1596 », qui est inscrite au dos et à la fin du document, est celle de la remise à Essex par Alonso Nuñez de Herrera d'une copie de la dite lettre (V. *infra*, p. 107).

and after these and this high amplified state, may she obtain goods and blessings that may come from all parts night and day!

We write these from our royal court of Moroccos — God preserve it! — Wee are — prayses be to God! — in all good, one after another — God be praised!

And the cause of writing this unto your high state is that the servaunts of our high housen, the merchant John de Marchona[1], humbled himself before our high presence about the matter of his nephew Alonso Nuñez de Herrara[2], whom your royal fleet carried with it amongst others from Caliz[3], as pledges for the quantity of money they agreed uppon with them[4], and hath helped himselfe of his service done in our royal gates and greatned state. And by this our royal letter we write unto you for his release, so that you let us know what belongs unto him[5] of the quantity of monie, which we will command to be given out of our royal treasure — God increase it! — for herein you shall respect our face, whereof he hath helped himself, and our honor shall shine over him.

And besides this, I require you would write him letters of security for his ships in their going and coming; for they goe in our service; and for this let there be written him letters for the protection of his shippes being met of them of yours.

December 1596.

Lambeth Palace Library, vol. 660, f. 191. — Traduction[6].
Hatfield House, Cecil Mss., 147, f. 200. — Copie.
British Museum. — Birch Mss., 4122, f. 143. — Copie du XVIIIe siècle.

1. Jean de Marchena, sujet du grand-duc de Florence, marchand établi au Maroc pour le service du Chérif. Les Espagnols l'utilisaient aussi comme agent, tout en le considérant comme suspect. V. *infra*, p. 108; *1re Série*, Espagne, aux années 1595-1602, *passim*.

2. Sur ce personnage, V. le Doc. XXXIV, p. 107. Le grand-duc de Toscane l'accréditait, le 16 février 1602, comme son agent à Rouen. V. *1re Série*, Dépôts divers, Florence, à la date indiquée.

3. *Caliz* : Cadix. Sur la prise de cette ville par les Anglais, V. *supra*, Doc XXVII, p. 93 et note 2.

4. *They agreed upon with them* : entendez : la contribution de guerre convenue entre les Anglais et les Espagnols. — Alonso Nuñez de Herrera expose lui-même (V. *infra*, p. 107) qu'il fut mis au nombre des otages emmenés par les Anglais, en garantie du paiement de 120 000 ducats par les Espagnols.

5. *What belongs unto him*, la part de la contribution de guerre dont il était garant.

6. Cette traduction est celle qui a été transmise par Alonso Nuñez de Herrera. V. *infra*, p. 107.

XXXI

REQUÊTE DE MARCHANDS DE LA BARBARY COMPANY

Leurs facteurs au Maroc sont contraints de laisser embarquer sur leurs navires les marchandises de Richard Tomson. — Celui-ci a introduit au Maroc de nombreux « interlopers ». — Il s'est fait donner le monopole des amandes, des dattes, des câpres, des mélasses. — Ses agents se sont emparés de sucres déjà achetés par les plaignants. — Ils ont un droit de préemption sur l'indigo. — Tomson obtient tous ces privilèges, parce qu'il fournit au Chérif des rames, des lances, des mousquets, des arquebuses, des cordages de navires, des lames de sabre, des balles, etc.

[Avant le 24 septembre 1596 ?[1].]

Au dos, alia manu : The inconveniences susteyned by Richard Thompsons[2] meanes amonges the Company of Barbary merchantes.

[1]. Le présent Document est postérieur aux *Lettres patentes* du 15 juillet 1585 « incorporant » la *Barbary Company* et lui conférant le privilège exclusif du commerce avec le Maroc, car il accuse Richard Tomson d'avoir introduit en ce pays de nombreux « interlopers », expression qui ne se justifie que si le dit privilège existe, au moins nominalement. V. 1re *Série,* Angleterre, t. I, Introduction critique, p. 453. Pour la même raison, il est antérieur à la date à laquelle devait expirer ce monopole accordé pour douze ans, c'est-à-dire au 15 juillet 1597. Il reproche à Tomson de fournir au Chérif des armes, des munitions, des rames et des cordages pour des galères. Or, le négociant espagnol Balthasar Polo, résidant à Merrakech, nous apprend qu'en 1594-1595, le Chérif s'employait très activement à réunir et à armer des galères, pour lesquelles il ne recrutait pas moins de 2 000 soldats, et que les Anglais lui procuraient à cet effet tout le nécessaire, rames, escopettes, munitions... V. *ibidem,* p. 504 et note 1. Il est à supposer que Richard Tomson était au nombre de ces Anglais. Il se peut enfin que le présent Mémoire se rapporte aux démêlés entre Tomson et la *Barbary Company,* que mentionne le document suivant et qu'il soit une des pièces produites par cette dernière pour sa justification. C'est pour ces diverses raisons que la date ci-dessus lui a été hypothétiquement attribuée.

2. Le *Dictionary of National Biography* mentionne un Richard Tomson, dont la mère était originaire d'Anvers et qui s'a-

The inconveniences that are come to your suppliantes by Richard Thompsons meanes.

Our servauntes and factors chardged, uppon paine of the Kinges displeasure and the restraint of shippinge our gooddes from theare in one whole yere, not to deny Thompson and his consortes to lade in our shippes at their pleasures.

Thompson hath brought in of enterlopers nere as many moe persons as wee of the Company, who have byn at grete chardges and susteyned grete losses there, and they never any.

Thompson and his consortes have procured the intire licences of almondes, dates, capers and mallasses whollie to theymselves. In which commodity your suppliantes have furnished 200 tonnes lading in one yere, and nowe not any by that meanes.

donna, pendant plusieurs années, au commerce dans la Méditerranée. En 1582, il était en procès avec la *Levant Company*. Il était un des armateurs du navire « the Jesus », qui fut capturé et emmené à Alger, où lui-même se rendit en 1583, pour racheter les prisonniers. On le trouve en Flandre en janvier 1588. Il semble avoir correspondu confidentiellement avec Walsingham. Dans l'été de 1588, il était lieutenant du navire marchand « the Margaret and John », commandé par le capitaine John Fisher, et prit une part active à divers engagements contre l'invincible Armada, notamment à la bataille de Gravelines, dont il écrivit pour Walsingham un intéressant récit. Vers la fin du siècle, il vivait à Londres et était en correspondance avec Robert Cecil. Ce Richard Tomson est, selon toute probabilité, le personnage dont il est ici question, bien que la fréquence du nom n'autorise pas une certitude absolue. Les documents où il figure ci-après permettent d'ajouter quelques traits à sa biographie. Ils confirment ses relations avec Robert Cecil. On voit aussi qu'il savait bien l'espagnol (V. *infra*, p. 166), ce qu'expliquent l'origine de sa mère et ses séjours en Flandre. Il comptait parmi les riches marchands de Londres et exerçait au Maroc un commerce très actif. Le premier en Angleterre, il procura au Chérif « des marbres et autres choses agréables à ce prince » (V. *infra*, p. 140). Les services ainsi rendus à Moulay Ahmed et ses hautes relations en Angleterre rendaient vaines, sans doute, les plaintes portées contre lui par la *Barbary Company*, dont il ne faisait pas partie. Son activité d'*interloper* pouvait se donner libre carrière. On trouve trois personnages à Merrakech employés par lui comme ses agents : Arnold Tomson, George Tomson, Jasper Tomson. Les deux premiers étaient ses frères et le troisième, sans doute, un parent. Arnold Tomson était à Merrakech en 1588. Il y prit part à une manifestation organisée par ses compatriotes pour célébrer le triomphe de la flotte anglaise sur l'invincible Armada et fut blessé dans une rixe à laquelle elle donna lieu avec des Espagnols (V. *infra*, pp. 252-253, et cf. *supra*, p. 13 et note 1). Il était mort avant 1599 (V. *infra*, p. 141). A cette date, Jasper et George Tomson se trouvent au Maroc, et le dernier y était encore au mois de novembre 1603. V. *infra*, pp. 143, 165, 173, 186, 230. Jasper Tomson avait vécu plusieurs années en Turquie ; il avait même suivi Mahomet

Thompsons factors hath wrounge from us per force our sugers after wee have inpapered theym, made theym upp and paide for theym longe before.

His factors have licence to goe to the place where aneal is made, and to have his first choice, restrayninge your suppliantes till they be furnished, beinge a commodity that your suppliantes have yerelie bestowed a grete some of money in.

All which favors he hath and doth obteyne by reason he furnisheth the King with ores for gallies, launces, muskettes, muskett arrowes, caleveres, poldaves, cordage for gallies, sorde blades, gret shott and such like; which wee will not do, beinge an unchristian thing and a grete sclaunder to this her Maties realme.

Signé: Edward Holmeden. — Richard Gore. — John Susans. — Robart Bowids[1].

British Museum. — *Lansdowne Mss., 112, f. 120.* — *Original.*

---

lll dans une expédition contre la Hongrie (V. *infra*, p. 143 et note 1).

[1]. Edward Holmeden, John Suzan et Robert Bowyer figurent au nombre des membres de la *Barbary Company*. Richard Gore était sans doute un des fils de « Jerard Gore the elder », qui sont aussi mentionnés collectivement dans les *Lettres patentes*. V. *1re Série*, Angleterre, t. I, p. 469 et notes 2 et 12, p. 470 et note 3.

XXXII

LETTRE DE BILLINGSLEY, HARVYE ET CARMERDEN
A BURGHLEY

Ils ont constaté l'exactitude des renseignements fournis par Tomson sur le navire arrivé dans la Tamise avec une cargaison de produits marocains. — Néanmoins, les marchands de la Compagnie du Maroc s'opposent au débarquement de cette cargaison. — Leurs arguments, qui s'insoirent plus de leurs intérêts particuliers que de ceux de l'État, ne méritent pas d'être rapportés à Burghley, qui avisera.

14 [n. st. 24] septembre 1596.

Au dos : To the right honorable and our verrye good Lord, the Lord Highe Treasorer of England. — *Alia manu :* 14 September 1596. — Mʳ Billingley, Mʳ Harvey, Mʳ Carmarthen to my Lord — Certeficat towching the informacion of Mʳ Thompson.

Our duties to your Lordship most humbly commended, — According to a letter of the 9 of this present receaved from your Lordship in the behalf of this bearer Mʳ Thomson[1], we have examined his information exhibited to your Lordship tooching a ship called « the Marget George », laden with goods at Barbary and now arrived in the river of Thamis, and doo find by testification of the master owner of the said ship (being examined openly before us in the Custome-house) the same to be true. We have also acquaynted the Gooverner and others of the Barbary merchants with the cause, and have mooved them, as from your Lordship, that they would, for the said respect, permitte the said goodes to

---

1. V. *supra*, p. 101, note 2.

be here customed and landed[1]; but they will not by any meanes be therunto drawen. They alledg many reasons to the contrary, which, for that in our opinions they have a reference rather to theyr owne private commodity then to the preserveng of her Maties custome, we forbeare to troble your Lordship therewith, referring the farther consideration thereof to your Lordships most honorable grave wisedome.

And so we commit your Lordship to the protection of the Almighty.

From the Custome-house, 14 September 1596.

Your Lordships most humbly to command,

Signé: Henry Billingsley. — Robert Harvye. — Richd Carmerden.

Hatfield House, Cecil Mss., 44, f. 91. — Original.

---

[1]. On a vu, 1re Série, Angleterre, t. I, p. 474, que les marchandises en provenance du Maroc ne pouvaient être inscrites à la douane anglaise et admises au débarquement que sur l'autorisation de la Compagnie du Maroc.

XXXIII

LETTRE DE WILLIAM LILLY A ESSEX

(Extrait)

Envoi d'un ambassadeur français au Chérif pour préparer une guerre contre l'Espagne, qui a soutenu Moulay en-Nasser.

Aumale, 13 décembre 1596.

Au dos : To the most honorable my lord and master the Erle of Essex, at the Court. — *Alia manu :* William Lillye, 13 December 1596, at Aumale.

My Lorde,

I have ben at Rouen this last weeke past.

. . . .

At this tyme the King is in hande to send to the great Seriphe, what is the King of Morockes, to treate a conclusion of a warre against Spaigne, for that the King of Spaigne hath assisted his brother against him[1]. I know the present he will send him is redy, and his ambassador named, and the instructions wrytten[2].

. . . .

Your Lordships most humble servant,

Signé : William Lylle.

Omall, this 13 of Decembre 1596.

Hatfield House, Cecil Mss., 47, f. 21. — *Original.*

---

1. Sur la lutte entre Moulay Ahmed el-Mansour et Moulay en-Nasser, son neveu et non son frère, comme le prétend Lilly, V. *supra*, p. 90 et note 4. — Il est inexact que Philippe II ait assisté Moulay en-Nasser. Il se contenta de lui permettre de quitter l'Espagne pour retourner au Maroc.

2. Dès la fin de 1595, il était question de faire revenir Arnoult de Lisle en France, en lui envoyant un remplaçant. V. 1re Série, France, t. III, Introduction, p. xvi. Étienne Hubert, qui fut désigné pour aller au Maroc, s'y rendit en 1598. V. *ibidem*, p. xxii.

XXXIV

LETTRE D'ALONSO NUÑEZ DE HERRERA A ESSEX

Il envoie à Essex la copie d'une lettre écrite en sa faveur par le Chérif à la Reine. — Il n'est pas sujet du roi d'Espagne, mais du grand-duc de Toscane; son oncle est un marchand aux gages du Chérif et réside au Maroc; lui-même s'y est rendu pour servir ce prince, qui l'a envoyé à Cadix pour acheter divers articles; il n'y a donc pas lieu de le détenir comme otage. — Ces faits sont attestés par un certificat que lui ont délivré les otages espagnols. — Il offre néanmoins de payer une rançon, mais demande qu'on le sépare des Espagnols et qu'on le laisse venir à Londres, où il s'engage à rester jusqu'à ce qu'Essex en décide autrement.

Ware[1], 26 décembre 1596 [n. st. 5 janvier] 1597.

Au dos, alia manu : An English coppie of the letter from Alonso Nuñez de Herrera unto the right honorable the Earle of Essex.

Right honorable and moste excellent Lord,

The Kinge of Berberye writte a letter in my behalf unto the Queenes Ma[tie][2], wherin he intreated her yt might please her to grante me liberty, as by the coppie thereof here inclosed your Honor may see. Which being given her Ma[tie], answer was made that I, being one of the pleadges for the hundreth and twenty thousand ducketts[3], yt behooved that this matter should be conferred of with the right honorable Generalls[4].

Wherfore, fynding myselfe amonge those that are att your Honors disposicon and command, it behooveth me moste humbly to beseech you yt may please your good Honor to understand that I was not borne in Spayne, nor am subjecte thereof, and that my father hath dwelled in the state of the Great Duke of Toscana (whereof he, my

---

1. Ville à 30 km. au nord de Londres.
2. V. *supra*, Doc. XXX, p. 99.
3. V. *supra*, p. 100 et note 4.
4. Les chefs de l'expédition de Cadix, le comte d'Essex et Lord Howard. V. *supra*, p. 93, note 3.

uncles and myselfe are subjectes) and at this present is at Venice. My uncle[1] is the Kinge of Barberyes merchant resident in that kingdome, whether I went from Florence in the same Kinges service, and from thence to Cales, in noe other sorte but as merchant stranger factor for my uncle.

So that the state of pleadge supposing a man to be subjecte to some enemy prince, your Honor may voutsafe, of your speciall favor and greate clemency, to judge that I canot be pleadge for any Spanish or other mater, my soverayngnes being in league of amitye with her Matie; the which I doe the rather declare, bycause assuredly I knowe it canot any waye be prejudiciall to your Honors right, specially for that the Spanish pleadges have given me certificate, according to truth, in writing, that I was not borne in Spayne, nor am subjecte of that King, and that my father and parentes dwell in the state of Florence, from whence I went to Maroccos in the service of the King of Barbery, whoe sent me to Cales, wher I bought him sundrey thinges, resyding ther but as a merchant stranger.

Which notwithstanding, I doe moste humbly submitt myselfe unto your Honors favor to paye for ransome what (my state and habilety considered) your Honor shall judge and comand ; moste humbly beseeching your Honor that yt would please you, of your courteous bounty, seeinge I am not subjecte of Spayne and so canne be no pleadge for Spanish affayres, you would comand me to be separated from that company, and that I maye be in London with some frend, givinge sufficient surety not to absent myselfe untill I have other order from your good Honor.

And so, moste humbly submitting myselfe unto your Honors good favor, I rest beseeching the Almighty alwayes to increase yt in all honor and felicity for many and happie yeares.

From Ware, this 26th of December 1596.

Your Honors moste humble servant, that kisseth your honorable handes,

Alonso Nuñez de Herrera.

Lambeth Palace Library, vol. 660, f. 140. — Original.
Hatfield House, Cecil Mss., 174, f. 60. — Copie.

1. *My uncle* : Juan de Marchena. V. *supra*, p. 100 et note 1.

XXXV

MÉMOIRE DE PEDRO FERREIRA[1] POUR ESSEX

Ferreira rappelle les services qu'il a rendus à la Reine, lors de l'affaire du docteur Lopes. — Il a pris part à l'expédition de Cadix, d'où il a été envoyé au Maroc. — Le Chérif a manifesté sa joie de la prise de Cadix et a demandé des renseignements sur le comte d'Essex. — Il a appris le départ de la flotte anglaise pour Terceira et a déclaré que la prise de cette île ruinerait le roi d'Espagne, en interceptant les envois d'argent. — Il met toutes les ressources de son royaume à la disposition de l'Angleterre. — Il demande réponse à la lettre qu'il a écrite à la Reine au sujet d'un marchand.

20 janvier 1596 [n. st. 30 janvier 1597].

Au dos : Ferrara. Sa memoyre au comte d'Essex, le 20me de janvier 1596.

Que Votre Excellence se souvienne de la parolle qu'elle me disoit en la Tour[2] sur la confession de Dr Lopes[3].

---

1. Pedro Ferreira, captif au Maroc, avait été racheté par Balthasar Polo et s'était rendu en Angleterre avec D. Christophe en 1592. Son père, Estevão Ferreira, s'étant trouvé mêlé à la conspiration du docteur Lopez, fut exécuté en 1594, et il résulte du présent document que Pedro Ferreira avait été l'un des dénonciateurs de cette conjuration. On a vu *supra*, p. 94, note 1, que Pedro Ferreira avait été envoyé de Cadix avec des lettres de D. Christophe et d'Essex pour le Chérif. Arrivé à Merrakech le 16 août, il reçut son congé à la fin de septembre. V. 1re Série, Espagne, lettre de Balthasar Polo des 30 août, 15-26 septembre 1596. Pedro Ferreira revint l'année suivante au Maroc, où il arriva le 25 avril. V. *ibidem*, lettres du même du 30 avril, de Diego Marin du 3 mai 1597. On ignore le but de cette seconde mission et ce qu'il devint ensuite. C'était, dit Balthasar Polo (V. *ibidem*, lettre du 19 mai 1597), un mauvais sujet, « un perdido ».

2. La Tour de Londres.

3. Sur la conjuration du docteur Lopes, V. *supra*, p. 65, note 3.

Que le roy du Portugal est mort[1] et que le roy de Espaigne a pardonné à tous les Portugais ausquels la Royne avoit fait mercy, et à moy non.

J'ay perdu mon père et ma mère et moy-mesmes[2], pour ce fait de Dr Lopes et le service que j'ay fait à la Royne.

Que je me suis trouvé avec Son Excellence en Calez, aussy bien sur la mer que sur la terre, et de Calez je suis allé en Barberie.

Celles-cy sont les choses que le Roy m'a demandé.

Que la prise de Calez luy avoit donné plus de contentement, que s'il eust eu la valeur de ce qu'estoit perdu en la ville, pour le mal que le roy d'Espaigne lui avoit fait[3].

Il m'a demandé si le Comte General feust vieus homme ou jeune, et s'il estoit le principal de ce païs d'Angleterre, s'il estoit marryé et avoit des enfants.

Je luy a fait responce qu'il estoit de 26 ans[4], marrié, avoit des enfants et estoit le plus grand seigneur[5] capitaine de tout ce païs.

Le Roi dit qu'il avoit gaigné grand honneur par la clemence qu'il avoit usé vers les subjets de son ennemy et en son propre païs.

Il m'a demandé où estoit allé l'armée. Je luy respondois : à la Tercera[6]. « Ma foy, dit le Roy, si elle prend la Tercera, le roy d'Espaigne n'aura remede pour recevoir d'argent[7] et sera bientost pauvre homme. »

Il a dit que toutes les choses qu'estoient en son païs necessaires

---

1. D. Antonio, roi titulaire de Portugal, qui avait quitté l'Angleterre pour se retirer en France auprès de Henri IV, était mort à Paris, le 26 août 1595.

2. Pedro Ferreira veut dire qu'il a été ruiné.

3. L'impression produite sur Mouley Ahmed el-Mansour par la prise de Cadix fut si vive, qu'il en conçut le projet de conquérir l'Espagne de compte à demi avec les Anglais. La première ouverture de ce projet fut faite, en juin 1599, par le caïd Azzouz, au nom du Chérif, à un marchand anglais de Merrakech, Jaspar Thomson (V. infra, Doc. XLIX, p. 142). La proposition formelle en fut faite, le 23 septembre 1600, par l'ambassadeur Abd el-Ouahed el-Anouri, qui fut envoyé en Angleterre spécialement à cet effet (V. infra, Doc. LXXI, p. 177).

4. Le comte d'Essex, né en 1567, avait alors 29 ans.

5. Au-dessus de ces mots, en interligne, on lit le mot : « guerrier ».

6. L'île de Terceira, qui était à cette époque considérée comme la principale des Açores. — En réalité, la flotte anglaise avait regagné directement l'Angleterre.

7. Les Anglais, une fois maîtres de cette île, auraient intercepté la flotte des Indes.

pour ce païs d'Angleterre et que, si elle en avoit besoign, qu'il la les fairoit avoir. Et que de ceste sorte il avoit escrit al seignor Don Christophero[1].

Il demande responce de la Royne à la lettre du Roy[2] escrite en faveur du merchant[3], et que je la porte, et en ce voyage puisse mener le cheval.

Lambeth Palace Library, vol. 654, f. 174. — Original[4].

1. V. *supra*, Doc. XXIX, p. 96.
2. V. cette lettre du Chérif, *supra*, Doc. XXX, p. 99.
3. Alonso Nuñez de Herrera. V. le document précédent.

4. Une analyse de ce document a été publiée par Thomas Birch, *Memoirs of the Reign of Queen Elizabeth*, t. II, p. 269. Il confond Pedro Ferreira avec son père Estevão. V. *supra*, p. 109 et note 1.

XXXVI

INSTRUCTIONS POUR MATTHEW BREDGATE[1]

Il prendra soin des marchandises qui sont à bord du « True Love » et de celles qui y seront embarquées au Maroc et il veillera à la bonne conservation du navire. — Il exécutera scrupuleusement au Maroc toutes les conventions stipulées avec les marchands dans sa charte-partie. — En croisant sur la côte espagnole, à son retour du Maroc, il évitera les galères ennemies. — S'il capture un navire, il l'enverra en Angleterre ou l'amènera au Maroc pour y vendre sa cargaison. — Les articles de grande valeur seront transportés à bord du « True Love » et inventoriés. — Bredgate acceptera comme second, dans la direction du voyage, le serviteur de Robert Cecil, Joseph Maye.

25 février 1596 [n. st. 7 mars 1597].

Au dos, alia manu : 25 February 1596. Instructions for Captain Bredgat into Barbery.

Instructions for Captayne Mathewe Bredgate for a voyage into Barbary, 25 February 1596.

1. Yow shall take charge of our good shippe « the Trewe Love », laden as she is by the marchauntes, and shall have due care as well to preserve the marchaundizes nowe on board, and suche goodes

---

1. Le Lord Amiral Howard et Robert Cecil, armateurs du « True Love », avaient frété leur navire à des marchands trafiquant au Maroc et voulaient, en même temps, utiliser le dit navire pour la guerre de course. Dans une lettre datée de juillet 1597 (*St. Pap., Dom., Eliz., vol.* 264, n° 37), Robert Cecil demandait à Essex, qui venait de recevoir le commandement d'une nouvelle expédition maritime, destinée à opérer contre la flotte des Indes, que, s'il rencontrait le « True Love », on ne visitât pas le navire et qu'on ne réquisitionnât pas les « pains de sucre ».

as shalbe laden into her from Barbarye, as also the shippes owne tackle, seastoare, furniture, powlder and munition from wast and spoyle of the Companye, or any other disorderlie usage.

2. Yow shall perfectlie instructe yourself in your charter partie, and, accordinge to the same, shall shape your course for Barbarye, and shall staie there, and doe there all manner of thinges that in the said charter partie is expressed and requyred, so as the marchaunts maie have noe just cause of grevaunce, whom espetiallie wee woulde have sattisfied with due performaunce of all covenauntes agreed uppon.

3. When yow have unladen att Barbarye and doe seeke adventures on the coast of Spayne, yow shall have care to keepe yourself out of the daunger of the gallies, which are wounte ever att that tyme of the yeare to be stirringe there.

4. Yf God blesse yow with any prise, and that shee be of good strengthe and hable to sayle home, yow shall put Maie into her, or, if he should miscary, then some honest and skillfull men into her, and shall sende her for Englande, if yow can do it with safetie; and, if she be not worth the sending for England, yow may then carry her for Barbery, if her commodites be fytt to be solde there.

5. The shorte endes of most valewe and such goodes as shall not neede to pestor your shippe with stowage, yow shall them, with the pryvitie of your maister and the substantiallest of your companye, take on board the « Trewe Love », and shall make a just inventorie therof to be avowed under the handes of the chefest of them.

6. Lastlie, bycause wee must referre manye thinges to your owne discreation, wee hope yow will order all thinges with that due respect as maye gyve us lykinge of your doinges and cause to imploye yow in like sorte hereafter.

Signé : Howard[1].

---

1. Charles Howard of Effingham (1536-1624), grand-amiral d'Angleterre en 1585, créé comte de Nottingham au retour de l'expédition de Cadix.

Yow shall suffer Maye, the servant of me, the Secretarie, to be acquainted with all such thinges as yow shall take or doe in your vooag; and, if the wyndes will serve yow, yow shall bestowe some tyme on the coast of Spaine as yow goe out, both for intelligence and purchase. And hereby we do comaund the sayd May to be obedient in all things to your government as captain and master.

Signé: Ro. Cecyll.

Hatfield House, Cecil Mss., 38, f. 59. — Original.

XXXVII

LETTRE DE JOSEPH MAYE[1] A ROBERT CECIL

Ses compagnons et lui ont capturé un navire du Brésil: la cargaison de sucre a été vendue au Maroc aux marchands Sothering et Tomson; les nègres et les balles de coton ont été également vendus sur place. — Prise d'un flibot chargé de sucre et de vins des Canaries, qui a été dirigé sur l'Angleterre.

Safi, 27 juin [n. st. 7 juillet] 1597.

Au dos : To the right honorable and his verye good master Sir Robert Sycill, Knight, her Majesties Principall Secritarye. — *Alia manu :* 27 Junii 1597. Your Honors servant Mr May, from Saphea, in Barbery.

Right Honorable,

Acording to my bounden duty, these ar to signifie unto youe our good successe, which we resevid un the ii of Maye in the mouthe of Tangust[2]. We toucke a Brasill man of 60 tune ; her sugers were whitte and others, to the number of 250 chests ; and for so much that they were weat and ill counditione, we caried them for Barberye, assuring ourselfes it was our best course ; wher we sold them to Mr Sothering[3] and Mr Thomsone[4] for 7^{li} the chest. And as we thinke,

---

1. V. le document précédent. Le « True Love » était encore en Angleterre le 21 [n. st. 31] mars. Matthew Bredgate écrivait, à cette date, à Robert Cecil que son départ avait été retardé par des perquisitions faites à bord de son navire, qu'on disait chargé de grosses sommes d'argent. *Hatfield House, Cecil Mss., vol. 7, f. 124.* Dans une lettre en date du 15 [n. st. 25] avril, Maye annonçait à son maître qu'il était arrivé à Safi le 9 [n. st. 19] du même mois. *Ibidem, vol. 50, f. 19.*

2. Estuaire à 3 lieues N. de Santa-Cruz.

3. Ce marchand, mentionné ultérieurement dans deux lettres d'Élisabeth à Moulay Ahmed el-Mansour, mourut au Maroc peu avant le 24 juin 1599. V. *infra,* pp. 141, 147 et 148.

4. Sur les Tomson, V. *supra,* p. 101, note 2.

theye wold have eldid no more in England. The money is to be paid by Mr Richard Thomson, of London, by biles of exchange; whose brother we have found most carfull of our busnes and frindly to us in the cuntrye; the captayne and master ordering me, by your articles, that I should staye in Barbery and tacke charge of the sugers with delivering them by acount to the marchant; which acordingly I have performed.

Since which tyme, they « Trew Love » hath taken another of 120, being a flibout loden with Canary sugers and Canary wyne; but is Spaniars goods, which by Gods help we will bring for England.

In the first prise, ther wear negros, which the captayn sold for 60^u, and 4 bages of coten woll, which eldid 30^u. The shipp I have fraightid with thinges of small valew, being Mr Thomson brothers goods, for your better profit and, I hopp, to your liking.

The master of the « Sollonia », of London, at our first arivall at Saphea, disuadid us from taken a ship of which we writ yow; but I have found by enquirye that the goods did belonge to the Duck of Florence subjects, and that the weare not they Spaniars of Morocus, untle she wear in horbored.

The report is geiving out of the death of the King of Spayne and the rising of the Portingals. The Spaniars report the flett to be bond for Seland.

This having nothinge els to advertize your Honor, but praing to the Almighty for the preservation of your prosperous helth with all prosperity long to countinewe.

From Saphea, 27 of June 1597.

Your Honors most bounden servant,

Signé : Josephe Maye.

Hatfield House, Cecil Mss., 52, f. 74. — Original.

XXXVIII

LETTRE DE CHRISTOPHER PARKINS[1] A [ROBERT CECIL][2]

Il envoie les deux projets de lettres d'Élisabeth au roi du Maroc et au vice-roi de Fez, son fils, qu'on l'avait prié de rédiger. — Il les a fait traduire en espagnol. — Parkins donne son avis sur la langue et le protocole dont il convient d'user avec le Chérif et son fils.

1er [n. st. 11] juillet 1597.

En tête : 1597. — Barbary.

Right Honorable,

Concerning the letters for Barbarie, I was first requiered to write them in Latin. Afterward I was informed that the last letters coming thence were written in the toungue of that countrie, with a copie of them in Spanish. Wheruppon I thought it agreeable that theis letters should have been written in Latin, with a copie also in Spanish. But at the length, I found a president of her Maties letter to that King written in the Spanish languadg, wherein her Highnes title usuall in the begyning of her letters was omitted, and wordes of speciall courtesie as Matie, Serenitic and Highnes, etc., weare, as it were, of purpose avoided. And, the marchauntes[3] urdging me verie much, I sought your Honors servant whome yow use in that tounge; but finding him to be absent from the Courte, I drew a forme of the letters in English, the which I send your Honor heare inclosed[4], and caused them to be tourned into Spanish by a verie sufficient man; afterward, for the titles and pointes, conferring

---

1. Sir Christopher Perkins ou Parkins (1547?-1622). Il entra, étant à Rome, dans la Compagnie de Jésus (1566) et s'en sépara par la suite. Revenu en Angleterre en 1589, inculpé de trahison, puis reconnu innocent, il fut employé comme agent diplomatique, notamment pour les affaires commerciales, en Danemark, en Pologne, près de l'Empereur, près de la Ligue Hanséatique. Il fit fonction quelque temps de « Latin Secretary » de la Reine.

2. On a cru pouvoir rétablir le nom de Robert Cecil, qui n'est pas indiqué, d'après la teneur de la lettre et les titres donnés au destinataire.

3. Thomas Bramley et Henry Farrington. V. *infra*, p. 120.

4. V. *infra*, Doc. XXXIX, p. 119 et n. 1.

them with Sir Edward Hobbie[1] his servaunt Hieronimo, counted the best Spaniard in England.

The merchauntes urdg verie much, as the matter ymporteth them, and to that effect they gave their supplication to your Honor, and since have much solicited the matter. So that now it remaineth in your good favor to give some order in aunswere of this their humble suite, as it shall please yow best, both for the manner, matter and writing.

Pleasing it your Honor to knowe my opinion, yf presidentes be no gospells nor above reason, I thinck that, as other kinges, by reason of state, use to begynn their letters to whomesoever with their owne stile, yt may seeme fitt for her Matie so to doe in theis letters, as she useth in others to the Emperor, the Greate Turke, etc. I thinck also it is with disadvantadg, both in substance and reputacion, to write in any other lounge hence to forraine princes then in English or Latyn, and that the courteous terme of Matie be used with the King of Marocus, who writeth himself Emperor of the Moares, and of Alteza with the King of Fez his sonne[2]. I would also consider if it were fitt, by this occasion, to make some honorable mention of the armie now sett forth.

Thus much for duties sake, leaving the use hereof to your Honors better censure, whearwith, as most readie for all occasions of service to your content, I take my leave.

This first of Julie 1597.

Your Honors ever at commandment,

Signé: Ch. Parkins.

British Museum. — Cotton Mss., Nero B. XI, f. 300. — Original.

1. Il avait été question d'envoyer ce personnage auprès du Chérif, lors de l'expédition de Cadix. V. *supra*, p. 94, note 1.

2. Parkins a constaté qu'en écrivant au Chérif, la Reine évite l'usage des titres royaux, soit pour elle-même, soit pour Moulay Ahmed. Cette constatation est exacte, comme le prouve la comparaison d'une lettre d'Élisabeth au Grand-Seigneur avec ses lettres antérieures au Chérif. V. *supra*, Doc. I, X et XI, pp. 1, 34 et 40. Ces questions de protocole ont toujours eu une grande importance dans la correspondance entre princes chrétiens et musulmans. Cf. H. DE CASTRIES, *La diplomatique des princes de la dynastie saadienne* (en préparation) et *Moulay Ismaïl et Jacques II*, p. 59, note 2, p. 61, note 1. — Le fils de Moulay Ahmed mentionné par Parkins était Moulay ech-Cheikh, institué vice-roi de Fez et désigné comme héritier présomptif en 1579. EL-OUFRÂNI, p. 149.

XXXIX

LETTRE D'ÉLISABETH A MOULAY AHMED EL-MANSOUR[1]

Thomas Bramley et Henry Farrington, marchands de Londres, ont à Larache un facteur, James Rives, qui détient pour 60 000 onces de marchandises leur appartenant. — Un de leurs navires étant allé prendre à Santa-Cruz soixante et quelques caisses de sucre et ayant touché à Larache pour compléter son chargement, James Rives y a fait débarquer le sucre, qu'il s'est approprié, et a fait repartir le navire sur lest. — Élisabeth prie Moulay Ahmed de faire restituer leurs biens à Bramley et à Farrington.

[11 juillet 1597.]

En tête : Barbary.

To the King of Moroco.

Most excellent King, — As the divine Providence foreseeth the weaknes of men to be such that they are like sometyme to declyne to unjust dealinges, so hath it appointed in all places governors and princes by whose just wisdome and authoritie wronges committed by the evill disposed may orderly be redressed. Wherfor, as we have long since intertayned mutuall amitie with your Highnes for the free trade of our subjectes, to the publique good of both our dominions, and have now many yeares performed all things on both sides accordinglie, for the furder following of those good courses,

---

1. V. le Document précédent et *infra*, Doc. XLI, p. 122. — Le projet de lettre à Moulay ech-Cheikh, qui vient à la suite de la présente lettre, sur le même folio, et qu'on n'a pas jugé utile de publier, recommande également à ce prince Thomas Bramley et Henry Farrington. Le préambule que l'on trouve dans le présent document a disparu : on passe directement des mots : « To the King of Fez. — Most excellent Prince », à un exposé des faits analogue à celui de la lettre à Moulay Ahmed. Comme ce dernier, Moulay ech-Cheikh est appelé : « your Highnes ».

it is now consequent that we frendlie and confidentlie requier your just favor for the remedieng an untollerable unjustice offered of late to some of our subjectes trading in your dominions.

Amongest the which two marchantes of our cittie of London, Thomas Bramley and Henrie Farrington[1], have ben verie much misused by a servant and factor of theirs in Barberie, named James Rives, having much of their goods now in his hands, to the value of aboute threescoare thowsand ounces, and offering to convert the same to his owne use. For the said marchantes, sending divers shipps this last yeare into Barberie, gave order for one of them to goe first to the porte of Suz and there to take in threescoare and odd chestes of sugar for parte of her lading, and then to goe to porte Alarach for other commodities, the which the said James Rives signified by his letters to be in a redinesse theare. But at the comming of the said ship to the said porte Alarach for the rest of her lading, by the practice of James Rives, the sugars were gott a shoare under pretence that the other comodities were more fitt to be stowed under them. The which being don, the ship was dismissed emptie, with declaration that the said James Rives intended to settle himself a state of lief with those his masters goods, a thing altogether untollerable and, being passed without redresse, sufficient to discouradg our men from trade.

In consideration wherof our frendlie request is that, at the suite of the bearer hereof, your Highnes will give some order wherby theis our subjectes may recover their owne from their unfaithfull servant. The which your most just favor wilbe agreable to our former amitie, a testimonie of your justice, an example for the evill disposed not to truste in their lewednes, and finallie an encouradgmente of honest marchauntes to follow their trade with the publique good of both our kingdomes.

And thus doubting nothing but that yow will have reguard of justice in this respect, the rather at our request, we pray God graunt your Highnes all true hapines.

British Museum. — Cotton Mss., Nero B. XI, f. 301. — Minute.

1. Ces deux marchands étaient membres de la *Barbary Company*. V. les lettres patentes du 15 juillet [n. st.] 1585, *1re Série*, Angleterre, vol. I, p. 469, n. 8 et 19.

XL

MÉMOIRE ANONYME ADRESSÉ A ROBERT CECIL

(Extrait)

Il conviendrait que la Reine envoyât un messager au Chérif, pour le prier de faire détruire les blés autour des places espagnoles du Maroc et d'interdire à ses sujets de vendre des grains aux Espagnols.

[1597 ?][1]

Au dos, de la main de Robert Cecil: A project for the sea.

Right Honorable,

Wheras of late I made unto your Honor a certeyne proffer or proposition of a warr againstt Spayne, such as hetherto hath not bin attempted :

. . . .

Further itt is requisitt thatt her Matie send a messinger in tyme convenientt to the King of Maroko, requesting him to appoynt som of his Mores to burne and spoyle the Spaniards corne adjoyning to their fortts and garisons in Barbarie, and streightlie to prohibitt his subjectts from bartring of corne with them; which the More, in regard of his antientt amytie, will not bee unwilling to yield unto. Not (I protest) that I would have those dogs to insultt ovir the Christian name, butt thatt hir Matie mightt make so sound and unresistable a warr on all sydes against the King of Spayne.

. . . .

Public Record Office. — State Papers, Domestic, Elizabeth, vol. CCLXV, n° 100. — Original.

---

1. Ce mémoire paraît avoir été rédigé en vue de l'expédition maritime projetée contre l'Espagne, qui partit en juillet 1597, sous les ordres du comte d'Essex.

XLI

ACTE DU CONSEIL PRIVÉ[1]

(Extrait)

Un certain James Rives, facteur au Maroc de Thomas Bramley et de Henry Farrington, son gendre, leur a soustrait une somme de six mille livres. — La Reine a écrit au roi du Maroc et au vice-roi de Fez pour faire rendre justice aux plaignants. — Henry Farrington, s'étant rendu au Maroc avec les dites lettres, a fait emprisonner James Rives et est mort au cours du procès. — Le Conseil prie les marchands anglais résidant au Maroc de venir en aide à ceux que Thomas Bramley chargera de poursuivre ce procès.

Whitehall, 15 mars 1597 [n. st. 25 mars 1598].

Wednesday forenoone. At the Court at Whitehall, 15° Martii, 1597.

Present: Lord Archbishopp, Lord Keper, Erle of Essex, Lord Admyrall, Lord Chamberlain, Lord Northe, Lord Buckhurst, M.r Comptroller, M.r Chauncellour of the Exchequer.

A letter to Sir Robert Cecill, Knight, Principall Secretary to her Majestie, and at this instant sent in ambassage from her Majestie to the French Kinge.

. . . .

A letter to the English merchauntes resydent in Barbary[2].

---

1. Sur l'affaire dont traite le présent acte, V. *supra*, Doc. XXXIX, p. 119.

2. Avant de passer à la présente lettre, le Conseil vient de décider d'écrire à Robert Cecil, qui se trouvait alors à la Cour de France, en faveur de Thomas Bramley, à qui des marchandises ont été saisies à Marseille, il y a environ six ans, pour une valeur de 11 000 livres, et qui n'a pu obtenir ni restitution ni indemnité. Il a, depuis, subi de lourdes pertes au Maroc. Il se propose d'envoyer un homme à Cecil pour lui ex-

Wee are enformed, as well by letters from the Lord Maior and moste of the Aldermen of the cytty of London, that, besides divers great losses that Thomas Bramley and Henry Farrington, his sonne in lawe, have sustained, a servaunt of theirs named James Ryves, whome they put in trust in Barbary with theire busynes, went awaie with the somme of 6 000^{li}. Hereuppon her Majesty, beinge moved with this unfaithfull lewde parte of theire factor, did very gratiously wryte her letters to the Kinge of Barbary and Kinge of Fesse, to procure the staie of theire said servaunt and that restitucion might be made unto thes merchaunts of the goods and money in his hands.

Farrington himselfe, repayringe with her Majestys letters into that countrey, procured theire lewd servaunt to be apprehended; and, beinge overtaken with greefe and sickness, died in prosecucion of the cause.

This case beinge well knowne unto you and concernynge as well the said Bramley, an honest and dyscret cyttyzen, as the poore wyfe and children of Farrington, uppon earnest suite made unto us, wee could doe no lesse then recommend earnestly this matter unto you, and doe pray and require you, in so pyttiful a case as this ys, to give your best ayds and assystaunces to soche as shalbe sent thether or appointed by the said Bramley to followe this cause, that the badd fellowe maie be detayned in pryson till he shall have made a perfect accompt and the goodes recovered that remayneth in his hands, or els that he maie be sent over hether to answere his lewd dealing.

Wherein wee doubt not but you will doe your best indevours, consideringe the unfaithfull and lewde dealinge of this badd fellowe, and that the lyke maie conscerne you or any other that of necessyty must put his servaunt in trust. So, etc.

Public Record Office. — *Privy Council Register, Elizabeth, vol. XVI, p. 198*[1].

pliquer l'affaire, dans l'espoir que celui-ci interviendra en sa faveur auprès du roi de France. Le Conseil recommande le cas à Robert Cecil.

[1]. Publié par DASENT, *Acts of the Privy Council of England*, t. XXVIII, p. 362.

XLII

LETTRE DE JOSEPH MAYE A ROBERT CECIL

Ses compagnons et lui ont capturé un flibot qui est envoyé en Angleterre. — Un autre flibot, chargé de grains, qu'ils avaient également pris, leur a échappé, en s'échouant à Mogador. — Robert Cecil aura à examiner si la cargaison du premier navire est de bonne prise. — Grande mortalité au Maroc: 34.000 décès par jour à Merrakech; le bruit court que le Chérif serait mort.

[Du Maroc], 20 [n.st.30] mai 1598.

Adresse : To the right honorable and my very good master, Sir Robert Cecill, Knight and her Majestyes Princippall Secretary etc., geve these in London.

Right Honorable,

My duty in all humbleness remembred, — This is to geve yowe to understand that, upon the first daye of Maye, we touck this flibott which is heare sent home by my Lord Admirals servant Thomas Meredith. Out of him we have taken sertayne unlawfull goods to the valew of twelfe or sextine hundreth ponds or therabouts; which goods remaneth in our shipp, the one halfe without impeachment. And this goods we had not taken out, but that ther was present with us at her taken a ship of Apsome caled the « Dolfyne », and a small pennise, of which one Captaine Lench was commander, of Hanton.

At that very instant, we touck another flibott loden with corne; which ship, as we wear raden in the harborrowe of Mogadore, cut both here cables and put herselfe throughe such a sandy shollowe rocky plase, that we durst not adventure your shipp thorrow; wherby we lost here.

The letters I have sent your Honor, praing that some onne inhabiting about Anserdam maye peruse them; for by the confession of a Portingall, which came in her as passinger, most part dothe belong to Spaniards of Anserdam and Bressels and other plaseis ther adjuning, and some other goods ar sent unto Duchmen dwelling in Spayne for the retorne of wyne and other goods, as will be known by the letters. If your Honor fynd by prove that any goods be not lawfully ours, that is taken out of the shipp, if it stand with your likyng, I thinke it convenient that, in the horborrowes wher these shipes shall aryve, yowe cause stay to be maid, before it be partid to ther companyes, for here the men of the captayne of the « Dolfynes » weare marvelus unorderly. The marchant of this flibott was a conseler in the going away of the other flibott.

We cold not learne of any flett aprovidinge in Spayne, but that sertayne of the shipes and gallies loden with munition and vittayles wear cast awaye.

There hath beane such a mortallity in many plasies in Barbary, that the have dyed in Morocus day by day 34000 thousand[1]; and now newes in these plasies is geve that the Kynege is dead, but not of certayne it is not knowne[2].

This, committing yowr Honor to the Allmightyes protexion, for the preservation of whose life, as my bounden duty, I will contynually pray for.

The xx of May 1598.

Your Honors most bounden servant,

Signé: Josephe Maye.

Hatfield House, Cecil Mss., 61, f. 31. — Original.

---

1. Ainsi répété dans le ms.
2. Sur la mortalité au Maroc à cette époque, V. *infra*, pp. 126, 129 et 130. Dans une relation publiée par Purchas et intitulée *The Voyage of Oliver Noort round about the Globe...* on lit: « October the fourth [1598], they met foure shippes, one of Amsterdam, another of England and two French, comming out of Barbarie, which related of the terrible pestilence in that countrey, of which two hundred and fiftie thousand men in short space had died in Morocco... » Purchas, *Hakluytus Posthumus or Purchas his Pilgrimes*, t. II, p. 71.

XLIII

AVIS DU MAROC

La peste fait de tels ravages que le Roi doit vivre sous la tente. — Le désordre est général. — Moulay Ahmed a dû renforcer sa garde avec des prisonniers. — Les révoltes sont nombreuses et les sucreries que les travailleurs abandonnent risquent d'être saccagées. — 230 000 morts ont été enterrés aux portes de Merrakech. — Les marchands anglais, qui résident dans le fondouk, n'ont pas encore souffert du fléau, bien que les Maures essaient de le leur communiquer. — Dans une ville, depuis quarante jours, 5000 habitants sur 10 000 sont morts et les cadavres sont dévorés par les bêtes, les vivants ne suffisant pas à enterrer les morts. — Les navires anglais reviennent sur lest en raison des troubles.

10 [n. st. 20] juin 1598.

En tête : July. — Advise from Barbery. — A furious plague, 230000 buried out of the gates of Morocco, the King constreined to live in tents, etc. — English, though in the middle of the cytye, free. — An abstract of letters from Barbery of the 10th of June 1598.

The plage [1] dispersed through the country so extremely that the King is forced, for his better securitye, to live in tents in the fields, and there is such an uproare in the countrie, by meanes of the infection, that none can passe unrobed and spieled [2]; the Kings strength, that kept the countrye in subjection, so weakened that he hath been forced to send for captives to strenghten the guard of his person.

Rebellions is in many places, and they threaten the ransacke and spoyle of the inginies [3] ; so the masters and laborers, through

---

1. Sur cette peste, V. le Doc. précédent, p. 125 et note 2.
2. *Spieled*, pour *unspoiled*.
3. V. *infra*, p. 135, note 1.

[eare of rebells and sickeness that is begun in some of the ingenies, are fallen away and leave all disforced, and no preparation for the next yeare.

There hath been caried by good [report][1], out of the gates of Moroccos to be buried, to the number of 230 thousand dead bodyes and more. Yet, the alffandica[2] being in the misdst of the cityc, over [which] our English merchantes are resadent, not any of them as yet infected, notwithstanding the Mores have used meanes to infectt the place, by layinge dead bodeyes at the dores and the streth, which [vermin][3] have eaten ; whereas the Mores say this plage only aperteineth to themselves.

In a towne, where, thought 40 [days][4] be not past, 5 thousand persons is proved to have died ; 10 thousand[5], and verment feedeth of their bodies, for that the rest liveing are not able to bury the dead.

There are in those partes diverse English shippes which will come home unladen, by reason of this trouble; there is reporte the sickness to be in some of them.

These two shippes[6] which are now come are said to be cleare, and will be, so soone as they cann, upp the River.

I thought good, Right Honorable, to give this adveise for that plage, as your Honour will think it requisit order be taken to prevent danger that may happen by those shipes which hereafter may come from thence inffected.

Oxford — All Souls College Mss., 222, f. 98. — Copie du XVIIe siècle.

1. En blanc dans le ms.
2. *Alfandica*, les fondouks.
3. En blanc dans le ms.
4. Mot oublié.
5. Mots mal lus ou phrase incomplète.

6. Les deux derniers alinéas sont une note personnelle émanant de celui qui a rédigé « l'avis » ; elle est adressée à Robert Cecil, comme le prouvent les titres *Right Honorable* et *your Honour.*

XLIV

LETTRE DE GEORGE TOMSON[1] A ROBERT CECIL

Il proteste de son zèle à instruire Cecil de ce qui se passe au Maroc. — Il avait réussi à connaître les nouvelles venant d'Espagne par un serviteur de Balthasar Polo. — Mais la peste qui sévit au Maroc, faisant périr jusqu'à 4500 personnes par jour, a emporté cet agent et son serviteur. — Moulay Ahmed s'était réfugié dans sa mahalla pour échapper au fléau. — Manquant de soldats pour la garde de sa personne, il se rapproche maintenant de Merrakech. — Une conspiration a été découverte, qui était ourdie par le caïd Moustafa, renégat espagnol, favori tout puissant de Moulay ech-Cheikh, vice-roi de Fez. — Il avait promis de livrer Larache au roi d'Espagne. — Il conseillait à Moulay ech-Cheikh de tuer ses frères et semait la discorde entre eux. — Moulay Ahmed a ordonné à Moulay ech-Cheikh de le mettre à mort. — Moulay ech-Cheikh, qui l'avait envoyé lever des impôts, l'a rappelé auprès de lui. — Dédaigneux de cet ordre, Moustafa s'attardait près de la place qu'il voulait livrer. — Sur un nouvel ordre, il s'est mis en marche avec cinq cents cavaliers. — Averti de son arrivée, Moulay ech-Cheikh est allé à sa rencontre, en commandant qu'on le tuât quand il viendrait lui baiser les pieds. — Moustafa, laissant derrière lui ses cavaliers, s'est approché seul avec un parent. — Tous deux ont été décapités.

Merrakech, 9 [n. st. 19] août 1598.

Au dos, alia manu: To the right honorable Sir Robert Cecill, Knight, her Maties Principall Secretarie, etc., at the Courte. — ..... 9 August. George Thomson to my master. Advyses from Moruccos.

1. Sur les Tomson, V. *supra*, p. 101, note 2.

In Morocus, the..... 9th August 1598.

Right Honorable,

Althoughe I knowe your Honour sufficiently advertized, from all places, of all matters worthy the writinge, as well from these partes of Barbery as from all other places wher the English nation houldeth trade, myselfe, as altogether insufficient, yet imbouldned throughe your Honours excedinge fame for good acceptance of every meane present, I have presumed to present these few for proffer of my meane service, which ever more contineueth at your Honours commandement to my uttermoste; and yf in any sorte yt maye seme gratious, I account myselfe fortunate.

In regard of the dayly newes brought out of Spaine into these partes, I have indeavoured to become conversant with some of truste of that nation, to understand the certenty what passed, and what ther newes was. Which was longe before I could compasse; but, findinge one fittinge my desires, servaunt to the Spanish imbassador[1], I thought yt moste for my credite to make some profe of his reportes before I would undertake the presentinge therof to your Honours perusinge, leaste in my first attemptes I became attainted for untruths. But such was the true tryall of his discoveries as I wishe him lyveinge, that your Honour might make use of his bewrayes, althoughe I knowe your Honour wanteth not. But in the time of this great mortallytie in this country, haveinge dyed to the nomber of 4500 a daye[2], which to your Honour maye be knowen before this by other mens reportes, the Spanish imbassador dyed, and many captives his retainers[3], amongst which my professed frind was one; soe that my first indeavours cann add nothinge to your Honours lykeinge.

Through this great mortallitye, the Kinge Mully Hammett hath

---

1. Balthasar Polo. V. *supra*, p. 89, note 1. Tomson annonce la mort de cet agent quelques lignes plus bas. Il l'appelle ambassadour, mais il était, plus exactement, *correspondiente* d'Espagne auprès du Chérif. Au mois de novembre 1598, on s'occupait, à Madrid, de lui trouver un successeur. V. De Castries.

1re Série, Espagne, 11 novembre 1598.
2. Sur cette poste, V. *supra*, p. 125 et note 2, pp. 126-127.
3. Ces captifs de la suite de Balthasar Polo étaient, sans doute, des Espagnols rachetés par l'entremise de cet agent ou mis gracieusement en liberté par le Chérif.

continewed abrode in his tentes[1], but now is drawinge nerer Morocus, through want of souldiers to gard his person, greatly fearinge some invation by the Great Turke, as also fearinge invation by the Spaniard: but that conspiracye is come to light, and the partie, who was the Vize-Kinge of Fesse and soe muche honoured by Mully Sheck, Kinge of that place, as all men admired therat. He was called Alcade Mustapher[2], a Spaniard borne, but torned Moore, and borne in Cevell, his father a cutler; but he in such estimation with the Kinge as often times he would overrule the Kinge, and evermore rode in as great pompe as the Kinge himself. This Alcade had promised to delyver into the Kinge of Spaines handes a porte towne called Allaroche, besides other hainous matters, as geveinge counsell to Mully Sheck to kyll his brothers, haveinge wrought such enmitye betwixt the Kinges sonnes as the Kinge cannot make peace betwixt them.

For these cawses, Mully Hammet cawsed Mully Sheck his sonne to behead him, and to send his head to his almahalla, wher yt is yet extant. The manner of his death was thus. The Kinge Mully Sheck had sent out the said Alcade Mustapher to receave in the graines or duties dewe to be paid by the Kinges subjectes. In the meanewhile, the Kinge, understandinge of his pretended treason, sent for him; but he so lightly regarded the Kinges sendinge as he delayed the time, haveinge with him 5 or 6 hundred men lyeinge neare the place which he purposed to have surrendred. But the Kinge, seinge him to defferr of time, sent him word that he had of importance to talke with him, and then he should retorne againe. Wheruppon he came with 500 horsmen and, sendinge the Kinge word of his comminge, the Kinge went out to mete him,

---

1. On trouve dans El-Oufrâni (pp. 298-305) une lettre écrite de Fez, le 1ᵉʳ septembre 1602, par Moulay Ahmed à Moulay Abou Farès, et dans laquelle le Chérif expose les précautions à prendre contre la peste. On y relève le conseil de quitter Merrakech dès le plus léger indice d'épidémie et de ne jamais rester plus de deux jours dans le même campement. D'après le même historien (p. 305), l'épidémie aurait duré presque sans interruption pendant dix années (1598-1608). El-Kadiri (Trad. Graulle, t. I, p. 109) rapporte qu'en 1598, « la mort emporta chaque jour à Fez de 500 à 2000 personnes; il périt cette année dans la ville plus de 6000 chérifs, fakihs ou notables ».

2. L'exécution du caïd Moustafa est confirmée par la *Relation de Ro. C. V. infra*, Doc. CVII, pp. 331-332.

but gave order that, when he came to kisse his fete, to laye handes one him and presently to dispatch him, geveing only in chardge to the executioners not to disfigur his head nor face, for that he purposed to send the same to his father. The forces he had of horsemen he lefte them in gardens nere adjoyninge, and came to the Kinge, only accompaned with a kindsman of his, and soe, by order of the Kinge, they were both beheaded.

And thus your Honour have heard the present newes and estate of this country; and what herafter shall happen, your Honour shall not want intelligence therof. Cravinge pardon at your Honours handes for my unbesceminge presumtion in offeringe such tedious trobles of noe vallewation.

And soe prayinge for the longe continewance of your Honours health with all happines, I committ your Honour to the Almighties protection.

Your Honours bounden servaunt,

Signé : George Thomson.

Public Record Office. — State Papers, Foreign, Barbary States, vol. XII. — Original.

XLV

LETTRE D'ÉLISABETH A MOULAY AHMED EL-MANSOUR

Elle a coutume de mettre en liberté les captifs maures qui se réfugient en Angleterre. — Elle en renvoie présentement deux au Maroc. — Elle demande, en retour, au Chérif la mise en liberté de deux sujets des Pays-Bas détenus dans son royaume, Engel Adriansz. et Karel van Vingermey.

1598.

Au dos : Al muy alto muy poderoso y muy eccelente rey Muley Hamet, Xarif.

En tête : Loores a Dios Nuestro Señor Todo Poderoso, criador del cielo, tierra y mar, etc.

Elizabeth, por la divina gracia, natural reyna de sus reynos y de sus subjetos, tanto amando y defendiendo los suyos quanto es entrañablemente, con toda felicidad dellos amada y obedescida, escrive esta su real carta al muy alto, muy poderoso, muy eccelente, etc., Muley Hamet Xarif, a quien el soberano Dios de continuacion de la paz y sossiego que al dia de oy tiene, siendo de los suyos temido, y dellos y de todos amado, acatado y honrrado como lo meresce, etc.

Assi como amamos los nuestros, no podemos hazer menos que de amar a nuestros vezinos y a los que buscan nuestro amparo. Los Moros que alcansan llegar debaxo de nuestra jurisdicion, luego son libres y los mandamos a vuestras tierras con buen trattamiento, como al dia de oy van dos y tambien un Turco o dos. Assi vos abemos bien querido visitar con estos pocos renglones para pediros la libertad de dos pobres Flamencos cattibos en vuestra tierra, el uno llamado Angelo Adrianson, de Berga, el otro Carlo de Vingermey, de Flissinga, ambos nascidos en las Tierras Baxas en lugares que yo tengo en mi amparo y en mi possession[1], y assi no dudo me ottorgareys de darles libertad, como continuare de dar libertad a los vuestros, quantos tuvieron tan buena ventura de escapar de manos de los que los cattiban y vendan y compran.

Guarde Dios, etc.

De mi real Corte, a los... de ...... 1598 años de nuestra quenta.

Vuestra hermana y pariente segun ley de corona y ceptro[2].

Public Record Office. — State Papers, Foreign, Barbary States, vol. XII. — Minute.

[1]. L'année suivante, Élisabeth écrivit une nouvelle lettre à El-Mansour pour lui demander la mise en liberté d'un autre captif hollandais, Cornelis Jansz. (*Public Record Office, State Papers, Foreign, Royal Letters, vol. II, n° 22.*)

[2]. Depuis 1585, des troupes anglaises occupaient plusieurs villes des Pays-Bas, entre autres Flessingue, pour les protéger contre les Espagnols.

XLVI

REQUÊTE DE J. NEWTON ET TH. OWEN[1] A ROBERT CECIL

Une somme de près de 8 000 onces en monnaie marocaine a été enlevée par une troupe de Maures à leur facteur Thomas Serocold, entre Merrakech et le Sous. — Bien qu'un caïd du Chérif ait retrouvé la totalité ou la plus grande partie de cette somme, les requérants n'ont pu en obtenir la restitution. — Ils sollicitent une lettre de la Reine au Chérif à cet effet. — Ils exposent également que le Chérif leur doit, depuis 1595, une somme de 11 000 onces environ, payable en sucre, et prient la Reine de leur en obtenir le paiement.

[1598[2].]

Au dos, alia manu: The humble petition of John Newton and Thomas Owen for her Maties letters to the Kinge of Barbery, for recovery of money taken frome theme vyolently by his subjectes and for payment of a debte which the Kinge oweth unto theme three yers olde.

To the right honourable Sir Robert Syssell, Principall Secretary to the Queenes Matie.

Humbly besechethe your Honour your daylye suppliants, John Newton and Thomas Owen of London, marchants, that your Honour wilbe pleased to be meanes for them unto the Queenes Matie for the

---

1. Ces personnages font partie des marchands énumérés dans les *Lettres patentes* du 15 juillet [n. st.] 1585. V. *1re Série*, Angleterre, t. I, p. 470 et notes 4 et 5.

2. La spoliation dont se plaignaient les marchands avait eu lieu en avril 1598 à Mentenitt (Imi n-Tanout). V. *Hatfield House, Cecil Mss., Petition 149.*

obtayneing of her favorable letters directed to the Kinge of Barbary on ther behalfes to this effect:

That, wheare in the moneth of Aprill last past, one Thomas Serocold, factor for your said suppliants in Barbary, did send downe from Morocus, to have bene carryed unto Susse, neare viii thowsand ownces Barbary money, beinge the greatest parte of your said suppliants welths, and sent downe in company of xiij Englishmen, the said Christians weare set uppon by ij^e Moores or more, and your said suppliants money vyolently robbed and taken by those Moores; the takers and possessors of all which money be very well knowne, and (as your suppliants be informed) men of good habilyty; and that all or the greatest part of your suppliants moneyes be recovered againe by an Alcado which the Kinge sent to take order for this and other lyke cawses. Notwithstanding which recovery, and also that the lawes of Barbary be that the cuntry in which any robbery is done shall make full restytution to the partye from whome it was taken, yet your said suppliants nor there saide factor Thomas Serocold cannot to this daye obtayne restytution of there said greate losse nor any parte thereof; which cawse your suppliants moste humbly beseche her Matie, by her letters, to recommend unto the Kinge. As also wheare the Kinge oweth to your said suppliants, for goods and money delyvered him in anno 1595, whereof is owinge the some of xj thowsand ownces or thereabouts, which should have bene paid them in sugers that yeare; the forbearance whearof hath greatly impoverished your suppliants, besids other great losses of good shipinge, which they had, and the excessyve charges in followinge the suite for the Kings payment, and yearely renewinge ther bills, which the Kings officers puts on suche ingenewis[1] as yealds not commodyty any thinge neare the satisficinge of the Kings saide debt, and soe cateth all out in charges.

Your suppliants distresse by the delayes considered, they most humbly besech that her gratious Matie will in pitty be moved to recommend this cawse; also that he will be pleased to appointe

---

1. *Ingenewis* : ingenios. Sur ce mot, V. 1re Série, Angleterre, t. 1, p. 555, note 1. Il faut entendre que chaque année, en leur faisant payer les frais de l'opération, on renouvelait aux requérants leurs effets, payables sur des sucreries dont le revenu était tout à fait insuffisant pour éteindre la dette du Chérif.

paymente of this said debt in sugers unto your suppliants apart by itselfe, seperated from other mens debts, as beinge men unto whome her Matie hath an espetiall regarde. And we shall be most bownde, as neverthelesse we are dayly, to praye to the Allmightie God for your Honours longe contynewance in helth and all happines etc.

Hatfield House, Cecil Mss., Petition 908. — Original.

XLVII

LETTRE D'ÉLISABETH A MOULAY AHMED EL-MANSOUR

Elle prie le Chérif, à la requête des États de Hollande et de Zélande, d'autoriser le rachat de certains de leurs sujets prisonniers au Maroc.

10 [n. st. 20 mai] 1599.

Au dos, alia manu: To the King of Morucco, for release of certain prisoners of Holland and Zealand. — 10 Maii 1599.

Muy alto...,

The people of the countries of Holland and Zealand and some others are and have ben a long tyme in our protection, who, with exceeding great charges and losse of the lyves of our subjectes, have protected them against the malyce of our and your common ennemie the Spanyard. The Estates governors of those countries have very humbly and earnestly besought us to employ that creditt, which they suppose the correspondency that hath long ben betweene you and us doth cause us to have with you, for the lybertie of certaine subjectes of theirs by dyvers chaunces being prysoners within your domynions, whose names are[1].....

Which their sute seemed so reasonable to us, and so sutyng to the care which persons sytting in place of governement ought to have over their subjectes, as wee did assure ourselfs that it would

---

1. C'est à la présente lettre que fait allusion John Waring dans celle qu'il écrit à Robert Cecil, le 20 juin 1600. V. *infra*, Doc. LVI, p. 161. On y lit que les captifs des Pays-Bas étaient au nombre de neuf. Leurs noms ont été laissés en blanc dans la présente minute. Leur mise en liberté est annoncée par Moulay Ahmed dans sa lettre à Élisabeth du 27 mars 1600. V. *infra*, Doc. LI, p. 149.

not seeme unreasonable to you, to whome Almightie God hath comytted the government of manie people, whereby you cannot but knowe the compassion that prynces have of theire subjectes calamyties. And forasmuch as also they are joyned with us both in lyke profession of relygion and in the same condition of having the Spanyard our comon ennemie, we were moved to employ our credit with you on the behalf of those poore men, whome we earnestly pray you for our sake to permitt to be redeemed by theire freindes and brought away, as we have heretofore, uppon lyke occasion, graunted lybertie to some of yours, and will ever hereafter, yf anie such chaunces shall cast them into our power.

Public Record Office. — *State Papers, Foreign, Royal Letters, vol. II, n° 24.* — Minute.

XLVIII

LETTRE D'ÉLISABETH A MOULAY AHMED EL-MANSOUR

Elle expose à Moulay Ahmed les raisons qui l'ont obligée de différer la mise en liberté d'Alonso Nuñez de Herrera. — Elle lui en donnait déjà avis dans une lettre en date du 2 avril 1598. — Le porteur de cette lettre, voyant, à son arrivée au Maroc, les ports dépeuplés par la peste, et apprenant que Moulay Ahmed avait quitté Merrakech pour se préserver du fléau, est revenu sans accomplir sa mission. — Richard Tomson, qui se montra toujours empressé à fournir au Chérif les marbres ou autres marchandises dont celui-ci avait besoin, craint d'être lésé par les exécuteurs testamentaires de Gilbert Sothering, mort récemment au Maroc. — Il conviendrait que le Chérif assurât la remise à George et Jasper Tomson, facteurs de Richard, de tout ce qui serait trouvé par eux appartenir audit Richard, et qu'il renvoyât devant la justice anglaise les réclamations que produiraient les exécuteurs testamentaires. — Élisabeth prie Moulay Ahmed d'accueillir avec bienveillance la requête que lui présenteront à cet effet George et Jasper Tomson.

Greenwich, 14 [n. st. 24] juin 1599.

Au dos, alia manu : xiii° Junii 1599. Copie of her Maties lettre to the King of Marueccos concerning Richard Tomson[1].

Muy alto y muy poderoso Sennor,

Dos annos ha que recevimos vuestra real carta escritta a la instancia de Juan de Marchena[2], sobre la libertad de Alonso Nuñez de Herrera, que fue traydo poco antes prisionero en nuestra armada de Cadix. A la qual en el mesmo instante no podiamos responder como desseavamos, a causa que los prisioneros que trayan de alla

---

1. Sur les Tomson, V. *supra*, p. 101, note 2.

2. Sur ce personnage, V. *supra*, Doc. XXX, p. 100 et note 1.

como rehenes (de los quales el dicho Alonso Nuñez era uno de ellos), para cumplir ciertas conditiones que avian assentado con nuestros Generales, desconciertaronse en gran manera sobre el aiuntamiento y repartimiento de la cantidad de moneda en que se avian obligado ; y en este desconcierto (mientras embiavan a España y aguardavan rispuesta) se passaron muchos meses, ni consentieron ellos en el interim que alguno fuesse libertado, hasta que se hiziesse acuerdo y tassa desta moneda, quanto cupiesse a cada uno. Lo qual con justicia no hemos podido negarla, estando ellos obligados todos de mancomun.

Desto dimos aviso por nuestras cartas del segundo del mes de Avril de mil quinientos noventa y ocho años[1], la qual mandavamos con un criado de nuestra real corte, para que las diesse a vuestra alta presencia. Y llegandose a la costa de Barberia, viendo de que manera los puertos estavan despoblados, y la muy gran mortandad que avia por todos vuestros reynos[2], juntamente con el peligro que en aquel tiempo corrian por los caminos, y oyendo por verdad que vuestra real persona, aviendo salido de vuestros altos palacios de Marruecos, a causa de la enfermidad, estava con vuestro exercito en los campos, mudandose cada rato de una parte a otra para la conservacion de vuestra muy desseada salud, tuvo por bien buelverse con las dichas cartas. Las quales si uvieran venido a vuestras manos, no dubdamos que no fuerades muy satisfecho, ansi en lo que nos fue pedido sobre el negotio de Alonso Nuñez de Herrera, como del salvo conductto para los navios de Juan de Marchena, a saberlos que yvan empleados en vuestros reales servicios. Porque es muy manifiesto, por lo que hemos hecho, el desseo que teniamos, y quan prestos estavamos siempre satisfaceros con los efetos de entera amistad en todas las cosas que nos fuessen demandadas, en el qual desseo y presteza al presente insistimos y perseveramos.

En confiança dello, hemos sido movidos pedir a vuestra real clementia, de parte de Richart Tomson, mercader de nuestra ciudad de Londres, el qual, siendo el primero y principal que a su gran costa y riesgo ha procurado llevar marmoles y otras cosas agra-

---

1. Cette lettre n'a pas été retrouvée. 2. V. *supra*, p. 125 et note 2.

dables a vuestro real servicio, ansi en la vida de su hermano Arnao Tomson como en la de Gilberte Sothern [1], que murio poco ha en vuestros reynos, se recela y teme de recivir danno y fraude de los albaceas del dicho Gilberte, ansi en las deudas a el devidas como en sus mercadarias que quedavan para vender al tiempo de su fallecimiento, de manera que le sera conveniente favorescerse de vuestro alto amparo y clementia, y para que con mas voluntad y gana acudiesse a las cosas tocantes a vuestro real servicio, fuessedes servido mandar que todo lo que sus fattores George Tomson y Gaspar Tomson haran prueva ser suyo y aver venido del se buelva y entregue a ellos o su valor, y que los dichos testamentarios o qualquier otro pretendiendo algo del dicho Richarte que los sea devido (pues que son todos Ingleses y vassallos nuestros) concediessedes sean remetidos con sus cuentas y demandas a seguir su justicia dentro de nuestros reynos, donde mandaremos que les sea dada con toda brevidad y derecho. Lo qual, aunque sabemos que de vuestra grandeza y accustumbrada justicia no le sera negado, todavia esperamos que le sera mas de effeto y provechoso, pidiendoselo nosotros a vuestro alto Estado, y por esto rogamos que, quando sus fatores George Tomson y Gasper Tomson se umillaren delante de vuestra alta presencia y suplicaren muy ahincadamente vuestra real clemençia y gracia para remedio de los agravios, fuessedes servido otorgalla, como se espera aver lo mismo de nosotros en lo que tocare de vuestros subditos y vassallos.

Fecha de nuestro real palacio de Grenewich, a quatorze de Junio de mil quinientos noventa y nueve.

Public Record Office. — State Papers, Foreign, Royal Letters, vol. II, n° 26. — Minute.

1. Gilbert Sothering. Sur ce personnage, V. *supra,* p. 115 et note 3.

2. Il existe dans le même volume, n° 25, une minute en anglais de la présente lettre, datée du 10 [n. st. 20] mai 1599 et beaucoup plus brève. Pour expliquer le retard apporté à la libération d'Alonso Nuñez de Herrera, on relève seulement cette circonstance qu'il n'était pas un simple prisonnier de guerre, mais « un otage parmi d'autres remis par la ville de Cadix en garantie de l'accomplissement de certaines conventions passées entre les généraux anglais et les habitants, lesquelles restèrent longtemps sans exécution ». On fait aussi allusion à une lettre antérieure d'Élisabeth, mais on attribue au naufrage du navire qui la portait, et non aux appréhensions que causait la peste au messager, le fait que cette lettre ne parvint pas au destinataire.

XLIX

LETTRE DE JASPER TOMSON A RICHARD TOMSON[1]

Moulay Ahmed, ayant appris que Tomson avait suivi en Hongrie l'expédition commandée par le Grand Seigneur, l'a fait venir dans son camp, à dix lieues de Merrakech, pour le questionner sur cette campagne. — Retenu, au dernier moment, par des lettres importantes de Moulay ech-Cheikh, il a fait raconter l'expédition par Tomson à son secrétaire, qui transcrivait le récit en arabe. — A l'approche de la nuit, Jasper Tomson s'était retiré dans sa tente avec George Tomson, promettant de finir sa narration le lendemain. — Mais, à minuit, le Chérif l'a mandé près de lui pour la terminer. — Depuis, le caïd Azzouz a interrogé Tomson plusieurs fois sur les affaires de Turquie. — Tomson, ayant appris la défaite du Grand Seigneur à Bude, en a informé Azzouz. — Celui-ci a transmis immédiatement la nouvelle au Chérif, à qui les échecs des Turcs causent un vif plaisir. — Azzouz a demandé à Tomson pourquoi Élisabeth avait requis l'aide du Grand Seigneur contre l'Espagne. — Tomson a démenti ce fait. — Parlant de la prise de Cadix, Azzouz a dit qu'avec sept ou huit mille cavaliers, Élisabeth aurait pu conquérir l'Espagne. — Tomson a répondu que la Reine n'en avait pas l'intention. — Azzouz a demandé si Élisabeth serait disposée à se joindre à Moulay Ahmed pour entreprendre cette conquête. — Tomson a dit qu'il l'ignorait et a conseillé l'envoi d'un ambassadeur à Londres. — Azzouz a prié Tomson de savoir les intentions de la Reine sur cette proposition. — Tomson engage son correspondant à faire connaître l'offre à la Reine, bien qu'il n'y attache aucune importance. — Le Chérif lève son camp tous les dix ou douze jours, par crainte de la peste. — Nouvelles de Cadix. — Le caïd Djouder vient d'arriver de Gago avec d'immenses présents pour le Chérif: poudre d'or, poivre, cornes, bois de teinture, chevaux, nains, esclaves, sans compter quinze filles du roi de Gago destinées au harem du Chérif.

---

1. Le destinataire de cette lettre est évidemment Richard Tomson, parent de Jasper. Sur cette famille, V. *supra*, p. 101, n. 2; cf. *infra*, pp. 126 et n. 4, 146 et n. 1.

De la mahalla, 24 juin [n. st. 4 juillet] 1599.

Au dos, alia manu: 1599. — Barberye.
En marge: 24 June 1599.

The Kinge, havinge intelligence that I had benn imployed some yeares in Turkie, and that, in this last journy into Hongarie which the Gran Seignor made in person[1], I was present and went withall, beinge verye desyrous to understand the greatnes of that campe and the trewe relation of all that succeeded in the said journy, sent for me to his tent, beinge with him all his court, and 5 or 6000 horse, tenn leagues from Morocos, for his gard, nere unto the ryver Tanseffe[2]. A lytle before I came, letters were come from his sonne, the Kinge of Fesse, of importaunce, whereby his Ma[tie] could not have oportunitie to conferre with me himself, but sent Alcaide Asuz[3] with the Kinges principall secretarie to carrie me into a chamber within the Kinges pavillion. And then the Vicerey departinge requested me to declare at large the discourse of the Turkes viage unto the secretarie, whoe would sett yt downe Larbie tonge, and left with us the Kinges cheiffe interpretour for the Latine and Spanish tongues. Where we spent 6 howres together till the night approched; and then I requested leave to goe unto my owne tent, untill the next morninge that I would retourne to fynish the said discourse. Whereuppon they made me and your brother George Tomson[4] a collacion; and soe, takinge our horses to goe to our tent, beinge night, the hackam[5] was commaunded with 30 horse to conduct us to our lodginge.

Beinge at our rest, for that we had travelled all the night before,

---

1. Il s'agit de la campagne de 1596, à laquelle prit part le sultan Mahomet III. Les Turcs s'emparèrent d'Erlau et remportèrent à Caresto (23-25 octobre) une grande victoire sur les Impériaux. L'ambassadeur anglais Barton avait accompagné le Sultan.
2. *Tanseffe:* l'oued Tensift.
3. Sur le caïd Azzouz. V. *supra*, p. 48, note 2. Il est appelé vice-roi dans la suite du document.
4. George Tomson était le frère de Richard Tomson.
5. *Hackam:* mot arabe حاكم chef, le chef de l'escorte.

at midnight the Kinge called to the secretarie for the writinges; whoe answearinge that they were not fynished, and that I was retired to my tent till the morninge, the King fourthwith sent his muschuary[1], which ys as much as his Lord Chamberlaine, to intreat me to come and finish that which was begonn. And soe I went alongst with him, and consumed all the hole night in endinge the same.

Alcayde Azus hath sent for me sondry tymes since, and hath examined me uppon many particularities concerninge the Gran Siegnor and his proceedinges (for I see nothinge ys more pleasinge to the Kinge then to heare that the Turkes afaires succeded not well). And I, havinge a lytle before receved a letter from my frend Mr John Bate of a great overthrow the Turkes had receaved about Buda[2], advertized the Vicerey thereof; which he went presently and informed the Kinge of, and since hath benn very earnest with me to gett advise from tyme to tyme of the Turkish occurrences, which I pray yow to remember.

Now yow shall note that, uppon this, the Alcayde hath had privatt conference with me of matters of state, and desyrous to knowe what reason or wherefore the Quene had required ayde of the Turke ageinst the Spaniard.

I made him answeare that her Matie had never required any such thinge, butt that in my tyme the Kinge of Fraunce requested yt ageinst Marcelia[3], and that her embassador was sewtor for the same, beinge theerunto requested by the French Kinges letter; but for the Quene, never any such thinge was demaunded.

Much talke we had about this and the Quenes army that tooke

---

1. *Muschuary*, mot arabe مشوار. L'identification de ce fonctionnaire avec le « Lord Chamberlaine » ne donne qu'une idée incomplète des attributions de cet officier. La charge du caïd el-Mechouar était l'une des plus importantes de la cour chérifienne. Outre sa fonction de maître des cérémonies, il était chargé de l'exécution de missions exigeant autant de tact que de vigueur, comme celle d'arrêter, sur un signe du Chérif, un caïd important, voire un vizir.

2. Les Impériaux, dans l'automne de 1598, avaient vivement pressé Bude et infligé de sanglants échecs aux Turcs. Toutefois, la mauvaise saison les contraignit de lever le siège de la place.

3. Sur le secours des galères turques demandé par Henri IV en 1596 pour recouvrer la ville de Marseille et pour soutenir les Maures contre l'Espagne, V. *Lettres missives de Henri IV*, t. IV, pp. 475 et 495; HAMMER, t. II, p. 287.

Cales¹, sayinge that, yf with those forces her Matie had sent 7 or 8 thowsand horse, yt had benn easie for her to have overrunne all Spaine.

I answeared there was no such intencion in her Matie to attempt any matter of such consequence as the conquest of Spaine, butt, with a fewe of her shippes and a small nomber of men, to assalt the towne of Cales and to sacke the same, and destroy such shippinge as was founde there, the rather bicause the Kinge of Spaine had, with his huge army of anno 1588, attempted her coastes in warlick manner, and with a preparation of many yeares gatheringe and yet was repulsed in such sort as not one of his men set foote ashore in her kingdome, but such as at the sea were taken and brought in prisoners.

In the end, his speech tended to this purpose, whither I thought the Quene would be content to make such another army to land in some port in Spaine with 20 thowsand footemen, and with vessels to transport 20 thowsand horses and men from Barberie, and soe to joyne together in conquest of the contrye; whereof, said he, there ys noe doubt but yt may be performed, yf her Matie and his Kinge should joyne together in the action.

My answeare was that I knewe nothinge howe farre her Matie did mynde to procede ageinst the Kinge of Spaine; butt yf the Kinge had any such desyre, yt were good he sent an embassadour to her Matie, about the negotiacion of whome I was assured he should have a princelye answeare; and thoe the offer should not be accepted, yet the messenger should be honorabley intreated and answered.

He asked me yf I had not frendes that could procure by worde of mouth to move the Quene therein, and that of me he might be informed of her inclination that way, requestinge me veric earnestlye to wryte concerninge yt, that he may be satisfied of her meaninge; which by reason of his importunitie I promised to doe. And althoe I am well assured her Matie will not accept of any such offer, yet it ys not amisse to make Mr Secretary², or my Lord Admirall³, or some one of her Maties Councell acquainted with this

---

1. V. supra. p. 93 et note 2.
2. Robert Cecil.
3. Lord Charles Howard, V. supra, p. 113, note 1.

motion, that at some convenient tyme may impart yt to the Quene (thoe yt be but to lawgh at yt). Uppon which she will not lett to gyve answeare; whereof I praye yow advertise, that yet I may performe with the Vicerey, that soe much insisteth in yt.

All this hath passed since the Kinge came into his almahala, where he removeth every 10 or 12 dayes from place to place, alongst the ryver of Tansyffe, for feare of the infection; where I am forced to contynew with your brother, attendinge till the Pasquall be paste, that we may have the Kinges bils for the payment of the marbles[1].

Newce from Cadix of 70 shippes and certaine galleis to be in the baye for the better securitie of the towne, beinge in great feare that the Flemish fleete ys purposely sent to surprise the same; and, nowe they have taken theire course to the westwardes, the shippes and gallies are apointed to be imployed in gardinge the coast.

Six dayes past, here aryved a nobleman from Gago, called Judar Basha[2], whoe was sent by this Kinge 10 yeares past to conquere the said contrye, wherein many people of this contrye have lost theire lyves[3]. He brought with him thirtie camels, laden with tyber[4], which ys unrefyned gold (yet the difference ys but six shillinges in an ownce weight betwene yt and duccattes); also great store of pepper, unicornes, hornes and a certaine kynde of wood for diers[5], to some 120 camels loades; all which he presented unto the Kinge, with 50 horse, and great quantitye of eanuches, duarfes, and weomen and men slaves, besydes 15 virgins, the Kinges daughters of Gago, which he sendeth to be the Kinges concubines. Yow must note all these be of the cole black heyre, for that contry yeldeth noe other.

Signé: Per me: Jasper Thomson.

This gold may amount to 604 800^{li} sterlinge. I say six hondred and fower thowsand eight hondred poundes.

Public Record Office. — State Papers, Foreign, Barbary States, vol. XII. — Original.

1. Richard Tomson avait procuré des marbres au Chérif. V. *supra.* p. 140.
2. Sur le pacha Djouder, V. *supra,* p. 66, note 1.
3. Sur la conquête du Soudan, V. *supra.* pp. 66 et 83-88.
4. Sur l'or de tibor, V. 1re *Série*, France, t. II, p. 359, note 2. Cf. *infra*, p. 224 et n. 1.
5. Probablement du brésil; ce bois était un article fréquemment importé au Maroc.

L

LETTRE D'ÉLISABETH A MOULAY AHMED EL-MANSOUR

Elle le remercie de la bienveillance qu'il témoignait à Gilbert Sothering, mort récemment au Maroc. — Gilbert Bradog et John Waring, qui ont payé toutes les dettes de Sothering au Maroc, éprouvent les plus grandes difficultés à recouvrer ce qui lui était dû. — A la requête de certains marchands de Londres, dont Sothering était le facteur au Maroc, Élisabeth prie le Chérif d'ordonner que ses sujets s'acquittent entre les mains de Bradog et de Waring des sommes qu'ils doivent aux dits marchands et à Sothering.

Richmond, 24 février 1599 [n. st. 6 mars 1600].

Au dos: Al muy alto y muy poderoso señor Muley Hamed, Xarife, Emperador de Marruecos, Rey de Fez y de Sus. — *Alia manu:* xxiii[th] of February 1599. — Copie of her Maties letter to the King of Barbary in the behalfe of her subjects their, to whom there is a great summe of mony due by that Kings subjects.

El buen tratamiento que hallan mis subditos en vuestros reynos y la mucha largueza que aveys usado con ellos, especialmente la liberalidad real en particular mostrado a Gilberto Sothern[1], uno de mis subditos, que pocos dias ha murio en aquel reyno, ha sido tan grande y de animo tan real procedido que no puedo dexar de reconocerlo. Y porque, quedando por caudal de los negocios del dicho Sothern Gilberto Bradog y Juan Waring[2] y tomando a su cargo las quentas y los negocios del con mucha fee y llaneza, an hecho pago de todo lo que el devia a vuestros subditos, y hallan

---

1. V. *supra*, p. 115, note 3.
2. C'est à ce personnage que fut envoyée la présente lettre, pour qu'il la remît au Chérif. Elle lui parvint à Merrakech, peu avant le 20 juin [n. st.] 1600. V. sa lettre de cette date, *infra*, p. 161.

tan grande difficultad en la cobrança de muchos dineros que vuestros subditos deven al dicho Sothern que se duda mucho no se cobraran sin especial favor vuestro, ha me parescido dar oydo a la peticion y ruego de ciertos mis subditos, mercaderes de mi ciudad de Londres, cuyos negocios hizo alla el dicho Sothern como fator dellos, y pediros, como os pido y ruego muy de veras, que, con la misma justicia y favor que asta agora aveys mostrado a mis subditos, acudeys a su justa demanda y mandeys que los dichos subditos vuestros paguen al dicho Bradog y Waring las sumas que a ellos y al dicho Sothern quedan deviendo.

En lo qual hareis que la fama de vuestra bondad y justicia se derame por el mundo, y dareys a mis dichos subditos poder y voluntad para con mas abondancia y comodidad continuar el trato y comercio en vuestros reynos y estados, los quales el Dios Todo Poderoso guarde y mantenga.

Deste nuestro real palacio de Ricomonte, a veyente y quatro de Hebrero de 1599, mill y quinientos y noventa y nueve años [1].

Public Record Office. — *State Papers, Foreign, Barbary States, vol. XII.* — *Copie contemporaine.*

1. Le 26 février [n. st. 8 mars], Robert Cecil envoyait la présente lettre à Thomas Windebank, l'un des secrétaires du sceau, en le priant de la faire signer par la Reine. Elle concerne, remarquait-il, beaucoup de malheureux sujets d'Élisabeth, dont les biens sont entre les mains du roi du Maroc, et qui vont être complètement ruinés, si le nom de la Reine, « dont les brises de l'Océan lui portent la renommée », n'incline pas ce prince à la pitié. *St. Pap., Dom., Eliz., vol. CCLXXIV, n° 49.*

LI

LETTRE DE MOULAY AHMED EL-MANSOUR A ÉLISABETH[1]

Les serviteurs du Chérif qui emportent la présente lettre ont ordre de se rendre à Alep en quittant l'Angleterre. — Moulay Ahmed prie Élisabeth d'assurer leur passage à destination et leur retour au Maroc sur des navires anglais. — Il a mis en liberté les esclaves des Pays-Bas pour lesquels Élisabeth avait intercédé.

Merrakech, 12 Ramadan 1008 [27 mars 1600].

SIGNE DE VALIDATION.

هذا الكتاب الكريم والمدرج الجسيم صدر عن المقام العلى الامامى المولوى الهاشمى الحسنى المنصورى دام اقبال دولته ولا زالت جهات البسيطة مشرقة بانوار معدلته

الى الاصالة التى لها فى الافطار النصرانية القدر الشامخ المكان والعز الباذخ الثابت الاركان والمكانة التى يعترف لها من اهل ملتها الفاصى والدان

---

1. Ce document est une copie, faite par un orientaliste du xviie siècle, d'une écriture gauche, et est remplie d'incorrections. Il existe de la présente lettre une traduction espagnole (*State Pap., For., Eliz.*, vol. CXLI, n° 982) et une traduction anglaise, probablement établie d'après l'espagnole (*State Pap., For., Royal Letters*, vol II, n° 23). Le protocole, dans ces deux traductions, est tout autre que dans la copie arabe. La traduction espagnole commence ainsi :

« Por mandado del siervo de Dios soberano, el conquistador por su causa, a quien todos los Moros siguen, el vitorioso por Dios, enperador de los Moros, hijo del enperador de los Moros, Xarife Aseni — ¡Dios de vitoria a sus heseritos!

« La que tiene, entre los que seguieron al Mesias, altos fundamentos en su reyno y poder anpleficado y estado con honrra engrandesido y arraygado en sus prensi-

اصالة السلطانة الاصيلة الجليلة المثيلة الاثيلة الاثيرة الخطيرة الشهيرة السلطانة
ازبيل لازال فدرها فى الملل النصرانية عزيز الجناب سامى الهضاب
امابعد فكتابنا هذ اليك من حضرة مراكش حاطها الله وصنع الله تعلى
متصل الامداد مزهر الاغوار والانجاد لله المنة هذا والذى اوجبه لمكانك
المكين انه يرد على ممالكتك خدامنا حملة هذا الكتاب الكريم الذين وجهناهم
الى حلب لفضاء بعض مآرب بنا وما عنّ من اغراضنا وقد اخترنا لهم ان يكون
مرورهم على بلادك للمحبة التى بيننا وبينك والصداقة التى تفردت بين جنابنا
وجنابك وحمّلناهم هذا الخطاب الكريم الى مكانك المكين نحب ان تستوصوا
بهم خيرا واحسانا فى طلوعهم مع سبن بلادك الى تلك الجهة توصى بهم
اهل السبن ليستلزموا منهم ويعتبروهم لوصايتك فى جميع احوالهم كما زيد
منكم ايضًا ان تعطوهم كتابك فى ايديهم الى تجار بلادك الذين يسافرون الى
تلك الجهة بانه اذا رجعت هذه السبن التى يطلعون فيها من قبل ان يستوبوا
اغراضهم كل من وجده الحال هنالك من سبن تجار بلادكم يحملهم حتى

pios ; la que es conosida entre los que seguieron al Mesias, los que della estan lexos y los que serca, la reyna enoblesida y afamada y ensalsada, la reyna Ysabel.

« Despues de los loores a Dios que es solo en suma grandeza alto y omnipotente, a cuya omnipotensia si humillan los altos sielos y encumbrados montes ; despues de la precativa por este alto estado, a quien todos los Moros sighen y obedesen — ¡ que le haga vitorioso ! — escrivimos esta de nuestra real Corte — ¡ que Dios prospere !

« Y la causa porque escrevimos esta nuestra real carta es para que.... »

Cette traduction espagnole se trouve classée parmi des documents de l'année 1576. Ce classement s'explique par une mention erronée écrite au dos de la dite traduction : « Translation of the King of Morocco his letter to her Majesty, delivered by his Ambassador the 20th August, at Nonesuch, 1576 ». Le même fait s'est produit pour le texte arabe d'une autre lettre de Moulay Ahmed du 3 juillet 1602 (V. infra, p. 210), qui porte cette mention : « Received October 16, 1576 ».

يبلغهم الى مملكتنا الشريفة ان شاء الله تعلى وتوصى عليهم فى ذلك كله اجمل الايصاء على نحو ما هو الظن بمكانك المكين واعلمى ان النصارى الهولاماتك الذين كتبت بيهم لعلىّ مفامنا وكانوا فى اسرنا هاهم يصلونكم صحبة خدامنا و قد امتننا عليهم لاجل رغبتك ورعاية جنابك ثم ان جميع مايكون لكم من الاغراض فى بلادنا وفى مماكنا الشريمة ويجمل شانه بعلّ مفامنا فهو مفضى وملتفى عندنا بوجه القبول والاقبال والرعى والاهتبال للمحبّة والصداقة التى بينا وبينكم وبهذا وجب الكتب اليكم فى ثانى عشر رمضان المعظم من عام ثمانية والف

British Museum. — Cotton Mss., Nero B. XI, f. 77 v°. — Copie.

LI bis

LETTRE DE MOULAY AHMED EL-MANSOUR A ÉLISABETH

(TRADUCTION)

Merrakech, 12 Ramadan 1008 [27 mars 1600].

Signe de validation.

Cette lettre noble, ce pli illustre émane de la Majesté élevée imamienne, moulouienne, hachémienne, hassénienne, mansourienne. Puisse durer la prospérité de son règne, et puissent les horizons de la terre demeurer éclairés par les lumières de sa justice !

A la Seigneurie dont la considération dans les contrées chrétiennes est haut placée, la puissance élevée sur des assises bien solides, et la gloire connue de ses peuples voisins et éloignés, Seigneurie de la reine qui est noble d'origine et de haute lignée, l'excellente, la noble, la distinguée et considérable reine Élisabeth. Puisse sa renommée ne jamais cesser, parmi les peuples chrétiens, d'être forte et élevée !

Ensuite, nous vous écrivons cette lettre de notre capitale Merrakech — Dieu l'entoure de sa protection ! — tandis que les bienfaits de Dieu Très-Haut ne cessent de resplendir et de se répandre par les monts et les vallées, grâce à Dieu !

Voici la raison pour laquelle nous adressons cette lettre à votre haute Seigneurie. Nos serviteurs, porteurs de ce noble message, sont envoyés par nous à Alep, avec la mission d'y accomplir certaines affaires que nous avons en vue, et aborderont prochainement dans votre royaume[1]. Si de préférence nous les faisons pas-

---

1. D'après le marchand Juan de Marchena (V. *supra*, p. 100 et note 1), ces Marocains

ser par votre pays, c'est à cause de l'amitié qui existe entre nous et vous, et des liens qui unissent notre Seigneurie et la vôtre. Nous les chargeons de ce noble message pour votre inébranlable Seigneurie, dans l'espoir qu'ils seront, pendant leur voyage vers la dite ville, bien recommandés par vous aux équipages des bateaux de votre pays, qui, grâce à votre recommandation, assureront leur bien-être et auront pour eux de la considération en toute circonstance. Nous désirons de même que vous leur remettiez en mains propres une lettre, signée de vous, destinée aux commerçants de votre pays qui voyagent dans ces parages-là. Il se peut, en effet, que les vaisseaux qui auront amené nos serviteurs s'en retournent avant que la mission de ces derniers ne soit terminée. Dans ce cas, tout autre navire appartenant aux commerçants de votre pays et se trouvant éventuellement dans ces parages, sera tenu de les embarquer à destination de notre noble royaume, s'il plaît à Dieu Très-Haut. Que votre recommandation à ce sujet soit faite de la meilleure façon, selon les espérances que nous fondons sur votre inébranlable Seigneurie.

Vous saurez que les chrétiens flamands, au sujet de qui vous avez écrit à notre haute Seigneurie et qui se trouvaient être nos captifs, vous parviendront bientôt en compagnie de nos serviteurs. La faveur que nous leur avons accordée est due à votre intervention et à la considération que nous avons pour votre Seigneurie. D'ailleurs, tout ce qui dans notre pays, dans nos États chérifiens, peut faire l'objet de vos désirs, et dont Notre Seigneurie aura connaissance, nous nous empresserons de vous l'offrir, comme témoignage de notre dévouement et de notre considération, aussi bien que par égard pour l'amitié sincère qui existe entre nous et vous.

Voilà pourquoi nous vous écrivons cette lettre, le 12 du mois respecté de Ramadan de l'année mil huit.

étaient envoyés en Angleterre, pour se rendre de là à Alep et y acheter des pierres précieuses. V. 1re Série, Espagne, lettre au duc de Medina-Sidonia, 1er septembre 1600. Mais ce n'était qu'un prétexte, acha-

que ; l'ambassadeur Abd el-Ouahed le dit formellement. Il ajoute que le but de la mission était de proposer à Élisabeth une alliance pour faire la guerre à l'Espagne. V. infra, Doc. LXI, p. 177.

LII

LETTRE D'ÉLISABETH A MOULAY AHMED EL-MANSOUR

Elle le prie de mettre en liberté Cornelis Jansz. et Engell Adriansz., habitants de Flessingue, qui sont captifs au Maroc.

Richmond, 31 mars [n. st. 10 avril] 1600.

Au dos, alia manu : March 1600. — Copie of her Maties letter to the King of Maruecos for Cornelis Janson and Engell Adrianson, inhabitants of Flisshing, and for John Newton and Tho. Owen, English merchants.

Muy alto y muy poderoso Sennor,

Siendo la piedad y clemencia virtudes muy propias a los reyes y grandes sennores, y siendo los principes tenidos de dar ayuda a los vassallos miseros y affligidos, nos, aviendo recebido informacion que Cornelis Janson y Engell Adrianson, moradores en Vlissinga, tierra que es aora del amparo de nuestro govierno[1], fueron presos y son tenidos cautivos en los reynos de V[ra] Mag[nd], vos rogamos y pedimos que se contente de darles libertad, si como nos en nuestros reynos dexamos libres todos sus subditos y vassallos, embiandoles a sus tierras. Esta sera obra muy piadosa y digna de su real grandeza y muy convenible para muestra de la buena amistad y confederacion que ay entre nuestras coronas.

Dios guarde la muy alta y muy illustre persona de V[ra] Maj[ad].

Al nuestro palacio real de Richmond, 31 de Março de 1600 annos.

Elizabetta R.

Public Record Office. — *State Papers, Foreign, Barbary States, vol. XII.*
Ibidem. — *State Papers, Foreign, Royal Letters, vol. II, n° 28.*
British Museum. — *Cotton Mss., Nero B. XI, f. 74.*

1. V. *supra*, p. 132 et p. 133, notes 1 et 2.

LIII

LETTRE D'ÉLISABETH A MOULAY AHMED EL-MANSOUR

Elle le prie de faire restituer à John Newton et Thomas Owen une somme dérobée par des Maures sur la route de Merrakech au Sous.

Richmond, 31 mars [n. st. 10 avril] 1600.

Muy alto y muy poderoso Sennor,

Aviendo entendido las supplicaciones y quexas de nuestros sudditos y vassallos Juan Newton y Thomas Owen, mercaderes[1], como, dos annos passados, treze Ingleses, caminando debaxo del seguro de V^{ra} Mag^{ad} de Marruecos a Suz, fueron assaltados y robados de ciertos Moros subditos de V^{ra} Mag^{ad}, algunos de los quales fueron despues conocidos, y, aviendo V^{ra} Mag^{ad}, entendido las quexas de nuestros dichos sudditos, prometido restitucion conforme al derecho de su real justicia, la qual pretenden no ser agora interamente cumplida, nos, por el obligo de justicia que todos reyes deven a sus sudditos, rogamos y de veras pedimos a V^{ra} Mag^{ad} que se contente dar orden que sea hecha restitucion a nuestros dichos sudditos ; lo que sera digno de vuestra real grandeza y conforme a la amistad y confederacion de nuestras coronas.

Dios guarde la muy alta y muy illustre persona de V^{ra} Mag^{ad}. Al nuestro palacio real de Richmond, 31 de Marzo de 1600 annos.

Elizabetta R.

Public Record Office. — State Papers, Foreign, Barbary States, vol. XII. Ibidem. — State Papers, Foreign, Royal Letters, vol. II, n° 27. British Museum. — Cotton Mss., Nero B. XI, f. 74.

1. Le fait s'était passé en avril 1598. V. *supra*, Doc XLVI, p. 134 et note 2.

LIV

REQUÊTE DE D. PHILIPPE D'AFRIQUE[1] A PHILIPPE III

Il expose de quelle manière et sur quels revenus publics il voudrait que lui fussent payées, avec leur arriéré, les gratifications accordées par le Roi.

[20 avril 1600][2].

Don Phelipe de Africa, infante de Marruecos, supplica a Su Mag.^d le haga merced que, en la provision que le mandar dar para que cobre los ocho mil cruzados y lo corrido que se le deve, desde primero de Junio del año de noventas ocho asta veinte de Otubre del año de noventa y nueve, en que Su Mag.^d le hizo merced que de nuevo se le pagassen en las rentas de los puertos secos de Portugal ; se declare que Su Mag.^d tiene por bien que los oficiales de la casa de la Yndia o contadores de los derechos de las naves le paguen, en virtud desta provision, sin otro recaudo alguno, la quantia que se le debiere, y con ella y su carta de pago o de su procurador, [de las] haciendas de las dichas naves, que los derechos dellas monten la dicha quantia, para hacerse pagado della en esta forma. Y recibira merced.

British Museum. — *Additional Mss., 28422, f. 387.* — *Original.*

1. Ce prince, fils de Moulay Mohammed el-Mesloukh, se nommait, avant sa conversion, Moulay ech-Cheikh. V. 1re Série. Angleterre, t. I, p. 256, Pl. III, le Tableau généalogique des princes de la dynastie saadienne, n° 30. Cf. *supra*, p. 90, note 9.
2. La présente requête fut transmise pour examen, le 20 avril 1600, par le duc de Lerme à D. Juan de Borja. D. Philippe étant revenu à la charge, le duc écrivait de nouveau, au mois de mai, à D. Juan de Borja, de tâcher de donner satisfaction au prince marocain. *Addit. Mss., 28422, ff. 386. 391.* Sur les nombreuses requêtes de D. Philippe d'Afrique, V. encore *ibid., f. 292* et *Addit. Mss., 28423, ff. 211, 212. 264.* La dernière requête de ce prince est datée du 19 octobre 1600.

LV

LETTRE DE MOULAY AHMED EL-MANSOUR A ÉLISABETH

Il a chargé son envoyé Abd el-Ouahed ben Messaoud d'exposer de vive voix et secrètement certaines questions à la Reine.

Merrakech, 3 Dou el-Hiddja 1008 [15 juin 1600].

هذا الكتاب الكريم والمدرج العلي الجسيم صدر عن المقام العليّ الامامى المولوى الهمامى السلطانى الهاشمى الاحمدى المنصورى الحسنى دام اقبال دولته ولازالت مشرفة جهات البسيطة بأنوار معدلته

الى الاصالة التى لها فى الاقطار النصرانية القدر الشامخ المكان والمكانة التى لها فى امها المسيحية العز الثابت الاركان والجخر الذى يعترف له من فومها القاصى والدان اصالة السلطنة الجليلة الاصيلة المثيلة الاثيرة الشهيرة الخطيرة السلطانة ازبيل لازال قدرها فى قومها رفيع الجناب سامى الهضاب

وكتابنا هذا اليكم من حضرة مراكش حاطها الله وعناية الله تعلى متصلة الامداد ومواهبه الجميلة مزهرة الاغوار والانجاد والسعادة الربانية بحمد الله فى الاصدار والايراد نشكره سبحانه على مامنح من ذاك شكرا يتكفل بالحسنى والازدياد

هذا وانه يرد على مكانك المكين حامل هذا الخطاب الكريم خديم مقامنا العلي الكاتب الانجد الاثير عبد الواحد بن مسعود بن محمد عنوري و قد حملناه من الا مور ما يلقيه اليكم ان شاء الله مشا فهة ويبثه عليكم مكالمة ومواجهة وعرفناكم لتعلموا اننا حملناه القاء ذلك اليكم وامرناه ببثه عليكم والمراد ان تصغوا الى ما استودعناه تبليغه انشاء الله جملة وتفصيلا حتى يتقرر لديكم ذلك تقررا اصيلا فتطالعونا حينئذ ان شاء الله بما لديكم الى ان نكون على بصيرة من كل ما عندكم

وبهذا وجب الكتب اليكم في ثالث شهر ذى الحجة الحرام متم عام ثمانية والف للهجرة النبوية الكريمة

British Museum. — Cotton Mss., Nero B. XI, f. 78. — Copie[1].

1. L'original du texte arabe n'a pas été retrouvé. Cf. *supra*, p. 149, note 1.

LVbis

LETTRE DE MOULAY AHMED EL-MANSOUR A ÉLISABETH

(TRADUCTION)

Merrakech, 3 Dou el-Hiddja 1008 [15 juin 1600].

Cette noble lettre, ce pli auguste et estimé émane de la Majesté élevée, imamienne, moulouïenne, magnanime, sultanienne, hachémienne, ahmédienne, mansourienne. Puisse durer la prospérité de son règne ! Puissent les horizons de la terre demeurer éclairés par les lumières de sa justice !

A la princesse qui jouit dans les pays chrétiens d'une considération élevée et dont la gloire est réputée parmi ses peuples, les voisins comme les plus éloignés, la seigneurie de la reine de haute lignée et d'illustre origine, la noble, l'excellente, la distinguée, la considérable, la sultane Élisabeth. Puisse sa renommée se perpétuer au milieu de ses peuples, planant sur les sommets de la puissance !

Nous vous adressons cette lettre de notre capitale Merrakech — Dieu l'entoure de sa protection ! Actuellement Dieu Très-Haut ne cesse de nous être secourable par sa providence, répandant sur nous ses grandes faveurs qui fleurissent les monts et les vallées. Que la faveur divine, grâces à Dieu ! se manifeste dans nos actions comme dans nos délibérations ! Nous remercions Dieu — qu'Il soit exalté ! — pour ces dons, comme nous le remercions des joies du Paradis, et plus encore.

Le porteur de cet auguste message, le serviteur de notre haute seigneurie, le secrétaire énergique et distingué Abd el-Ouahed ben Messaoud ben Mohammed Anouri[1] arrivera prochainement auprès

---

1. *Anouri.* Le texte arabe porte عنوري avec le ي en interligne. Il s'agit très vrai-

de Votre Haute Majesté. Nous l'avons chargé de traiter[1] avec vous certaines questions de vive voix et en secret[2]. Nous vous informons de cela, afin que vous sachiez que c'est nous-même qui lui avons donné mission de vous exposer ces affaires et qui lui avons enjoint de vous fournir à ce sujet des explications. Nous désirons que vous prêtiez attention à l'objet de l'ambassade que nous lui avons confiée et que vous l'examiniez à fond, dans l'ensemble comme dans les détails. Après quoi, vous nous ferez connaître votre manière de voir, afin que nous sachions exactement tout ce que vous en pensez.

Tel est le motif de cette missive écrite le trois de Dou el-Hiddja sacré, complétant l'année mil huit de l'hégire prophétique et illustre.

semblablement d'un ethnique que le copiste européen aura mal transcrit. On retrouvera ci-dessous ce mot transcrit en anglais: *Anoone* et *Anone*. V. *infra*, pp. 162 et 169. Sur la personne de cet ambassadeur, V. *infra*, p. 165.

1. Il existe une traduction anglaise de cette lettre, commençant seulement à cette phrase. *Public Record Office, State Papers, Foreign, Barbary States, vol. XII.*

2. Cette affaire secrète était la proposition d'une alliance entre Élisabeth et le Chérif en vue d'une guerre avec l'Espagne. V. *infra*, Doc. LXI, p. 177.

LVI

LETTRE DE JOHN WARING[1] A ROBERT CECIL

Le Chérif, ayant reçu, il y a huit mois, la lettre de la Reine en faveur de neuf captifs des Pays-Bas, par l'entremise de Marchena, a soupçonné quelque intrigue et repoussé la requête. — Mais les instances de J. Waring ont dissipé les soupçons de Moulay Ahmed, qui a relâché les captifs. — Ceux-ci ont quitté Merrakech pour aller s'embarquer sur le navire « the Eagle ». — Ils partiront en compagnie des ambassadeurs que le Chérif se propose d'envoyer à la Reine. — Il ne reste plus qu'un captif hollandais, originaire de Flessingue. — Une lettre de la Reine lui obtiendra sa liberté. — Waring a reçu récemment la lettre que la Reine a écrite en sa faveur, à l'instigation de Cecil; mais il ne l'a pas encore remise au Chérif, qui est absent de Merrakech.

Merrakech, 10 [n. st. 20 juin] 1600.

Au dos, alia manu: To the right honorable Sir Robert Cissell, Knight, Principall Secretary to hir Matie and one of hir most honorable Privye Counsell. — *Alia manu:* 1600, June 10. John Waringe to my master, from Barbarie.

Right Honorable,

Itt hath pleased hir excellent Ma[tie], throwe your honorable favour, to efforde unto the Duche congregation at London and the magistratties at Amswerdam hir most gratious lettars[2] in the behalf of 9 Duchemen taken longe since captives by the Barbarians and became slaves to Mully Hamett, Kinge of Barbery; which lettar reseaved by the sayd magistrattes, they dyd simply commytt the

---

1. Sur ce personnage, V. *supra*, p. 147 et note 2.
2. V. cette lettre d'Élisabeth, *supra*, Doc. XLVII, p. 137.

same to bee sent heather by the handes of a Portingall resydent in Amswerdam; who sent hir Maties letter to one Marchena[1], a Spaniarde, to bee delivered to the sayd Kinge; who, receaving the same from the handes of a Spaniard, 8 monthes past, made doubt of some colewtion or descytt, and would nott effect the contentes in any respectt.

Which I perceavinge, dyd by peticion unportunar the Kinge very often to have aunswar of hir Magesties lettar, who, perceaving the veritie and direknes of the cause, dyd partly grant releasement of the forsayde captives. And so, untill now, havinge dayly sollicited the same, his Matie hath bin pleased to release them, and deliver them unto my handes to bee sent unto hir Matie in a good shipp of London called « the Eagle ». And so from hence they are departed to the place of imbarking. By whose means especially and your Honor, they are freed out of this heathen country, wherby they are bound dayllye to praye to God for hir Maties most longe and happye raygne, and the longe continewaunce of your favor with hir Matie and prosperows healthe, with all heavenly felicity.

And now, the Kinge beinge purposed to send in imbassage to hir Matie his secretary, by name Sidy Abdala Wahett Anone, and one All-Hage Messa, with one other of that name, togeather with there interpretter[2], yt is thought most meette that they sayd captives doe accompany the Moors, untell they come one with the other unto hir Matie or your Honors presenttes, to acknowlege hir Maties great bounty and liberallyty.

So now ther remayneth no more captives of that nation but only one of Flushinge; in whose behalf I have formarly writt to my very good lorde Sir Robart Sidnaye, and the magistrates there to bee peticioners unto your Honor for hir Maties gratious lettar; havinge often sollicited heare his liberty, and am aunswered that, yf itt please hir Matie to write for him or 100 more, they shalbe sent unto her, nottwithstandinge the Kinge douth houlde in bettar esti-

---

1. Juan de Marchena. Sur ce personnage, que Waring qualifie inexactement d'Espagnol, V. *supra*, p. 100, note 1.

2. Sur les membres de l'ambassade envoyée à Londres par Moulay Ahmed, V. *infra*, Doc. LVII, p. 164.

ation one Christyan then 100 of his owne nation and people.

And, as all these are bound to praye for your Honor etc., and myself especially for your formar gratious favours, and lastlye for your honorabell asystaunce to sertayne merchantes of London, in procuringe hir Maties princely letters [1] in my behalf and pertner to the aforsayd King of this countrye. Which latly cominge to my handes, for some especyall causes I have nott yeatt presented itt, and the rather by reason the Kinge is abroad in the feildes with his tentes, where I cannott so well sollicitt his Matie in my affaiers as if he weare in his cowart.

Right Honorable, I never have had meant to declar my good affection towardes you, and lesse expectacon of great thinges in my estate, yeat hath there nott wanted good will to wishe well with the best; and so wishinge that ther myght occation bee mynestred to declar with what devocion I desier to doe you servize, most humbly beseeching your Honor to command mee, as one desirous to doe yow what service itt shall please you to impose upon mee, in these partes wher my profession douth detayne mee.

These countryes effordes no newes to enlarge of. And therfore will humblye take leave and crave pardone for my boulde tediousnes, beseechinge God to continewe your prosperous healthe with all happines.

Written in Morocus, the 10th of June anno 1600.

Your Honors humbly at commandment,

Signé : John Waring.

Hatfield House, Cecil Mss., 251, *f.* 5. — *Original.*

1. V. *supra.* Doc. L, p. 147.

LVII

NOTE DE GEORGE TOMSON POUR RICHARD TOMSON[1]

Sidi Abd el-Ouahed, qui va comme chef de l'ambassade envoyée à Londres par le Chérif, est un Maure, mais de la race des Fasi, et, partant, de basse extraction. — Il est apprécié pour son esprit subtil, mais les affaires les plus secrètes sont confiées à un caïd plus en faveur que lui. — Il s'entend à flatter ceux qui servent ses intérêts. — Il est d'un caractère si bas qu'il demande à tout le monde, à Merrakech, des lettres de recommandation pour l'Angleterre. — Tomson, qui n'a pu lui en refuser une, a voulu la rectifier par la présente note confidentielle. — Le second ambassadeur est Sidi el-Hadj Messa. — Il a déjà rempli de nombreuses missions, mais il était, dit-on, tombé en disgrâce, et y était resté jusqu'à maintenant, pour avoir dissimulé deux rubis qu'il avait achetés à l'étranger et qu'il fut contraint d'envoyer au Chérif, à la suite d'une perquisition faite dans sa maison. — Il est très connaisseur en pierres précieuses. — Le troisième ambassadeur est Sidi el-Hadj Ba Ahmed. - Sidi el-Hadj Messa et lui doivent aller trafiquer, comme marchands, dans une certaine ville, mais le plus grand secret est gardé, sur ce point, à Merrakech. — Le quatrième personnage est un Andalou appelé Sidi Abdallah Dodar, qui va comme interprète. — C'est un ami de Tomson, qui le recommande à son frère comme un très honnête homme. — Sidi el-Hadj Messa et Sidi el-Hadj Ba Ahmed ont mission de recevoir pour le Chérif des sommes importantes qui lui sont dues par les marchands Hambden, Field et Stokeley, en vertu de marchés passés avec lui. — Ils achèteront volontiers des pierres précieuses. — Moulay Ahmed ne parle jamais à des étrangers que par interprète. — Il ne sait guère que sa propre langue. — Les ambassadeurs ont ordre d'exposer leur message en secret à Élisabeth.

---

1. L'auteur et le destinataire de cette note sont indiqués (V. *infra*, p. 166), par les mots suivants : « our brother Arnold Tomson ». Sur les différents membres de la famille Tomson et sur leur rôle au Maroc, V. *supra*, p. 101, note 2.

[Du Maroc, 20 juin [n. st. 1ᵉʳ juillet] 1600¹.]

Au dos, alia manu: An ambassador sent from Barbery.

If Mʳ Secretarie² be pleased to have knowledge of the birth, behaviour and creditt that Side Abdala Wahed³ hath in these partes, because he goeth as cheiffe in this imployment, you may signifie to his Honour thus :

First, he ys a naturall Moore borne, but of the race of the Fessians, which the naturall Moore houldeth basenes, yet in creditt by his sharpenes of wytt and guift of penn, beinge not imployed in matters of greatest secreates, for that there ys another of greater estimation⁴. His nature ys to speake well of such as are most bountifull unto him, and to such he will showe a merye countenaunce. What his behaviour may be there, I knowe not; but here no gentility apeareth in him, and such ys his basenes of mynde as he desireth a letter from everye one in his behalfe, and asketh the same in manner that everie one should wryte to his master or frend to be beneficiall to him above the rest, bycause he ys in place here to deserve yt; but he cann doe nothinge more then what Alcayde Asuz comaundeth him. He much relieth one Warens⁵ frendes, and noe dowbte but the merchants which trade to this place wilbe liberall unto him. I knowe not uppon what occasion, but he desireth my letter earnestlye unto yow, which I cannot denye. And therefore I wryte yow secreatlie in this, the twenty⁶, of his birth and condicion, and his ordenarie behaviour here, for that in my other I must extoll him above any deserts ; wherefore keepe this secreat to yourself, least some pickthanke goe to congraciar with him by revealinge.

There goeth with him the old man Side al-Hage Messa, who was thowght should have gonn for principall ; but the Kinge ys otherwize

---

1. La date est donnée dans le corps du document, V. plus loin, note 6.
2. Robert Cecil.
3. Sur le nom de ce personnage, V. *supra*, p. 159 et note 1.
4. Le caïd Azzouz, nommé plus loin. V. *supra*, p. 48 et note 2.
5. John Waring. V. Doc. précédent.
6. Cette mention a permis de rétablir la date du document.

determined nowe. He hath gonn one messages many times, and, as the report goeth, the Kinge tooke displeasure ageinst him the last tyme uppon small occasion, since which he hath lyved in some disgrace untill nowe; onely imployed him in affaires as before wrytten of him. And for as much as I cann gather from such as are nere about the Kinge, his Maties displeasure grewe uppon knoweledge of two ballast rubies[1] (called diacotes[2]), which the said Side al-Hage Messa bought at his beinge abroad, and kept them secret from the Kinge a great while, untill, dayes past, he sent his cheiffe capado[3] to search his howse, soe that he was constreyned to send the Kinge his 2 diacotes, which he valewed in thirtie thowsand ownces[4]. This Side al-Hage Messa hath great skill in all manner of pedreria, as in diamondes, rubies and such lyke.

Besides, there goeth another, called Al-Hage Bahanet, whose father was a verie ritchman of this countrey. He with Side al-Hage Messa goeth (as yt ys here reported) as marchaunts to trade in some place[5], as yow shall better understand when thee embassadge ys knowen soe. Here yt ys soe secreat that none knoweth the grounde of theire goinge[6].

The fourth person ys called Side Abdala Dodar, an Andoluz[7], who goeth for trudgman or interpretor, who telleth me he will speake Italian to her Matie; butt I take yt he will use the Spanish tonge, beinge his naturall language, before Italian. He ys a frende of myne, and did greatly favour our brother Arnold Tomson, when he lyved, and, understandinge how well yow have the Spanish tonge, he desireth to be familiar with yow and craveth my letter. He ys of more sence then all the rest and a verie honest man, and yt wilbe pleasinge unto him to conferre with yow.

Side Abdala Wahed speaketh a lytle Spanish, after the manner of the Moores, butt he wilbe ashamed to use the same, except it be in privatt conference with his inferiour.

---

1. *Ballast rubis*, rubis balais.
2. *Diacotes*, de l'arabe ياقوت rubis.
3. *Capado* : mot espagnol : eunuque.
4. On lit en marge : « 2600 £ str. ».
5. Il s'agit d'Alep. V. *supra*, p 152.
6. L'achat de pierres précieuses à Alep n'était qu'un prétexte. V. *ibidem*, note 1; cf. p. 160 et note 2.
7. Ce personnage, au dire de Juan de Marchena (V. *1re Série*, Espagne, 1er septembre 1600), avait été soldat en Italie.

The old man Side al-Hage and the other Al-Hage goe to trade in some place; they are to receave much money there of Mr Hambden, Field and Stokeley, one the money dewe uppon the parthydos[1] or bargeines they have made with the Kinge. Yf yow knowe of any jewels to be sould, make yow full account they will buy them of yow, or any frend of yours may be preferred therein, by your meanes and conversation with the trudgman.

The Kinge Muley Hamet doth never speake to any strannger but by an interpretor, and yt ys accompted with him a greatnes of majestie, for he knoweth very lytle of any language but his owne.

They have in charge to delyver theire embassage, yf they cann be permitted, in secrett with her Matie, and in Italian, althoe I knowe he ys farr more perfect in Spanish.

This title Al-Hage ys noe part of theire name, butt all such as become penitent for theire evill lyvinge, and in token thereof doe travaill in pilgrimage to Meca, where the tombe of Mahomett ys[2], and there doe vowe more puritie and integritie of lyfe afterwards, these men are, in regard of theire daungerous and chardgeable travaill and devocion, solye dignified with the tytle of Al-Hage, and none other.

Public Record Office. — State Papers, Foreign, Barbary States, vol. XIII. — Original.

1. Mot espagnol : « partido », parti, marché conclu avec un gouvernement.

2. Le tombeau de Mahomet est à Médine, et non à La Mecque.

LVIII

LETTRE DE THOMAS BERNHERE A EDWARD WRIGHT[1]

Moulay Ahmed s'intéresse beaucoup à l'astronomie. — Wright pourrait lui vendre à bon prix sphères, montres, cadrans, sextants, instruments magnétiques, astrolabes. — L'un des ambassadeurs qui partent maintenant du Maroc pour l'Angleterre, Sidi Abd el-Ouahed, a quelques notions de cette science. — Pate, le porteur de la présente, et Robert Kitchen amèneront cet ambassadeur à Wright, qui fera bien de lui montrer ses instruments et ses dessins. — Wright pourrait faire fabriquer des instruments en cuivre ou en argent et y laisser une place pour les mots et les chiffres arabes, lesquels seraient gravés au Maroc, ou bien en Angleterre, d'après des modèles dessinés par Abd el-Ouahed. — Les expériences sur l'aimant feront un vif plaisir à ce dernier. — Bernhere demande à Wright d'envoyer des dessins et des explications sur toutes ces matières, soit à lui-même, soit à John Wakeman, qui pourra les communiquer au Chérif et à ses fils. — Wright fera plaisir aux ambassadeurs en leur montrant quelque instrument qui puisse servir à diriger à travers le Sahara la caravane envoyée annuellement par le Chérif au Soudan.

Merrakech, 24 juin [n. st. 4 juillet] 1600.

To his loving brother, Master Edward Wright.

This King Muley Hamet is much delighted in the studie of astronomie and astrologie, and valueth instruments serving for the course of the sunne and moone that are of rare device, exceedingly; wherefore your spheare, your watch, your mundane diall and your sextans, your new magneticall instrument for declination, or any

---

1. Edward Wright (1558?-1615), mathématicien et hydrographe. Il appliqua les mathématiques à l'art de la navigation, auquel il fit faire de grands progrès. Il écrivit, entre autres ouvrages: *Certaine Errors in Navigation...* (1599); *The Description and Use of the Sphære* (1613); *A Short Treatise of Dialling* (1614).

astrolable that hath somewhat extraordinarie in it, will be accepted; and you might sell the same at good prices.

Now with the « Eagle » there goe from hence certaine ambassadors, and one of them is the Kings secretarie, named Abdala Wahed Anoone[1], who hath some insight of such matters. This bearer, my friend Master Pate[2], and Robert Kitchen, the master of the ship, I thinke, will bring him unto you, unto whom I would have you shew all the varietie of instruments that you have, either in your owne hands, or have sold and lent to others; that hee may choose some for the Kings use and his owne. You may shew them also the draughts and lineaments of whatsoever you have in paper; all which I know will make them admire and be desirous to have some that they can understand how to use.

You may cause to be framed some instruments in brasse or silver, leaving the spaces for Arabique words and figures, yet drawing the pictures of them in paper exactly, and setting downe the Latine figures and the words in Latine or Spanish, which is farre better. There will be found here that can grave the same in Arabique upon the instruments, having some direction from you about the matter; or Abdala Wahed, being a perfect pen-man, can set the Arabique letters, figures and words downe very faire; and so any of your gravers can worke the same in metall, having his writing before them. Master Cyprian[3] would be a good interpreter betweene you and them, or some that understandeth and speaketh both Latine and Spanish, and knoweth what the words of arte meane.

The experiments mathematicall of the load-stone will content the Ambassadour much. Make no scruple to shew them what you can; for it may redound to your good. I desire to heare more of magneticall workes and the discovery of the North Passage. Write to me thereof, and send any maps or draughts of instruments, or what you thinke fit about dyalling, or the course of time, and the motions of the heavens, which you thinke I can understand; but direct the same either to me, or to one Master John Wakeman[4], servant to

---

1. Sur cet ambassadeur, V. *supra*, p. 165.
2. Thomas Pate, marchand. V. *infra*, Doc. LXXXV, p. 236.
3. Sur ce personnage, *alias* Juan de Cardenas, V. t. I, 1re *Série*, Angleterre, p. 530, note 1.
4. Marchand anglais au Maroc. V. *infra*, pp. 210 et note 1, 237 et note 2.

Master Alderman Hamden; who, though he have small skill in such things, yet is desirous to see and learne, and can preferre such matters to the view of the King and his sonnes, who all are exceeding studious of matters tending this way. So that, if I had skill myselfe, or but some of your instruments, whereof I could make demonstration for their use, I could give great content and be a meanes to pleasure you much. But conferre with Master Pate and Master Kitchen, who will direct you in the businesse, and from whom you may receive money before hand, for making any instruments that the Ambassadours would have for themselves or the King.

Your magnetical instrument of declination would be commodious for a yeerely voyage, which some make for the King over a sandy sea (wherein they must use needle and compasse) to Gago. If you question about the matter, and shew them some instrument serving for this purpose, it will give great content. Other directions I might adde unto you; but from the parties above named you may receive the same fully.

And thus with my good will, hoping and wishing to see you shortly, I take my leave.

This 24 of June, 1600. From the citie of Maroco.

From Maroco in Barbary.

Your loving brother-in-law,
Thomas Bernhere.

Samuel Purchas. — *Hakluytus Posthumus, or Purchas his Pilgrimes...* — Londres, 1625, t. II, p. 852 [1].

1. Purchas, ayant republié au tome II de son ouvrage (pp. 851-873) la relation intitulée : *A True Historicall Discourse of Muley Hamets rising to the three Kingdomes of Moruecos, Fes, and Sus...* et parue en 1609 sous la signature Ro. C., a inséré dans le texte de cette relation, à la fin du chapitre 1 (V. *infra*, p. 327 et note 2), la lettre de Thomas Bernhere, en la faisant précéder de la phrase d'introduction suivante : « Touching this Muley Hamet, I thought good to insert this letter of master Bernhere, the sonne of that worthy Augustine Bernhere, as I have heard, which is so commended by master Foxe for his zeale in Queene Maries days, in the Historie of Bradford, Carelesse, Glover, etc. »

LIX

ACTE DU CONSEIL PRIVÉ

(Extrait)

Attendu qu'une autorisation a été demandée au Conseil d'exporter au Maroc certains articles peu importants, destinés uniquement au Chérif, et que les marchands requérants espèrent, par ce moyen, obtenir le recouvrement de ce qui leur est dû par le dit Chérif, les douaniers et agents du port de Londres laisseront Rowland Healyn embarquer, sans payer de droits, les objets dont l'énumération suit.

Greenwich, 20 [n. st. 30] juillet 1600.

Sonday. At the Courte, at Greenewich, the xxth of July 1600.
Present: Lord Treasorer, Lord Admyrall, Lord Chamberlain, Lord North, Mr Comptroller, Mr Secretary Cecill, Sir John Fortescue, Chauncellour of the Exchequer.

. . . .
An open letter to the Customers and other her Majestys officers of the port of London and to every of them and to all others to whome yt should appertaine.

Whereas request hath bene made unto us to give permyssion for certaine necessaries to passe into Barbary, for the provicion and onlie store of the Kinge of the said country, being matters of small importance, in regarde the same hath bene provided for the use of the said Kinge and the hope conceaved the merchauntes maie by that meanes recover certaine debttes owinge them by the said Kinge, and, beinge recovered in sugars and other comodyties of that country, yt ys intended they shalbe transferred and brought into this realme to the benefitt of her Majestys customes, wee doe, for thes respectes, hereby will and require you to suffer Rowland Healyn, merchant of London, to make entry with you of the parcell of goodes hereunder wrytten, and to permytt him to shipp the same in the « Amytie » of London, or any other shipp, without payinge any custome or sub[s]idie for the same. And thes shalbe your warrant.

A wynde instrument.

Eight paire of latten candlestickes.

Three perfumynge pannes of latin[1].

Seaventy and five course sables.

Eight guilt murryons.

One armour parcell guilt.

Fyftie bastard muskettes stocked and inlayed with mother-of-pearle.

Two cases of enamelled pistolls.

Tenne buffe jerkyns plaine.

. . . .

Public Record Office. — *Privy Council Register, Elizabeth, vol. XVI,* p. 286[2].

---

[1]. *Latin,* et plus haut *latten,* laiton ou cuivre jaune.

[2]. Publié par Dasent, *Acts of the Privy Council,* t. XXX, pp. 521-522.

LX

LETTRE DE GEORGE TOMSON A ROBERT CECIL

Des navires marseillais ont apporté à Salé la nouvelle que deux vaisseaux anglais avaient été pris et emmenés à Cadix par les Espagnols. — Ils disent encore qu'une flotte espagnole de 14 voiles a quitté Cadix et serait allée guetter les Anglais et les Hollandais traversant le Détroit. — Depuis lors, sept navires qu'on avait vus au large de Safi sont descendus jusqu'à Santa-Cruz. — Apprenant qu'ils venaient d'Espagne, les gens de la kasba ont tiré sur eux. — Le Chérif a appris qu'ils avaient dessein de capturer tous les navires anglais rencontrés dans les ports du Maroc et qu'ils guettaient le navire « the Eagle », sur lequel se sont embarqués ses ambassadeurs. — Mais ils sont arrivés trois jours après le départ de ce navire, qui eut lieu le 17 juillet. — Moulay Ahmed a quitté son camp pour rentrer à Merrakech. — Il est fort soucieux ; il a congédié des renégats espagnols de son entourage qui révélaient ses secrets. — Il renforce beaucoup de places, où il envoie ses principaux chefs militaires. — Parmi eux, le caïd Moumen Bou Kourzia, son beau-frère, qui commande le plus fort contingent, est désigné pour le Sous. — Le bruit court que le Chérif s'y rendra en personne. — Celui-ci a des raisons d'être inquiet, car son royaume a été très dépeuplé par la dernière épidémie, ses sujets sont très remuants et ses trois fils ne s'entendent pas, malgré les efforts du caïd Azzouz pour maintenir l'accord. — Bien que l'aîné, Moulay ech-Cheikh, ait été proclamé roi à Fez, Moulay Zidân, alléguant sa qualité de fils légitime, cherche à se rendre populaire et déclare bien haut qu'il règnera ou qu'il mourra vaincu. — On croit qu'à la mort de Moulay Ahmed, le peuple se partagera entre Moulay ech-Cheikh et Moulay Zidân. — Moulay Abou Farès, frère utérin de Moulay ech-Cheikh, fait cause commune avec lui. — Comme il réside avec son père, il escompte les avantages de cette situation au point de vue de la succession. — La mère de Moulay Zidân appartient à la plus grande famille du royaume.

Safi, 21 [n. st. 31] août 1600.

Au dos : To the right honorable Sir Robert Cecill, Knight, Principall Secretarie to her Matie, etc. At the Courte. — *Alia manu :* 21 August 1600. George Thomson to my master. Ffrom Saphia.

Right Honorable,

Since my laste, littell or nothinge hath bene offered worthy the presentinge; yet, ffor I knowe your Honours clemencye such as to accept of the meanest, I imbolden myself not to omitt the present conveiance offered ffrom hence, although I doubt with myself that my knowen insufficiency cannot lesse then make me censured by your Honour to presumptious. But howsoever your honorable ffame taketh awaye all suspition, I have often times determined in my best understandinge to acquainte your Honour how this country hath bene generallye governed since my arryvall, as alsoe with the heathenest observations, which althoughe not in ffull, yet in parte; but, haveinge dewly considered, I hould your Honour cannot be unffurnished of more sufficienter advise in each perticuler; in which perswation I have withheld my penne ffrom that tardynes.

Now concerninge what hath passed, of late ther hath come Marcillian shipps ffrom Cales to Sallye, a porte of trade nere unto Fes, which bringeth newes of 2 Englishe shipps taken by the Spaniardes, comminge out of the Straightes, which were brought into Cales beffore ther departure thence. But, what shipps they are, they canne geve noe certaine knowledge.

And more reporteth that ther were 14 sayle of great shipps men of warr, well appointed, which departed thence duringe ther abode ther; and, as they understood, they went to awaite such English shipps or Fleminges as might goe or come ffor or ffrom the Straightes. In which shipps ther went an English man, commander called Gripse, as they saye. These shipps departed ffrom Cales the 13th June, by ther account.

Since which time ther was sene in Saphia seaven sayle, which bare allooffe; and saylinge some smale distance of, to the mouth of a ryver called Tansiste[1], they came to an ankor wher shipp beffore never ankored; and, contineweing but awhile, costed alonge and

1. *Tansiste,* l'oued Tensift.

came to anckor againe at a place called Tammora[1], nighe unto the plea of S[ta] Cruse; and soe the 10th July they came to the plea of S[ta] Cruse, and were vewed to be 4 great ſlylbotes and 3 Spanishe shipps. The admerall, beinge a greate ſlyebote, bare an Englishe ſlagg, and came soe neare the shore as the other shipps were enſſorced to send ther botes to towe her out againe. Ther were Englishe marchauntes which spake with them ſſrom the shore; and demandinge whence ther shipps were, they answered in Englishe: « of Spaine ». The castle shott at them in the best manner they were provided, and soe they departed without molestation.

The Kinge hath newes that they came to take all such Englishe shipps as might be in any porte, and purposely they awaited the « Eagle » to have taken her, with the embassadors which went ſſrom hence. But they came 3 dayes to short; ſſor the « Eagle » departed the 7th July. At which time the Kinge was abrod with his almahalla or campe; and hearinge this newes, ys himself come in to Morocus, but leaveth his tentes and ſſorces abrod, dreading, as yt semeth, some invation.

The Kinge ys much greved in minde, and, uppon some late intelligence, hath dismissed certaine calches attendantes about him, being Spaniardes torned Moores, which he ſſound reavelers of his seacresyes; and would have put them to death, had not bene great entreatye made ſſor them.

He ys now busied about dispedinge his principall men of ſſorces to many places, amongst which Alcade Mommen Bockency[2], whome the Kinge married his sister, beinge the chefest of force in all this land; he ys appointed to goe ſſor Sus with all his ſſorce, that yf any attempt should be ther, which port ys most ſſeared, he ys the moste sufficientest to deffend. And the rumor goethe the Kinge will goe in person thither.

The Kinge hath reasonne to ſſeare, ſſor his country ys much weakned by the late great mortallitie[3]; and although his nomber

1. *Tammora*. Tamarakht.
2. Moumen Bou Kourzia. Sur ce caïd, V. 1re *Série*, France, t. II, p. 209, note 4. Il prit, d'abord, parti pour Moulay Zidân dans les luttes qui éclatèrent à la mort de Moulay Ahmed; puis il passa dans le camp de Moulay Abou Farès et périt en juin 1604 à la bataille de Lektaoua, où les troupes de ce dernier furent battues par Moulay Zidân. V. *infra*, p. 351.
3. Sur cette peste, V. *supra*, p. 125 et note 2, pp. 126-127 et 129.

of peopell be much demineshed, yet hath he much troble to kepe them in subjection.

Besides, his 3 sonnes are still at varience, that the pollecye of Alcade Asus, who governeth all, ys not sufficient to bringe them to an unitye; flor they would be all Kinges, which ys impossible. And although the eldest[1] be proclaimed Kinge and governeth as Kinge in Fes, yet the third brother, alleadinge to be the legittimate[2], through his bountye seketh to winne the hartes of the peopell and feareth not to reporte his resolution, that ys, to be Kinge, yf he lyve, or to dye conquered. And, when yt shall please God to send an alteration, yt ys supposed of all that, although the one be proclaimed, the other will not be reffused of the whole commenaltye, although many be sworne to the contrarye.

The seconde sonne[3] ys brother to the proclaimed Kinge, by mother, and therffore he houldeth with the elder, and, continewing with his ffather, hopeth to be made Kinge by better deservinge or otherwise by survivorshipp. And the third sonne, by name Mully Sedann, he cometh of an other woman, which ys of the greatest house in the land; which makethe him to stand one pointes with his brothers.

I could inlardg much hereof, but, knowinge tediousnes cannot but make my simple laboure of lesse worth, I stopp my penne for the present, promisinge that, yf this ffind but ffavour, my herafter endeavours shalbe more answerable to your Honours desires.

And soe I committ your Honour to the good protection of the Almightye, who send yow all health and happines.

From Saphia, the 21th of August 1600.

Your Honors servaunt,

Signé : George Tomson.

Public Record Office. — *State Papers, Domestic, Elizabeth, vol.* CCLXXV, n° 50. — *Original.*

1. Moulay Mohammed ech-Cheikh el-Mamoun, appelé abréviativement Moulay ech-Cheikh.
2. Moulay Zidân avait pour mère Lella Aïcha bent Abou Beker, de la tribu des Chebâna, épouse légitime de Moulay Ahmed *el Mansour*, tandis que ses deux frères aînés étaient fils d'une concubine de race noire. V. *infra*, p. 269, note 1.
3. Moulay Abou Farès.

LXI

MÉMORANDUM D'ABD EL-OUAHED[1]

Abd el-Ouahed, envoyé en Angleterre sous couleur de s'y embarquer pour Alexandrette, est chargé d'une mission secrète pour la Reine. — Il rappelle l'hostilité et la perfidie qui caractérisent la politique de l'Espagne. — Il propose une alliance entre Élisabeth et le Chérif contre cette puissance. — Le Chérif porterait la guerre en Espagne. — Il possède une armée nombreuse, des munitions de toutes sortes, des vivres en abondance, du bois pour construire des navires, du fer. — Il approvisionnerait toute place espagnole voisine du Maroc, dont s'emparerait Élisabeth. — L'Angleterre et le Maroc unis pourraient enlever à l'Espagne les Indes orientales et occidentales. — Moulay Ahmed pourvoirait à tous les besoins de la flotte anglaise en blé, en munitions et en hommes. — La conquête d'un puissant royaume en Guinée, avec ses 86000 cités, a prouvé l'endurance des soldats du Chérif aux climats chauds. — Si la Reine veut adresser un ambassadeur au Chérif pour conférer sur l'alliance proposée ou la conclure en Angleterre avec un nouvel envoyé de ce prince, Abd el-Ouahed se rendra à Alexandrette. — Si la Reine préfère renvoyer, avec un ambassadeur anglais, Abd el-Ouahed lui-même au Maroc, celui-ci est à ses ordres. — Il serait bon de trouver un navire pour le conduire à Alexandrette et le ramener au Maroc, afin de mieux dissimuler l'objet de sa mission.

13 [n. st. 23] septembre 1600.

Au dos, alia manu : 13 September 1600.

El Embaxador ha venido a esta tierra en achaque de buscar navio para andar al Levante a Scalderon[2] y, con esta ocasion, vino

---

1. Ce personnage n'est pas nommé dans le Mémorandum, mais on a vu ci-dessus (pp. 159, 165) qu'il était le chef de la mission envoyée par le Chérif en Angleterre.

2. *Scalderon*, Alexandrette, dont le nom turc est Iskanderoun, est le port d'Alep. — Abd el-Ouahed devait donner comme prétexte à sa mission un voyage à Alep pour acheter des perles (V. *supra*, p. 51, n. 1), et, dans ce but, demander un navire anglais.

a hablar a Su Ser^ma Mag^d en secreto y en provecho de Su Ser^m Mag^d, y en provecho del Su Mag^d del Emperador su señor, y en provecho del genero humano. Y dize que no ay cosa encubierta de Su Ser^ma Mag^d de los tratos y malevolas cosas que el rey de España usa y usara, y tambien de sus trayciones, que siempre acostumbra, y que no es menester fiarse en el ni sus malas inclinaciones. Pero bendito sea Dios, que la ha hecho siempre del vencedora y victoriosa, porque, por qualquier buelto que ha entendido hazer a ella alguna traycion, que Dios la ha discubierta y buelto en su propria cabeça. Empero, uno que tiene estas mañas y condicion, que dessea siempre de hallar algun descuydo en su enemigo, como sabe Su Mag^d fiarse del? Y qualquiera que tiene pujança para ordenar una traycion, la hara prolongando el tiempo.

Y ansi, si Su Ser^ma Mag^d se servira de acetar la amistad perpetua entre ella y el Ser^mo Emperador su señor contra el, sera obra de misericordia, que se hara para todo el genero humano, porque es enemigo de todos en particular. Y el Ser^mo Emperador su señor no demanda de Su Ser^ma Mag^d mas que sean de acuerdo en ello. Y el Ser^mo Emperador dize que el le dara a entender que hazer en su tierra propria, y la causa es que nuestra tierra sta mas cercana de la suya. Y allende de esto, tenemos mucha cavalleria y infanteria y muchas municiones de todas maneras, assi de polvora y de todo lo que es menester para la guerra, y mucho trigo y lo demas perteneciente a vittuallas. Tenemos tambien bosques para hazer navios, y hierro por todo lo necessario para ellos, que es lo que pertenece al arte militar. Y si se offreciere de que Su Ser^ma Mag^d ganare algunas fuerças o ciudades de España, que sean cerca de nosotros, que quisiere prepararlas con gente de guerra o de municiones o de dinero, que sera todo aparejado de la parte del Emperador su señor, porque, todo lo que demandara Su Ser^ma Mag^d del Emperador, acetarlo-ha con mucho amor, por la antigua amistad que ay entre ellos.

Y si acetaren esta liga los dos Serenissimos, tambien se lo pueden quitar las Indias del Oriente y del Poniente, y aprovechara y multiplicara a Su Ser^ma Mag^d y al Emperador y afloxara al rey de España, porque su fuerça del rey de España no es sino las Indias.

Y de lo que tuviere menester la armada de Su Ser^ma Mag^d, lo bastecera el Emperador de trigo, de municiones, de polvora, de mantenimientos, y mas de infanterias y dineros. Y no monta la infanteria, sino porque es su gente de calidad caliente, como las Indias, y esto porque ha ganado Su Majestad del Emperador un reyno muy poderoso, que es del rio Niger en Guinea. Ha ganado en aquel reyno camino de noventa jornadas en contorno, y en este reyno ha tomado ochenta y seis mil villas y ciudades, y las ha bastecido de todo perteneciente, assi de soldados como de municiones, y la gente ha sufrida la callidad de la tierra, aunque es muy caliente[1].

Y si pareciere a Su Mag.^d que la liga sea por las Indias, y por lo demas mentado, y de embiar algun embaxador que hable con el Emperador en secreto en este negocio, y mire en la liga, como ha de ser, y si le pareciere a Su Ser.^{ma} Mag.^d que el mismo embaxador escriva al Emperador su señor, que embie de alla algun embaxador que venga aqui a ligar esta liga, que el señor Embaxador andara su viage a Scalderon. Y sobre esto vea la Ser.^{ma} Mag.^d lo que le pareciere mandar al Embaxador, y el lo hara y estara debaxo de su amparo y mando.

Y si Su Ser.^{ma} Mag.^d mandare al Embaxador que torne a Berberia con algun otro de la parte de Su Mag.^d para la liga que importa, que el estara en ello al parecer de Su Mag.^d, con tal que la Reyna escriva al Emperador que ella le ha mandado bolver a Berberia, por lo que importa al provecho de ambos a dos Reyes, para que otros no entiendan el secreto.

Y dize el Embaxador que sera de mucho provecho para el negocio, que se halla algun navio que vaya para Scalderon y toque en la Berberia, para mejor encubrir el secreto, y cumplir con lo que ha mandado el Ser.^{mo} Emperador.

Public Record Office. — State Papers, Foreign, Spain, vol. VII. — Original[2].

1. Sur la conquête du Soudan par Moulay Ahmed, V. *supra*, pp. 66 et 83-88.
2. Il existe de ce document une traduction anglaise. *State Pap., For., Barbary States*, vol. *XII*. On lit au dos, de la main de Robert Cecil : « 15 sep. 1600. The Barbarie Embassadors proposition to the Queen, delivered to Mr Secretarie Harbart and me. »

LXII

MÉMORANDUM D'ABD EL-OUAHED

Abd el-Ouahed a reçu la réponse de la Reine et remercie Robert Cecil de la lui avoir fait tenir si promptement. — Il prie la Reine d'adresser au Chérif un de ses agents les plus sûrs, pour négocier et conclure l'alliance proposée. — Si la Reine le renvoie directement au Maroc en compagnie de cet agent, il fera partir pour Alexandrette deux marchands venus avec lui en Angleterre. — Il demande qu'on lui réponde par le porteur du présent mémoire.

Après le 15 [n. st. 25] septembre 1600.

Au dos, alia manu: Memoriall of the Barbary Embassadours.

El Embaxador dize que besa las manos del señor Secretario, y le suplica que diga a Su Mag.^d que besa la tierra debaxo de sus rreales pies, y que a recevido la substancia de la respuesta de Su Mag.^d, y entiende lo que ay en ella ; y que agradece al señor Secretario de que se acordava del con tanta brevedad de embiarle la respuesta. Y dize que todo lo que ha dicho Su Ser.^{ma} Mag.^d tiene mucha razon. Y suplica a Su Ser.^{ma} Mag.^d que embie algun señor de los mas secretos (aunque no sea embaxador), que trate con el Emperador sobre el concierto que se hara en este negocio, y haga la liga conforme a la voluntad de Su Mag.^d y del Emperador.

Y el Embaxador, en lo que toca a su viage a Scalderon o su buelta a Berberia, se governara conforme a lo que Su Mag.^d mandare. Y si Su Mag.^d fuere servido de escrivir al Emperador, que ella le ha mandado, por el conviniente del negocio, que buelva a Berberia, en compañia del cryado de Su Mag.^d, el lo hara, y embiara a Scalderon dos mercaderes[1], que tiene en su compañia. Y en esto, vea Su Mag.^d lo que fuere servido mandarle, y la suplica que, por boca del que trae este memorial, se le embie con toda brevedad la respuesta.

Public Record Office. — State Papers, Foreign, Barbary States, vol. XII. — Original.

1. Sidi el-Hadj Messa et El-Hadj Ahmed Mimoun. V. *supra*, pp. 165-166, et *infra*, p. 202.

LXIII

ORDONNANCE DU CONSEIL PRIVÉ[1]

Certains marchands de Londres trafiquant au Maroc ont signalé les abus commis en ce pays à leur propre préjudice et à celui de l'État par d'autres marchands. — Le Chérif ayant attribué aux plaignants, en remboursement de leurs créances, les produits de certaines de ses sucreries, les autres, en offrant un prix plus élevé, se les font adjuger. — Les plaignants n'ayant aucun pouvoir de réprimer eux-mêmes ces abus, par voie d'ordonnances, puisqu'ils ne forment pas une corporation, le Conseil interdit à tout marchand d'entraver l'exécution des contrats passés par eux avec le Chérif, en mettant une surenchère sur le sucre. — Une copie de la présente ordonnance sera envoyée à tous les intéressés.

22 septembre [n. st. 2 octobre] 1600.

Order for the Barbarie marchants, ordered the 22 of September in Counsaile, there being present the Lord Keeper, Lord Tresorer, Lord Admirall, Lord Chamberlaine, Mr Comptroller, Mr Secretary Cecyll, Mr Secretary Harbert.

Whereas, by an humble peticion and complainte exhibited by

---

1. La présente Ordonnance accompagnait une lettre du Conseil Privé, en date du 23 septembre-n. st. 3 octobre 1600, adressée à « Mr Alderman Holmden and the rest of the Barbarie marchauntes ». Le Conseil accusait réception de la requête par laquelle les marchands lui signalaient une pratique injuste de renchérissement du sucre au Maroc et les dommages qui en résultaient pour eux. Il constatait que cette pratique, en produisant une hausse sur le sucre en Angleterre, était également contraire à l'intérêt général. Les marchands lésés n'ayant, d'autre part, aucun moyen de la réprimer, le Conseil, en attendant qu'il plût à la Reine de leur en donner le pouvoir en les constituant en corporation, avait rendu une Ordonnance qu'il les invitait à faire connaître et à faire rigoureusement exécuter, sous peine d'être tenus responsables des infractions commises. *Privy Council Reg., Eliz., vol. XVI*, p. 378.

certaine merchantes of the citty of London that trade into Barbarie, it hath bin declared that divers other merchantes usinge the same trade have committed and do usually committ a great abuse and disorder in buyinge of sugars in the said countrey of Barbarie, procuringe thereby great losse and hinderance unto the rest of the merchantes and no small hurte and damage to this whole realme by enhauncinge the price of sugars. Which said abuse and disorder is particularlie expressed and delivered in this manner that the Kinge of Barbarie, being indebted in great summes of money unto divers of the said marchantes complaynantes, and for the payement and satisfaccion thereof having taken good order to assigne unto them certaine sugar howses with the sugars in them made and to be made untill the said debtes be acquited, which sugars should be so reasonablie rated and prized unto them (if they were not impeached by others their fellow marchauntes) as might give them good satisfaccion and prove beneficiall to this realme, the other marchauntes, through a greedie and imoderate desire of advantage to themselves, do use to offer greater prices and to overbidde their fellowes. Whereby the said marchantes unto whome the Kinge is indebted are disappointed and the prices of sugars are thereby advanced here in Englande.

And whereas the said complaynantes being of themselves not able to redresse this disorder, because the merchantes tradinge into Barbarie are not incorporated into a lawfull societie whereby they might be enabled to make lawes and orders amonge themselves[1], have made humble suite unto the Lordes and others of her Majestys Privie Counsaile that they wilbe pleased to prescribe some order for redresse of the said abuse.

Forasmuche, as their Lordships have considered that the same is a matter appertayning, not onely in particular to the complaynantes, but to this whole realme and State, and for that cause meete to be looked unto and ordered by them in the behalfe of her Majestie and for the good of the State, it is therefore, upon good consideracion of the premisses, ordered by the said Lords and others of her

---

1. La *Barbary Company*, constituée par les lettres patentes du 15 juillet 1585 pour une durée de 12 années, n'avait pas, à l'expiration de son privilège, été reconstituée comme « corporation ». V. *1ʳᵉ Série*, Angleterre, t. 1, pp. 445-454.

Majestys Privie Counsaile that no marchant or marchantes servantes or factors tradinge into Barbarie shall intermeddle, molest, hinder or impeache any of the said complaynantes, or other of the marchantes tradinge into Barbarie, or any of their servantes or factors, by any such abuse as is before mencioned, or by any subornation, prevencion or undue practize, to defeate or disapointe the contracte or bargaine of any other, and to enhaunce the price of sugar, but shall quietlie suffer every one of those unto whome the Kinge hath assigned or shall assigne for payementes any sugar howse or howses with the sugars made in them, to enjoye and take benefitt of the same; as they and every of them will answere to the contrarie and for breache of this order uppon payne of makinge restitucion, according to the value of the losse, unto the partie wronged, upon due proofe made thereof, or abidinge such other punishment for the same, as uppon complaint and proofe shall by the Lords and the rest of her Majestys Counsaile be thought meete; and that all and every one of the said marchantes shall take notice of this order by a true coppie of the same to be sent by a messenger of her Majestys Chamber unto them and every of them abidinge in London, and by such other meanes as the said marchantes shall thincke good to the rest, either merchantes or their factors abidinge in Barbarie.

Public Record Office. — Privy Council Register, Elizabeth, vol. XVI, pp. 378-379[1].

[1]. Publié par DASENT, *Acts of the Privy Council*, t. XXX, pp. 687-689.

LXIV

ACTE DU CONSEIL PRIVÉ

Les marchands de la « Levant Company » prendront leurs dispositions pour transporter à Alexandrette l'ambassadeur marocain et sa suite et le ramener à Tétouan, où leurs navires font habituellement escale.

22 septembre [n. st. 2 octobre] 1600.

22 September. Signed *ut supra*.

A letter to the Governour and Company of the Turkie marchauntes.

Whereas the Kinge of Barbari hath of late (as you know) sent his Ambassadour unto her Majestie in such sort as honour hath bin donne to her by the ambassage, it is her Majestys pleasure to shew her princelie acceptance thereof by yealding the said Ambassador such respect and favour as his occasions do require. And therefore, as he found the meanes to comme hither out of Barbarie by the helpe of Englishe shipping that appertaine to somme of your Company, so now, being in readynes to depart hence and having cause to make his voyadg unto Scandarona[1] before he returne to Barbarie, he is desirous to take the opportunity of the shipping for his passage that your Company very shortlie is to sende thither. And it is her Majestys good pleasure that he shall both have the aide, opportunitie and benefite of passage by that shipping unto Scandarona where he meaneth to lande, and also of returne from thence into the kingdome of Fesse when the shipping commeth backe, because he may be conveniently landed at Tuana in the

---

1. *Scandarona*, Alexandrette. V. *supra*, p. 177, note 2.

kingdome of Fesse, where the shipping doth usuallie towch for watering and refreshing in their returne.

Wee do therefore heereby give you notice of her Majestys pleasure in that behalf, and do praie and require you to take order accordinglie for the bestowing and disposing of the said Ambassadour with his retynew in the said shipping and in such good and convenient manner as may be agreable to him ; and, when you have resolved how to order the same, to give him notice thereof, that he may prepare himself to take the opportunity of the passage. And heereunto not doubting but you will have dew regard, wee bidd, &c.

Public Record Office. — Privy Council, Elizabeth, vol. XVI, pp. 375-376[1].

[1]. Publié par DASENT, *Acts of the Privy Council*. t. XXX, pp. 679-680.

LXV

LETTRE DE GEORGE TOMSON A ROBERT CECIL

Moulay Ahmed, qui craignait une attaque des Espagnols contre ses ambassadeurs, a reçu avec joie les lettres écrites par ces derniers, en vue de Douvres, pour annoncer leur arrivée. — La nouvelle de la mort d'Élisabeth, que les Espagnols avaient répandue à Merrakech, ayant été reconnue fausse, Moulay Ahmed a vivement encouragé les réjouissances des Anglais. — Le Soudan, d'où Moulay Ahmed tire annuellement de la poudre d'or, est en paix. — Le pacha Sliman, envoyé par Moulay Ahmed au Soudan avec la mission secrète d'emprisonner ceux qui y commandaient, a fait savoir qu'il a exécuté ses ordres. — Tomson ignore encore les raisons de cette mesure, mais espère bientôt les connaître. — Moulay Ahmed a mandé les principaux chefs de ses troupes, campées auprès de Mazagan. — Il a donné à chacun d'eux un cheval, leur a adressé des encouragements, et il va les renvoyer immédiatement à leur poste, car il se défie des Espagnols.

Merrakech, 26 septembre [n. st. 6 octobre] 1600.

Au dos : To the right honorable Sir Robert Cissell, Chefe Secretary to her Maieste and of her Highnes Prevye Counsell, deliver thes. — *Alia manu :* 26 September 1600. M' Thomson to my master. From Moroccos.

Right Honorable,

From Saphia, by a shipp called the « Jonethame », I wrote your Honour. Since which time ther ys arryved the « Amity », who hath brought letters from the Kinges Ambassadors, which were written abord the « Eagle » of Dover, which have signiffied to the Kinge of ther salf arryvall. With which newes the Kinge ys very much contented, as dubtffull beffor, through the fflyeinge reportes of the Spanish men of warre, that some hard accident might have befallen them. Haveinge ffrendes continewall attenders one his Majestye, I understand he rejoyced more then ordinarie.

And, ffor the Spaniard here reported that our Quene (whome the Lord longe preserve!) was dead, we, haveing that joyffull newes which our hartes prayed ffor, desired of Alcad Asus, the principalest man in this land, to procure ffor us leave from the Kinge to make our rejoysment ffor soe blessed newes, which the Lord had geven us. Whome gave us answer that the Kinge willed us to rejoyse more then ordinarie.

Thus much I thought good to write your Honour to noe other end but that your Honour maye understand the outward shewe of love in this Kinge towardes her Majestie. God longe increase his blessinge uppon her to his glorie and all mens comffortes!

Since my comminge to Morocus, ther ys come newes ffrom Gago, whence the Kinge hath yearly quantitye of tiber brought him, that the country ys in peace. Only he gave order to Bashaw Sillman[1], which was the last which went ffor that place with a powre of souldiers, to apprehend and imprisonne those which beffore had government of his powres; which charge he had in seacresye. And newes ys come he hath perfformed the Kinges command[2], see that the Kinge hath seased one ther howses and goodes. But the reason why, as yet not knowen; haveing labored to know the certentye, but the newes comminge soe lately, I cannot learne ffor that none hath any light therof. Beffore long I shall knowe the same, but not soe sone as my desires are to ffurnish your Honours exspectations, which I would doe by this conveiance but cannot, craving your Honours patience in this as in all other.

The Kinge hath called ffor all the principall Moores which had in chardg his fforces, which continewallie lie against Mazegaunt to incounter with the Christians which hould that place. Whome at presant are here, and the Kinge hath geven them every one a horse,

1. Sur le pacha Sliman, V. *infra*, p. 367 et note 2, et p. 371.
2. Le pacha Sliman, arrivé à Tombouctou le 18 mai 1600, fit arrêter le pacha Ammar et le caïd Mostafa el-Fil. Le Chérif reprochait à Mostafa ses violences et au pacha Ammar sa faiblesse envers Mostafa. Es-Sadi, pp. 288-290.

besides ffurther incouradgmentes, soe that ther abode here will not be above a daye or 2, beinge to retourne presently; ffor the Kinge hath noe trust in the Spaniardes.

What shall passe ffrom time to time, as conveiance shall serve, I will advertise your Honour; and, ffor at present ffurther I cannot, I committ your Honour to the merciffull protection of the Almightye.

From Morocus, the 26th September 1600.

Your Honors servaunt,

Signé : George Tomson.

Public Record Office. — State Papers, Foreign, Barbary States, vol. XII. — Original.

LXVI

ACTE DU CONSEIL PRIVÉ

Le Conseil informe la « Levant Company » qu'il admet les raisons pour lesquelles elle s'excuse de ne pouvoir transporter en Turquie l'ambassadeur du Chérif et qu'il la tient quitte des ordres qu'il lui avait donnés à cet effet.

Oatlands, 28 septembre [n. st. 8 octobre] 1600.

At the Courte at Oatelandes, the 28 of September 1600.
Present: Lord Keeper, Lord Admirall, Lord Chamberlaine, Mr. Comptroller, Mr. Secretary Cecyll, Mr. Secretary Harbert.

28 September 1600.

A letter to the Governour and Companye of Marchantes trading Turkey.

Wee have considered of your answere made to our letter concerning the passage of the Ambassadour of Barbarie in some of your shipping that is to goe for Turkeye. And, because your excuse seemeth unto us very just and reasonable, wee do intende to move her Majestie for some other course to be taken; and therefore you maie holde yourselves freed from our former direccion for the provision of passage for the said Ambassadour. And so, etc.

Public Record Office. — *Privy Council Register, Elizabeth, vol. XVI, p. 380*[1].

1. Publié par DASENT, *Acts of the Privy Council*, t. XXX, p. 691.

LXVII

ACTE DU CONSEIL PRIVÉ

Le Conseil prie le capitaine Prynne d'étudier les mesures à prendre pour le retour au Maroc de l'ambassadeur du Chérif et de sa suite sur un vaisseau de guerre que la Reine veut bien mettre à leur disposition.

29 septembre [n. st. 9 octobre] 1600.

29 September. — Lord Admirall, Lord Chamberlaine, Mr. Comptroller, Mr. Secretary Cecill, Mr. Secretary Harbert.

A letter to Captaine Primme[1].

Forasmuche as it is her Majestys good pleasure that wee shall take somme order for the convenient passage of the Ambassadour of Barbarie in his returne and wee are accordinglie mindfull of the same, it is needfull, for the better accomplishing thereof, that wee receave informacion what the number is of the retinew of the said Ambassadour and what provisions are intended to be taken with him, as also what other particularities there are to be thought on and provided for, appertayning to their passage, to the ende that (her Majestie being pleased to do the Ambassadour the favour that a shippe of warre shall be expreslie appointed and taken up for that purpose) order maie be taken for it accordinglie. For which cause wee have sent this bearer unto you, that you, receaving knowledge from the Ambassadour, maie conferre with him, the said bearer, and sett downe an accompte of the provision that is to be made of the shippe and other thinges thereto belonging, which being donne, he shall forthwith goe in hande to putt the shippe in readynes. And so, etc.

Public Record Office. — *Privy Council Register, Elizabeth,* vol. XVI, p. 382[2].

1. Edward Prynne. V. *supra,* p. 2, note 1.

2. Publié par Dasent, *Acts of the Privy Council,* t. XXX, p. 697.

LXVIII

ACTE DU CONSEIL PRIVÉ

L'ambassadeur du Chérif ayant renoncé à retourner au Maroc sur un vaisseau de guerre, le Conseil prie le Lord Trésorier de rembourser au capitaine Kinge les dépenses qu'il avait faites pour l'armement de son navire.

8 [n. st. 18] octobre 1600.

8th of October.
Lord Admirall, Mr. Secretary Cecill, Mr. Secretary Harbert.
A letter to the Lord Buchurst, Lord High Treasurer of England.
Whereas your Lordship is authorised by her Majestys Privie Seale, bearinge date of the 28th of September last, to satisfie out of her Highnes Receipt of the Exchequer all such charges as should be expended, as well for the dyettes of the Ambassadour of Barberie as also for his transportacion homewardes, being allowed by us and so satisfied under our handes. Forasmuch as this bearer, Captaine Kinge, was by us lately directed to prepare a shippe of his of warre to transport the said Ambassador and his company and for that occasion made diverse expences; but since, the said Ambassadour having signified to bee unwilling for some respectes to passe in any shippe of warre, but rather in a marchantes shippe, her Majestie is willing to give him contentment therein; and therefore, because order is given accordinglie for the discharging of the said shippe of Captain King and it is reasonable he should be remboursed such expences as hee hath made for the said preparation, which amounteth to the somme of twentie poundes, theise are to pray your Lordshipp to make allowance unto him of the said somme of twentie poundes. Which being agreeable with her Majestys Privy Seale, theise shalbe unto your Lordship a warrant and discharge, etc.

Public Record Office. — *Privy Council Register, Elizabeth, vol. XVI p. 390*[1].

---

1. Publié par Dasent, *Acts of the Privy Council*, t. XXX, p. 715.

LXIX

LETTRE DE JOHN CHAMBERLAIN[1] A DUDLEY CARLETON[2]

(Extrait)

Les ambassadeurs du Maroc vont prendre congé et rentrer dans leur pays. — Marchands et marins ont refusé de les conduire en Turquie, regardant comme scandaleuse une trop grande amitié pour des infidèles. — Il n'en est pas moins flatteur pour les Anglais de voir que des gens viennent admirer leur reine de si loin.

Londres, 15 [n. st. 25] octobre 1600.

Au dos: To my assured frend Mr Dudley Carleton geve these at Englefeld. — 15 October 1600.

. . . .

The Barbarians take theyre leave sometime this weeke to go homeward; for our marchants nor mariners will not carrie them into Turkie, because they thinck yt a matter odious and scandalous to the world to be too frendly or familiar with Infidells. But yet yt is no small honor to us that nations so far remote, and every way different, shold meet here to admire the glory and magnificence of our Quene of Saba.

. . . .

And so I commit you to God.
From London, this 15th of October 1600.
Your most assuredly.

Signé: John Chamberlain.

Public Record Office. — *State Papers, Domestic, Elizabeth, vol. CCLXXV, n° 94.* — *Original*[3].

---

1. John Chamberlain (1553-1627), épistolier remarquable et savant distingué.

2. Sir Dudley Carleton (1573-1632), ambassadeur à Venise (1610-1615), à la Haye (1616-1625 et 1626-1628), en France (1626), vicomte de Dorchester (1628), premier secrétaire d'État (1628-1632).

3. Publié par Sarah Williams, *Letters written by John Chamberlain...* (Camden Society), 1861, p. 90.

LXX

LETTRE D'ÉLISABETH A MOULAY AHMED EL-MANSOUR

Elle a reçu les lettres de Moulay Ahmed. — L'amitié que lui témoigne ce prince lui donne la ferme assurance que les trafiquants anglais qui n'ont pu recouvrer leurs créances au Maroc recevront satisfaction. — Elle le remercie d'avoir fait mettre en liberté, sur sa requête, certains captifs des Pays-Bas. — Quant aux navires qu'il demandait pour transporter ses ambassadeurs à Alep, cela n'aurait pu se faire sans de très graves inconvénients. — Elle a donc pris sur elle de renvoyer directement au Maroc les dits ambassadeurs, qui, après une longue résistance, ont accepté sa décision. — Elle loue la manière dont ils ont accompli leur mission.

[20 [n. st. 30] octobre 1600[1].]

Muy illustrissimo y poderoso Rey y Sennor,

Avemos recebido de las manos di vuestros ambaxadores, las muy reales y agradescidas cartas di V^{ra} Mag^{d} [2], con tantas muestras di su real amistad, che seamos forzada di reconocer, con estas nuestras cartas, los muy altos effetos imprimidos en nuestro corazon, para assegurarle del mismo agradecimiento en todas las occasiones che se presentaran. Porque, como siempre avemos tenido muy cierta resolucion de la gran stima che V^{ra} Mag^{d} haze della correspondencia establecida y firmada muchos annos con los tratos y contrataciones entre nuestros sudditos, assi aora, siendo en tal manera acertada por vuestros ambaxadores dell' intento y desseo che tiene V^{ra} Mag^{d} di

---

1. La présente lettre, ainsi que la suivante, était destinée à être remise au Chérif par Henry Prannell. Toutes les deux sont donc de la même date que la lettre de De Castries.

créance de colui-ci. V. *infra*, Doc. LXXII, p. 198.

2. V. *supra*, Doc. LI et LV, pp. 149 et 157.

mantener la misma libertad y seguridad di tratos y trafagos perfettamente y enteramente, esta real manera di V^ra Mag^d nos accrescienta mucho la confiança y contentamiento nuestro. Por lo che, aviendo giusta razon di declarar y monstrar a V^ra Real Mag^d los duros tratamientos en estos postreros annos offrecidos a nuestros sudditos por la detencion de muchos dineros devidos a ellos y sus criados[1] tratantes en vuestros bienaventurados puertos debaxo della confiança y dell' amparo di V^ra Real Mag^d, con la qual se tiene muy seguro, creemos de veras, no solamente che todo lo antespassado acaescido por las faltas de los ministros a los quales todos grandes principes en semejantes casos se confian, mas agora seamos persuadido che, por esta nuestra recomendacion, di ellos y sus razonables desseos seran mas assegurados di recebir giusto descuento y satisfacion para todas cosas passadas y favorable respeto en los tiempos a venir.

Agora aviendo V^ra Mag^d querido, a nuestra requesta, compadecerse, para tener misericordia di ciertos Christianos sudditos di nuestros confederados[2], los quales avemos con mucho gasto amparados y defendidos lungo trempo della violencia di nemigos comunes a nuestros estados, podemos bien dezir che, como la tenemos cosa muy aventurada poder procurar el bien de los che con nosotros reconocen el nombre di Giesus el Redentor y Salvador di todos hombres, assi recebimos muy mas grande contentamiento della certeza della real amistad di V^ra Mag^d; pues che todo el mundo podra por esto intender y veer no solamente los effetos di vuestra giusta y sincera negociacion, mas tambien los frutos de vuestra piadosa dispusicion a los che vienen debaxo de vuestro poder, con infinita honrra presente di V^ra Mag^d y eterna memoria sua.

In quanto a la requesta di V^ra Mag^d de navios para la imbarcacion di vuestros ambaxadores por Aleppo, avemos tenido buena consideracion, y nos pesaria mucho di niegar a esta o alguna mas grande cortesia di esta calidad ; mas siendo informada y acertada de muchas inconveniencias y difficultades che di esto podria seguir,

---

1. Il s'agit très probablement des marchands qu'Élisabeth avait déjà recommandés au Chérif dans une lettre antérieure. V. supra, Doc. L et LIII, pp. 147 et 155.

2. Ce sont les captifs des Pays-Bas dont il a été question, supra, pp. 132, 133, 155.

no solamente a nuestros navios, mas agora a los ambaxadores mismos, por rispeto di muchas y muy grandes dependencias, avemos prendido atrevimiento di governar vuestros ambaxadores en esta particularidad y assegurarlos che V^ra Mag^d no imputaria a ellos alguna tacha por aver hecho segun nuestra voluntad y direccion. Benche despues di aver resistidos muy importunamente, han finalmente consentido. Los progressos de los quales, en esto y en todas otras cosas, despues de aver allegado a nuestros regnos, fueron a nos tan agradables che no podemos hazer menos, seno de certificar a V^ra Mag^d lo contentamiento che havemos recebido di ellos.

¡Dios guarde la muy alta y muy illustre persona de V^ra Mag^d !

British Museum. — Harleian Mss., 1582, f. 222. — Minute[1].

---

[1]. Il existe de la présente lettre deux minutes en anglais, *State Papers, Foreign, Royal Letters, vol. II*, n°s 74. 78 et 80. On a cru voir, par erreur, deux documents distincts dans la seconde, qui a reçu deux numéros.

LXXI

LETTRE D'ÉLISABETH A MOULAY AHMED EL-MANSOUR

Elle envoie deux réponses aux deux lettres du Chérif. — La présente a trait aux ouvertures que lui a faites de vive voix l'ambassadeur marocain. — L'affaire en question est trop importante et trop complexe pour se traiter par écrit. — Élisabeth a donné pouvoir et envoyé des instructions à Henry Prannell, qui réside au Maroc, pour la négocier avec le Chérif. — Elle suspend toute décision en attendant le résultat des pourparlers.

[20 [n. st. 30] octobre 1600[1].]

Au dos, alia manu : Lettera della Regina al re di Morocco, Octubre 1600. — Queens Letter to the King of Morocco.

Muy alto y muy poderoso Señor,

Avemos guardado con V[ra] Mag[d] la misma forma que aveys usado con nosotros, escriviendoos dos cartas, pues que hallamos que mas gusto os daremos, tomando el mismo camino y siguiendo vuestras pisadas. En la una, respondimos a la substancia de vuestra carta general[2], la qual, por ser llena de mucha real cortesia y amistad, nos dio grandissimo contento y satisfacion y seremos siempre prestas de conservar y reconocerlo. En esta, nos parecio avisaros que entendimos los particularidades recebidas de la boca de vuestro embaxador con la sola ayuda de su interprete. Los quales, a nuestro parecer, an tratado estos negocios con mucha discrecion, segun la confiança que aveys puesto en ellos. Y a lo

---

1. V. *supra*, p. 193, n. 1.
2. La lettre précédente d'Élisabeth répondait à celle du Chérif en date du 27 mars 1600. V. *supra*, Doc. LI, p. 149. La présente lettre répond à celle du 15 juin. V. *supra*, Doc. LV, p. 157.

que toca al negocio mismo, que, por ser muy largo y dependiente de muchas circumstancias, no permite que se le haya la respuesta por escrito, lo hemos examinado muy a menudo y particularmente, y dado a entender a vuestro embaxador lo que nos a parecido sobre ello.

Y para que mejor entendeys nuestro intento, avemos dado comission y poder a Henrico Pranel, que reside en vuestros reynos, para tratar con V^{ra} Mag^d conforme a las instructiones que le hemos embiado[1] ; a quien os rogamos que deys entera fe y credito, porque, hasta que entenderemos lo que se tratara con el, nos sera menester de suspender todas las resoluciones que pertenecen a este negocio, en lo qual V^{ra} Mag^d ha mostrado tan buena voluntad.

¡ Dios guarde la muy illustre persona de V^{ra} Mag^d !

Escrita en nuestro real palacio de Ricomonte, a los... de Octubre, en el anno de Nuestro Señor el Messias redemptor del mundo 1600.

Public Record Office. — State Papers, Foreign, Royal Letters, vol. II, n° 30. — Minute.

[1]. Ces instructions n'ont pas été retrouvées. Elles étaient datées du 19 [n. st. 29] octobre 1600. Prannell avait reçu mission à cette date de remercier le Chérif d'avoir remis en liberté quelques captifs des Pays-Bas, ainsi que la Reine le lui avait demandé, et de présenter les excuses de sa souveraine de ne pouvoir accepter les propositions qui lui étaient faites. *Public Record Office, St. Pap., For., Barbary States, vol. XII, n° 123.*

LXXII

LETTRE D'ÉLISABETH A MOULAY AHMED EL-MANSOUR

Elle accrédite auprès du Chérif Henry Prannell, qu'elle a chargé d'exposer à ce prince son opinion sur les propositions apportées par l'ambassadeur marocain.

20 [n. st. 30] octobre [1600 [1]].

Au dos, alia manu: October 20 ..... . — Mynute of her Matie lettre to the King of Marocco, to give Prannell creditt.

Accordinge to our promise made unto you by your Embassadour, we have given instruccions [2] to the bearer hereof, Henry Prannell, to deliver unto you our mynde concerninge that negotiacion wherein your Embassadour dealt with us by authority from you. We pray you therefore to give him creditt in such thinges as he shall deliver to you on our behalfe, and to make us understand with convenient speed how you doe like our answeare and resolution in all such matters as your Embassadour hath propounded unto us.

Public Record Office. — State Papers, Foreign, Royal Letters, vol. II, n° 31. — *Minute*.
Ibidem. — State Papers, Foreign, Barbary States, vol. XII. — *Copie*.

1. Le présent document, rédigé en même temps que les deux précédents, fut envoyé comme lettre de créance à Henry Prannell, qui résidait au Maroc. V. *supra*, p. 197.
2. Sur les instructions de Prannell, V. *ibidem*, note 1.

LXXIII

LETTRE DE JOHN CHAMBERLAIN A DUDLEY CARLETON

(Extrait)

*Les ambassadeurs du Maroc ont eu leur audience de congé ;
le plus âgé d'entre eux est mort.*

Londres, 21 [n. st. 31] octobre 1600.

Au dos : To my very goode frend Mr Dudley Carleton geve these at Englefeild. — 21 October 1600.

Good Mr Carleton,

I had aunswered your letter this morning, but for your cousen Lytton, who, being to go out of towne, not only trifled out the time himself, but made me such a trifler that I doubt I shall come short of your messenger.

. . . .

The Barbarians were yesterday at Court to take theyre leave and wilbe gon shortly; but the eldest of them[1], which was a kind of priest or prophet, hath taken his leave of the world and is gon to prophecie *apud inferos* and to seeke out Mahound theyre mediator.

. . . .

Thus hoping to see you shortly, I take a short leave.
From London, this 21 of October 1600.
Yours most assuredly,

Signé : John Chamberlain.

Public Record Office. — *State Papers, Domestic, Elizabeth, vol. CCLXXV, n° 100.* — *Original*[2].

1. Sidi el-Hadj Messa. V. *supra*, pp. 165-166 et *infra*, p. 203 et note 3.
2. Publié par Sarah Williams, *op. cit.*, p. 93.

LXXIV

MÉMOIRE DE PHILIPP HONYMAN

(Extrait)

L'ambassadeur du Maroc a fait de belles phrases pour offrir à la Reine l'assistance de Moulay Ahmed. — Il lui a amené des captifs de Hollande et de Zélande. — Mais son dessein véritable, sous couleur d'ambassade, était de se renseigner sur l'état du commerce et sur les bénéfices que rapporte aux Anglais le sucre du Maroc, afin de relever le prix en conséquence. — Sa visite n'a pas fait grand plaisir aux marchands.

[Londres,] octobre 1600.

Au dos, alia manu: 1600 October. — A relacion of her Ma[ty] proceadinges with the King of Spayne in the matter of peace. — Hunnyman.

En marge, alia manu: He of Barbary used great woordes of offer in generall of any assistance to the Queen; he brought her also certain captives of Holland and Zeland; but his dryft was, under colour of thir formall voyadge, to lerne here how merchandize went, and what gaine we made of their sugers, that he might raise the prices accordingly. The merchants took little pleasure in his being here.....

Here hath bene an Embassador from Barbarie to the Queene [1].....

Public Record Office. — State Papers, Foreign, Spain, vol. VII. — Original.

---

1. « MDCI. Regina, anno inchoante, vacat legationibus honore plenissimis. Ab austro enim Hametus, rex Mauritaniæ Tingitanæ... » G. Camden, *Rerum Anglicarum et Hibernicarum Annales, regnante Elisabetha*, Leyde, 1639, p. 781.

LXXV

LETTRE DE NICHOLAS MOSLEY[1] A ROBERT CECIL

La somme de 230 livres qu'il a payée au capitaine Prynne pour les dépenses de l'ambassade marocaine ne couvre pas la totalité de celles-ci. — Ratcliffe, chez qui logeait l'ambassadeur, s'attend à une indemnité. — Il ne faut pas oublier non plus le maître d'hôtel et les portiers. — Mosley attend de nouvelles instructions.

Londres, 1er [n. st. 11] novembre 1600.

My dewtie to your Honour remembred, — I have thought good, before the departinge of the Barberie Imbassador, to let your Honour understande that, apon your Honours letters for repaiment, I have caused to be delivered unto captaine Primme, at sundrie times, the some of 230^{li} toward the defrayinge of the Imbassador his charges, which will not discharge all that is owinge. And Mr Ratlefe, in whose howse he is lodged, expecteth some consideracon for the use of his howse, and spoile made by them. Besides, there hath bin a steward and porters daylie attendinge, who are to be considered, to whom captaine Prime will not consent for theire allowance, before your Honours pleasure be knowne. And therefore, for the better satisfyinge of your Honour, and to knowe your Honours farther pleasure, I have thowght good to send the Chamberlin of London, who can better satisfie your Honour then I can write.

And so, scasseinge to troble your Honour any farther, I rest,

At your Honours comandement,

Signé : Nycholas Mosley.

London, the first of November 1600.

Hatfield House, Cecil Mss., 250, f. 101. — Original.

---

1. Sir Nicholas Mosley, lord-maire de Londres en 1600. V. *supra*, p. 64.

LXXVI

NOTE SUR L'AMBASSADE MAROCAINE

Entrée des ambassadeurs à Londres, escortés par les principaux marchands trafiquant au Maroc. — Ils sont logés chez l'alderman Ratcliffe. — La Reine les reçoit en audience. — Malgré les égards qui leur ont été témoignés, ils se sont abstenus, par haine des Chrétiens, de toute aumône aux pauvres. — Ils sont venus sous le prétexte de demander à la Reine la continuation de ses bonnes grâces envers le Chérif, mais, en réalité, pour se renseigner sur les prix courants des marchandises en Angleterre, sur les poids et les mesures. — On suppose qu'ils ont empoisonné leur interprète et un autre membre âgé de l'ambassade, pèlerin de la Mecque, qui faisaient l'éloge de l'Angleterre. — L'opinion générale est qu'ils étaient des espions.

[Après janvier 1601[1].]

Ambassador from the King of Barbary.

On the 8th of August, there arryved at Dover Mully Hamet Xarife, Secretarie and Principall Ambassador from Abdola Wayhet Anowne[2], King of Barbary, and with him in commission two marchants, to wit are Al-Hadg el-Messy and Al-Hadg Hamet Mimon[3]. These, with thirteene others, by Sir Thomas Gerard, Knight Marshall, divers gentlemen, and the chiefe Barbary marchants, were brought to London, the 15th of the same moneth, being carefully provided and lodged neere the Royall Exchange, in Alderman Ratcliffes house.

Within five dayes after that, they delivered their letters and had

---

1. La présente note fut rédigée après le départ des ambassadeurs, qui ne dut pas avoir lieu avant le mois de janvier 1601, puisqu'il est dit qu'ils restèrent six mois en Angleterre.

2. Interversion de noms propres, due, sans doute, à une erreur d'impression.

3. Sur ces trois membres de l'ambassade et sur l'interprète mentionné ci-après (p 203), V. supra, Doc. LVII, p. 164.

audience, the Court being then at Nonsuch[1]. The tenth of September, they received answere, the Court being then at Otelands. The 17th of November, being the Queenes day[2], the Queene being then at Whitehall, a speciale place was builded onely for them neere to the Parke doore, to beholde that dayes triumph.

Notwithstanding all which kindness shewed them, together with their dyet and all other provision for sixe moneths space wholly at the Queenes charges, yet such was their inveterate hate unto our Christian religion and estate as they could not endure to give any manner of almes, charitie or reliefe, either in moneie or broken meate, unto any English poore, but reserved their fragments and solde the same unto such poore as would give most fort them.

They kild all their owne meate within their house, as sheepe, lambes, poultrie and such like, and they turne their faces eastwrad when they kill any thing. They use beades, and pray to saints.

And whereas the chiefe pretence of their embassie was to require continuance of her Majesties favour towardes their King, with like entreatie of her navall ayde, for sundry especial uses, chiefly to secure his treasure from the parts of Guynea, etc., yet the English marchants helde it otherwise, by reason that, during their halfe yeeres abode in London, they used all subtiltie and diligence to know the prises, wayghts, measures and all kindes of differences of such commodities, as eyther their country sent hither or England transported thither. They carried with them all sortes of English wayghts, measures and samples of commodities.

And being returned, it was supposed they poysoned their interpretor, being borne in Granado, because he commended the estate and bountie of England. The like violence was thought to be done unto their reverend aged pilgrime[3], least he should manifest Englands honour to their disgrace. It was generally judged, by their demeanors, that they were rather espials then honorable ambassadors; for they omitted nothing that might damnifie the English marchants,

John Nichols. — *The Progressions and Public Processions of Queen Elizabeth.* — *Édition 1823, t. III, p. 516.*

1. Palais bâti par Henry VIII à Cuddington, comté de Surrey.
2. Le 17 novembre était l'anniversaire de l'avènement d'Élisabeth.
3. Sidi el-Hadj Messa. V. *supra*, p. 199 et note 1.

LXXVII

LETTRE DE MOULAY AHMED EL-MANSOUR A ÉLISABETH

Les ambassadeurs marocains sont revenus auprès de Moulay Ahmed et lui ont fait un rapport favorable sur l'accueil qu'ils ont reçu d'Élisabeth pendant leur séjour et à leur départ. — Le Chérif accepte les excuses de la Reine, qui n'a pas fait transporter ses serviteurs à Alep. — Le mémoire ci-joint contient ses réponses à celui de la Reine.

23 Chabàn 1009 [27 février 1601].

Au dos, alia manu : Emperor of Morocco to Queen Elizabeth, From the Emperor of Morocco, 1601.

En tête : Este es una traduccion de una carta rreal missiva del rrey Mully Ahmet, enperador de Maruecos, rrey de Fez; es dirijida a la mag^t de la rreyna Elissabet, rreyna de Ingallatera, cuyo tenor, traducido *de verbo ad verbum*, es este que sigue :

El que es.

Esta rreal carta alta, ensalçada y engrandecida, procede del estado alto a quien siguen los Moros, el señoreador de grand ser, el profetico, el Fatemi, el Haceni, el vencedor — ¡ Dios le de el proceder con victoria en todos los sucessos, tarde y mañana !

A la que procede del estado que tiene, en las tierras que siguieron al Mejias, poder engrandecido y honrra cumplida, cuyos fundamentos son firmes, el estado que rreconocen de los Cristianos los que del estan cerca y los que lejos, y lo engrandecen con honrra y nombre, la rreyna de grande procession, engrandecida, affamada, la rreyna Elisabet — ¡ sea siempre su poder entres las naciones cristianas de grande honrra y nombre !

Y despues escrivimos esta de la pressencia de Marruecos — ¡ Dios la guarde y la obra de Dios soberano en este alto estado a quien siguen los Moros, el estado señoreador, Fatemi, con prosecucion de bienes floreciente, y su honrra ensalçada en esta cumbre proffetica siempre la conocemos — ¡ bendito Dios soberano en todos los sucessos y disignos ! — y nos anparamos con su perpetua sombra todos nuestros rreynos, jarifes, cibdades y villajes, con la honrra de Dios soberano y su ayuda divina !

Y esto por rrazon de que vinieron ante nuestro alto estado nuestros criados que aportaron de vuestra parte, los quales contaron de vuestro grande estado lo bien cumplido y buena obra, y alabaron lo que con ellos hizo vuestra gran procession, del miralles con bien, lo qual conocieron en todos los sucessos, assi en la estada alla como en la partida. Y supimos dellos la cierta amistad que Vuestra Grandeza tiene a este alto estado, a quien siguen los Moros, lo qual siempre conocimos en todos los sucessos, y todo esto es alabado en Vuestra Grandeza y la perseveracion en l'amistad clara y manifiesta.

Y en quanto a la escusa que Vuestra Grandeza pone en no enbiar nuestros criados a las partes de Halep, rrecibimos la escusa y la elejimos y por bien trobimos y la tenemos por la mejor via de amistad.

Y todo lo que tenemos que rresponder en quanto a los articulos contenidos en el memorial que vino ante nuestro alto estado con la carta de Vuestra Grandeza van especificados, con el aiuda de Dios, en el memorial[1] que va con esta nuestra rreal carta, de manera que todo se entienda en jeneral y en particular y lo entienda Vuestra Grandeza claramente.

Y esta es la rrazon desta, qu'es escrita en los veynte y tres del mes de Jaben del año de la procession de la lei de mill y nueve años.

Concuerda la ffecha desta carta con los veynte y cinco[2] del mes de Febrero del año de la hera del Mezias de mill y seiscientos y uno.

Public Record Office. — State Papers, Foreign, Royal Letters, vol. II, n° 32 B. — Traduction[3].

1. V. le document suivant.
2. En réalité, le 27 et non le 25.
3. La traduction anglaise est conservée sous la cote 32 A.

LXXVIII

MÉMOIRE DE MOULAY AHMED EL-MANSOUR POUR ÉLISABETH

Moulay Ahmed partage l'opinion d'Élisabeth qu'il vaut mieux, pour elle et pour lui, conquérir les Indes, d'où Philippe II tire ses ressources, que l'Espagne. — Il a pleine confiance dans les garanties que lui offre Élisabeth pour le remboursement de la somme de 100000 livres qu'elle lui demande de fournir secrètement à l'entreprise. — Il tient cette somme toute prête; mais, comme elle est considérable, il juge dangereux de la confier à un navire marchand et il demande qu'Élisabeth envoie pour la prendre un vaisseau à elle bien armé, en tenant caché le but de son voyage. — Il faudrait décider comment se fera l'occupation des Indes après leur conquête, si l'armée du Chérif et celle d'Élisabeth s'y établiront ensemble, ou seulement la première, qui a l'habitude des pays chauds. — Il faudrait encore s'entendre sur le partage de la conquête et de ses revenus. — Élisabeth devra donc envoyer quelqu'un au Maroc pour traiter tous ces points. — Elle retirera beaucoup d'avantages de l'occupation des Indes; car ces pays d'Orient sont voisins de nombreuses nations qui suivent la religion de Moulay Ahmed et qui, voyant unies les forces de l'Angleterre et du Maroc, entreront dans leur alliance.

23 Chabàn 1009 [27 février 1601][1].

Au dos: 25[2] February 1600. — Articles or a Memoriall from the King of Marruccos.

In the name of the gracious and merciful God.
This proceedeth from our high estate, which the Moores obeye

---

1. Ce mémoire était joint au document précédent. V. *supra*, p. 205 et note 1.

2. On retrouve ici l'erreur de date déjà signalée. V. *supra*, p. 205, note 2.

— Almightie God increase it! — to be Queene exalted upon strong foundations, the renowned Princesse and of great counsayle, Queene Elizabeth — God make her estate perpetuall among the Christian nations, in highe estate and being!

Whereas your Matie sayeth that, in the affaire with the Spaniard, to oppresse him and conquere him in any the kingdomes and citties adjoyning to our kingdomes and countries, yow are not of opinion that any profit can ensue to yow and us, and that which seemeth unto yow best and most nedefull and of greatest reputation ys to conquer him — by the help of God — in his countries of the Indies, as well because by this meanes his power, by which he fortefieth himself and from whence his succors come, shall be infeebled, as also for that this waye the more profitt will ensue to us both. Your high estate and great knowledge may be assured that this order which yow have layed, and this opinion which yow have conceaved, is the very same which wee covett and desire and to which we direct our intentions. For our dominion over those countries (by the help of God) shall be more profitable for us and yow, and of greater reputation, and of more welth and honour; and hereupon wee will resolve — by the help of God.

And, where yow saye that the fleet to be employed in that action shall need thresure for the chardge to the value of one hundred thowsand poundes, and that wee shold assist yow therewith in secrett, that the Spanyard may not come to the knowledge thereof and prepare himself for defence, and that this thresure which yow require shall be the first that shall be taken and devyded from the prizes and purchases that shall be made in those countries — by the help of God — and that then the division of the rest shall be made according to such order as shall be geven, and yow require that this threasure may forthwith be sent, and that wee repose our-selves on your fayth and credit and the performance of with this high estate of all that yow saye; your high estate skall knowe that, all that which yow saye concerning our securitie and the perform-ance of your word, wee hold it for sure and certeyne, and that there is noe doubt to be made thereof. For your word is held with us for very certeyne, and wee will build upon it and will make no doubt at all of it; for yow are a Queene and it is a lawe that the words of princes shold be credited, and that noe doubt shold be made of them, and that they be performed and beleaved.

As touching the threasure, it is the thing which wee have neerest at hand and which is most easye for us, in such sort as there is no difficultie at all in sending this sume; for it is readie and provyded. And wee doo not forbeare speedely to send it, but in respect of certeyne reasons which fall into our consideracion.

The one is that this sume of monie is a grosse sume; and it is not fitt it shold be endaungered by sending in every ship of merchandize; for so shold we put it in perill, the merchantes shipp being not of strength to defend and keepe it. And therefore it will be necessarie that some shippe of your owne come for it, that may be a strong and tall shippe, and some person of accompt take chardg of it, untill it arrive, and that this shippe come in such sort as it be not knowen that it comes to this purpose.

The second point is that it is necessarie that wee first treat of this affaire with your high power, upon all the distinction thereof from the begynning to the ending — by the help of God.

Besides, we must treat of your armie and of our armie, which shall goe to those countries, of peopling the land, after that — with the help of God — we shall have subdued it. For our intent is not onely to enter upon the land to sack it and leave it, but to possesse it and that it remayne under our dominion for ever, and — by the help of God — to joyne it to our estate and yours. And therefore it shall be needfull for us to treat of the peopling thereof, whether it be your pleasure it shall be inhabited by our armie or yours, or whether we shall take it on our chardg to inhabite it with our armie without yours, in respect of the great heat of the clymat, where those of your countrie doo not fynde themselfes fitt to endure the extremitie of heat there and of the cold of your partes, where our men endure it very well by reason that the heat hurtes them not.

Furthermore, it shall be necessarie that wee treat of the division of the countrie betwene us and yow — by the assistance of Almightie God — that it may be understood howe the rentes and profittes thereof may be devyded, that every one of ech syde may knowe his part, and that all thinges may be cleare betweene us and yow concerning our partes.

And of all those matters it is needfull for us, as yow well knowe, to discourse untill it be cleered betweene us and yow — by the help of God — in a playne and manifest manner. And therefore it shall of force be needfull to send from yow some speciall person with whome we may treat of all those matters.

In this there is nothing wherein any opportunitie shall be slipt; and that which is not done this yeare — by the help of God — shall be done in the next; and no opportunitie at all shall passe.

And your high estate shall knowe that, in the inhabiting of those countries by us and yow, yow shall have a great benefite: first for that those countries of the East are adjoyning to many Kinges Moores and infinite nations of our religion; and further, if your power and command shall be seene there with owre armie, all the Moores will joyne and confederate themselves — by the help of God — with us and yow.

Public Record Office. — State Papers, Foreign, Barbary States, vol. XII. — Traduction.

LXXIX

LETTRE DE MOULAY AHMED EL-MANSOUR A ÉLISABETH[1]

C'est par son ordre que le marchand John Wakeman a acheté à Safi certaines marchandises apportées par des navires anglais.

Merrakech, 13 Moharrem 1011 [3 juillet 1602].

Au dos: Received October 16 1576[2].

SIGNE DE VALIDATION.

هذا الكتاب الكريم والمدرج العلى الجسيم صدر عن المقام العلى المولى الامامى السلطانى الاحمدى المنصورى الحسنى وصل الله له اطراد عوائد الاقبال وسوابغ العوارب المنثالة بى البكر والاصال

الى الاصالة التى لها بى الافطار المسيحية الذكر الشهير والقدر الجليل الخطير اصالة السلطانة الجليلة الاصيلة المثيلة الاثيلة الاثيرة الخطيرة الشهيرة السلطانة ايزبيل التى نحب ان لا يزال قدرها معتدًا من ملتها المسيحية بالتعظيم والتبجيل ومرجعًا اليها عند اهل فطرها بى كل دبير وفبيل

---

1. Cette lettre fut remise par Richard Wakeman, en même temps qu'une pétition par laquelle il demandait mainlevée de la saisie des biens de son frère John, opérée à la requête d'un Français, qui réclamait les marchandises achetées pour le compte du Chérif. *Hatfield House, Cecil Mss., Petition 155.* — V. un fac-similé de cette lettre, p. 212, Pl. IV.

2. Mention erronée. V. p. 149, note 1.

اما بعد فكتابنا هذا اليكم من حضرة مراكش حاطها الله وصنع الله تعالى لايالتنا العليه مشرف الانوار منهر الانجاد والاغوار هذا والذى لمكانك المكين إعلامك ان ما كان اشتراه خديمكم احد تجار بلادكم جوان وتمّان من السلعة الخارجة بمرسى اسفى من ثغورنا المحمية بالله على يد بعض اهل سفن بلادكم انما استند فى ذلك الى اذنا الكريم وبامرنا العلى اقدم على شراء ما اشتراه لاجل ان تلكم السلعة لمّا نزلت على يد سفن بلادكم واعتدنا ان ما ياتى من بلادكم لا تتعلف به مرية ولا يلحقنا بيه ريب سوغنا له شراء ما تولاه من ذلك واذنا له فيه لما ظهر لنا فى ذلك من المصلحة وعرّفناك كى تكونى على بصيرة ويحصل ان شاء الله بهذا التعريف الامان والاطمئنان لخديمك التاجر المذكور من جانبك وهذا موجبه اليكم و فى ثالث عشرة المحرم متم عام احد عشره والف

Public Record Office. — State Papers, Foreign, Elizabeth, vol. CXLI, n° 981. — Original.

LXXIXbis

LETTRE DE MOULAY AHMED EL-MANSOUR A ÉLISABETH

(Traduction française)

Merrakech, 13 Moharrem 1011 [3 juillet 1602].

Signe de validation.

Cette noble lettre, ce pli sublime et substantiel émane de la seigneurie élevée, moulouienne, imamienne, sultanienne, ahmédienne, mansourienne, hassénienne — Dieu lui assure un bonheur sans interruption et lui accorde largement ses bienfaits depuis le matin jusqu'au soir !

A la noble dame qui, dans les pays de la Chrétienté, possède une renommée célèbre et un pouvoir entouré de gloire et de respect, la grande sultane, la révérée, d'origine illustre, le modèle, celle dont les vertus laissent des traces, la majestueuse, la fameuse, la sultane Élisabeth. Nous formons des vœux pour que son pouvoir ne cesse pas, appuyé de gloire et de considération, parmi toutes les sectes de la Chrétienté, que ce pouvoir soit reconnu par les habitants de son pays dans tous les temps et tous les lieux !

Nous vous adressons cette lettre de notre capitale Merrakech — Dieu la protège et qu'Il assiste notre magnifique empire par l'éclat des lumières et par les parfums des monts et des vallées ! A Dieu la louange !

Nous portons à la connaissance de Votre Altesse que l'achat des marchandises qui ont été débarquées dans le port de Safi, l'une de nos villes frontières[1] — Dieu la défende ! — achat, qui a été fait

---

1. Le texte porte من ثغورنا.

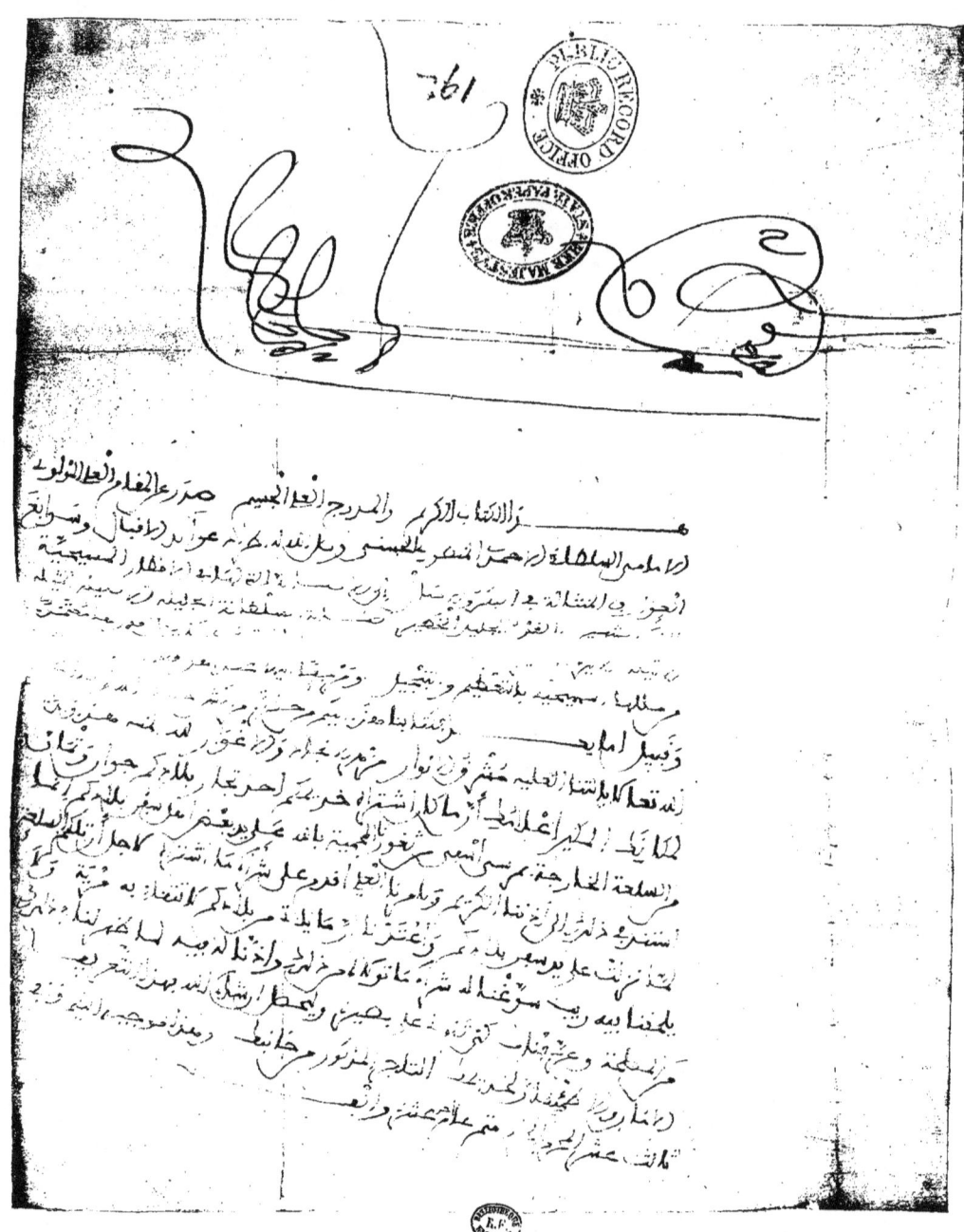

LETTRE DE MOULAY AHMED EL-MANSOUR A LA REINE ÉLISABETH
13 MOHARREM 1011 (3 Juillet 1602).
D'après l'original conservé au Public Record Office.

à quelques matelots de votre pays par votre sujet, le marchand de votre pays, Juan Wakeman[1], a été effectué, conformément à notre autorisation bienveillante et à notre ordre auguste. S'il est venu procéder à cet achat, c'est que nous pensions, comme d'habitude, qu'on ne pouvait avoir ni doutes, ni soupçons au sujet de marchandises venues sur des navires de votre pays et provenant de votre pays. C'est pourquoi nous avons accordé à Juan Wakeman autorisation et permission. Il nous a paru ,en effet, que cette opération pouvait présenter quelque avantage. Nous vous en avisons pour que vous examiniez vous-même la question ; et le résultat de cette explication sera, s'il plaît à Dieu, que votre sujet, le marchand susnommé, soit en sécurité et tranquillité de votre côté.

Tel est l'objet de la lettre que nous vous écrivons.

Le 13 Moharrem commençant l'année 1011.

1. Le texte arabe et la traduction contemporaine (V. *infra*, p. 215) portent : Wateman.

LXXIX ter

LETTRE DE MOULAY AHMED EL-MANSOUR A ÉLISABETH

(Traduction anglaise)

Merrakech, 13 Moharrem 1011 [3 juillet 1602].

Au dos, alia manu: Copie of the Kinge of Barbarys lettere to her Matie. — Tempore Elizabethæ.

This is a coppy, well and faithfully translated, of a letter missive written in the Arabian tounge and letter, written by Mully Hamett, Emperour of Moroco, Kinge of Fesse, Susse, Cyuta, directed to the Matie Royall of Queene Elizabeth, Queene of England and Fraunce, and whose tenour, beinge translated *verbatim*, is this that followeth. The which is :

This high, coroborated and exalted letter Royal proceedeth from the conquoring and victorious Estate, whome the Moores of the State of Mully Hamett, Chareife Hacene, do followe. God give you the accustomed prosperity and increase of honour, by day and by nighte.

To that Estate which you hould in thouse countryes which followed the Mesias, the highe fame and highe and compleate power of the Estate of the greate and reverensed, the prosperous and high Queene, the Queene Elizabeth, whome we desire that her power be alwayes advaunced and augmented in those lawes which followed the Mesias, and that all her nations be to her obediente and subjecte in all partes and places.

And after this, wee write thus from our Royall Courte of Morocos — God save it with the worke of the soveraigne God upon it and upon our highe Estate and Royal power, beautefyinge it with his guiftes and blessinges! His divyne Matie be praised!

I have written for reason of letting you understand that the merchandize which your servaunte and one of your marchauntes, John Wateman, had boughte of the goodes that were unladen in this our citty of Safye, one of our garisons defended by the power of the soveraigne God, the which merchandize he boughte att the handes of some of the menn of some of the shippes of your kingdome, he went not about it but by our order and comaundemente, and for us, by reason that those goodes came in shippes of your countrey. And we did understand that in the like shippes there would not be any susspicion of evell, nor any thing to doubte of. Therefore wee commaunded him and gave him order that he should buy of itt that which was fitt for us, for so wee sawe that it behoved us. Therefore wee do advise you of itt, because you maye take notice and be enformed thereof, and because that, with the helpe of God, the saide your servaunte maye be assured and defended, by this informacion, of your parte.

And this is the reason of this our letter royall, which is written the 13th of the moneth of Moharron of the yeare of 1011.

This date of this letter agreeth with the 21th of June[1] of 1602, of the date of the Mesias. The which I, Abdrugman Escata[2], did translate and signed itt.

Abrugman Escata.

This translated out of Spanishe, according to the litterall sence.

Public Record Office. — State Papers, Foreign, Royal Letters, vol. II, n° 29. — Traduction.

1. Concordance erronée.
2. Il faut rétablir Abd er-Rahman el-Kattan. C'était un Andalou; on le retrouve à Merrakech en 1609, comme traducteur auprès de Moulay Zidân. V. 1re Série, Pays-Bas, t. I, p. 644.

LXXX

AVIS D'ESPAGNE

(Extrait)

Les forces espagnoles venues d'Italie sont destinées à une seconde expédition contre Alger, à laquelle doit collaborer le roi de Fez Moulay ech-Cheikh. — Celui-ci opérera sur terre, tandis que la flotte espagnole bloquera le port. — Il a envoyé au roi d'Espagne un otage en garantie de l'exécution des conventions passées entre ce prince et lui. — Il a déjà vingt mille hommes en campagne et il a mis le siège devant Tlemcen.

6 [n. st. 16] août 1602.

Au dos: Advertisements out of Spaine and the Low Contreis. — 1602.

Abstract of an advertisement out of Spayne of the 6 of August 1602.

The soldiers and galleis which are come hether out of Italy are now to be imployed against the Turk, in a second entreprise upon Algier, wherein the King of Fez is become a partner with Spayne; the one being bound to keepe the seas against any succours to come from the Turk; the other with his Moores to proceed on by land. To which purpose the King of Fez hath sent into Spayne one of his principall men, to remayne as pledges for the performance of certain articles agreed betwixt them [1], and hath already

---

1. Ces nouvelles d'une entente conclue entre Philippe III et Moulay ech-Cheikh contre Alger se retrouvent dans plusieurs autres documents : un avis d'Espagne du 5 août (*State Pap., Foreign, News Letters. Spain and Portugal, vol. XC, n° 48*), un avis de Lisbonne du 23 août (*Ibidem, n° 53*), un avis de Venise du 13 septembre (*Hatfield house, Cecil Mss. 184, n° 124*), deux lettres des 3 et 10 octobre, écrites de St-Jean-de-Luz par William Palmer (*State Pap., For., Spain, vol. VIII, nos 60 et 61*). Samuel Brunault, résident de France en Espagne, les transmet également à Villeroy, de Valladolid, le 16 août. V. *1re Série, France*, t. II, p. 318.

putt into the field some 20000 men and besiedged Tremissen, a strong place near Oran[1]. The duke of Parma, is sayd, shalbe an actor for the King of Spaine in theis desseing, and shall have the cheef command over the Kings forces.

. . . .

Public Record Office. — State Papers, Foreign, News Letters, Spain and Portugal, vol. XC, n° 50.

1. La nouvelle était inexacte. S'il est vrai que Moulay ech-Cheikh avait formé le projet de se rendre à Tlemcen, ce n'était pas pour combattre les Turcs, mais au contraire pour demander leur appui contre son père Moulay Ahmed. Ce projet, d'ailleurs, ne se réalisa pas. EL-OUFRÂNI, p. 290.

LXXXI

LETTRE DE THOMAS WILSON[1] A ROBERT CECIL

(Extrait)

Le roi d'Espagne, d'accord avec le roi de Fez, ferait une expédition contre Alger. — Elle semble insensée, étant donné que l'on ignore les desseins de la France. — On fait néanmoins de grands préparatifs. — D. Juan de Cardona n'est pas de taille à mener à bien cette entreprise.

Venise, 20 [n. st. 30] septembre 1602.

Au dos : To the right honourable Sir Robert Cecyll, Knyght, Principal Secretarye to her Matie.

It may please your Honour not to take ill that I am not yett onward of my viage.

. . . .

For other matters, I have, by letters of Spain of August 20, that the army was to depart within 2 days, and the enterprise published for Algire ; but a captain and commander of galleys wrytes to my frend of Genoa he is astonished at the madness of the enterprise, that, upon confederation with a poor King of Cucco[2] and I know

---

1. Thomas Wilson (1560?-1629). Créature des Cecil, il fut chargé d'une mission d'observation à Florence, à Ferrare et à Venise en 1601-1602, puis fut consul en Espagne en 1604-1605. Nommé en 1606 « Keeper of the Records », il exerça ces fonctions jusqu'à sa mort.

2. Une expédition se préparait en Espagne sous le commandement de D. Juan de Cardona, dans le but d'aider le roi de Kouko (Grande Kabylie) alors révolté contre les Turcs. Une attaque combinée devait avoir lieu sur Alger, Bougie ou une autre ville maritime. La flotte se réunit à Majorque et fut disloquée presque aussitôt en novembre 1602, l'entreprise paraissant avoir peu de chances de succès. Fernandez Duro, *Armada española*, t. III, pp. 242-243.

not what other Moors, they shold undertake such an enterprise without means, they not having for certain mor than 5000 land soldiers in the army.

In confirmation, therof, notwithstanding, it is written me from Florence, this daye, that the Great Duke certainly believes it is for Algire, and that the Kings of Fez and Spain have agreed to beseege it, the one by see, and the other by land, with condition that the Seriffe shall hold the town if he can get it, and render into the King of Spain a fortified harbour within the Strayght upon the coast of Africa[1].

But these are but vanities; the Council of Spain walks in a nett and thinks they are hidden. No man of sound judgement but sees there is noe thing purposed but to hover, as I wrote before, upon the see till they see whatt France will do, and therefore the whole army of 2000 and odd vessells, shipps, caravells and gallies are to come to Majorca, where all kind of provision is made for them. The King of Spain may be out feare confident his cautelous, wary and timorous general Don Gio. de Cardona[2] will do neither great hurt nor good.

. . . .

Your Honour most humble servant,

Signé : Tho. Wilson.

Venice, 20 September 1602.

Hatfield House, Cecil Mss., 95, *ff. 98-99.* — *Original.*

1. Allusion au bruit qui courait en Europe d'une alliance de Moulay ech-Cheikh, vice-roi de Fez, avec l'Espagne contre les Turcs. V. *supra*, Doc. LXXX, p. 216 et note 1.

2. D. Juan de Cardona avait commandé l'avant-garde de la flotte de la Sainte-Ligue à la bataille de Lépante en 1571. Vice-roi de Navarre, il venait d'être nommé en 1602 conseiller d'État et capitaine général de mer et de terre. Il mourut en 1609, âgé de 90 ans.

LXXXII

LETTRE D'ÉLISABETH A MOULAY AHMED EL-MANSOUR

Elle a coutume de mettre en liberté les captifs maures qui se réfugient en Angleterre. — Elle demande, en retour, au Chérif la mise en liberté de Cornelis Jansz., sujet anglais, qui habita quelque temps Flessingue.

[Avant le 3 avril][1] 1603.

Au dos : Al muy alto, muy poderoso, muy eccelente rey Muley Hamet, Xarif, rey de Marruecos, de Fez, de Suz, etc. — *Alia manu* : Emperor of Morocco, 1603.

En tête : Loores a Dios Nuestro Señor Todo Poderoso, criador del cielo, tierra y mar, etc.

Elizabeth, por la divina gracia, natural reyna de sus reynos y de sus subjetos, amparadora de todos los virtuosos que se recogen debaxo de su amparo, escribe esta su real carta al muy alto, muy poderoso y de muy clarissima progenie, el escogido rey y gobernador del imperio de la Morisma, Muley Hamet, Xarif, a quien el Soberano Dios de continuacion de paz y sossiego entre los suyos.

Nos, amando los nuestros y siendo entrañablemente dellos amado y obedescido, no podemos menos que de ampararlos. Todos los Moros que alcançan llegar debaxo de nuestro mando luego son libres y los mandamos a vuestras tierras con buen trattamento, como muchas vezes abemos hecho a Moros y a Turcos. Assi vos abemos bien querido visitar con estos pocos renglones por pediros

---

1. La reine Élisabeth mourut le 24 mars [n. st. 3 avril] 1603.

la libertad de un pobre cattybo vuestro, Cornelis Janson[1], natural subjecto mio, nascido en este mi reyno de Ingalaterra, aunque algun tiempo morado en Flissinga, lugar de Zelanda. Assi no dudo me otorgareys de darle libertad, como con toda buena affection continuare de dar libertad a los vuestros quantos tuvieren tan buena v[entura] de escapar de manos de los que los cautivan y venden y compran.

Guarde Dios, por su divina clemencia, a vuestra real persona con su ceptro, poder y fuerte, con los vuestros, muchos años en paz.

De mi real corte de...., a los.... del mez de.... de 1603 años de la quenta de nuestro calendario.

Vuestra hermana y pariente segun ley de corona y ceptro.

Public Record Office. — *State Papers, Foreign, Barbary States, vol. XII.* — *Minute.*

[1]. Élisabeth était déjà intervenue en faveur de ce personnage dans une lettre du 31 mars [n. st. 10 avril] 1600. V. *supra*, p. 154 et note 1.

LXXXIII

MÉMOIRE DE HENRY ROBERTS[1] A JACQUES Ier

Henry Roberts a passé trois ans et demi au Maroc comme agent de la reine Élisabeth. — Il soumet à Jacques Ier un projet pour la conquête du pays et sa conversion au christianisme. — Richesses du Maroc : céréales et plantes diverses ; cire, salpêtre, poudre d'or amenée de la Guinée ; animaux. — Forces militaires du Roi : 4 000 Renégats, ce sont ses meilleurs soldats, 4 000 Andalous, 1 500 Zouaoua, des Turcs et d'autres soldats, le tout formant un effectif de 40 000 hommes, auxquels on peut ajouter 200 000 Arabes, troupe sur laquelle on ne peut compter. — Pour affaiblir ces forces, il faudrait proclamer que ceux qui feront leur soumission seront libres, que ceux qui se convertiront au christianisme conserveront leurs biens et seront bien traités ; quant à ceux qui refuseront de se convertir, il leur sera accordé un délai, pendant lequel ils garderont la jouissance de leurs biens et le libre exercice de leur religion. — La plupart des Marocains se soumettront, les autres se réfugieront dans la montagne ; ils sont maltraités par leur roi et l'espérance de jouir du fruit de leur travail les détachera de lui. — Si le Maroc n'est pas conquis par un prince chrétien, il sera occupé par les Turcs. — Si le roi d'Angleterre s'en empare, il pourra pénétrer en Guinée aussi loin qu'il le voudra ; il contiendra les Turcs et agira à volonté contre l'Espagne, le Portugal, la France et l'Italie. — Les Espagnols devront être tenus dans l'ignorance de ce projet, car ils pourraient y mettre obstacle ; ils n'aspirent à la paix avec l'Angleterre que pour s'emparer du Maroc. — La conquête devra commencer par l'occupation des places que les Espagnols possèdent sur la côte, Tanger, Ceuta, Mazagan, ainsi que le fort d'Arguin, d'où ils tirent une grande quantité de poudre d'or et trafiquent avec la Guinée ; il sera facile de s'en emparer avec l'aide du roi des Maures. — Jacques Ier pourra faire alliance avec les Pays-Bas qui

---

1. Sur ce personnage et sur sa mission au Maroc, V. 1re Série, Angleterre, t. I, p. 500 et note 1 et p. 510. On rappelle qu'il arriva à Safi le 14 [n. st. 24] septembre 1585 et qu'il quitta le Maroc le 2 [n. st. 12] novembre 1588; il était de retour en Angleterre le 1er [n. st. 11] janvier 1589.

fourniront des vaisseaux. — Les Irlandais et les Hébridais sont les meilleurs soldats pour cette conquête. — Le trésor du roi de Maroc pourvoira plus de six fois aux frais de l'expédition. — Cette entreprise, par les richesses et par la gloire qu'elle rapportera, fera cesser les dissensions civiles entre l'Angleterre, l'Irlande et l'Écosse. — Henry Roberts a tenu son projet secret pendant quinze ans, ne trouvant pas l'occasion de le révéler ; mais l'avènement de Jacques Ier, prince zélé pour la gloire de Dieu et de son Église, est une circonstance favorable. — Henry Roberts rappelle ses services et demande une pension ou un logement à Windsor pour reposer sa vieillesse.

[Après le 3 avril 1603 [1].]

Your Highnes faithfull subject, Captaine Henry Roberts, who was her Maties sworne servante, Squier to the bodye and so desireth to bee to your Matie, and whoe was ymploied as Agent for her Highnes with the Kinge of Marockos three yeares and a half, duringe which tyme giveinge his best endeavour to knowe the state of these countreis, beinge verie great and riche with many great comodities, and how godly and christianlike yt weare to subdue the same from Mahomet to the knowledge of Christ, and the which hee well perceiveth may bee accomplished to the great glorie of Godd, profite and increase of your Maties domynions, trafique of marchantes, ymployments of navies and people, and to the universall good of all Christendome, most humbly submitteth a true and plaine project thereof to your Maties good likinge, to bee considered of, when as best shall please your Highnes.

The comodities that this countrey dooth yeilde.

The soile verie fertile, and good and more better then Spaine or any other countrey knowne. Wheate, barley and pease, aboundance and verie good anniseeds and sugar, verie good dates, anneeles, wynes, oyles, raisons, hides, goatskinnes, waxe, honye and

1. La date résulte d'un passage du texte (V. *infra*, p. 227 et note 1), où il est dit que le présent Mémoire a été rédigé quinze ans après le départ de Henry Roberts du Maroc (V. p. 222 et note 1) et peu après l'avènement de Jacques Ier.

rawe silke. Saltpeeter more plenty and better then in any countrey.

A great trade to Genne over land throughe the Sand Sea, as they call yt, whereas your Matie may make it by sea, for they have noe shippinge to doe so; from whence they bringe goulde called tyber[1], and being refined wee call yt fine Barbery gould, and of this the Kinge hath great store, oystriches feathers, great store of graines and many other commodities. And this countrey of Genney woulde utter many of our commodities, as lynnen, cloth and course wollen clothes, so that this woulde bee made a good comodious trade for our countrey.

Of Beasts.

Oxen, kine greate and lardge, and many sheepe, greate store of goates, horsses very light and great store cammuells, moiles, asses, wilde swyne, connyes, hares, deares, roebuckes, aboundance lyons and many other animales.

Fowles.

Eagles, hawks, busterdes, storkes. Genney hennes, Turkey hennes, pidgeons, partridges, turtle-doves, hennes and capons, of all theis aboundance, and many other sortes of fowles.

All sortes of fruites, as orenges, leamondes, pomegranards, potatoes[2], muskemillions and palmites, and all other sorte of fruites or hearbes as in Spaine, Ffrance or England, and more better and more plentie. And yt is well knowne that there are riche mynes of goulde and silver, but the Kinge will not have yt knowne, for feare least his lande shoulde bee invaded for yt by others.

The forces of men that the Kinge can make.

Of Ellches, being runnegades, the best solduares, 4000. Of Andoloustes, being runnegade Moores out of the mountaines of

---

1. La poudre d'or appelée or de tiber. V. 1re Série. Angleterre, t. I, Introd., p. IV.

2. Patates douces, qu'il ne faut pas confondre avec les pommes de terre.

Granado, 4 000. Of Swagostes[1], that are Moores of the Mountaines, 1 500. And of Turkes and others, to make upp them above fortie thowsand.

The Kinge hath of theis above in paie 40 000, which hee calls his Maganisies[2], which is as much as to saie his guardes. But of theis, there ys not 20 000 good menn.

But the Kinge may have of his Larbies twoe hundred thowsand, but they bee of noe force, for they will never come neare any fight, but run awaye, so that they will doe them more hurte then good, for they will disorder their armye and breake their orders.

And to weaken their forces there ought to bee proclaimed at the arivall that there shalbee noe captives, but all shall bee free that will come in and submitt themsealves to your Matie. And, as many as will tourne and bee Christians, they shall not only enjouy all their owne goodes, but your Matie will give them that they and theirs shall live ever heerafter very well. And they that will not tourne Christians, they shall have leave to use their owne conscience for a tyme, so that they come in and submitt themsealves to your Matie, and they shall enjoy their goodes also, and that they shalbee better governed by the Christian goverment then ever they weare before.

And this will make a great nomber of them to come into your Matie, ffor there be many captives and Neagroes and Christians, and theis Elches, which weare Christians and tourned Moores, which wee call Runnagates, will most of them come in, and theis bee his best solduares that hee maketh most accompt of. So the most parte of them will come in, and the rest runn awaye to the Mountaines. For theis people bee very unstable and changeable in their mynde, and will bee drawne with faire wordes and good promises, for indeed the King dooth so keepe them under subjection and so grane them, taske, use and keepe them ever as captives. And, thinkinge to be freed of theis, and that they may enjoye the fruites of their labour to them and theirs, will make them to tourne from the Kinge.

---

1. *Swagostes*, les Zouaoua, tribu de la Kabylie, en espagnol Açuagos.

2. *Maganisies*, mekhaznia, soldats du makhzen.

And this countrey is easie to be wonne by your Maties owne forces; and, if this countrey bee not wonne in tyme by some Christian Prince, the Turkes will have yt, and then hee will bee to neere a neighbour to Spaine, Ffraunce and Christendome.

And your Matie haveinge possessed this countrey, you may invade and goe as farre as you please into Genney, which is very rich both of goulde and other great riches comodities.

Also your Matie may greatly annoy the Turke, to the great rejoysinge of all Christendome. And also your Matie may goe into Spain, Portugal, Ffraunce and Italy and annoy all of them at your Maties pleasure.

But this must be kept verie secrett and from the knowledge of the Spaniards, for, if they should knowe of it, they woulde hinder yt all, if they might. And also, if the Spaniard have peace with your Matie, they themsealves woulde seeke to wynne this countrey; and therefore they would bee glad to have peace the soner, for this countrey is many tymes richer then all Spaine.

The Spaniard houldes certen ffortes in Barberye on the coast, as Tangir, Suta, Massagon and one or twoe more[1]; and some of theis must bee wonne, and then, by Goddes helpe, all the rest are wonne. Also the Spaniard houldes a castle in Genneye called Erganic[2], from whence the Spaniards hath much gould and there makes a good trade with the Negroes; and this castle is to be wonne with smale force, ffor the King of the Moores dealt with me to write to her Matie for 3 shipps, to transporte his soldaures thether to take yt, for hee is desirous to have this castle.

Yf yt please your Matie, you may doe this with your owne forces and with the Lowe Countries, for they may spare your M^tie as many shipps as yow please to transporte your armye.

Your Maties Irishe solduars and they of the Out Isles[3] bee the best solduars in the worlde for this service of that countrey of Africa, and your M^tie may drawe from thence twenty or thirty thousand; and the countrey wilbee the better to bee ridd of them, for they bee but idle and will never fall to worke but steale as longe as

---

1. Il faut ajouter à cette énumération Melilla et le Peñon de Velez.
2. *Erganie*, Arguin. V. 1re Série, Angleterre, t. I, Introd., pp. iv et v, et *supra*, Doc. XIII, p. 44 et note 2.
3. *The Out Isles*, les Hébrides.

they remaine in Ireland. And in their places there would bee sent over good subjects of trades and occupacions, and so this would make Ireland a good countrey.

I knowe that the Kinge of Morockoes treasure is sixe tymes more then the chardge of the army will come unto.

And yet I know there wilbe some that will not like of it, and they will do all they maye to diswade your Matie from yt; but they are they that have litle care to wynne many thowsand soules to God and to make your Matie to bee the greatest potentate next under God on earth.

Yt woulde, through the great riches, honour and fame of so glorious an enterprise, which thereby coulde not but of necessitie growe and succeed, keep his M^{ties} subjectes in England, Ireland and Scotland from intestine inovacion, conspiracies, treasons and rebellion, which naturally springe and are nourished through idleness, lacke of maintenance and discontented humours wanting whereupon to worke or materially to bee ymploied, as in the reignes of Kinge Henry the 3, Edward 3 and Henry 5, when, through glorious, gainfull and lawfull warres of Ffraunce, noe treasons weare imagined against the Kinges person.

I have kept this seacret to myselfe theis fivetenn yeares[1], for I sawe noe tyme to reveale yt. But yt hath pleased God to send us your Matie, whoe seekes the advannce of Godes glorie and the increase of his Churche; and hee that dooth so maye doe muche, for God will assist him and bee allwaies with him. If it please God, yt maye bee done with litle bloudshed, as hath bein before declared.

To the Kinges most excellent Matie.

In all humblenes sheweth unto your most excellent Matie that:

Whereas your suppliant, Captaine Henry Robertes, was sworne servant unto her late Matie, Squier to the bodie, and being by her said late Highnes commaundment imployed in service to the Kinge of Morockoe, where he remained three yeares and a half, and before that and since in divers other her services, in which hee

---

1. Cette indication a permis de dater approximativement le document.

hath spente all his best tyme of yeares and twoe thowsand five hundred poundes out of his pursse, and haveinge bein a suitor unto our said late Queene for some recompence towardes his relief and mantenance now in his droupinge yeares, and, notwithstandinge her many gracious grauntes and bountifull promises, hee hath bein allwaies crossed and hindered by some that loved noe followers of the late Earles of Leicester and Essex; your subject, by his experience and travelles, beinge able to disclose good services, as hee hath mede knowne to his good Lord the Earle of Cumberland[1].

Humblie therefore hee beseecheth your Matie to bestowe some smale pencion uppon him, or a poore knightes roome in Windsor, to relive him, nowe in his oulde aidge. And hee will, accordinge to his bounden duety, daily praie for your Maties happie and longe reigne and of your most royal issues, etc.

British Museum. — Additional Mss., 38 139, f. 33. — Copie du temps.

1. George Clifford, 3ᵉ comte de Cumberland (1558-1605). De 1586 à 1598, il ne fit pas moins de onze expéditions contre les Espagnols, comme flibustier.

LXXXIV

LETTRE DE GEORGE TOMSON A ROBERT CECIL[1]

Sa dernière lettre annonçait la mort de Moulay Ahmed, qui, en 1602, avait marché sur Fez contre son fils Moulay ech-Cheikh, devenu intolérable par ses excès, et l'avait fait prisonnier. — Moulay Ahmed, ayant rétabli l'ordre dans le gouvernement de Fez, s'apprêtait à rentrer à Merrakech, quand il mourut. — Depuis lors, le Maroc est en proie à des troubles que l'on prévoit de plus en plus graves. — Moulay Ahmed avait divisé son royaume en deux parts : Fez et la région jusqu'à l'oued el-Abid pour Moulay Zidân, Merrakech et le Sous pour Moulay Abou Farès. — Moulay ech-Cheikh est entre les mains de ce dernier. — Moulay Zidân et Moulay Abou Farès, tous deux proclamés dans leurs royaumes respectifs, se défient l'un de l'autre et se préparent à la guerre. — Moulay Zidân veut être seul roi ou ne pas régner du tout. — Leur hostilité remonte à la prise par Abou Farès du Tadla, qui est situé sur le territoire de Moulay Zidân. — Les Maures, en général, font des vœux pour ce dernier, qui est le plus habile et le plus martial. — On le préfère surtout comme né d'une femme libre, les deux autres frères étant fils d'une négresse. — Abou Farès, qui détient le trésor de Moulay Ahmed à Merrakech, cherche à s'attacher les troupes par des largesses ; Moulay Zidân réclame en vain la moitié de ce trésor. — Il s'est approprié, grâce à sa mère, les richesses que Moulay Ahmed, à sa mort, avait avec lui. — La plupart des soldats qui étaient au camp de Moulay Ahmed ont abandonné Moulay Zidân et sont rentrés à Merrakech pour toucher la solde due par le feu roi. — Les caïds Azzouz, Moumen Bou Kourzia Abd es-Seddik, Abd el-Ouahed, Djouder, Ahmed ben Mansour, tous puissants personnages, ont pris parti pour Moulay Zidân et sont à Fez. — Moulay Ahmed avait épousé la sœur du plus considérable d'entre eux, Moumen Bou Kourzia. — Djouder, le conquérant du Soudan, commande aux Renégats. — Ahmed ben

---

1. Sur les faits et les personnages mentionnés dans la présente lettre, cf. ci-après la *Relation de Ro. C.*, pp. 335-340 ; 1re Série, Pays-Bas, t. I, p. 82, Sommaire ; Espagne, à la date de 1603 ; El-Oufrâni, pp. 289-310.

Mansour est le chef des Andalous, lesquels sont à Merrakech, mais sont favorables, pour la plupart, à Moulay Zidân. — Les principaux caïds partisans de Moulay Abou Farès sont Messaoud en-Nebili, le frère de celui-ci, et Sidi Gouaia, qui a pris le Tadla. — Le Juif Brahim ben Ways est très écouté de Moulay Abou Farès et l'entraîne à des pratiques violentes et malhonnêtes contre les marchands. — Les sucreries, qui sont la base du commerce au Maroc et une grosse source de revenus pour le roi, ont été détruites à la mort de Moulay Ahmed. — Tomson a sauvé celle d'Azrou. — Abou Farès les a abandonnées au pillage. — Tomson vient de lire des lettres de Merrakech qui annoncent que Moulay Zidân a repris le Tadla, où il a installé le caïd Moustafa, et qu'il est entré en campagne avec toutes ses forces. — Moulay Abou Farès a envoyé aussitôt demander la paix à son frère.

Santa-Cruz-du-Cap-de-Guir, 30 octobre [n. st. 9 novembre] 1603.

Au dos : To the right honorable the Lord Cyssell, Cheffe Secretary to the Kinges Majestie, in London or at the Court. By the waye of France. — *Alia manu :* 30 October 1603. Advertisementes from Barbarie.

Right Honorable,

I have sondry times written your Honour ffrom hence, to my best capacetye, of all such newes as the times have afforded. And my last was soe overtaken with the time as infforced to geve my ffyrst penninge to a ffrend of trust, to be copied at home, and after to be presented your Honour; which went by the shipp called the « Tomazen », whome departed hence the 6th September, conteininge the newes of the death of the Kinge of this country, Mully Hammett; whome, in anno 1602, went to Fes to subdewe or deprive his eldest sonne, Mully Sheck, ffrom ffurther governinge, whome he made kinge of that place and partes. He governed, by account of some of best memory, twenty one yeares; and his ffather, ffull with complaintes of his abuses and habominations, could endure noe longer, went with his almuhalla and fforce, and tooke him prisoner in manner as my fformer made yt knowen.

The Kinge, after a twelfe months staye[1] ther and more, puttinge order ffor the well governinge of those partes, and haveinge his sonne prysoner, was in the waye to retorne for Morocus; but death overtooke him; and, since his death, the country in reboultes and soe contineweth; dayly exspectation of greater trobles, and noe hope of peace in longe time.

The certentye is that, beffore the Kinge dyed, he made a divition of his country into two partes, to be governed by two of his sonns. The governement of Fes and all those partes, and soe ffarr towardes Morocus as to a ryver called Wed Labide[2], was geven to Mully Sydan. And ffrom that ryver to Morocus and thes partes of Sus, was geven Mully Befferris, whome the Kinge lefte to governe Morocus in his absence. This Mully Befferris, younger brother to Mully Sheck, whome was taken prisoner, and, by order of Mully Hammett, sent to Morocus to be kept prisoner ther by his brother Mully Befferris[3]; and soe he contineweth, both prisoner and made blind[4] by a devise used, soe reported.

Mully Sydan and Mully Befferris, uppon the death of ther ffather, proclaimed themselves Kinges[5] in manner as ther ffather lefte by will, and from that time have and doe governe accordingly. But neither of them endeavoureth to make such peace in ther country as the estate and time requireth, beinge, as yt semeth, ffearffull one of other. They are both of them preparinge for warr; and the rumor goeth they will one against annother ffor the victorye. And, as yt ys spoken, Mully Sydan resolveth to be sole Kinge or noe Kinge; and that agreeth with the conditions of the peopelle to have but one Kinge. Somethinge beffore longe will passe. God guide all ffor the best!

What hath made the difference betwixt the two brothers ys that,

1. Onze mois au plus, puisque, d'après El-Oufrâni, Moulay Ahmed partit pour Fez dans la seconde quinzaine d'octobre 1602 et qu'il mourut le 25 août 1603.

2. Wed Labide, l'oued el-Abid.

3. Moulay Zidân donna l'ordre de se saisir de la personne de Moulay ech-Cheikh, qui était prisonnier à Meknès; mais le pacha Djouder déjoua cette tentative en emmenant à Merrakech ce prince, qu'il remit à Moulay Abou Farès. EL-OUFRÂNI, p. 310.

4. Ce fait est inexact; on ne creva pas les yeux à Moulay ech-Cheikh.

5. Moulay Zidân fut proclamé à Fez le 25 août; Moulay Abou Farès fut proclamé à Merrakech le 29. EL-OUFRÂNI, p. 309.

dayes past, Mully Befferris sent a fforce to take a place called Tedula, within Mully Sydan his country, and the same taken and held ffor Mully Befferris. The other, ffor the losse of a place of his domineon, will have a kingdome. Yt ys not lesse thought by the moste, and wished generally by all; ffor he ys the most wisest and moste warlikest, and best beloved of the peopell ffor many respectes, and cheflly becawse he ys the sonne of a ffree woman, and Mully Sheck and Mully Befferris both brothers and sonnes of a negra woman, which Mully Hammett, ther ffather, bought with his mony, calling them ther slaves, and therffor of noe such estemation and honour as Mully Sydan.

Mully Befferris hath this advantadge: possession of his ffathers tresore in Morocus, which was held to be very great, and doubtles in ffeinte; and with that he seketh to gett frendes and to winne the souldiers hartes, by geveing them good paye. Uppon his proclaimeinge Kinge, he paid the souldiers eightene months paye, which his father owed, and sixe months paye befforehand, and added to every ones paye thre shillinges per month, amounting to much. Mully Sydan demandeth the halffe of that tresore, but yt ys denyed; which will bring enmitye betwixt them some time or other. All the tresore the Kinge had about him at his death came to the handes of Mully Sydan, by how much his mother was with the Kinge at his death, and ffewe other weomen which could challendg or take therof.

Mully Sydan, after the death of his ffather, seeinge the souldiers doubtffull to staye or to retorne to Morocus, gave command to have yt proclaimed, that whosoe ever would staye should be entertained and have paye, and whome would depart might; soe that the most part went, the rather to gett ther paye oweinge by the deceased Kinge and to geve maintenance to ther wiffes and children.

For the cheffe and princepall men which were greatly ffavoured of Mully Hammett in his lyffetime, namely, alcade Asus[1], Mommen Buckkersia[2], alcade Bencus, alcade Abdala Sadick[3], and alcade Abdala

---

1. Le caïd Azzouz. V. *supra*, p. 48, note 2, p. 143, et p. 165.
2. Moumen Bou Kourzia. V. *supra*, p. 175, note 2.
3. Abd es-Seddik. V. *infra*, p. 285 et note 4.

Wahed¹, his brother, basha Judare², and alcade Hammett Mounsor³, thes of the Kinges counsell : alcade Asus alwaies kept wher the Kinge kept, and beloved for his wisdome and seacrecye, Mommen Buckkersea, Bencus, and Abdala Sadick, and his brother, all men of great howses and have continewally, he that least, 150 horse, and the 2 ffirst named have now with them twenty thowsand horsemen in a reddines. All thes are in Fes and about Fes, with Mully Sydan; and the newes ys now currant they are in felde with all ther fforces.

Alcade Asus hath bene sick ever since the Kinges death, but thought a fained sicknes, only to staye with Mully Sydann. Mully Hammett marred the syster of Mommen Bokersea, and he ys the greatest subject in this land. Basha Judare conquered the country of Gago for the Kinge, ffrom whence the Kinge had yearly much gould. He ys commander of all the Kinges elches⁴, which are the best souldiers; and alcade Hammett Mounsor, commander over the Andolozes. And although the be in Morocus with Mully Befferris, yet they most of all favoure and love Mully Sydan.

What cheffe men are with Mully Befferris are, namely, alcade Imsoud Imbylla⁵, and his brother, whome marred alcade Asus his daughter, and one Sydde Gawe⁶, younger brother to alcade Mommen Bokersea. He was sent with a fforce by Mully Befferis against Tedula, and tooke yt. Thes two are the counsell to the Mully. Ther ys a Jewe called Brihem ben Wash⁷, with whome the Kinge hath much

---

1. Abd el-Ouahed ben Messaoud, qui était venu en ambassade à Londres en 1600. V. *supra*, p. 159 et note 1; p. 165, et *passim*.

2. Le pacha Djouder. V. *supra*, p. 66, note 1. — Il est inexact, comme Tomson le dit quelques lignes plus loin, que Djouder ait pris le parti de Moulay Zidân. Ce fut lui, au contraire, qui, à la tête des troupes de Moulay Abou Farès, défit complètement, le 8 janvier 1604, Moulay Zidân, à la bataille d'El-Mouata. EL-OUFRÂNI, p 311; et *infra*, p. 242 et note 2, p. 345 et note 1.

3. Le caïd Ahmed ben Mansour, renégat. Après la mort de Moulay Ahmed, il entraîna une partie de son armée à Merrakech et se prononça pour Moulay Abou Farès. EL-OUFRÂNI, p. 310.

4. *Elches*, renégats.

5. Le caïd Messaoud en-Nebili. EL-OUFRÂNI, p. 299. Il était neveu du caïd Azzouz. Dans une relation du gouverneur de Mazagan du 27 novembre 1603, il est appelé Maçoude Nebille. V. *1ʳᵉ Série*, Espagne, à cette date.

6. A identifier avec Sidi Gouwy (*1ʳᵉ Série*, Pays-Bas, t. I, pp. 476-477) et avec « alcaide Gowie ». V. *infra*, p. 341, note 1. Dans la Relation citée à la note précédente, il est appelé Cide Guaia Malluco.

7. Brahim ben Ways. V. *1ʳᵉ Série*, Pays-Bas, t. I, p. 343, note 3, p. 500,

seacrett confference and followeth soe much his counsell ffor commonwealth matters, as the peopell doe greatly complaine of wronges. And ffor such marchauntes as have dealt with his ffather, he calleth them to new accountes[1] and, by takeinge awaye in price of goodes longe since sould, and price cutt by Mully Hammett, he maketh men indebted unto him, wheras in right and justice he ys to paye what his ffather owed them; soe he useth plaine tyranny.

The engenewes of this country, which yeuldeth him yearly great rentes, and the ground of trade here, they, uppon the death of Mully Hammet, were all destroyed, only one called Azerew[2]. The same engenew, at the request of a ffrend here, I tooke to chardge to governe and looke unto; and in respect those about the same affected me, they stad with me and soe preserved the same, although mulltitudes came to ruenate the same. Although they be very beneficcall to the Kinge, yet he noewaye provideth ffor them, but permitteth them to be more and more spoyled, ffor he sendeth none to resiste the evell-minded. Hitherto he seketh the undoeinge of marchauntes, and littell hope ffrom him of better. God amend all! And, yf he continew Kinge, the country will never be in quiettnes.

At instant, I red letters from Morocus, of the 19th, wherin they write such newes as Tedula is ffor Mully Sydan againe, and that ther ys in Tedula one alcade Mustepha[3], servaunt to Mully Sydan, with 1800 choise shott, and the sonne of one alcade Boteras[4] lyeing nere about with 3 thowsand men, the sonne of Mommen Bukersea, with a great almahalla, and the Kinge, with all his fforces, abrode. The moste of the souldiers which went with Sydde Gawe have taken sanctuary, and, as they terme yt here, horme, and will neither goe fforward nor backward, unles they maye have more paye.

Mully Befferris, hearing his brother in ffelde, hath sent a nomber of his saintes about him to Fes, to entreat peace. What wilbe the

---

note 1 et *passim* ; Espagne, à la date de juillet 1608.

1. Un exemple des procédés employés par Moulay Abou Farès envers les marchands est fourni par le Document suivant, qui expose le traitement infligé à John Wakeman. V. *infra*, p. 237.

2. Azrou, nom trop répandu pour pouvoir être identifié.

3. Le caïd, depuis pacha Moustafa, V. 1re Série, Pays-Bas, t. I, pp. 259, 297, 469, 471, 474 et *passim*; cf. *infra*, p. 331 et n. 4.

4. *Alias* : Abuluct Butueira. V. 1re Série, Espagne, 27 novembre 1603.

issue hereof, time as yt bringeth out the truth, your Honour shalbe, God willing, ffurnished with the certenty.

In the meanewhile, I humbly take my leave of your Honour, praying ffor continewall health and happenes, and that every stepp maye be noe lesse then a degree of honour to yourself.

From the plea[1] of Sta Cruse, in Sus, this 30th October 1603.

Your Honours servaunt to command,

Signé : George Tomson.

Public Record Office. — *State Papers, Foreign, Barbary States, vol. XII.* — *Original.*

1. *Plea,* transcription du mot espagnol *playa* (en portugais *praia*), plage. On désignait parfois sous ce nom la ville basse d'Agadir ou Santa-Cruz, appelée plus généralement Fonti. V. *1re Série,* France, t. II, p. 269, note 2.

LXXXV

REQUÊTE DE THOMAS PATE[1] A JACQUES Ier

Le marchand John Wakeman, établi depuis longtemps au Maroc, était devenu le fournisseur du feu roi Moulay Ahmed. — Il s'adressait à Thomas Pate, qui envoyait au Maroc les articles demandés par le Chérif. — En garantie de ces fournitures, Moulay Ahmed avait affermé à Wakeman, pour la présente année, plusieurs sucreries. — Le Chérif, au moment de sa mort, se trouvait être le débiteur de Wakeman. — Or, les sucreries ont été saccagées et Wakeman pillé. — Bien loin de protéger et d'indemniser Wakeman, le roi actuel, Moulay Abou Farès, l'a emprisonné et a saisi ses biens, ainsi que des marchandises appartenant à Thomas Pate, pour se payer des fermages dus par ledit Wakeman, évaluant, d'ailleurs, à très bas prix les biens saisis et augmentant de neuf cents livres le fermage fixé par Moulay Ahmed. — Ces violences ont rendu Wakeman insolvable et atteignent, par suite, Thomas Pate, qui doit lui-même de grandes sommes à divers marchands. — Ces derniers se joignent à Thomas Pate pour implorer la protection du Roi en faveur du requérant, qui veut se rendre au Maroc pour tâcher d'y rétablir ses affaires. — Il sollicite une lettre de Jacques Ier à Moulay Abou Farès, priant ce dernier de réparer les dommages causés par ses sujets, d'exécuter le contrat relatif aux sucreries passé par son père avec John Wakeman, et d'estimer, d'après les prix convenus, les biens confisqués audit Wakeman, lequel, en obtenant justice, sera mis en mesure de rembourser Thomas Pate. — Il demande également une lettre du Roi à Moulay Zidân, invitant ce prince à intervenir auprès de son frère en faveur de Wakeman et de Pate.

[Londres, vers la fin de 1603[2].]

To the Kings most excellent Matie.

The humble petition of your Maties distressed subject Thomas Pate, of London, merchant.

1. Sur ce personnage, V. *supra*, p. 169.   2. Ce Document est postérieur à la mort

REQUÊTE DE THOMAS PATE A JACQUES Ier   237

The peticioner[1] humblie sheweth that John Wakeman[2], English merchant, by meanes of his long residence in Barbarie, became the late decessed King of Maroccus merchant, and delt with hym for diverse particular imployments, and specially in supplying from hence necessaries and furnitures for his owne use ; wherein the said Wakeman used the help of your said subjects servant and factor there, and by his directions your subject provided the same and caused them to be hence transported uppon everie occasion, as is partly knowne to the Lords of your Maties privie Counsell, to whome he was lately suitor for transportation of a coach and bedd for the same late King.

In respect whereof and of the great intercourse of dealings betwene the said Wakeman and the said King and that he might be the better secured for payment, the said Wakeman had of the King for this year ingenewes, at a certain rent, being matters of exceeding great value. And, for the maintenaunce and supplie thereof, your said subjects factor, having continuall dealings with the said Wakeman, did, amongst others, furnish hym with sondrie merchandize sent from hence from tyme to tyme ; so as said Wakeman became indebted to your said subject in divers great somes of money yet unsatisfied.

But soe it is, dread Soveraigne, that in the midst of theis great imployments, whilst a great stock lay in the hands and charge of the said Wakeman, the King died, and the common unruly people breaking forth, did presently runne uppon, spoile and ransack the ingenews, and robbed the said Wakeman of his goods, to so great a value that he is in no sort able to satisfie your said subject. The rather for that the nowe King Mully Beferis, notwithstanding he aught, both by the ordinarie justice and equitie of that cuntrie

---

de Moulay Ahmed (25 août 1603), qui y est mentionnée. On y lit, d'autre part, que Moulay Ahmed avait affermé à Wakeman des sucreries « pour cette année-ci ». Ce bail n'était donc pas encore expiré quand Thomas Pate rédigea sa requête.

1. Au dos de la présente requête se trouve un résumé, qui a dû être rédigé pour les membres du Conseil privé, à la suite duquel on lit : « The Lords do think this case so full of æquity, as they wish that his Matie be moved to be so gracious as to yeld the petitioner a protection. — Ro. Cecill. »

2. Sur ce marchand, V. *supra*, p. 169 et note 4, et Doc. LXXIX, p. 210 et note 1.

and the warrant of the Kings letters[1], be either protected from suche violences or sufficiently recompenced by hym for his losses therein, did not onely not recompence hym being thereto intreated, but imprisoned the said Wakeman, and by his officers seized uppon and made havock both of the said Wakemans and divers of your said subject's goods and merchandize, taking at unreasonable rates and underprizes the full debt due by the said Wakeman for the said dispoyled goods to the decessed King, with an overplus, taxed beyond the first agreement, of about £ 900.

Whereby and by meanes of other charges, wrongs and hyndraunces unjustlie putt uppon the said Wakeman since the late Kings death, which this King ought in justice to releive and recompence, your said subject is greatly indamaged, driven to returne his shipps back, emptie of lading, and forced to suche other extremities as that his whole state and credit is greatly hazarded yf not overthrowne, being indebted to divers merchants here in great somes which he knoweth not howe to discharge.

But forasmuche as this hard and unexpected exigent, happening uppon the alteration of a kingdome, is well knowe and greatly pittied by those merchantes to whom your said subject is most indebted[2], and for the greatest somes of import; and that they are desirous he should take some available course for his relief and their speedier payment, which is not to be compassed but by your Ma[ties] pittifull regard and gracious clemencie in furthering the reabling of the said Wakeman, they have therefore joyned with your said subject in this humble petition.

Whereby he beseecheth that your Highnes wilbe pleased not onely to protect him and his goods for one yeare, that he may goe thither and seek to redeeme his estate, otherwise like to be quite subverted; but also, in tendering the same, to write your favorable letters unto the said King Mully Beferis, that, seeing he hath receaved his fathers debts, rent and profitts by the benefitt of his succession, he will make good the spoile done by his people, accord-

---

1. Entendez : les lettres de Moulay Ahmed. Dans le résumé (V. supra, p. 237, note 1), on lit : « *their* Kings letters ».

2. On lit dans le résumé, après *indebted*, les mots suivants placés entre parenthèses : « even full vii parts of viii ». Il faut entendre que les 7/8 des dettes de Pate sont dus aux marchands signataires.

ing to his bills of securitie and the ordinarie justice and equitie of that cuntrie to Christians; permitt the said Wakeman to enjoy his first bargaine in the ingenews, and accept of those goods and merchandize so seized by his officers at suche rates as in suche cases was by his father accustomed, the rather for that he was one whome his father so speciallie favored and ymploied. By righting of whome, your subject shall recover his debts, otherwise most assuredly lost, and shalbe enabled to doe further good to your Matie and his cuntrie in all ductifull service and love, having in a short tyme, since your Highnes raigne, paid alredie to your Matie in custome above £ 420.

And also that your Matie, for the better furtherance hereof, so neerly concerning your poore subject, will likewise be pleased to direct other letters to Mully Sydon, King of Fesse, his brother, that, in regard of his fathers honor, he will write to the said King of Morocus, in the behalf of the said Wakeman and of your said subject, to have respect of merchants so necessarie and beneficiall to his cuntrie, least so hard and unusuall a president discourage and drive others from that course of traffique, and therein to use suche perswasions to hym as may be most available for your poore subjects good. And, as his vowed and bounden duetie is, he will daily praie for the long and happie raigne of your royall Matie and princely progenie, whilest he liveth.

Signé : Thomas Jacksoune. — Frauncys Dent. — Thomas Havers. — Thomas Fletcher. — Humffrye Walweyne. — Edward Davenant. — Thomas Flukely. — Richard Deane. — Thomas Brampton. — Edmund Palmer. — John Sturry. — Humffrey Handsorde. — Humfrey Slany. — Per me Thomas Dent, for my master William Eaton. — Edward Horell. — John Dyke, for Thomas Sercowlde[1]. — Nicholas Tobey.

Public Record Office. — *State Papers, Foreign, Barbary States, vol. XII.* — Original.

1. Sur ce personnage, V. *supra*, p. 135.

LXXXVI

LETTRE D'ANTONIO PEREIRA[1] A PHILIPPE III

Moulay Zidân, roi de Fez, prétendant être seul héritier du royaume, a déclaré la guerre à son frère Moulay Abou Farès, roi de Merrakech, et fait envahir le Tadla par le caïd Moustafa. — A cette nouvelle, Moulay Abou Farès a fait partir le pacha Djouder, qui a rejeté Moustafa sur la rive droite de l'Oumm er-Rebia. — Sur ces entrefaites, Abou Farès a tenté un accord, par l'intermédiaire de cinq marabouts. — Zidân a refusé de négocier et s'est porté en avant avec des renforts venus du Gharb. — Sur le conseil de Djouder, Abou Farès a remis en liberté son frère Moulay ech-Cheikh, qu'il détenait à Merrakech. — Celui-ci, à la tête de 100 cavaliers, a rejoint Djouder dans le Tadla. — L'armée de Djouder franchit l'Oumm er-Rebia et engage le combat. — Zidân vaincu s'enfuit à Fez, mais, poursuivi par l'ennemi, il doit s'échapper de la ville; les uns disent qu'il s'est retiré dans la direction du Peñon, les autres dans celle d'Alger. — Moulay ech-Cheikh, entré en vainqueur à Fez, a fait arrêter les caïds de Zidân et les a envoyés, chargés de fers, à son frère à Merrakech. — Il y a maintenant quatre prétendants au Maroc, sans compter le fils de Moulay Abd el-Malek, qui depuis longtemps est à Alger, attendant une occasion.

Tanger, 23 février 1604.

Au dos: Copia de carta del capitan de Tanjar, Antonio Pereira, para Su Mag[d], de 23 de Hebrero 1604.

Oy, que son 23 de Hebrero, amanecio un Moro a las puertas desta fuerça, con carta de otro, que llego Alcassar, por mandado de Mulei Xeque, a tomar posesion de la hacienda y bienes del

---

1. Antonio Pereira Lopes de Berredo succéda à Ayres de Saldanha dans le gouvernement de Tanger, le 22 août 1599; il fut remplacé, le 22 septembre 1605, par Nuno de Mendoça. MENEZES, *Hist. de Tangere*, pp. 101-118.

alcaide Amette, que lo fue de aquella ciudad mas de 20 annos[1].
Por este Moro que digo, tuve aviso de ciertas personas de mucha
confiança, porque las tengo bien experimentadas, y si, hasta aora,
no lo hizieron, fue por la gran vigilancia y cuidado que se tenia en
que esto ne acaesesse. Las nuevas son las seguientes, y V^{ra} Mag^d las tenga por ciertas.

Mulei Zidan intento hazer guerra a Mulei Buferes su ermano, diziendo ser el solo el heredero d'aquellos reinos, y mando de Fez a un alcaide llamado Mustafa[2] a Tedula, con seis mil hombres de cavallo y d'a pie, adonde, en el mes de noviembre pasado, hizo grandes estragos. Luego que supo la nueva Mulei Buferes, mando de Marruecos al alcaide Jaudar[3], arrenegado y hijo de una pobrecilla mujer, natural de aqui[4], con otra copia de gente, con la qual echo de aquella parte al Mustafa, y le obligo a pasar el rio Morbea; y assi quedo cada uno de los campos de su parte del dicho rio.

Tanto que Mulei Zidan tuvo nueva deste sucesso, en trese dias se apresto, y, antes de Pasqua de Navidad[5], echo su almahala fuera de Fez, y en quinze dias ayunto ocho mil tiradores y seis mil cavallos, y mando que el alcaide de Alcassar le seguiesse con toda su gente. Estando las cosas en este estado, le mando Muley Buferes por sinco Morabitos cometer grandes partidos y dizir que no quisiesse dar occasion a muertes ni guerras en aquellos reinos. Y lo qual ne quiso conceder, respondiendo que el era el ligitimo eredero dellos, y les embio luego. La ultima otava del Nascimiento[6], empeço a marchar la buelta del Jaudar; y en el camino se detuvo hasta dia de los Reis, en que llego el alcaide de Alcassar con mil y quinientos cavallos. Tanto que le tuvo consigo y aver llegado veinte y dos pieças de artillaria, fue demandar el inimigo muy desordenadamente, que assi fue desbaratado[7].

---

1. Moulay ech-Cheikh voulait punir le caïd Ahmed, qui avait suivi le parti de Zidàn et qui était venu renforcer l'armée de ce dernier sur la rive droite de l'Oumm er-Rebia. V. *infra*, p. 242, note 1.

2. V. *supra*, p. 234, note 3.

3. *Jauder*, le pacha Djouder. V. *supra*, p. 66, note 1.

4. Le pacha Djouder, originaire du royaume de Grenade, avait été élevé à la cour du Chérif depuis son enfance. V. H. DE CASTRIES, *La conquête du Soudan par El-Mansour*, dans *Hespéris*, 1923, pp. 433-438.

5. *Pasqua de Navidad*, la fête de Noël.

6. L'octave de Noël, le 1er janvier 1604.

7. *Que assi fue desbaratado*, ce qui fut cause de sa défaite (racontée plus loin).

En llegando los Morabitos al Jaudar, temiendo el poder de Zidan, escrivio a Buferes que, si no soltava a Muley Xeque, que hiziesse quenta que no tenia reino. Vista su carta, mando luego que fuesse libre; y, con cien cavallos, vino la buelta de Tedula, adonde estava el Jaudar.

El Zidan llego a su Mustafa quasi el mismo dia, aviendo marchado tan a prissa y con tanto dezorden que la artillaria le quedo atraz quatro o cinco leguas. Luego mando reconoscer el campo del inimigo y, por lengua que tomo, supo como Mulei Xeque era alli llegado, y como venia en su seguimiento mucha gente. Por lo que procuro que, antes que llegasse, venir con el a la batalla, como lo hizo, llevando consigo ya en este tiempo diez mil arcabuzeros y doze mil cavallos, con que se la presento. Mulei Xeque con su alcayde Jaudar passaron el rio con seis mil infantes y quatro mil cavallos, y rompieron uno con otro, durando el conflito como tres oras, en las quales se levanto una voz : « ¡ Viva Mulei Xeque! »[1] con que la gente de Zidan volto huyendo, no queriendo mas pelear contra el, perdiendo la batalla[2]. Morieron, de parte a parte, cosa de tres para quatre mil hombres. El Xeque mando que no siguiessen el alcance, pero los Alaraves robaron todo el excercito por donde pudieron, y mataron mucha gente.

Mulei Zidan llego a Fez muy desbaratado, adonde estuvo sinco dias, en fin de los quales empeçaron de llegar los que venian en su seguimiento. El se partio de aquella ciudad a toda priça con sinco criados solamente, dizen que en la vuelta del Piñon, y otros que Argel[3]. Muley Xeque entro luego, y fue recibido con grande aplauso de la gente de aquella ciudad, adonde empeço a prender alcaides, siendo el de Alcassar el primero que mando con otros a Marruecos a su hermano, cargados de hierros.

Al fin, estan estos reinos con quatro pretençores : Mulei Xeque, y Mulei Buferes, y Mulei Zidan desbaratado, Mulei Nassar, otro ermano, que esta en el reino de Sus, con alguna gente junta[4] ; y,

---

1. Ce cri fut poussé par les contingents du Gharb qu'avait amenés le caïd d'El-Ksar et qui firent défection. EL-OUFRÂNI, p. 311.

2. La bataille fut livrée au lieu dit El-Mouata. *Ibidem.*

3. Moulay Zidân se réfugia d'abord à Oudjda, puis à Sidjilmassa, d'où il passa dans le Sous. EL-OUFRÂNI, pp. 311-312.

4. Sur cet autre fils d'El-Mansour, qui mourut en 1604, V. *infra*, pp. 337-338,

mas, el hijo de Maluco, que esta en Argel[1], esperando otra ocasion, ha muchos dias segun se tiene entendido. Y, conforme a esto, avra bien que hazer entre ellos.

Aviendo de nuevo cosa de que deva avisar a V^{ra} Mag^d, no me descuidare en lo hazer.

Dios guarde la catholica persona de V^{ra} Mag^d, etc.

British Museum. — Additional Mss., 28425, ff. 206-207. — Copie.

et cf. *1re Série*, Angleterre, t. I, p. 256, Pl. III, *Généalogie des princes de la dynastie saadienne*, note 26.

1. Sur Moulay Ismaïl, fils de Moulay Abd el-Malek, V. *ibidem*, note 21, et *supra*, p. 27, note 3.

LXXXVII

LETTRE D'AFFONSO DĖ NORONHA[1] A PHILIPPE III

(Extrait)

Les ports du Maroc ont été fermés en raison des guerres entre les prétendants. — Il y a eu rencontre entre Moulay Zidân et Moulay ech-Cheikh, remis en liberté par son frère Moulay Abou Farès. — Zidân, battu, s'est enfui vers Alger. — Les principaux caïds du Gharb, parmi lesquels celui d'El-Ksar, ont été mis aux fers et envoyés à Merrakech.

Ceuta, 23 février 1604.

Copia de la carta para Su Mag^d del general de Ceuta. — *Alia manu* : 23 de Hebrero de 1604.

Estando los puertos serrados por causa de Mulei Zidan aver salido de Fez con su campo la buelta de Tedula, procure saber el sucesso que tuviera. Y, teniendo armada una fregata para se ir tomar lengua, el alcayde de Tetuan me corrio las tranqueras, de que no uvo daño. Por la gente que con el venia, assi Judios como Moros, supe averse dado batalla entre Mulei Zidan y Mulei Xeque (que, hasta aora, estuvo preso en Marruecos en poder de su ermano Mulei Buferes), de la qual quedara desbaratado Mulei Zidan, que huyo para Argel. Los principales alcaides de Berberia (en que entra el de Alcassar[2]) fueron presos en hierros y llevados a Marruecos. Con la qual estan de presente quietos, que me parece durara poco, por estar el reino dividido en parsialidades, y quereren los demas que Muley Xeque quede con el. De lo que mas succediere, avisare a V^{ra} Mag^d.....

British Museum. — *Additional Mss. 28425, f. 208.* — *Copie.*

1. Gouverneur de Ceuta de 1602 à 1605.   2. V. *supra*, p. 241, note 1, et p. 242.

LXXXVIII

LETTRE DE JUAN DE BORJA[1] AU DUC DE LERME[2]

Antonio Pereira, gouverneur de Tanger, demande l'autorisation de venir informer Philippe III de la situation des affaires du Maroc. — D. Juan de Borja est d'avis de lui accorder sa demande. — D'après les renseignements qu'il donnera, on pourra juger de l'opportunité d'occuper Larache.

Valladolid, 4 mars 1604.

Despues de aver cerrado este pliego, he recebido este despacho de Antonio Pereyra, general de Tangere. Por lo que me escrive, entiendo que pide licencia a Su Mag^d para poder venir por la posta a dar cuenta a Su Mag^d del estado en que estan las cosas de Berberia y las occasiones que hay para poder Su Mag^d tener muy buenos sucessos. Y, aunque ha muchos dias que Antonio Pereyra pide esta licencia y se la a ydo dilatando el darsela, aora la pide con mas justa occassion, y assi no pareze que seria de inconveniente el darse, para intender bien el estado supuesto en las cosas de Africa, con la guerra que entre si tienen los Xarifes. Y si, en esta ocasion, pudiessemos quedar con Larache en los manos, seria de harto provecho. Lo que de presente se offresce es ver si sera bien oyr a Antonio Perreyra, para despues determinar lo que mas conviene. Supplico a V. Ex. lo trate con Su Mag^d, y mande responder a estas cartas. El correo que les trajo queda aqui, sperando la respuesta.

1. D. Juan de Borja, chevalier de Saint Jacques, commandeur d'Azuaga, fut ambassadeur en Allemagne. Le duc de Lerme avait épousé sa sœur.

2. D. Francisco de Sandoval y Rojas, duc de Lerme (1555-1625), premier ministre de Philippe III de 1598 à 1618, cardinal en 1618.

¡Guarde Nuestro Señor a V. Ex. como desseo y he menester!
De Valladolid, 4 de Março 1604.

Signé : Don Juan de Borja.

RÉPONSE DU DUC DE LERME[1].

Antonio Pereira ne devra quitter son poste sous aucun prétexte.
Il transmettra avec célérité tous les renseignements.

Arganda, 8 mars 1604.

A Su Mag^d le paresce que Antonio Pereyra, en esta occasion, hara mas falta en aquella plaça que en ninguna otra, y que, assi, conviene que, por ninguna cosa, falte en ello ; y que V. S. le scriva que, con mucha particularidad y brevedad, avise lo que se le ofresce, y con esso podra Su Mag^d resolver lo que convendra a sa servicio.

Dios guarde a V. S.

En Arganda, 8 de Março 1604.

(*Paraphe.*)

British Museum. — *Additional Mss. 28425, f. 203.* — *Original.*

1. Cette réponse est en marge de la lettre de D. Juan de Borja.

LXXXIX

LETTRE DE MOULAY ABOU FARÈS A JACQUES Ier

L'objet en or qui avait été apporté à Moulay Ahmed et dont le prix était demeuré en discussion, a été payé par Moulay Abou Farès, après quelque réduction ; le porteur n'a plus rien à réclamer.

[1604][1].

Au dos, alia manu : King of Marocco his letter to the King.

Muly Bu Fez, Emperor of Marocco, King of Fez and Guinea, unto the Kings Matie of England.

The beginning of the letter and so forward untill the latter end is nothing but barbarous titles and complement, with acknowledgement of the receit of his Ma[ties] letters, with thanks for the contentment his Ma[ty] shewes to have received for this Kings quiet establishing in his kingdomes of Morocco and Fez. Afterward it followeth thus :

Concerning that which your Ma[tie] writes touching the piece of gold which came to this our royall Court in the lifetyme of our father, who had given unto him that brought it a warrant that, if they agreed not of the price, that it should be returned againe to the owner, and that this was upon our hand ; so it fell out that, in the meanetyme, our father died, and wee afterward retranched somewhat from the price of it, when he brought it us, and paid him accordingly, out of our royal treasure ; so that he hath no more to challenge at our hands, for he was payd royally. And so endeth.

Public Record Office. — *State Papers, Foreign, Royal Letters, vol. II, n° 79.* — *Traduction.*

---

1. Le présent document est une réponse à une lettre de Jacques Ier, où celui-ci félicitait Moulay Abou Farès de son avènement au trône, et qui n'a pas été retrouvée.

XC

RELATION DE GEORGE WILKINS[1]

(Extrait)

Moulay Ahmed el-Mansour, devenu roi, se venge de ceux qui, sous le règne de son frère Moulay Abdallah el-Ghâlib, avaient conseillé sa perte. — L'un d'eux, le caïd Azzouz, reçoit son pardon. — Moulay Ahmed hésite quelque temps sur le choix à faire de son principal conseiller. — Un instant, il songe à un des renégats de sa cour. — Mais, ayant considéré le danger de confier les intérêts de son royaume à un Chrétien de naissance, il finit par choisir Azzouz. — Gloire et prospérité de son règne. — Rixe provoquée dans les rues de Merrakech entre Anglais et Espagnols par les nouvelles relatives à l'invincible Armada: le marchand Arnold Tomson est blessé; d'autres sont tués. — Histoire d'un Anglais qui se fait musulman. Procédure suivie dans de tels cas: le renégat comparaît devant une assemblée de Chrétiens et de Maures; les Chrétiens lui demandent s'il persiste dans son intention; ils sont libres d'argumenter avec lui pour le ramener. — Trois fois convoqué, l'Anglais maintient trois fois son apostasie; sa fin misérable. — Les trois femmes préférées de Moulay Ahmed: Lella Aïcha, mère de Moulay Zidân; Lella Djaouher, une négresse, mère de Moulay ech-Cheikh et de Moulay Abou Farès; Lella Meriem,

---

1. George Wilkins, auteur salarié de peu de considération, n'est connu que par des écrits de circonstance et des pièces de théâtre. Après avoir rédigé la relation publiée ici, intitulée *Three Miseries of Barbary*, et qui paraît avoir été écrite en 1604 (V. infra, p. 249, note 1), il s'associa à la *King's Company*, dont Shakespeare était le principal membre. La première pièce qu'on ait de lui est intitulée: *The Travels of the three English Brothers, Sir Thomas, Sir Anthony, Mr Robert Sherley*, Londres, 1607. La dédicace: *To honour favourites and the entire friends of the familie of the Sherleys, health*, est signée John Day, William Rowley, George Wilkins. La pièce fut représentée pour la première fois le 29 juin 1607. Outre quelques écrits sans valeur, on attribue à Wilkins une part dans la composition de deux des dernières tragédies de Shakespeare, *Timon of Athens* et *Pericles*, représentées en 1608. Il ne paraît pas être allé au Maroc, mais on sait qu'il était en relation avec les membres de la « Barbary Company », comme le prouve la dédicace du présent document; il était spécialement lié avec les Tomson. V. infra, pp. 252-253.

autre négresse, mère de Moulay Bel-Hassen, lequel fut tué par un jeune homme qu'il avait offensé. — Moulay Ahmed partage son royaume entre ses trois fils : à Moulay Zidân, un tempérament de soldat, il donne le Tadla et le Tafilelt ; à Moulay Abou Farès, caractère sensuel, le Sous ; à Moulay ech-Cheikh, le royaume de Fez, avec Moustafa, un renégat, comme principal conseiller. — Allégorie contée à Moulay Ahmed par Lella Aïcha, qui avait rencontré, un matin, le Chérif en compagnie de Lella Djaouher : l'alouette, oiseau du matin, et le corbeau, oiseau de nuit. — Exemple de la crainte que Moulay Ahmed inspirait à ses sujets : le fils du caïd Sidi Abd el-Kerim, s'étant introduit dans le harem du Chérif, est découvert ; Moulay Ahmed, irrité, jure de le mettre à mort ; puis, ayant pitié de son père, il déclare à celui-ci qu'il fait grâce ; mais Sidi Abd el-Kerim, ne pouvant croire à la sincérité de ce pardon, fait étrangler son fils sous ses yeux et dresser procès-verbal de l'exécution. — La fortune vient mettre un terme à la prospérité de Moulay Ahmed ; le Maroc est ravagé par la peste. — Le Chérif fuit la contagion de place en place. — Son entourage est décimé ; il est contraint de remplacer ses serviteurs par des esclaves pris sur les galères. — Les vivants ne parviennent plus à enterrer les morts. — A Merrakech, sept cent mille Maures et sept mille sept cents Juifs meurent dans une année ; quatre mille sept cents habitants succombent dans une seule journée. — A Fez, la même année, on compte cinq cent mille victimes. — Les Maures se réfugient en foule dans les montagnes. — Les moissons ne peuvent être récoltées. — Moulay Ahmed succombe au fléau. — A la peste succède une terrible famine. — Ce sont maintenant les guerres civiles qui désolent le pays.

[1604][1].

Titre : Three Miseries of Barbary : Plague, Famine, Civil Warre ;

1. Cette relation (in-4°, sans pagination) a été écrite, sans nul doute, en raison de l'actualité de la peste qui sévit à Londres en 1602-1603. Cf. J.-B. Collier, A bibliogr. Account..... Cette peste désola aussi le Maroc, où elle se fit sentir, dès l'année 1006 de l'hégire (1597-1598). El-Kadiri, Nachr el-Mathani, Trad., t. I, p. 109 ; cf. supra, pp. 125 et 126. A l'époque où écrivait Wilkins, il y avait sept ans qu'elle régnait dans ce pays (V. infra, p. 262), ce qui donne l'année 1604. D'autre part, cette même Relation a été rédigée peu de temps après l'époque où parvint à Londres la nouvelle de la mort de Moulay Ahmed el-Mansour (25 août 1603) et la guerre entre les prétendants Zidân et Abou Farès (octobre 1603-janvier 1604).

with a relation of the death of Mahamet[1] the late Emperour, and a briefe report of the now present wars betweene the three brothers.

To the right worshipfull, the whole Company of the Barbary Merchants[2].

Having drawn certaine collections together of some the best and maine occurrents which have now lately (and not many years past) hapned in Barbary, and they being digested into a volume (although little for quantity, yet delightfull to be perused for the raritye), I thought they could not better be bestowed than upon such as holde commerce with that countrey and know the state and condition of the people. Amongst which number I make bolde to present these my labors to you onely, because you are all brothers and men that most worthily can judge of the relation and the truth thereof. The chiefe and farthest point that my intention seeks to arrive at in this, is to describe the horrour and unheard-of misery that hath falne upon that kingdome by a plague: to the intent that, by comparing our sins with theirs (being altogether as greet if not greater) and the hand of mercy which Heaven hath stretcht forth over our nation, above theirs, we may be allured to looke into our soules betimes, least the like viols of wrath bee powred downe uppon us. It is my love that bestowes this uppon you, which I pray receive with such good acceptation, as with my best affection it comes unto you. And thus referring myselfe to your censure I take my leave.

    Devoted yours,
            Geo. Wilkins.

Barbary.

This is a story, like a briefe chronicle, conteining various and much matter in few lines. It is but a little bottom of tyme, which you may holde and hide in your hand, yet, being unrolled to the length, it reacheth to the beginning of many yeares past. A word

---

1. C'est Moulay Ahmed *el-Mansour* que l'auteur désigne ainsi.

2. Sur la « Barbary Company », V 1re Série, Angleterre, t. I, pp. 445-454.

now must stand heare, as in a map, for a citty, and a few sheetes for the chart of a spacious kingdome.

Understand therefore that Abdela the Emperor being dead, Muly Mahamet, his brother, succeeded[1], and was crowned King of Barbary. No sooner was this dignity conferred uppon him, but he revenged himselfe on those that in Abdelaes raign loved him not, and therefore by their counsels ded what in them lay, to draw his brothers the Emperors affection from him, yea so far that they perswaded either to have his eyes put out, or bee sent to death[2]. Of these counsellours, these three were chiefe, alcade Azus[3], alcade Mussa and alcade Bardu, from two of which he commaunded their lives. But because his state needed the heads of wise men to hold it up, and for that he was not generally beloved of the nobility and some of the bloud royal, he gave alcade Azus his life, and of a prisoner and a man in disgrace, advanced him up to higher honours than before, receiving him every daie into his bosome for his counsell. Which he did the rather because he knew that Azus would bee provident and carefull to increase the Emperors Bitt el-Mell[4], that is to say his treasury. Much and often was his mind perplexed with thoughts about settling his empire; his cogitations fought within themselves, when sometimes hee would, in his owne pryvate judgment, make such a man fit to be of his secret and chiefest counsels, and sometimes another; this he would like to-day, and to-morrow utterly distast him.

At length, he resolved to trust none of his owne countrymen, but lay his hart in the brest of one of his Elkes (that is to say a Chrestian turned Moore); yet, upon sounder contemplation, him hee rejected too. He would put the health of so great a kingdome into no such dangerous physitians hands; for he delivered that Mahamet,

---

1. Moulay Ahmed el-Mansour, que l'auteur appelle Mully Mahamet, succéda, non à son frère Moulay Abdallah, mais à son autre frère Moulay Abd el-Malek, qui régna de 1576 à 1578.

2. Pour assurer sa succession à son fils, Moulay Abdallah (1557-1574) voulut se débarrasser de ses frères. Trois furent mis à mort, deux s'enfuirent du royaume, Moulay Abd el-Moumen et Moulay Abd el-Malek ; le plus jeune, Moulay Ahmed, fut épargné, contrairement aux avis, d'après ce que dit Wilkins, de certains conseillers de Moulay Abdallah.

3. Sur ce caïd, V. supra, p 48, note 2.

4. Le Trésor.

his God, would take all favor from him, if he should doe so. Besides, he that had forsaken his owne law and religion, could not have the temper of constancy, to serve one of a contrary religion : « Nay, however in outward shew those Elkes or Renegadoes, quoth hee, seeme saints and holy ones, to me they may prove divels, and hold it no conscience to betray my bloud and kingdome. » Azus therefore was the man culled out from the rest by the Emperor.

This prince flourished in as great glory as the greatest of his predecessors; the blessed fruites of sweete peace tooke away the sourenesse of any warre, either forren or domesticke, that was served in against him; his subjects were infinite, his citties filled with nations. He had more wives then any of his forefathers; his concubines were fairer and more in number. He was as happy as ever was any King in Barbary, in the flourishing multitudes of his people, and as infortunate as ever any before him, in beholding their misery. Fortune twice had her pleasure upon him, first in lifting him uppe hygh in her love, lastly in pursuing him and his subjectes with her tyrrany.

Many noble and notable occurrentes presented themselves to the eye and care of the world, during his raigne; of which to write as they deserve were to adde a large volume to the chronicles of that countrey. I will therefore, as one having been at a royall banquet, reserve some of it to myselfe, and bestow some uppon others, such as I thinke will be sweetest in going downe : of wich take this as part.

It was in his time, when that great Armada, that brought terror in her wombe from Spain, was delivered of it, in the narrowe seas of England. At the birth (but indeed the buriall) of which invincible navy, the Spaniards that laythen in Barbary and attended on the Spanish Embassadour[1], beguiling themselves with a false rumor that this land was conquered, prepared for triumphs, as, if their joy had bin tamely begot, they had reason. But one Maister Arnold Tomson[2], an English marchant, certifying to the Emperour the

---

1. Il y avait à cette époque deux agents de Philippe II au Maroc, Francisco da Costa, ex-ambassadeur du cardinal Henri, roi de Portugal, et Diego Marin. Ce dernier, dont il est question ici, avait un caractère plutôt officieux. V. *supra*, p. 7, n. 4, et p. 13, n. 1.

2. Sur ce personnage, V. *supra*, p. 101, note 2.

truth and certaine defeature of the Spanish fleete, the Englishmen that were there hadde likewise leave of Mahamet to expresse their joy in bone-fires and other triumphs; for the King did ever love the nation of our countrey, and did many favors to our marchantes.

The English embassadour[1] lying in the same streete where the Spanish embassador lay, and our marchants gathering togither, determining to ride into the fielde, and there, having put themselves into some gallant order, to come back into the citty in a triumphant and civill manner, to doe honour to their countrey for so happy and unheard-of a victory : behold, before the Spanish embassadors gate[2], by which our countrymen determined on horsebacke to passe, stood a company of Spaniardes, with some Moores whom they had hired, armed with pike and shot to stop their passage. Betweene whom what happened, those English marchantes that then were hurt, of which Maister Arnold Tomson was one, can, if they be yet living, testifie; and, for those that were then slaine outright, the Emperour, in indignation, swore not onely that they who did execute this trechery uppon the English nation should have iron given them (that is to say should have their throates cut), but hee would also certifie the King of Spaine of this abuse; so willing was hee to doe justice even to strangers.

Another accident, because it is worthy note for the example, and may be a warning to our countreymen, will I set downe ; and this is it. An Englishman, fallen out and struck by his maister, desperately resolved, whilest the fire was in his bloud, to revenge those blowes on his body by giving wounds to his own soule ; and thereupon he presently went and denyed his religion, forsooke Christ to follow Mahomet, and from a Christian turned Moore.

It is the custome of that countrey, when any man will do so, to observe, amongst others, these ceremonies. It is signified to those Christians that are in the citty, towne, etc., that such a one

---

1. Il n'y avait pas alors d'ambassadeur ou agent officiel d'Angleterre au Maroc. Henry Roberts, qui en avait exercé les fonctions de 1585 à 1588, en était reparti le 28 août 1588 (V. *1re Série*, Angleterre, t. 1, pp. 510-512), c'est-à-dire avant que la nouvelle du désastre de l'Armada ait pu parvenir au Maroc, car, en Espagne même, on n'en fut informé qu'à la fin d'août.

2. La maison de l'agent espagnol Diego Marin. Sur cette affaire, V. *supra*, p. 13, note 1.

will be an Elke, or turne Moore. A certaine equall number therefore, as wel Barbarians as Christians, are assembled in a place fit for such purposes, one part sitting like judges on the one side, the other opposite directly against them; the turnecoate just in the middle of the roome betweene them and in presence of both. He is there then demaunded whether he will deny the law of his owne religion and embrace theirs or no. It is offered unto him his free liberty to take the one or the other; nay it is lawfull, for those that sit there on the contrary part, being Christians, to use all the power of argument to winne him from this delinquishment. Thus did they serve this man; thus was he, three severall times, convented before them; and, three several times, did he most stifly defend what he had done, and defie Christ. No physicke or spirituall counsell doing good uppon him, they gave him over. But note the judgment of that Captaine, the Lord of Hoasts, whose colours of salvation he had forsaken. Within a short time after this apostasy and rebellion of his soule, this traytor to God happened to kill a man. For which fact he was adjudged by the cadies of that countrey not to loose his life, but, wich was worse, to live. But how to live? As the first murderer that ever drew bloud of man, as Cayne lived, wandering up and down with none, on paine of death, to keep him company, but his owne thoughtes, which were tenne thousand executioners; none to give him bread, so that he fed upon despaire; none to quench his thirst, so that he drunk the poison of an infected conscience. He knew he had killed a man, and therefore even Infidels abhorred him; he knew he had forsaken his religion, and therefore Christians would not pitty him. In thes wretched state he went up and downe, in thes misery he pyned, till hee dyed. Let that death of his teach others how to live.

But leaving this, let us againe fire our eyes upon Mahamet the Emperor, who, thinking it would be as great a glory to him to create others Kings, as to be a Kinge himselfe, did, by the advice of his Counsell, but most of all out of the working and height of his owne spirit, determine to divide his large and fruitful empire amongst his sonnes.

Of all the wives and concubins that this Emperor had, three onely, above the rest, had a soveraignty over his amorous affections; and, of those three, he did still prefer one before the other. Lelia Isa[1] was the fairest, and her did he love dearest; she was Empresse over the rest, yet were the rest Queenes over others. Shee had the supreame commaund of the Kinges house, and none commaund her but the King. Lilia Ageda[2] was a negro, yet had she a second place in his heart. Lilia Myriem[3] had the third. Of Lilia Myriem, being a blacke woman likewise, did hee beget a son, called Muly Shem[4], being one of the fairest children that ever he had; but this Muly Shem, offring some offence to a youth that attended on him, was by him slaine; the young man afterward, knowing the Emperours wrath, killing himselfe. Lilia Ageda was mother to Muly Beferris and Muly Sheck, the youngest brother; Lilia Isa, mother to Muly Sidan, the eldest. Betweene these three were these late civell warres in Barbary.

And thus did Mahamet make division of his kingdome, which afterwarde bred division amongst his people, and set all in a combustion: to Muly Sidan, who was given to armes and to love a souldier, gave he the kingdome Tadula and Taphalet. To Muli Befarris, whose soule lusted after nothing but sensuall pleasure, gave he the kingdome of Sus; to Muly Sheck, the kingdome of Fez, appoynting Mustapha, that was born a Christian and turned Moore, but a souldier and a gentleman of a noble spirit, to attend on Sheck as his guardian, because he was but young.

Before we step any farther, it shall not be amisse, because I would draw this Barbary picture with as much life and delightfull colours as I could, to set downe a pretty combat betweene two of the Emperours wives, played before the Emperour himselfe. Thus it was: Mahamet sitting one morning with Lilia Ageda, the Negro, by him, talking mearily, for hee tooke pleasure in her speech, because shee was wise, in comes Isa, his fairest bedfellow, and seeing the blacke one so neere her beloved, she blushed and shewed anger even in her eyes. For what woman would not be angry to see another robbe her of the love of an Emperour? At

---

1. Lella Aïcha. V. *supra*, p. 176, note 2.
2. *Ageda*, El-Djaouher (la perle), concubine du Chérif. V. *infra*. p. 269, note 1.
3. Lella Meriem.
4. Moulay Abou el-Hassen. V. *supra*, p. 88 et note 3.

length bowing to the earth, she fell at the Kings feete, and, with a pretty smile, beganne to tell a tale of the larke and the crow : the shutting uppe of her morrall being, that the larke was the bird of the morning and of the day, and therefore might be bold to challenge the mornings due and all rytes of the day; but the crow was the bird of the night, and had nothing to do with the morning.

The Emperor, understanding her sweete witty bitternesse, that by the larke shee ment herselfe, and by the crow, Lilia Ageda, because of her blacknesse, was so delighted with the comparison, that hee gave charge none should ever after presume to give the Emperour his good morrowe till Lilia Isa had bin with him; and thereupon was Isa called the Emperors larke, or his bird of the morning.

Let us loose one poynt more of our compasse, and sayle a little out of our intended way, to finde out in what feare and awful reverence the subjectes of this kingdome hold the anger of their soveraigne; to understand which, receive this only as a tast. One of the Emperours officers of his custome, whose name was Cidde Abdela Creme[1], being an olde man, had one sonne onely, called Enhamet[2], whom he tended as his life, being the hope and health of his age; him had the father put into his owne place. The young man, comming in a morning betimes to the custome-house, but the rest of the officers being not present, he could not enter; for every one hath a severall key, and unlesse all be there together, not one can get in. He determined within himselfe to spend an houre, till the rest met, in reveewing the Emperors pallace, where his concubines lived, because he was told it was a rare and rich place, and that it was not lawfull without great meanes to enter. That report more inflamed his desire, insomuch that in the end, watching his time, by stealth he got in.

Where being and staring up and downe, it chanced that one of the women saw him, who presently screeked out and ranne crying : « A man ! a man ! » For you must note that, if any one of

---

1. Sidi Abd el-Kerim ben Touda, l'un des principaux caïds de Moulay Ahmed; Il mourut avant le 23 septembre 1601. V. 1re Série, Espagne, années 1599-1601.
2. Faute d'impression; il faut rétablir Mahamet.

them spy a man, except the eunuches that attend them, and doe not call for helpe, it is death to her ; and what man soever rudely presume to have a sight of them, it is death to him. It was knowne by inquiry, upon her noyse, that is was Enhamet, the customers sonne, who had thus offended the lawes. The Emperor, being given to understand so much, made an oath he should dye for it.

Immediately upon this, by occasion of some busines, comes the olde man, Enhamets father, to the King ; who, supposing it hadde beene about his sonnes pardon, and his indignation being now a little cooler, suddainely demaunded of him what that man deserved, that durst breake into the place where his Emperours concubins were. Cid Abdela, not suspecting the offender, answered that he deserved the sharpest sentence of death, for so the law would adjudge him. « Be thou then, quoth the Emperor, thine owne sonnes condemnation ; as thou hast judged him, so let it be. » But the King, beholding death sitting in the olde mans face at that doome, grew pittifull, and, for love he bare the father, forgave the sonne.

Which mercy, notwithstanding, Abdela Creme not truely laying holde of, but mistaking the noble spirit of a prince and imagining that this favor so strangely extended was but a snare to intrap his owne life, because offences of that nature were never before pardoned in any, home hee comes, with sorrow in his afflicted looks, and his heart even murdered within him by the cruelty of his owne thoughtes. His sonne demaunded the cause of this so strange and suddaine distemperature ; but his father, giving no answer, sends for cordes, shewes them onely insteade of speech, and, to make this dumb tragedy fall in the end, he causeth him, before his owne eyes, to bee strangled. Great were the lamentations of the sonne, and abounndant were the teares he let fall to soften his fathers heart. A mighty conflict was there in the poore old mans bosome, betweene naturall piety to a child and naturall feare of a soveraigne ; but the last of the two prevailed. And, having bestowed upon the dead body the ceremonies of the grave, according to the custome of the countrey, hee caused the act to bee registred downe for his owne safety, alledging that howsoever the Emperor, when he heard this blacke and unnaturall deed reported, would happily bee moved unto wrath, yet inwardly he would be highly contented with it.

Mahamet being thus feared and loved of his subjects, wanted nothing that, according to humane judgement, could make a prince happy. Pleasure was his slave and waighted on him whensoever he lusted for her company; riches flowed in to his houses of treasure in large and golden streams; his court was full of counsellors, his cittyes full of merchants, his castles full of souldiers. He was a mightie King himselfe, and had sonnes that were as mightie as hee; their dominions were ample, they were full of men, and full of all thinges that maintaine men. It seemed that the father lost much of his imperiall state and dignitie, when hee placed his three sonnes, like three great lights, to shine equally in his kingdome, considering that all the beames of majestie that came from them might, if he had pleased, have been sent foorth from the centred glory of his owne head. But even this borrowed reflexions of theirs made his brightness the greater ; and his sonnes yeelding acknowledgement of all their royaltie to flow from him, did, like rivers paying tribute to the sea, seeme not a whit the lesse for such homage and fealtie.

Fortune having turned the wheele of this Emperours fate a long time with steddie hand, had now brought it about to the uppermost point and highest on which she meant hee should sitte ; he should be no more her darling, and therefore shee tooke her favours from him. Or, to speake of a power that controlls fortune, and whose very finger throwes downe kingdoms to utter confusion, or holdes them up in their greatnesse, whether the generall sinnes of the whole nation deserved it, or whether the people were punisht for the particular faults of the King and his courtiers, as many times it falls out, and as it hapned to the Grecians, for

<blockquote>Quicquid delirant reges, plectuntur Achivi[1],</blockquote>

or for what other faultes soever, the rodde of vengeance was made readie. It is in man to thinke uppon and feare, but not to examine ; yet sure it is, that as a fire catching hold at first but of

---

1. HORACE, *Épitres*, I, 2, 14.

some meane cottage, in some one end or corner of a cittie, hath oftentimes, ere the furie of it could bee put out, swallowed up in his flames the goodliest and most beautifull buildings that stoode even fardest out of reach, so did the clowdes of infection burst open their vaines, and let fall the poyson of them on this kingdom of Barbary[1].

If ever the plague in any place got his true name, there he had it. At the beginning, it strooke, like an arrowe, on the head but of one citty, but in a short time after, it flewe from cittie to citty, and in the end stucke in the very hart of the whole kingdome, insomuch that Death came, like a tyrannous usurper, to the Court gates, and threatned to depose the Emperour himselfe.

Hee that before sate in his throne of majestie, greatly feared of other nations round about him, and strongly garded by his owne, is on the suddaine daunted, and, beeing accounted one of the mightiest amongst the Kings of the earth, is ready to submit to him with whom even infants doe every howre fight hand to hand.

See the authoritie, fame and terror of that invader, Death : hee strooke but up an allarum in this Emperours pallace, and the Emperour himselfe trembled through feare thereof ; his conceites, that stood before like so many aged oakes, bowed presently to the earth like so many ranks of young willowes ; yet his citties shooke at the voyce, no lesse then if it had beene at an earth-quake. And so hardly did the pestilence pursue Mahamet, that he durst not sleep for it in one place twice together ; every night was he compelled, for safety, to flye unto a contrary lodging.

As his Court removed, so did the plague : whersoever the one kept his standing house, there the other pitched up his pavilion as a proud and daring challenger to all commers, insomuch that sicknesse in the end, though weake of himselfe, wrastled with so many that were neere and about the princes person, and still got the better of them, that Mahomet had not men to remove those tents, which hee was inforced to carry up and downe with him for his owne household to lye in, fourescore Barbarians, being all attendants and officers in Court, falling every night, in this mortal

---

1. Sur la peste qui ravagea le Maroc à cette époque, V. *supra*, p. 249 et note 1.

and pestiferous massacre. So that the Emperour, for want of servants, was glad to take chained slaves from the oare, out of their gallies[1], and to make them his guard.

What a strange alteration is here of a Court! He that had seene this prince so royally attended, so majestically attyred, with such godlike reverence kneeled unto, so guarded, so followed, so circled round with a nation in number infinite, would that man have ever thought that such a prince could have been driven out of his stately pallaces, and beene glad to lye abroade in the fields, or that he shold ever submit to such humility as to put his life into the hands of slaves and miserable captives, the onely dispised wretches of his kingdome, the beggerliest, the most discontented, the worst-minded to him and his nation, yea, such whom he knew could have been glad to cut his throat, to ransome themselves from the bondage and hell of the gally? Yet even these most forlorne creatures, which before like oxen were yoaked by the neckes with iron, was this great monarch faine to make much of, and to turne them into his best and fayrest courtiers; so easily and so low can the hand of Heaven pull downe the mightiest upon earth, and make them stoope even to the weakest!

The hart being thus sicke, was not the whole body, thinke you, in danger to perish? The eye of the kingdome being so much blemished, did not the universal land dwell in darkenesse? Was it possible that the Court should pyne, and that the citties should flourish? No, no, alasse! full houses were emptied there of whole families, whole streetes of their housholds; yea, even the citties themselves were left desolate of inhabitants.

Had all the artificers in the land layde by all other worke, onely to have made coffins, they could not all have builded roomes fast enough for the dead to dwell in; for sicknesse was even weary of throwing downe bodies, and death even glutted with killing them. Doe but imagine how the world shewed, when all creatures that were drowned in the universall Flood lay heaped together, after the waters were shrunke into the earth; such a Mount Calvary was

---

1. Moulay Ahmed entretenait à Salé sept ou huit galiotes, qu'il employait à la course contre les Espagnols. V. *1re Série*, Angleterre, t. I, p. 504 et note 1.

Barbarie. The carkases of unburied men were so many, that afar off they might be taken for hills; yea, so numberlesse were they, that it seemed as if all the nations uppon earth had sent their dead thether, and that Barbarie had beene the common churchyard.

When Vespasian besieged Jerusalem, famine fed upon the cittie within and warre without, yet did the Jewes choose rather to steale forth and trust the doubtfull mercy of an enemie, then to perrish under the crueltie of their owne countrymen. At length, such multitudes of them got daily through the gates, that Tytus, to be ridde of them and fright them from comming, crucified them all, and fixt the bodies so put to death round about the cittie, before their walls, as a terror to those within; so that in the end, they pressing forth for all this continuallie uppon him, there coulde be found neither wood enough for crosses to nayle them upon, nor ground enough whereon to set crosses.

The like miserie fell upon this royall kingdom of Barbarie; for the people in it were strooke downe so fast by the pestilence, that the living were not able to inter the dead, neither could there be found ground sufficient enough, about theyr citties, to affoord them buriall, so that the earth did not, as in other countries, cover and burie them, but they buried and covered the earth.

Let us muster the dead together, and take a view of this disordered armie. In Morocco, the cheefest cittie of Barbarie, died in one yeere seaven hundred thousand Moores and seaven thousand seaven hundred Jewes, as by bills daily sent to the Emperour did appeare.

What nation in the worlde would not have trembled, hearing of such an invincible host marching against them, yet Death with one arrowe slew all these. In the cittie of Faz died, the same yeere, five hundred thousand, beside those that fell in the country[1].

Yea, so terrible and fierce was Death in his execution of those in Morocco, that, in the space of one day and a night, hee slewe there, with his owne handes, foure thousand seaven hundred and odde: a mercilesse and tragicall conquest, an inglorious victorie, for he

---

1. Exagération manifeste.

made them away in their beddes. O, what a number of graves must have beene opened, if all these thousands should have had their rites of buriall! Howe many fathers for children, wives for husbands, sonnes and daughters for parents, and kinsfolkes for friends should heere have wept, if the dead had beene paid their due lamentations! But mourning heere had so wasted itselfe, that it quite forgot truly nowe to mourne. Sickness and griefe grew so familiar with men that, to be ridde of such lothsome company, they sought out death, when they knewe not where to finde a grave.

O thou, beautiful Kingdome, how couldest thou chouse but looke unlovely, having so many children dead in thy wombe? How could thy body be otherwise then unwholesome, having so mortal a disease running uppon thee, yea, all over thee, seven years together[1]? And, o you, Citties that were the fairest daughters to so noble a mother, what shrikes and soule-afflicting passions did not you breath forth, seeing all your marchants, that had wont to court you bee your loves, and forsaking you to see your buildinges stand in their wonted height, but robbed of their wonted ornamentes, to see foxes and wilde beastes, instead of men, inhabiting in your goodliest streetes and meeting daily upon your exchanges? A more than widdow-like lamentation must you needes put one, to behold yourselves utterly bereaved of those that were your best-beloved. What kingdome, though never so farre removed, is not heavy at the heart, hearing these sad stories of your sorrow?

        Quis, talia fando,
Mirmydonum Dolopumve, aut duri miles Ulissi,
Temperet a lachrymis?[2].

Your enimies cannot bee so barbarous as not to yeeld to your condolement. We will therefore no longer let out your teares withindoores, nor no more stand wondring to see all your buildinges shew like so many hearses; but will survay your filds abroad, and try if they can afford any better consolation. Alasse! they cannot. Calamity there travels up and downe in the same wretched habilyments that she weares within the walled citties; people fly

---

1. Ce renseignement a contribué à restituer la date du présent document. V. *supra*, p. 249, note 1.
2. Virgile, *Énéide*, II, 6 sqq.

in numbers up to the mountaines, to dwell amongst beastes and
to dispossesse them of their inheritance. They flie, thinking Death
would not follow them, but hee, like a politick generall, lay so
close in ambush at their returning backe to their citties, that he
cut them off faster then at the first, and left their bodies to be a
pray to those beasts who not many daies before ranne into their
caves as beeing afraid of them.

O what a miserie was it, to see highwayes strewed with dead
and infected carkases, as if the whole kingdome had beene sacked,
and the enemie had had all the people in execution! A rich and
abundant harvest covered the face of the earth, but the husbandmen, insteade of filling their barnes, were busied in filling
up graves; the fruites which the ground brought forth, shee herselfe did again devoure. A strange harvest was it; for corne was
had in without reapers. It was gathered and sowed againe all at one
time, for the earth did now play the good huswife; shee saved all
to herselfe, yet, even in saving it, did she spill all. There were not
handes enough to gather the foode, which she, out of her plenteous
lappe, bestowed among her children, nor mouthes enough to eate it.

The country-lasse sate not nowe singing by her milking-payle,
for the poore beastes ran bellowing up and downe with swolne
udders, mourning before their maisters doores, because they could
not be eased of their burdens.

The pestilence having thus, like a mercilesse invader, destroyed
both citties and villages, and having oftentimes made the greatest
lords in the kingdome stoope to his commaund, and determining to
conclude his conquest with taking the generall over so great a nation
prisoner, did at the last set upon the Emperour Mahamet himselfe,
and with her venemous breath kild him. Which glorious victorie
beeing gotten, Death and his liefetenant, Sicknes, beganne to sound
a retraite, to march from their walls and to let them live in quiet.

No sooner were their backes turned, but againe in multitudes
came the people downe from the mountaines; and, as all rivers,
when land-waters have opprest them, flie to the bosome of the sea
for safety, so did the nation of this great empire from all parts
thereof come marching joyfully, and yet fearefully, to fill up and
make good againe theyr disinhabited houses. What stories are now

tolde of lamentable funeralls! What friends and kinsfolkes are missing! What sorrowe there is for so much acquaintance lost! What gladnes to meete with any whom they heard or doubted were in their graves! Their citties doe now looke with cheerefull countenaunces, streetes are filled with men, houses with families; every one applies himselfe to his former labour, every merchant to his trafficke. But behold, in the heate of all this sunshine, when no wrinkle could be seene in the browe of Heaven, when all was calme and that men lay safely snorting on their secure pillowes, a second storme burst out of the clowdes, a second and a more fearefull. God poured another vengeance on the heads of this people; he sent famine to breath upon them, and to suck the life-blood out of theyr bosoms; so that they that before durst not come neere one another, for feare of being infected with the pestilence, are now ready to lay hold each of other and to turne their owne bodies into nowrishment. The plague was mercifull to them, in dispatching them quickly out of the world, but this tyrant put them to lingering deaths. They had once more meate then mouthes, now they had many mouthes and no meate[1].

. . . .

But was the terrible Judge of the world satisfied with punishing this people twice in this manner, had their offences towardes him deserved no more blowes? It seemes they had run into a most proude rebellion, and that he had sworne in his indignation to be revenged uppon them for it. For loe, the spirit of his rage comes nowe in a consuming fire: it is wrapt up in clowdes of lightning and the thunder of it breakes into civill warre. The three sonnes of so great an Emperour shine now like three meteors in the firmament, all in steele; their courts now are campes, and none are courtiers but souldiers. Three brothers, beeing all three Kings, are up in armes, only to make of three but one, miserie upon miserie. They that escaped the stripes of the pestilence were eaten to death by famine, they that saved themselves out of the jawes of famine are now in danger to perish on the sword[2].

1. Wilkins interpelle ensuite la Faim et la Famine dans une prosopopée qui sent son euphuïsme.

2. Vient ensuite une évocation des

. . . .

This fire of discension hath now taken holde of Barbarie, a kingdome full of people, abundant in riches, flowing with arts and trafficke with all nations. How happy therefore are we, that have peace in our citties, and plentie in our fieldes! Yet, doubtlesse, our sinnes are in number infinite, in nature abhominable, wee deserve as little pardoning as they, yet is our wickednes as blacke and detestable as theirs. Let us therefore stray aside awhile, and by comparing the heavy afflictions which the divine Justicer hath layd upon other countries in times past, acknowledge an incommensurable love and mercy of his to this iland of ours, nowe in these present dayes[1].

. . . .

Yet you see howe the Great Father of nations keepes us under his wing; he is loth to chide, more loath to strike us; let us not therefore, like foolish haire-braind children, provoke him too often and too much to anger, least he take up his triple mace of hote vengeance, and with it bruze our people, as hee hath already stretcht out his arme to smite those of Barbarie.

FINIS.

British Museum. — Printed Books, Press Mark : 1046. D. 24. — Three Miseries of Barbary...[2]. — Londres, sans date, in-4°.

malheurs récents de la France et des Pays-Bas.

1. Suit une description des pestes antérieures en Europe.

2. Au dessous du titre, tel qu'il a été reproduit plus haut (V. pp. 249-250), est une gravure en forme de cercle, dont la moitié gauche représente des oiseaux de proie et la moitié droite un rayon de soleil. Sous la gravure, on lit : « Post tenebras lux », et au bas de la page : « Printed by W[illiam] I[ones] for Henry Gosson, and are to be sold in Pater Noster Rowe, at the signe of the Sunne. »

XCI

RELATION DE JOHN SMITH[1]

(Extrait)

Description de Merrakech. — Il n'y reste guère debout que le palais royal et l'église des Chrétiens. — Les trois boules d'or. — Le fondouk; le quartier juif. — Universités jadis fameuses transformées en écuries. — Nombreuses maisons en ruines. — Jardin autrefois splendide et aujourd'hui abandonné. — Grand nombre de fontaines, de portes, de tours, de temples, restes d'une splendeur déchue. — Mort de Moulay Ahmed el-Mansour, empoisonné par sa femme; guerres civiles entre Moulay Zidân et ses frères. — Portrait physique et moral de Moulay Ahmed. — Il entretenait à sa cour des artisans anglais, orfèvres, plombiers, sculpteurs, polisseurs de pierre, horlogers. — L'horloger anglais Archer, emprisonné à la suite d'une querelle avec un marabout, est délivré par la garde royale. — Histoires de lions. — Description de Fez. — Les deux villes. — Le grand temple et ses innombrables lampadaires. — Écoles, auberges, moulins, etc. — Sept cents temples et chapelles. — Le bazar. — Le palais royal. — Marchands anglais en Guinée. — Les Maures sont supposés tirer leur or des mines de Gago et de Tombouctou. — Progrès de la piraterie.

---

1. John Smith (1580-1631) s'en vint, en 1596, chercher fortune dans les rangs de l'armée française, puis, la paix venue, parmi les insurgés des Pays-Bas. En 1600, il était de retour en Angleterre; il voyagea ensuite en France, en Italie et en Dalmatie, et entra au service du prince de Transylvanie. Capturé par les Turcs, il réussit à s'échapper, traversa la Hongrie, l'Allemagne, la France et l'Espagne. C'est de là qu'il se rendit au Maroc (1604). De retour en Angleterre en 1605, il ne tarde pas à en repartir pour l'Amérique (1606). Colon en Virginie, il est, en 1608, élu président de cette colonie. Revenu encore une fois dans son pays natal, il fait ultérieurement un nouveau voyage de découvertes en Amérique, puis se consacre à Londres à faire des brochures et des cartes pour encourager la colonisation. Parmi ses œuvres sont les *True Travels*, parus en 1630, où il raconte ses divers voyages, non sans y mêler quelques invraisemblances. Sur sa vie et ses œuvres, V. la réédition de celles-ci par E. Arber (Édimbourg, 1910, 2 vol. 8°).

[1604][1].

Chap. XVIII.

The observations of Captaine Smith, Mr Henrie Archer and others in Barbarie.

Being thus satisfied with Europe and Asia, understanding of the warres in Barbarie[2], hee went from Gibraltar to Guta[3] and Tangier, thence to Saffee, where growing into acquaintance with a French man of warre, the captaine and some twelve more went to Morocco, to see the ancient monuments of that large renowned city. It was once the principal citie in Barbarie, situated in a goodly plaine countrey, 14 miles from the great mount Atlas, and sixty miles from the Atlanticke sea; but now little remaining but the Kings palace[4], which is like a citie of itselfe, and the Christian church[5], on whose flat square steeple is a great brouch of iron, whereon is placed the three golden balls of Affrica[6]: the first is neere three ells in circumference, the next above is somewhat lesse, the uppermost

---

1. La date est fournie par le passage suivant du chap. xix de la Relation, qui se rapporte à 1604 : « ... But, not to trouble you too long with those rarities of uncertainties, let us return again to Barbary, where the wars being ended, and Bofferes possessed of Morocco and his fathers treasure, a new bruit arose amongst them, that Muly Sidan was raising an army against him, who after took his brother Befferes prisoner; but by reason of the uncertainty, and the prefidious, treacherous, bloody murthers rather than war, amongst those perfidious, barbarous Moors, Smith returned with Merham and the rest to Saffe, and so aboard his ship, to try some other conclusions at sea. »

2. On lit dans Playfair, A Bibliography of Morocco, n° 173, p. 251. « Smith offered his sword to Abd el-Aziz. » Il n'y a eu aucun souverain ou prince de ce nom au Maroc à cette époque.

3. Mauvaise lecture pour : Ceuta.

4. Le palais d'El-Bedi. V. 1re Série, Pays-Bas, t. IV, pp. 570-584.

5. Lapsus ou erreur difficile à expliquer, car il ne peut s'agir que d'une mosquée et vraisemblablement de la Kotoubia. — John Smith exagère, d'autre part, les ruines de la ville de Merrakech; toutes les belles mosquées de la ville étaient debout, lors de son voyage.

6. Cet ornement architectural, appelé *djamour* ou *tafafih*, se voit sur les minarets de presque toutes les mosquées, mais le djamour de la Kotoubia, sur lequel circulent beaucoup de légendes, est célèbre par la grandeur de ses proportions. Cf. Gallotti, *Le Lanternon de la Koutoubia*, dans *Hespéris*, 1923, p. 37.

the least over them, as it were an halfe ball, and over all a prettie guilded pyramides. Against those golden bals hath been shot many a shot; their weight is recorded 700 weight of pure gold, hollow within; yet no shot did ever hit them, nor could ever any conspirator attaine that honor as to get them downe. They report the prince of Morocco betrothed himselfe to the Kings daughter of Æthiopia; he dying before their mariage, she caused those three golden balls to be set up for his monument, and vowed virginitie all her life.

The Alfantica is also a place of note, because it is invironed with a great wall, wherein lye the goods of all the merchants securely guarded. The Juderea is also, as it were, a citie of itselfe, where dwell the Jewes. The rest, for the most part, is defaced; but by the many pinnacles and towers with balls on their tops, hath much appearance of much sumptuousnesse and curiositie.

There have been many famous universities, which are now but stables for fowles and beasts, and the houses in most parts lye tumbled one above another, the walls of earth are with the great fresh flouds washed to the ground, nor is there any village in it, but tents for strangers, Larbes and Moores.

Strange tales they will tell of a great garden, wherein were all sorts of birds, fishes, beasts, fruits and fountaines, which for beautie, art and pleasure, exceeded any place knowne in the world, though now nothing but dunghils, pigeonhouses, shrubs and bushes. There are yet many excellent fountaines, adorned with marble, and many arches, pillers, towers, ports and temples; but most only reliques of lamentable ruines and sad desolation.

When Mully Hamet reigned in Barbarie, hee had three sonnes, Mully Shecke, Mully Sidan and Mully Befferres; he a most good and noble King, that governed well with peace and plentie, till his Empresse[1], more cruel than any beast in Affrica, poysoned him[2], her owne daughter, Mully Shecke[3], his eldest sonne, born of a Por-

1. Aïcha bent Abou Bekor, de la tribu des Chebana, mère de Moulay Zidân. V. supra, p. 255, et note 1.

2. Fait inexact. Moulay Ahmed el-Mansour mourut de la peste; mais la mort naturelle d'un sultan est un fait si rare, que le bruit courut qu'il avait été empoisonné par Moulay Zidân. Cf. El.-Oufrâni, p. 306.

3. Moulay ech-Cheikh fut assassiné en 1613. Ibidem, p. 323.

tugall ladie¹, and his daughter, to bring Mully Sidan to the crowne, now reigning², which was the cause of all those brawles and wares that followed betwixt those brothers, their children, and a saint³ that started up, but he played the devill.

King Mully Hamet was not blacke, as many suppose, but molata, or tawnie, as are the most of his subjects; everie way noble, kinde and friendly, veric rich and pompous in state and majestie, though hee sitteth not upon a throne nor chaire of estate, but crosse-legged upon a rich carpet, as doth the Turke, whose religion of Mahomet with an incredible miserable curiositie they observe. His ordinarie guard is at least 5000; but, in progresse, he goeth not with lesse than 20000 horsemen, himselfe as rich in all his equipage as any prince in Christendome, and yet a contributor to the Turke⁴.

In all his kingdome were so few good artificers, that hee entertained from England goldsmiths, plummers, carvers, and polishers of stone, and watchmakers, so much hee delighted in the reformation of workmanship; hee allowed each of them ten shillings a day standing fee, linnen wollen, silkes and what they would for diet and apparell, and custome-free to transport or import what they would; for there were scarce any of those qualities in his kingdomes but those of which there are divers of them, living at this present in London. Amongst the rest, one Mʳ Henry Archer, a watch-maker, walking in Morocco, from the Alfantica to the Juderea, the way being very foule, met a great priest or a Sante (as they call all great clergymen), who would have thrust him into the durt for the way; but Archer, not knowing what he was, gave him a box on the eare. Presently he was apprehended, and condemned to have his tongue cut out and his hand cut off; but, no sooner it was knowen at the Kings court, but 300 of his guard came, and broke

---

1. Moulay ech-Cheikh était fils d'une concubine noire, nommée El-Kheizouran, la liane, ou El-Djaouher, la perle. El-Oufrâni, p. 312. V. *supra*, p. 255 et note 2.

2. Moulay Zidân mourut en 1627, donc avant la publication de la présente relation (1630).

3. Abou Mahalli. Sur ce perturbateur, V. *infra*, Doc. CXXXII, p. 465.

4. Moulay Ahmed *el-Mansour* envoya plusieurs ambassades au Grand Seigneur, porteurs de présents, mais il ne se reconnut jamais son vassal. V. *Nefcha el-Meskia*, Trad., p. 120, note 2.

open the prison, and delivered him, although the fact was next degree to treason.

Concerning this Archer, there is one thing more worth noting. Not farre from Mount Atlas, a great lionesse, in the heat of the day, did use to bathe herselfe and teach her young puppies to swimme in the river Cauzeff[1] of a good bredth; yet she would carrie them one after another over the river. Which some Moores perceiving, watched their opportunitie; and, when the river was betweene her and them, stole foure of her whelps; which she perceiving, with all the speed shee could, passed the river, and comming neere them, they let fall a whelp and fled with the rest; which she tooke in her mouth, and so returned to the rest. A male and a female of those they gave Mr Archer, who kept them in the Kings garden, till the male killed the female; then he brought it up as a puppy-dog, lying upon his bed, till it grew so great as a mastiffe, and no dog more tame or gentle to them he knew. But, being to return for England, at Saffee he gave him to a merchant of Marseillis, that presented him to the French King, who sent him to King James, where it was kept in the Tower seven yeeres. After, one Mr John Bull, then servant to Mr Archer, with divers of his friends, went to see the lyons, not knowing any thing at all of him, yet this rare beast smelled him before hee saw him, whining, groaning and tumbling, with such an expression of acquaintance that, being informed by the keepers how hee came thither, Mr Bull so prevailed the keeper opened the grate, and Bull went in. But no dog could fawne more on his master than the lyon on him, licking his feet, hands and face, skipping and tumbling to and fro, to the wonder of all the beholders. Being satisfied with his acquaintance, he made shift to get out of the grate; but when the lion saw his friend gone, no beast by bellowing, roaring, scratching and howling, could express more rage and sorrow, nor in foure dayes after would he either eat or drinke.

In Morocco, the Kings lyons are alltogether in a court, invironed with a great high wall. To those they put a young puppy-dogge: the greatest lyon had a sore upon his necke, which this dogge so

---

1. *Cauzeff*, l'oued Tensift.

licked, that he was healed : the lyon defended him from the furie of all the rest, nor durst they eat till the dog and he had fed ; this dog grew great, and lived amongst them many yeeres after.

Fez also is a most large and plentifull countrey ; the chiefe citie is called Fez, divided into two parts : old Fez, containing about 80 thousands housholds, the other 4000, pleasantly situated upon a river, in the heart of Barbarie, part upon hil. part upon plaines, full of people and all sorts of merchandise. The great temple is called Carucen[1], in bredth seventeene arches, in length 120, borne up with 2500 white marble pillars ; under the chief arch, where the tribunall is kept, hangeth a most huge lampe compassed with 110 lesser ; under the other also hang great lamps, and about some are burning fifteen hundred lights. They say they were all made of the bels the Arabians brought from Spaine. It hath three gates of notable height, priests and officers so many that the circuit of the church, the yard and other houses, is little lesse than a mile and an half in compasse.

There are in this citie 200 schooles, 200 innes, 400 water-mils, 600 water-conduits, 700 temples and oratories ; but fiftie of them most stately and richly furnished. Their Alcazer[2] or Burse is walled about, it hath twelve gates, and fifteen walks covered with tents, to keepe the sun from the merchants and them that come there. The Kings palace, both for strength and beautie, is excellent, and the citizens have many great privileges.

Those two countreyes of Fez and Morocco are the best part of all Barbarie, abounding with people, cattell and all good necessaries for mans use. For the rest, as the Larbes or mountainers, the kingdomes of Cocow, Algier, Tripoli, Tunis and Ægypt, there are many large histories of them in divers languages, especially that writ by that most excellent statesman, John de Leo[3], who afterward turned Christian.

The unknowen countries of Ginny and Binne[4], this six and twentie yeeres, have beene frequented with a few English ships, only

---

1. *Carucen*, Karaouin.
2. *Alcacer*, El-Caïceria اﻟﻘَﻴْﺼَﺮِﯾﺔ, le bazar central de Fez. V. 1re Série, France, t. II, p. 279, et Massignon, pp. 232, 233.
3. Jean Léon l'Africain.
4. Guinée et Bénin.

to trade, especially the river of Senega, by captaine Brimstead, captaine Brockit, Mr Crump and divers others; also the great river of Gambra, by captaine Jobson, who is returned in thither againe, in the yeere 1626, with Mr William Grent, and thirteene or fourteene others, to stay in the countrey, to discover some way to those rich mines of Gago or Tumbatu, from whence is supposed the Moores of Barbarie have their gold, and the certaintie of those supposed descriptions and relations of those interiour parts, which daily, the more the are sought into, the more they are corrected; for surely those interiour parts of Affrica are little knowen to either English, French or Dutch, though they use much the coast; therefore wee will make a little bold with the observations of the Portugalls.

. . . .

Chap. XXVIII.

The bad life and conditions of Pyrats; and how they taught the Turks and Moores to become men of warre.

..... Now, because they grew hatefull to all Christian princes, they retired to Barbary, where, although there be no many good harbours but Tunis, Argier, Sally, Mamora and Tituane, there are convenient rodes on the open sea, which is their chiefe lordship. For their best harbours, Mass al-Queber, the townes of Oran, Mellila, Tanger and Çuta, within the Streights, are possessed by the Spaniards; without the Streights they have also Arzella[1] and Mazagan; Mamora likewise they have lately taken[2] and fortified. Ward[3], a poore English sailer, and Dansker[4], a Dutchman, made first here their marts, when the Moores knew scarce how to saile a ship;

---

1. Erreur. Arzila fut évacué par les Espagnols en 1589.
2. El-Mamora fut pris par les Espagnols en 1614. V. 1re Série, France, t. II, p. 566.
3. Ce pirate, d'abord associé à Simon Danser, s'établit ensuite à Tunis. E. van Meteren, *Histoire des Pays-Bas*, f. 622.
4. Simon Danser, célèbre pirate néerlandais établi à Alger. En 1609, il passa au service de la France.

Bishop[1] was ancient and did little hurt ; but Easton got so much as made himself a marquess in Savoy ; and Ward lived like a bashaw in Barbary ; those were the first that taught the Moores to be men of warre. Gennings, Harris, Tompson died at Wapping[2]. Hewes, Bough, Smith, Walsingam, Ellis, Collins, Sawkwell, Wollistone, Barrow, Wilson, Sayres, and divers others, all these were captaines amongst the Pirats, whom King James mercifully pardoned. And, was it not strange, a few of these should command the seas. Notwithstanding the Malteses, the Pope, Florentines, Genoeses, French, Dutch and English, gallies and men of warre, they would rob before their faces, and even at their owne ports, yet seldome more than three, foure, five or six in a fleet. Many times, they had very good ships, and well manned, but commonly in such factions amongst themselves, and so riotous, quarrelous, treacherous, blasphemous and villanous, it is more than a wonder they could so long continue to doe so much mischieve ; and all they got, they basely consumed it amongst Jewes, Turks, Moores and whores.

John Smith. — The True Travels and Adventures and Observations... — Londres, 1704[3].

1. *Alias* Bisschop, nommé par E. VAN METEREN, *loc. cit.*, parmi les principaux pirates de son temps.

2. Paroisse à l'est de Londres. C'est là que l'on pendait les pirates et les matelots criminels.

3. D'après la réimpression de CHURCHILL dans *A Collection of Voyages and Travels*, in-f°. vol. II, pp. 394-396. — Dès 1625, PURCHAS, dans *His Pilgrims*, 1625, vol. II, avait donné un résumé des voyages de John Smith. L'ouvrage lui-même parut en 1630, sous le titre : *The True Travels and Adventures and Observations of Captaine John Smith in Europe, Asia, Affricke and America, from anno Domini 1593 to 1629*... Londres, Thomas Slater, in-f°, 60 pp. Les extraits publiés ici se trouvent pp. 34-37 et 58.

ANTHONY SHERLEY ET LE MAROC[1]

(1605-1606)

Le grand règne d'Élisabeth, traversé par des intrigues de toute nature, vit surgir un certain nombre d'aventuriers qui allèrent courir le monde, mettant au service de toutes les causes leur humeur belliqueuse et leur imagination fertile en projets politiques plus ou moins chimériques. L'un d'eux, Anthony Sherley[2], né en 1565, appartient à l'histoire du Maroc, car, de 1605 à 1606, il exerça sa turbulente activité dans l'empire chérifien.

Ce fut en 1586, dans l'armée du comte de Leicester venu pour seconder les Pays-Bas dans leur lutte contre l'Espagne, et où son père remplissait les fonctions de trésorier, qu'Anthony Sherley fit ses premières armes. En 1591, il va rejoindre en Normandie l'armée qui soutenait Henri IV et sert jusqu'en 1593 sous les ordres du comte d'Essex, dont il devient un admirateur enthousiaste, voulant, disait-il, le prendre pour modèle dans toutes ses actions. Nommé chevalier de Saint-Michel par Henri IV, il est emprisonné à son retour à Londres pour avoir accepté cette dignité sans l'autorisation de la Reine et il n'est relâché qu'à la condition de se démettre de l'ordre.

Mal vu de la Cour, néanmoins, pour son intimité avec Essex, Sherley quitte l'Angleterre et se fait flibustier; il part en 1596 avec six navires pour les Antilles et l'Amérique Centrale. Au cours de ce voyage, il passe devant Maza-

---

1. V. au frontispice du présent volume le portrait d'Anthony Sherley, dessiné par Gilles Sadeler et gravé en 1612 par Marc Sadeler. — Il existe des exemplaires de cette gravure non signés, dans lesquels Anthony Sherley est représenté, la face tournée à droite; il est revêtu d'un pourpoint avec le collier d'un ordre indéterminé, tandis que sur la gravure des Sadeler, il porte une cuirasse sans aucun ordre. Ces exemplaires ont dû être exécutés sur les indications de Sherley lui-même, car on les retrouve en tête de la relation de son voyage en Perse, publiée à Londres en 1613.

2. Ainsi que l'indique le titre, on ne donne pas ici la biographie complète d'Anthony Sherley. On la trouvera dans les ouvrages suivants: The Three Brothers, or the Travels and Adventures of Sir Anthony, Sir Robert and Sir Thomas Sherley in Persia, Russia, Turkey and Spain, with portraits. Londres, 1885, 8°. — The Sherley Brothers, by one of the same House [Evelyn-Philipp Shirley], Chiswick, 1848. — Stemmata Shirleiana, Londres, 1841, réédition en 1873 par le même auteur. — La publication des Sources inédites de l'Histoire du Maroc a fourni sur le séjour au Maroc du célèbre aventurier un grand nombre de documents nouveaux de diverses provenances, qui ont permis de compléter les biographies antérieures et sont la raison d'être de la présente notice.

gan, touche à l'île de Mogador, longeant les côtes de ce Maroc où il devait venir en mission dix ans plus tard[1].

Malgré l'intérêt que peut présenter la vie aventureuse de Sherley, nous ne saurions le suivre dans ses courses à travers le monde : à Venise (1599), à Constantinople, en Perse, où, sur les instructions du comte d'Essex, il arrive avec son frère Robert et trente-cinq gentilshommes anglais. Il en revient par Moscou, Arkhangel, Stettin, Prague, où l'empereur Rodolphe II lui fait le meilleur accueil, et se rend à Rome, où il est reçu par le pape Clément VIII en 1601. Son imagination en travail lui suggère partout des combinaisons et des plans politiques, ce qui lui donne une vague allure de conspirateur. En 1603, se trouvant à Venise, il entre en relations avec le roi d'Espagne Philippe III et le gouvernement anglais prend ombrage du personnage, qui est arrêté par ordre de la Seigneurie de Venise.

Il est remis en liberté à l'avènement de Jacques Ier, mais n'est pas autorisé à rentrer en Angleterre. Il obtient seulement une « licence », en date du 8 février 1604, l'autorisant « à prolonger son séjour outre mer » et le recommandant à la considération des princes et des étrangers des pays où il pourrait passer. Au printemps de 1605, il retourne à Prague et c'est alors qu'il suggère à l'empereur Rodolphe II, en guerre avec le Grand Seigneur, un plan consistant à faire opérer une diversion par le Maroc. Sherley devait se rendre auprès du Chérif régnant et lui persuader d'attaquer les Turcs dans la régence d'Alger. Le roi d'Espagne, également intéressé à cette offensive, devait vraisemblablement entrer dans la combinaison et, par conséquent, commanditer le négociateur. En outre, quelques éleveurs autrichiens le chargèrent d'achats de chevaux et lui remirent des lettres de crédit pour 14 000 ducats[2]. A ces ressources il faut encore ajouter « une lettre du roi d'Angleterre l'autorisant à lever sur les marchands anglais autant d'argent qu'il lui faudra[3] ». L'ambassade était donc très largement dotée, et l'on ne saurait ajouter foi au dire du duc de Medina-Sidonia prétendant que Sherley n'était que « médiocrement argenté[4] ». Il faut également récuser sur ce sujet le témoignage de Sherley lui-même, écrivant à l'empereur Rodolphe, à la date du 5 octobre 1605 : « Me dispiache de essere tanto male fornito como sono[5] ». Un bourreau d'argent, comme l'était Sherley, devait fatalement se trouver parfois dans des situations critiques.

---

1. La relation de ce voyage a été publié par HAKLUYT, The Principal Navigations... 1598-1600, t. III, pp. 598-602, sous le titre : A True Relation of the Voyage undertaken by Sir Anthony Sherley. Knt, in anno 1596, intended for the Isle of San Thomé..., with the memorable exploytes atchieved in all this voyage.

2. Lettre de P. M. Coy aux États du 16 décembre 1605. 1re Série. Pays-Bas, t. I, p. 109.

3. Ibidem.

4. « Antonio Scherley, ingles, creo que lo an ya conoscido en Marruecos, y su poco caudal do hazienda. » Lettre du duc de Medina-Sidonia à Philippe III du 23 avril 1606. 1re Série. Espagne, à cette date.

5. V. 1re Série, Dépôts divers, Florence.

Voulant donner au Chérif une haute idée du souverain qu'il allait représenter, et estimant, d'ailleurs assez justement, que le prestige était un facteur de réussite dans sa mission, Sherley ne négligea rien de ce qui pouvait contribuer à relever son ambassade. Il emmenait avec lui treize personnes, toutes de nationalités différentes, pouvant, à l'occasion, lui servir d'interprètes [1]. Le plus distingué de ses compagnons était Sir Edwin Rich, cadet de grande famille [2].

Il s'embarqua à Gênes. Surpris par la tempête, force lui fut de se réfugier à Alicante, d'où il se dirigea sur Cadix, en passant par Madrid. Arrivé dans cette dernière ville, il remit à l'ambassadeur d'Autriche une lettre que l'empereur Rodolphe II lui avait confiée [3]. Le roi d'Espagne, auquel sa présence fut signalée, ne lui accorda pas d'audience, voulant sans doute éviter de donner à ce négociateur un caractère officiel. Toutefois Sherley, à son arrivée à Cadix, ayant eu à se plaindre des procédés discourtois du gouverneur de cette place, Philippe III n'hésita pas à envoyer le duc de Bragance pour lui présenter des excuses et le complimenter en même temps au sujet d'une mission qui intéressait à un si haut point la Chrétienté [4].

Ayant trouvé à louer un navire pour 700 écus, Anthony Sherley débarqua à Safi, le 2 octobre 1605. La situation du Maroc était alors des plus troublées. Moulay Ahmed *el-Mansour* était mort le 25 août 1603 et, depuis cette date, ses trois fils Moulay Zidân, Moulay ech-Cheikh et Moulay Abou Farès se disputaient le pouvoir souverain. Moulay Zidân, après avoir été proclamé à Fez, avait dû s'enfuir poursuivi par Moulay ech-Cheikh, qui était entré dans la ville sur ses derrières. Quant à Moulay Abou Farès, son autorité était bien reconnue à Merrakech, mais il s'attendait, d'un jour à l'autre, à être attaqué par Moulay ech-Cheikh. C'était cependant auprès de lui qu'était accrédité Anthony Sherley. Ce dernier, rendant compte à l'empereur Rodolphe, le 5 octobre 1605, de son arrivée à Safi, trace des trois prétendants des portraits qui doivent être très exacts, car nous en retrouvons les traits principaux dans les historiens marocains.

Moulay Abou Farès était un caractère pusillanime et peu guerrier, se montrant généreux, quand il s'agissait de sa sécurité. Il était obèse et de mauvaise santé ; Sherley prévoyait qu'il ne vivrait pas.

Moulay ech-Cheikh était adonné à la débauche et à l'ivrognerie ; il manquait d'esprit politique, mais avait des qualités guerrières.

Quant à Moulay Zidân, Sherley le représentait comme un prince très généreux, d'une grande bravoure, instruit et capable de grands desseins ; il visait au pouvoir souverain, saisissait tous les moyens pour y parvenir ; il serait vraisemblablement, un jour, le roi de tout le Maroc.

---

1. V. *infra*, p. 357.
2. Sir Edwin Rich était le quatrième fils de Richard, Lord Rich, et frère de Robert Rich, comte de Warwick.
3. Lettre de Sherley à l'empereur Rodolphe II du 5 octobre 1606. V. 1re Série, Dépôts divers, Florence, à cette date.
4. Lettre d'Arnoult de Lisle à Villeroy, Merrakech, 29 janvier 1606. V. 1re Série, France, t. II, pp. 331-332.

Appréciant à leur valeur les chances des prétendants, Sherley crut prudent de demander à l'Empereur une lettre de créance pour Moulay Zidàn, avec lequel il se faisait fort de traiter, s'il rencontrait des difficultés auprès de Moulay Abou Farès [1].

En attendant, il écrivit à ce dernier pour l'informer de son débarquement à Safi. Moulay Abou Farès lui répondit, le 23 octobre, pour lui souhaiter la bienvenue et lui annoncer qu'il avait donné l'ordre au caïd de Safi de lui procurer toutes les facilités possibles ; il ajoutait qu'il enverrait bientôt un caïd pour le conduire à Merrakech, où lui serait faite une réception solennelle [2].

Cependant, le débarquement à Safi de Sherley avait fait sensation au Maroc et fortement intrigué les agents et marchands chrétiens. A la date du 16 décembre 1605, P. M. Coy, le représentant des Pays-Bas, écrit de Merrakech aux États-Généraux : « Il y a environ deux mois, il est arrivé à Safi un certain sieur Anthony Sherley, en qualité d'ambassadeur de Sa Majesté Impériale. Personne ne sait ce qu'il vient faire ici. Les opinions diffèrent. Je suppose que c'est pour chercher à exciter ce roi [Abou Farès] contre le Grand Turc, ce qui, à mon avis, ne lui réussira pas. A la cour d'Angleterre, on était au courant de sa venue ici, car il apporte des recommandations pour quelques Anglais..... Il est également porteur de lettres de crédit pour une valeur de 14 000 ducats, qui lui ont été fournies en Autriche par des éleveurs de chevaux. Ce personnage se trouve encore à Safi. Il ne peut venir ici, à cause de l'insécurité des routes [3]. »

D'autre part, Arnoult de Lisle, envoyé par Henri IV au Maroc pour traverser les desseins de l'Espagne, arrivait à Safi en janvier 1606 ; il y trouvait encore Sherley et il cherchait à pénétrer l'objet de la mission de ce fastueux personnage : « J'ai trouvé à Safi, écrit-il à Villeroy, le comte Anthoine Serlay, Anglais, qui estoit, il y a environ quatre ans, ambassadeur de l'Ampereur et du roy de Perse vers le Pape, venu vers le roy de Fez de la part de l'Ampereur, avec force presens et argent, entre aultres dont j'ay eu advis, une anseigne de la valleur de plus de douze à quinze mille escus, faite de diamans, et un rocher de corail fort ingenieusement faict. Et voiant le nombre de gens de guerre qu'il a à son train et l'excessive despence qu'il faict, et aiant sceu par les marchandz cretiens qu'il avoit vingt mil escuz à deppendre, tant sur ung Espagnol faisant sa demeure icy à Marroque que sur d'autres Crestiens, j'ay creu qu'il avoit d'aultres desseins que pour l'Ampereur ; quy m'a incité l'envoyer visiter par un gentilhomme qui m'a accompagné icy, nommé le sieur de Masseilles, qui a servi monseigneur de Montpensier, pour recognoistre quelque chose ; ce qu'il a faict. » Le sieur de Masseilles apprit, en effet, les détails du voyage de l'Ambassadeur, mais la curiosité d'Arnoult de Lisle ne fut pas satisfaite et, pour en savoir plus long sur le « négoce » d'Anthony

---

1. Lettre d'Anthony Sherley à l'empereur Rodolphe II, Safi, 5 octobre 1605. V. *1re Série*, Dépôts divers, Autriche, à cette date.

2. V. le texte de cette lettre chérifienne, *infra*, Doc. XCII, p. 284.

3. V. *1re Série*, Pays-Bas, t. I, pp. 108-109.

Sherley, il eut recours à une femme du harem chérifien, Lella Safia [1], fille de Moulay Ahmed el-Mansour. Il apprit d'elle « que ledit ambassadeur venoit principalement de la part du roy d'Espagne, offrant d'unir ses forces à celles dudit roy de Fez, pour faire ensemblement la guerre au Turc, le long de la coste d'Affricque quy regarde la mer de Levent, pour le chasser des places qu'il tient sur ledit rivage, comme sont Tlemcen, Argel, Bone, Bizerte, bref de toutz les lieux maritimes, où il y a portz, plaies, baies, rades, au dessus de Tramelen située au dessus du destroit de Gilbaltar, jusques par delà Tunis, à condition que tout le dedans de la terre demeureroit au roy de Fez et tout le rivage de la mer au roy d'Espagne, affin de rendre les costes de Castille, d'Aragon, Sardagne, Naples et Sicille exemptes des continuelles courses desdits Turcz. » Arnoult de Lisle, bien entendu, promettait d'employer l'expérience qu'il avait du makhzen pour contrecarrer l'alliance projetée entre le Chérif et l'Espagne [2].

L'insécurité du pays, d'une part, et, d'autre part, l'habitude quasi protocolaire d'imposer aux ambassadeurs chrétiens, même les plus qualifiés, un stage de purification dans le lieu de leur débarquement, obligèrent Sherley à prolonger pendant cinq mois son séjour à Safi. Ce retard apporté à l'accomplissement de sa mission ne le préoccupa pas autrement. Certes, il n'en perdait pas de vue l'objet, puisque lui-même en avait eu l'initiative. Mais, dans son imagination d'aventurier, il était persuadé que, pour réussir, il importait surtout de hausser son personnage et d'arriver à la cour chérifienne précédé d'une réputation de magnificence. Aussi le voyons-nous mener à Safi une existence fastueuse, portant au col l'ordre du S' Esprit et de S' Michel, voire même, assurait-on, la Toison d'or [3]. Il tenait table ouverte, invitant journellement tous les marchands chrétiens à dîner et à souper [4], distribuant des largesses aux indigènes. « Il n'a laissé ny petit ny grand à qui il n'ayt fait de presens [3]. » Un trait extravagant de son séjour à Safi fut l'achat qu'il fit, sans même débattre le prix, d'un navire de 160 tonneaux avec sa cargaison de blé ; il versa, séance tenante, à son vendeur une avance de 200 onces, s'engageant à payer le reste dans les dix jours de son arrivée à Merrakech [6]. On estimait que, pendant son séjour à Safi, il avait dépensé plus de 25 000 livres de Flandres [7]. Quand l'argent lui manquait, il empruntait à des Juifs, au taux de 50 %, remettant toujours le payement à son arrivée à Merrakech [8].

1. Sur cette princesse, V. 1re Série, Angleterre, t. I, p. 256, Pl. III, le Tableau généalogique des princes de la dynastie saadienne, n° 28.

2. Lettre d'Arnoult de Lisle à Villeroy, Merrakech, 29 janvier 1606. V. 1re Série, France, t. II, pp. 331-332.

3. Lettre de M. de Barrault à Puisieux, Madrid, 16 novembre 1606. V. ibid., p. 350.

4. V. infra, p. 357.

5. Lettre d'Arnoult de Lisle à Villeroy, 10 avril 1606, V. 1re Série, France, t. II, p. 337.

6. V. infra, p. 357.

7. Lettre de P. M. Coy, Merrakech, 18 mars 1606, V. 1re Série, Pays-Bas, t. I, p. 134.

8. V. infra, p. 357.

Au commencement de mars 1606, l'escorte envoyée par Moulay Abou Farès vint chercher Sherley pour le conduire à Merrakech ; elle était composée de 500 hommes et commandée par deux caïds. Saisissant l'occasion de faire une fois de plus montre de sa magnificence, Sherley fit présent d'un turban à chacun des cavaliers de l'escorte[1]. L'entrée d'Anthony Sherley à Merrakech se déroula suivant le cérémonial habituel, mais l'éclat en fut rehaussé par la personnalité de l'Ambassadeur et par la réputation de richesse et de générosité qu'il s'était faite. Moulay Abou Farès le fit loger dans « une magnifique maison[2] », et Sherley continua à Merrakech le train de vie luxueuse qu'il avait mené à Safi.

Arnoult de Lisle, qui avait éventé en lui « un ambassadeur d'Espagne soubz le nom de l'Empereur », se confirme de plus dans son opinion. « Il le tesmoigne assez, écrit-il à Villeroy, par tous ses discours et ses actions. Il a fait icy un agent espagnol..... Il a cent escuz pour jour du roy d'Espagne, et, quand il marche, deux cens. Et, pour tesmoigner que le fondz de sa dence vient d'ailleurs que de l'Empereur, le roy d'Espagne luy a baillé deux pièces : l'une un ruby oriental[3] extrêmement beau et grand, qui poise deux onces moins un huitième, qui n'est point en œuvre, qu'il porte à son chapeau à l'audience qu'il a devant le roy de Fez... ; l'aultre est un dyament qui poise une once..... Il a dict au sieur de Masseilles, quy est icy avec moy, qu'il a, outre tout cela, quarante mil escuz à dependre et dit partout que le roy d'Espagne, son maître, a des millions à donner[4]. »

L'agent des Pays-Bas, P. M. Coy, de même qu'Arnoult de Lisle, présumait que Sherley était soutenu par l'Espagne. « J'ai, d'ailleurs, appris, écrivait-il aux États-Généraux, qu'il était en correspondance avec les principaux personnages de la Cour de ce pays. Le motif de sa venue ici est, selon toute vraisemblance, de provoquer une guerre entre le roi d'ici et le Grand Seigneur, comme celle que le Persan ou Sofi fait contre ce dernier, guerre dont on dit que cet ambassadeur a été l'instigateur. On présume qu'il s'occupe des affaires de l'Espagne. Il a eu deux audiences du Roi, mais, jusqu'à présent, je n'ai pu en apprendre rien de positif[5]. »

Sherley avait, en effet, eu audience de Moulay Abou Farès, deux jours après son arrivée à Merrakech. Contrairement aux usages et bravant toutes les défenses, il avait traversé à cheval le méchouar, où les fils du Chérif eux-mêmes

---

1. V. *infra*, p. 358.
2. Lettre de P. M. Coy du 18 mars 1606, déjà citée.
3. Ce rubis provenait, disait-on, du Trésor de l'abbaye de Saint-Denis. Lettre de M. de Barrault, Madrid, 16 octobre 1606, V. *1re Série*, France, t. II, p. 346 et note 3. En vertu d'un arrêt du Conseil du 28 mai 1590, un rubis, estimé 20000 ducats, avait été extrait du Trésor de cette abbaye, qui avait été transporté à Sainte-Croix de la Bretonnerie, et vendu pour la défense de Paris. D. Michel Félibien, *Histoire de l'abbaye de Saint-Denis*. p. 416.
4. Lettre d'Arnoult de Lisle du 10 avril 1606, *loc. cit.*, pp. 336-337.
5. Lettre de P. M. Coy du 18 mars 1606, déjà citée.

ne pénétraient qu'après avoir mis pied à terre. Il fut reçu en grande pompe et, après avoir remis ses lettres de créance, il revint escorté par les principaux personnages de la Cour. A la seconde audience, qui lui fut accordée cinq jours après, Sherley trouva le méchouar barré par une chaîne, pour l'empêcher d'y pénétrer à cheval. Irrité, il tourna bride et rentra chez lui. Le Sultan dut lui envoyer trois caïds pour arranger l'affaire ; mais Sherley ne voulut rien entendre, déclarant que l'affront atteignait non sa personne, mais celle de l'Empereur, qui saurait venger l'injure faite à son représentant. On rejeta la faute sur le bouab (portier) du méchouar, qui fut battu en présence de Sherley et mis en prison [1].

Sherley eut plusieurs conférences avec Moulay Abou Farès, ou plutôt avec ses ministres, dans lesquelles il dut exposer le projet qu'il avait conçu d'une offensive du Maroc contre les Turcs, offensive qui servait à la fois la politique de l'Empereur et celle du roi d'Espagne. Les renseignements directs sur cette négociation font défaut, mais son résultat négatif ne saurait être mis en doute. Sherley, dès son arrivée à Safi, avait appris le départ d'un vaisseau affrété par Abou Farès, pour porter au sultan de Constantinople une somme de 300 000 onces d'or [2] ; bien loin de se liguer contre lui, le Chérif aurait plutôt recherché son alliance. Si l'on tient compte, en outre, de l'état très précaire où se trouvait Moulay Abou Farès, menacé par Moulay ech-Cheikh, on comprend facilement que ce chérif n'ait pas acquiescé à la proposition qui lui était faite au nom de l'Empereur et du roi d'Espagne [3].

Malgré l'insuccès de sa mission, Sherley n'en continuait pas moins à vivre à Merrakech en grand seigneur. Non seulement il ne payait pas ses dettes de Safi, mais il contractait de nouveaux emprunts ; sa superbe, sa générosité, son langage lui assuraient un tel crédit que deux marchands espagnols rivalisaient à qui lui prêterait la plus forte somme [4]. Néanmoins, voyant sa situation obérée s'aggraver de jour en jour, il fit partir pour Safi son compagnon Sir Edwin Rich, qui était le mieux en fonds, avec commission d'acheter un autre navire, de 300 tonneaux [5], et il se décida à demander au Chérif son audience de congé ; elle lui fut accordée au commencement de juin 1606 [6]. Mais l'Ambassadeur avait à liquider un fort passif, avant de se mettre en route. Force lui fut de recourir à une transaction très dure : il laissa deux personnes de sa suite comme caution de 250 000 florins, somme qui ne représentait sans doute que

1. V. infra, pp. 358-359.
2. V. la lettre d'Anthony Sherley à Rodolphe II, Safi, 5 octobre 1605, déjà citée. Cette somme était portée par un ambassadeur, qui partit de Safi le 22 juin 1605, à bord d'un vaisseau des États-Généraux, et était de retour dans ce port le 12 décembre suivant. V. 1re Série, Pays-Bas, t. I, p. 89 et note 2, et p. 116.

3. Cf. la lettre de M. de Barrault à Henri IV, Madrid, 12 novembre 1606. V. 1re Série, France, t. II, p. 348.
4. V. infra, p. 358.
5. Lettre d'Arnoult de Lisle à Villeroy, 10 avril 1606, loc. cit., p. 340.
6. Lettres de P. M. Coy aux États, 18 mai et 21 juin 1606, 1re Série, Pays-Bas, t. I, pp. 148 et 151.

le montant de ses dettes vis-à-vis des Juifs, car il restait redevable de 70 000 florins à des marchands chrétiens [1].

Mais Sherley avait un autre compte à régler avec le trésor chérifien. Désireux de sanctionner par un acte généreux la paix qui existait entre l'Angleterre et l'Espagne, il avait manifesté l'intention de racheter deux seigneurs portugais, Pedro Cesar d'Eça et Antonio de Saldanha [2], ainsi que trente captifs espagnols. Perdu de dettes, il se trouvait dans l'impossibilité d'acquitter la moindre rançon. Des négociations pénibles s'ouvrirent en vue d'un arrangement. Il fut convenu que Sherley remettrait en gage au Chérif son fameux rubis et signerait une reconnaissance de 160 000 onces, soit 16 000 livres sterling, somme fixée pour le montant des rançons. Sherley fut obligé, en outre, de donner des présents pour une somme de 6 000 livres sterling. De son côté, chacun des captifs rachetés lui signa une reconnaissance de la somme fixée pour sa rançon personnelle [3].

Il est difficile d'admettre que Sherley ait dénoncé à Moulay Abou Farès, au moment de son départ de Merrakech, les trafiquants chrétiens comme frustrant son trésor des taxes et droits de douane. Une pareille vilenie, que lui reproche P. M. Coy, l'agent des Pays-Bas [4], se concilie mal avec la générosité, plutôt excessive, du caractère de Sherley.

Ce fut au commencement d'août 1606 [5] que, sous la conduite d'un fonctionnaire du Palais, Sherley se mit en route pour Safi. Son escorte était de 400 arquebusiers, commandés par le caïd Abdallah Sinko, renégat portugais. Toujours prodigue, malgré sa situation obérée, Sherley, en arrivant à Safi, récompensa le fonctionnaire du Palais qui l'avait accompagné, en lui jetant son chapeau orné d'un bijou de grande valeur, et rémunéra largement les cavaliers de l'escorte. Deux navires, celui qu'il avait acheté pendant son premier séjour à Safi et celui qu'avait affrété Sir Edwin Rich, l'attendaient en rade ; mais, avant de s'embarquer, il dut encore entrer en composition avec les créanciers qu'il avait laissés à Safi : on lui réclamait une somme de 35 000 onces ; un marchand chrétien consentit à lui en faire l'avance.

Au moment de faire voile, un incident faillit retenir Sherley à Safi. Le caïd Abdallah Sinko, le renégat portugais, désirait rentrer dans sa patrie. Pour dissimuler son évasion, il s'entendit avec Sir Edwin Rich pour se faire enlever par les matelots de son bord. Dès que la disparition du caïd Abdallah Sinko fut connue à Safi, la population s'émut ; on arrêta cinq hommes de l'équipage du navire de Sherley, qui se trouvaient à terre ; ils furent chargés de fer et envoyés à Merrakech. Sherley écrivit à Moulay Abou Farès pour se justifier et il resta à Safi quatre jours après le départ de Sir Edwin Rich. Il aurait attendu

---

1. Lettre de P. M. Coy aux États, 3 octobre 1606, loc. cit., p. 161.
2. Sur ces deux captifs portugais, V. infra, p. 290, note 2.
3. Lettre d'Anthony Sherley à Salisbury, 7 [n.-st. 17] septembre 1606, infra, Doc. XCVII, p. 294.
4. Lettre de P. M. Coy aux États, 3 octobre 1606, citée ci-dessus, note 1.
5. V. ibidem.

la mise en liberté de ses matelots, s'il n'avait été informé de la présence de vaisseaux de guerre néerlandais croisant au large ; ceux-ci auraient pu s'emparer des captifs rachetés par lui, tous sujets du roi d'Espagne, avec qui les Pays-Bas étaient en guerre.

Le lendemain du départ de Sherley, arriva une lettre du Chérif, lui annonçant la relaxation de ses matelots, pour lesquels les marchands anglais de Merrakech avaient dû payer au Trésor chérifien une somme équivalente à la rançon du caïd Abdallah Sinko [1].

Dans les premiers jours de septembre 1606, Sherley débarqua à Lisbonne [2]. Les autorités portugaises ne semblent pas avoir pris très au sérieux le personnage, sur lequel couraient des bruits contradictoires, les uns le représentant comme un faiseur et un charlatan [3], les autres le donnant comme un ambassadeur extraordinaire « suivy et accompagné et ayant force argent [4] ». C'est en vain qu'il fit des démarches pour se faire rembourser les rançons des deux gentilshommes portugais qu'il avait avancées [5]. Néanmoins, à Madrid, où il alla présenter ses réclamations, il fut reçu avec grand honneur ; il portait au col « l'ordre du St Esprit et de Saint Michel avecq un ruban bleu, mais sans croix au manteau, moings encores à la bource [6] », écrivait à Puisieux M. de Barrault, ambassadeur de France en Espagne.

Cependant les vastes projets politiques hantaient toujours Sherley. A la suite de conférences qu'il eut avec D. Pedro Franquezza [7], secrétaire d'État de Philippe III, il parvint à se faire donner une commission d'amiral des mers du Levant, avec charge d'équiper une flotte pour combattre en Orient les Turcs et les Maures. Cette mission l'obligea à aller à Naples et à visiter les villes d'Italie, pour réunir des approvisionnements (1607-1608). Entre temps, il poussa jusqu'à Prague et rendit compte de sa mission à Rodolphe II, qui le nomma comte de l'Empire (1607). En 1609, la flotte du Levant étant équipée, Sherley partit de Sicile pour l'île de Mitylène, où il opéra une descente infructueuse. Cet insuccès entraîna sa révocation.

Discrédité, il revint en 1611 de Naples à Madrid, où Philippe III lui accorda une pension de 3000 ducats, laquelle fut presque absorbée par le payement de ses anciennes dettes. Une plainte, en effet, avait été portée contre lui ; il était accusé d'avoir abusé du titre d'amiral, que lui avait conféré le roi d'Espagne,

---

1. Sur le retour de Sherley de Merrakech à Safi et sur son départ pour Lisbonne, V. *infra*, pp. 359-360. Sur l'évasion du caïd Abdallah Sinko, V. aussi *1re Série*, France, t. II, pp. 398-399, la Relation de Jean Mocquet, qui appelle ce caïd Abdela Cinthe.

2. V. *infra*, Doc. XCV et XCVI, pp. 290 et 292.

3. V. *infra*, Doc. XCIX, p. 299 et n. 2.

4. Lettre de M. de Barrault à Henri IV, Madrid, 13 septembre 1606. V. *1re Série*, France, t. II, p. 342.

5. V. *infra*, Doc. XCVII, p. 294.

6. Lettre du 16 novembre 1606. V. *1re Série*, France, t. II, p. 350.

7. Lettre de M. de Barrault à Puisieux, 16 novembre, et à Henri IV, 26 novembre 1606. V. *ibidem*, pp. 350 et 352.

pour acheter un navire qu'il n'avait pas payé[1]. Bien déchu de ses splendeurs passées, dans un état voisin de la gêne, mais portant beau quand même, Sherley vivait à Madrid, se faisant appeler le comte de Leste[2]. Il fréquentait Sir Francis Cottington, l'ambassadeur d'Angleterre, qui écrit à son sujet : « Le pauvre homme vient souvent chez moi ; il est aussi plein de vanité que jamais, se figurant qu'il sera un jour un grand prince ; mais, pour le moment, il manque de souliers[3]. » Ce dénûment n'empêchait pas son imagination de travailler, et il adressait au Conseil d'État mémoires sur mémoires au sujet de la politique mondiale ; l'un d'eux, daté de 1622, n'a pas moins de 144 folios et porte le titre « Pesso polytico de todo el Mundo[4] ».

Sherley, à côté de plans chimériques, s'appliquait parfois à des questions pratiques et d'un intérêt commercial, ainsi qu'en témoigne un acte daté de 1627, dont voici le titre : « Cédule royale de contrat avec D. Antonio Sherley, comte de Leste, pour l'exploitation des pêcheries et du commerce de la côte occidentale de Barbarie et pour la fortification des ports de Fedala et de Mogador, sous condition d'entretenir 50 vaisseaux de guerre et marchands du port total de 20000 tonneaux[5]. »

Un écrivain anglais, qui visita l'Espagne à cette époque, nous a laissé de Sherley le portrait suivant : « Parmi les réfugiés anglais à la cour d'Espagne, le premier et le plus en vue est Sir Anthony Sherley, qui se faisait appeler comte du Saint Empire Romain, et reçoit de Sa Majesté une pension de 2000 ducats par an, ce qui, étant donnée sa prodigalité, est aussi peu que rien. C'est un grand conspirateur et faiseur de projets politiques, qui cherche par des plans maritimes à préparer l'invasion et la ruine de son propre pays. Il faudrait un volume entier pour raconter ses actions[6]. »

L'accusation portée contre Sherley de travailler contre sa patrie, accusation qui ne repose sur aucun fondement, mise de côté, le caractère de Sherley semble assez bien retracé.

On ignore la date exacte de la mort d'Anthony Sherley ; on ne trouve plus de mention de lui après 1635.

---

1. Lettre de Cottington à Salisbury du 12 [n. st. 22] janvier 1610 [n. st. 1611]. *State Papers, Foreign, Spain*, vol. XVIII.

2. V. *ibidem*, lettres de Cottington des 22 février [n. st. 4 mars] et 20 [n. st. 30] mars 1610 [n. st. 1611] ; et vol. XXIII. lettre du même à Dudley Carleton du 22 mai [n. st. 1er juin] 1618.

3. Lettre de Cottington à Naunton du 12 [n. st. 22] décembre 1619. *Ibidem*.

4. V. un extrait de ce Mémoire, *infra*, Doc. CLVIII, p. 543.

5. V. 1re Série, Espagne, à la date de 1627. — On sait que la côte atlantique du Maroc est très poissonneuse et que des pêcheries s'y sont établies depuis le Protectorat français. Cf. BERTHELOT, *La pêche sur la côte occidentale d'Afrique*. Quant à Fedala, son importance a été reconnue et il s'y est créé un port.

6. WADSWORTH, *English and Spanish Pilgrim*, 1629 et 1630.

XCII

LETTRE DE MOULAY ABOU FARÈS A ANTHONY SHERLEY[1]

Il a reçu la lettre par laquelle Sherley lui annonce son arrivée et il lui souhaite la bienvenue. — Il a ordonné au caïd de Safi de se mettre à la disposition de Sherley. — Il enverra bientôt quelqu'un pour le conduire à Merrakech et lui fera une réception solennelle.

10 Djoumada II 1014 [23 octobre 1605].

Au dos, alia manu: King of Mar[occo] to S[ir] A[nthony] S[herley].

Esta escritura noble y el estilo señoril altissimo procede del alto mando sagrado, al-Ffarasy[2], equitable Xarife — ¡ que Dios mantenga la buena ventura en sus dias y ensalce con su favor sus pendones y vanderas !

Al privado de noble extraction, cuya presencia y aspecto se dessea de todos, el noble, illustre, el privado Don Anthonio Xerleyo — ¡ que Dios continue su grandeza entre los suyos, y mantenga su prosperidad !

Por en quanto nos allego vuestra noble carta, que nos hizo saber vuestra venida y allegada en buen hora a nuestras altas Puertas sagradas y a nuestra presencia sublime, xarifica, sabed pues que llegastes a lugar vuestro y alcançastes a Corte favorable y, con ayuda de Dios, de buen accatamiento.

Y hemos mandado al governador dessa ciudad para vuestra

---

1. Ce document était une copie annexée à la lettre de Sherley à Barvitius du 10 décembre 1605 ; il fut intercepté en même temps. V. Doc. XCIV, p. 287 et note 3.

2. *Al-Ffarasy*, El-Faresi, c'est-à-dire émanant d'Abou Farès. Sur ce qualificatif, V. 1re *Série*, Pays-Bas, t. I, p. 125, note 6. Cf. *supra*, p. 22, note 1.

buena y ample pozada, y le encomiendamos que os provea de todos menesteres a contento y que uze toda beneficencia convosco.

Y en estos dias, con favor de Dios, os yran, de parte de nuestro, por la gracia de Dios, alto estado, quien os trayga a nuestra alta presencia, con ayuda de Dios, en mucho estima, respecto y benevolencia, accompañandoos en vuestro alojar y desalojar.

Y llegando, en buen hora, a nuestras altas cazas y sagradas Puertas, luego sereys recebido con todo genero de bien, nobleza y buen trattamiento, con favor de Dios, tanto que alabareys a Dios muchas vezes, por aver venido a nuestras altas Puertas.

Fecha en diez de Jamad, año de 1014[1].

Public Record Office. — *State Papers, Foreign, Royal Letters, vol. II, n° 34*. — *Copie*[2].

[1]. La date ne précise pas Djoumada I ou Djoumada II, mais il ne peut y avoir de doute, vu l'arrivée de Sherley à Safi le 2 octobre 1605.

[2]. Ce document est une copie, comme le dit Sherley lui-même (V. *infra*, p. 288), faite sans doute sur une traduction espagnole qui accompagnait un texte arabe. Il existe, dans le même volume des *Royal Letters*, sous le n° 33, une traduction anglaise de la présente lettre, qui a été publiée par [E.-P. Shirley], *The Sherley Brothers*, p. 52.

XCIII

LETTRE DE CHARLES CORNWALLIS[1] A SALISBURY[2]

(Extrait)

Anthony Sherley et Edwin Rich, arrivés récemment à Cadix, y ont loué un navire pour passer au Maroc, accompagnés de dix serviteurs.

Valladolid, 18 [n. st. 28] octobre 1605.

A lettre to the Earle of Salisbury, Principall Secretary to his Matie, from Valiadolid.

Maie it please your Lordship, — I am this day certeinely advertized that Sir Anthony Sherley and Sir Edwyn Riche[3] were lately at Cales, and there hired a ship to passe over into Barbary, being attended with ten servaunts. They there reported that either of them have of the Lordships here[4] a pencion of 200 crownes a month. What the intention of their journey is I cannot learne, but thought fitt instantly to advertize it. They have both shaped their religeon for this state.....

18 October 1605.

Your Lordships humble and affectionate servaunt and assured poore freind,

Ch. Co.

British Museum — *Harleian Mss, 1875, f. 200.* — *Copie.*

1. Sir Charles Cornwallis, ambassadeur en Espagne de 1605 à 1609, mort en 1629.
2. Robert Cecil, qui avait été nommé vicomte Cranborne le 20 août 1604, venait d'être créé comte de Salisbury, le 4 mai 1605.
3. V. *supra*, p. 276 et note 2.
4. Les ministres espagnols.

XCIV

LETTRE D'ANTHONY SHERLEY A BARVITIUS

Moulay Abou Farès ne veut pas faire venir Sherley à Merrakech, avant d'y avoir lui-même affermi son pouvoir. — Il sera très probablement vainqueur, car il est déjà en possession du royaume et du trésor; tous les notables, en outre, sont pour lui. — La bataille doit se livrer dans le royaume de Fez avant deux jours. — Moulay ech-Cheikh se tient à Larache, prêt à se réfugier, en cas de défaite, auprès du grand-duc de Toscane. — Moulay Abou Farès redoute les Turcs et il n'a pas confiance dans l'Espagne. — Le prestige de l'Empereur triomphera des hésitations de ce prince. — Sherley envoie à l'Empereur copie de la lettre qu'il a reçue de Moulay Abou Farès.

Safi, 10 décembre 1605.

Au dos : Sir Anthony Sherley to Barvitius[1], the Emperors[2] secretary, 10 December 1605. From Zaffye. — Out of Italian[3].

Most renowned Sir,

The tyme hath ben such an enemye to the speedy dispach of his Maties busines that, wher I hoped to have bene retorned before this, I have not yett attayned to the Kinges presence; who desyreth to knowe himselfe sure in his state before he will hazard my person att the arbitrement of an other vanquisher, as he hath lett me

---

[1]. Johann Barvitius, secrétaire privé de l'empereur Rodolphe II, depuis 1594 jusqu'à la mort de ce prince en 1612.
[2]. Rodolphe II.
[3]. Cette lettre et son annexe (V. *supra*, Doc. XCII, p. 284) furent interceptées par le gouvernement anglais et traduites de l'italien par la même personne qui rédigea la Relation des guerres civiles publiée *infra*, Doc. C, p. 301 et note 1.

understand divers tyme by the governor of this place. But I make litle doubt of his fortune, he being alredy in possession of the kingdome and the tresor, and holding al the great ones att his devotion. Two dayes cannot pass before every discorse wilbe concluded in effect, the battaile being apointed in the kingdome of Fez[1]. His Matie may vouchsaffe to be contented with the necessitye of thes accidents, which were not possible in mans judgment to be prevented, and, for the rest, to be confident in the enterprise as much as all discource of reason can persuade his high wisdome.

We have a Kinge rich in treasure, oppressed by a potent neybor, the Turke[2], ill assured of the Kinge of Spayne; and, if he[3] shall remayne vanquisher of Mulley Xeque, he[4] will retyre himselfe presently to the Great Duke, having made his waye and keeping a shipp of warr of the Great Dukes[5] ready for that purpose in the port of Laracha, wherin is alredy putt the treasure of jewells which he hath. Yourselfe may discourse of the rest, whither the great name of the Emperor will not be of force to take away all future feares from the Kinge[6], and whither he will not be content to doe more then ever he thought. For my part, my lifetyme and fortune shall not be spared to accomplish the sincear loyaltye and affeccon which I beare to the service of his Ma{tye}, nether shall ther want any sort of art or industrye.

This is all I can say for the present upon this occation. God shall geve happie success unto all for His owne glorye. Meanewhile your patience cann not be greater in expectinge the ende then myne in procuringe it.

The copie of the Kinges lettre[7] to me I send unto his Matie. The

---

1. Les deux armées étaient commandées par les fils des deux prétendants: celle de Moulay Abou Farès par Moulay Abd el-Malek, celle de Moulay ech-Cheikh par Moulay Abdallah. La première, qui s'était avancée jusqu'à Meknès, affaiblie par des défections et des révoltes, se replia sans combattre, et rentra à Merrakech le 18 décembre 1605. V. 1re Série, Pay-Bas, t. I, pp. 466 et 476, et infra, p. 355.

2. Sur les sentiments de Moulay Abou Farès à l'égard des Turcs, V. supra, p. 280.

3. He, Moulay Abou Farès.

4. He, Moulay ech-Cheikh.

5. Le grand-duc de Toscane, Ferdinand Ier de Médicis, entretenait des relations avec Moulay ech-Cheikh, par l'intermédiaire de deux agents, Nicolo Giugni et Bastiano Acquisti. V. 1re Série, France, t. II, p. 338 et note 7; Dépôts divers, Florence, aux années 1603-1606.

6. The Kinge, Moulay Abou Farès.

7. La lettre de Moulay Abou Farès à Sherley. V. supra, Doc. XCII, p. 284.

duble therof shall not be necessary, sith all passeth by your owne handes; unto whom from Heaven I wish all happiness.

From Zaffia, 10 December 1605.

Your Lords most devoted to serve you,

Anth. Sherley.

To the Lord Barvitius, of his Maties Privy Consell and his Principale Secretarye.

Public Record Office. — State Papers, Foreign, Barbary States, vol. XII. — Traduction[1].

---

1. Publié par [E.-P. Shirley], *The Sherley Brothers*, pp. 51-52.

XCV

LETTRE DE HUGH LEE[1] A SALISBURY

(Extrait)

Anthony Sherley est arrivé du Maroc, où il était allé pour le service de l'Empereur. — Il en a ramené divers captifs portugais, dont deux lui doivent près de cinquante mille couronnes pour leur rançon. — Son attitude lui fait honneur : il est très aimable pour ceux de ses compatriotes qui professent de leur attachement pour Jacques Ier, très froid pour les autres. — Il compte se rendre à la cour d'Espagne.

Lisbonne, 8 septembre 1606.

Au dos, alia manu : Mr Hugh Lee to my Lord, from Lisbonn. — Advertisements.

Right Honorable my very good Lorde,

My humble dutie remembred, — My last unto your Lordship was the 8 of August, and was also my vijth written unto your Lordship, sence my comynge to this place.

. . . .

Sir Ant° Sherley ys here aryved out of Barbery, wher he hath benn ymployed by the Emperour, as he sayeth. He hath brought with hym dyvers Portingales, that were captives there; whereof 2 men of good accompt[2], which are to yeld hym neere 50 thousand

---

1. Consul d'Angleterre à Lisbonne.
2. Ces deux captifs étaient Antonio de Saldanha et Pedro Cezar d'Eça; ils avaient été faits prisonniers à Tanger dans une sortie, le 17 octobre 1592. Fernando de Menezes, *Historia de Tangere*, p. 94. Sur les conditions de leur rachat par Anthony Sherley, V. *supra*, p. 281, et *infra*, p. 295. Cf. 1re Série, France, t. II, p. 398 et note 3.

crownes for theyr ransome. He laboureth the inlargement of Hugh Gurganey[1] very earnestly with the Vizroy, and hath recevid good wordes, which gyveth hym hoape he shall obtayne his desyre; God grant he maye.

His carryage here ys very honorable, and sheweth hymselfe very kinde unto all his cuntrymen that professe to be frindes to his Ma[tie], and to others the contrary. His purpose ys from hence to travell unto the coorte of Spayne; whither I have advised unto my Lord Ymbassador[2] the troubles of Gurgany with the needfull.

. . . .

Praying for the longe preservacion of your Lordships health, with increase of honnor, I most humbly take my leave, this 8 of September, in Lyzborn, where I remayne.

Your Lordships in all humble dutie at comand,

Signé : Hugh Lee.

Public Record Office. — *State Papers, Foreign, Portugal, vol. III.* — *Original*[3].

1. Marchand anglais, emprisonné à Lisbonne par l'Inquisition.
2. Charles Cornwallis, ambassadeur à Madrid. V. *supra*, p. 286, note 1.
3. Publié par [Evelyn-Philipp Shirley], *The Sherley Brothers*, p. 53.

XCVI

LETTRE DE CHARLES CORNWALLIS AU CONSEIL PRIVÉ

(Extrait)

Anthony Sherley est arrivé à Lisbonne. — Il s'arroge le titre d'ambassadeur de l'Empereur et il veut être traité d'Excellence. — Il rapporte qu'il a offert au Chérif de lui vendre un rubis valant cinq cent mille ducats. — Le Chérif ayant montré des soupçons sur la manière dont ce rubis avait pu venir en la possession de Sherley, celui-ci proposa de lui en faire présent en échange de captifs. — Sherley a ramené ainsi à Lisbonne de nombreux Portugais et des Juifs, tous fort riches.

S. l. 6 [n. st. 16] septembre 1606.

To the Lords of the Counsell, the 6th of September — By Browne aforesaid.

Maie it please your Lordshipps, — I received your letters of the 11th of July, the 20th of August.

. . . .

Sir Anthony Sherley arrived at Lisbon some 14 dayes sithence, where he arrogates to himself the name and title of Ambassador to the Emperor, by whome he sayeth he was sent to the King of Marocco. Lesse than Excellencie he willinglie receives not from any; and, as I heare, my countrymen there are content to geve it him. From a man of myne in that citty he received onely an English Sir, wherewith he seemes not to be well pleased. Noe niggard, as it appeares, he is of his owne accions and purposes.

Hee reporteth that he offered to sell to the King in Barbary a rubie of greate perfection, of the weight of twoe ounces, the same being esteemed at 500000 ducates[1]. The King, being in possession, was content, as he had reason, to suspect that the jewell belonged to some greate prince and was not soundly comen by, by so meane a subject. Hereupon Sir Anthony, put to the proofe of his wittes, suddainely resolved to make a frank gift of it to the King[2], and to drawe in recompence the libertie of so many Spaniardes as might countervaile the value[3].

In this, as I heare, he hath succeeded, having brought to Lisbon many Portugalles of greate wealth, and some rich Jewes, to whome he hath promised here an obtayninge of habitacion and libertie of their conscience.

. . . .

British Museum. — Harleian Mss., 1875, f. 607. — Copie.

1. Sur ce rubis et sur sa provenance, V. *supra*, p. 279 et note 3.

2. Sur cette affaire, cf. *I*ʳᵉ *Série*, Pays-Bas, t. I, pp. 151, 161; Franco, t. II, pp. 337, 345-348.

3. Ce récit est fantaisiste. Sur les conditions du rachat des captifs par Sherley, V. *supra*, p. 281, et le document suivant.

XCVII

LETTRE D'ANTHONY SHERLEY A SALISBURY

Sherley a remis en gage au Chérif, pour la rançon de deux gentilshommes portugais et de trente autres captifs, un rubis de grande valeur et a fourni de l'argent et des cautions. — L'agent de France, Arnoult de Lisle, a donné à entendre au Chérif qu'il risquait de perdre à la fois le rubis et la rançon. — Sherley, pour lever les soupçons, a dû laisser le rubis dans les mains du Chérif et s'engager personnellement pour la somme de 160 000 onces ; il a, en outre, été obligé de faire des présents pour 6 000 livres sterling. — Les gentilshommes portugais, Pedro Cezar d'Eça et Antonio de Saldanha, ont signé aux marchands un engagement pour une partie de ces sommes ; mais, une fois arrivés à Lisbonne, ils refusent de payer. — Sherley demande l'intervention de Salisbury.

Lisbonne, 7 [n. st. 17] septembre 1606.

Au dos, alia manu : 7 September 1606. — Sir Anthony Sherley.

Right Honorable,

I beseetche yowr Lordeshipes pardone in that I trooble yow with a history, which I thought should have beene bothe honorable unto mee and of good satisfaction ; and, throughe the disposition of this people, yss fallen owt so contrary thatt I ame forced to beeseetche your Lordships favour to helpe mee in that discharge, which my owne good mind and intentions and vyld naturs of thos which I have given lyf and libertye too have cast mee unto. My most honorable Lord, the Emperour, having imployed mee into Barbary, I found to gentlemenne Portugeses[1] ther, which had benne prisoners

---

1. Antonio de Saldanha et Pedro Cezar d'Eça. V. *supra*, p. 290, note 2.

15 years, and the country likwise full of Spannishe captives. The consideration of the nue peace[1] betweene Britaine and Spayne and the yll proceedings of soome partes mad mee desirous to shew soome extraordinary honnour to be in our hartes, and to draw one besyde a perticular obligation and reputation to our nation, so that I resolved to deliver those prisoners, which I knew allso wear well able to pay mee, and with them thirty other captives[2].

For the gentlemen, I impawned a ruby[3] to the King of 2 ownces weyght, to bee redeemed withine half a year. For the other captives, I gave mony and credit. And, after the gentlemen wear sent home to my house, a certayne Frentch malicious dealour, agent for his Ma^{ty} with that King[4], tould the King that hee should be cosened in the rannsome of those gentlemen, I being resolved to intitle the Emperour with thatt stoane ; and so, they beeing out of his handes, hee should bothe loase stoane and the rannsome. My juell was already in the Kinges hand, and the gentlemen wear to bee returned to prison ; and I was forced to give grat presente to the King and his principall counselours, to bee contented with my pawne, to receave allso part mony, part security for the rannsome. So that I ingadged myself and my frends for one hundred and three score thousand ownces, which amountethe to sixteene thousands pound sterling, besyde my gyftes which I was forced to give for their beeing once in my house, to save them from returning to prison againe and my owne reputation ; and those are of no les weayght thenne six thousand poundes, besyde my juell.

Thes gentlemen, whereof the one ys named Pedro Cæsar d'Essa, the other Antonyo de Saldanha, sygned with mee to the papers of divers perticolar marchants, of the payment of part of thes soomes att too shillinges the ownce, which yss currant so amongst all marchantes. And beesyde I mad myself eeven naked to deliver them to ther frends and country. And, now I am comme hear, they doe not only deny to pay, butt persecut mee ass mutch ass they dare and

---

1. La paix conclue entre l'Espagne et la Grande-Bretagne en 1604.
2. Sur le rachat de captifs opéré par Anthony Sherley. V. *supra*, pp. 281-282.
3. V. *supra*, p. 293 et note 1.
4. Arnoult de Lisle, envoyé au Maroc par Henri III et Henri IV, amassa pendant ses deux missions « richesses et autres commodités », ce qui explique le terme de « dealour » appliqué à cet agent.

canne, with all the vyld usadge thatt canne bee devysed. And, since the act yss so inhumane, barbarouse and against nations, beeing layed beefor so generous a mynd ass your Lordships, I know ytt will breed bothe pytye and disdaine, and, as I implor your Lordships favour and helpe, so I doe most constantly assur myself of ytt, protesting to your Lordshipe thatt I am your true servant, and under that title I will ever live, and do beseetch God from my hart thatt your Lordshipe may longe live with alle prosperity [1].

From Lisbon, this 7 of September 1606.

Your Lordships most humble and faythfull servant,

Signé : A. Sherley.

Public Record Office. — State Papers, Foreign, Spain, vol. XIII. — Original [2].

[1]. Il semble qu'il fut donné suite à cette requête de Sherley, car il existe une lettre de Charles Cornwallis, ambassadeur à Madrid, au président de Castille, D. Juan de Zuñiga y Avellaneda, et un mémoire du même, demandant qu'il soit fait justice en cette affaire. *British Museum. Cotton Mss., Vespasian, C. V, ff. 83 v° et 93.*

[2]. Publié par [Evelyn-Philipp Shirley], *The Sherley Brothers*, pp. 53-54.

XCVIII

LETTRE DE HUGH LEE A THOMAS WILSON[1]

(Extrait)

Les captifs rachetés au Maroc par Antony Sherley refusent de lui payer leur rançon. — Ils nient la validité d'engagements contractés par des prisonniers et en terre païenne. — Sherley sera contraint de se plaindre au roi d'Espagne. — Il se prépare à partir pour cette Cour.

Lisbonne, 8 octobre 1606.

Adresse: To the worshipfull Thomas Wilson, gentleman, at Salisbery Howse, nere the Strand, at London. By the conveyance of a frind. — *Alia manu*: From Mr Lee, the Consul of Lisbone, 8 8^{ber} 1606. Receyved this 27 October.

Laus Deo. Anno 1606, the 8 October, in Lishborne.

Worshipfull,

Though unacquainted by myselfe, yet by my frind, Mr John Dorington, I ame encouraged to pray your favour.

. . . .

Sir Ant° Sherley ys very badly dealt withall by the captives which he redemed in Barbery, he bountifully trusting unto theyr lyberall promises, without any note of theyr handes[2]; and they nowe, lyke Jewes, deny all they promysed, and plead all dishonest advantages for good payment: alleaging fyrst that they weare cap-

---

[1]. Sur ce personnage, V. *supra*, p. 218, note 1.

[2]. Erreur. Ces captifs avaient signé un engagement. V. *supra*, p. 295.

tives, and therefore bounde to performe no promyse, but by any meanes seeke theyr lybertye ; secondly that, what promyse was made in a heathen cuntrey, they are not tyed to performe. So that they will dryve hym to complaine to the Kinge, who must right hym ; otherwise he hath small redresse. He ys preparing hymselffe to the Courte of Spayne, as speedelye as he maye, there to seeke his remedye.

. . . .

And so for this tyme I bid yow hartely farewell, remayninge Your Worships in all good affection at comande,

Signé : Hugh Lee.

Public Record Office. — *State Papers, Foreign, Portugal, vol. III.* — *Original.*

XCIX

LETTRE DE CHARLES CORNWALLIS A SALISBURY

(Extrait)

Sherley a exécuté au Maroc de nombreux tours de charlatan. — Certains marchands de Londres pourraient bien en sentir les fâcheux effets. — Ceux de Lisbonne, qui ont Sherley en grande vénération, ne manqueront pas d'être ses dupes. — Il a produit un singulier passeport de Jacques Ier, où celui-ci le recommande à tous les souverains et à ses sujets.

[Madrid, octobre 1606[1].]

Another lettre to my Lord of Salisburie, sent to my Lord Ambassador in the Low Countreys, inclosed in a lettre of Thomas Freeman to his father, which was to be enclosed before the former lettre.

. . . .

That I neede not certefie his Lordshipp much of Sir Anthony Sherley, being so well knowne to him, but doe understand by one that attended him in Barbarie that he hath there played many partes of mountebankerie[2], which I feare some merchauntes factors in London will bitterly taste of; that those of Lisbone will hardly escape him, who hold him either in the accompt of a saint or a great

---

1. La date, qui n'est pas écrite sur le document, est fournie approximativement par comparaison avec la lettre de Cornwallis, citée dans la note suivante.

2. Dans une lettre du 29 septembre [n. st. 9 octobre] 1606, le même Charles Cornwallis écrit à Henry Wotton : « Le charlatan que mentionne en chiffre Votre Seigneurie a extrêmement bien joué son rôle au Maroc ; mais il n'a, semble-t-il, d'autre souci que de monter la baraque, sans tirer lui-même un bénéfice durable de ses onguents et de ses poudres ». *Harleian Mss., 1875, f. 562 v°.*

sorcerare, soe apt is the confused and promiscuous multitude to worshippe rather in Samaria than in Jerusalem ; that here hath shewed an inexampled maner of license[1] or pasport from the King, my master, desireinge all princes to geve him passage thorough their countreyes, to assist and supply him in all necessities that might occurre, which he would accept as a favor to himself, and concludeing, what he desired of forraigne princes, he straightly comaunded to his owne subjectes.

. . . .

British Museum. — Harleian Mss., 1875, f. 634. — Copie.

1. Sur cette licence, en date du 8 [n. st. 18] février 1604, V. *supra*, p. 275.

C

RELATION DES GUERRES CIVILES DU MAROC[1]

Il ne savait rien de plus sur le Maroc que ce que disaient les dernières lettres d'Anthony Sherley à l'Empereur et à Barvitius traduites par lui de l'italien, mais il vient de causer avec un marchand qui a reçu des lettres datées de Safi. — Il remonte aux origines de la guerre civile au Maroc, en consultant les notes qu'il a prises en Espagne. — Moulay Ahmed en mourant laissa trois fils. — Ayant déshérité et emprisonné l'aîné, Moulay ech-Cheikh, il partagea ses royaumes entre les deux autres : Merrakech et le Sous pour Moulay Abou Farès, Fez pour Moulay Zidân. — Ce dernier déclara la guerre à Moulay Abou Farès, qui lui opposa Moulay ech-Cheikh, après l'avoir remis en liberté. — Moulay ech-Cheikh, ayant vaincu Moulay Zidân, s'est fait proclamer roi à Fez, malgré ses promesses à Moulay Abou Farès. — Moulay Zidân s'est réfugié dans le Sous, où, avec l'appui d'un marabout, il s'est fait reconnaître roi. — Moulay ech-Cheikh, effrayé des préparatifs de Moulay Abou Farès contre lui, se préparait à fuir en Europe sur un navire du grand-duc de Toscane, mais les événements ont tourné en sa faveur. — Les troupes de Moulay Abou Farès, commandées par son fils Moulay Abd el-Malek, ont été vaincues. — Moulay Abd el-Malek est mort de la peste. — Le caïd Azzouz a réussi à opérer un rapprochement entre Moulay Abou Farès et Moulay Zidân, qui se préparent à attaquer Moulay ech-Cheikh. — Au moment où Sherley est arrivé au Maroc, Moulay Abou Farès a envoyé un ambassadeur au Grand Seigneur, qui, après avoir favorisé Moulay ech-Cheikh, soutient maintenant, à ce qu'on pense, son rival. — Moulay Abou Farès fait bon visage à Sherley, mais il ne lui accordera rien.

1. La forme de cette Relation anonyme porte à croire qu'elle a été écrite par le rédacteur de la Relation de Ro. C., publiée ci-après (Doc. CVII, pp. 322-408), à savoir par George Wilkins. On peut même la considérer comme un avant-projet de cette dernière. — Le destinataire de la présente Relation est évidemment Salisbury, comme le prouvent les titres qui lui sont donnés.

[Après le 4 janvier 1607][1].

Au dos, alia manu: Barbary. — Historicall Narration of the Civill Warrs betweene 3 Brethren there Kinges.

It pleased your Lordshipp yesterdaye to aske me what I knewe of the present busines of Barbarye, and of the warres of those Kinges and brothers.

I then knewe no more then what the late letters from Sir Anthony Sherley to the Emperor and Barvitius his Secretary did import[2], which I translated out of Italian by your Lordshipps comandement; but since, I have talked with a marchant, who had letters of advice from thence, dated in Zaffi, the fortenth of Maye last.

It is truly said that *nihil de rebus ipsis scit, qui rerum causas nescit;* and therefore, to relate the present debate of thes three barbarian or barbarous brothers, it shall not be amiss to reach a little backe to ther fathers death and to the beginning of this dissention betwixt them, which I fynd out of my notes, which I gatt of that busines att my being in Spayne.

The old Kinge died about three yeares since[3], and left behind him 3 sones, the eldest caled Mully Shecke, the second Mully Buffarez, and the third Mully Zedan: the 2 elder borne of slavish wemen, the yongest of one of his Queenes, yett (accordinge to the custome of that contrye) all alyke legittimate.

The eldest sone he disinherited for his unnaturalnes in taking armes against him, and, having vanquished him, comitted him prisoner to his second sone, and soe gave to his two yonger sones his three kingdomes. To Mully Buffarez he gave Marocco and Zus, and to Mully Zedan the kingdom of Fez.

Mulley Zedan, fynding himselfe agreaved that his brother, borne

1. L'auteur de la Relation, après avoir rappelé qu'il a quitté l'Espagne, il y a eu un an le jour de Noël, soit le 25 décembre 1605 [n. st. 4 janvier 1606], rapporte ensuite comme postérieurs des événements marocains survenus en 1606, tels que la mort de Moulay Abd el-Malek, qui eut lieu le 8 mai 1606. V. *infra*, p. 304 et note 4.

2. La traduction de la lettre de Sherley à l'Empereur n'a pas été retrouvée; celle de la lettre adressée à Barvitius est le Doc. XCIV. V. *supra*, p. 287.

3. A l'époque où le présent document fut rédigé, il y avait trois ans et demi que le « vieux roi », Moulay Ahmed *el-Mansour*, était mort. V. *supra*, p. 231 et note 1.

of a slavish woman, shold have 2 kingdomes and he but one, and knowinge that he was noe soldier nor man of corage, or for what other causes I knowe not, made warr upon his brother. He, fayintinge in his owne strength, durst not goe against him in person, but sent his brother that was his prisoner ; who, gladd of any conditions to undergoe any perills to be out prison and feare of secret murthering, tooke the warr upon him, having first sworne to his brother not to medle with the kingdome, in case he overcame, but to content himselfe with such recompence as he shold make him. He proceeds, overthrowes his brothers army, takes the kingdome of Fez from him, and drives him into the mounteynes, but retornes noe more to Morrocco, as he had sworne. Heer he is once againe Kinge of Fez, as he was in his fathers tyme, which he hoped to maintayne better against his 2 brothers then he had don against his father ; and soe he doth yett [1].

This Mulley Sheck, the eldest brother, being in possession, Mulley Buffarez of Marocco, the second, seekes to displace him, and prepares against him a strong army ; and heer ryseth the epitasis of all this busines.

Whilst thes 2 wer weakinnge on another, the weakest of the three getteth strength, and comes downe into the kingdome of Zus out from the mountaynes. Ther he joyned himselfe to one of the holly men [2] of that cuntrye, which the people doe adore as demigods, and call them saints. By the help of this man, he gat the love of the people, and in short tyme was by them proclaymed Kinge of Zus. Heer have the three brothers ech one a kingdome, if they can keep them.

Mully Buffarez of Marocco, seing himselfe soe hard besett by his 2 brothers on ech syde, of 2 evells tooke that most patiently which was after most remediable ; he suffred his yonger brother Mully Zedan to enjoy Zus as a tributary kingdome holden of Marrocco, and bent all his force against Mulley Sheck of Fez. The preparacion was soe great that it terrified him, in soe much that he

---

1. Sur les événements rapportés plus haut, V. *supra*, Doc. LXXXIV et LXXXVI, pp. 229 et 240.

2. Abou Mohammed sidi Abdallah ben Embarek, marabout d'Akka. Sur ce personnage, V. *infra*, p. 352 et note 2.

sought remedyes against all extremityes. He made frendshipp with the Turkes in Algire, Tunis and other places, and, if the worst shold fale, provided shipps reddy from Italy, wherof, for his mony, by the Jewes meanes in Livorne and Pisa, he had one good one of the Great Dukes[1] to imbarke himselfe, and his treasure and jewells, and soe to save himselfe in Christendome. The feare was worse then the harme, as it fell out afterwards; but in this state stood ther busines att my departure out of Spayne, att Christmas[2], was a twelmonth.

The springe followinge, the armyes mett. The King of Morocco his sone, leading that of his father, was vanquished, his army wholly defeated, and himselfe hardly escaping[3].

After all, the somer, the Kinge of Morrocco providing to reenforce himselfe, his sone dieth of the plague, which was gotten into his campe[4]. Heer was a stopp from armes for want of a generale.

In this tyme, a great man of authority with all the three brothers, especially with Buffarez and Zedan, caled alcaide Zus[5], seeketh to make a perfect accord betwixt the said 2 brothers Buffarez and Zedan, the one as yett but temporizinge with the other untill the third were brought to weaker termes. This alcaide persuads Buffarez of Morrocco that, he having nowe noe children, he cannot doe better then, for want of issue, to establish the kingdoms upon his brother Zedan. This matter hath ben long in treating. Nowe, by this last advise of the 14 May last, it is written that thes 2 are soe agreed as the alcaide propounded, and that they are nowe both joyned, and preparing ther forces against Mulley Sheck of Fez; and thes are the yrons that are ther nowe in the fyre[6].

---

1. Sur les relations de Moulay ech-Cheikh avec Ferdinand Ier de Médicis. V. supra, p. 288 et note 5.

2. Le 25 décembre 1605. C'est cette date qui a permis, par déduction, de fixer celle de la présente Relation. V. supra, p. 302, note 1.

3. D'après P. M. Coy (V. 1re Série, Pays-Bas, t. I, pp. 466 et 476), Moulay Abd el-Malek ne fut pas vaincu, mais, après s'être avancé jusqu'à Meknès, il fut forcé, par la révolte et la défection d'une partie de son armée, de rentrer à Merrakech, le 18 décembre 1605. V. supra, p. 288, note 1.

4. Moulay Abd el-Malek mourut de la peste, le 8 mai 1606. V. 1re Série, Pays-Bas, t. I, p. 146.

5. Le caïd Azzouz.

6. La paix entre Moulay Abou Farès et Moulay Zidân fut conclue en août 1604,

About the tyme that Sir Anthony Sherley came to Morrocco from the Emperor, the Kinge sent an Ambassador[1] to the Great Turke, who, though he favored Fez whilst he was weake, and untill he had sett both kingdomes in hot combustion, yett nowe 'tis thought he favour Marocco most, albeit the Kinge outwardly makes fayre wether with Sherly, the Emperors Ambassador, but doth but temporise, and, as is thought, when he sees his tyme, will geve him a figg[2].

Public Record Office. — *State Papers, Foreign, Barbary States, vol. XII.* — *Original.*

par l'intermédiaire du caïd Azzouz (V. *infra*, p. 352), mais de nouvelles négociations entre les deux frères eurent lieu vers le milieu de 1605 (V. *infra*, p. 354).

1. Sur cet ambassadeur, V. *supra*, p. 280 et note 2.

2. On voit que l'auteur de la Relation considère Anthony Sherley comme étant encore au Maroc. Or, Sherley était de retour à Lisbonne dans les premiers jours du mois de septembre 1606. V. *supra*, pp. 290 et 292. Les renseignements de l'auteur s'arrêtent au 14 mai 1606, comme il le dit lui-même. V. pp. 302 et 304.

CI

LETTRE DE HUGH LEE A SALISBURY

(EXTRAIT)

Moulay Abdallah, fils de Moulay ech-Cheikh, a vaincu Moulay Abou Farès, qui a été contraint de s'enfuir dans la montagne. — On dit que cette victoire est due surtout à un contingent de six cents Anglais. — Les vainqueurs n'étaient que cinq mille contre trente mille. — On espère, pour les marchands, que le pays sera maintenant plus tranquille.

Lisbonne, 4-5 février 1607.

Au dos, alia manu: 1607. Mʳ Hugh Lee, from Lisbonn.

Right Honorable, my very good Lord,

My humble dutie remembred, — may yt pleaze your good Lordship to be advertised hereby that my last to your Lorship was of the 23 December past.

. . . .

Lizborne, this 4 February 1607, where I rest
    Your Lordships in all humble dutye at comand,

Signé: Hugh Lee.

Post-scriptum: Kept till the 5, and this day departid to sea 3 great carreks for the East Indies.

. . . .

Here ys late newes out of Barbery, that the Kinge of Fesse hath gotten the victory of the King of Marrocus, and forced hym to flye¹; the old King of Fesse hymselfe in person not being in the battayle, but sent his sonne² of 24 yeres of age as generall, hymselffe being very sycke. The report goeth of 600 Englishmen, such as were rovers uppon the coast, dyd one the part of the King of Fesse great service, and by whom cheifly he obtayned the victory, though the oddes was very unequall against hym. This King ys repported to have but 5 thousand souldyars, besydes the ayde of the English; and the other was 30 thousand stronge; and yet he and his forces forced to flye into the mountains.

Whereby there ys nowe hoaped a more setled quietnes to followe in thos countries, for the trade of merchandizes; which God graunt! For this hath ben a very hard tyme, by reason of much shipp-wrak; as within this 6 weekes space, in these partes, hath ben lost eleven English shipps, besides on in Byskaye.

Public Record Office. — *State Papers, Foreign, Portugal, vol. III.* — *Original.*

1. Sur cette bataille, livrée à Mers er-Remâd, à 3 ou 4 lieues à l'est de Merrakech, le 8 décembre 1606, et sur les Européens enrôlés dans l'armée de Moulay Abdallah, V. *infra*, p. 362 et note 1.

2. Moulay Abdallah, fils de Moulay ech-Cheikh. Sur ce prince. V. *1re Série*, Angleterre, t. I, p. 256, Pl. III, Tableau généalogique des princes de la dynastie saadienne, n° 31.

CII

LETTRE DE R. COCKS A [THOMAS WILSON][1]

(Extrait)

Un pirate anglais ayant capturé un navire de Bayonne et l'ayant conduit au Maroc pour y vendre l'équipage, Moulay ech-Cheikh s'est emparé de tous, Anglais et Français, et les a enrôlés dans son armée, leur promettant une bonne récompense, s'il remportait la victoire sur son frère. — Les Français, après la victoire, ont été relâchés par les soins de l'agent de France au Maroc. — Le fils d'un avocat de Bayonne, M. de Moisset, a écrit à son père tous les détails de cette affaire.

Bayonne, 31 mars 1607

Au dos, alia manu: Cox. — 31 March 1607.

Sir,

Som 3 dais past I wrot yow of the recept of your paket dated in London, the 5th ultimo.

. . . .

Ther was an other shipp of this place taken by an English pirat, and carid into Barbary, men and all, wheare they thought to have sould them for slaves; but by meanes of these trowbls amongst the brothers, which is happened by the death of the King of Morocus, on of the brothers ceazed upon all these people, both English and French, and took them to serve hym in the warres, promising them good recompence, yf he obtayned the battell against his brother.

---

[1]. Le destinataire n'est pas indiqué; mais les autres lettres de R. Cocks sont adressées : « To the most worshipfull Thomas Wilson, at my Lord of Salisbury's. »

Which cominge to effect[1], they demanded ther liberty (I meane the Frenchmen); which, by meanes of the French agent in those partes, they obtayned. And on Monsieur de Moisets sonne[2], an advocat in this place, hath writ his father of the whole cercomstance of this matter, when they of these partes thought the shipp and all had byn cast away long tyme past.

I have byn somthinge lardge in this matter, because I would geve yow well to understand of the continewall abuses which are daily offered by these mercyles English pyrats; for ther is noe mercy yf they meete with an Englishman, and very littell yf they meete with a stranger.

. . . .

For other matters, I comyt me to my former, and soe take my leave, restinge
    Yours most ashewred at comand,
          Signé : R. Cocks.

Bayon, the 31th Marche 1607.

Public Record Office. — State Papers, Foreign, Spain, vol. XIII. — Original.

1. La bataille de Mers er-Remåd (8 décembre 1606). V. *supra*, p. 307 et note 1. P. M. Coy mentionne en effet la présence à cette bataille de onze Français capturés par les Anglais. V. *1re Série*, Pays-Bas, t. I, p. 210.

1. Ce personnage est recommandé dans une lettre de Henri IV à Arnoult de Lisle, agent de France au Maroc. V. *1re Série*, France, t. II, p. 367.

CIII

LETTRE DE HUGH LEE A SALISBURY

(Extrait)

Le fils de Moulay Mohammed el-Mesloukh a quitté la cour d'Espagne et se tient près de Lisbonne. — Cela donnerait à penser que les préparatifs qui se font actuellement ont pour objet une descente au Maroc.

Lisbonne, 12-13 juillet 1607.

Au dos, alia manu: 13 July 1607. — Mr Lee to my Lord, from Lisbonne.

Right Honorable, my very good Lord,

My humble dutie remembred, — May yt pleaze your good Lordship to be advertised that my last to your Lordship was the 25 of June.

. . . .

I most humbly take my leave, remayning
    Your Lordships in all humble dutie at comand,
            Signé : Hugh Lee.
Lixboa, the 12 July 1607.

Post-Scriptum : Sence the fynishing of the former part hereof, here ys newes come out of the Straights.

. . . .

Further yt ys secretly reported that the Black King[1] of Barbery his sonne[2], which hath benn long in the courte of Spayne, ys secretly

1. Moulay Mohammed *el-Mesloukh*, qui était mulâtre. V. *1re Série*, Angleterre, t. I, p. 202 et note 1.
2. Moulay ech-Cheikh. A la mort de son

come from the Courte, and kepeth hymselfe closse in the cuntrey, some small distance from this cytty; which should ymport thes forces nowe in preparing here and in Spayne to be pretended for Barbery. The tyme will further declare; and, as I cane further understand, according to my duty, I will, God willing, advertise your Lordship thereof. Hoping your Lordship will pardon thes peeced woorkes comyng to my knowledg after the closing hereof, and even uppon the departure of this bringer, as knoweth the Allmighty, who preserve your Lordship to your harts desyre.

Kept till the 13 July 1607, in Lixboa, where I rest
 Your Lordships in all humble dutie at comand,

      Signé : Hugh Lee.

Public Record Office. — *State Papers, Foreign, Portugal, vol. III.* — *Original.*

père, qui périt, noyé dans l'oued Loukkos, à la bataille d'El-Ksar (4 août 1578), il s'était retiré en Espagne, où il se convertit au christianisme en 1593 et prit le nom de D. Felipe de Africa. V. *supra,* Doc. LIV, p. 156 et note 1.

CIV

LETTRE DE HUGH LEE A THOMAS WILSON

(Extrait)

Moulay Zidân aurait fait sauter la ville de Merrakech, qui est détruite. — Il reste maître du pays, mais Moulay Abdallah lève des troupes contre lui. — Le capitaine Giffard a été tué dans une précédente bataille.

Lisbonne, 20 avril 1608.

Au dos : To the worshippfull my very good frind Thomas Wilson, Esquire, geve these att Salisburye House, in the Strand, at London. By a frind, who God preserve. — *Alia manu :* Mr Lee from Lysbone. ...[1] April 1608.

Mr Thomas Wilson. — Laus Deo. — Anno 1608, the 20 Aprill, in Lixboa, new stile.

Worshipfull,

In my last, bearing date the 23 November last, I signifyed unto yow the occurants of that season.

. . . .

The newes of Barbery ys that Marrocus ys distroyed by poulder that was within ytselffe, by the practize of Mully Sedan[2], who remayneth King thereof[3]; though yt ys thought he shall not longe

---

1. Le manuscrit est déchiré à l'endroit où se trouve cette date.
2. Cette nouvelle était erronée.
3. Le 23 mars 1608, Moulay Zidân avait vaincu un nouveau prétendant, Moulay Ahmed ben Abou Hassoûn, qui venait de s'emparer de Merrakech. V. *infra*. p. 379 et note 3.

hold yt, for that Mully Abdala ys raysinge of a power against hym. Capitaine Gyfford[1] was slayne in a former conflict; the cuntrey at present in great trobelles.

. . . .

And thus, craving pardon for my overbouldnesse herein, leave yow to the protection of the Allmighty, who graunt unto yow both health and happines. I rest
        Your Worshipps at comand,
                Signé : Hugh Lee.

In hast, unperused.

Public Record Office. — *State Papers, Foreign, Portugal, vol. III.* — Original.

1. Sur le capitaine John Giffard et les autres Anglais enrôlés dans l'armée de Moulay Zidân, V. *infra*, pp. 372-375. Il fut tué à la bataille de Ras el-Aïn, 6 décembre 1607, à la suite de laquelle Moulay Abdallah s'empara de Merrakech.

CV

LETTRE DE HUGH LEE A THOMAS WILSON

(Extrait)

La flotte espagnole, commandée par Don Luis Fajardo, est destinée à la prise de Larache. — Moulay Zidân aurait promis de livrer cette place, à la condition d'être lui-même secouru contre ses concurrents. — Mais les gens qui connaissent les Maures prétendent qu'au dernier moment ils se mettront d'accord contre les Chrétiens. — Don Luis Fajardo aurait l'intention de capturer tous les navires de commerce sur la côte du Maroc.

Lisbonne, 4 septembre 1608.

Au dos, alia manu : Lettre. — Lisbon, 4 September 1608.

Worshippfull Sir,

Wisshing yow health with much happines, — My last unto yow was of the 18 of the last, by the conveyance of M⁺ Arthur Jackson ; wherein I was somwhat tedyous, hoaping yow will beare with my infirmity therein. And sence which, here ys small allteration but that the generall report, as well from Sevyll as in this citty, ys that Don Luis Fashardo[1], with the armada, ys to joyne with the gallyes of Italye for the takinge of Alarach in Barbery[2]. I recevid letters,

---

1. D. Luis Fajardo, capitaine général de la flotte et de l'armée de la mer Océane, mort en 1617. Ce ne fut pas lui qui commanda l'expédition contre Larache en septembre 1608. V. *infra*, p. 316 et note 2.

2. Dans une lettre du 18 août 1608, Hugh Lee annonçait déjà le but de l'expédition qui se préparait : « Navires et galères transportent un grand nombre de soldats et d'armes ; ils doivent se rendre à la côte du Maroc, ou, pour mieux dire, à Laracho, sur quelque espérance que l'on a de trouver de l'aide dans le pays, selon de grandes promesses qui ont été faites. »

4 dayes past, from Sevill, whereby I understand that those gallyes weare at Cartagena and are dayly expectid in Spayne. The report ys further that Mully Sedan[1], one of the Kinges in Barbery, hath promised to be the meanes for the delyvery of Alarach into the possession of the Spanyards, with condicion hymselffe to be ayded against the other Kinges in Barbery by the Spaniarde. But the opinions of the best acquainted with the natures of those people ys that, when they shall perceyve that the Christians shalbe ready to enter the towne, they will suddenly growe to ane accorde within theymselves, and joine togeather against the Christians. What will sucede thereof, tyme will manyfeste; and as I shall understand further, you shall have notice thereof[2].

I here also that Don Luis Fashardo with his sonne Don John, who ys his Vizeadmyrall, have in purpose to make good prize of all such shipps and goodes as they shall finde tradinge uppon the coaste of Barbary, of what nation soever being; warranted thereunto by the edicte lately published, which I have heretofore sent unto his Lordship.

. . . .

I leave yow to the protection of the Allmighty, and remayne
Your Worshipps ever at comaund,

Signé : Hugh Lee.

Lixboa, the 4 September 1608, newe stile.

Public Record Office. — State Papers, Foreign, Portugal, vol. III. — Original.

St. Pap., For., Portugal, vol. III. — Philippe II avait déjà négocié, de 1578 à 1585, avec Moulay Ahmed *el-Mansour* pour obtenir la cession de Larache. V. *1re Série*, France, t. II, pp. 30-123, *passim*, et Espagne aux dates ci-dessus. Les négociations avaient été reprises, en 1605 et 1606, avec Moulay ech-Cheikh, par l'intermédiaire d'un Génois, Gianettino Mortara. V. *infra*, pp. 381-383.

1. C'est Moulay ech-Cheikh, et non Moulay Zidân, qui négociait alors la cession de Larache. V. la note précédente.

2. Sur les préparatifs de l'expédition de Larache, V. *1re Série*, France, t. II, pp. 435-440.

CVI

LETTRE DE CHARLES CORNWALLIS A THOMAS EDMONDES[1]

(Extrait)

Les Espagnols, arrivés devant Larache, ont été reçus à coups de canon par les Maures et sont repartis sans rien tenter.

Madrid, 17 [n. st. 27] septembre 1608.

Au dos, alia manu: 17 of September 1608. — From Sir Charles Cornwallis.

My verie good Lord,

By your last of the 21th of August, I perceyve that thinges walke on there in a more uncertaine pathe then ever, and therein I finde myselfe nothinge at all deceyved in the opinion I have allwayes held of them.

. . . .

I doubte not but before this your Lordship hath hearde that our great disseigne by sea, which hath made soe great a noise in the world, hath ended onlie with makinge an approache and takinge a veiwe of Allerache[2]. Comminge thether they founde the sea soe distempered, and the Moores soe furious, as, havinge shott of a cannon of peace, they founde themselves immeditelie aunswered with three of warre; whereuppon, thinkinge not good to approache

---

[1]. Sir Thomas Edmondes (1563?-1639), ambassadeur à Bruxelles (1604-1609), puis à Paris (1610-1617 et 1629).

[2]. C'est le 6 septembre 1608 que la flotte espagnole, commandée par Alvaro de Bazan, marquis de Santa-Cruz, arriva en vue de Larache. V. *1re Série*, France, t. II, pp. 441-442; Espagne, à la date du 18 septembre 1608 et; *infra*, p. 383 et note 1.

nearer, they turned themselves homewarde, and weare (as I heare) by a Moore, who stoode uppon a watche-tower, brandishinge his sworde, saluted for a farewell with the basest of his backeside.

. . . .

And soe, my good Lord, for this time, I leave your Lordship and all yours with noe worse wishes then to myselfe.

Madrid, this 17th of September 1608, *stilo Angliæ*.

Your Lordships assured lovinge freind to doe you service,

Signé : Charles Cornwaleys.

British Museum. — Stowe Mss., 170, f. 165. — Original.[1]

1. Ce ms. fait partie de la correspondance de Sir Tho. Edmondes, douze vol. in-f°.

LA RELATION DE RO. C.

NOTE BIBLIOGRAPHIQUE.

La Relation intitulée : *A True Historicall Discourse of Muley Hamets Rising...* pose un problème bibliographique ; si, en effet, elle n'est pas tout à fait anonyme, son auteur ne s'y révèle que par les initiales Ro. C., placées à la fin d'une épître dédicatoire[1] adressée à Sir Robert Cottington of Cunnington. Avant de formuler une hypothèse plausible sur l'identification du personnage, il paraît rationnel de commencer par la description matérielle de l'édition de son œuvre et par une analyse de son contenu.

La Relation, que nous appelons, pour plus de commodité, Relation de Ro. C. ou Relation de 1609, est constituée par une plaquette de 74 pages in-4°, non numérotées ; ses dimensions sont de 12×17 cm. ; elle a été imprimée en 1609 à Londres sous les presses de Thomas Purfoot, pour le libraire Clement Knight[2]. Le titre fait connaître les divisions principales de l'ouvrage :

1° Règne de Moulay Ahmed *el-Mansour*.
2° Guerres civiles entre ses enfants.
3° Religion et Gouvernement.
4° Aventures d'Anthony Sherley.

La dédicace, sur laquelle nous aurons à revenir, est brève et conçue dans des termes empreints d'amitié plutôt que de condescendance ; on n'y remarque pas la déférence obséquieuse qui caractérise le plus souvent ces hommages littéraires.

La Relation qui vient ensuite est divisée en chapitres. Le premier est consacré aux origines de la dynastie saadienne ; le second retrace le grand règne de Moulay Ahmed *el-Mansour* ; les chapitres III à XVII sont la partie principale de la Relation ; ils embrassent l'histoire des cinq années de troubles qui suivirent la mort d'El-Mansour. Le chapitre XI tout entier et une partie importante du chapitre XVII contiennent le récit des aventures d'Anthony Sherley au Maroc. Les dix autres chapitres traitent de la religion et du gouvernement ; l'auteur n'a pas jugé utile de les numéroter[3].

---

1. V. cette épître dédicatoire, *infra*, p. 322.
2. V. ci-contre, Pl. V, un fac-similé du titre de cette relation.
3. L'érudit Purchas, dans *His Pilgrims*, t. II, 1625, in-fol., pp. 851-873, a publié

A
True Historicall

discourse of *Muley Hamets* rising to the three Kingdomes of *Moruecos, Fes,* and *Sus.*

The dis-vnion of the three Kingdomes, by ciuill warre, kindled amongst his three ambitious Sonnes, *Muley Sheck, Muley Boseres,* and *Muley Sidan.*

The *Religion* and *Policie* of the *More,* or *Barbarian.*

The aduentures of Sir *Anthony Sherley,* and diuer other English Gentlemen, in those Countries.

With other Nouelties.

AT LONDON,

Printed by Thomas Purfoot for *Clement Knight,* and are to be sold at his shop in *Paules* Churchyard, at the Signe of the Holie Lambe.
An. Dom. 1609.

FAC-SIMILE
DU TITRE DE LA RELATION DE RO. C.

La partie historique, à l'exception du chapitre I sur les origines de la dynastie saadienne, est très exacte. On peut s'en convaincre, en la rapprochant de la correspondance si précieuse de P. Maertensz. Coy, agent des Pays-Bas au Maroc, où il résida de 1605 à 1609[1]. Les deux sources se complètent l'une par l'autre et font de cette époque l'une des mieux connues du Maroc.

Mais si P. Maertensz. Coy, qui suivait parfois dans leurs déplacements les mahalla chérifiennes, a été un témoin oculaire des événements qu'il raconte, il n'en est pas de même de l'auteur de la Relation de 1609. La lecture attentive de son œuvre nous fait reconnaître qu'il n'a pas résidé lui-même au Maroc : il n'écrit pas *de visu* mais *de auditu*, se bornant à coordonner des lettres et des documents qui provenaient d'agents anglais ayant une longue pratique du pays. Il ne cherche pas, d'ailleurs, à s'en faire accroire et il indique lui-même, à plusieurs reprises, qu'il écrit d'après un informateur qu'il appelle « my author »[2] ou bien « our own countryman »[3]. Il arrête son récit à la date de juin 1608, parce que, dit-il, « écrire sans renseignements, c'est voyager à l'aventure »[4].

Quel a été l'écrivain qualifié, à qui l'on a confié des lettres et des documents, ayant parfois un caractère officiel, pour en tirer la Relation semi-anonyme qui nous occupe ? Une comparaison attentive avec la Relation de George Wilkins[5] autorise à penser que celui-ci fut l'homme choisi pour cette mise en œuvre.

George Wilkins, littérateur de second plan, quoique ayant collaboré avec Shakespeare[6], était obligé, de par sa situation précaire, de vivre de sa plume. Or, il s'intéressait au Maroc, comme le prouvent la Relation qu'il écrivit en 1604, *Three Miseries of Barbary*[7] et celle de 1607, *Historicall Narration of the Civill Warrs*, que nous lui avons attribuée[8]. Il avait, en outre, des rapports avec les membres de la *Barbary Company*[9] et connaissait particulièrement Arnold

---

la Relation de Ro. C. sous le titre : *Collections of Things most Remarkable in the History of Barbarie, written by Ro, C*. Ce récit forme le chapitre II du livre VI. La division de la Relation en chapitres n'a pas été conservée ; Purchas l'a divisée en cinq paragraphes. Dans le premier, il a inséré (pp. 852-853) la lettre de Thomas Bernhere à Edward Wright du 24 juin [n. st. 4 juillet] 1600, qui a été publiée dans le présent volume à sa date. V. *supra*, p. 170 et note 1. Cf. *infra*, p. 327 et note 2. L'ouvrage qu'indique PLAYFAIR dans sa bibliographie (n° 148, p. 247), à la date de 1617, n'est autre que le premier paragraphe de la réédition de PURCHAS, auquel il a conservé son titre. Il est à noter que la date de 1617 est inexacte, car la Relation de Ro. C., rééditée par Purchas, se trouve dans le t. II de *His Pilgrims*, paru seulement en 1625.

1. V. les dépêches de l'agent P. Maertensz. Coy à leur différente date, dans 1re Série, Pays-Bas, t. I.
2. V. *infra*, pp. 382, 387 et 406.
3. V. *infra*, p. 408.
4. V. *infra*, p. 384 : « To write without advice is to saile at random. »
5. Sur George Wilkins, V. *supra*, p. 248, note 1.
6. DELIUS, *Shakespeare Jahrbuch*, 1867.
7. V. *supra*, Doc. XC, p. 248.
8. V. *supra*, Doc. C, p. 301 et note 1.
9. George Wilkins leur a dédié sa Rela-

Tomson[1], marchand anglais à Merrakech, l'un des frères de George Tomson[2], le correspondant de Robert Cecil. A ces titres, George Wilkins était tout désigné pour composer, avec des matériaux qu'on lui remettrait, le récit de cette période troublée de l'histoire du Maroc.

Si, maintenant, l'on compare, en tenant compte de la différence de genre et de sujet, la Relation de 1609 avec celle de 1604, on est frappé des caractères communs qu'elles présentent toutes deux, tant pour la composition que pour le style : mêmes traits humoristiques, mêmes citations latines[3], identité absolue d'un certain passage[4].

Il est donc vraisemblable que George Wilkins a été le *rédacteur* de la Relation de 1609. Mais, à côté, ou plutôt au-dessus de ce rédacteur, il y a eu celui qui a été l'animateur et l'inspirateur de l'œuvre, mais qui, ne se reconnaissant pas néanmoins la qualité d'auteur, n'aura voulu la signer que des initiales de son nom : Ro. C. Cet homme paraît être Robert Cecil, comte de Salisbury, secrétaire d'État de Jacques Ier.

Robert Cecil suivait attentivement les affaires du Maroc, non seulement au point de vue de la politique anglaise, mais encore à raison de ses intérêts privés. On le voit, en 1597-1598, envoyant au Maroc un navire lui appartenant, le « True Love », pour faire à la fois le commerce et la course[5]. George Tomson, son correspondant, lui écrivait régulièrement, le renseignant sur tous les événements du Maroc[6]. Ces lettres sont vraisemblablement la principale source utilisée pour la rédaction de la Relation de 1609 et George Tomson doit être celui que Ro. C., au cours de son récit, appelle « my author ».

Enfin, on peut ajouter à ces arguments une preuve tirée de l'épître dédicatoire placée en tête de la Relation de 1609. Elle est adressée, comme on l'a vu, à Sir Robert Cottington, et elle implique par ses termes l'existence d'un commerce amical entre celui-ci et l'auteur. Or nous voyons, en 1605, Robert Cecil

---

tion de 1604. V. l'épître dédicatoire, *supra*, p. 250.

1. V. *supra*, pp. 252-253.

2. Sur George Tomson et sa famille, dont plusieurs membres séjournèrent au Maroc, V. *supra*, p. 65, p. 101 et note 2, pp. 140-141.

3. Le vers d'Horace : « Quicquid delirant reges, plectuntur Achivi » est cité dans les deux Relations de 1604 et de 1609. V. *supra*, p. 258 et note 1, et *infra*, p. 370

4. Le passage relatif au caïd Azzouz. V. *supra*, pp. 251-252; *infra*, p. 380 et n. 2.

5. V. *supra*, Doc. XXXVI, XXXVII et XLII, pp. 112, 115 et 124.

6. V. *supra*, les lettres de George Tomson à Robert Cecil des 19 août 1598, 31 août et 6 octobre 1600, 9 novembre 1603, pp. 128, 173, 186 et 224 ; la lettre de Jasper Tomson à Richard Tomson du 4 juillet 1599, et la note de George Tomson à ce dernier du 1er juillet 1600, pp. 142 et 164. Ces deux derniers écrits devaient être communiqués à Robert Cecil, comme cela est dit explicitement. Il est à remarquer que l'on ne trouve plus de lettres ni de notes émanant des Tomson après 1603, quoiqu'il soit vraisemblable que leur correspondance se soit prolongée au delà de cette date. Ces documents, après avoir été utilisés dans la Relation de 1609, n'auront sans doute pas été conservés.

recommander le jeune Francis Cottington à Charles Cornwallis, qui l'emmène comme secrétaire, pendant son ambassade à Madrid [1].

Les bibliographes ne semblent pas avoir cherché jusqu'ici à identifier l'auteur de la Relation de 1609. Anthony Wood [2] attribue à Anthony Sherley un ouvrage intitulé : *Account of M. Hamet's Rising in the Kingdom of Morocco, Fez*, etc., Londres, 1609, in-4°, ouvrage qui est, sans aucun doute, la Relation qui nous occupe. Cette indication bibliographique erronée est reproduite par Niceron, qui se contente de traduire inexactement le titre [3]. Enfin, Lambert Playfair [4] donne, comme auteur de la Relation, Sir Robert Cottington, qui se serait ainsi dédié l'ouvrage à lui-même.

1. V. *infra*, p. 423, note 1. Cf. l'article du *Dictionary of National Biography*.
2. Anthony Wood, *Athenæ Oxonienses*, t. I, p. 551.
3. Niceron, *Mémoires*, t. XXIII, p. 113. Ce bibliographe a sans doute lu *Riding* au lieu de *Rising*, car il donne à la plaquette le titre suivant : Sherley Anthony, *Voyage de M. Hamet dans le royaume de Maroc, Fez, etc.* (en anglais). Londres, 1609, in-4°.
4. Playfair, *A Bibliography of Morocco*, n° 124, p. 244.

CVII

RELATION DE RO. C[1]

Londres, 1609.

Titre[2]: A true historicall discourse of Muley Hamets rising to the three kingdomes of Moruecos, Fes and Sus. — The disunion of the three kingdomes by civil warre kindled amongst his three ambitious sonnes, Muley Sheck, Muley Bo Feres and Muley Sidan. — The religion and policie of the More or Barbarian. — The adventures of Sir Anthony Sherley, and divers other Englishe gentlemen in those countries, with other novelties.

Dédicace: To the right worshipful Sir Robert Cottington of Cunnington, Knight.

Sir, I entreate you, patronize this smal treatise, if in your judgment it can either pleasure, or in small measure profite, by being divulged to the open view of the world. If otherwise, lay it by you as a bundle of waste paper. In so doing, I shal thinke myselfe much obliged unto you, if, in suppressing the originall, my weakenesse may rather take a private checke of a friend for being too bolde, then an open scorne of a multitude for being too foolish. Thus relying wholy upon your wonted favour, discreete and judiciall censure herein, I rest ever

At your service.

Ro. C.

---

1. La présente relation, généralement très exacte, contient de nombreuses erreurs pour les débuts de la dynastie saadienne (chap. 1). Ces erreurs, que l'analyse ne pouvait pas ne pas reproduire, seront signalées en note.

2. V. *supra*, p. 318, Pl. V, un fac-similé de ce titre.

Titre de départ : The true historicall discourse of Muley Hamets rising to the three kingdomes of Moruccos, Fes and Sus.

Cap. I.

How the Kingdome of Barbary came to Muley Hamet Xarif, the late deceased King.

Moulay Ahmed, venant du Draâ avec de nombreux Berbères, enlève Merrakech et Fez au sultan mérinide et s'empare de tout le plat pays depuis l'Atlas jusqu'au détroit de Gibraltar. — Il tenait à attribuer ses succès à son origine chérifienne. — Ayant appelé des troupes turques à son aide pour réprimer une révolte du Sous, il est massacré par elles à son entrée dans ce pays. — Ces troupes, après avoir pillé le Sous, sont anéanties par les indigènes en traversant les montagnes pour regagner Tlemcen. — Moulay Abdallah, frère et successeur de Moulay Ahmed, est en guerre constante avec les Mérinides. — Son fils aîné, Moulay Abdallah el-Ghalib, devenu roi, fait périr tous ses frères, à l'exception de Moulay Abd el-Malek, qui s'enfuit en Turquie, et de Moulay Ahmed, qui est épargné. — Il laisse trois fils, Moulay Mohammed el-Mesloukh, qui lui succède, Moulay ech-Cheikh et Moulay en-Nasser, qui se réfugient par la suite en Espagne. — Moulay en-Nasser, ayant plus tard envahi le royaume de Fez, sous le règne de Moulay Ahmed el-Mansour, est vaincu et tué. — Moulay Abd el-Malek, à la tête de quatre mille soldats turcs, détrône son neveu Moulay Mohammed el-Mesloukh. — Celui-ci va demander secours au roi de Portugal. — D. Sébastien débarque au Maroc avec trente mille hommes : il est défait et meurt dans la bataille, ainsi que Moulay Mohammed el-Mesloukh et Moulay Abd el-Malek. — Un fils de ce dernier vit encore en Turquie. — Avènement de Moulay Ahmed el-Mansour.

The familie of the Marcines[1], beeing Larbies[2], were long times Kings of Barbary, untill a plaine Haly[3], some hundred yeres agoe[4],

---

1. *Marcines,* les Mérinides.
2. On lit en marge : « Any one which is not of the tribe of Mahemet is so tearmed. » Cette définition est inexacte : le mot « Larbies » (Arabes) s'oppose avec plus ou moins de précision au mot « Brebers » (Berbères). En réalité, la dynastie des Mérinides était d'origine berbère.
3. *Haly,* pour *ouali* ولي, saint, marabout.
4. La date est sensiblement exacte. Ce fut en 1513 que les chérifs saadiens commencèrent la guerre sainte dans le Sous et dans le royaume de Merrakech.

calling himselfe Muley Hamet Xarif[1], came out of the countrey of Dara[2], lying beyond the mountains of Atlas, with a great number of montaniers called in their owne language Brebers. These, with their strength, got Moruecos from the Mareins, and going forwarde, following the fertilnes of the soyle, drave the Mareins out of Fes, getting into his power all the flat countries comprised under the titles of Sus, Moruecos and Fes, from the hilles of Atlas to the straits of Gybraltar. Being thus growne great, he would prove himselfe a Xarif, one of the kindred of the Prophet Mahomet, desiring his birth might be held answerable to his new acquired fortunes. But within a little time after this his sodaine invasion, Sus rebelling refused his governement; wherefore he sent to the bordering Turkes for ayde[3], who fulfilled therein his request.

Aided with these Turkish auxiliary forces, he set forward, and, at his enterance into that kingdome, the Turkish souldiers through treason killed him, and cut of his head[4], sacked Taradant, and running over the whole countrey, spoyled it by the space of twoo moneths. Which done, they would gladly have returned to Trimasine. Yet fearing their owne strength to return the same way Hamet had brought them, it was helde their better course and shorter journey to passe over the mountaines; but the montaniers knowing this their new done bloody sack, and seeing them have good store of pillage, set upon them, so that few or none escaped their handes, but were all slaine.

After this Hamet Xarifs death, who raigned some eight yeares[5],

---

1. Le véritable fondateur de la dynastie saadienne, celui qui établit sa domination sur le Maroc tout entier, fut Moulay Mohammed ech-Cheikh. Son frère aîné Moulay Ahmed el-Aaredj, qui n'avait régné qu'à Merrakech, fut déposé en 1544. V. 1ʳᵉ Série, Angleterre, t. I, p. 256, Pl. III, Tableau généalogique, nᵒˢ 3 et 4.

2. On lit en marge : « or Drawe ».

3. Le Chérif Moulay Mohammed ech-Cheikh ne fit pas appel aux Turcs, dont il fut toujours l'ennemi juré, mais il accueillit et incorpora dans sa garde quelques janissaires d'Alger, qui se donnèrent comme des déserteurs et qui avaient reçu mission de Hassan ben Kheïr ed-Din de l'assassiner.

4. Sur l'assassinat de Moulay Mohammed ech-Cheikh par sa garde turque, V. El-Oufrâni, pp. 78-80; Marmol, II, 40.

5. En prenant comme point de départ du règne de Moulay Mohammed ech-Cheikh, la date de son entrée définitive à Fez (janvier 1549), l'évaluation de l'auteur est exacte, puisque ce Chérif mourut le 23 octobre 1557. Mais, en réalité, Moulay Mohammed ech-Cheikh régna depuis 1544, date de la déposition de son frère aîné Moulay Ahmed el-Aaredj.

succeeded his brother Muley Abdela¹, having all his lifetime great warre with the Mareins, to keepe that his brother had conquered. Hee, having raigned some fifteene yeares, died, leaving behind him thirteene sonnes, the eldest Muley Abdela², who, at his entrance to the kingdome, commaunded all his brethren to bee killed; but the second brother, Abd el-Melech, fearing hard measure, fled presently upon the death of his father into Turkie, and so saved his life. The third brother, Muley Hamet, of whome we are hereafter to entreate, beeing held a great churchman, simple and humble spirited, not any way addicted unto armes, was spared alive as lesse feared. The other ten were all put to death in one day at Taradant, in Sus, where they were kept in their fathers lifetime. This Abdela raigned fortie yeares³, and dying, left behind him three sonnes, Muley Mehamet, Muley Sheck, Muley Nassar⁴. Muley Mehamet beeing King, his twoo yonger brethren ranne away into Spaine⁵; the elder whereof named Muley Sheck is yet living, and there turned Christian⁶.

The yonger brother, called Muley Nassar, returned into Barbary in the fourteenth yeare of Muley Hamets raign⁷, who died last. At this Muley Nassars landing in the country of Fes, much people favoured him and his title; two thousand of Muley Shecks souldiers, who now liveth and then governed Fes for his father⁸, revolted from him to Nassar, insomuch as Muley Sheck was in mind to

---

1. Le règne de ce chérif est purement imaginaire. Ce fut Moulay Abdallah el-Ghalib, dont il est parlé ci-après, fils de Moulay Mohammed ech-Cheikh, qui succéda directement à son père.
2. Moulay Abdallah el-Ghalib. Sur le massacre de ses frères, cf. supra, p. 251.
3. Moulay Abdallah el-Ghalib régna de 1557 à 1574.
4. L'auteur commet une erreur. Moulay Abdallah el-Ghalib n'eut que deux fils : Moulay Mohammed el-Mesloukh et Moulay en-Nasser. Moulay ech-Cheikh était fils de Moulay Mohammed el-Mesloukh. Sur tous les princes cités ici, V. 1re Série, Angleterre, t. I, p. 256, Pl. III, Tableau généalogique des princes de la dynastie saadienne.

5. Ce n'est pas sous le règne de Moulay Mohammed el-Mesloukh, mais après la défaite de l'armée portugaise à El-Ksar el-Kebir, que ces deux chérifs se réfugièrent en Espagne. Moulay en-Nasser avait passé dans le camp de D. Sébastien la veille de la bataille.
6. Sur la conversion de ce Moulay ech-Cheikh, qui prit le nom de D. Felipe de Africa, V. supra, p. 310 et note 2.
7. Sur l'incursion de Moulay en-Nasser, dans le royaume de Fez, en 1595-1596, V. supra, p. 90 et note 4.
8. On sait que Moulay ech-Cheikh, fils aîné de Moulay Ahmed el-Mansour, avait été institué vice-roi de Fez du vivant de ce dernier, en 1579. V. supra, p. 118 et note 2.

have fled unto his father, but that alkeyd Hamet ben Jau[1], being a very wise captaine, and there placed to helpe Muley Sheck by his councell, who was very yong, kept him from running away and Muley Nassar with a dilatory warre; with whome, if the souldiers had staied, he might peradventure have gotten the country. But their Lent approaching, the souldiers tolde Nassar they would go keepe their Easter at their owne houses. Wherupon Nassar, thinking, if they were once gone, they would never returne to him againe, would give present battaile; and so was this Nassar slaine.

Abd el-Melech, being second brother to Abdela, got such favor in Turkie where he lived, as entering Barbary with foure thousand Turkish souldiers, he got the kingdome from his nephew, Mehamet, the eldest son of Abdela[2], and their raigned yeares. Muley Mehamet, thus deprived of his kingdome, fledde for succour to Sebastian, then King of Portugale, who came in person into Barbarie to helpe him with thirtie thousand men. Giving battaile, the Mores fled, and the Christians retired, hoping the Mores would returne, that so the Christians might make the greater slaughter of them. According to this expectation, Abd el-Melech with his armie returned, and the Christians charged the formost of their horsemen very hotly, who would have fledde. But such was the aboundance of Abd el-Melechs horsemen, following the foreward which were discomfited, as they could not have fieldroome to flie, but were forced to fight it out[3]. This was a bloody battaile, wherein three Kings lost their lives, Don Sebastian, King of Portugale, Muley Mehamet, unto whose ayde Sebastian came over, and Abd el-Melech, who came out of Turkie, being second brother to Abdela. This Abd el-Melech left behind him a sonne yet living at this day in Turkie, whose name is Muley Smime[4].

After the death of these twoo, Abdelas third brother, Muley

---

1. Ce caïd est nommé Hamou Bijau dans la Relation de Pierre Treillault (V. *I*re *Série*, France, t. II, p. 209 et note 1, et pp. 224-225), Hamu Beja dans une Relation espagnole du 5 juin 1596 (V. *ibidem*, Espagne) et Hamu Beya par GUADALAJARA f° 86 v°.

2. Sur l'avènement de Moulay Abd el-Malek et le concours que lui prêtèrent les Turcs, V. *supra*, p. 49 et notes 3 et 4.

3. Sur cette bataille d'El-Ksar el-Kebir (4 août 1578), V. *I*re *Série*, France, t. I, pp. 375-697, et Angleterre, t. I, pp. 312-321 et 329-338.

4. Moulay Ismaïl. V. *supra*, p. 27 et note 3, p. 49 et note 4.

Hamet Xarif, was made King, raigned about twenty-seaven yeares[1] in great peace and felicity, untill he went to take his sonne Muley Sheck at Fes, where the father dyed, whose death hath caused all these warres, as yee may reade hereafter[2].

Cap. II.

The course of Muley Hamet Xarifs governement during his 27 yeares raigne.

Moulay Ahmed, à son avènement, choisit ses conseillers et les commandants de ses troupes parmi les plus capables. — Comme il régnait sur deux peuples, les Arabes et les Berbères, il institua un double système de gouvernement. — Les Arabes, cultivateurs pacifiques, reconnaissaient volontiers son autorité et payaient l'impôt. — Les Berbères, race indomptable, parlant une langue à eux, habitant des montagnes inaccessibles, étaient plus difficiles à gouverner. — Moulay Ahmed, pour les affaiblir, les employait dans des expéditions, notamment dans ses longues guerres contre les Noirs du Soudan. — Chargés d'accompagner les caravanes qui allaient chercher le tribut annuel à Gago, ils périssaient en grand nombre dans la traversée du Sahara et étaient mis à mort pour tout acte d'indiscipline. — Moulay Ahmed divisa leur pays en districts commandés par des caïds qui y résidaient avec des troupes. — Moulay Ahmed voulut toujours vivre en paix avec les Chrétiens. — Il aimait particulièrement les Anglais et admirait leur reine, à qui il écrivit de nombreuses lettres et envoya une ambassade en 1601. — Il acquit d'immenses richesses par le tribut que payaient les Arabes, par son commerce avec les Noirs, à qui il vendait contre de l'or le sel de Teghazza, par ses sucreries qui lui rapportaient annuellement au moins six cent mille onces. — Il aimait les artisans étrangers. — Il fit reconstruire son palais à Merrakech et orner magnifiquement son harem.

Obtaining the scepter, he first provided himselfe of the gravest men he could finde in his kingdomes to be counsellors of Estate, then of the most experienced and valiant souldiers for commanders over his campe and garrison townes. And whereas hee was

---

[1]. Moulay Ahmed *el-Mansour* régna en réalité 25 ans, de 1578 à 1603.

[2]. Purchas, dans sa réédition, intercale ici, avec quelques lignes d'introduction, la lettre de Th. Bernhere à Edw. Wright. V. *supra*, p. 170 et note 1.

monarch over two nations, the Larbies and Brebers, hee found it requisite to use a twofolde governement. The Larbies, dwelling in the best plaine champion country of his three kingdomes, Moruecos, Sus and Fes, were easily governed, being of mild and peaceable nature, given to thrift and tillage of the ground, sought no alterations, but receiving from him a due forme of justice executed by his ministers, protecting them from the Montaneirs, which are robbers, willingly obeyed his regall authoritie, and yearly payed their tenths towards their Kings maintenance.

As for the Brebers or Montaneirs, beeing of an untamed and fierce disposition, speaking the Tamiset tongue[1], which is as much different from the Larbee as Welch from our English, dwelling in places by nature defensible and almost inaccessible, he could not so well governe, neither had ever such absolute power over them, nor received the fift pennie of profite from them as he did from the Alarbeis. Therefore he sought by all meanes to diminish their strength of people, drawing them alwayes into foraigne expeditions, especially into that warre against the Negros, which continued a long time, thereby extending his empire farre that way, as by camell it was sixe monethsjourney from Morruecos to the farthest parts of his dominion[2]. Likewise, he used this people to go with the carabans[3] to Gago to fetch home his yearely tribute and monie, whereby manie were consumed in travailing over the Saharas. For anie offence or robberie committed by them, his sword should punish severely, that the rest might feare. Dividing their countrey into severall divisions or cantons, in everie which he placed an alkeyd with souldiers, to suppresse any suddaine uprores, much like our lieutenant set over our severall countyes, but that the alkeyd is continually resident, and hath greater power in executing marshall law. And lastly, as pledges of their loyalties, hee would get their chiefest mens sonnes into his hands, bringing them up in his Court to a more civill and delicate kinde of life.

---

1. La langue Tamachek.
2. Sur la conquête du Soudan par Moulay Ahmed *el-Mansour*, V. *supra*, p. 66 et note 1, et pp. 83-88.

3. On lit en marge : « A company of marchants going together for trading, with a great number of horses, camels and mules, laden with commodities. »

He was alwayes of minde to keepe peace with Christendome, with Spaine, who was his next potent neighbour, but above all loved the English nation, and admired the late Queenes happie governement, willing to entertaine trading with us, witnesse his manie letters written to that worthie Ladie of happie memorie, and his embassage sent unto her anno 1601, performed by Abdala Wahad Anowne and Hamet al-Hadg, their great travailer to Mecca and other places[1].

Towards his subjects, he was not too tyrannicall, but sweetned his absolute power and will with much clemencie. By diverse wayes he got excessive store of gold. First, by seeing his tenths truly payed from the Larbees. Secondly, by trading with the Negroe, taking up the salt at Tegazza[2] and selling it at Gago, having from thence returne in good golde. Thirdly, by husbanding his mascraws[3] or ingenewes[4], where his sugar canes did growe, though nowe all spoyled with these warres[5]: for it is sufficiently knowne all of them about Morruecos, Taradant and Mogador were yearely worth unto him sixe hundred thousand ounces at the least. I omit his love he tooke in entertaining forraigne artisans[6], the reedifying of his house in Morruccos, getting Italian marbles, the richest that could bee bought for money, and workmen hired from thence at great wages[7], his sumptuous provisions for his saraile[8] and maintenance of his women, not so much delighting in the sinne, as his predecessors had done before, as to shew his glorie, because the fashion of the countrey is such to shewe their riches and greatnesse upon that fraile sexe and their attendances. For his chiefest pleas-

---

1. Sur cette ambassade, qui eut lieu en 1600, V. supra, pp. 165-167 et 177-205.

2. Teghazza, grande mine de sel gemme située à deux jours de marche au nord de Taodeni. Sur les revenus que les chérifs saadiens tiraient de cette saline, cf. H. DE CASTRIES, La conquête du Soudan par El-Mansour, dans Hespéris, 1923, pp. 442 et 448.

3. Mascraw, de l'arabe معصرة pressoir.

4. On lit en marge : « Sugar gardens. » — Sur le mot ingenewes, V. supra, p. 135, note 1.

5. Sur la destruction des sucreries au Maroc après la mort de Moulay Ahmed, V. supra, p. 234.

6. Les artisans étrangers étaient en grande faveur auprès de Moulay Ahmed el-Mansour. V. 1re Série, Angleterre, t. I, p. 436, et supra, pp. 168-170 et 269.

7. Sur le palais d'El-Bedi, V. Pays-Bas, t. IV, pp. 572-577.

8. On lit en marge : « The place where his women are kept. » Le harem, d'après cette définition.

ures were to see the gallantrie of his kingdome managing their good Barbarian steedes, and the falcons upon their wing making faire flights after the heron ; for these sports hee was provided, no man better, from which hee was recalled by certaine discontents which as clowds forerunned his owne sunset.

CAP. III.

Moulay Ahmed el-Mansour laisse en mourant cinq fils : Moulay ech-Cheikh et Moulay Abou Farès, tous deux fils d'une concubine noire, Moulay Zidân, né d'une femme légitime, Moulay en-Nasser et Moulay Abdallah, nés de concubines. — Moulay Ahmed, de son vivant, avait donné à Moulay ech-Cheikh le gouvernement de Fez, à Moulay Abou Farès celui du Sous, à Moulay Zidân celui du Tadla. — Moulay ech-Cheikh remet toutes les affaires aux mains du pacha Moustafa, renégat espagnol. — Les caïds de l'entourage de Moulay Ahmed accusent Moustafa de donner à Moulay ech-Cheikh l'habitude du vin et de vouloir s'emparer du trésor de ce prince, pour l'emporter en pays chrétien. — Moulay Ahmed, ayant accueilli ces accusations, envoie plusieurs fois à Moulay ech-Cheikh l'ordre de mettre à mort Moustafa ; celui-ci finit par obéir à contre-cœur. — Du vivant de Moustafa, Moulay ech-Cheikh avait donné toute satisfaction à son père par sa conduite. — Moulay Abou Farès reste peu de temps dans le Sous, à cause de la peste et du caractère indiscipliné des habitants, et revient auprès de son père. — Moulay Zidân demeure au Tadla, où il montre de grandes qualités de gouvernement. — Il châtiait sévèrement tous les voleurs, et surtout les coupeurs de routes. — D'un caractère ambitieux, il refusait toute marque de respect à ses frères aînés et il se prétendait, par sa naissance, l'héritier légitime du royaume, contrairement à l'usage des Maures, qui ne tiennent aucun compte de la condition de la mère en matière de succession.

Muley Hamet Xarif, the late deceased King and father of these three brothers now living that strive for the kingdome, at the time of his death, left five sonnes alive: the eldest, Muley Mahemet, commonly called Muley Sheck, a title given alwaies to the eldest of the Kings sonnes [1]; the second, Muley Bo Feres, which two sons

---

1. Ce nom de Moulay ech-Cheikh, qui a été retenu par l'histoire, n'était pas, comme le prétend l'auteur, un titre porté par le fils aîné. Le nom complet du prince dont il est ici question était Moulay Mohammed ech-Cheikh *el-Mamoun*.

were both by one woman, a negra [1], one of his concubines; the third sonne, Muley Sidan, whome he had by one of his wives [2]; the fourth sonne, Muley Nassar, who was about the age of nineteen yeares; and the fift, Muley Abdela, about fourteene yeares old at the time of the old Kings death; and these twoo last were not legitimate, but the sonnes of twoo severall concubines. This deceased King, in his lifetime, had placed his three elder sons in severall parts of his kingdome, to governe for him in them. To Muley Sheck, his eldest, he had given the kingdome of Fes, which kingdome hath in former times continually been allotted by the late Kings of Barbary to their eldest sonnes. Muley Bo Feres he placed in his kingdome of Sus. To Muley Sidan he gave the province of Tedula, which lyeth in the midway betweene Moruecos and Fes [3]. His two yonger sonnes, Muley Nassar and Abdela, remained with him in his house, whome, by reason of their yong yeares, he had not as yet placed in any part of his kingdomes.

The eldest sonne Muley Sheck in his yonger yeares governed Fes and those partes of Barbarie with great approbation of his father, through the counsell of Basha Mustepha [4], a Spanish renegado; which Basha, in continuance of time, grewe in such favour with him, that the whole government of the kingdome of Fes was wholly by Muley Sheck put into his hands. Wherupon the alkeyds of the countrie, that were naturall borne Mores, continuall attendants upon the old King, envying the greatnes of the said Basha, raised divers accusations against him, complaining to the King that he learned Muley Sheck to drinke wine (a thing unlawfull to the Mores, being forbidden them by their Prophet Mahomet), and that now, having the whole government of the kingdome of Fes in his hands under the Kings sonne, he purposed, after he had possessed

---

1. Sur les noms de cette concubine, V. *supra*, p. 269, note 1.
2. Aïcha bent Abou Beker *ech-Chebania*, V. *supra*, p. 176, note 2, p. 255 et n. 1.
3. Ce partage eut lieu en 1584. El-Oufrâni, p. 175. D'après cet historien, un autre fils de Moulay Ahmed, nommé Abou el-Hassen Ali, eut Meknès, mais ultérieurement il reçut le Tadla et Moulay Zidân passa à Meknès. Abou el-Hassen Ali fut assassiné en 1594. V. *supra*, p. 88 et note 3.
4. Sur ce personnage et sur sa mort, V. *supra*, p. 130. Il ne doit pas être confondu avec un autre pacha Moustafa, au service de Moulay Zidân (V. *supra*, p. 234 et note 3) et qui sera fréquemment mentionné ci-après.

himselfe of Muley Shecks treasure, to flie and carry it with him to some partes of Christendome. Which accusations the old King, upon some probabilities and likelihoods, conceiving to be true, these alkeyds procured at last with him that he should send to his sonne Muley Sheck, commaunding him to send the head of the said Basha. Which commaund, howsoever Muley Sheck, who greatly loved and favoured the said Basha, at the first delayed to performe, yet, after divers messages, the old King sending at the last a principall servant of his to see the execution done, he was forced, much against his will, to see fulfilled.

In these yonger yeares of Muley Sheck, whilest this Basha was alive, none of the Kings sonnes was more dutifull to their father than he, neither any of their actions so contented the old King as his; insomuch as the whole kingdomes hope for a successor, after the old Kings decease, was onely in Muley Sheck. Whereupon, and by the Kings voluntary motion, all the principall alkeyds and men of commaund that were in the kingdomes by solemne oath vowed allegeaunce to Muley Sheck after the olde Kings decease[1].

And at that time Bo Feres, the second sonne, by reason of the great plague in Sus, and other discontents he received from that rebellious people, stayed not long there, but returned againe to his father in Moruccos, where he stayed with him untill his fathers departure to Fes in September[2] 1602.

Muley Sidan, the third sonne, continued in Tedula (a province fruitfull and situate in the flat of Barbarie, the midway betweene Fes and Moruecos, as I have told you), who governed those parts in great peace and quietnes, even in the cheife times of the tumults that were in the bordering dominions of his eldest brother Sheck, whereof you shall read hereafter; insomuch that he was generally commended and liked both of his father and of all the kingdome for his government, being strict in seeing the execution of justice to be done in those parts that he governed, not sparing his kindred or nearest followers in those cases. From his infancy, he naturally hated all manner of theeves whatsoever, especially those which robbed by

1. Le serment de fidélité fut prêté à Moulay ech-Cheikh, en qualité d'héritier présomptif, en 1579, 1581 et 1584. El.- Oufrâni, pp. 149 et 174-175.
2. Il est dit plus loin (p. 335 et note 1) que ce départ eut lieu en octobre.

the highwayes, and without any favour or mercy severely punished them. Howsoever he carryed himselfe very dutefull to his father, whilest he was living, yet, from his childehoode, he was alwayes of an aspiring and ambitious nature, which could never be brought to subject itselfe to any awefull respect to his elder brethren, but to hazard his whole estate in obtaining the kingdome, accounting himselfe his fathers lawfull heire, in that hee was his fathers eldest sonne which he had by any of his marryed wives; in this point not regarding the custome and lawe of the Mores, who, in title of inheritance or succession, respect not the mother, whether shee be marryed wife or concubine bought with money, so that her sonne be the eldest in birth.

Cap. IV

Après la mort du pacha Moustafa, Moulay ech-Cheikh, adonné à l'ivrognerie et à la débauche, laisse son royaume en proie aux exactions de ses serviteurs et aux pillages de bandes qui rendent tout voyage impossible autrement que par caravanes de trois ou quatre cents personnes. — Les Arabes, ne pouvant plus récolter en paix leurs moissons, refusent le tribut et se mettent eux-mêmes à piller. — La prodigalité de Moulay ech-Cheikh s'exerçait avec si peu de discernement qu'un Juif musicien acquit par les dons de ce prince une fortune de quatre cent mille ducats. — Moulay Ahmed, très affecté du changement survenu chez son fils et n'ayant pu réussir par ses nombreuses remontrances à le corriger, marche sur Fez, au mois d'octobre 1602, pour le détrôner et rétablir l'ordre, laissant à Moulay Abou Farès le gouvernement de Merrakech et du Sous. — Moulay ech-Cheikh, surpris par la brusque arrivée de son père, veut s'enfuir dans le Tafilelt, mais, serré de près, il est contraint de se réfugier dans un sanctuaire. — Comme il refusait d'en sortir, Moulay Ahmed ordonne d'y pénétrer de force et de s'emparer de lui. — Il refuse de le voir et le remet au pacha Djouder, qui l'emmène à Meknès. — Il fait venir Moulay Zidân de Zidania, ville fondée par ce dernier dans la province de Tadla, pour le mettre à la place de Moulay ech-Cheikh. — Comme il se mettait en route pour regagner Merrakech, en août 1603, il tombe malade et meurt en quelques jours.

But to returne againe to Muley Sheck, the Kings eldest sonne, who, after the death of his Basha Mustepha, beheaded by his fathers commaund, soone shewed unto all men the want of government that was in him; for, in his latter times, giving himselfe over to drunkennes and other detestable vices, which amongst the Mores commonly accompanieth that sinne, regarded not at all the government of his kingdome, but suffered his servants, followers and souldiers to doe what they would, in robbing and spoyling the goods of his honest minded subjects without controllment; and through want of justice duly executed, the whole country in short time swarmed so with theeves and robbers by the highwayes, that there was no travelling through his dominions, but in caffilas or companies of 300 and 400 persons at a time, and they hardly sometimes escaped the hands of theeves.

The Alarbies, who continue to this day in tribes and kindreds, being the husbandmen of the countrey, living in the fields and tents, by tilling of the ground and breeding up of cattell, whenas they could not quietly gather in and peaceably enjoy the corne and fruits of the ground, denyed to paye the King their accustomed dutie, and in the fields followed the courses of Muley Shecks servants in the citie, in robbing of all passengers that came within their power. And such was his lavishing manner of spending and consuming of his treasure, that in his humors hee neither regarded what hee gave nor to whome; in so much that a Jew, who was a musitian and used to play before him in his drunken fits, what with the gifts given him by the prince and what else he gotte out of his house, had gotten, together in money and jewels, in the space of foure or five yeares, to the value of foure hundred thousand duckets, which is about fortie thousand pound sterling.

This dissolute life and carlesse government of Muley Sheck greeved the old King not a little, especially to see such a change or alteration in him, whose forwardnes in former times had beene the staye of his age, and had mooved him to cause the alkeyds of his kingdome by oath to confirme their allegeance after his owne death. Many wayes he sought to amend what was amisse in those parts, and to draw his son to a more stricte course of life and more carefull kind of government, as well by his letters as by sending divers principall alkeyds to be counsellors unto him. Yet such was the small accompt he made either of the one or the other, that the old King, in the end, seeing no amendment, but the estate of that kingdome to grow dayly worse and worse, determined to go to Fes in his owne person with an armie, as well to displace his sonne, who had denyed to come unto him upon his sending for, as also to put in order all matters in those parts, which through the ill government of his sonne were all out of frame. And so, about the beginning of October 1602[1], he set forwards from Moruecos, with an armie of eight thousand horse, towards Fes, leaving his second sonne Muley Bo Feres to governe Moruecos and Sus in his absence untill his returne, making such speedy journeyes, that he was with his forces within one dayes journey of Fes, before his sonne Muley Sheck was certainly advised of his setting forth from Moruecos. Who, when hee understood of his fathers being so neere, and himselfe every waye unprovided to resist him, would have fled towards Tafilet; but, being followed by Basha Mustefa[2], hee was constrained to take sanctuary[3] with five hundred of his best souldiers being very good shotte and well provided. The old King, the father, seeinge his sonne take the priveledge of the place (which is much respected in that countrey), willed him to come forth and submit himselfe to his mercy. But Muley Sheck refused, either obstinate in not obeying, or fearefull he could not render a good accompt of his twenty-five yeares government in Fes. Therefore Muley Hamet commaunded Mustefa, a Basha of Sidans, though then in the old Muleys service, to take three thousand men, and perforce to enter the place, which he performed, bringing Sheck prisoner and the rest of his company which were left alive after the conflicte. The old man would in no wise admit him into his presence, but committed him to the charge and custody of Basha Judar, one of the greatest place about the King, who carryed Sheck to Mickanes, a strong garrison towne, and there remained untill the time of his fathers death, which was some five moneths after.

The olde King, in his journey to Fes against his eldest sonne, passed by the province of Tedula, and from thence tooke alongst

---

1. Cette date en vieux style est exacte. V. EL-OUFRÂNI, p. 291.

2. Distinct du pacha Moustafa exécuté en 1598. V. supra, pp. 234 et n. 3, 331 et n. 4.

3. C'est dans la zaouïa de Moulay Bou Cheta que Moulay ech-Cheikh se réfugia le 31 octobre 1602. V. EL-OUFRÂNI, pp. 291-297.

with him his third son Muley Sidan, whom he commaunded to remove his houshold to Fes from Sidania¹ (a citie which he had begunne to build in Tedula, and called it after his owne name), intending to leave him Vizeroy of those parts, in the roome of his eldest sonne, whom he purposed to carrie with him from Mickanes, where he was prisoner, to Moruecos. Which hee had also performed, if hee had not beene prevented by suddaine death²; for, in August 1603, hee, having set all matters in order in those parts of Fes, providing for his returne to Morruecos, put out his tents without Fes gates; but, being abroad, hee suddainly fell sicke, and his sicknesse so sore increased, that, on Thursday falling sick, on Sunday morning, beeing the fourteenth of August 1603, he died³.

CAP. V.

Muley Sidan proclaimeth himselfe King in Fes, Muley Bo Feres in Morruecos. Muley Nassar would have done the like in Taradant, but is hindered; the death of Nassar.

Informé par sa mère de la mort de Moulay Ahmed, avant qu'elle fût ébruitée, Moulay Zidân va saisir au camp le trésor du Chérif et se fait proclamer à Fez roi du Maroc. — La mère de Moulay Abou Farès envoie en toute hâte un message à ce dernier. — Dès qu'il apprend la mort de son père, Moulay Abou Farès, qui campait près de Merrakech avec son frère Moulay en-Nasser et Moulay Abdallah, fils de Moulay ech-Cheikh, rentre dans la ville et s'empare de la kasba et du trésor. — Le lendemain, il publie la mort de Moulay Ahmed et se fait proclamer roi. — Il est également reconnu à Taroudant. — Au moment de rentrer à Merrakech à la suite de Moulay Abou Farès, Moulay en-Nasser essaye en vain d'exciter contre ce prince les défiances de Moulay Abdallah

---

1. Sur la rive gauche de l'Oumm er-Rebia, à 5 kilomètres en amont du confluent de l'oued Derna. — Cette ville n'était qu'une kasba; elle eut la destinée de toutes les kasba au Maroc : agglomération importante, tant qu'y réside un chef (kholifa, pacha, caïd, etc.), ruine, quand la disgrâce atteint ce chef. Elle fut détruite à la fin de 1603 par le pacha Djouder. V. *infra*, p. 341.

2. Sur la déposition de Moulay ech-Cheikh et la mort de Moulay Ahmed el-Mansour, cf. 1ʳᵉ Série, Espagne, à la date du 27 novembre 1603, une relation du gouverneur de Mazagan.

3. Nouveau style : dimanche 24 août 1603. La relation citée à la note précédente donne la même date. EL-OUFRÂNI, p. 305, dit que le Chérif tomba malade le mercredi 20 et mourut le lundi 25.

et de le décider à la fuite. — Il s'enfuit alors seul dans les montagnes, auprès de la famille de sa mère, d'où il passe dans le Sous avec un millier de gens. — Le caïd de Taroudant ayant refusé de le reconnaître, il est abandonné par ses gens, qu'il ne pouvait payer, et il retourne vivre dans la famille de sa mère. — Il meurt, quelques mois plus tard, de la peste, ou secrètement empoisonné.

Muley Sidan, by reason his mother Lilla Isha governed the old Kings house, understood of his fathers death before it was noysed abroad. Whereupon he presently went forth into his fathers campe and tents, from whence he carried away all such jewels and treasure as he found there. And after his fathers death, he caused himselfe in Fes to bee proclaimed King of Barbarie[1], as lawfull heyre of his deceased father.

Lilla Johora[2], mother to Muley Sheck and Muley Bo Feres, seeing her eldest sonne in prison and voide of all meanes to helpe himselfe at that instant, was not unmindfull of her second son Bo Feres, whom the old King had left to governe Morruecos during his absence, to whom shee dispeeded presently letters by one of the Kings eunuchs; who made such hast that in foure dayes he came from Fes to his tents, which were some two leagues from Morruecos, where he had lien, all the summer before, to avoyd the infection of the plague which had beene that summer in Morruecos; and with him was his younger brother Muley Nassar, and his eldest brothers sonne Muley Abdela. Muley Bo Feres, understanding of his fathers death, presently entred Moruecos, and gat possession of the alcasava, his fathers house, before the newes of his fathers death was noysed abroad and generally knowne, fearing how the alkeyds and people of Morruecos might stand affected unto him, and knowing that, if he had once possession of the alcasava and of his fathers treasure, he had the best part of the kingdome. And the next day after his entrance, hee caused to bee published generally thorow the whole citie the newes of his fathers death, and withall himselfe to be proclaimed King[3], writing letters to the Vizeroy of Sus to doe the like in

---

1. Moulay Zidân fut proclamé à Fez le jour même de la mort de son père (25 août 1603). EL-OUFRÂNI, pp. 308-309.

2. *Lilla Johora*, Lella Djouher, V. *supra*, p. 269, note 1.

3. Moulay Abou Farès fut proclamé à Merrakech le 29 août 1603. EL-OUFRÂNI, pp. 308-309.

Taradant, the chiefe citie of that kingdome; the which he accordingly performed.

Muley Nassar, the fourth sonne of the deceased King, having beene all the summer abroad with his brother Bo Feres, when now hee understood of his fathers death, followed his brother afarre off as though hee meant to have entred Morruccos with him. But comming to the gates of the citie in companie with Muley Abdela his nephew, being sonne to Muley Sheck, with whome hee was familiar, conferred with him about their flying into the mountaines, perswading Muley Abdela that hee might no wayes put any trust in Bo Feres, since his father and he were the chiefest impediments that hindered Bo Feres from claiming the kingdome by course of justice, his father Muley Sheck being the old Kings eldest sonne, and he the eldest sonne of his father. Besides, his father being in prison so neere Fes, where Muley Sidan was, it was to be doubted that Muley Sidan had alreadie gotten him into his power, and, it might be, had made some agreement with him alreadie to joyne both against Muley Bo Feres; which, if it should so fall out, would cause Bo Feres to deale more cruelly with him. But these perswasions moved not Abdela, who rather chose to enter the cittie and follow his uncle on whose curtesie he would relie; though Nassar, fearing how Bo Feres would deale with him, with all speede fled into the mountaines to the kindred of his mother, from whence, after a few daies, with some eight hundred or a thousand of those people whome he joyned together, he passed into the plaines of Sus, sending to the alkeyd in Taradant to proclaime him King, or else to suffer him quietly to depart. But the alkeyd, having alreadie proclaimed Muley Bo Feres, withstood him; and he having no meanes wherewith to pay his souldiers and people that he had gathered togither, was soone left of all and so returned againe to his mothers kindred, and lived privatly there about seven moneths[1], and then dyed of the plague, or, as some reported, secretly poysoned, was brought to Morruecos and there buryed.

[1]. D'après cette indication, la mort de Moulay en-Nasser aurait eu lieu en mars 1604, au lieu de mars 1605, date portée dans le Tableau généalogique des princes de la dynastie saadienne (*1re Série*. Angleterre, t. I, p. 256, Pl. III).

Cap. VI.

The revolt of alkeyd Hamet Monsore. Muley Sheck prisoner delivered to Bo Feres. Muley Sidan rayseth forces against his brother Bo Feres, and the like doth Muley Bo Feres against Sidan.

Les soldats campés près de Fez, qui réclamaient seize mois de solde et voulaient retourner à Merrakech, se mutinent. — Envoyé par Moulay Zidân pour les apaiser, le caïd Ahmed ben Mansour attise leur révolte et convient de revenir avec eux à Merrakech. — Djouder, qui gardait à Meknès Moulay ech-Cheikh, se joint aux révoltés et part avec eux pour Merrakech, amenant son prisonnier à Moulay Abou Farès. — Moulay Zidân, que d'autres caïds ont encore abandonné, envoie dans le Tadla deux mille fusiliers et des cavaliers sous les ordres du renégat Moustafa. — Il fait lui-même à Fez de grands préparatifs militaires. — Les caïds Azzouz, Bou Kourzia, Abd es-Seddik et d'autres lui restent fidèles. — Moulay Abou Farès fait partir pour le Tadla Djouder avec cinq mille fusiliers, des cavaliers et quatre canons. — Moustafa se retire devant lui. — Djouder détruit Kasba ez-Zidania et ravage la contrée. — Moulay Zidân rassemble une armée de neuf mille fusiliers, douze mille cavaliers et vingt canons. — Il donne le commandement de son artillerie à deux canonniers anglais. — Mais le terrain détrempé par la pluie empêche les canons d'arriver pour la bataille.

But, to returne to Fes and those parts, after the death of the old King, Sidan being now proclaimed King in Fes, Bo Feres in Morruecos and Sus, and Muley Sheck prisoner in Mickanes in the keeping of Basha Juda, the souldiers, being abroad in their tents without Fes gates, began to be in a mutenie, as well for sixteene monethes pay which the old King owed them, as also about their returne to Morruecos, where most of them had left their wives and children. To appease this mutenie, Muley Sidan sent out of Fes unto them alkeyd Hamet Monsore[1], their chiefe commaunder in the olde Kings time, to promise them as well content in payment, as also a speedie returne to Morruecos with Muley Sidan himselfe. But Monsore, instead of pacifying, laboured to increase their mutenous humours,

---

1. Le caïd Ahmed ben Mansour. V. *supra*, p. 233, note 3.

and at last agreed with them suddainly in the night to take up their tents and to march with him to Morruecos, alleadging unto them both the uncertaintie of Muley Sidans pay, and the small likelyhoode of any speedie journey hee meant to take to Moruecos[1]. And being to passe within a little of Mickanes, were the Basha kept Muley Sheck prisoner, hee wrote unto the said Basha to know his intent, whether hee would goe to Moruecos or no with him.

To whom the Basha came and brought Muley Sheck with him, whom they brought along as a prisoner to Moruecos and delivered him up to his brother Bo Feres, who kept him close prisoner in his house some 4 or 5 moneths, untill the comming of Muley Sidan against him in battaile; by this meanes thinking to have established the whole kingdome to Muley Bo Feres, who now, besides the possession of the city of Moruecos and his fathers treasure, had brought unto him the greatest part of his fathers forces, and his elder brother put prisoner into his hands.

Muley Sidan, being thus deceived by Monsore, and likewise by divers other principall alkeids, who had secretly departed from Fes and left him, forthwith dispeeded one Mustefa, a renegado of his owne, whome hee made a Basha, with two thousand shot and some companyes of horses to Tedula, as well to receive from the Alarbies those duties which they always pay unto their King, as also to stoppe and returne to Fes whomsoever he should finde flying from thence to Moruecos, keeping possession of the province for his use. He made likewise great preparations both of horse and foote in Fes, to bee alwaies ready to accompany himselfe in person, if neede should so require, having with him in Fes of principall alkeids: Azus, cheefe counsellor to the late deceased King and lord over his Bitlemel[2], Bo Crazia[3], Absadiks[4] and divers others.

Muley Bo Feres likewise in Moruecos foreslacked no time in making preparations to send forth against him, sending first alcaide

---

1. Le caïd Ahmed ben Mansour annonça son arrivée par une lettre qui arriva à Marrakech, le 31 août 1603. V. 1re Série, Espagne, à la date du 27 novembre 1603.

2. *Bitlemel*, pour Bit el-Mal. L'auteur a donné en marge la traduction « Treasurio », qui est exacte.

3. Bou Kourzia. Sur ce caïd, V. *supra*, pp. 175, note 2, et 232.

4. *Absadiks*. Abd es-Seddik. C'est le caïd appelé par George Tomson Abdallah Sadik. V. *supra*, p. 232.

Gowie[1], with some six hundred men, to make provision of corne and other victuals amongst the Alarbies; and after he had certaine news of Muley Sidans forces to be in Tedula, he sent out his Basha Juda, with five thousand shot choyst men, foure peeces of artillary and certaine companies of horse to enter Tedula, and to give battaile to Mustefa, the generall of Sidans forces, or perforce to drive him out of that country.

At whose comming thither, Mustefa, seeing himselfe no waies strong enough to encounter with Judar, retyred backe againe with his armie out of Tedula, and Judar destroyed the foundations of Sidania[2] (which Muley Sidan at his being in Tedula had begunne to build upon the river of Morbaie[3] and called it Sidania after his owne name), likewise wasted and destroyed the country thereabout, at least so many of the kindreds of the Alarbies as he knew to be friends to Muley Sidan, or those that would not acknowledge Bo Feres for King.

Sidan, understanding what Juda had done in Tedula, and likewise of the great preparations that his brother in Moruecos daily made to send out against him, forthwith put forth his tents, and joyned together his whole forces, which were some eight or nyne thousand shot and some twelve thousand horse, with two and twentie peeces af artillery, himselfe in person going along with them[4]. And, because he was altogether unprovided of skilfull gunners for his ordinances, he procured from Salie, out of certaine English men of warre who at that instant were there, twoo English gunners, to whome hee committed the charge of his artillery ; but by reason of much raine that had fallen, it being in the moneth of January 1604, the ground in many places was so soft that they could not march with their artillery so fast as neede required. So that his artillery never came at the battaile, which was thought to be a chiefe cause of his overthrow.

1. Ce caïd, appelé Guaia Malluco dans les documents espagnols, était frère cadet du caïd Moumen bou Kourzia. V. supra, p. 233 et note 6. Le 25 octobre, il était à sept lieues de Merrakech, marchant contre le pacha Moustafa. V. 1re Série, Espagne, à la date du 27 novembre 1603.

2. V. supra, p. 336 et note 1.
3. Morbaïe, Oumm er-Rebia.
4. Moulay Zidân fit partir de Fez sa mahalla, le 25 décembre 1603, et se mit lui-même en route pour la rejoindre, le vendredi 1er janvier 1604. V. supra, pp. 241 et 242.

Cap. VII.

Fokers sent to entreat of peace from Muley Bo Feres to Sidan. Muley Sheck set at libertie. The battaile betwixt Muley Bo Feres and Muley Sidan.

Moulay Abou Farès envoie des marabouts offrir la paix à Moulay Zidân. — Il n'en prépare pas moins activement un envoi de renforts au pacha Djouder. — Impropre lui-même à conduire une armée et sentant la nécessité d'opposer à Moulay Zidân un prince du sang, il délivre Moulay ech-Cheikh et l'envoie rejoindre Djouder, lui offrant, en cas de victoire, son ancien gouvernement de Fez, à la condition qu'il se contentera du titre de vice-roi et qu'il laissera comme otage son fils Moulay Abdallah. — Djouder reçoit secrètement l'ordre de ne confier aucun commandement à Moulay ech-Cheikh, de le montrer seulement aux troupes et d'avoir l'œil sur lui pour le ramener prisonnier en cas de victoire. — Moulay ech-Cheikh a connaissance de ces instructions. — Moulay Zidân, apprenant les préparatifs de son frère, repousse ses offres de paix. — Il rassemble en toute hâte deux mille mulets et chevaux, pour transporter des soldats au camp de Moustafa, dressé près de l'oued Oumm er-Rbia, en vue de Djouder qui est posté sur l'autre rive. — Lui-même part à la tête de sept ou huit mille cavaliers, dans l'espoir d'attaquer Djouder à l'improviste ou avant l'arrivée de Moulay ech-Cheikh. — Mais ce dernier a déjà rejoint Djouder. — Moulay Zidân, averti de sa présence et ne voulant pas laisser à ses troupes le temps d'en être informé, livre sans tarder bataille. — Les premières décharges de l'artillerie de Djouder mettent en fuite les troupes de Moulay Zidân, qui, après avoir résisté avec quelques soldats d'élite, abandonne lui-même le champ de bataille. — Il avait eu le tort de perdre plus de deux heures, au lieu de fondre sur l'ennemi dès son arrivée au camp, avant le jour. — Moulay ech-Cheikh a peu d'hommes tués et Moulay Zidân en perd au plus six cents. — On avait prévu que la bataille ne serait ni acharnée, ni longue, car les combattants étaient tous Maures, de même pays, de même religion, et il n'y avait presque pas de caïd qui n'eût un frère, un fils, un ami dans le camp opposé.

Whilest these preparations were in hand on either side, Muley Bo Feres sent certaine Fokers [1], held of great estimation amongst

---

1. On lit en marge : « Fokers are men of good life, which are onely given to

the Mores, to his brother Muley Sidan to treate conditions of peace[1]; howbeit, after their dispeeding from Moruccos, he omitted no time and diligence in sending foorth newe armies and fresh supplies, both of souldiers and provision, to Judar Basha that was in Tedula. And understanding for certaine that his brother Sidan was in the field in person (because hee himselfe had never beene inbred to travell, and knowing it would be no small discouragement to his side, and encouragement to the other that Sidan should be in person in the field, and no other his equall in bloud in his armie to withstand him), he concluded a colourable peace betweene himselfe and his eldest brother Muley Sheck, whome untill that time hee kept close prisoner in his house, agreeing with him that he should go forth into his armie, and joyne with Judar to fight against Muley Sidan; whome if he overthrow in battaile, he should enjoy the kingdome of Fes and so much of those easterne parts of Barbarie as he enjoyed in his fathers time, on condition that, at his enterance into Fes, hee should proclaime Muley Bo Feres King, and himselfe onely Vizeroy, and so should still acknowledge his government there, as derived from Bo Feres. And to the intent Muley Sheck should the better observe these conditions according to their agreement, hee was to leave his eldest sonne[2] in pawne with Muley Bo Feres in Moruccos. On these plausible conditions, Muley Sheck was set at libertie, a happy turne for himselfe as he thought, who never looked for any better but perpetuall imprisonment with much misery. But the truth is Basha Judar had secret advertissement from his master Bo Feres (yet not so secret but it was knowne to Muley Sheck and closely carryed of him by interception of letters betwixpt Moruccos and the campe in Tedula) that he should abridge Muley Sheck of any commaund in the campe or matter of counsell in ordering of the fight, onely shew him to the souldiers under his canopy[3], that the Fezes, who were the strength of Sidans armie, might know Sheck was in the campe of Bo Feres, whome they loved in regard partly

peace. » — *Foker*, en arabe فقير faquir, ascète musulman. Ici le mot est synonyme de marabout.

1. Sur l'arrivée à Fez de ces marabouts et sur l'accueil que leur fit Moulay Zidân, V. *1re Série*, Espagne, à la date du 16 décembre 1603.

2. Moulay Abdallah.

3. *Canopy*, le parasol impérial.

of his long abode amongst them, but especially of his great liberality, or rather prodigality formerly shewed unto them, which wrought much in their minds at the ensuing battaile. And withall the Basha had a speciall charge sent and his guard to watch him, that, if he got the battaile, he should bring Muley Sheck in yrons, as safe a prisonner from the camp to Moruecos, as once hee had done from Mickanes. But, this being discovered, Muley Sheck so shufled his game, that, though Judar wonne the field, Muley Sheck escaped unto Fes, and was lovingly entertained of the citizens, proclaiming himselfe King of Barbarie.

But returne we to the Fokers treating about conditions of peace in Fes with Muley Sidan, who by intelligence understoode from Moruecos of the fresh supplies of souldiers daily sent out by his brother to the Basha; whereby hee greatly suspected those offers of peace to be a device to prolonge the time whilest his whole forces were in readines and then sudenly to have come upon him unawares, before he should be provided for him. And therefore hee returned the Fokers with denials of the offered conditions of peace; and himselfe thinking to take the opportunity and advantage of the time before either his brothers new forces should come to the Basha, or Muley Sheck his eldest brother be set at liberty, he caused with all diligence to be gotten together some two thousand mules and horses, and upon every mule to be set two souldiers with their furniture, and so, without any stay for the reballing of tents or carrying along of his artillery with him, to bee with all hast possible sent[1] and joyned by the almohalla[2] of alkeid Mustefa, which lay hard by the river of Morbaie[3] in the sight of the almohalla of Basha Judar, the river onely betweene them.

He himselfe likewise in person went along[4] with some seaven or eight thousand of his horsemen, thinking by this meanes to come with his best forces upon Basha Judar before the Basha should expect him, or before the comming of Muley Sheck, who for his

---

1. Ces forces furent expédiées le 25 décembre 1603. V. *supra*, p. 241 et note 5, et p. 341, note 4.

2. On lit en marge : « Almohalla is a campe. » Ce mot a un sens plus étendu et s'applique à une armée en campagne.

3. *Morbaie*, l'Ouimm er-Rbia.

4. Moulay Zidân partit de Fez le vendredi 1ᵉʳ janvier 1604. V. *supra*, p. 241 et note 6.

liberality and bounty in former times was greatly beloved of all the souldiers both of Fes and also of Moruecos.

But this pollicy of his herein tooke no place, for Muley Sheck, after he was set at liberty, made such speedy journeyes that he came to the almohalla of the Basha before that Muley Sidan had certain intelligence of his liberty; and yet he entered the almohalla but on the Tuesday, the battaile being fought upon the Fryday following. Muley Sidan, understanding for certaine that his eldest brother was come into the Basha his almohalla, thought it no time for him to deferre giving battile, least it shold be knowne amongst his souldiers, many of whome in former times had served the sayd Muley Sheck. And therefore on Fryday, the first of January 1604[1], the forces of each side met and joyned together[2]; between whom there was no long fight, for, uppon the discharging of foure peeces of artillery, which Judar Basha had with him, some 3 or 4 times, a great part of the souldiers of Muley Sidan began to flye, except some choyce men which were in that part of the battaile where the Muley[3] himselfe was, by reason of the resolution of their commaunder, continued somewhat longer, but in the end fled whenas the canopy over Muley Sidans head was shot down with a piece of ordinance. At which mischance and not before, the Muley himselfe began to leave the field; who, in the managing of this battaile, was something to be blamed, for, as he had used the celerity of a wise generall, comming with all speed to Mustefa, after he heard Muley Sheck should be set at liberty, setting two souldiers upon every mule, and every horseman, for the speedier march, to take a souldier with his piece up behinde him, being come to his campe an hour before day, hee should not have delayed two howers and more the present onset, gazing in his enemies face and giving them time to ready themselves to fight, whome otherwise he might have taken at the disperview, and his Fezzes, whome he half mistrusted, no premeditation to revolte or runne away.

---

1. La date est donnée d'après le calendrier grégorien, mais elle est erronée. Ce n'est pas le vendredi 1er janvier 1604, mais le vendredi 8 qu'eut lieu la bataille. On a vu (p. 344) que la date du 1er janvier est celle du départ de Fez de Moulay Zidàn.

2. Les mahalla se rencontrèrent au lieu dit Mouâta, sur les bords de l'Oumm er-Rebia. EL-OUFRÂNI, p. 311.

3. *The Muley*, Moulay Zidàn.

On Muley Shecks side few were slaine, and of Muley Sidans side the greatest number was some sixe hundred men or thereabout. Neither was it ever thought that the battaile would be sore or endure long, but that the one side would presently flye. First, for that they were all Mores of one country and one religion, and, howsoever the Kings might be affected one to the other, yet, between the cominality of each side, was no hatred; onely for their paye came into the field to fight one against the other. Secondly, by reason of the olde Kings death in Fes, there was almost no alkeide of Muley Shecks side, but had either his brother, sonne or chiefest friend on the other side. As alkeid Mumen Bo Crasia was a cheefe commaunder on Muley Sidans side, and his brother, alkeid Gowie, of the like commaund on the other side. Alkeid Absadok was chiefe counsellor with Muley Sidan; his brother[1] was the like with Muley Bo Feres, to whome also was sworne alkeid Absadocks son. Alkeid Hamet Monsore was on Muley Bo Feres side, and his brother alkeid Ally Monsore on the other side. And so of divers others.

Cap. VIII.

Sidans justice done uppon the Larbees for robbing. His flight, after the battaile lost, to Trimasine.

La guerre civile engendre au Maroc une anarchie et une insécurité auxquelles Moulay Abou Farès est, par nature, incapable de remédier. — La tribu des Oulad Entid, forte de quinze mille cavaliers, étend ses brigandages jusqu'aux portes de Merrakech. — Pendant qu'il était le maître de Fez, Moulay Zidân avait fait, sur un douar de cette même tribu, un sanglant exemple. — Moulay Zidân, après sa défaite, est rentré à Fez et a envoyé le caïd Azzouz offrir la paix à Merrakech. — Lui-même se préparait de nouveau à la lutte, lorsque l'approche de Moulay ech-Cheikh et de Djouder le contraint à prendre la fuite. — Il est serré de si près qu'il ne peut aller reprendre à Larache les neuf cent mille ducats qu'il y avait déposés et qu'il s'enfuit directement vers Tlemcen. — La plupart de ses caïds l'abandonnent, entre autres Moumen Bou Kourzia. — Le caïd Abd es-Seddik lui reste fidèle, malgré les objurgations de son frère,

---

1. *His brother*, Abd el-Ouahed Anouri. V. *supra*, p. 159, note 1.

le caïd Abd el-Ouahed, et de son fils. — Moulay Zidân, harcelé dans sa fuite, perd une grande partie de son trésor, bien qu'à de nombreuses reprises il fasse front contre l'ennemi avec une vingtaine d'hommes au plus. — Le caïd En-Nebîli, saisi d'admiration et de pitié, finit par abandonner la poursuite. — Moulay Zidân continue sa marche vers Tlemcen.

The three brethren thus striving for the golden ball of soveraignty, justice was trodden downe. The Larbees robbed one another, the strongest carrying away all. Quarrels betwixt families and tribes, which durst not be talked of in old Muley Hamets time, came to be decided with the swoord. After this battaile, all wayes were stopped with robbers, no trading from the porte townes to Moruecos without great strength of men. Muley Bo Feres, who had the imperiall seate, was neither so fit for action or to do justice as Muley Sidan, who had lost the day. And that the kindred called Weled Entid¹ well knew, which presuming upon the soft nature of Bo Feres and their owne strength, which consisted of fifteene thousand horse, foraged up to Moruecos gates, foreclosed all passages for travellers, making marchants goods their prizes; whereas an exemplary punishment executed uppon them for their robbing in Fes by Muley Sidan, whilest hee raigned there, made them thinke the countrey too hot. For Sidan commaunded alkeid German² with twoo thousand souldiers, in hostile manner, to fall upon the next dwarre³ of tents belonging to that tribe, to burne man, woman, childe, kyne, sheepe, and, whatsoever belonged to them, not to spare it, uppon his owne life, from fire and sword; which fully executed and so bloodily, that Muley Sidan sighed hearing the true report; yet it made Fes the peaceable part in Barbarie.

But returne we to Sidans fortunes. After he lost the field, having the overthrowe, retyred backe to Fes; and forthwith was alkeid Azus, the onely man, in the latter daies of the old King, favoured by the whole countrey, dispeeded towards Moruecos to treate of a peace; and himselfe beganne to make head againe to resist such forces as should follow him. But, before hee could bring his forces

---

1. *Weled Entid*, peut-être : Entifa.
2. Le caïd Grimân. V. EL-OUFRÂNI, p. 110; 1ʳᵉ Série, Angleterre, t. I, p. 179 et note 3; France, t. II, p. 48, note 3.
3. On lit en marge : « Dwar is a towne of tents. »

together againe, newes was brought unto him that his brother Muley Sheck was neare at hand, with certaine companies of horsemen, and that the whole almohalla of the Basha was not farre behinde. So that then hee was rather to consider of and to provide for his escaping by flight, then anywayes to resist; and having before put some nyne hundred thousand duckets in Allarocha, for the which money he had send one of his alkeids after his returne from the battaile, he thought it his best course to passe that waye and to take that money along with him; but he was followed so hardly by alkeid Abdela Wahad and alkeid Umsoud Umbilie¹, Bo Feres servants, that he was forced to flye directly towards Trimasine, and to leave that treasure behinde him, which was taken by his brother Muley Sheck.

In these his frowning fortunes, the most of his alkeids left him, and amongst others Mumine Bo Crasia flying to Moruecos, in whome hee put no small trust; and, more then the servants of his house, he had no man of accompt but forsooke him; onely alkeid Absadik, Hado Tabid² and Mustepha, the twoo latter of them being his household servants, and belonging to him in his fathers time, left him not in his adversitie. So that, any alkeid of the cassas or castes in Barbarie, hee had no more then Absadicke, who rather then he would leave him (although allured by the perswasions of his brother alkeide Abdela Wahad, and entreated by the theares of his sonne to returne, both of them then beeing in the pursuite of Muley Sidan, and in a playne overtooke the sayde Absadocke), yet hee left his house and children at the mercie of Muley Bo Feres, his maister and enemie.

The alkeids who followed in pursuite of Muley Sidan followed him so hard that, besides the treasure of Allarocha, they likewise tooke much of the Muleys treasure that hee carryed along with him, although, with that small companye of horses, which were no more then twentye horsemen or thereabout, hee returned many times and fought with those who pursued him in person, beeing still one of the foremost in these skirmishes; untill alkeide Umbilie, who pur-

---

1. *Umsoud Umbilie*. Messaoud en-Nebili. V. *supra*, p. 233 et note 5.

2. *Hado Tabid*. Le caïd Haddou Tebib.

En 1607-1609, on le retrouve vice-roi de Merrakech. V. *1ʳᵉ Série*, Pays-Bas, t. I, pp. 473, 639, 640 et 643.

sued him, admiring his resolution, and pittying his miserable estate, requested his Majestie to keepe on his way and save himselfe by flight, he not purposing to persue him any further. And so the Muley, in this miserable estate, forsaken almost of all, kept on his way to Trimasine, a towne bordering upon the Turkes in the frontiers of the kingdome of Argiers; and the alkeids who pursued him returned again to Fes[1].

Cap. IX.

Muley Sheck proclaimeth himselfe King in Fes. Sidan goeth to Tafilet, from thence to Sus. A skirmish wherein Mumine Bo Crasia is slaine. Peace concluded between Muley Bo Feres and Muley Sidan.

Moulay ech-Cheikh entre à Fez et s'y fait proclamer roi. — Moulay Abou Farès envoie des mahallas dans toutes les directions pour pacifier les Arabes. — Celle que le caïd Ahmed ben Mansour conduit dans le Sous est contrainte à la retraite par la peste et l'hostilité des habitants. — Moulay Abou Farès, au mois de juin 1604, rappelle toutes ses troupes, pour les envoyer contre Moulay Zidân, qui vient de passer dans le Tafilelt. — Instruit des dispositions du Sous, où les Chebana refusent de reconnaître Moulay Abou Farès et où l'appellent presque toutes les tribus, Moulay Zidân se prépare à y entrer. — Cependant, Moulay Abou Farès envoie des troupes dans le Draâ, sous le commandement de son fils Moulay Abd el-Malek, pour fermer le passage à Moulay Zidân. — Escarmouche de cavalerie au Lektaoua, dans laquelle périt le caïd Moumen Bou Kourzia. — Ce dernier n'est pas regretté des Maures, qui lui reprochent sa trahison envers Moulay Zidân. — Celui-ci, trop faible pour lutter contre l'armée ennemie, est contraint d'entrer dans le Sous par le Sahara. — Après une marche très pénible, il arrive à Akka, près du marabout Sidi Abdallah ben Embarek, dont l'influence est prédominante dans la région. — A la suggestion de ce marabout, le caïd Azzouz est envoyé par Moulay Abou Farès, en août 1604, pour conclure la paix avec Moulay Zidân. — Ce dernier obtient le royaume du Sous, qui, après avoir été la région la plus tumultueuse du Maroc, en devient la seule paisible et bien administrée. — Mais Moulay Zidân soumet le pays à de lourds impôts, que désapprouve Sidi Abdallah ben Embarek et

---

[1]. Ces faits se passèrent dans la seconde quinzaine de janvier 1604.

qui provoquent les révoltes des montagnards de l'Atlas. — Les gens des plaines sont maintenus sous le joug.

After Muley Sidans flight in this manner, Muley Sheck entred Fes, where he was joyfully receaved of them, proclaymed himselfe King, and not governour under his brother Bo Feres. And it being in the time of Rummadan[1], all the almohallas of Moruecos returned home against the Pascua[2]; from whence, after the celebration of the feast, they were sent forth to all parts of the countrie against the Larbies, among whome were as great civile wars as among the brethren; for, in this time of so many Kings, they would acknowledge none, or pay duty to any of the three brethren. Whereuppon Hamet Monsore, with three thousand souldiers, was sent into Sus in the moneth of Aprill 1604; but his men dying of the plague (which was very hot at the time) and thereby the Larbies, little regarding his power, would bring him no victuals; so that, with remainder of his men, hee was constrayned to returne towardes Moruecos.

Diverse other almohallas were sent abroad into severall parts of the countrey. But, in the beginning of June, newes comming of Muley Sidans returne from Trimasine to Tafilet, they were all sent for by Bo Feres to returne to Moruecos, and bee joyned together the second time against Muley Sidan; who, having some fewe moneths lived about Trimasine with some fiftie souldiers, went towards Tafilet, about which part lived the cassa or caste of alkaid Absadok, who was master of the hawkes to Muley Hamet, and brought to Sidan of his caste some twelve hundred horses, with which force he entered Tafilet, the alkeid of Muley Bo Feres flying to Dara or Draw with his souldiers.

In Tafilet, Muley Sidan stayed some fortye daies, where he understood perfectly of the estate of Sus and had letters from divers of his wellwillers there, understanding of alkeid Hamet Monsores departure from thence, and that the Shebanites[3], which is the

---

1. On lit en marge : « Rummadan is Lent. » — Le mois de Ramadan 1012 correspond à la période 2 février-2 mars 1604.

2. *The Pascua*, la fête de l'Aïd es-Seghir, qui se célèbre après le Ramadan.

3. *Shebanites*, les Chebana, puissante tribu au sud de Merrakech. Sur les Che-

greatest cast in all Barbarie and the casse or cast of the Muleys mother[1], would not acknowledge Bo Feres for King, and likewise how most of all the casts in Sus desired his comming thither. Whereupon he prepared what forces hee could there get to go into Sus.

Muley Bo Feres, upon the first newes of his brothers comming to Tafilet, called in all his almohallas, and joyning some foure thousand shotte of them, besides horse, sent them from Moruecos to Dara, under the commaund of his sonne Muley Abd el-Melech, with whome went divers principall alkeids, as alkeid Gowie[2], Umbilie[3] and Mumine Bo Crasia, who, in the first battaile of Muley Sidan, was a principall man of commaund on his side, and after his overthrow fled from him to Moruecos with divers others. The chiefe intent of these forces was to stop the passages from thence to Sus; which Muley Sidan perceiving, before the comming of their whole forces, he passed by Alcatouy[4], where the horsemen on each side skirmished, the footmen not being able to come up, and some slaine of either side, but no man of account, save onely alkeid Mumine Bo Crasia, who, as some reported, dyed with thirst being overheated (the battaile being fought in the middest of July), or, as others reported, being wounded and returning to his tent, calling for water, after hee had drunke it, presently dyed ; whose death was little lamented or pittyed by the Mores, they saying he was justly rewarded for being a traitour to Muley Sidan, his master, who was not onely contented to leave him in his misfortunes and to flye to his brother, but also to goe forth into the field against him.

Muley Sidans forces were so small that he was not able to match in strength the forces of his enemies, and therefore was constrayned to passe into Sus by the waye of the Sahara[5], and durst not passe by Draw. In which sands, for want of water, both he and his whole company had almost perished ; and, after much misery indured in

---

bana, V. 1re Série, France, t. III, p. 579, note 2.

1. Sur la mère de Moulay Zidàn, V. supra, p. 268 et note 1.

2. Gowie, le caïd Gounïa. V. supra, p. 341 et note 1.

3. Umbilie, le caïd Messaoud en-Nebili. V. supra, p. 348 et note 1.

4. Alcatouy, le Lektaoua, district méridional de l'Oued Draâ.

5. On lit en marge : « Sahara, the countrey or desert of sands. »

that journey, he arrived at Aca[1], where Sidie Abdela Imbark[2], the great Foker[3], dwelleth; the friendshippe of whome obtained, he knewe that all his brothers forces could not dispossesse him of the kingdome of Sus, in such great reverence is that churchman held in those partes that the people will obey none but whome hee commaundeth them.

He being come thither, the Foker, by letters to Muley Bo Feres then at Moruecos, procured that there might be a treatie of peace betweene the two brethren. Whereuppon in August following, anno 1604, alkeid Azus was sent to Muley Sidan to Aca, where, by the endeavours of the said alkaid and the Foker, a peace was concluded betweene Muley Bo Feres and his brother Muley Sidan, this to enjoy the kingdome of Sus, and the other the residue of the empire. Whereupon Sidan peaceably entered Taradant, the chiefe citie in that kingdome; uppon whose entrance thither, Sus, which in all former times had been the most unquiet and rebellious part of all Barbarie, through his execution of justice became the onely peaceable and well governed countrie of that kingdome, all other parts of Barbarie that were under the government and belonging to the other two brethren as then remaining very unquiet and full of all tumults. Neither was his government any way to bee misliked, but that, scarce setled, he charged the country with greater impositions then his father ever demaunded; insomuch as Sedie Abdela Imbark, who was the onely man who first brought him thither, reproved his courses, and the montaniers of Atlas being good souldiers, excellent shott, and their dwelling by nature defencible, finding his yoke too heavie, the lesse regarded him or his power; which humor of theirs was nourished by secret practises of Bo Feres, lothe that Sidan should either grow great in friends or treasure. But the inhabitants of the plaine and lower regions felt the smart of his rodde, knowing their throats lay at his mercey, whenas the mon-

---

1. *Aca*, Akka, sur l'oued Akka, à son débouché du Djebel Bani.

2. Sidi Abdallah ben Embarek, marabout très influent dans la région du Sous, de l'oued Noun et du Draà. C'était un de ses ancêtres, Mohammed ben Embarek, qui avait contribué à l'avènement de la dynastie saadienne. V. EL-OUFRÀNI, pp. 22-24 et 32. Cf. *1re Série*, Portugal, t. 1, aux années 1513 et 1525.

3. Sur le sens de ce mot, V. *supra*, p. 342 et note 1.

laniers defended themselves with open armes, and oftentimes gave the new King his hands full.

Cap. X.

Abdela, Muley Shecks sonne, escapeth from Bo Feres. Sidan is sent for to go in battaile against Muley Sheck; he refuseth. Abd el-Melech, Bo Feres sonne, goeth. His bad successe.

Moulay ech-Cheikh intrigue secrètement avec des princes étrangers, pour se ménager leur appui contre Moulay Abou Farès. — Son fils Moulay Abdallah s'échappe de Merrakech, où il était détenu comme otage. — Le caractère entreprenant de ce dernier le rend très populaire à Fez. — Moulay Abou Farès envoie le caïd Azzouz prier Moulay Zidân de marcher en personne contre Moulay ech-Cheikh et son fils. — Moulay Zidân réunit ses forces et s'avance jusqu'à une demi-journée de Merrakech, sans vouloir entrer dans la ville, par défiance de son frère. — Il demande à choisir lui-même les commandants et à fixer le nombre des soldats qui marcheront contre Fez. — Moulay Abou Farès, quoique peu satisfait de cette demande, répond par des lettres remplies d'affection et de compliments. — Moulay Zidân, ayant découvert par une ruse les vraies dispositions à son égard de Moulay Abou Farès, se retire dans le Tafilelt et le Draâ. — Moulay Abou Farès donne le commandement de ses troupes à son fils Moulay Abd el-Malek. — A une journée de marche de Fez, trois mille hommes se révoltent au cri de : « Vive Moulay ech-Cheikh ! ». — Moulay Abd el-Malek décide de rentrer à Merrakech sans combattre.

The peace concluded betwixt Bo Feres and Sidan by the meanes of Abdela Imbark and Azus, the wisest counseller that Barbarie hath, we will leave Sidan at Sus, seeking his owne ende once more to become maister of Morruccos, and returne to Bo Feres, who was troubled which waye to contrive the regaining of Muley Sheckk, who, like a bird, had broken cage and was flowne to Fes, making a faire pretence to governe but as Vizeroy, yet secretlie practised with forain states[1], either to make them his friends whereunto he might

---

1. Sur les relations du chérif Moulay ech-Cheikh avec le grand-duc de Toscane, Ferdinand Ier de Médicis, V. *supra*, p. 288 et note 5, et 1re *Série*, Dépôts divers, Florence, aux dates des 25 février et 15-24 octobre 1604.

flie, if Muley Bo Feres by force should drive him out of Fes, or, rather then he would loose footing in Affrike, determined to bring in foraine power for his ayde. Wherefore Bo Feres, fearing a Christian storme which might haile bullets, was carefull to keepe Abdela, Muley Shecks eldest sonne, the safer, to keepe the father surer from doing mischiefe. But it happened the plague[1] was sharpe in Moruecos; therefore Bo Feres sent his sonne Muley Abd el-Melech some five miles forth of Moruecos with his tents, and Muley Shecks sonne with him; but either his keepers were negligent and corrupted, or else young Abdela too wilie, for one night he made escape out of the campe, and, having horses ready layd, poasted to his father at Fes.

This gallant, being at liberty, sought all meanes to defend his title, being the eldest brothers sonne. His stirring spirit and youth-full hope drue all the minds of the Fezzes unto him; insomuch as Muley Bo Feres, sore afflicted with his escape, but more with the newes of his preparations[2], dispeeded Azus unto Muley Sidan, then in Sus, with request hee would go personally to battaile against Sheck and Abdela his sonne. Muley Sidan well entertained this message, and, with all convenient speede drawing his owne forces together, he came within halfe a daies journey of Morruecos, there pitching his tents, but not determined to hazard his fortune or trust the price of his owne head under his brothers hands; yet daily hee sent letters by his servants of great credit, wherein hee was willing to undertake the charge of warre against Abdela, so that he might make choyce of captains and commanders and such proportion of souldiers as he thought fit to undergo an action of such import. This proposition was neither liked of Bo Feres or his counsell; yet making faire weather to Muley Sidan, letters passed from him daily of great love, farced with many complements, much misliking his brothers mistrust, not daring to jeopard his person within Moruecos.

Muley Sidan, meaning to proove what corespondency his brother Bo Feres heart caryed with his hand, framed a letter which was sent as from the chiefest man in those mountaine countries of Atlas

1. La peste, qui avait commencé en 1597 (V. *supra*, p. 125 et note 2, et pp. 126-127), dura à l'état endémique jusqu'en 1608. Cf. EL-KADIRI, *Nacher el-Mathani*, Trad., t. I, p. 109; EL-OUFRÂNI, p. 305.

2. Sur les préparatifs de guerre de Moulay Abou Farès, V. 1re *Série*, Espagne, à la date du 30 juin 1605.

to Muley Bo Feres, full of dutie and services, offering withall to send him Muley Sidans head, who was encamped within his countrey at the foote of the hilles. Answere to this letter was returned with great thankes, and a large rewarde of gold promised, if a businesse of that high and important service would bee performed. When Sidan by this had confirmed his brothers meaning, he raysed campe, went to Tafilet and remained in the country of Dara, gathering in of money and men, after twoo monethes spent with his brother to no effect at all.

Bo Feres seeing Sidan departed, and destitute of his helpe for Fes, committed his campe to Abd el-Melech, his owne sonne [1], who was to be advised by the counsels of Basha Judar, alkeyd Hamet Monsore, Sedy Gowy and alkeyd Bo Kerse [2] (thorow whose hands passed all busines of Christian marchants, so well dispatched and so good regard thereof taken, that hee was well liked of everie man for his good dealing). This campe being come within a dayes journey of Fes, which is twentie dayes march from Morruecos, there the souldiers fell to a mutenie, and three thousand of them revolted unto Sheck, crying openly: « Long live Muley Sheck [3] ! ». Hereupon Abd el-Melech called a counsell of warre, wherein it was concluded, though their number were twise as many, to returne, without blow given, backe to Morruecos, perceyving indeed their souldiers hearts quite alienated from them.

Cap. XI.

Sir Anthonie Sherleys ambassage from the Emperour of Germanie to Muley Bo Feres performed. Anno Domini 1605.

Au commencement d'octobre 1605, Anthony Sherley, envoyé par l'empereur d'Allemagne, arrive à Safi. — Sir Edwin Rich fait partie de sa

---

1. Moulay Abd el-Malek marcha sur Fez en septembre 1605 avec une armée de 15000 fantassins, 20000 cavaliers et 30 pièces d'artillerie. V. *1re Série*, Pays-Bas, t. I, p. 98, et Dépôts divers, Autriche, à la date du 5 octobre 1605.

2. Il est dit plus haut (p. 351) que le caïd Bou Kourzia avait été tué dans une escarmouche, en juillet 1604.

3. Sur la rencontre des armées de Moulay ech-Cheikh et de Moulay Abd el-Malek, qui ont lieu près de Meknès, le 8 décembre 1605, V. *1re Série*, Dépôts divers, Florence, aux dates des 18 décembre 1605 et 25 janvier 1606; Pays-Bas, t. I, pp. 466 et 476.

suite, qui comprend environ treize personnes. — Sherley demeure quatre mois à Safi, où il tient table ouverte pour tous les marchands chrétiens et emprunte aux Juifs à gros intérêts. — Il achète un navire anglais avec toute sa cargaison de blé. — Moulay Abdallah s'empare de Salé, mais échoue devant la kasbah. — Le caïd de la kasbah demande à Moulay Abou Farès des ravitaillements et des renforts. — A la requête de Moulay Abou Farès, Sherley envoie son navire pour approvisionner la place; mais celle-ci succombe avant l'arrivée du dit navire. — Cinq cents hommes sont envoyés à Safi pour escorter Sherley à Merrakech. — Sherley s'acquiert un immense prestige en donnant à chacun d'eux un turban. — Moulay Abou Farès lui écrit des lettres très élogieuses. — Deux jours après son entrée solennelle à Merrakech, Sherley se rend à la Cour avec sa suite et, contrairement à tous les usages, traverse à cheval le Mechouar. — Le Chérif lui fait une réception très cordiale. — Revenant cinq jours après pour une nouvelle audience, Sherley trouve le Mechouar barré par une chaîne et, ne voulant pas descendre de cheval, il tourne bride fort mécontent. — Moulay Abou Farès lui envoie trois caïds pour l'apaiser. — Sherley se plaint de l'injure faite en sa personne à l'Empereur. — Les caïds rejettent le blâme sur le portier du Chérif, qui est bâtonné devant Sherley. — Durant ses cinq mois de séjour à Merrakech, Sherley s'entretient à diverses reprises avec Moulay Abou Farès sur les moyens pour celui-ci de se maintenir contre ses frères et de chasser les Turcs d'Alger et de Tunis. — Sherley revient très satisfait de Merrakech, avec deux seigneurs portugais qu'il a rachetés à Moulay Abou Farès et dont l'un est fils du vice-roi des Indes orientales. — En quittant l'officier du palais qui l'a reconduit à Safi, Sherley lui donne son chapeau orné d'un joyau de grand prix. — Le caïd Abdallah Sinko, renégat portugais, qui commandait l'escorte de Sherley, s'enfuit sur le navire de Sir Edwin Rich et part pour l'Espagne. — Sherley, qui était resté en rade sur un autre navire, envoie cinq hommes à terre pour un approvisionnement. — Ces hommes sont arrêtés par représailles et envoyés à Merrakech. — Sherley écrit à Moulay Abou Farès pour se disculper et réclamer les prisonniers. — Il met à la voile, avant d'avoir reçu la réponse de Moulay Abou Farès, qui a ordonné l'élargissement des captifs.

About this time, being the beginning of October, arrived at Saphia Sir Anthonie Sherley[1] as Ambassador from the Emperour

---

1. Sherley arriva à Safi le 2 octobre 1605. Sur ce personnage, V. *supra*, pp. 274-283.

of Germanie to the King of Morruecos; his attendance was better then a private man, though somewhat wanting of the person from whom he was sent. Few of note were in his companie, being in all about thirteene persons, of every Christian language one, because hee would bee fitted for interpretation of tongues. Amongst these was Sir Edwin Rich, whose behaviour was good and well spoken of in everie place were he came, not strayning his credite to borrow money, but well provided to serve his own turne, answering to his birth, state and disbursments for the time.

Sir Anthonie then taking the title of Ambassadour, during foure moneths[1] aboad in Saphia, kept open house, invited all Christian marchants dayly both to dinner and supper. To supplie his owne turne for money, he got credite of Jewes to take up money and pay them in Morruecos at excessive rate, almost fiftie for a hundred. He bought likewise of an English marchants factor, being at dinner with him, at two or three words, a ship of a hundred sixtie tonne with all her lading beeing wheat, paying him in hand two thousand ounces, and, if he were not payed the rest of his money within tenne dayes after his arrivall in Morruecos, then the buier to lose his earnest. But before hee went up, Abd el-Melech returning from Fes by reason of his soldiers treason, the King of Fes[2] marched towardes Morruecos some foure dayes journey, and there gave siege unto a port-towne called Sally, and tooke it, but the castle he could not win. So the alkeyd of the castle wrote to Muley Bo Feres, that, though the towne were lost, the castle hee woulde keepe for him, if he sent three hundred quarters of corne to vittaile his men, and a fresh supplie of fiftie souldiers. Bo Feres loath to loose the place, and hearing Sir Anthonie had bought a ship of corne, writ to Saphie, and willed him to send his shippe to Sallie, and there to unlade her corne for the reliefe of the castellan and his souldiers. Sir Anthonie, willing to doe the King a favour, sent for the captaine and marchant of the shippe, willed them to goe for Sally, and paying them for three hundred quarters, delt so that thither they went;

1. Anthony Sherley resta cinq mois à Safi, d'octobre 1605 à février 1606. V. *supra*, p. 278.

2. Entendez : Moulay Abdallah, fils du roi de Fez. Cf. 1re *Série*. Dépôts divers, Florence, 25 janvier 1606.

but, the castle being yeelded before they came, the captaine and marchaunt landed neither men nor corne, but returned to Saphie.

By this time were sent, for the conduct of the Embassador, five hundred men under the commaund of two alkeyds. Unto every souldier Sir Anthonie gave a turbith[1] as a livery of his love, which made them respect and honour him exceedingly, insomuch as one of the two alkeyds, not hastning to conduct the Embassador up to Morruecos, but to provide himselfe of corne, it being exceeding deare at Morruecos, Sir Anthonie desirous to set forward, and the souldiers willing to pleasure him, fell to mutenie in regard of the alkeyds stacknesse, killing twoo of his men to hasten their maister forwarde. After his foure moneths abode in Saphie, wherein his bountie was extraordinarie, not to his countrymen onely, but to Flemish, French and Spanish, admired of his souldiers, hee was received into Morruecos with great state[2], having by the way, as also during his abode in Saphie, diverse letters from the King, extolling his honourable endevours and approved valiantnesse in his far adventures both by sea and land, not omitting any courtship to winne his love or make him doubt his welcome.

After two dayes stay in the citie, the King made preparation for his entertainment at Court, whither he went, suting his followers as well as the shortnesse of time could suffer, and his credite with the Christian marchants could afford, which was good, for two Spaniards were so rapt with admiration of his worth, and by his speeches allured with so strange hope, that they fell in emulation whether should doe him more services or helpe him to more money. Reasonably attended, he rode to Court, not lighting from his horse where the Kings sonnes usually doe, but rode therew the Mushward[3] (which is the Kings great hall wherein most of his lords, gentlemen and chiefe sort of people doe attend, when they come to Court), which none but the King himselfe doth. Being come into the Kings presence, his letters of credite were receyved with great shewe of kindnesse, and himselfe entertained with all gracious respect, not onely at the Kings hands, but of the principallest men

---

1. *Turbith*, pour turban.
2. Sherley arriva à Merrakech au début de mars 1606. V. *supra*, p. 279.
3. *Mushoard*, Mechouar.

in office or favour about the Court, and so, for that time, was dismissed, the chiefest men attending him backe to the place where he tooke horse.

Some five dayes after, Sir Anthonie Sherley comming to audience and thinking to have ridden in as he did before, a chaine was hung crosse the entrance of the Mushward ; which he perceyving onely done to hinder his passage, would not alight from his horse, but returned backe verie discontented. This being certified to Bo Feres, presently three of his chiefest alkeydes were sent to qualifie the matter.

But Sir Anthonie tooke the disgrace not as his owne, but his whole person he represented, telling the alkeyds his maister the Emperour was able and would requite the injury, neither did he feare, though now within the power of Bo Feres, knowing the greatnesse of him in whose service hee was imployed so farre surpassing the King of Morruecos, as, maugre the proudest, he would be fetched from thence and bee fully revenged of the least injurie done unto him. The three alkeyds layde the blame uppon the Kings porter, offering Sir Anthonie the porters head, if he would have it, so spending an houre to pacifie his choller and bring him backe ; the porter before his face was sore beaten and imprisoned, neither ever after was he hindered of riding thorow the Mushward.

During his abode in Morruecos, which was five moneths, Bo Feres and he had diverse private conferences, as it was generally thought, which way to keepe him in the kingdome against his two brethren Sheck and Sidan, as also to give the Great Turke a blow to drive him out of Argiers and Tunes.

From Moruecos Sir Anthonie departed[1] with great content to himselfe and good liking of Bo Feres, of whom he bought two Portingall gentlemen for a hundred and fiftie thousand ounces, which amounteth to some ten thousand pound sterling. These two had beene captives in Morruecos almost 16 yeares, the one sonne to the Viceroy of the East Indies[2], the other of a noble house in Portingal[3]. The first had his resgat thrise sent for to ransom him out

---

[1]. Au commencement d'août 1606, V. supra, p. 281.

[2]. Antonio de Saldanha. V. supra, p. 290 et note 2. Il était fils d'Ayres de Saldanha, vice-roi des Indes de 1600 à 1604.

[3]. Pedro Cezar d'Eça. V. ibidem.

of the East Indies; but twise it was taken, by the English, once by Flemings during our late warres with them; the other his brethren drive him of for his resgat, either to save so much money, or not able to pay so great a fine.

To accompanie him from the Court to Saphie, was sent one of the Kings gentlement ushers, to whom at his parting he threw him his hat, which hee wore, from his head, with a jewell of great value, rewarding largely all the ushers followers. For his guard, the wayes being then very dangerous, was sent downe with him foure hundred shot, under the commaund of alkeyd Abdela Sinko, a Portingall renegado (which is a Christian turned Moore). This man, whether by perswasion or voluntarily, desiring to see his native countrey, in the night gat aboard of the ship Sir Edwin Rich was in, not Sir Anthonies; the ship presently weying anchor made saile for Spaine, but the other remaining with Sir Anthonie in the harbour.

This dealing was taken in ill part, insomuch that five of his men being sent to shore for certaine provision which they lacked, were clapped up in prison, and sent in chaines to Morruecos, but afterward released. Sir Anthonie writing to the King, both to cleare himselfe of the fact, and desiring remedie for these his new sustained grievances, set a good shew upon the matter, stayd foure dayes after the ship which had carried away the alkeyd, and would have tarried untill hee had his five men againe, but that he was written unto to bee gone, from an especiall friend ashore, advising him he did not well to ride so long in the port, divers Flemisch men of warre being abroad, and, if any should chaunce to come in there, as seldome it is without, they finding these two gentlemen as prize would scase uppon them : and then was there left thertie five thousand ounces, which a marchants factor had lent Sir Anthonie Sherley to cleare him out of the countrey, for which the factor had the two Portugales bound to pay this debt at their arrivall in Lisbon. Upon this advertisement, hee departed, and the next day Bo Feres sent him a letter to cleare his men [1].

And so I returne to the file of my continued history.

[1]. Sherley arriva à Lisbonne dans les premiers jours de septembre. V. *supra*, p. 282.

Cap. XII.

Muley Abdela goeth in person against Muley Bo Feres, driveth him out of Moruecos. Putteth to death Basha Judar and other noblemen.

Moulay ech-Cheikh, dans l'attente d'une bataille décisive, avait mis son fils Moulay Abdallah à la tête de ses troupes ; il tenait trois navires italiens à Larache pour s'enfuir à Florence, en cas de défaite. — La rencontre n'ayant pas eu lieu, il modifie ses dispositions, fait saisir tous les navires étrangers à Larache, Salé et autres ports, débarquer leurs canons, enrôler de force les équipages à son service. — Moulay Abdallah marche sur Merrakech et, grâce aux artilleurs chrétiens, il défait Moulay Abou Farès, près de cette ville, le 8 décembre 1606. — Moulay ech-Cheikh attendait l'issue de la lutte près des navires italiens, alors mouillés à El-Mamora. — Moulay Abou Farès traverse en hâte Merrakech et s'enfuit dans les montagnes. — Ses caïds, qui amenaient derrière lui son trésor, sa femme et ses enfants, sont attaqués par des Arabes et les femmes sont violées. — Les caïds tournent bride et reviennent se réfugier dans un sanctuaire à Merrakech. — Moulay Abdallah, qui leur avait promis le pardon, les fait exécuter et envoie leurs têtes à Fez. — Ainsi périssent le pacha Djouder, Sidi Gouaïa, le fils du caïd Azzouz et plusieurs autres notables.

Muley Sheck, putting his sonne Abdela forward to the whole commaund of the armie, himselfe meaning to save one, kept in Allarocha three Italian ships, purposing, if matters prospered not well, with treasure sufficient to go to Florence[1] ; but the battaile not fought, his determination altered, for hee presently seized all strangers ships which came either to Laratch, Salie or other parts, as also some marchants ships of Fes, robbing them of their goods,

---

1. A la demande de Moulay ech-Cheikh, le grand-duc Ferdinand Ier avait envoyé à Larache un vaisseau commandé par le capitaine Pompilio Peretti, à bord duquel le Chérif devait s'embarquer et se retirer en Toscane, dans le cas où ses troupes auraient été défaites. Le capitaine Pompilio Peretti arriva à Larache, le 17 septembre 1605. Mais sa mission fut rendue inutile par suite de la retraite de Moulay Abd el-Malek, dont les troupes refusèrent de combattre, le 8 décembre 1605. V. supra, p. 355 et note 3. Cependant, le séjour du capitaine Peretti se prolongea, à Larache d'abord, puis à El-Mamora. V. 1re Série, Dépôts divers, Florence, aux dates des 24 septembre et 8 octobre 1605, 25 janvier et 6 mai 1606.

making the marriners land their pieces, and all the men either to serve him or else to have the yron given them. Hereby he fitted himselfe of captaines and souldiers, being English, French and Dutch, with 27 pieces of ordinance and shot thereunto sufficient, and so fired the minde of his sonne Abdela with hope of winning Moruecos (being of himselfe drunken with the ambitious desire of a kingdome) that Abdela, about the latter ende of November 1606, marched to Moruecos with his troupes being some ten thousand horse and foote, besides his Christian marriners, whose helpe wonne him the field, fought some sixe myles south-east from Moruecos, on the eight of December 1606 [1].

Sheck bore his sonne company no farther then Salio, from whence three houres riding is a river called Mamora, into which by the Italian shippes put in. Sheck went thither, and hard by the shippes uppon the shoare pitched his tent, wherein he lay, part of his treasure beeing shipped, himselfe determining there to stay and expect the event of his sonne; if it passed well with him, then Affricke should hold him; otherwise to visite the Great Duke of Thuscane, on whose courtesie he much rested [2].

But the Christian gunners so well observed their times of shooting and placing their ordinance, as they gotte Abdela the field, hoping thereby to have obtained both libertie and pillage; of which most of them, poore men, fayled, as afterward you shall read.

When Sheck hears Abdela has gotte Moruecos, hee grew careles to send provision or supplie the wants of his three Italian shippes, wherefore they set saile from Mamora homewards, taking such treasure for their pay as were in their custodies [3].

Bo Feres lost in this battaile about six hundred men, fled into the

---

1. Sur la bataille du 8 décembre 1606, à la suite de laquelle Moulay Abdallah entra à Merrakech, le 10 décembre, V. *1re Série*, Pays-Bas, t. I, pp. 173, 210-211 et 467, et *supra*, p. 307 et n. 1. La rencontre eut lieu dans une localité nommée Akelmim, suivant les uns, ou Mors er-Remâd, suivant d'autres. EL-OUFRÂNI, p. 313.

2. Il y a confusion dans l'exposition des faits. Les événements mentionnés dans ce passage se rapportent à avril 1606, époque où l'on s'attendait à la marche de Moulay Abd el-Malek sur Fez. V. *supra*, p. 361 et note 1 ; *1re Série*, Espagne, à la date du 20 avril 1606, et Dépôts divers, Florence, à la date du 6 mai 1606.

3. Le capitaine Pompilio Peretti ne revint d'El-Mamora à Livourne que le 6 décembre 1606. V. *ibidem*, aux dates des 9 novembre et 6 décembre 1606.

citie to save his treasure and his women; but, for feare of being surprised, durst not tarry to take his treasure away with him, but in all hast poasted toward the mountaines, willing the alkeids and chiefest men of his court to bring it after him with the rich swoord the like whereof is not in the world, committing also to their conduct his daughter and the chiefest of his women, amongst whome was the wife of Ben Wash[1], the Kings marchant. At the entrie of the hilles, a kindred of the Larbies, being five hundred horsemen, seized uppon these people[2], pillaged their cariages, rifled and dishonoured the women, not sparing Bo Feres daughter; whome Abdela determined to have married, but hearing divers Mores to have lyen with her, and also that shee was suspected to have lived in incest with her father, after his enterance into Moruccos he never enquired farther after her.

The alkeids, being well mounted, by the swiftnesse of their horses, returned backe to Moruecos, and there tooke sanctuarye. Abdela uppon their submission promised them pardon, on whose princelie word they relying came foorth, the Foker of the place presenting them.

But Muley Abdela, whether incited by envious counsell, or on his owne bloody minde, putteth them so secretly to death, that, sending all their heads in one sacke to Fes for a present for his father, their deaths were not fullie known in the citie of Moruccos, before their heads were set uppon Fes gates. Here was the end of Basha Judar[3], a great souldier in olde Hamets time, a faithfull commaunder during his life to Bo Feres, accompanyed with Sedy Gowie[4], alkeid Azus his sonne, alkeid Moden the Cassemie[5], and some foure great men more[6].

---

1. Ibrahim ben Ways. Sur ce personnage, V. supra, p. 233 et note 7.

2. Sur la capture de la smala de Moulay Abou Farès, qui se réfugia dans la kasba du caïd Azzouz, V. EL-OUFRÂNI, pp. 318 et 371; 1re Série, France, t. II, pp. 403-404; Pays-Bas, t. I, p. 210 et note 8. Sur le sort ultérieur de Moulay Abou Farès, V. infra, p. 379 et note 1.

3. Basha Judar. Sur le pacha Djouder, V. supra, p. 66 et note 1, et passim.

4. Sedy Gowie. Sidi Gouaïa, frère cadet du caïd Moumen Bou Kourzia. V. supra, p. 233 et note 6, p. 341 et note 1.

5. Moden the Cassemie, nom trop défiguré pour pouvoir être restitué.

6. Onze caïds furent exécutés. V. 1re Série, Pays-Bas, t. I, p. 212 et note 6.

Cap. XIII.

Muley Sidan commeth against Muley Abdela, getteth Moruecos from him, killeth eight thousand of his men, and, upon colde blood, causeth 3000 thousand Fezees to bee slaine, yeelding uppon good composition.

L'exécution des caïds et les exactions commises par les troupes de Moulay Abdallah font fuir beaucoup d'habitants de Merrakech vers Moulay Zidân et mécontentent ceux qui restent. — Moulay Zidân, qui se trouvait à mi-chemin entre Fez et Merrakech, marche sur cette dernière ville. — A son approche, ses partisans délivrent les prisonniers dans la ville et, au milieu du tumulte, introduisent un fort détachement de ses troupes, qui est repoussé par Moulay Abdallah après un vif engagement. — Le lendemain, Moulay Abdallah se porte à la rencontre de Moulay Zidân, campé au nord de la ville. — Moulay Zidân l'attaque avec ses meilleurs cavaliers. — Moulay Abdallah fait avancer par des chemins étroits, entre des jardins, son artillerie, qui repousse la charge. — Les cavaliers de Moulay Abdallah, lancés à la poursuite de l'ennemi, viennent masquer l'artillerie. — Saisissant cet avantage, Moulay Zidân ramène des troupes fraîches contre l'adversaire, qui se replie en désordre sur l'artillerie. — Les canonniers chrétiens, qui voulaient tirer quand même, en sont empêchés par le Maure qui les commande. — Moulay Zidân s'empare des canons. — Dans le carnage qui dure environ quatre heures, sept à huit mille hommes sont massacrés. — La plupart des soldats chrétiens périssent dans l'action ou sont exécutés ensuite. — Moulay Abdallah s'enfuit à Fez avec moins de cent hommes. — Moulay Zidân entre dans Merrakech. — Trois mille hommes des troupes de Fez, qui tiennent encore la kasba, refusent de la rendre ; mais, surpris par l'escalade soudaine de cinq cents hommes, ils se réfugient dans la mosquée dépendant de la kasba. — Sur la promesse d'être épargnés, que leur apporte le caïd Sliman, ils rendent les armes ; mais ils sont immédiatement mis à mort par ordre de Moulay Zidân, qui veut venger la mort des caïds.

This tyranny of Abdela shewed uppon these valiant and woorthy men, and the spoyle which the Fezees had made, as well in robbing the alkeids houses as in ryfling the citizens goods and committing al outrages which follow war, caused many to flie to Muley Sidan, and the rest which remained in Moruecos grewe discontented, so that the sunneshine of Abdelas happines scarce lasted two monethts;

for Sidan, resting in the halfe way between Moruecos and Fes, taking oportunity of this uproare of the townsemen, marched toward Moruecos on the north side of the towne, determining to give present battaile, hearing by the scowts that Muley Abdela his campe was lodged in the great garden or orchard called the Almowetto[1], being some two English myles about. The first night of Sidans approach, the prisoners were released and prisons broken open, so that these men, getting liberty, ran halfe mad up and downe the cittie, crying: « Long live Sidan! », which troubled the citizens not a little. And in this uproare, Sidans faction let into the citie, at a secret gate, many of his souldiers, which made a sally upon the regiment of Zalee, meaning to have surprised Abdelas campe; but himselfe, comming to the rescue with two thousand men, continued a hotte skirmish against the Sidanians, in which the Christians fought valiantly to recover their peeces of artillery which were lost, untill the Sidanians were forced to retyre.

The next day, being the 25 Aprill[2] *stilo novo*, Abdela remooved towards Muley Sidan, who was encamped on the north side of the citie, not daring to come on the south side for feare of the shot which galled his men from the battlements of the Kings house[3]. Therefore, he hearing of Abdelas remove, and intending to venture his fortune upon a present battaile, set forward to meete him with a regiment of his best horse. Abdela, perceaving this, caused his canoniers to march formost, which could but place five peeces of their artillery in a brest, because the orchards and gardens made the passages very narrowe and straight whereas the armies should meete. Sidans horsemen gave a very gallant charge, but the canoniers made them retyre, which Abdelas horsemen perceiving, being encouraged, and too eager of the chase, some thousand horse galloped before their own ordinance and followed their enemie close to Sidans campe, their peeces of artillary being drawne after them. Muley

---

1. *Almowetto*, nom mal transcrit. Il s'agit du jardin d'El-Menara, situé à 3 km. à l'ouest de Merrakech.

2. La bataille de Djenan Bekkar, que l'auteur va raconter, eut lieu le 25 février 1607, d'après P. M. Coy et Arnoult de Lisle qui se trouvaient sur les lieux. V. 1re Série, Pays-Bas, t. I, pp. 213-216, et France, t. II, p. 429.

3. La kasba de Merrakech, renfermant le palais du Sultan, se trouve à l'extrémité sud de la ville.

Sidan, well knowing the advantage of the place, seeing his enemies deprived of the benefit of their great ordinance, which he most feared, encouraged his men to keepe their ground, and bringing with his owne person fresh supplies to second them, gave his adversaries the Abdelians so hotte a charge, that they were faine to retire in great disorder upon the mouths of their owne artillary. This disarray perceived by the Christian gunners, it put them in minde to discharge uppon their owne men the Abdelians, holding it better to kill five or sixe hundred of their owne side then to loose the battaile. But the More who was captaine over the canoniers and other commaunders would not suffer it. Therefore the Sidanians, following in good order and very close, fell to the execution with their swoords, surprised the artillery and slew the men.

The slaughter continued some foure houres, betwixt seaven or eight thousand killed, and fewe to speake on left alive; for, what the souldiers spared, the citizens, in revenge of their disorders, pillages and villanies done to their women, bereaved them of their lives: who being dead were not suffered to bee buried, but lay above the ground as a prey to the dogges and fowles of the ayre. Heavie likewise was the conquerors hand uppon the Christians which tooke Abdelas part; most of them, for their five moneths service to Abdela, were either slaine in the fury of battaile, or after had his throat cut. And this was the ende of them who had lived in the Streights of Gibraltar and the Mediterranean Sea, not as marchants by honest trading, but having committed spoyle upon divers seafaring men, felt the bloody hande of a barbarous nation, as a deserved punishment sent from God, to execute justice for their manifold committed wrongs and outrages [1].

This battaile being lost with the greatest bloodshed that any hath been since these warres beganne, Muley Abdela fledde to Fes, a hundred persons of his whole armie not left alive to beare him company; and Sidan, maister of the field, entered the citie of Morruecos, having another taske to take in hand, ere hee could settle himselfe quietly in his owne nest. For the Kings house being

---

1. D'après P. M. Coy, quarante-cinq Anglais, dont les capitaines Peres et Foydts, périrent dans cette bataille. V. 1re Série. Pays-Bas, t. 1, p. 217.

castle-wise builded, and severed from the citty with a defencible and a stronge wall, lacking no kind of munition for the defence thereof, had within it, besides souldeirs of Morruecos, three thousand Fezees, who were not at the last battaile, but left there to guard the place for Abdela.

These presuming on their owne valour and strength of the place, denyed to render it uppon any tearmes to Sidan, though they were sollicited during the space of two dayes by all faire meanes thereunto. Sidan, bringing his artillary to the walles, yet delayed, as loath to deface a building so strong, costly and beautifull. So that, in the meanetime, a captaine, whose house joyned to the wall, by stealth, with five hundred men, scaled and wonne the top of the wall, crying: « Victory for Muley Sidan! » which so amazed the souldiers within, thinking the forces which were entered farre greater than they were, without more adoe or offering to resist, they tooke sanctuary in the great church[1] belonging to the Kings house, every man with his peece and furniture about him.

Muley Sidan upon this sent Basha Seleman[2], willing them to deliver up their armes, with promise they shuld be pardoned: which presently they did, yeelding and delivering both swords and peeces[3]. Thus disarmed, they seely soules came forth, when, presently after, message came from the King to butcher and cut the throates of them, which was executed. A pittiffull matter, in my judgment, so many men yeelding upon good composition after furie of battaile, upon cold blood to be made so pittifull a spectacle. It was bootlesse for them to alledge either law or reason in defence of their lives; such is the miserie and slaverie of that people, whose goods and lives lieth alwayes in the will of the King, either to save or destroy at his pleasure. Some colour Sidan had for his tyrannie, thinking these Fezees would never be woonne wholy to be his, but upon fit

---

1. La mosquée d'El-Mansour, près de Bab Agnaou, construite par le sultan almohade Yacoub el-Mansour.

2. Le pacha Sliman avait été maître de la cavalerie de Moulay Ahmed el-Mansour. Il fut gouverneur du Soudan, du 18 mai 1600 à juillet 1604. Es-Sadi, pp. 289-291; cf. supra, p. 187 et note 2. Il fut assassiné le 12 mai 1607. V. infra, p. 371 et note 1.

3. Cette capitulation, avec promesse de la vie sauve, n'est pas mentionnée par P. M. Coy, dans le récit qu'il fait du massacre des gens de Fez, qui eut lieu les 26 et 27 février (V. 1re Série, Pays-Bas, t. I, p. 216, n. 1 et p. 467), mais d'après Guadalajara (f. 94 v°), il y eut bien capitulation.

time and everie little occasion revolt from him. Secondly, he meant to requite Abdela *lege talionis*, for putting so many commaunders to death, prizing everie one of their lives worth three hundred common souldiers.

Cap. XIV.

Sidan sendeth great preparations against Abdela, who, after composition, murdereth verie neare three thousand Sidanians. Sidans bloodie decree against the Shraceis for their offence.

Moulay Zidân, à Merrakech, extorque l'argent des notables et devient impopulaire. — Il envoie contre Fez une armée sous les ordres du caïd Moustafa et reste lui-même à Merrakech, craignant qu'en son absence la ville ne se soulève. — Moulay ech-Cheikh se rend à Larache, prêt à s'enfuir sur un navire néerlandais. — Moulay Abdallah rencontre près de Meknès les troupes de Moulay Zidân. — Celles-ci refusent de se battre; le plus grand nombre prennent la fuite; d'autres, trois mille soldats de Merrakech, s'étant livrés avec confiance à Moulay Abdallah, sont mis à mort. — Trente à quarante canonniers Anglais, qui étaient au service de Moulay Zidân, sont faits prisonniers; d'autres s'enfuient à Merrakech. — Moulay Zidân envoie ses caïds lever de nouvelles troupes et de l'argent parmi les Arabes. — Six cents Cheraga, sur les douze cents que Moulay Zidân avait à sa solde, font partie du détachement commandé par le pacha Sliman. — Ils mettent à mort leur chef et portent sa tête à Moulay Abdallah. — Moulay Zidân ordonne un massacre général de tous les Cheraga, soldats ou autres, résidant sur son territoire. — Beaucoup d'entre eux, gens riches, qui habitaient Merrakech, périssent; d'autres se sauvent ou se cachent. — Ce n'est qu'en apprenant la venue de Moulay Abdallah que Moulay Zidân, effrayé, donne l'aman aux survivants. — Moulay Abdallah, vivement poussé par les meurtriers du pacha Sliman, qui lui ont amené des renforts de leurs tribus, se met en marche pour Merrakech vers la fin d'août. — Son armée compte près de quinze mille hommes.

Now is Sidan setled in Morruecos, but scarce secure, for the chiefest men in the citie wished an alteration because their King, to get their money and wealth to maintaine his owne estate, began to picke quarrels with them, making some, who began to speake and to repine at his doings, lose their heads, *quoniam canis mortuus non latrat*. The common people, whose naturall condition is alwayes to desire novelties, wished for a newe King, feeling his oppression and the famine[1], whereof many dyed, grewe carelesse of peace, thinking everie change would bring a remedie, when indeed it was like the incision of an unskilful surgion, not curing the maladie, but making the wound wider, gangrened and incurable.

Sidan, purposing to purge this malecontented humour of the comminalitie, raised an armie of twelve thousand foote and sixe thousand horse, determining to take Fes. The chiefe men of commaund over this armie were these : basha Mustefa, alkeyd Hamet ben Breham[2], alkeyd Ally Tahila, alkeyd Gago and alkeyd Hadoe Tobib[3], with divers other ; Muley Sidan not going in person with this armie, least in his absence Morruecos, the seate of the empire, should revolt.

Muley Sheck, hearing these newes, went to Allarocha, there tooke a great Flemish ship from the marchant, with all the goods in her, therein shipping his treasure, determining to run away, if his sonne Abdela should lose Fes[4]. Abdela omitted no time to gather new forces, so that in small he thought himselfe sufficient to meete the Sidanians in open field, and so hee did neare to Mickanes[5], where the people on Sidans part, missing their King on the field, or any one of the blood royall, refused to fight, and, instead of striking, fell to parley that, if Abdela would pardon them, they would yeeld ; and so they did. Yet most of them ranne away, except three thousand Morruekyns, who, presuming upon Abdelas gentle nature, stayd with him, hoping kind entertainment into his pay ;

---

1. Sur cette famine, qui régna au Maroc en 1606-1608, V. *1re Série*, Pays-Bas, t. I, pp. 147 et 471.

2. Le caïd Ahmed ben Brahim es-Soflani. V. *infra*, pp. 374 et 396.

3. Sur le caïd Haddou Tebib, V. *supra*, p. 348 et note 2.

4. C'est à El-Mamora que Moulay ech-Cheikh comptait se réfugier, en cas de défaite. Deux vaisseaux espagnols devaient venir le chercher, mais ils ne partirent qu'en janvier 1608, et la tempête les força de revenir à San Lucar. La victoire de Moulay Abdallah et son entrée à Merrakech rendaient dès lors ce projet inutile. V. *1re Série*, Dépôts divers, Florence, aux dates des 22 janvier et 20 février 1608.

5. La bataille eut lieu le 2 octobre 1607 sur les bords de l'oued Tifelfelt (oued Tiflet), à 70 km. à l'ouest de Meknès. V. *1re Série*, Pays-Bas, t. I, pp. 260 et 469 ; Guadalajara, f. 95 ; El-Oufrâni, p. 315.

instead whereof Muley Abdela commaunded all their throats to bee cut, graunting them onely this favour, first to bee stripped for fowling their cloathes. Thus we may see mercilesse Sidan butcher poore soules at Morruecos, pittilesse Abdela murder these unfortunate slaves at Mickanes, both verefying the old proverbe:

Quicquid delirant reges, plectuntur Achivi[1].

In this battaile were taken betwixt thirtie and fortie Englishmen, who served Muley Sidan as canoniers, yet not any of that companie which served Abdela at Morruecos, when he lost the citie and field[2], but other voluntaries. Part of these fledde with the bodie of the armie backe to Morruecos, part were taken, whome Abdela spared as well in regarde of former services the nation had done him, as also for the present use he was to employ them in.

This expedition of Sidans comming to so unlooked a disaster, made him send forth his commanders with divers companies to the Alarbies, for fresh supplie of men and treasure; amongst which as chiefe was dispeeded Basha Seleman[3], maister of the old Kings horse, for Tafilet, there to governe the countrey, carrying with him some fifteene hundred shot, of which sixe hundred were Shracies[4], people of the King of Chaus or Coucocs country[5], who hath alwayes warrs with Algers or Argiers.

These Shraceis were borne in the mountaines of Atlas, being of a fierce and bloodie nature, not respecting the Turkes might or government no more than the montaniers of Morruecos will acknowledge the soveraintie of the Barbarian[6]. Some twelve hundred of these had Sidan in his pay, halfe whereof he kept at Morruecos, the other was sent with Seleman. These amongst themselves

---

1. Vers d'Horace déjà cité par George Wilkins dans sa relation de 1604. V. *supra*, p. 258 et note 1.

2. V. *supra*, p. 365 et note 2.

3. Sur le pacha Sliman, V. *supra*, p. 187 et note 1, p. 367 et note 2. C'est au Soudan, d'après Es-Sadi (p. 295), et non au Tafilelt, comme il est dit plus bas, qu'il aurait été envoyé.

4. *Shracies*. Cheraga. V. *infra*, p. 472, n. 3. Moulay Ahmed el-Mansour avait dans son armée deux divisions de Cheraga. El-Oufrâni, p. 197. V. *1re Série*, France, t. II, p. 215, n. 3; Pays-Bas, t. I, p. 463, n. 6.

5. Il s'agit du royaume de Couco, qui correspondait à la Grande Kabylie d'aujourd'hui.

6. *The Barbarian*, le roi du Maroc.

fell into a mutenie, neither for want of pay or ill usage, but in desire to doe a mischiefe, by force cutt off the Bashas head, carrying it with them as a trophie of their victorie, and a fit present to winne Abdelas favour, who was then at Fes, whither they went for entertainment [1].

Sidan herewith moved made proclamation that, for three moneths, what Shracee soever, souldier or any other, were to bee found in Morruecos or elsewhere in his dominions should be put to the sworde; and to have it better and more fully executed, it was proclaimed that the manqueller should have the goodes of the Shracee so killed. Many rich men of this nation or kindred, resiant in Morruecos, felt the furie of the sworde for the follie and foule fault of their tribe. Such as could get packing ran away, others of the better sort their friends hid them in their houses, untill Sidan, scared with the newes of Abdelas comming towards him, proclaimed generall pardon for the remainder left alive, and free passage of trading or commerce for any Shracee which would venture to Moruecos; yet few durst come upon these goodly termes, or those who lay hid in Morruecos, if they were worth anything, shew themselves in publique, for feare this were a pretence to bring the residue unto the halter.

Those Shracees who were sole causers of this massacre, beeing with Abdela at Fes, dayly moved him to goe towardes Morruecos, vowing every man to die in his cause, and for revenge for their wives, children and friends who had smarted for their sakes. Abdela, something animated with their offers, yet delayed, knowing his forces farre inferior unto Sidans, untill still urged by the Shracies, which had brought from the mountaines some store of their kindred, verie able and resolute men, to his ayde, he set forwards about the latter end of August towards Morruecos, determining to give battaile once more to Muley Sidan. Of what strength Abdelas armie consisted is not knowe, but ghessed to be very near fifteene thousand horse and foote.

---

1. Le pacha Sliman partit le 10 mai 1607, et fut massacré par ses soldats à deux journées de Merrakech. 1re Série, Pays-Bas, t. I, p. 468. Ce fait est donc antérieur à la bataille de l'oued Tifelfelt, qui vient d'être racontée.

Cap. XV.

Sidan flieth. The death of the valiant captaine John Giffard and divers Englishmen. Abdela regaineth Morruecos.

L'armée de Moulay Zidân, qui était très forte, comptait, outre les propres soldats de ce prince, huit mille hommes de Merrakech, deux cents Anglais, soixante pièces de campagne. — Le contingent chrétien était commandé par le capitaine John Giffard. — Celui-ci avait reçu en présent de Moulay Zidân un sabre de grand prix et un manteau brodé de perles, offerts autrefois à Moulay Ahmed par la reine Élisabeth. — Il touchait vingt-cinq shillings par jour, sans compter les libéralités du Chérif. — Avec lui servaient son parent Philip Giffard, le capitaine Jaques, le capitaine Smith, un des meilleurs ingénieurs de l'Europe, et plusieurs autres. — La plupart touchaient douze shillings par jour, les simples soldats douze pence. — Les devins de Moulay Zidân lui prédisent qu'il sera vaincu et chassé dans le Sous, mais qu'il reprendra Merrakech dans cinq mois et règnera sa vie durant. — Moulay Zidân, en conséquence, fait partir sa mère, ses femmes, ses enfants, et charger son trésor sur des mulets. — La bataille s'engage à seize milles environ de Merrakech : les canonniers de Moulay Zidân déchargent leurs pièces trop tôt; les Cheraga de Moulay Abdallah attaquent avec furie; les troupes de Moulay Zidân se débandent au premier choc. — Moulay Zidân fait dire aux Anglais de battre en retraite; ils s'y refusent; le capitaine Giffard est tué; trente Anglais au plus survivent à la bataille, dont deux capitaines. — Quarante Maures à peine périssent. — Les habitants de Merrakech, qui ne regrettent pas Moulay Zidân, accueillent sans enthousiasme Moulay Abdallah. — Celui-ci ne trouve aucun trésor au palais royal et ne peut récompenser ses troupes. — Pour les faire patienter, on répand le bruit qu'un trésor a été découvert dans un puits. — Trois mille Cheraga, constatant qu'ils ne sont payés qu'en bonnes paroles, se retirent. — Moulay Abdallah demeure environ deux mois à Merrakech, cherchant tous les moyens de contenter ses troupes et de les retenir.

Muley Sidan was verie strong, for beside his owne souldiers, the Morruecans ayded him with eight thousand men, and divers tribes sent supplies to augment his forces. He had twoo hundred English, the most of them voluntaries, sixtie field-peeces with sufficient shot and powder. Over the English and all the Christians was generall Captaine John Giffard¹, a gentleman of a worthy spirit, and discended from the auncient and honourable stemme of the Giffards in Buckinghamshire. Upon his first entertainment and welcome into this countrey, Sidan bestowed upon him a rich sword valued at a thousand marks, and a scarlet cloake richly imbrodered in pearle, sent as a present to Muley Hamet, the Kings father, from our late soveraigne of famous memorie Queene Elizabeth, besides manie other extraordinarie favours of good value, and often conversing familiarly, yea, sometimes visiting Captaine Giffard at his owne tent.

His entertainment was twentie five shillings *per diem*, besides many supplies proceeding from the Kings bountie. With him, as secondarie men in charge, was one maister Philip Giffard, his neare and verie deare kinsman, Captaine Jaques, a verie valiant souldier, Captaine Smith, one of the most exquisite engineers in Europe, Captaine Baker, an ancient Brytaine souldier, Captaine Tailer, Captaine Faukes, Captaine Chambers, Captaine Isack, men everie way able to undergoe their severall commaunds. These were dayly stipendaries at twelve shillings a man, except the two sea captaines Isack and Chambers, who had foure shillings a day, and everie common souldier twelve pence truly payed them.

These preparations considered, Muley Sidan had small reason to leave the field or feare Abdelas forces, being nothing in respect of his. But certaine it is, the Muley sending for his wisards, soothsayers, willing them to foretell, that hee might foreknow the successe of his embattailed armie, their answere was that he should loose the battaile, be driven into Sus, within five moneths should regaine

---

1. Le capitaine John Giffard avait servi dans les Pays-Bas, sous les ordres de Sir Francis Vere. Ayant encouru la disgrâce de Jacques Iᵉʳ, il entra au service de Ferdinand Iᵉʳ de Médicis, grand-duc de Toscane, prit part à l'expédition d'Alger en 1604 et pénétra dans le port pour incendier les vaisseaux des pirates. Le Grand-Duc, pour le récompenser, lui confia le commandement d'un navire marchand. Après un premier voyage dont il avait rendu bon compte, il s'enfuit avec le navire, sa cargaison et une somme de 12000 écus appartenant au Grand-Duc. 1ʳᵉ *Série*, Dépôts divers, Florence, aux dates 26 septembre et 19 octobre 1605; Van Meteren, liv. XXXI, f. 623. L'historien Godard commet à la fois une erreur et un anachronisme en disant (p. 480) que ce personnage fût envoyé par Charles Iᵉʳ, à la demande de Moulay Zidân, pour soumettre Salé, et que les troupes auxiliaires qu'il commandait concoururent à l'extermination prétendue des pirates de cette place.

Morruecos, and there during life enjoy the kingdom. Upon this answere, the Muley, giving great credit therunto, as the nature of a Barbarian is verie suspicious, commanded Basha Mustefa with 3000 souldiers to convey away his mother, wives and children. To alkeyd Hamet ben Breham and Hado Tabib he commended the charge of his treasure, who laded sixtie mules with gold, garding them and the muleters with two thousand of his choysest shot.

These dispeeded, it may appeare Sidan but hovered and would follow, yet the battailes met the 26 of November 1607, some sixteene miles from the city of Morruecos[1], the canoniers of Muley Sidan part having in the forefront discharged, there enemies being somewhat farre off; but before they could charge again, the enemie was with them.

The Shracies did not once discharge a peece, great nor small, but joyning themselves close to the Abdelians[2], charged the Sidanians verie fiercely with their sables, revenge of Sidans tyrannie shewed uppon their kindred enraging their minds and courages. Or their faithfull promise, which they sought to make good, to Abdela, made them put the Sidanians to flight, or els it was Sidans feare, that hee shoulde not make good his soothsayers prophecie, which made his men to runne away. For, at the first encounter, his Moores fell into a disarraay and presently into a dishonorable flight; wherupon Muley Sidan fled, sent to the English captaines to be gone, and to Captaine Giffard a good horse to save himselfe.

The English returned word that they came not thither to run, but rather die an honourable death. Captaine Giffard encouraged his men, telling them there was no hope of victorie, but to prepare and die like men, like Englishmen, and then asking for his Jaques, whom he loved dearely, and taking a pike in his hand, thought to have rode unto him, being told he was not six score from him, and to have died together.

---

1. La bataille eut lieu à Ras el-Aïn (50 km. au N.-E. de Merrakech) le 6 décembre 1607 (26 novembre vieux style), d'après P. M. Coy. V. *1re Série*, Pays-Bas, t. I, pp. 268 et 469. Arnoult de Lisle donne la date du 8 décembre. V. France, t. II, pp. 428-429; EL-OUFRÀNI, p. 315. GUADALAJARA, ff. 95 v°-96, offre un récit détaillé de cette rencontre, mais il la place erronément « aux fêtes de Noël 1607 ».

2. *Abdelians*, partisans de Moulay Abdallah.

But, in the way, Captaine Giffard being charged by eight Abdelians, one behinde him shot him thorow, and so was he there slaine[1]. Few of al the English nation were left alive, the number not exceeding thirtie, and none of the commaunders escaped, except Captaine Isack and Captaine Faukes. Of the Mores were not slaine in all fortie persons.

Sidan being gone, as loath to tarry, spend bloud and winne a field, Abdela got the ground his enemyes marched uppon, but no great victory, entered Morruecos[2] without applause or rejoyce of the citizens, some yet feeling his late done injuryes, nether sory for the losse of Sidan, who had proved a tyrant, nor welcomming Abdela upon hope of amendment, but with policy and patience fitted themselves to the misery of the time.

Abdela, once againe maister of Moruecos, got the Kings house, but found no treasure to releeve his wants. Great were his promises to rewarde the Shraceis with bounty and enrich his followers when the citty was recovered. Now hee having it, there fayled of his expectation, and his souldiers lacking both meat and money. Yet to keepe them still in hope, and so in government, it was bruited the yong King had found a well full of treasure within the house, which Muley Hamet Xarif had layed up for a deare yeare. But this good newes quicklye vanished, the well not yeelding water to refresh their fainting stomacks. Therefore the Shraceis having released their kindred, recovered their wives and children which had escaped the fury and bloody decree of Sidan the last King, they tooke good words and kind usages of Abdela in lieu of payment, seeing Moruecos neither afforded them meat nor Abdelas fortune further maintenance; and so three thousand of them departed at one time. Muley Abdela with the residue of his forces kept Moruecos, labouring by all possible meanes to give his souldiers content and keepe them together. So with much ado he lived in Moruecos some two monethes, during which time Muley Sidan was gathering a fresh army in Sus.

1. Sur la mort de John Giffard, cf. E. van Meteren, liv. XXXI, f. 623, qui le représente luttant en chemise et refusant de se rendre, quand Moulay Abdallah voulait lui faire quartier.

2. Moulay Abdallah entra à Merrakech, le 10 décembre 1607. *1re Série.* Pays-Bas, t. I, p. 470.

Cap. XVI.

Muley Hamet Bosonne commeth against Abdela, and causeth him to flie to his father. Bo Feres, like to bee taken, flyeth to Salie. Muley Sidan commeth against Muley Hamet Bosonne, who flieth and is poysonned by old Azus.

Un cousin des trois prétendants, Moulay Ahmed ben Abou Hassoûn, réunit près de vingt mille hommes dans les montagnes et s'avance contre Merrakech. — Moulay Abdallah, sentant la résistance impossible, se retire à Fez. — La mère de Moulay Zidân, s'imaginant que Moulay Ahmed ben Abou Hassoûn opère pour le compte de son fils, envoie pour l'aider des gens de sa garde et de sa tribu. — Ceux-ci reviennent annoncer que Moulay Ahmed ben Abou Hassoûn s'est fait proclamer roi lui-même. — Ce prince autorise une trentaine d'Anglais à aller s'embarquer à Safi. — Il gouverne avec justice et honnêteté. — Sa mère, venant des montagnes pour le rejoindre, investit la forteresse où s'était réfugié Moulay Abou Farès, lequel s'enfuit dans la nuit et gagne Salé. — Le lendemain, entrant dans la place, elle met à mort l'un des principaux serviteurs de ce chérif, le caïd Messaoud en-Nebîli, puis rejoint son fils à Merrakech. — Moulay Zidân sort du Sous avec une puissante armée et rencontre, près de Merrakech, les troupes du prétendant. — Il refuse au cheikh des Ksima l'honneur de donner l'attaque. — Ce dernier ayant passé outre et allant être culbuté, Moulay Zidân lui envoie des renforts. — Les troupes de Moulay Ahmed ben Abou Hassoûn s'enfuient vers les montagnes. — Moulay Zidân rentre à Merrakech. — Moulay Ahmed ben Abou Hassoûn revient devant cette ville, comptant sur l'appui des habitants. — Nul ne bouge en sa faveur. — Vaincu et réfugié dans la montagne, il est empoisonné par le caïd Azzouz. — Ce caïd, qui, sous le règne de Moulay Abdallah el-Ghâlib, avait conseillé à ce prince de mettre Moulay Ahmed à mort, était devenu le principal conseiller de ce dernier. — A la mort de Moulay Ahmed, il se déclara pour Moulay Zidân. — Mais Sidi Abdallah ben Embarek et lui, rebutés par l'entêtement de ce prince, se sont retirés, le premier à Akka, et le second dans un château fort des montagnes, où il a amassé de grandes richesses et vit en sûreté.

But whilst Abdela and Sidan were contriving their owne endes, there arised a storme in the mountaines, which fell in the plaines of Moruecos. The tempest driver was one Muley Hamet Bosonne[1], cosine to the three brethren which have striven for the kingdome. This man, gathering treasure and temporising with them all three, so played their game, that, finding their weaknes which these quarrels had brought them unto, uppon a suddaine, seeing his time, went into the mountaines to his mothers kindred, mustered very neare 20 thousand able men. The Muley, being well provided of treasure, gave them due pay and large, winning them to his respect and service, so that, in lesse then two moneths space, hee gotte all thinges in readines, descended from the Tessevon[2] mountaines towards Moruecos[3].

This news brought to Abdela was very unwelcome; yet, calling his wittes and councell together, it was concluded, considering the Schraceis were gone, his remnant of souldiers feeble and out of heart, and the Moruecans daily fled to Hamet Bosonne, whose uprising like a blazing starre drew their eyes uppon him, that Abdela should travell to Fes, which he might well doe without a guide, having heretofore uppon like necessities often measured the myles. And, though he was determined so to doe, yet a small occasion hastened his journey; for some myle from Abdelas campe, upon a hill on the backside of Morruecos, a man being seen with a speare in his hand and a white linnen uppon it as a flagge, Abdela thought Hamet Bosonne to be with his whole forces behinde the hill, when hee was a full daies march from Moruecos. Therefore in all hast he tooke up some of his tents, but the greater part, left standing in a manner, being feared, ranne away[4]. And after-

1. *Muley Hamet Bosonne*, Moulay Ahmed ben Abou Hassoun, *alias* Mohammed. Sur ce personnage, V. 1ʳᵉ Série, Angleterre, t. I, p. 256, Pl. III, Tableau généalogique des princes de la dynastie saadienne, n° 29; France, t. II, p. 430; Pays-Bas, t. I, p. 267, note 5.

2. *Tessevon*, peut-être les montagnes d'où sort l'oued Tessaout.

3. Abou Hassoûn alla rejoindre au Djebel Guiliz les adversaires de Moulay Abdallah, qui s'y étaient rassemblés.

4. Si impossible que paraisse cette panique, elle est rendue vraisemblable par de nombreux exemples constatés en pays indigène. Il est probable qu'elle fut le fait, non de l'armée entière, mais de quelque détachement de troupes. D'après GUADALAJARA (f. 98), Moulay Abdallah envoya contre le prétendant le caïd Ali ben Mansour Gutierrez. Victorieuses une première fois, ses troupes se débandèrent dans une seconde rencontre; il dut, le 31 janvier 1608, évacuer Merrakech, qui ouvrit ses portes à Moulay Ahmed ben Abou Hassoûn. Cf. 1ʳᵉ Série, France, t. II, pp.

ward, when this matter was discovered, which Abdela held a token of his surprise, it was nothing else but a poore More washing his napery, and for the speedier drying used this meanes, which terrifyed Abdela from the seate of his empire to Fes, the safest place for his abode.

Lylla Isha, Sidans mother, hearing of Hamet Bossones approach, was perswaded his movements were onely to defend her sonnes right, knowing Bosonne of late favoured Sidans title, comming into his pay and in person serving the Muley at the last battaile when Sidan fled into Sus. Hereuppon shee sent divers captaines, part of her owne guard, others of her freinds and kindred, to his ayde, thinking he would have taken Moruecos for Sidan. But Bosonne, having entered the citie peaceably, proclaymed himselfe King, dismissed all Sidans favourers which were not willing to bee his servants, who returned to their lady mistresse, certifying her error and their successe.

His treasure he imparted largely to his followers, by strong hand desired no mans service but those who were willing. Some thirtie Englishmen remayning, wearie of their sustained misery and the state of the country, he gave them licence to imbarke, and writte to the governour of Saphia to give them their passe; notice whereof being given to the factor marine for the English, he disparted them into divers shippes with all conveniency, though to his cost and charges, charity to helpe the distressed soules, and love to his native country moving him thereunto. This Muley Hamet Bosonne, during the time of his government, was a very good and just man, offered no discourtesie or tooke away any mans goods, but payed the marchants trulie for the same, who liked well his currant and true dealing [1].

Bosonnes mother, hearing her sonne was setled in Morruecos, brought what strength shee could from the mountaines; and in her way, knowing Bo Feres, lodged in a fortresse whereunto he was fled, not to be well guarded, she beset the house, meaning to take the Muley prisoner; who being voyde of all means to resist, in the

---

429-430; Pays-Bas, t. I, pp. 270 et 469; El-Oufrâni, p. 317.

1. Les bons procédés de gouvernement de Moulay Ahmed ben Abou Hassoûn sont attestés par P. M. Coy. V. 1re série, Pays-Bas, t. I, p. 278 et note 4.

night, made a hole through the wall and so escaped privately to Salie, a porte towne within the jurisdiction of his brother Sheck, where at this day he remaineth[1].

On the morow betimes, Bosonnes mother with her men entered the fort, missing Bo Feres, cut off the head of Umsed Benbela[2], one of his chiefest servants and commanders; then went shee forward to congratulate her sonnes comming to the kingdome, beeing then in Moruecos. But an empire ill got is seldome seene of long continuance; for within lesse than two moneths, Muley Sidan came out of Sus with a great army, for whose ayde Lylla Isha sould her jewels and plate to furnish her sonne with swords, pikes, horsemen, slaves and other warlike munition.

On the other side, Hamet Bosonne prepared to welcome his cousine the Muley Sidan. So about the beginning of Aprill 1608, both their forces met hard by Morruecos[3], where a chiefe of a kindred, one grufe which came out of Sus, a great wyne-drinker, alwaies a favourer of Muley Sidan, though little valuing any of the three Kings, presuming uppon his owne strength and valour, desired the honour that hee might give charge uppon the enemy with five hundred horse, which was his owne regiment and of his owne kindred. Sidan refused to graunt him his request; therefore the Casima tooke his owne leave and gave the enemy a full charge uppon the body of his army; which receaving him very bravely, the Casima and his company were in great danger to bee overthrowen. But Sidan, to releeve him, sent five hundred horsemen of his owne; so, with these thousand, the Casima broke the ranks of Bosonnes battalions, then with their sables fell to execution, until the whole campe seeing the field lost, fled towards the mountaines.

Thus Sidan without further resistance entering Morruecos, resting therein quiet three moneths, untill Hamet Boson recovering new forces in July following, presented himselfe before the citie,

---

1. Moulay Abou Farès demeura désormais auprès de Moulay ech-Cheikh et de Moulay Abdallah, jusqu'au jour où celui-ci, craignant que son oncle ne voulût le détrôner, le fit étrangler en sa présence (août 1609). Cf. El-Oufrâni, pp. 318-319; Guadalajara, f. 112 v°.

2. *Umsed Benbela*, le caïd Messaoud en-Nebili.

3. D'après P. M. Coy, cette rencontre eut lieu le 23 mars. V. 1re série, Pays-Bas, t. I, p. 278.

trusting as well uppon his owne strength as the love of the citizens, hoping his good and gentle usage, when hee was amongst them, would have bred a liking in them of his milde and gentle government. But either the servile minde of the multitude little respected his forepassed kindnesse, or the feare of Sidan made them loath to shewe any signe of good will; for at his approach no man in the citie was knowen to drawe a swoord in his defence. So on the eight of July[1], Bosonne was discomfited with the losse of some thousand men, fledde to the mountaines, where, within foure dayes after, alkeid Azus got him poysoned[2], hoping thereby to winne the favour of Muley Sidan.

This Azus is aged and subtill, by long experience knoweth the secrets of that state, was brought up under Abdela, Muley Hamet Xarifs brother, and for his counsell to Abdela, willing him either to put out the eyes of Hamet Xarif or cut his throate, was in daunger to have lost his life, when Hamet Xarif came to be King, but the wisedome of the man wonne such respect with Hamet, that of a prisoner he made him his chiefest counceller and master of his treasury[3]. During whole lifetime, his behaviour was such as he wonne great love among the commons, nobility and many of the blood royall. When old Hamet dyed, he was in his campe neare Fes, and after his death rested all his love upon Muley Sidan, holding him the prime man and fittest of the three brethren to rule the kingdome, untill both he and Sidy Imbark[4] could not counsell and rule Muley Sidan for his owne good and benefit of the commonweale, being headstronge, and would take no mans counsell but to his owne liking and hurt[5]. Therefore Sedy Abdela Imbark went to his contemplation of Aca, and Azus to a castle in the mountaines, which hee had stored with treasure against a storme, or to refresh the winter of his age; from whence he will not come

---

1. P. M. Coy place cette seconde rencontre de Moulay Zidân et de Moulay Ahmed ben Abou Hassoûn, qui se produisit à Aghmat, à la date du 24 mai 1608. V. 1re Série, Pays-Bas, t. I, pp. 282 et 470-471.

2. P. M. Coy annonce la mort de Moulay Ahmed ben Abou Hassoûn dans une lettre du 4 juillet. V. ibidem, p. 286.

3. Ces mêmes détails sont donnés, en des termes presque identiques, dans la Relation de George Wilkins. V. supra, pp. 251-252.

4. Sidi Abdallah ben Embarek. V. supra, p. 352 et note 2.

5. Went to his contemplation of Aca. Entendez: il revint à Akka mener sa vie ascétique.

downe untill he see some hope of peace, having at this instant more treasure in his coffers then all the three brethren besides, and hopeth to keepe it, beeing in the middest of his friends and kindered, and in place as well fortified as any in Barbarie.

Cap. XVII.

Muley Sheck sendeth John Etyna[1] into Spaine; the Mores are against their landing.

Moulay ech-Cheikh, effrayé des revers de son fils et des succès de Moulay Zidân, envoie un marchand italien, Gianettino Mortara, offrir à Philippe III Larache, Salé, El-Ksar et d'autres places, en échange des secours de l'Espagne. — La négociation aboutit ; Gianettino Mortara reçoit promesse d'une rente de deux mille ducats à la remise des ports marocains. — A la fin d'août 1608, une flotte espagnole de cent navires, avec des pionniers, fait voile vers Larache. — Trente mille Arabes accourent au rivage pour s'opposer aux Espagnols. — Le caïd de Larache offre à ceux-ci les clefs de la ville, mais leur fait observer qu'ils sont venus trop tôt et n'ont pas laissé le temps de préparer l'opération. — Les Espagnols repartent sans débarquer. — D'aucuns pensent qu'Anthony Sherley, qui a été magnifiquement récompensé par Philippe III de sa mission au Maroc, faisait partie de l'expédition. — Il est certain que Sherley a une grande expérience du Maroc et sait prendre les habitants. — Mais il est probable qu'il n'était pas sur la flotte, car il eût fait réussir l'expédition, ou tout risqué pour cela. — L'auteur, que ses informations ne mènent pas plus loin, arrête son récit, laissant Moulay ech-Cheikh et Moulay Abdallah à Fez, Moulay Abou Farès à Salé ou sur la côte,

1. *John Etyna*, Gianettino Mortara. Ce gentilhomme génois était venu à Fez pour offrir des diamants et autres bijoux à Moulay ech-Cheikh, qui en était un amateur passionné. Rojas, f. 11. Dès l'année 1605, il était ouvertement l'agent de l'Espagne auprès du Chérif. V. *1re Série*, Espagne, aux dates 15 et 30 juin 1605. Une rivalité d'influence s'établit entre lui et les Florentins Nicolo Giugni et Bastiano Acquisti, mandataires du grand-duc de Toscane. V. *supra*, p. 288 et note 5. En 1606, Gianettino, ayant été informé de la correspondance de Moulay ech-Cheikh avec le Grand-Duc, en avertit le duc de Medina-Sidonia et donna au Chérif le conseil de saisir les biens de Giugni et d'Acquisti. V. *1re Série*, Dépôts divers, Florence, aux dates 20 décembre 1606 et 20 février 1608. En 1606, il avait détourné Moulay ech-Cheikh de se retirer en Toscane (*Ibidem*, à la date du 2 juillet 1608), et Philippe III, pour supplanter le Grand-Duc, avait écrit au Chérif, le 25 janvier 1607, pour lui offrir des navires, afin de gagner l'Espagne, en cas de nécessité. Guadalajara, l. 96 v°.

Moulay Zidân à Merrakech, tandis que l'Espagne médite un agrandissement en Afrique et garde sous sa main l'héritier légitime du trône marocain.

Muley Sheck, seeing his sonne Abdela returned to Fes, his souldiers part lost, the residue wearied with travels and out of heart, his treasure all spent, nothing left, Sidan chasing Bosonne to the mountaines, who was there dispatched of his life, recovering the citie and likely to keepe it against them all, fearefull lest Sidans next enterprise would bee to rowze him out of Fes, fell in conference with an Italian marchant, named John Etina, making him his agent to go into Spaine, there to conclude that, if the Catholique King would ayde him with men and money to recover his right, there should be delivered up in his handes Allaroche, Saly, Alcasar, and other townes lying fit for his mouth[1].

This negotiation was well entertained, and John Etina was promised, for his labour in this businesse and bringing it to effect, uppon the delivery of the porte-townes, to have yearely paied him twoo thousand duckets during his life. In June last past, this matter was first mooved; since which time, in the latter end of August, as my author telleth mee, seaven gallions and the gallies of Naples, in all a hundred sayle, well manned with store of pyoners to raise forts, went to Alaroche, thinking to bee receaved. But thirtie thousand Alarbees came downe to the shore, not allowing any such neighborhoode, though they holde the Andelusian halfe their bloud. It is reported the governour offered them the keyes of Allaroche, if they would land, but tolde them they came somewhat to soone, before matters were ripe or could bee effected as Sheck did desire for the King of Spaines benefite. Thus

---

1. Au commencement de l'année 1608, Gianettino, porteur de lettres de Moulay ech-Cheikh, se trouvait en Espagne, où sa présence est constatée à Madrid le 15 mars. V. *1re Série*, Dépôts divers, Florence, à la date ci-dessus. Sa mission ne consistait nullement à négocier une cession de ports marocains à Philippe III ; il devait informer le roi d'Espagne de la victoire de Ras el-Aïn (6 décembre 1607), et demander un sauf-conduit pour Moulay ech-Cheikh, dans le cas où les événements obligeraient le Chérif à passer en Espagne. Toutefois, Gianettino traita de la remise de Larache à Philippe III avec le duc de Medina-Sidonia, mais ce fut à l'insu de Moulay ech-Cheikh. GUADALAJARA, ff. 96-97 ; ROJAS, ff. 11 v°-12. Gianettino repartit pour le Maroc en juin 1608. *1re Série*, Dépôts divers, Florence, à la date du 2 juillet 1608.

are they returned, missing of their designes, and for this yeare likely to fayle of making their maister the onely commander of both sides the Streights of Gybralter[1].

Whether Sir Anthonie Sherley was ymployed in this service is not certainely knowen : some are of opinion that he was induced thereunto, because they have formerly hearde the King of Spain hath royally rewarded him for his travailes with Bo Feres, by giving him the places and pay of two captaines in the Indies, made him admirall of all the Levant seas, and next in place to the Vizeroy of Naples, having for his entertaynment five hundred duckets a moneth. Without question, hee knoweth well the state of that uncivill and barbarous nation, having an apprehending and admirable witte to conceave the disposition of any people with whom he shall converse. Whilest he was amongst them, he behaved himselfe very well toward the better sort, winning credit whith them, and gayning the love of the poorer sort exceedingly by his larges ; for if a More or slave gave him but a dish of dates, hee should receive a reward as from an Emperour ; and, howsoever some may holde this a vice, counting him a lavisher, yet by this meanes he came to the knowledge of that which otherwise hee never should have attained unto. The more credible fame is Sir Anthonie was not with this fleete ; therefore they sped never the better, for had hee beene in company and had commaund, hee would either have taken footing or ventured all, scorning to returne with nothing doing and so bee laughed at. This may bee a *caveat* for great men not to undertake great matters and exploits, but uppon certaine ground and weighty reason ; for else the envious eye of the world, looking uppon them

---

1. A la suite des négociations de Gianettino avec le duc de Medina-Sidonia (V. *supra*, p. 381, note 1), Philippe III envoya une expédition sous les ordres du marquis de Santa-Cruz pour occuper Larache, que Gianettino avait dit être dépourvue d'hommes et de munitions. La flotte espagnole arriva devant Larache, le 6 septembre 1608, et débarqua 200 hommes sur la plage, mais l'état de la mer obligea de les rembarquer, et deux jours après la flotte était de retour à Cadix. V. *supra*, p. 316 et note 2 ; 1re Série, Dépôts divers, Florence, 5-8 septembre 1608. Moulay ech-Cheikh, qui n'avait nullement alors l'intention de livrer Larache, se montra très irrité de la tentative espagnole, fit emprisonner Gianettino et ne le remit en liberté qu'après la défaite qu'éprouva son fils Moulay Abdallah sur les bords de l'oued Bou Regrag, le 27 janvier 1609. GUADALAJARA, ff. 100 v°-102 v° ; ROJAS, ff. 12-13 et 16.

and marking their actions, will deride if they see them faile in their enterprizes[1].

Now, gentle reader, must I, with these galleys, returne to the safe and calme harbour of your favour and gentlenes. Seeing the sunne declyneth towardes the winter tropike, the seas will beginne to runne high and rough ; if they should lanshe further into the maine, perchance they might bee weatherbeaten. Even so for me to write without advice is to saile at randome, which would quickly be found in your wisedome how I ventured without my seacard, and might, without more directions, easily make shippe-wracke of my smale burden, not valuable, I confesse, yet will be better prised if it passe your friendly censure. Therefore here will I strike sayle, leaving Sheck with his sonne Abdela in Fes, Bo Feres either at Salie or uppon the sea-coaste, redier to flye then to fight, Sidan holding the sterne at Morruecos, hoping to guide his tossed barke during the prophecy[2], Spaine a great monarch[3], desiring to take better hold in Affrique then Tituan, having at this instant Muley Sheck, commonly called Prince de Morruecos[4], the right heyre in discent from the stemme of Hamet Sheck Xarif[5], in his safe keeping, who was the first man which gotte the empire from the Marines and translated it into his owne family.

[Cap. XVIII[6].]

The damnable Religion of the incredulous More or Barbarian.

Comment Mahomet fonda l'Islam ; sa doctrine sur le Christ. — Mahomet

1. A cette époque (1607-1609), Anthony Sherley, nommé par Philippe III amiral des mers du Levant, parcourait les villes d'Italie. V. supra, p. 282.
2. V. supra, pp. 373-374.
3. *Monarch*, monarchy.
4. Ce prince avait été baptisé sous le nom de Felipe de Africa. V. supra, p. 156 et note 1 ; p. 310 et note 1.
5. Entendez : Moulay Mohammed ech-Cheikh, le vrai fondateur de la dynastie saadienne. Selon le droit européen, le fils de Moulay Mohammed el-Mesloukh était, comme le dit l'auteur, l'héritier légitime du trône. V. 1re Série, Angleterre, t. I, p. 256, Pl. III, Tableau généalogique des princes de la dynastie saadienne, n° 30.
6. La numérotation des chapitres s'arrête au chapitre xvii. Les chapitres suivants contiennent des renseignements généralement très exacts sur la religion, les mœurs, les institutions. On les rapprochera avec

envoyé par Dieu pour achever l'œuvre du Christ. — Le Coran, seul livre religieux qui soit autorisé, est interprété par les tolba, qui l'apprennent par cœur. — Cérémonie de la circoncision. — Il y a quatre principales fêtes : la première est la Pâque ou Aïd es-Seghir ; elle est précédée du Carême ou Ramadan, pendant lequel le jeûne est rigoureux ; exemple d'un Maure qui, insulté par la foule pour avoir étanché sa soif dans les rues de Merrakech, se tua de désespoir. — La seconde fête est l'Aïd el-Kebir, où l'on immole un agneau dans chaque famille ; le Roi en tue un de ses propres mains, le visage tourné vers l'Orient. — La troisième fête, dite El-Achoura, est célébrée après la rentrée des récoltes ; le Roi s'en autorise pour se faire payer la dîme ; les Maures s'affranchissent souvent de la dîme qui est due également aux églises à cette occasion, le clergé ne disposant d'aucun moyen de contrainte. — La quatrième fête, dite Aïd ech-Chemma, correspond à la Chandeleur ; d'immenses cierges, semblables à des mais ou à des tours, sont portés au Roi à travers la ville ; lectures publiques de la loi durant la nuit. — Ces lectures se font également au vendredi saint des Maures.

The false prophet Mahomet, calling to counsell a Jew and a fryer to make his lawe, extracted out of the Olde Lawe what he found for his liking, and likewise perverted places in the Newe Testament which, by a wrong and sinfull wresting, might seeme fit for his purpose. Out of these two and the fancies of his own braine, the Devill being register, Mahomet compiled his Alcoran. To please the Jew, hee told him Moses was Cillim Ulla[1], that is the word of God, because hee spake to the Israelites as God commanded him. To winne favour with the fryer, hee confessed our Saviour Christ was of great esteeme, calling Him Sedy Nysa[2], and withall sayd He was Roh Alla[3], that is, the breath of God, borne of the Virgine Marie after a strange fashion, whome he called Lylla Mariam, but not incarnate. Confessed that of her was borne a

---

fruit de ceux qui ont été donnés par Jean Mocquet, Le Gendre, Mouette, Dapper, Höst, etc. — L'appareil critique étant en français, on a dû donner les transcriptions françaises des mots arabes, sans vouloir prétendre qu'elles soient préférables aux transcriptions anglaises de l'auteur. On sait combien est vaine la recherche d'une transcription exacte. V. 1re Série, Angleterre, t. I, Introduction, pp. xvii-xx.

1. *Cillim Ulla*, Kalam Allah, la parole de Dieu.
2. *Sedy Nysa*, Sidna Aïssa, Notre Seigneur Jésus.
3. *Rohalla*, Rouh Allah, l'esprit de Dieu, l'Esprit Saint.

prophet to save the world, to whome all should have given care and have believed; but the Jewes, before he had finished the woorke of our salvation, would not heare, but sought to crucifie him. Whereupon Christ, seeing the Jewes so obstinate, ascended up into Heaven, putting another man in his place to be crucified, whom they did torment[1]; for which cause the Jewes are at this day slaves amongst them. That Christ shall come againe, and at His comming all shall be one, and gathered into one sheepfold.

Their false prophet Mahomet, whom they call Rosulla[2], that is the messenger of God, was but a Larbee as they were, but God gave unto him power and understanding to make an end of the Law, which the Jewes would not suffer Christ to doe; and most blasphemously alledge that place in the sixteenth of Saint Johns Gospel to be meant of Mahomet: *Expedit vobis ut ego vadam ; si enim non abiero, Paracletus non veniet ad vos ; si autem abiero, mittam eum ad vos*[3]. Images they disallow, either in churches or private oratories, holding this principle: none can forgive sinnes but God onely.

Other booke of religion then their Alcoran none may use, neither anie explains by writing the meaning of any place therein, be he never so learned. Therefore if any doubt, he must goe to the priest called talby[4], and of him be resolved. Smal learning maketh a talby, which is onely to learne the Alcoran without booke; and it is thus learned: first, he hath written to him a lesson upon a boord like unto a hornbooke; when he hath learned that *memoriter*, then is it wiped out; so a third, so a fourth, untill he hath learned it all; and then hee may be made a talby.

Circumcision they use and a kind of baptisme, but at their owne houses, not in the churches, because women used about the lavature may not enter the sinagogue: first, because of their often uncleanesse; secondly for their offence, because Eve incited Adam

1. On lit en marge : « Judas is the man who, they say, was crucified instead of Christ; which error might grow of this, that Simon Sireneus carried His crosse. »
2. *Rosulla*, Rassoul Allah.
3. Ce verset de Saint Jean (xvi, 7) annonce, d'après les Musulmans, la venue de leur prophète; ils ont transformé le Paraclet, παράκλητος (le Consolateur, l'Esprit-Saint), en περικλυτός (illustre), mot qui serait exactement rendu en arabe par celui de Mohammed.
4. *Talbi*, taleb, pluriel tolba, proprement : savant.

to sinne (the like custom for their women is amongst the Jewes). Therefore the Moore, when a sonne or daughter is borne, the eight day after their birth the parents send for a talby and some old men and women ; where, after a fewe prayers said, the women wash the childe all over with water, and so give the name, making a banket according to the mans abilitie. But it may be the child shall not bee circumcised of two, three or eight yeares after, according as the father doth thinke good, for then he maketh great bankets, and usually, to save cost, hath a child marryed, or some of his kindred upon that day.

They have foure principall feasts. The Easter, which is called Rumedan[1] ; preceding this feast is their Lent, about the constitution of which their Prophet, finding it hart to fast fortie dayes together, abated them tenne, so they fast but thirtie ; yet is it verie hard, for after day breaketh, they take no manner of sustenance in the world, not so much as a sup of water, before night that the stars doe appeare. So strict are they when their Lent falleth high in the yeare (which it must needes doe, because their yeare is shorter than ours by ten dayes, reckoning by the moone, not by the moneth) as many grow faint with fasting ; and my author saith he hath seene divers layd before the church doore, readie to give up the ghost for drought, and some have died, holding it, no question, something meritorious to die in seeking to fulfill their law. And once the same gentleman, travailing to Morruccos with certaine Moores in his companie, in their time of Lent, one of the Moores being thirstie with heate and travaile, went to a conduit in the streetes of Moruecos to drink a little water, but the people so wondered at him and reviled the poore slave, crying out hee knew not God for breaking in publique their lawe (though it doth admit one may breake the fast for great necessitie a day or two in his travaile, so hee take upon his conscience to fast as many dayes as hee hath missed before the next Rumedan come againe), that the poore slave, seeing himselfe condemned of his owne people, and dishonoured before the Christian travailers, in a desperate minde, which may be counted zeale, killed himselfe with his owne

---

1. Erreur. Le Ramadan est le jeûne qui précède la fête, et non la fête elle-même.

dagger. The Jewes in that countrey observe a Lent in remembrance of their fortie yeares journey in the wildernesse, but divide the fortie dayes of this their Lent equally, in every moneth some.

Their second feast called Lidlaber[1], celebrated about our Whitsontide, is kept in remembrance of Abrahams obedience in sacrificing his sonne Isaac : therefore the Moore, be he poore or rich, for himselfe and for everie sonne he hath, will buy a sheepe against the day, when every one must kill his sheepe with his owne hands. And the King doth the like, flaying one with his owne hand, turning the head into the east. The Jewes in their church or synagogue, three or foure times when they are at prayers, do blow a sheepes horne in remembrance of this feast, but no every one bloweth it, only the greatest Raby or High Priest for solemnitie sake doth it.

Their third feast is like to our Michaelmasse, called Lashour[2], which the Jewes keepe as the Feast of Tabernacles. The Moore celebrateth it after his inning of corne and fruits. The King maketh use of this positive lawe, strengthning it with his authoritie, as also with the habite and cloake of religion and conscience, thereby to make his subject pay the tenths, due to bee payed at that time, of all his corne and cattle, both young and old, with greater alacritie ; all which commeth unto the Kings coffers. Likewise at this time the common people should pay the tenth of their money to the poore and church ; something indeed they give, but, if the King bee payed, that oftentimes is winked at, their church having no command to compell the laitie to pay their due. For the temporall sword, since Augustines time (who, as many do report, hath preached in Morruecos, and not farre from thence lieth buried[3]), hath beaten downe the key of the prelacie ; the beautie of which being taken from them, no doubt is the greatest cause of their barbarisme and slaverie.

1. *Lidlaber*, El-Aïd el-Kebir ; elle se célèbre 70 jours après l'Aïd es-Seghir et c'est pour cette raison qu'elle est comparée à la Pentecôte. L'Aïd es-Seghir et l'Aïd el-Kebir sont, en réalité, les seules fêtes musulmanes essentielles, celles qui sont mentionnées ci-après n'ont qu'une importance secondaire.

2. *Laschour*, El-Achoura, se célèbre le 10 du mois de Moharrem et ne correspond nullement à la Saint-Michel. Sur cette fête, V. DOUTTÉ, *Magie*, pp. 526 et ss.

3. Sur la légende qui confond Saint Augustin avec Sidi bel Abbès es-Sebti, V. Ire *Série*, France, t. III, p. 213, note 4, pp. 733 et 739.

There fourth feast is their Candlemasse day, called Lidshemaw [1], when every one must have a candle for himselfe, and for every sonne in his house. The King, that day, hath candles carried to him thorow the citie, some like maypoles, other like castles, sixe or eight men carrying one of them; they are so great and heavie, made so fine with devices, as some are in making sixe moneths. That night the King doth heare all his law read, and the like is done in all other churches.

Likewise, upon their Good Friday, in Lent, the law is read over, and the talby which cannot read it over in one night, is held insufficient for his place and function. Many of their learned men sit up all that night, because many of the devotest Moores will watch the night thorow to heare their lawe. Not in remembrance of our Saviour Christ is this meeting, but rather to suppresse the sparkes of Christianitie in the mindes of their owne people, and darken the remembrance of His most bitter death and passion.

[Cap. XIX.]

The Manner of Going to Prayer.

Les Maures prient six fois par jour et font, auparavant, des ablutions. — Le premier temps de la prière se place deux heures avant le jour; éveillés par le muezzin, ils peuvent rester chez eux pour prier. — Ceux qui vont à la mosquée enlèvent leurs chaussures à l'entrée; ils se tiennent en rangs, debout ou assis; les plus zélés se prosternent à terre. — Deux heures plus tard, au jour, ils retournent à la mosquée, puis vont à leur travail. — Le troisième temps de la prière est à midi. — Le quatrième vient tout de suite après quatre heures. — Le cinquième est à l'heure du crépuscule. — Deux heures plus tard, les uns vont à la mosquée, les autres prient chez eux, pour obtenir une bonne nuit. — Leur mode d'ablutions. — Le vendredi, qui est leur jour de sabbat, ils ne cessent pas le travail, mais fréquentent plus assidûment la mosquée. —

---

1. *Lidshemaw*, El-Aïd ech-Chemma عيد الشمع « la fête des Cierges », connue sous le nom d' « El-Mouloud », c'est-à-dire « la Nativité », où l'on commémore la naissance de Mahomet; elle se célèbre le 12 du mois de Rebia el-Aouel. Elle est appelée « fête des cierges », parce qu'il est d'usage d'illuminer en ce jour les mosquées et les maisons.

Les mosquées n'ont pas de sièges, ni d'ornements ; le sol est couvert de nattes et très propre ; il n'y a pas de cloches ; la voix puissante du muezzin en tient lieu. — Le clergé est pauvre et se contente de peu ; il pratique la polygamie. — Aucune église n'est riche, sauf la principale mosquée de Fez, dont le trésor ne peut être employé qu'à repousser une invasion des Chrétiens. — Ils n'ont aucune liturgie, aucune formule de prière ; chacun suit son inspiration.

They go to service sixe times in twentie-foure hours, washing themselves quite over before prayer, either *post concubitum uxoreum*, or going to stoole or urine, so much respecting the saying : « Wash and be cleane », as by washing they are perswaded to bee cleansed of their sinne.

Their first time of prayer is two houres before day, which is salie[1], when the sexton or mouden cryeth from the top of the steeple : *Helo caber ; helo helelow Hula*[2], which is : Oh Thou Great God, and none but one God. Then every man awaketh, washeth himselfe, and desireth God to send him the day. After this crie, no man may touch his wife, but prepare himselfe to serve God, which he may doe by his bed side, if he will not goe to the church, but first to wash, or his devotion is no way acceptable. Those that come to the church, either at the entrance must leave their shooes behind them, or carrie them in their handes. During their prayers, either they stand all arow, one row before another, or sit so ; but they are held most devote, who prostrating themselves bow their foreheads to the verie ground. After their praier, it may bee some desire to confer about some poynt of religion. Then both the talby sit downe and his auditours about him in a ring or circle, to whom he declareth what they desire to be resolved upon, and within halfe an houre dismisseth them, this being all they have instead of preaching.

---

1. *Salie*, sala, la prière. Il doit exister une lacune soit dans la rédaction, soit dans le texte imprimé. L'auteur a vraisemblablement pensé à nommer cette prière, comme il l'a fait pour les autres. Il faut rétablir : « which is salie [el-fedjer] », c'est-à-dire « qui est la prière de l'aurore ».

2. Il est impossible de reconnaître sous cette transcription, d'ailleurs très écourtée, la formule d'annonce à la prière (adan), qui est la suivante : *Allah akber ! Allah akber ! La ila illa Allah. Mohammed rassoul Allah. Haï ala es-sala ! Haï ala el-Felah !* « Dieu est le plus grand ! Dieu est le plus grand ! Point de dieu, si ce n'est le Dieu. Mahomet est l'envoyé de Dieu. Accourez à la prière ! Accourez au salut ! »

Some two houres after, when it is day, they goe to church againe, thanking God he hath sent them the day, after which every one goeth to his labour. And this time of prayer is called subelhall[1].

The third time of prayer is at noonetyde, giving thankes the half day is passed, which they call dehour[2].

Presently after foure of the clocke is churchtime againe, desiring the sunne may well set upon them; and this is called lasour[3].

Being twilight, they give God thanks after their dayly labors, desiring his blessing may prosper them; this they terme mogrube[4].

And two houres after this is their time of prayer called lasha[5] ell-hara, when some go to church, but most say prayers at home, desiring God to send them good night and quiet rest, provided alwayes before saying of prayers they wash themselves, though not starke naked, yet their hands, head, feete and nether parts betweene their legges; for which cause they hold it unseemly to eat any meate with their left hand, or touch any thing therwith, but all with their right hand, the other accounted as uncleane.

As we celebrate the Sabbath upon Sunday, in remembrance of Christs resurrection, the Jewes uppon Saturday, so the Moores upon Fryday, who will doe any worke upon their Sabbath, onely that day they goe more duely to the church then on other dayes.

Their churches[6] are not so goodly builded as ours in Christendome, neither have seates to sit in, or decked up with any ornaments, but all the floore is matted and keept verie cleane, because no man may enter with shooes or any thing to defile them. Bels they have none in their steeples, but the mouden or sexton, being a big voyced knave, chosen for the purpose, standeth in the top of the steeple, and calleth them to their sallies or prayers.

Their churchmen are verie poore and contented with a little, may have as many wives as the layman, neither is there any church of great foundation or rich in treasure, except the chiefe

---

1. *Subelhall*, sabah, la prière du matin.
2. *Dehour*, dohor, la prière de midi.
3. *Lasour*, el-aasser, la prière de l'après-midi.
4. *Mogrube*, la prière du maghreb, c'est-à-dire du coucher du soleil.
5. *Lasha*, el-acha, la prière du soir. L'épithète *ell-hara*, placée à la suite, a sans doute le sens de *pure*, mais n'est pas d'un usage courant.
6. On lit en marge : « Churches and their service ».

church in Fes, which is thought to have treasure a million of crownes, which may not bee spent except the Christians should come to invade.

Their church service or lethargie is nothing at all in respect, nor in any set forme, not so long as the Lords prayer and the Beleefe. Therefore everie one prayeth according to his owne devotion. So I thinke our men of the newe learning, which would overthrowe church service, have the minister live upon almes and mens good willes, forsaking their tenths, pray according to the spirit, preach *ut dabitur in illa hora*, hold ringing of belles unnecessarie, wishing them turned into morters and great peeces, have the selfe same chimeras in their heads which the Devill forged in Mahomets.

[Cap. XX.]

Concerning Marriages.

La loi permet aux Maures d'avoir quatre femmes et un nombre illimité de concubines. — Réglementation du rapport des femmes avec le mari. — La femme négligée par son mari le poursuit devant le juge, qui le condamne à payer le douaire de la plaignante et à la renvoyer dans sa famille. — L'obligation de constituer un douaire à la femme fait que seuls les riches en ont trois ou quatre, tandis que les pauvres n'en ont qu'une ou rarement deux. — Le mari traite bien sa femme, parce qu'il sait qu'il devra lui payer son douaire, s'il la renvoie. — Formalités suivies pour le mariage: l'homme ne doit pas voir sa future épouse; il envoie près d'elle sa mère, sa sœur ou une autre parente, et, sur un rapport favorable, il va faire sa demande au père. — En cas d'accord, le contrat est immédiatement rédigé par deux taleb. — Six mois plus tard environ, la femme est amenée au mari sur une mule, cachée à tous les regards. — Si elle n'est pas vierge, le mari la renvoie sans payer le douaire.

The More may have by his lawe foure wives, concubines as many as he will keepe, either captives or slaves bought with mony; for being his owne proper peculium, they are to be at his disposing; but with these hee may not lye withall in the night, which the wives clayme as their interest, unlesse by stealth. If the husband have many wives, none will loose their turne, so nightly the husband by course must lye with one, then with another. If in this case any be defrauded of her night and the husband pleasure one more than another with his company, the wife injured complaineth to the magistrate that shee is despised and neglected, wherunto the husband must answere. If the judge rest not satisfied, the husband shall bee forced to pay the woman her dower and send her home to her father, if he be alive (marrying againe if shee will), if not, to the next of her fathers kindred; and this bill of divorce they call a shyed [1].

Though the liberty of poligamie be granted, yet not one amongst a hundred hath foure; the reason is the wives friends will never suffer any to marry their kinswomen without first they have a bill of dowry sufficient for the maintainance of her. Therefore the great and rich men have three or foure wives, but the poore most but one, few two, because of their disability to maintaine. Also this bill of dower keepeth their husbands in great awe, and maketh the women have the better life, which otherwise would live in great slavery: first, because the womans friends will bee sure to see shee have a stay of maintenance, for feare of after-charge to themselves; secondly, the justice of the country is so strict, if a man turne away his wife without reason, he shall pay her dower, though he sell the cloathes of his backe. Otherwise, every day for change of pleasure and yonger game, me [2] would turne away their wives faster then horscosers tainted jades.

Their fashion of wooing or marrying is thus. The man never seeth the woman hee shall marry till shee commeth to his bed, but hearing her to be a proper maide, beautifull and commendable, sendeth his mother, sister or kinsewoman to see her. Uppon this report the mans liking and affection resteth; if he proceedeth, then must he go to the father of the woman to demaund his daughter. They two agreeing, presently twoo of their talbies or learned men are sent for to write downe her portion, his endowment. So, some halfe yeare after, is the wedding day, which is onely a day of feasting, when the friendes of the bride bring her home to the

---

1. *A shyed*, شاهد un témoin, c'est-à-dire une attestation.

2. *Me*, pronom archaïque, équivalant à *one* ou à *they*; en français: *on*.

bridegroome riding uppon a mule, inclosed, like a blackebird, within a cage for the purpose covered over with silke, and great store of musicke going before her, yet in such sort riding thorough the streets as shee is seene of nobody, no not of her husband untill her bed her, for then were shee held of small accompt, and the jest spoyled. If that night the bridegroome finde her a virgine, then is there great joy of her friends; if not, the next day he turneth her home, and by law may keepe her portion.

[Cap. XXI.]

Concerning Buriall.

Les morts sont immédiatement lavés, portés sans délai au cimetière, hors de la ville, lavés de nouveau et inhumés, les riches seuls dans un cercueil. — Les femmes se réunissent à certaines dates pour pleurer les morts de la famille et rappeler leurs vertus.

Their manner of buriall is in this sort. When one is dead, presently hee is washed, and, with all speede, preparation is made to put him in the ground, for, the countrey being hot, it is not possible to keepe the corse above ground. Therefore with the kindred accompanied to the grave (which is without their citie, for within their citie or synagogues no person may be buried), he is there againe washed, and if hee be a man of ability, is put into a coffine, if not, buryed without one, the talbie saying a short prayer.

Besides, the people have a custome, the women of every kindred to meete by themselves at certaine convenient times and there make memoriall of such of their kindred as be dead, making great lamentations in remembring the vertues and good dispositions of them who are deceased, being perswaded this maketh the living have especiall care of leaving a good name and fame behinde them.

Cap. [XXII.]

The Policie of Barbarie.

Le Maroc renferme des esclaves et des hommes libres. — Les esclaves des-

cendent des Chrétiens ou des Noirs; les hommes libres sont les Arabes, gens de la vallée, et les Berbères, gens de la montagne. — Le Roi, monarque absolu, gouverne par le glaive et par les tribunaux. — La classe militaire comprend les moulays, personnages de sang royal, les pachas, les caïds, les faris, les kiahia, les biak-bachi, les thoubjia, les rouma ou simples soldats. — Moulay Ahmed el-Mansour avait à sa solde cinquante mille cavaliers, les uns armés de la lance ou de la sagaie, les autres de l'arbalète, et seize mille hommes de pied, la plupart des fusiliers. — Les principaux personnages du Maroc étaient, dans ces derniers temps, les caïds Azzouz, Ahmed ben Ibrahim es-Sofiani, Ahmed ben Bou Beker, Abd el-Ouahed, l'eunuque Ahmed, le caïd Moustafa el-Fil, le raïs commandant les galères de Salé. — Ces personnages ne peuvent transmettre la noblesse à leurs enfants, lesquels doivent conquérir les honneurs par leurs propres mérites. — Le titre de cheikh est donné au chef de chaque tribu, et le fils aîné du Roi ne dédaigne pas de le porter. — Les cheikhs ont un grand prestige. — Un seul d'entre eux peut mettre en campagne dix mille cavaliers ou plus de sa tribu. — Il est important pour le Roi de surveiller leurs dispositions.

Every kingdome consisteth of men, not of buildings. Therefore the kingdome of Barbary consisteth of bond and freemen. The naturall bondmen are such as are descended either from Christians or Negroes, the freemen ar Larbies or Brebers, which may be termed the valley and mountaine men. Over all, as absolute monarch, is the King, who maintaineth his seate by the sword and power of justice. The swordmen, according to their degrees, are thus placed:

1. The Muleys[1] are the Kings children, and all other who are of the bloud royall are tearmed by this nome.
2. Bashas[2] are captaine generalles over armyes.
3. Alkeyds be the lords set as well over garrison townes as countries, to rule and keepe the people in subjection.
4. Ferres[3], gentlemen who carrie armes, yet lesse commanders than alkeids.

---

1. Le titre de Moulay est donné aux chérifs, qu'ils soient ou non de sang royal.

2. Les Turcs ayant été les instructeurs des armées du Maroc, le vocabulaire militaire est, en grande partie, emprunté à la langue turque.

3. Ferres, de فارس cavaliers.

5. Bahaia¹, lieutenant to an alkeyd.
6. Brak-bashi², a sergeant at armes.
7. Debushi³, a captaine over thirtie.
8. Romie⁴, the common souldier of these men of war.

There were kept in daily paye, in the old Kings time⁵, to the number of 50 000 horsemen, part serving with the launce, others with the speare⁶, called spahaias⁷, and some, especially the horsemen of Fes, serve with the crose-bowe on horsebacke, bending it as they ryde, shooting a strong shot and sure, and 16 000 footemen ; the Alarbies beeing fitter for horsemen, but the Brebers the stronger footemen, most of them shot.

The chiefest men in commaund in the latter times were these :

1. Alkeyd Azus⁸, chiefe counsellor of State.
2. Hamet ben Breham Sefiani⁹, maister of the horse and ruler over the alkeids.
3. Sedi Hamet ben Bouker.   ⎱ These two
4. Sedi Abdela Wahad Anoune¹⁰. ⎰ were treasurers.
5. Alkyd Hamet, a capatho¹¹ or enuche, governor over the women and enuches.
6. Alkeyd Mustefa File¹², maister of the ordenance.

---

1. *Bahuia*, pour kahaïa, كاهية, lieutenant.
2. *Brak-bashi*, pour biak-bachi. Sur les biak, V. EL-OUFRÂNI, pp. 196-198, et 1ʳᵉ *Série*, France, t. I, p. 603, note 1.
3. *Debushi*, pour thoubji, artilleur.
4. *Romie*, les tireurs, de رمى tirer.
5. Sous Moulay Ahmed *el-Mansour*.
6. *The speare*, la sagaie.
7. *Spahaias*, les spahis.
8. V. *supra*, p. 48, note 2.
9. V. *supra*, p. 369 et note 1, et p. 372.
10. V. *supra*, p. 159 et note 1.
11. *Capatho*, castrat.
12. Le caïd Moustafa el-Fil avait été envoyé au Soudan avec le caïd Abd el-Malek el-Bortougali, pour remplacer le pacha Djouder ; ils arrivèrent à Tombouctou à la fin de 1598, mais furent presque aussitôt remplacés par le pacha Ammar el-Feta. Néanmoins le caïd Moustafa el-Fil resta au Soudan, et, le 30 Ramadan 1007 (26 avril 1599), il débloqua la ville de Djenné assiégée par le roi de Melli. Le caïd Moustafa était un homme tyrannique et violent, qui domina le pacha Ammar. Aussi le Chérif irrité les rappela tous les deux et les remplaça par le pacha Sliman (V. *supra*, p. 187 et note 2), qui arriva à Tombouctou le 5 Dou el-Kada 1008 (18 mai 1600). Moustafa el-Fil fut arrêté et renvoyé chargé de chaînes au Maroc. ES-SADI, pp. 277, 278 et 289.

7. Rishavan [1], admirall over the gallies at Saly [2].

Note: though these bee enobled, taking priorrity or precedency before others, yet is not this noblenes hereditary; for the children of these men must clayme no honour by birth-right but what they get by their service and honour of their sword, live unrespected unlesse they bee valiant; and so prooving, the King will take them into his service, wherupon, by desert, the son may obtaine his fathers fortune and honour.

There is another title of dignitie termed Sheck, attributed to the chiefe man of everie familie or cast. Neither doth the Kings eldest sonne scorne the title, signifying that he is the prime or best blood of his royall kindred. These Shecks are much respected, because it is the nature of the people, the whole kindred to follow their head, insomuch as one of these Shecks can bring into the field ten thousand horsemen of their owne cast or kindred, and some more. So that it is a matter of great consequence, the King to have an eye over such a man, and to know how his affection resteth towards him, either in love or hatred.

[Cap. XXIII.]

Officiers of Justice.

Le Roi rend la justice une fois par mois : il reçoit les appels ; les étrangers ont plus libre accès que ses propres sujets à son tribunal. — Les juges inférieurs sont pris parmi les prêtres ou taleb les plus intègres. — Le premier juge après le Roi est le mufti, qui reçoit les appels : il y en a trois, un à Merrakech, un à Fez et le troisième à Taroudant. — Le mufti de Merrakech siège avec le Roi, et seul tous les vendredis. — Les juges ordinaires siègent tous les jours : on en trouve un dans chaque grande ville ; les habitants des villes et les Arabes de la campagne viennent devant lui ; il rend son arrêt immédiatement après l'audition des parties ;

---

1. *Rishavan*, Raïs Chaban. En 1612, il avait à Salé 4 navires sous ses ordres. V. 1re *Série*, Espagne, 13 juillet 1612.

2. Moulay Ahmed *el-Mansour* entretenait à Salé sept ou huit galiotes pour la course contre les Espagnols. V. 1re *Série*, Angleterre, t. I, p. 504, et *supra*, p. 260 et note 1.

mais, si l'une d'elles veut produire des témoins, trois jours lui sont accordés pour les amener, et la partie adverse a trois jours pour les réfuter. — *Un débiteur poursuivi en justice doit payer, ou aller en prison, ou fournir un gage. — Au-dessous des juges ordinaires sont les notaires, des taleb, qui rédigent les actes entre parties sans phrases inutiles. — Procédure en usage : les contractants concluent leur marché en présence de deux témoins, puis se rendent avec ces derniers devant le notaire, qui dresse l'acte en quelques lignes. — Les Sitari sont chargés de faire exécuter les lois et les arrêts du juge et d'amener devant le tribunal ceux qui refusent de répondre à une citation. — Le Mohatasseb inspecte les poids et mesures et châtie les fraudeurs. — Le Hakem juge au criminel : le meurtre, le vol, l'adultère ; certains actes interdits par proclamation royale, selon les circonstances, sont punis de mort. — Les Mokaddem sont les substituts du Hakem. — Les fakirs ou marabouts offrent l'hospitalité aux voyageurs, donnent l'exemple d'une vie intègre, secourent les pauvres, règlent les différends ; leurs maisons sont considérées comme des sanctuaires.*

The King, once in a moneth, on Frydaies in the afternoone, after prayers, either in his house or church, sitteth to doe justice, hearing complaints or appeales from subalterne ministers, from whom the grieved persons do appeale to his royall person. When the King sitteth, the stranger shal have freer accesse to plead his cause before the King then his owne borne subject.

All inferiour judges and ministers are their churchmen or talbies, and those are soonest chosen into offices, which are of stricktest life, being free from avarice and such other sinnes as may pervert and hinder the course of equitie and justice.

The chiefest man for judgment under the King is the Muftie, to whome the partie greeved may appeale from any other ordinary judge. There be three of these men, one in Moruecos, another in Fes, the third at Taradant in Sus.

The Muftie of Moruecos sitteth with the King in judgement, and everye Frydaye in the afternoone by himselfe, to heare and determine causes of the subject and the stranger. Though he be in eminent place, he is a poore man, in respect what he might bee if hee would sell justice and take bribes.

The ordinary judge sitteth all the yeare long twoo houres before noone and two houres after noone. In every great towne throughout the three kingdomes is placed one of these judges, to whome not onely the inhabitants of every towne and citie do repaire, but the countrey people or Larbees uppon differences come thither to have their causes decided. Every one must tell his owne tale and plead his owne matter. When both parties have spoken, then giveth the judge sentence, so that in one day the cause is brought into court and the same day ended. If either part have witnes to produce, then the judge giveth three dayes respite to bring them in, which being brought, the adverse partie shall have other three daies respite to disproove them. And if he can proove the witnesses either infamous in manners, or given to detestable sinne as drunkennesse, adultery or such like, and can proove the witnes saith not his prayers sixe times dulie in foure and twenty houres, then shall he be utterly disabled to beare witnes, and thus in seaven daies the longest sute shall be ended. If an obligation, or rather bill of debt, bee brought into court, the obligee must either pay the debt, goe to prison, or to pawne the value of the debt or better; which pawne may be kept *in deposito* nine daies uppon great reason, to see if the debtor can redeeme it at the nine daies end. If he doth not, then is it solde, and the partie who should pay the money must sustaine the losse.

As coadjutors to these judges, and next in place to them, bee the *scrivanos,* who, uppon death or other remoove, are commonly made judges. These are talbies, which make writings between partie and partie, short and plaine, without multiplication of words, and they are of opinion : *abundans cautela nocet.* In their obligatorie bils, they put neither forfeit nor condition, having for the making thereof twoo pence English, and no more. They use no long draughts in matters of purchase, or these tripartite indentures, with such large and long implicite and explicite covenants, but thus the people deale in matters of contracts and bargaines : I buye of you a vyneyard, house, marchandize, at such a prize, to be payed at such a time, calling two honest men, wherof one shall be a talbie, if I can get him, to witnes this our bargaine. We foure go to the scrivener, who likewise is a talbie, and have this set downe in writing; and if our bargaine be for twenty thousand pounds, it is set downe in ten lines, and the justice of the country will allow me my bargaine with as great reason as if I had a great ingrossed booke of convenience as big as the map of the whole world in the newest edition.

Next in this nature to these be the Stereys[1], which have small fees to see the execution of lawes and sentence of the judge fulfilled. These likewise fetch men to answere their adversary, which would delay and not come before the judge, either upon perversenes or badnes of their plee, or any other cause whatsoever. Wherefore to be alwaies readie, these are continually attendant in the house of the judge, and waighting uppon him whethersoever he goeth.

Muttiseb[2] is an officer to see true weights and measures; if any bee faultie, all the wares in such a mans shop he giveth to the poore, the party proclaimed an unjust man and sore whipped.

The Hackam[3] is the Lord Marshall in every citie, who judgeth uppon life and death. As soone as the partie delinquent is taken, and his offence prooved, presentlie his throate is cut. Murder there is death; so is manifest theft, adultery likewise, prooved by very good witnes. And sometimes it is death for a man to weare a sword, who is not an officer, yea, though hee be a souldier. Other offences, according to the necessity of the time and pleasure of the King, by proclamation are made death, which the Hackman must see executed upon losse of his owne head.

Muckadens be substitutes to the Hackam, seeing his judgement fulfilled, and in his absence hath his authoritie.

Fokers[4] or Saints dwell in the best places of the country, keepe great hospitalitie for all travellers, whither any man may come for a night, and be gone in the morning. Much good these doe in the country by their example of morall living and bestowing their

---

[1]. *Stereys*, à identifier avec les « cetaires » de Torres, « que son lacayos » (*Relacion.... de los Xarifes*, cap. 88 et 105), les « citeros » de J. Mocquet, « sergens à pied armés de bastons et d'alfanges ou cimeterres » (*1re Série*, France, t. II, p. 401), et les « citairis » de Th. Le Gendre, « especes de sergens » chargés des exécutions de la justice (*Ibidem*, t. III, p. 730). — Ce mot (en arabe سْتَائِرِي) n'est plus employé aujourd'hui avec ce sens. Cf. Dozy, *Dict., Supplément*, t. I, p. 632.

[2]. *Muttiseb*, mohatasseb.

[3]. *Hackam*, hakem.

[4]. *Fokers*. V. supra, p. 342 et note 1.

owne goods in their lifetime to helpe the needie and distressed, compromising differences betwixt parties, and repressing all disorders, winning great love and respect, for their houses are held as sanctuaries, whose priviledges the King will not violate but upon great and weighty reason.

[Cap. XXIV.]

The Manner of Fight.

La plupart des Maures combattent à cheval, dans la proportion de trois cavaliers pour un fantassin. — Le Roi dispute rarement la bataille: celui qui a le dessous au premier choc s'enfuit immédiatement. — Armes offensives et défensives. — Les Arabes combattent tous à cheval; ils se battent avec plus d'acharnement pour leurs querelles intestines que pour leur Roi; une jeune fille montée sur un chameau, un drapeau à la main, les précède dans le combat. — Ils vengent les meurtres des leurs, non seulement sur le meurtrier, mais sur le premier homme de sa tribu qu'ils rencontrent. — Les Berbères luttent également entre eux: les femmes suivent les combattants et lancent sur les fuyards du henné, ce qui les marque d'infamie. — Les combats singuliers.

The King, nobility and souldiers desire to serve on horsebacke, which most commonly they doe, for in any army there be three horse for one foote. The King will seldome venture to fight out a battaile, but as you may perceive by the precedent, it was and is the usage amongst the three brethren, when they meete in a field, whosoever getteth at the first onset the advantage, maketh the other presently leave the field and flie unto some place of strength. They fight with no armor except a buffe jerkin for the better sort, and a leather hide tanned for the meaner, and some coates of male. Their armes is a horsemans staffe, target and swoord, or a horsemans piece and sword.

The Alarbies serve all uppon horse, will fight sorer battails to mantaine their deadly fewde than in service of their King; insomuch that, upon losse of any great lord or cheefe man of their bloud, cruell battailes have ensued, wherein ten thousand men have beene slaine at one time. And it is their fashion the fairest virgin to ride upon a camel with a flag in her hand, decked all in pompe to sollicite her kindred to revenge, and goeth formost in the field, encouraging them to follow; uppon which incitement much blood is spilt, her kindred as loath to loose their virgin and not revenge their injuries, the other side striving to win her and the field, holding that a continuing glory to the seaventh generation[1].

When a man is killed, his tribe seeketh not revenge only uppon the man which killed the party, but the first man of the tribe hee meeteth withall, him will hee kill if hee can, and so thinketh hee hath satisfied his kinsmans death.

The Brebers or montaniers likewise maintaine this fewde, who are most shot and swoord men. Uppon the day of battaile, their women follow hard behinde them with a colour in their hands called hanna[2]. And if they see any of their side offer to run away or retyre, presently they will throwe some of this hanna uppon their clothes, which will stayne, and the party ever after is held for a coward and a dishonoured Jew. For feare of this infamy, few forsake the field, but either conquer their enemyes or dye like men, who are presently stripped and buried by these women which follow them.

The single combatte is performed with the short sword, lapping about the left arme his uppermost garment, which is worne lose. Seldome the field is appointed, but either the men fight upon their falling out, or at their next meeting by chance. If a man bee set upon by more persons than one, hee fighteth winking, laying about him with all his might, not charging his adversarie *punctum*[3], or after the rapier fight, but *cesim*[4], edgewise, either in battell or single quarrell.

[CAP. XXV.]

The Trading of the Moores into Guinee and Gago for Gold Ore, or Sandie Gold.

Moulay Ahmed résolut de s'emparer du Soudan, conquête qu'il jugeait

1. Cf. TORRES, cap. 86.
2. *Hanna*, henné.
3. *Punctum*, pour *punctim*, d'estoc.
4. *Cesim*, pour *cæsim*, de taille.

facile et fructueuse. — Des mines d'or avaient été découvertes dans les montagnes de l'Atlas, mais il aima mieux aller chercher ce métal au loin, craignant que les dites mines, si elles étaient riches, n'attirassent des Chrétiens en armes, et il fit mettre à mort ceux qui les avaient trouvées. — Le pacha Djouder, mis à la tête de l'expédition du Soudan, s'empara de Gago, où il établit un fondouk et une douane. — Les marchands mettent six mois pour aller de Merrakech au Soudan, dont deux pour traverser le désert, où les conduisent des pilotes, comme en mer. — Ils voyagent par caravanes de deux ou trois cents personnes et transportent de l'eau sur des chameaux. — Ils apportent aux Noirs beaucoup d'étoffes, de l'ambre, du corail, et surtout du sel qu'ils achètent à Teghazza et qu'après avoir payé les droits de douane à Gago, ils vont vendre plus loin à une race de Noirs contrefaits. — Manière dont s'opère l'échange du sel et de l'or entre ces Noirs et les marchands. — Cet or ressemble à du sable fin agglutiné par la pluie.

Muley Hamet, being at peace with his neighbours, at quiet with his subjects, determined to warre upon the Negroes, knowing the conquest easie, because the people are undisciplined in warre, and the profite would be exceeding great by bringing their gold into his countrey, exchanging for it salt and other commodities. And howsoever certaine miners had found rich mynes of golde in the hilles of Atlas, yet he held it better policie to fetch his gold farder of, then to digge that which was found in the centre of his owne kingdome, fearing, if the mines proved rich, the golden ore would draw thither Christian armes ; therefore he cutte the throats of all such as were the authours, and gave the maisters of the workes death for their hire. But, to perfect his other designe, he chose Judar Basha, sent him with great store of souldiers, who entred farre into the Negroe countrey, depriving them of a great citie called Gago, which standeth upon the river of Synega[1], three hundred leagues within the firme land, builded there an alpandeca[2] for Barbarian marchants, and a custom house for the King.

The marchants make it six moneths journey from Morruecos thither ; of which two moneths they passe thorow the sandie deserts, where no people dwell, neither any roadway, but directed

---

1. La ville de Gago (Gao) est située sur le Niger et non sur le Sénégal.

2. *Alpandeca* pour *alfondeca*, un comptoir.

by pylots, as ships at sea, observe the courses of sunne, moone and stars, for feare of missing their way. If they lose themselves, they meete with famine and die for lacke of water; whose dead carkasses consume not, but maketh munna[1] or otema[2] flesh, every way as phisicall or medicinable as that which commeth from Alexandria. They never travel under two or three hundred in companie. It may bee not meeting with water in twelve or fifteene dayes space, but carrie water by camels, both for them and their beasts to drinke; which failing, to save their own lives, they kill their camels and drinke the blood. If the wind blow at north-east, they cannot unlade their camels, least the sands should cover them.

The marchandise carried from Morruecos to the Negroes is much cloath, amber beades, corall. But the chiefest commoditie is salt, which is bought at Tegazza,[3] and other places, for foure shillings a camels lading, which is sixe hundredweight, and payeth at Gago five poundes for custome to the King of Barbarie, afterward sould farre within the countrey to a kinde of deformed Negroes, who will never bee seene in the commerce of trading with the Barbarians or any stranger. Wherefore they lay their salt in the fields and leaveth it. Then commeth the deformed Negro, and laieth, against every mans prizall of salt, as much of his gold as he thinketh the salt is worth, and goeth his way, leaving his gold with the salt. Then returneth the Moore; if he like the gold, taketh it away; if not, detracteth so much from his heape as he will sell to the Negro for his gold. The Negro returning, if he like the quantitie, putteth to more gold, or else will not barter, but departeth. Yet they seldome mislike; for the Moore maketh a rich returne, and his King a full treasure. Wherefore the deformed Negro is praysed for the truest dealing man in the world. The gold which they have is not coyned, but like small gravell or sand gathered after gluts of raine, in the drie bankes of mountaines and rivers.

---

1. *Manna*, pour *mummi*, chair de momie, qu'on employait à certains usages médicaux. Cf. Jacques SAVARY, *Dictionnaire universel de commerce*.

2. *Otema*, mot non identifié.

3. V. *supra*, p. 329, note 2.

[Cap. XXVI.]

Of the Grasshoppers which come into Barbarie from Guinee.

Les sauterelles apparaissent au Maroc sept ans de suite et disparaissent pour sept ans. — Elles viennent à la fin de février, dévastent tout, et partent à la fin de mars, après la ponte. — Avant la ponte, elles sont bonnes à manger. — Elles ne volent que dans la journée, et sont si denses qu'elles voilent le soleil. — Leurs larves, en se développant, font encore plus de ravages qu'elles et s'en vont à la fin de juin, portées parfois par le vent en Espagne. — Le grain est cher au Maroc dans les années de sauterelles et très abondant dans les autres. — Grande fertilité du sol.

The grashoppers come seaven yeares together, and other seaven yeares they come not. Their comming is about the end of Februarie, from the parts of Benie or Genie [1], as the countrey people imagine, in such abundance, that, where they light, for five or sixe myles compasse, all grasse and corne newe sowed is eaten up. And if they light upon a tree, they eate up all the leaves, buds and barke of the smaller twigs, which is tender or greene. Thus remaine they in Barbary untill the end of March, when they spawne their young, then flie away, as is thought, further into Turkie. Before spawning, they are good meate, the poore of the countrey being relieved with them; yea, the people will come a dayes journey to fetch two or three horse, bull or mules laden of them.

All the night they lie on the ground, untill nine or ten a clocke in the morning, because, before their wings be drie, which are moystened with the evenings dew, they cannot flie, so that one man will gather of them foure or five bushels in a morning. When they rise, they flie untill foure of the clocke in the afternoone, so thicke, that like to a cloude they hinder the light of the sunne from you. Carried they are with the wind out of the countrey, none but God knoweth certainly whither, leaving behind them their young which they have spawned, five times more in number then the old are at their first comming, and doe more hurt then

[1]. *Benie or Genie*, le Bénin ou la Guinée.

they have done; for, though the old have eaten the corn at their first comming, when it was greene, yet is it not utterly destroyed, for much of it recovereth and commeth to good; but the young, after twentie dayes that they are spawned, begin to creepe, and corne then growing ripe, are more perilous to destroy it, and so famish the country. Wherefore thousands of people, all the day long, do nothing but kill these young ones, putting them in sacks, but cannot destroy them all, being innumerable. The juyce of these young grashoppers is poyson; therefore the countrey people take great care least the juyce touch man or beast; for if it should, all the skinne would presently go off. These young ones flye away foorth of the country in the end of June, no creature knoweth whither. Sometimes, if a strong gale of a south-east winde take them, they are carryed over the Streits into Spaine, making dearth by destroying their corne.

The 7 yeres they come into Barbary, corne is deare, the other seaven yeres most commonly corne is plentifull. In my authors remembrance, wheat hath been sold for foure pence a bushell, and barly for twoo pence, insomuch the countryman would not bestow the labor of reaping his corne to have it, but let his cattle eat it standing upon the ground. Such plenty God doth send and the fertilenes of the soyle doth yeeld, being black in colour as in garden earth much manured; and, though the ground is not so often ploughed as here in England, being once turned over or ploughed when they sowe it, yet it giveth as great increase either in corne, hearber or rootes for mans sustenance as the soyle of any countrey in Europe whatsoever.

[Cap. XXVII.]

Recreations of Pleasure.

Les Maures chassent au faucon. — Ils chassent le cerf, l'antilope, le chevreuil, le lièvre, le renard, le chacal, le sanglier, le chat sauvage et le léopard. — Comment ils prennent les autruches.

Hawking with the long winged hawke, of which they have

greater store and better then we have in these parts of the world; their game is the kawde¹, a land fowle like unto a drake, and so ryseth the curwan², tigernute³, which we have not in England, the bustard, Ginne hen, pheasant, partridge, ducke and mallard. Hunting of the stagge, antilop, roe-bucke, hare, fox, debe, halfe a dog halfe a fox, wilde bore, tiger wilde cat, leopard.

In the sandie countries, where the best horses are bred, which ordinarily will drinke milke and can fast from water 4 daies, there they hunt the estridges, marking when they come to water, which they doe at set times in flocks or companies. Then the horsemen disperse themselves, and first one troope of horse set upon the heard of estridges, which the birds perceiving betake them to the wing, not flying aloft from the ground, but making a running flight so fast, as it tryeth their horses at their full speede, and most commonly tryeth three companies of horses, one after another, ere they bee taken. The birds have at the end of their wings a horne growing, which in running and moving of their wingges, in manner of a spur, pricketh them, as it were to make speede, and therewith are sore gauled, as may be perceaved at their taking. These birds some hunt for plesure, others for profite of their feathers, their carkasses not anywise good to be eaten.

[Cap. XXVIII.]

Of the Lyon.

La plus belle espèce de lion habite la région montagneuse et boisée qui s'étend vers l'Atlantique. — Les lionceaux peuvent s'apprivoiser. — Il suffit de menacer le lion du regard pour le faire fuir. — Il poursuit ceux qui ont peur de lui. — Comment on le tue.

The fairest for shape or noblest for courage is bred in the

---

1. *Kawde*, mot défiguré sans doute par une mauvaise lecture du manuscrit. Celui-ci devait porter « rawde ». L'oiseau, d'après la description qu'en donne Ro. C., serait la petite outarde, appelée aussi poule de Carthage, canepetière, et en arabe raad رعد.

2. *Curwan*, peut-être « carwan », espèce de perdrix. Cf. Eguilaz, *sub voce* « alcaravan » et les dictionnaires espagnols.

3. *Sic*. La signification de ce mot n'a pu être établie.

mountaine and woddy country of Barbarie, toward the Atlantike sea. The lionesse hath seldome above two whelpes at a time, which are in great perill of death when they put forth their great teeth, whereof many die uppon very paine of tooth-ach. The young ones may be brought up very tame, as a mastife, and will continue so if you keepe him from bloud; but if he have once tasted thereof, he waxeth angry and cruell. The country people where the lyons most breed, when they meet with one, looketh sternly and angerly in the lyons face, miscalling and rating him; in so doing the lyon will run away like a dog. But upon the sight of the lyon, let a man as affraid run away, he will make after and worry the party if he once catch him.

The countryman killeth the lyon with his piece, by making a pit neere to the place where he thinketh the lyon will resort to his prey, the man standing in the same, having nothing open but a little hole to put forth the end of his peece, and to take his marke to shoote at him. Others who go upon pleasure to hunt him with their horse-peeces, being wel mounted, give promise one not to forsake another in extreamities; for our own countryman hath shot a lyon and killed him when 4 men have beene slaine outright, made a buffe jerkin of his outside, not desiring Hercules fame for wearing the Neemeian mantle, but to let the world know an English traveller taketh a great content and pleasure to weare the trophie of his owne manhoode, as a milkesoppe gallant the favour of his amorous mistres.

British Museum. — Printed Books, Press Mark: 1198. C. 20. — A True Historicall Discourse[1]..... *— Londres, 1609, in-4°.*

1. V. le titre complet, *supra*, p. 322.

CVIII

LETTRE DE HUGH LEE A THOMAS WILSON

(Extrait)

Moulay ech-Cheikh, chassé de Larache par Moulay Zidân, a débarqué en Portugal et s'est rendu, dit-on, à la cour d'Espagne. — Moulay Zidân est tranquille possesseur de Merrakech. — Ces nouvelles sont accueillies avec déplaisir par les Espagnols.

Lisbonne, 26 mars 1609.

Au dos : To the worshippfull Thomas Wilson, Esquier, secretary to the right honorable the Earle of Salisburye, Lord High Treasorer of England, at Salisbury Howse, in the Strond, nere London. By a frind, whom God preserve. — *Alia manu :* Mr Lee, 28 March.

Lixboa, the 26 March 1609, newe stile.

Worshippfull Sir, my last to you was the last moneth, under cover to Mr Arthur Jackson, by Samewell Dove, to which I refer me.....

Of late there hath ben a conflicte in Barbery : Mully Shek put cleane from Alarach, and forced to flye, who aryved in the Algarvas, and nowe ys seyd to be gone to the coorte of Spayne[1]. And Mully Sedan remayneth with Alarach, who ys also said to be quietly in posession of Marrocus. The Spaniard ys nothinge pleased with the newes, for nowe theyr hoape of Alarach ys quayled.....

I comend unto you my love, resting yours at comand,

Signé : **Hugh Lee.**

Public Record Office. — State Papers, Foreign, Portugal, vol. III. — Original.

---

1. Le 27 janvier 1609, Moulay Zidân avait défait complètement, sur les bords de l'oued Bou Regrag, les troupes de Moulay ech-Cheikh, commandées par son fils Moulay Abdallah et par Moulay Abou Farès. Sur cet événement et sur la fuite de Moulay ech-Cheikh en Portugal, d'où il passa en Espagne, V. *infra*, p. 410 et note 1, et pp. 412-413 ; 1re *Série*, Pays-Bas, t. I, pp. 306-307, 463 ; France, t. II, pp. 444-454.

CIX

LETTRE DE HUGH LEE A THOMAS WILSON

Moulay ech-Cheikh n'a pas été chassé de Larache par Moulay Zidân, comme on l'avait dit d'abord. — Il est venu de son plein gré, pour offrir aux Espagnols de leur livrer Larache, où il a laissé son fils. — Les Espagnols ont décidé l'expédition, mais ils craignent que Moulay Zidân ne surprenne la place avant leur arrivée. — Philippe III fait à Moulay ech-Cheikh une pension de deux cent cinquante cruzades par jour. — Il a ordonné en conséquence la levée d'une taxe sur les vins en Portugal.

Lisbonne, 4 avril 1609.

Au dos : To the vorshipfull Thomas Wilson, Esquier, secretary to the right honorable the Earle of Salisbury, Lord High Treasorer of England, gyve these at Salisburye Howse, in the Strand at London. — *Alia manu :* M‍r Lee. From Lisbon, 1609.

Worshippfull Sir,

My last to you was the 30 of the last month but 5 dayes past. Sence which the gallyes of this place are departid for Cales uppon the same service I therein wrote you; the which ys nowe more lykely, by comon judgment, to prove worthy the attemptinge, for that matters have ben carryed very seacrett and with pollicy. For though the generall report, at the first comyng over of Mully Sheke from Alarach, yt was gyven out that he was by the forces of Mully Cedan forced from thence, nowe yt appeareth that he came voluntaryly[1] from thence, and hath there lefte his sonne to hould the

---

1. Moulay ech-Cheikh dut s'embarquer, le 4 mars 1609, pour éviter de tomber dans les mains du pacha Moustafa, qui fit occuper Larache le même jour; il arriva à

possession thereof[1], and that his comyng hether ys to assure the Kinge of Spayne that yt shalbe delyverid unto hym[2], sending forces to hould the same. For which ys this sudden provizion made, and they goe with a full resolution to have the same performed unto theym. All the dowghts they have of theyr prevention ys that yf, before theyr comyng thether, Mully Cedan with his forces doe not surprise the same ; the which ys by them somwhat doughted.

The Kinge gyveth 250[3] of Portingall money dayly unto Mully Shoke for his charge, so long as he shall remayne in this kingdom, and for the performance thereof hath comanded 2 res to be ymposted upon every canada of wine that shalbe drawne and tapped out to be soulde in Portingall.

Having present conveyance, I hould yt my duty not to omytt to signify my knowledge briefly, which I pray you to accept as tyme will afoorde.

And so for the present I leave to the protection of the Allmighty, resting

   Yours ever at comand,

        Signé : Hugh Lee.

Lixboa, the 4 Aprill 1609, new stile.

Public Record Office. — *State Papers, Foreign, Portugal, vol. III.* — *Original.*

Villanova de Portimão, en Algarve, le 8 mars. V. *1re Série*, Espagne, aux dates des 8, 9 et 11 mars 1609 ; GUADALAJARA, f. 104 v°; ROJAS, ff. 16-17.

1. Moulay Abdallah, après sa défaite, était revenu à Larache auprès de son père, mais celui-ci l'on avait fait partir, avant sa fuite en Espagne, pour tenter de reformer une armée. GUADALAJARA, f. 103 ; EL-OUFRÂNI, pp. 317-318. — Hugh Lee rectifia, du reste, son erreur dans sa lettre de [mai] 1609. V. *infra*, Doc. CXI, p. 415.

2. Moulay ech-Cheikh n'était nullement décidé à livrer Larache à l'Espagne. Cette question fit ultérieurement l'objet de longues et difficiles négociations. V. *infra*, p. 417 et note 5.

3. Sans doute 250 cruzades.

CX

LETTRE DE CHARLES CORNWALLIS A THOMAS EDMONDES

(Extrait)

Moulay ech-Cheikh est arrivé récemment en Portugal. — Il est accompagné, dit-on, de quatre cents hommes et il a de quoi en payer douze mille. — Il les demande à Philippe III pour pouvoir retourner au Maroc. — Il offre Larache à ce prince. — Le vice-roi de Portugal devait aller à sa rencontre en grande pompe pour le recevoir à Lisbonne, mais on a décidé, ensuite, de l'envoyer dans une ville voisine de Séville. — D. Luis Fajardo est parti pour Cadix. — Certains supposent que Philippe III prépare une expédition au Maroc en faveur de Moulay ech-Cheikh.

Madrid, 28 mars [n. st. 7 avril] 1609.

Au dos, alia manu : 28 March 1609. From Sir Ch. Cornwalleys.

My verie good Lord,

The last I receyved from your Lordship was of the 7th of Februarie.

. . . .

Here is latelie arrived in Portugall the Kinge of Fez, enforced, as appeares, to flie his countrie. It is sayd that he comes accompanied with 400 men and with treasure sufficyent to pay 12 000 ; which he requires of the King here for the enhablinge of his retourne into his countrie. He offereth deliverie of Allerache to become tributarie to this crowne, and manie other honorable and advantageous condicions [1].

[1]. Un certain John Jude écrit de Madrid, le 26 avril [n. st. 6 mai 1609], à Thomas Wilson : « La principale nouvelle, ici, est l'arrivée de Moulay ech-Cheikh, le

It was purposed that the Viceroy of Portugall[1] should have gone out of Lixbone with great companie and much pompe and applause to have receyved him; but as I heare, that determination is altered, and the Barbarian Kinge and his companie are to remove to a towne not farre from Sevill[2], there to expect the Kinge of Spaine his further resolution.

Don Luys Fajardo[3], Capitan Generall of the Kinges armada by sea, is in some hast dispatched hence to Cales, and, as is sayd, is to be followed verie shortlie with all the gallions that remayne at the Groyne[4] or in Biskay. Some thinke this motion may be for some enterprise to be performed against Barbarie in favor of this Kinge[5].

. . . .

And soe, my good Lord, with my best wishe of all health and happines to you and yours, I comitt your Lordship to God, and remaine

    Your Lordships assured to doe you service,

        Signé : Charles Cornwallys.

Madrid, the 28th of Marche 1609, *stilo veteri.*

British Museum. — Stowe Mss., 171, f. 1. — Original.

---

roi maure, qui a débarqué en Portugal, il y a quelques semaines. Il est accompagné de quatre cents Maures, et il a apporté, dit-on, son trésor. Il demande secours au roi d'Espagne contre son frère cadet, Moulay Zidân, qui, après avoir vécu longtemps dans les montagnes, est maintenant au pouvoir et l'a chassé de son royaume de Fez ». *St. Pap.. For., Spain, vol. XVI.*

1. D. Christovão de Moura, marquis de Castel-Rodrigo. V. *supra*, p. 44 et note 1.

2. Moulay ech-Cheikh fut envoyé à Carmona, à 35 kilomètres à l'E.-N.-E. de Séville. V. *infra*, p. 417 et note 4.

3. Sur ce personnage, V. *supra*, p. 314, note 1.

4. *The Groyne*, La Corogne.

5. La flotte de D. Luis Fajardo, qui partit de Cadix le 14 juin 1609, avait, en réalité, pour objet la capture du célèbre corsaire Simon Dancer, qu'elle chercha vainement. Fernandez Duro, *Armada española*, t. III, p. 324. Il n'y eut du reste aucune expédition sur Larache en 1609, mais le bruit en courut plusieurs fois. Cf. *British Museum, Stowe Mss., 171, f. 41.*

CXI

LETTRE DE HUGH LEE A THOMAS WILSON

(Extrait)

Préparatifs des Espagnols contre Larache. — 15000 hommes doivent prendre part à l'expédition, dont 10000 seraient fournis par Moulay ech-Cheikh. — Moulay Zidân étant maintenant seul maître du Maroc, le succès de l'entreprise demeure incertain. — En cas d'échec à Larache, les Espagnols tourneront leurs coups ailleurs.

[Lisbonne, mai 1609][1].

Suscription : To the worshipfull Thomas Wilson, secretary to the right honourable the Earle of Salisbury, Lord Highe Treasorer of England, at Salisbury House, in the Strond, att London.

Worshipfull Sir,

My last to you was the 16 of Aprill[2], under cover to Mr Thomas Bothby, merchaunt, which was accordinge unto the tyme, at that instant, whereunto I referr you. Sence which I have farther understoade, in the busynes of Africa, that the galleys of this place are gone into Andolozia, there to joyne with the forces out of Italy and others, to goe against Alarach. Yt ys serteinly reported. And that there shalbe 15 thousande men joyned to goe uppon that service,

---

1. La date n'est pas indiquée, mais elle est fournie par la mention dans le contexte des préparatifs de l'expédition de D. Luis Fajardo. V. *supra*, p. 413 et note 5. Le document est postérieur au mois d'avril 1609, comme le prouvent les mots : « My last to you was the 16 of Aprill » et antérieur au 14 juin, date du départ de Cadix de D. Luis Fajardo pour sa croisière en Méditerranée.

2. Cette lettre du 16 avril 1609 est sans intérêt pour les événements du Maroc.

whereof the report ys that 10 thousand to be furnished and payd by Mully Sheke, and 5 thousand by and at the charge of the Kinge of Spayne.

And where formerly[1] I wrote, according to the report of that tyme, that Mully Shek had lefte his sonne in Alarach, at his comynge for Portingale, yt was not soe. For, when he fledd hether, his sonne fled into the mountaines of Barbary, and only Mully Sedan remayned absolute Kinge of Barbery, as he yet remayneth ; whereby yt ys thought that Alarach will nott soe easely bee surprised by the Spaniardes. But yt ys supposed that, by the meanes of Mully Shek, the purpose ys not aloane for Alarach, but also for some other partes, yf they shall fayle of theyr purpose at Alarach.

Don Lewis Faxardo, with the armado which was at the Groyne, doe also repayre into Andolozia to joyn with those forces ; but from here goeth no further ayde then the 4 gallyes which are already gone, neyther any provizion for warrs for any other place; onely three newe carrekes are in buildinge for the East Indies.

. . . .

Not serving for others at present, doe, with my beste comendacions, betake you to the protection of the Allmightie, and remayne

Your Whorshipp's ever at comaund,

Signé : Hugh Lee.

Public Record Office. — State Papers, Foreign, Portugal, vol. III. — Original.

1. Dans la lettre du 4 avril 1609. V. *supra*, p. 411 et note 1.

CXII

LETTRE DE CHARLES CORNWALLIS AU CONSEIL PRIVE

(Extrait)

Mouvements de la flotte espagnole; Anthony Sherley doit, dit-on, se joindre à elle avec ses navires. — Le but doit être le Maroc, où un marabout, qui a déjà rassemblé vingt mille hommes, s'est levé récemment contre Moulay Zidân avec l'intention de restaurer Moulay ech-Cheikh. — Ce dernier a été envoyé à Carmona. — Si les Espagnols l'aident à rentrer au Maroc, ils tireront de lui des conditions avantageuses et notamment la possession de Larache, qui leur sera utile pour commander la mer et interdire aux autres nations le commerce avec la région.

Madrid, 1er [n. st. 11] juillet 1609.

Au dos : To the Lords of his Maties most honorable Privie Councell. — *Alia manu :* Primo Julii 1609. Sir C. Cornwaleis to the Lords.

May it please your Lordships.

. . . .

The Kinges armada by sea here I heare to be devided into two squadrons of gallions, of which Fajardo is sayd to be gone towardes the Streightes with tenne[1], and Ochendo[2] towardes the Cape St Vincent with six ; the whole number of their soldiers as yet but 1500. They are all verie shortlie to gather together ; and the gallies of this kingdome, which are in number about tenne, are to joyne with them ; and soe is likewise, as I understande, Sir Anthonie Sherley with

---

1. V. *supra*, p. 413, note 5.
2. D. Antonio de Oquendo, célèbre homme de mer (1577-1640). Il venait d'être nommé, le 7 janvier 1608, capitaine général de l'escadre de Cantabria, sous les ordres de D. Luis Fajardo.

LETTRE DE CHARLES CORNWALLIS AU CONSEIL PRIVÉ

his shippes[1], reported to be in number twelve or sixteene; and that some of the shippes that are at Dunkirke are also sent for.

The disseigne, as I suppose, is for Barbarie, where there hath of late a Moravites[2] of great wealthe and much anthoritie and credite amonge that people raised himselfe against the Kinge that is now in possession[3], and alreadie gathered about twentie thousande men, with purpose to restore againe the exiled Kinge that remaines here into his countrie and kingdome.

That Kinge is now latelie drawne downe to a village called Corea[4], some two leagues from Sevill. If by the armes of this Estate he recover his kingdome, there is noe doubte but they will here drawe from him verie proffitable and advantageons condicions[5]. Amongst the rest, I make noe doubte but the possession of Allerache wilbe one; which will, in my weake judgement, be a matter of noe small consequence towardes their desired comandement of those seas, and prohibitinge to other the traffique of that parte of the worlde.

. . . .

Madrid, the 1st of Julie 1609, *stilo veteri*.
Your Lordships most humblie at comandement,

Signé : Charles Cornwaleys.

Public Record Office — *State Papers, Foreign, Spain, vol. XVI.* — *Original*.

1. C'est en 1609 que Sherley partit de Sicile, comme amiral des mers du Levant, pour une expédition dans l'Archipel. V. *supra*, p. 282.

2. Sur ce marabout, nommé Sidi Brahim, qui s'était levé dans le Sous, V. *1re Série*, Pays-Bas, t. I, pp. 473-474.

3. Moulay Zidân, dont les troupes, sous le commandement du pacha Moustafa, avaient pris Fez le 5 mars, fut rappelé à Merrakech au commencement de juin par la révolte du marabout Sidi Brahim. Moulay Abdallah en profita pour marcher avec les Cheraga contre le pacha Moustafa; il le défit, le tua et réoccupa Fez le 16 juillet 1609. V. *1re Série*, Pays-Bas, t. I, pp. 473-474; France, t. II, p. 467; EL-OUFRÂNI, p. 318.

4. *Corea*, entendez : Carmona.

5. Sur les négociations poursuivies par la cour d'Espagne avec Moulay ech-Cheikh, par l'intermédiaire de Gianettino Mortara, V. *1re Série*, Espagne, 1609, *passim*. Elles aboutirent à un traité signé le 9 septembre 1609, par lequel Moulay ech-Cheikh s'engageait à remettre Larache à Philippe III, moyennant 200 000 ducats et 6 000 arquebuses. GUADALAJARA, ff. 107-110.

CXIII

LETTRE DE MOULAY ZIDÂN A JACQUES Ier

Des trafiquants anglais ont acquis au Maroc des sucres, qui ont été saisis par les Espagnols. — Ces sucres avaient été achetés à Moulay Zidân lui-même par voie d'échange. — Si Jacques Ier n'obtient pas réparation des dommages subis par ces trafiquants, ils prendront le parti de cesser tout commerce au Maroc, ce qui sera plus nuisible aux Anglais qu'aux Marocains. — Moulay Zidân, ayant reçu la plainte de ces marchands, les renvoie devant Jacques Ier, s'en remettant à lui pour leur faire obtenir justice.

Merrakech, 15 Rbia II 1018 [18 juillet 1609].

Au dos : The copie of the King of Barbaryes letter, touching merchants offended.

Regi potentisimo, prudentisimo, gloriosisimo, illustrisimo, magno pastori et oculatissimo observ[atori], regi Jacobo, qui semper observabitur a regibus potentissimis superbo oculo[1], loqu[entibus] tamen intra se quod corespondeat decori ordinis et gloriosæ potestati ejus.

In nomine Dei miseratoris, misericordis.

The grace of God be uppon our lorde and protector Mahamed; and upon God his ffr[iend] peace and the blessinge of good men!
From the servant of the high God of the nations, conqueror through the ayde [of God], the trew successor or Chaliph, the

---

1. On est étonné de ce membre de phrase péjoratif, placé dans une suscription où le roi Jacques Ier est, par ailleurs, loué avec les hyperboles du style oriental. Il faut, sans aucun doute, y voir une phrase arabe mal traduite. William Bedwell a reproduit son contre-sens dans la traduction anglaise. V. page suivante.

succorer, the Phatimi, governor of the nations, the helpe and ayde of nations, the Mahdi.

Mulley Zeydan, the sonne of Ahamed, of Mohamed the Mahdy, the Haziny.

God leadeth forthe with a mighty ayde, he compasseth the tents with a moste sure guard, [hee] exalteth in the execution of justice, hee continueweth in the remission of the [sins] and offences of the worlde, hee giveth ayde and enlargement victoriously, and even in the greatest darkenes!

Unto that Court which amongest all the Courtes is most magnifficent, most christian of wisdome and power, which descended into theire breasts by contempt of the wo[rld and] scorne of idolatrie, the Court I meane of that Kinge, whose memorie is fo[und] spread through the worlde, all whose coastes and coontryes are obedient at hi[m], the greate Kinge most wise, mighty and famouse, great Kinge Jeames, whoe i[s] continually observed of greate Kings with disdaintfull lookes, which notwithstanding [doe] speake within themselves those things that are corespondent unto the honor of h[im] and power.

Nowe, after praises and thanks given to God, the lorde of excellencyes and the restrain[er of the] same, the manifester of perfecktions and their beginings, grace and peace be upp[on the] lanthorne of essence and his morninge starre and uppon the light which exte[nds] itselfe from the brightnes of his cast unto our lorde and protector Mohamed, [and] unto God first begiven praises and thankes abundantly with exceeding much ho[nour and] glory without ende, as also upon his followers which doe conferme his judg[ment to] the openinge of his lawe, untill their doe arise one which shall bee the builder up[pon] justice by other lawes and statutes, and one that shall call unto this greate u[niverse], when it shall increase strongly and manifestly, hee that shall sett himselfe in the eye of all faces as the brightnes of the light.

Know you that wee have written these our letters confidently and joyfullye and have hereto our royall stampe endoobled as all men maye see — thankes bee given to God, whose name is o[nly] to bee praysed — from our Courte, the center of our princely dominions, the throne of the W[estern] Chaliffes, the pole that is fixed for the direcktion of the nations, Maroco, I me[an], which God keepe and enclose on every syde roundabout and defende with an outstretched arme mightely.

This letter I saye which I have sent unto your Hightnes is in cause of the marchaunts of your lan[d], which doe trade in this coontrye and have solicited there cause at our Court before our Hig[hnes], in zeale of our justice and good intencyons, and have certified our Majesty the emb[argadores] of Spaine have embargued certaine of their goods of sugars there of thers, fein[ing] them to belong to the marchaunts of Spaine, which indeed is not so ; these men hav[e] gotten them by the trew manner of tradinge, either bought out to rights, or by m[eans] of exchaunge.

And know you allso that this our coontry, by the goodnes of God, is kept, both the outcoastes and the inward champions, confirmed by good lawes and dilligent looking, unto that none maye offer wronge, but straight it must needs be spyed, and no man maye circomvent any marchant or other which come in hither to staye heere. And indeede these sewgars thus embargued there of those marchants and detayned, they had of our Excellencey by good and lawfull trading, accordinge to the trew form of traffick used amongest marchants, and this wee testifye that they had them of us by waye of exchange, according to the true accoostomed manner of tradinge used in all coontryes of the worlde ; and no man shall be able to gainesaye this thinge. And, as for your royall selfe, that you maye deliver these marchants from those greate wronges, they are constrained to flye to your protection rather then to the protection of aney other ; and indeede, when they shall see there good embargued from them, and yet shall have no remydie, but shall be forced to soostaine the losse, they will repent themselves greatly and will soorcease to trade any more into those quarters ; and so your coontry shall be much endomaged more then aney other.

For trewth it is that our coontry, by the goodnes of God, is bespred with divers sortes of marchants, which come theither from soondry quarters of the worlde, delightinge much in our justice so equallie executed and shrowdinge themselves under the coverture of our Courte, where they think themselves safe at all tymes ; and their they report allwayes whatsoever they have, and it is safely preserved night and daye. Moreover this owne coontrye — thancks be to God — standeth not upon the tradinge of aney one kinde of marchant whatsoever of so maney as thronge thether, nether hath it neede of them or that they shoulde proffit it by there cominge.

Wherefore they desired the light of our justice on this behalfe and our paines, as allsoe to take notice of their uprightnes in this vyolens and wronge done unto them, they beetooke themselves to our protection, they lodged in the saffest places, they lived securely by our clemency and compassion had to them, wheresoever they lived and tooke there rest.

Moreover, these, when they made their complaint and shewed us their greefe and injurye done unto them, nothinge doubting that their hope should be frustrate, wee shewed them that justice and favor which is used to be showed to our Highnes soobjects, and have sett thereunto our royall stampe for confermacion of that which hath bene sayde, that wee doe speeke in these our letters nothinge but the trueth concerning them, otherwise then, as it is falne out, that you maye knowe, if they shall certiffie your Highnes, the like unto this matter in trewth concerning the marchants, which are innocent and profitable to your coontrye and doe labour for the increase of your revenuewes and proffitt. But we leave those things unto your owne princely consideracion and care, for they knowe that, in whatsoever shall be good for them, you will not forsake or faile them.

Sent unto your Highnes and written this 15th daye of Rabie the Second, in the year after the Hegira one thousand and eightone.

This computation of theirs agreeth with the year after the byrthe of Christ 1609, Julye 11 [1].

Gu. Bedwell[2] transtulit.

British Museum. — Cotton Mss., Nero B. XI, f. 302. — Traduction.

1. Computation erronée.
2. William Bedwell, savant ecclésiastique anglais, versé dans les langues orientales, mort le 5 mai 1632 à l'âge de 70 ans.

CXIV

LETTRE DE HUGH LEE A THOMAS WILSON

(Extrait)

Le fils de Moulay ech-Cheikh s'étant emparé de Fez, ce dernier désirerait rentrer au Maroc; le roi d'Espagne y consentirait. — On pensait que les galères de Lisbonne avaient été envoyées en Andalousie pour transporter ce prince, mais on croit maintenant que leur destination est autre.

Lisbonne, 18 septembre 1609.

Au dos : To the worshipfull my especiall good frind Thomas Wilson, Esquire, secretary unto the right honorable the earle of Salisbury, Lord High Treasorer of England, give these, att Salisbury Howse, in the Stronde, London.

Worshipfull Ser,

My last to you was the 26 July last, under cover to Mr Thomas Bothby, to which I refer you. Sence here ys some alteracion uppon a reporte that Mully Sheck his sonne hath gotten Fesse [1]. Whereuppon Mully Shecke hymsellfe desyreth to retorne for Barbery: whereunto yt ys sayd this Kinge ys very willing. And, for the ayd of his transport, the gallyes of this place are sent away, 14 dayes past, for Andelozia; and sence theyr departure, yt ys thought theyr ymployment ys ment other wayes.....

Signé : Hugh Lee.

Lixboa, the 18 of september 1609, *stilo novo*.

Public Record Office. — *State Papers, Foreign, Portugal, vol. III.* — *Original.*

1. Sur les circonstances de la reprise de Fez par Moulay Abdallah, fils de Moulay ech-Cheikh, le 16 juillet 1609, V. *supra*. p. 417, note 3.

CXV

LETTRE DE FRANCIS COTTINGTON[1] A CHARLES CORNWALLIS

(Extrait)

Les Espagnols veulent empêcher les Anglais de trafiquer entre l'Espagne et le Maroc. — Cottington, qui s'en est plaint, a reçu pour réponse que c'était la volonté du Roi. — Prada lui a dit que les Espagnols n'étaient pas admis à trafiquer avec le Maroc sans autorisation spéciale ; que les Anglais pouvaient trafiquer à leur aise entre leur pays et le Maroc, mais que, le commerce entre l'Espagne et le Maroc étant interdit aux Espagnols, il n'y avait pas de raison de le permettre aux Anglais. — Cottington a répondu qu'en fait, les Espagnols avaient toute liberté de trafiquer avec le Maroc. — Il a rappelé des propos antérieurs de Prada, disant que l'Espagne était en paix avec le Maroc et que les Anglais étaient en droit d'y trafiquer à leur gré. — Il s'est étonné qu'en ce temps de paix générale, le duc de Medina-Sidonia prétendît s'enquérir d'où venaient les navires anglais. — Il a constaté l'hostilité du duc, qui a laissé bien peu d'Anglais trafiquer au Maroc sans leur créer des ennuis.

Madrid, 8 octobre 1609.

Au dos, alia manu : 1609, October 8, *stilo novo*. — Mr Cottington. — From Madrid.

My good Lord,

Twyse have I largely written to your Lordship since your depar-

---

[1]. Francis Cottington (1578 ?-1652), secrétaire de Sir Charles Cornwallis, ambassadeur en Espagne. Il lui succéda avec le titre d'agent (1609-1611), fut consul à Séville (1611-1612), ambassadeur en Espagne (1616-1622 et 1629-1631). Chancelier de l'Échiquier (1629-1642), il entra à la Chambre des Lords en 1631.

ture from hence, and directed both the pacquetes for Paris, in hope that you should ther find them at your arryvall.

. . . .

I perceave they are here directly resolved to prohibite all trade of his Matie's subjectes from Barbary hither, and from hence to Barbary, as neer as they can. The Duke of Medina now denies entrance in Cadiz unto certaine shipping of London that come from Barbary, consigned to John Skibow ; wherof I have here complayned to the Constable[1], the Duke of Infantado[2], and Secretarie Prada[3], who, wit one voyce, tell me yt ys his Matie's pleasure wit them all. I have much disputed yt, but espetiallay wit Prada, who sayes that his Matie suffers not any of his own subjectes to trade thither witout espetiall lycence ; that the subjectes of his Matie of Great Britaine might from theyr own cuntries use theyr trade thither at theyr pleysure (provided that they made not Spaine in theyr way); and that, yf here they found yt holsome for theyr estate to cutt of all trade from hence thither, they saw no reason why his Matie of Great Brytayn should purfiar[4] to have yt styll permitted to his subjectes.

I answered that I was hable to prove unto him (and so I am) that, from Cadiz and other portes adjoyning, all Spaniardes that would did freely trade into Barbary, and that the licence he speakes of ys but from the ordinary officeres of those townes ; that I remember himselfe tould me, not many menthes since (when your Lordship complayned hereof), that this King had peace wit the Moores and that he thought yt was lawfull for all English to use that trade at theyr pleasure ; and that, at your Lordship instance, his Matie then wrote unto the Duke of Medina about yt. I tould him that, peace being now generally made, I saw no reason why the Duke of Medina should so ernestly enquire from whence any English marchante's shipp came that brought no prohibited goodes. Hereuppon he confessed that that Duke had advertysed his Matie of many incon-

1. *The Constable.* D. Juan Hernandez de Velasco, duc de Frias, connétable héréditaire de Castille.
2. D. Juan Hurtado de Mendoza, duc de l'Infantado, marquis de Santillana (1555-1624), membre du Conseil d'État.
3. Andres de Prada, secrétaire d'État, mort en 1611.
4. Mot espagnol : *porfiar,* insister, s'opiniâtrer.

veniencies ; that he would seeke out the letters, and then say more unto me.

I tould him that your Lordship had ever noted that Duke to be a great ennymy to our nation, and that I had often heard you say you thought he had not yet so forgotten the voyage of 88[1], but that he had styll a remembrance of his disgrace then receaved, for very few of his Ma$^{tie's}$ subjectes have traded into those partes witout having receaved some agravio[2]; to which he aunswered not a word, but smiled at yt[3].

. . . .

And so, wit the remembrance of my humble dewty, I rest
  Your Lordship's obedient servant,
        Signé : Fra. Cottington.

Madrid, this 8th of October 1609, *stilo novo*.

Public Record Office. — *State Papers, Foreign, Spain, vol. XVI.* — *Original.*

1. L'expédition de l' « Invincible Armada », que le duc de Medina-Sidonia avait commandée en 1588.
2. Mot espagnol : tort, dommage.
3. Sur les vexations infligées aux commerçants anglais, qui trafiquaient entre le Maroc et l'Espagne, V. *supra*, Doc. CXIII, p. 418.

CXVI

LETTRE DE RALPH WINWOOD[1] A SALISBURY

(Extrait)

Il est venu à La Haye un ambassadeur du roi du Maroc, qui est parti depuis pour Amsterdam. — Il a apporté en présent des chevaux et des tapisseries sans grande valeur. — Il a prétendu qu'il venait négocier une levée de gens de guerre pour son maître. — Il annonce maintenant son départ et dit qu'il reviendra ou quelque autre à sa place. — Il a pour interprète un Juif qui parle espagnol.

[La Haye], 7 [n. st. 17] octobre 1609.

Au dos : To the right honorable the Earle of Salisbury, Lord High Treasurer of England.

Alia manu : 7 October 1609. Sir Raphe Winwood to my Lord. Received 16.

Right Honorable my good Lord,

By the copie of the lettres which herewith I sende, your Lordship may see with what ernestnes the princes at Dusseldorp doe presse my coming to them.

. . . .

Wee have had here an ambassadour from the King of Morocco[2], who now is gone to Amsterdam[3]; he brought with him certaine

---

1. Sir Ralph Winwood (1563?-1617), agent de la cour d'Angleterre aux Pays-Bas (1603-1613), secrétaire d'État de 1614 à sa mort.
2. Cet ambassadeur s'appelait Hammou ben Bachir. Sur sa mission, V. *1re Série*, Pays-Bas, t. I, pp. 357-499, *passim* ; France, t. II, pp. 485, 486, 490, 491.
3. Sur ce voyage à Amsterdam, V. Pays-Bas, t. I, pp. 367, 370, 371.

horses and hangings of that country for presentes to the States, and the count Maurice, all of no great valew. He made shew at first that his errand had ben to treate for a leavy of men of warre for the service of his King[1], and to that purpose he demaunded many questions; now he sayeth that he will returne, and, uppon report of his negociation, eyther he himself will come back hether, or some other shalbe sent in his place. He treateth by a trucheman, a Jew[2], who treates in Spannish.

And so I humbly take my leave and rest
  Your Lordships in all duety to be commaunded,
    Signé: Raphe Winwood.

Haghe, this 7th of October 1609.

Public Record Office. — State Papers, Foreign, Holland, vol. LXVI. — *Original.*

1. Sur l'objet de la mission de Hammou ben Bachir, V. *1re Série*, Pays-Bas, t. I, p. 369 et note 3.

2. Samuel Pallache. Il fut, de 1609 à sa mort, survenue en 1616, l'agent de Moulay Zidân dans ses relations avec les Pays-Bas. V. *ibidem*, t. I, *passim*, notamment p. 273 et note 1, et t. II, *passim*.

CXVII

LETTRE DE HUGH LEE A THOMAS WILSON

(EXTRAIT)

A la suite d'un complot qui a été découvert, les Moriscos ont été condamnés à être déportés dans les États Barbaresques. — La flotte espagnole se prépare à effectuer leur transport. — Anthony Sherley viendrait de Sicile se joindre à elle avec vingt navires. — On croit, en outre, à quelque dessein sur le Maroc, favorisé par Moulay Abdallah, qui règne actuellement à Fez; mais Moulay ech-Cheikh ne prendra pas part à l'expédition.

Lisbonne, 21 octobre 1609.

Au dos : To the worshipfull my very good frind Thomas Wilson, secretary to the right honorable the Earle of Salisbury, Lord High Tresorer of England, at Salisbury Howse, in the Strand, London. By the way of Bristoll, with a frind. — *Alia manu :* Mr Lee. Lisbone, 21 octobre 1609.

Worshipfull Sir,

My last to you was the 18 of the last moneth, under cover to Mr Bothby, whereunto I referr yow.

. . . .

Att present this state are wholly busied in the providing of shippinge to send into Andelozia for the transportinge of Moores into Barbary, by reason of a treason complotted by theym to gyve ane entrance unto the Great Turke into these kingdoms[1]; the which

---

1. Les Moriscos étaient entrés en correspondance, sinon avec le Grand-Seigneur, du moins avec Moulay Zidân. Ils promettaient de s'insurger et lui offraient de s'emparer de l'Espagne à la faveur de leur soulèvement. Ce fut la cause déterminante de

beinge discoverid, they are sentensed generally to be banished the kingdoms both of Spayne and Portingale, and to lease beath landes and lyvinges.

. . . .

Done Lewis Faxardo, with the whole fleete of gallions, ys at Cartagena, where are also sayd to be 30 sayle of gallyes, from whence shalbe transeported the Moores of Valencia and Murcia. Yt ys sayd here that Mr Anthony Sherly cometh from Sycyllia, with 20 sayle of shipps, and also the gallyes of Italy, with 12 sayles of shipps from Dunkerke with soldyers in theym. These goe all to joyne with Don Luis Faxardo. Yt ys thought that some other services ys purposed for Afryca besides the transporting of the Moores, by the meanes of Mully Abdela, the sonne of Mully Sheck, being nowe King of Fess; but Mully Sheck hymselffe shall not goe in the service.

. . . .

I humbly take my leave for thys tyme, wysshinge you helth with happines.

Your Worships ever at comaund,

Signé : Hugh Lee.

Lixboa, the 21 of October 1609, new stile.

And this day depart the shipping for Andolozia for the transporting of the Moores; they are sayd to be in the kingdoms of Valencia, Mursya, Grenada, Castile, Andolozia and Portingale 600 ℧ soules, ould and yonge [1].

. . . .

Public Record Office. — State Papers, Foreign, Portugal, vol. III. — Original.

leur expulsion. V. *1re Série*, Pays-Bas, t. 1, p. 369, note 3. Les Moriscos de Valence, atteints les premiers par un décret d'expulsion publié le 22 septembre, avaient cherché un refuge dans les ports barbaresques de la Méditerranée ; ceux de Castille, prévenant la sentence qui les menaçait et qui fut promulguée en janvier 1610, passèrent en grand nombre au Maroc, dès la fin de l'année 1609.

1. Dans une lettre au même, en date du 26 novembre, Hugh Lee annonce que les Moriscos ont déjà été déportés en grand nombre et que les expulsions continuent ; dans le royaume de Grenade, une révolte a éclaté et les Moriscos ont fui dans les montagnes. *State Papers, Foreign, Portugal. vol. III.*

CXVIII

LETTRE DE RALPH WINWOOD A SALISBURY

(Extrait)

L'ambassadeur de Moulay Zidân paraît peu pressé de partir des Pays-Bas, bien que les États, voulant lui enlever tout prétexte de prolonger son séjour, lui aient procuré à leurs frais un navire pour le ramener au Maroc.

La Haye, 17 [n. st. 27] novembre 1609.

Au dos: To the right honorable my very good Lorde the Earle of Salisbury, Lord High Treasurer of England. — *Alia manu*: 17 November 1609. Sir Raphe Winwood to my Lord. From the Haghe. Received 28.

Right Honorable my good Lord,

The affayres of Cleves stande for the present in this state.

. . . .

The ambassadour of Morocco yet is here; neyther doth he shewe any greate forwardnes to be gone[1], notwithstanding that the States have taken of him their last leave, and to take away all pretext of longer stay, have furnished him of a shippe at their chardge to transporte him into his country, which lies ready for him at Roter dam.

And so I humbly take my leave and rest
Your Lordships in all duety to be commaunded,

Signé: Raphe Winwood.

Haghe, this 17th of November 1609.

Public Record Office. — *State Papers, Foreign, Holland, vol. LXVI.* — *Original.*

---

1. Sur les raisons de ce peu d'empressement que montrait l'ambassadeur Hammou ben Bachir à retourner au Maroc, V. *1re Série*, Pays-Bas, t. I, p. 373, note 1. Il ne partit que le 30 janvier 1610. *Ibidem*, pp. 494 et 496.

CXIX

LETTRE DE FRANCIS COTTINGTON A SALISBURY

(Extrait)

Embarquement des Moriscos pour le Maroc. — Moulay ech-Cheikh est maintenant au Maroc. — On ignore la destination de la flotte espagnole.

Madrid, 21 [n. st. 31] mars 1610.

Au dos, alia manu : 21 March 1609. — Mr Cottington to my Lord, from Madrid. — Cottington.

My most honorable Lord,

.....We doe not suffer no more Moriscoes to pass into Fraunce, but have proclaymed that they which remayn repayre immediatly to Carthagena, wher they shall be embarked for Barbary.

The Moriscoe King that was lately in thes partes ys now in Xeuta in Barbary[1]. Our armado ys allmost redy to goe to sea, but no man knowes whither that enterpryse they have in hand.....

Your Lordship's most humble servant,

Signé : Fra. Cottington.

Madrid, 21° Martii 1609, *stilo veteri.*
My Lord Treasurer.

Public Record Office. — *State Papers, Foreign, Spain, vol. XVII, ff. 54-55.* — *Original.*

---

1. En réalité, Moulay ech-Cheikh se trouvait à Velez, où il avait débarqué le 20 février, étant parti de Gibraltar le 18. V. 1re *Série*, Espagne, 26 février 1610. — Suivant El.-Oufrâni (p. 320), ce chérif aurait débarqué à Velez pendant le mois de Dou el-Hiddja 1018 (25 février-25 mars 1610).

CXX

LETTRE DE FRANCIS COTTINGTON A SALISBURY

(Extrait)

Le roi d'Espagne a négocié la livraison de Larache avec Moulay ech-Cheikh et son fils.

Madrid, 27 mai [n. st. 6 juin] 1610.

Au dos, alia manu : 27 May 1610. — M\ Cottington to my Lord, from Madrid. — Received 16 June.
En marge : Alaracha.

My most honorable good Lord,

. . . .

I am now of opynion that the King wyll gett Alaracha, for that I am credably advertysed he hath dealt with the King of Fess, who was here in Spayn some few months since, and with the sonne[1] allso, to buy yt for money, and hath alredy disbursed upon yt 200000 duckettes, and that the father remaynes in Tanger as hostage for true performance on the son's behalfe[2].

. . . .

Your Lordship's most humble servant.
Signé : Fra. Cottington.

Madrid, 27° Maii 1610.

Public Record Office. — State Papers, Foreign, Spain, vol. XVII, ff. 96-98 v°. — Original.

---

1. *The sonne*, Moulay Abdallah, son fils aîné.

2. Ce renseignement était erroné. Moulay ech-Cheikh ne quitta Velez que le 10 juin 1610. Rojas, f. 30. C'étaient ses plus jeunes fils qui étaient retenus en otages à Tangor jusqu'à la remise de Larache. V. *infra*, p. 436 ; Guadalajara, f. 109 v° ; Rojas, *loc. cit.* ; Fernando de Menezes, *Historia de Tangere*, p. 124.

CXXI

LETTRE DE HUGH LEE A THOMAS WILSON

(Extrait)

Les troupes de Moulay ech-Cheikh ont vaincu Moulay Zidân, qui s'est enfui à Merrakech. — Le mauvais temps empêche l'expédition projetée sur Larache.

Lisbonne, 9 juin 1610.

Au dos, alia manu : Mʳ Lee, from Lisbon, June 1610.

Right Worshippfull,

My last to you was of the 26 Aprill, under cover of Mʳ Bothby, by Peter Kenton, master of a shipp of Dover, wherunto I referr you.

. . . .

Here ys also newes that Sir Anthony Sherley hath pilliged an iland of the Turke[1] and ys speedily expectid by his brother, the Persian ambaxador[2], at the courte of Spayne.

Also out of Barbery here ys newes that there hath ben a battell fought betwen Mully Sedan and Mully Shek, sence the going of Mully Shek from Spayne, and that Mully Shek had the victory, and caused Mully Sedan to forsake the feild[3] ; who fledd to Marrocus and was followed by Mully Abdala. And Mully Shek remayn-

---

1. L'île de Mitylène. V. *supra*, p. 282.
2. Robert Sherley.
3. Cette victoire, dont ne parle aucun historien arabe, fut remportée, le 5 mai 1610, par Moulay Abdallah ben ech-Cheikh sur Moulay Abdallah *ez-Zobda*. V. *1ʳᵉ Série, Espagne*, 19 et 26 juin 1610, Rojas, f. 39 et *infra*, p. 450.

eth in Fess¹ and ys thought that Mully Sedan will be forced flye to the mountaines.

. . . .

The Spanish gallyes have made three sallies with pretence to goe for Allarach, but have ben forced backe againe, every tyme, with fowle weather. They have now a fitt opportunitie by the victory of Mully Shek, and yet ys yt thought they shall hardly gett yt.

. . . .

And soe, with remembrance of my humble dutie unto his Lordship, I leave you to the protection of the Allmightie, resting Your Worshipp ever att comaund,

Signé : Hugh Lee.

Lixboa, 9 June 1610, new stile.

Public Record Office. — State Papers, Foreign, Portugal, vol. III. — Original.

1. Moulay Abdallah ne poursuivit pas les vaincus et rentra à Fez. ROJAS, *loc. cit.* Quant à Moulay ech-Cheikh, il était toujours campé près du Peñon de Velez (V. *supra*, p. 432 et note 2) et il ne vint pas à Fez.

CXXII

RELATION DE L'EXPÉDITION DE LARACHE[1]

Le marquis de San-German, arrivé devant Larache le 14 juin, est accueilli à coups de canon. — Après avoir opéré une démonstration, il rembarque ses troupes, sans avoir essuyé aucune perte, et revient à Tarifa.

Tarifa, 16 juin 1610.

Au dos : Relacion de la jornada que hiço el marques de San German Alarache.

Haviendo el marques de San German[2] dispuesto su partida para Alarache desde Tarifa, prosiguiendo lo tratado con el rey Muley Xeque y el medio que havia ofrecido para el entrego de aquella plaça, por los quatro alcaydes y un Judio[3] que invio a Gibraltar con horden para que, yendo sus hijos del dicho Muley Xeque y los dichos alcaydes, los recivissen sus vassalos y los Christianos que fuessen con ellos y se les hiciissen muy buena acogida, embiando juntamente titulo de alcayde de Alarache a uno de los dichos quatro alcaydes que enbio el Marques para que entregasse la plaça, partio sabado a 12 deste, a la una de el dia, la buelta de Tanjar, con 10 galeras y 10 vergantines y 21 lanchas y barcos luengos, por haver tenido aquella mañana carta de sobre Alarache de Juan Battista Reales[4] y las demas personas que, a son de mercaderes, havia

---

1. Cette relation était jointe à une lettre de Francis Cottington à Salisbury, en date du 26 juin [n. st. 6 juillet] 1610. *State Papers, Foreign, Spain, vol. XIII, ff. 113-114.* — Sur cette expédition, cf. 1re Série, Dépôts divers, Florence ; ROJAS, ff. 29-30 et GUADALAJARA, ff. 113 v°-114.

2. D. Juan de Mendoza, marquis de San-German et de Hinojosa, capitaine général de l'artillerie en 1607. Il fut ambassadeur en Angleterre, gouverneur de Milan et vice-roi de Navarre.

3. Nathan Ulel. ROJAS, f. 29 ; GUADALAJARA, f. 113.

4. En marge, de la main de Cottington : « John Baptista Reales, a priest whom

embiado el Marques a que le diessen noticia cierta del estado de aquella plaça, en que le aseguraban que, a los 10 deste, estavan con el mismo descuido y falta de prevencion que antes.

Y, haviendo llegado el dicho Marques a Tarifa el dicho dia 12 deste a las 5 de la tarde, con solo su capitana y otra galera, dexando horden a Don Pedro de Toledo[1] para que, siendo de noche, siguiesse a juntar con el Marques al salir de Tanjar la buelta del Cavo de Spartel, fue en tierra a visitar los hijos de Muley Xeque, y los truxo a embarcar en su capitana y con otros dos hijos de los mas importantes alcaydes de Muley Xeque, con toda decencia y regalo. Y, como a una hora de la noche, se le junto el dicho Don Pedro de Toledo, y se fue navegando seis leguas a la mar, mediendo el tienpo de manera que le amanecio el paraje de Arcila, emarados las dichas seis leguas y desarbolados, y estubo todo el dia en jolito, dispuniendo la desembarcacion y todo lo necessario para saltar en tierra en Alarache, con los Alcaydes y cartas de Muley Xeque, y ver la forma en que los Moros las obedecian y, en caso que hallasse occasion de apoderarse de la plaça, se hiciesse.

Y, estando dispuesto todo assi, dio orden a Don Antonio de Oquendo[2] de que con dos alconceres[3] hiciesse espaldas, y, resguardando a Juan Battista Reales para que aquella noche le havisasse lo que hiciesse en la fuerça, arvolaron las galeras, una hora despues de puesto el sol, y con algun poco de viento fueron con los trinquetes a la buelta de tierra, a reconocer al Cavo Blanco[4], donde havian de aguardar Don Antonio de Oquendo, para yr desde alli costeando, como se hiço. Y, haviendo encontrado el dicho Don Antonio a los dos de la mañana, dixo que aquella noche se havian visto unos fuegos desde Arcila a Alarache, y que de la fuerça se havian disparado 3 pieças, y que assi creia que se savia la yda del Marques, y que havia embiado en su busca un barco luengo con una carta de Juan Battista Reales, en que avisava particularmente de todo, el qual barco nunca encontro al Marques.

I know very well. » Sur ce personnage, cf. ROJAS, f. 35; et *1re Série*, France, t. II, p. 505, note 1.

1. D. Pedro de Toledo, marquis de Villafranca, capitaine général des galères d'Espagne en 1607.

2. V. *supra*, p. 416, note 2.

3. Le sens de ce mot n'a pu être fixé.

4. A une lieue au sud d'Arzila. Cf. B. RODRIGUES, *Anais de Arzila*, à l'Index.

Y haviendo passado en esto el Cavo de Mexilones, el mas vezino a Alarache, parecio al Marques que, si era sentido, no convenia intentar nada por fuerça, sino tan solamente dar las cartas de Muley Xeque por mano de sus alcaydes, y entender la novedad que havia y el socorro que havia entrado. Y conforme fue midiendo el tienpo de manera que llego de dia a Alarache con todas sus galeras, vergantinos y barcos junto, y con poco viento llevante, aunque con mucho mar de vaga. Y, llevando la capitana vandera blanca de paz, fue en esta buena horden y cercandose.

Y, en reconosiendole la fuerça de la punta de la barra, disparo dos pieças, y la del lugar tres, que era la seña que paresce que tenian de pedir socorro. Passo el Marques adelante y, llegandose mas cerca, le tiraron tres pieças con bala; y el mando responder con una sin bala, creiendo que en esto berian que venia de paz, y passo la buelta del Castillo de Genobeses[1], donde estava la saetia de Juan Battista Reales, para tomarla y que paresciesse que era enemigo nuestro, como se hiço, disparando la fuerça otras 3 pieças con bala en su defiensa y no respondiendo las galeras con ninguna. Y luego se vieron salir 300 o 400 Moros, los 30 o 40 dellos a cavallo con una bandera blanca, y los demas a pie, la buelta del Castill de Genobeses.

Y el Marques hordeno que los alcaydes y Judio con Jannetin[2] Mortara y Diego de Orea[3], y gente de guerra para su difensa, fuessen a dar las cartas a tierra y hablar y quietar al alcayde y gente della. Y los dichos alcaydes de ninguna manera querian yr, por decir que la tierra estava en arma y que ny serian admitidos, ni se atrevian a poner en riesgo semejante. Pero, con todo esso, a las persuaciones del dicho Marques, se embarcaron algunos dellos y el Judio y el dicho Jannetin para entrar por la varra a dar las dichas cartas. Y el Marques fue por su persona a reconocer el desembarcadero del Castil de Genobeses con Don Francisco de Varte[4] y algunos cava-

---

1. Construction en ruines avec une petite tour et quelques murs en pisé, qui se trouvait à proximité du port de Larache. GUADALAJARA, f. 226 v°.

2. En marge, de la main de Cottington : « Jannetin, a Frenchman. » — On a vu supra, p. 381, note 1, que Gianettino Mortara était Génois.

3. Diego de Urrea, interprète du roi d'Espagne pour les langues orientales. ROJAS, ff. 27 et 63.

4. D. Francisco Varte Ceron. Il était

lleros y a ver lo que mas se abian de hazer y a dar horden en ello, por venir la gente embarcada en los vergantines y varcos desde la tarde antes, por los Moros vinieron creciendo, assi la buelta del desembarcadero como en el Castillo de la voca de la varra y Castil Genobeses, de manera que parescia que abria mas de 500 Moros, haviendo, dos dias antes, menos de ciento en el lugar y fuerças.

Y, llegando a este punto Juan Battista Reales al Marques, le dixo que si havia recivido su ultimo aviso. Y respondiendole que no, le dixo que se le avia enbiado por mano de Don Antonio de Oquendo; y que la tarde antes, 13 deste, havia entendido del alcayde de Alarache el mayor y de un Judio y otras personas, que aquel dia havian tenido aviso del Anaqueci[1] de Tituan de como su muger, que estava en Ceuta, le escrivia que el Marques partio con su armada el sabado 12 deste y que sin duda estaria alli el domingo o el lunes, que se apersebiessen; y que este haviso se dio a los de Alcazar y todos los aduares conbicinos, y que toda aquella noche havian estado passando gente de a pie y de a cavallo del campo de Arcilla a Alarache, y de Alcazar benia mucha gente, y que para esto fueron los fuegos y las pieças de las fuerças de Alarache y de la costa; y que tan en particular savian los deseños del Marques que havia despachado a la Mamora para que un cossario de los de alli[2] viniesse a tomar la satia de trato del dicho Juan Battista Reales, por havisar a Hanacaci[3] que era enbiado por el Marques.

Con lo qual y ver la fuerça que los alcaydes habian en no saltar en tierra por verla en arma, y que los Moros crecian en numero y en desvergueça, arcabuzeando la gente de paz, parescio que era justo castigar aquel estero[4]; y assi ordeno que saltassen en tierra 300 o 400 infantes, a ojear aquellos Moros. Y assi lo hizo el

chargé des approvisionnements. ROJAS, f. 30 v°.

1. *Anaqueci*, En-Neksis, nom d'une famille notable de Tétouan, dans laquelle le pouvoir était héréditaire. Le mokaddem Ahmed en-Neksis était partisan de Moulay Zidân et s'était révolté en 1608 contre Moulay ech-Cheikh. V. *1re Série*, Pays-Bas, t. I, p. 299 et note 4; t. II et t. III, *passim*.

2. Des pirates européens, principalement anglais, s'étaient établis, vers 1610, à El-Mamora, à l'embouchure de l'oued Sebou; ils y restèrent jusqu'en 1614, date où les Espagnols occupèrent ce point. V. *infra*, pp. 442, 450, 462 et 503.

3. *Hanacaci*, En-Neksis. V. ci-dessus, la note 1.

4. *Estero*, pour estuario

duque de Fernandina¹, siendo el primero que se desembarco, y D. Rodrigo de Silva, hijo del duque de Medina Cedonia, aunque con tanta mar que salieron el agua a los pechos y desfondaronse dos barcos luengos y un eschife. Y, haviendo subido un repecho y cargado a las Moros, mataron 30 o 40 dellos, a que ayudo tambien la artilleria de las galeras; con lo qual no quedo Moro que no se retirase a gran priesa la vuelta de los castillos de la (sic) lugar.

Pero, como fuesse creciendo la mar y enposibilitandose la embarcacion, porque los soldados salian a nado, mojando las armas y municiones, fue el Marques a tierra en una chalupa de Don Antonio Oquendo, y al desembarcarse estubo para ahogarse, por yr armado y por ser grande el golpe de mar. Haviendo estado alli la gente 6 o 7 horas, la hiço retirar que se bolviesse a embarcar, con tan buena horden que no perdio un hombre, haviendo castigado aquellos Moros sin que se le matassen soldado alguno, y solo uno salio herido. Y, pareciendole que no estava el negocio para acometerlo por fuerça, pues con tan poca gente no se podia ganar la plaça tan fuerte y que estava ya soccorida, y que quedava mas viva la quexa que pudiera dar a Muley Xeque de lo mal que sus Moros le havian recivido, sin darles aun platica, sin recibir sus hijos, resolvio de estar alli hasta de las 6 a la tarde, y recoxer su armada y bolverse al amanecer a Tanjar, como lo hiço. Donde dexo a los hijos, alcaydes y criados embiados de Muley Xeque, y horden de que se cerrassen los puertos y no ubiesse por ay agora contrato con los Moros; y lo mismo aviso a Ceuta al marques de Villa Real². Y, por no dexar diligencia por hazer, le parescio despachar luego Jannetin Mortara al Peñon con cartas para el rey Muley Xeque, havisandole la inobediencia de sus vasallos y el sentimiento justo con que quedava, la causa que tubo para hazer aquell demostracion de castigo, y pidiendole que el suyo fuesse exemplar, y que, si pensava cumplir a Su Mag.ᵈ lo ofrescido, se beniesse en su persona Alarache y le entregasse o desengañasse deste caso, a que solo aguardaria su respuesta; y assi partio el dicho Jannetin Mortara.

---

1. D. Garcia de Toledo, duc de Fernandina, fils aîné de D. Pedro de Toledo, marquis de Villafranca. V. *supra*, p. 436, n. 1.

2. D. Luiz de Noronha e Menezes, marquis de Villa Real, gouverneur de Ceuta de 1606 à 1622.

Desde Tanger, el Marques vino con el armada a Tarifa, y desde aqui la embio a Gibraltar, y assi por ser mas seguro puerto, como por tenerla mas lexos de Berberia dellos (*sic*) y de los havisos que los Moros puedan tener.

Fecha en Tarifa, a 16 de Junio, año 1610.

Public Record Office. — *State Papers, Foreign, Spain, vol. XVII, ff. 101-103.* — *Copie.*

LES HUIT VOYAGES AU MAROC DE JOHN HARRISON

(1610-1632)

John Harrison était gentilhomme de la Chambre du prince de Galles[1], quand il fut désigné pour sa première mission au Maroc, sans que l'on puisse indiquer les raisons qui avaient présidé à ce choix. Il devait remettre au sultan Moulay Zidân une lettre de Jacques Ier, puis s'employer au rétablissement des relations amicales entre les deux États et demander satisfaction de plusieurs griefs. Parmi ces derniers, le plus sérieux était un litige concernant une somme d'argent considérable que le Juif Brahim ben Ways, trésorier de Moulay Zidân, avait saisie sur des négociants anglais, sous prétexte qu'ils voulaient l'exporter, contrairement à une ordonnance chérifienne[2].

Parti d'Angleterre, le 24 mai 1610[3], Harrison arriva à Safi au mois de juin[4]; il attendit longtemps, en raison des troubles du pays, l'autorisation de se rendre à Merrakech. On ne possède ni relation, ni renseignements sur cette première mission, dont le résultat semble avoir été de vagues promesses de Moulay Zidân relatives à la restitution de l'argent indûment saisi, ainsi qu'à la confirmation des privilèges accordés autrefois aux marchands anglais. Harrison était de retour à Safi le 28 avril 1611; un ambassadeur chérifien, porteur d'une lettre de Moulay Zidân pour le roi d'Angleterre[5], l'accompagnait, ainsi qu'un Juif, Samuel Pallache[6], agent du Chérif aux Pays-Bas.

A son retour en Angleterre, Harrison reprit ses fonctions auprès du fils de Jacques Ier et les conserva jusqu'à la mort de ce prince, survenue le 16 [n. st.] novembre 1612.

Cependant, la tension entre l'Angleterre et le Maroc, loin de diminuer, s'était aggravée: Moulay Zidân se refusait à remplir ses engagements; en outre, des naufragés anglais jetés sur la côte du Maroc avaient été maltraités et réduits en esclavage.

Harrison fut de nouveau désigné en 1613[7] pour aller porter au Chérif des

---

1. V. *State Papers, Domestic, Charles I*, vol. CLXXXV, n° 3.
2. V. 1re *Série*, Angleterre, t. III, Relation de J. Harrison, fin 1627. — Dans la présente notice, les dates ont été ramenées au calendrier grégorien.
3. V. *ibidem*.
4. V. *infra*, p. 449.
5. V. 1re *Série*, Angleterre, t. III, Relation de J. Harrison, fin 1627.
6. V. 1re *Série*, Pays-Bas, t. I, p. 623, lettre de Samuel Pallache.
7. V. 1re *Série*, Angleterre, t. III, Relation de J. Harrison, fin 1627.

lettres de Jacques Ier. Lors de son précédent voyage au Maroc, il avait, comme nous l'avons dit, fait la connaissance de Samuel Pallache. Une confiance irréfléchie dans l'esprit insinuant du personnage poussa Harrison à aller le rejoindre dans les Pays-Bas, afin de partir avec lui pour le Maroc. Mal lui en prit, car il dut attendre à La Haye sept ou huit mois et ne s'embarqua que le 18 avril 1614. Ils débarquèrent tous deux à Safi au mois de mai[1].

A cette époque, une flotte des Pays-Bas, commandée par Evertsen, croisait, à la requête de Moulay Zidân, devant l'embouchure du Sebou, à El Mamora, où des pirates européens, principalement anglais, avaient établi leur repaire[2]. Le dessein du Chérif était d'occuper et de fortifier ce point avec le concours des Pays-Bas; mais Samuel Pallache, toujours insinuant, avait donné à entendre aux États-Généraux que Moulay Zidân le leur céderait. Comme il fallait, au préalable, en déloger les pirates, Evertsen profita de la présence à Safi d'un ambassadeur anglais pour agir sur eux et les persuader de choisir un autre refuge. Harrison, à la demande d'Evertsen, écrivit donc, le 25 juillet 1614[3], à ses « chers compatriotes, les capitaines et gens de guerre anglais, dans El-Mamora » ; il leur représenta les relations d'amitié qui existaient entre les Pays-Bas et le roi d'Angleterre, les exhorta, sur le ton d'apôtre qui lui était habituel, « à chercher une situation meilleure et plus honorable » et à remettre El-Mamora à la flotte des Pays-Bas, en ayant la vie sauve et « sous de bonnes et honorables conditions ». Evertsen, rassuré du côté des pirates anglais, n'attendait plus que des ordres de Moulay Zidân pour occuper El-Mamora, quand, le 6 août, parut une flotte espagnole de cent vaisseaux, qui, sous ses yeux, s'empara de la place sans coup férir[4].

De Safi, Harrison se dirigea sur le camp de Moulay Zidân, établi à proximité de Merrakech, sur les bords de l'oued Tensift; il y arriva en novembre 1614. Le sultan lui fit le meilleur accueil; il célébra les louanges de Jacques Ier et s'engagea de nouveau à restituer la somme d'argent en litige et à libérer les captifs anglais; il remit à Harrison une lettre pour le Roi[5], l'accréditant pour un message verbal qui était relatif à un projet d'union de l'Angleterre et des Pays-Bas, en vue d'une action commune[6], qui devait vraisemblablement être dirigée contre l'Espagne.

Harrison, de retour à Safi, était sur le point de s'embarquer, quand on lui apporta deux nouvelles lettres chérifiennes. La première, datée du 14 janvier 1615[7], était adressée aux États-Généraux des Pays-Bas. Moulay Zidân leur

---

1. V. 1re Série, Pays-Bas, t. II, pp. 326-328, lettre de J. Harrison aux États; p. 272, Résolution des États; p. 305, lettre de Samuel Pallache.

2. V. ib., p. 225. Cf. supra, p. 438, n. 2.

3. V. cette lettre, ibidem, p. 320.

4. V. 1re Série, France, t. II, Relation de la prise d'El-Mamora, pp. 566-572, et Pays-Bas, t. II, lettre de Jan Evertsen aux États, pp. 334-341. Cf. supra, p. 438, note 2.

5. V. cette lettre de Moulay Zidân à Jacques Ier, infra, Doc. CXXXIV, p. 479.

6. V. 1re Série, Pays-Bas, t. II, pp. 506-507.

7. V. cette lettre de Moulay Zidân aux États-Généraux, ibidem, p. 460.

demandait d'intervenir auprès du roi de France pour obtenir la restitution de sa bibliothèque. Celle-ci avait été chargée sur un navire français, patron Castelane, affrété par le Chérif en juin 1612, lequel avait été capturé en cours de route par les Espagnols. Cette affaire était une des grandes préoccupations de Moulay Zidân ; déjà, en août 1612[1], les États avaient, à sa requête, fait une semblable démarche auprès du roi de France. La seconde lettre confiée à Harrison devait être remise par lui au roi Louis XIII, en mains propres ; il était recommandé, en outre, à l'envoyé anglais de profiter de sa présence à la cour de France pour appuyer l'intervention des États-Généraux des Pays-Bas[2].

Cette mission de Harrison, ainsi qu'on le voit, n'avait pas eu plus de succès que la première ; Moulay Zidân ne voulait rien restituer ; par contre, il entendait qu'on s'entremît pour lui faire rendre ses livres. Harrison, débarqué en Angleterre le 16 mars 1615[3], n'y fit qu'un très court séjour ; il passa en France, pour s'acquitter de sa mission auprès de Louis XIII, et repartit pour le Maroc en juin 1615[4].

Son voyage fut encore plus malheureux que les deux précédents. Il apprit, en débarquant, que Moulay Zidân s'était retiré près de Safi pour échapper au marabout Sidi Yahia révolté contre lui[5]. Le Chérif, dans sa grande détresse, fut réconforté par l'arrivée de cet envoyé, porteur de lettres d'Angleterre, de France et des Pays-Bas[6], et il fit publier que les souverains de ces pays lui offraient leur aide. Harrison reçut donc le meilleur accueil. Mais, le marabout Sidi Yahia n'ayant pas poussé ses avantages et s'étant retiré dans la montagne, la situation changea subitement. Le Chérif, rassuré, ne voulut plus entendre parler des satisfactions qu'il avait promis de donner à Jacques Ier. Bien plus, il envoya à Harrison, resté à Safi, l'ordre de se réembarquer.

Sous le coup de cet affront, Jacques Ier fit repartir presque aussitôt Harrison, qui, pour la quatrième fois, reprit le chemin du Maroc, à la fin de l'année 1616[7]. L'envoyé anglais, arrivé à Safi, écrivit à Moulay Zidân de la rade même. Ne recevant aucune réponse, il jugea prudent de ne pas descendre à terre. Cependant, pour attendre les événements, il demeura en vue des côtes du Maroc, profitant des navires anglais qui faisaient escale à Safi et passant d'un bord à l'autre. Après deux hivers d'expectative (1616-1617 et 1617-1618)[8], il revint en Angleterre. Le navire qui le ramenait ayant relâché à Tétouan[9], il entra en relations avec le mokaddem Ahmed en-Neksis[10], le gouverneur de la ville, et s'intéressa à la situation des Moriscos, qui, depuis leur

---

1. V. 1re Série, Pays-Bas, t. II, p. 138.
2. V. ibidem, p. 506.
3. V. ibidem.
4. V. 1re Série, Angleterre, t. III, Relation de J. Harrison, fin 1627.
5. Cf. EL-OUFRÂNI, pp. 342-387 ; 1re Série, Pays-Bas, t. II, pp. 124, 197, 214, 234 et 339.
6. V. 1re Série, Angleterre, t. III, Relation de J. Harrison, fin 1627.
7. V. ibidem.
8. V. ibidem
9. Sur le passage de Harrison à Tétouan en 1618, V. infra, p. 574 et note 6, et p. 575.
10. Sur ce personnage, V. supra, p. 438 et note 1.

récente expulsion d'Espagne, étaient venus en grand nombre se réfugier à Tétouan, où ils avaient trouvé bon accueil.

Les déceptions répétées de ses voyages firent momentanément renoncer Harrison à la vie errante. Fortement imbu de puritanisme, il s'adonna, en 1619, à des études de controverse religieuse et publia un ouvrage pour faire revenir les Juifs de « leur misérable aveuglement [1] ». On le voit ensuite prendre parti pour l'électeur palatin Frédéric V [2], puis, après la défaite de ce prince à Prague [3], chercher fortune en Amérique [4].

En 1625, un événement ramène ses pensées vers le Maroc ; la guerre vient d'éclater entre l'Angleterre et l'Espagne, une expédition se prépare contre Cadix. Harrison entrevoit la possibilité d'y jouer un rôle ; il adresse à Sir Albertus Morton un rapport sur la situation des Moriscos, qu'il montre animés de haine contre l'Espagne et susceptibles d'être utilisés comme auxiliaires dans les opérations contre Cadix. Il offre de lever au Maroc une armée de 10 000 hommes [5]. Sa proposition est acceptée et il est envoyé à Tétouan avec mission de sonder les dispositions tant des Moriscos que des Maures et de rassembler des approvisionnements pour la flotte. Le roi Charles Ier lui remet, pour le cas où il aurait à en faire usage, des lettres pour Moulay Zidân [6].

Harrison arriva, le 13 juin 1625, à Tétouan. Le mokaddem Ahmed en-Neksis venait de mourir ; ses quatre fils lui avaient succédé dans le gouvernement de la ville. Celui qui était alors en fonctions se montra d'autant plus favorable aux ouvertures de l'envoyé anglais, que les En-Neksis avaient toujours en vue de déloger les Espagnols de Ceuta. Harrison eut avec eux de fréquents entretiens, dans lesquels il donna carrière à son esprit de prédicant, leur expliquant la supériorité de la doctrine protestante sur le catholicisme espagnol. Quant aux Moriscos, ils accédèrent avec enthousiasme à l'idée de prendre part à une guerre contre l'Espagne et offrirent même de combattre à leurs frais [7]. Tout allait pour le mieux quand l'échec de la flotte anglaise, à la suite d'un débarquement malheureux (6 novembre 1625) [8], vint rendre inutiles toutes ces bonnes dispositions.

Ces relations avec les Moriscos eurent pour effet d'orienter définitivement la carrière de Harrison : désormais, il fut l'agent, le porte-parole de ces nouveaux venus sur la terre marocaine.

---

1. *The Messiah already come....* Harrison avait composé cet ouvrage au Maroc, en 1610.

2. Il avait épousé la princesse Élisabeth, fille de Jacques Ier.

3. Ce prince, défait à la bataille de Prague, le 8 novembre 1620, fut mis au ban de l'Empire.

4. Harrison déclare même qu'il fut nommé gouverneur des îles Somer (les Bermudes). *Calendar of State Papers, America and West Indies. 1574-1660*, p. 32. Cf. *infra*, p. 595.

5. V. 1re Série, Pays-Bas, t. IV, p. 284.

6. V. ces lettres, *infra*, p. 565.

7. V. 1re Série, Angleterre, t. III, Relation de J. Harrison, 11 septembre 1627.

8. Sur l'expédition des Anglais contre Cadix en 1625, V. Fernandez Duro, *Armada Española*, t. IV, pp. 63-79.

Sur ces entrefaites, les Salétins lui proposèrent de se rendre auprès d'eux, offrant de se révolter contre Moulay Zidân et de se mettre sous la protection de l'Angleterre. Harrison, sans nouvelles et sans instructions, se décide, « en désespoir de cause », à entreprendre ce voyage. Il quitte Tétouan au commencement de 1626 et, pieds nus, en costume de pèlerin, il se dirige sur Salé, par des voies détournées, car les Espagnols, au courant de ses démarches auprès des Moriscos, ont mis sa tête à prix. Chemin faisant, il passe par le camp de Sidi El-Ayachi, le Commandeur de la guerre sainte, qui lui offre toutes les ressources du royaume de Fez, si les Anglais veulent attaquer El-Mamora.

La ville où se rendait Harrison était celle de Salé-le-Neuf ou Rbat, qui avait été fondée par les Moriscos sur la rive gauche du Bou Regrag et que les Chrétiens appelaient ainsi pour la distinguer de Salé, sa voisine de la rive droite, appelée par eux Salé-le-Vieux. Enrichis par la course maritime, les Moriscos supportaient impatiemment les exactions du makhzen chérifien ; Moulay Zidân, sur leurs instances, venait de destituer leur caïd Ez-Zarouri, qu'il avait remplacé par un homme à lui, le caïd Adjib. Harrison arriva chez eux après un arrêt de quelques jours à Salé-le-Vieux. Les Moriscos, qui aspiraient à leur indépendance, entrèrent immédiatement en pourparlers avec lui : ils s'engagèrent à mettre en liberté leurs captifs anglais, en échange de canons et de munitions. Ces propositions parurent si avantageuses à Harrison, qu'il se mit en route presque aussitôt pour les transmettre à Londres ; il débarqua à Falmouth le 24 mai 1626[1].

En Angleterre, le Conseil se montra peu favorable à l'idée de traiter avec des pirates, mais les arguments d'Harrison finirent par l'emporter : il fit valoir que la mise en liberté des captifs anglais au Maroc, dont le plus grand nombre était entre les mains des Moriscos, ne pouvait être obtenue autrement ; il s'appuya, en outre, sur le précédent créé par l'accord que l'Angleterre avait conclu avec les pirates d'Alger.

Parti de Dartmouth, le 21 janvier 1627, pour son sixième voyage[2], Harrison arrive à Safi le 1er février ; il en repart le 4 mars pour Salé, où il débarque les canons et les munitions destinés aux Moriscos. Ceux-ci, escomptant déjà la protection de l'Angleterre, expulsent le caïd Adjib et proclament leur indépendance. Le 18 avril, l'envoyé anglais signe avec eux un traité *ad referendum*, par lequel ils s'engagent à servir le roi d'Angleterre, de leurs personnes et de leurs vaisseaux, en toute occasion. D'ores et déjà, ils donnent la liberté à 190 esclaves anglais[3]. Ce traité plaçant Salé sous la protection de l'Angleterre était

---

1. Sur le cinquième voyage de J. Harrison, V. *infra*, Doc. CLXVIII, p. 567, CLXX-CLXXI, pp. 571 et 573, et CLXXIX, p. 595 ; 1re *Série*, Angleterre, t. III, Relation de J. Harrison, 11 septembre 1627 ; Pays-Bas, t. IV, pp. 284-286.

2. V. 1re *Série*, Angleterre, t. III, Commission pour John Harrison, 15 décembre 1626. Il est qualifié dans ce document « Captain John Harrison ».

3. C'est le chiffre donné par Brahim ben Chaïb Vargas, caïd de Salé, dans sa lettre à Charles Ier du 18 avril 1627. 1re *Série*, Angleterre, t. III, à cette date.

déjà un résultat important; mais Harrison pouvait entrevoir par surcroît l'occupation d'El-Mamora, car Sidi el-Ayachi, le Commandeur de la guerre sainte, le chargea de renouveler sa proposition de concours pour enlever cette place aux Espagnols.

Le 20 mai 1627[1], Harrison, emmenant avec lui deux ambassadeurs des Moriscos porteurs du traité et les captifs anglais libérés, s'embarquait sur un navire de Pays-Bas et arrivait en Angleterre au mois de juin.

Le roi Charles Ier se refusa à ratifier le traité conclu par Harrison, pour la raison déjà invoquée qu'il était peu honorable de négocier avec des rebelles et des pirates.

Aucun accord définitif n'étant intervenu, les Anglais continuèrent la course contre les Salétins; un navire de Salé ayant été capturé par eux, l'équipage fut jeté par-dessus bord et la cargaison fut saisie. Par deux fois, les Moriscos envoyèrent des commissaires pour porter plainte au Roi. Harrison fut chargé officiellement de les recevoir.

La situation troublée du Maroc rendait difficile une négociation d'ensemble pour la liberté du commerce et pour le rachat des captifs : si le plus grand nombre de ceux-ci étaient au pouvoir des Moriscos devenus indépendants, d'autres se trouvaient dans les prisons du Chérif; il y en avait également à Iligh, capitale du Tazeroualt, le petit état autonome de Sidi Ali ben Moussa.

On pensa tout naturellement à utiliser l'expérience acquise par Harrison, au cours de ses précédents voyages, et il fut désigné pour porter les lettres de Charles Ier au divan de Salé, au chérif Moulay Abd el-Malek, successeur de Moulay Zidân, et à Sidi Ali ben Moussa. Pour la septième fois, il dut reprendre le chemin du Maroc. A son arrivée à Salé, le 8 avril 1630, les Hornacheros, qui occupaient la kasba, étaient en pleine hostilité avec les Andalous, fixés à Salé-le-Neuf (Rbat). Grâce à son entremise, l'accord se rétablit entre les deux partis. Les lettres de Charles Ier furent lues au Divan, et Harrison fit comprendre à cette assemblée que le roi d'Angleterre ne pouvait être tenu pour responsable d'agressions et de violences commises contre sa volonté.

Pendant son séjour à Salé, Harrison reçut une lettre de Sidi el-Ayachi; le Commandeur de la guerre sainte reprenait sa proposition de 1627 et insistait pour une action des Anglais contre El-Mamora; que si Charles Ier s'y refusait, il engageait Harrison à soumettre le projet aux Etats-Généraux des Pays-Bas.

Le 24 mai 1630, Harrison quitta Salé, se rendant à Safi, où il arriva le 1er juin et d'où il fit parvenir à Moulay Abd el-Malek la lettre de Charles Ier. Quant au voyage d'Iligh, force lui fut d'y renoncer, par suite de la mauvaise volonté du capitaine du navire anglais à bord duquel il se trouvait, et, après avoir touché à Santa-Cruz-du-Cap-de-Guir, à Ténériffe et à Madère, il dut revenir à Salé le 13 juillet 1630. Dix jours après son retour, arrivait dans ce

---

1. Sur le sixième voyage de John Harrison, V. 1re Série, Angleterre, t. III, sa Relation du 11 septembre 1627, et Pays-Bas, t. IV, son Mémoire du 26 mars 1631.

port une flotte française, commandée par MM. de Razilly et Du Chalard. Harrison offrit à ceux-ci ses bons offices et parvint à leur faire obtenir une réduction sur le prix de rançon des esclaves français; deux cents d'entre eux furent remis en liberté, et Razilly ne put mieux faire que de traiter magnifiquement à son bord l'envoyé anglais.

Cependant la situation sur mer au point de vue de la course restait mal définie; Harrison, saisi de différends surgis entre Anglais et Salétins, dut regagner l'Angleterre; il promit d'obtenir du roi les satisfactions demandées et de revenir dans un délai de quatre mois[1]. Dès son arrivée, le 24 septembre 1630, Harrison rendit compte à Charles Ier des propositions de Sidi el-Ayachi relatives à l'occupation d'El-Mamora par les Anglais, mais les pourparlers engagés avec l'Espagne en vue de la paix[2] empêchèrent le Roi de s'arrêter à ce projet. Se conformant aux instructions de Sidi el-Ayachi, Harrison soumit alors cette même proposition aux États-Généraux des Pays-Bas, le 26 mars 1631; ceux-ci décidèrent de renvoyer cette affaire à des temps plus opportuns[3].

Retenu en Angleterre par son souverain, malgré ses instances réitérées, Harrison fut empêché de tenir la promesse qu'il avait faite aux Moriscos de Salé de revenir dans un délai de quatre mois. Il ne put quitter l'Angleterre que le 3 septembre 1631. Sa mission eut alors pour objet[4] de régler à Salé les différends relatifs aux prises maritimes et d'obtenir la mise en liberté des captifs anglais; il devait, en outre, se rendre à Merrakech pour saluer Moulay el-Oualid, qui avait succédé à Moulay Abd el-Malek, et négocier avec ce sultan le rachat des esclaves anglais qui se trouvaient en son pouvoir.

Parti des Downs pour ce huitième voyage, Harrison arriva devant Salé le 25 septembre 1631; mais, ayant trouvé les Moriscos très surexcités à la suite d'une nouvelle prise faite par les Anglais, il s'abstint de débarquer et resta au mouillage jusqu'au 15 octobre, date où il repartit pour Safi. Contrarié par le vent, il fut poussé sur les côtes d'Espagne et n'arriva à Safi que le 15 novembre. Deux jours après, il se mit en route pour Merrakech, où il eut une audience de Moulay el-Oualid; le Chérif ajourna les diverses questions pendantes à la signature d'un traité, dont il chargea Harrison de porter le projet au roi Charles I[er][5].

De retour en Angleterre en 1632, Harrison présentait au Roi, le 14 mai[6],

---

1. Parti de Salé le 11 août, Harrison toucha à Safi le 13 et à Santa-Cruz le 19, d'où il fit enfin parvenir à Sidi Ali ben Moussa la lettre de Charles Ier. — Sur le septième voyage de J. Harrison, V. sa Relation du 8 octobre 1630, dans 1re Série, Angleterre, t. III.

2. La paix entre l'Angleterre et l'Espagne fut conclue le 15 novembre 1630.

3. V. le Mémoire de Harrison du 26 mars 1631, 1re Série, Pays-Bas, t. IV, p. 283.

4. V. le Mémoire de John Harrison du 25 juillet 1631, dans 1re Série, Angleterre, t. III.

5. Sur le huitième voyage de J. Harrison au Maroc, V. ses lettres à Andrew Carnwath des 9, 15 octobre et 16 novembre 1631, ibidem.

6. V. ibidem, lettre de J. Harrison au secrétaire Coke, 24 juin 1632.

les lettres de Moulay el-Oualid ; mais, malgré ses instances, réitérées de 1632 à 1634, il ne put obtenir que le traité fût ratifié.

Sa carrière aventureuse prit fin alors; il ne fut plus employé au Maroc. Utilisant les souvenirs que lui avait laissés ce pays, il publia en 1633 une plaquette intitulée *The tragical Life and Death of Muley Abdala Malek, the late King of Barbarie*, inspirée par un opuscule similaire paru en France en 1631 [1]. Ses nombreuses missions n'avaient eu pour l'Angleterre aucun résultat appréciable ; elles ne lui avaient personnellement rapporté que peu d'honneurs et nul profit, car nous le voyons, en 1638, réclamer aux Lords de l'Amirauté le paiement d'une partie des arrérages qui lui étaient dus [2]. Pour porter un jugement équitable sur la carrière de John Harrison, il faut se rappeler combien sont vains les engagements pris par la Cour des Chérifs, pour qui l'atermoiement tient lieu de toute négociation ; seules, des démonstrations énergiques auraient pu avoir raison de leurs procédés dilatoires et appuyer Harrison dans ses missions. Peut-être aussi ce zèle de prédicant que nous le voyons déployer, tantôt vis-à-vis des Juifs, tantôt vis-à-vis des Moriscos, le qualifiait peu pour être un agent politique.

---

1. *Bref et fidelle récit des inhumaines & barbares cruautez de Moley Abd el-Malec, empereur de Maroque....* V. ce récit dans 1re Série, France, t. III, p. 377-390.

2. V. 1re Série, Angleterre, t. III, Requête de J. Harrison du 31 octobre 1638.

CXXIII

LETTRE DE JOHN HARRISON A SALISBURY

Harrison est arrivé à Safi, porteur d'une lettre de Charles Ier pour Moutay Zidân. — Celui-ci, à la suite d'un échec, est en train de refaire ses forces. — Il est campé dans le Tadla, entre Merrakech et Fez, et sur le point de livrer bataille. — Sur le bruit faussement répandu par lui qu'il avait repris Fez, la région du Sous s'est livrée à lui. — Moulay ech-Cheikh est revenu d'Espagne au Maroc. — El-Mamora sert de repaire aux pirates, qui y vendent leurs prises à bas prix.

Safi, 10 [n. st. 20] juin 1610.

Suscription : To the right honourable the Earle of Salsburie, Lord High Treasurer of England, at the Court.
Au dos, alia manu : 10 Junii 1610. — Mr John Harrison to my Lord. — From Saphia in Barbary.

Right Honourable,

Being imploied as a messenger with his Ma^{tie's} letters[1] to the King of Barbarie in the behalfe of the Barbarie merchants[2], and arrived at Saphia, I thought it my dutie, both in respect of those honourable respects I found at your Lordship's hands when I was last present before your Lordship and tooke my leave, as also otherwise in regard of your honourable place and callinge, whom it chiefflie concerneth to understand all such offairs, to enforme your Lordship so much of the present estate of this troublesome countrie, as by a generall report passeth for currant. Which is that Mully Zidan is and hath been this long time in his almohalla, as they call it, or campe, at or neare to Tedula, between Fez and Marocco.

---

1. Ces lettres de Jacques Ier à Moulay Zidân n'ont pas été retrouvées.

2. Sur la première mission de John Harrison au Maroc, V. *supra*, p. 441.

Part of his forces, whearof his brother Abdela ben Hamet[1] was commander, not long since receaved an overthrowe; whearupon the King now sendeth to everie part for new supplies.

Mulley Abdela ben Sheck holdeth Fez; so that the former newes of Mulley Zidan his recoverie thearof holdeth not true. But, in this particular, they say he used a great pollicie, dispatching messengers to sundrie parts, as Marocco, Saphia and other places, with a false alarme of his recoverie of Fez (as was pretended); whearupon in triumphe they shott of theyr great ordinance in token of victorie; which they of Sus hearing of, presentlie yeelded themselves; by which pollicie he is become lord of Sus, but not yet of Fez, being as yet scarce in the midwaie to Fez, his enemies equall in strength, as it is thought; so that a battayle, or it be long, is expected to be fought betweene them. Also they say that Mulley Sheck is returned out of Spaine[2], and some forces expected thence for Allaroch.

In Mamora, a harbour of pyrats[3] upon the coast of Barbarie, the report is theare hath come in, at one time, but of late, to the number of twentie-two sayle pyrats, togither with theyr prizes, which they sell at soe reasonable a rate, as the merchants that escape theyr hands have little doings.

Rebus sic stantibus, I thought it my dutie to acquaint your Lordship with what I heare for the present, hoping your Lordship will pardon my boldnes, errors and infirmities whatsoever, in writing or otherwise.

And soe, in most humble maner, beseeching God to direct your Lordship in all your counsayles, as he hath donne hetherto, to his glorie, the good of his Matie and royal posteritie, with the generall good of Church and commonweale, I rest, as in duty most bounden,

Your Lordshippe's to be commaunded,

Signé : John Harison.

Saphia, the 10th of June 1610.

Public Record Office. — *State Papers, Foreign, Barbary States,* vol. *XII.* — Original.

1. Sur la défaite d'Abdallah *ez-Zobda,* V. *supra,* p. 433, note 3.
2. V. *supra,* p. 431 et note 1.
3. V. *supra,* p. 438 et note 2.

CXXIV

LETTRE DE FRANCIS COTTINGTON A SALISBURY

(Extrait)

L'expédition dirigée contre Larache aurait échoué. — La prise de cette place par les Espagnols serait préjudiciable au commerce anglais.

Madrid, 15 [n. st. 25] juin 1610.

Au dos, alia manu: 15 June 1610. — Mr Cottington to my Lord, from Madrid. Received 13 July.

My most honourable good Lord,

. . . .
It is here reported that the gallies are againe returned from Alaracha, without having doone anything. Myselfe have no such advertisment, in respect the ordinary of Andaluzia ys not yet come, but have understood, by divers lettres, that they went from Cadiz, some 16 dayes since, with confidence that place should have been delyvered unto them [1]. For myn own part, I am not sory for theyr evyll successes ther, as houlding yt prejudiciall unto the subjects of his Matie that the King of Spaine should be master of Alaracha; who, as your Lordship well knoweth, would gladly prohibitt all trade into Barbary unto any but his own subjects, and had, yf he durst, allredy so declared yt in playn termes...

Signé : Fra. Cottington.

Madrid, 15° Junii 1610, stile of England.
My Lord Treasorer.

Public Record Office. — State Papers, Foreign, Spain, vol. XVII, ff. 104-105. — Original.

1. Sur cette entreprise, V. *supra,* Doc. CXXII, p. 435 et note 1.

CXXV

LETTRE DE JOHN HARRISON A SALISBURY

Harrison est retenu à Safi depuis quatre mois, par ordre de Moulay Zidân. — Celui-ci, parti du Tadla, a occupé Fez. — Moulay Abdallah, revenu avec de nouvelles forces, lui a livré bataille ; Moulay Zidân, d'abord vainqueur, a été ensuite battu et se retire vers Merrakech. — Un caïd lui a amené de Gago 40 quintaux d'or. — Harrison vient d'apprendre que Moulay Abdallah aurait été tué par ses soldats mutinés.

Safi, 14 [n. st. 24] octobre 1610.

Suscription : To the right honourable the Erle of Salsbury, Lord High Treasorer of England, at the Court.

Au dos, alia manu : 14 Octobr 1610. — Mr John Harrison to my Lord, out of Barbary. — Received the 14th of November.

Right Honourable,

Having presumed heartofore, upon my arrivall heare and present imployment in this barbarous countrie of Barbarie, to write unto your Honour of such occurrents as for the present I could heare of, being then a shipboord and not landed ; since landed, but never a whit the further on my journey, by reason of the troublesome estate of this countrie, having ever since remayned heare in Saphia, by the King's appointment, now almost foure monthes, I have thought it a seacond part of my dutie (heare detayned upon these occasions much longer than I expected) to let your Lordship understand what further hath passed, or rather what we heare hath passed since, as touching this countrie affaires. For this countrie people is so gyven to noyse, false allarums, rumors and reports uppon every slight occasion, and the place, to wit Fez, wheare the two Kings have been all this while in armes one against an other, so far distant hence, that the true report of things hath been ofttimes eyther buried by the waie, our trotteroes[1] or messengers miscarying, or els quite altered by these Larbies into a different, many times a cleane contrarie report, by that time it come to us.

But that I be not tedious to your good Lordship, the King[2] having lingered some time at Tedula, about the midwaie betweene Marocco & Fez, wheare he was upon my arrivall, as in my other letter I gave your Lordship to understand, he marched thence towards Fez. The other, Mulley Abdela, hearing of his approch, left the citie and rehalled one rehalle[3] beyond Fez, among the Larbies, his chieffest strength. The King thearupon entred Fez, wheare leaving some of his forces, marched on towards him, no more but a river, as they say, betwixt them.

Since which time we have had seaven severale reports, one in the necke of an other, as touching this busynes: now that Mulley Zidan had got the daie, thearupon great rejoycing after the countrie maner; after a while, Mulley Abdela; and so successively, some affirming theare have been two battayles fought: in the first Mulley Zidan conquerour, and thearof we had letters from Marocco; but since that, Mulley Abdela, with a new supply of horse, hath encountered Mulley Zidan againe, at the gates of Fez, and given him a great overthrowe[4]. Which we have from some soldiours ranne awaie, who saie they left the King at Sallie, making towards Marocco; which report continueth constant and currant[5]. At this present, they say, Mulley Zidan hath an alkaid comming from Gago, now at the Drawe[6], with 40 quintals of gold; he had never more need of it.

This is all for the present I have to enlarge unto your Honour;

---

1. *Trotteroes*, pluriel de *trotero*, courrier, mot espagnol.
2. *The King*, Moulay Zidàn.
3. *Rehalled one rehulle*, transcription de l'arabe رحل رحلة واحدة « alla à une étape ».
4. C'était cette dernière version qui était exacte. V. 1re Série, Pays-Bas, t. I, p. 623, note 6.
5. Moulay Zidàn occupa Fez le 24 septembre et dut l'évacuer le 29, ayant été battu par Moulay Abdallah à Ras el-Ma. El-Oufrâni, pp. 399-400. Sur ces événements, cf. Rojas, ff. 37-38, 50-51 et 56-58.
6. *The Drawe*, le Draà.

which my hope is your Lordship will take in good part at my hands, as a testimonie onlie of my dutifull affection and thankefulnes to your Lordship, both for that honourable respect I found at your Lordship, upon my comming awaie, as also in an other particular, whearin I was once beholding to your Lordship for an allowance of twentie marks by yeare out of the King's cofers, till such time as our wages under the Prince[1] weare sett downe. Which though your Honour, perhaps, among other your infinite good turnes, have forgotten, yet it is my part to remember and acknowledge, as I do, with all thankefulnes. And soe, God willing, shall your Lordship ever find me readie upon all occasions further to expresse the same in all humble affectionate service to my power.

And so hoping your Lordship will pardon this my too much boldnes and tediousnes, I committe your Lordship in my humble praiers, with all your greater and waightier affaires, to the Almightie.

Saphia, this 14th of October 1610.

Your Lordship's most humble at commaund,

Signé: Jo. Harison.

May it please your Honour further to understand that, upon this instant, we have newes that Mulley Abdela, in a mutinie among his soldiours about the dividing of the spoyle of the last battayle, should be shott, and since dead[2].

Public Record Office. — *State Papers, Foreign, Barbary States, vol. XII.* — *Original.*

1. Henry, prince de Galles. V. p. 441.   2. Cette nouvelle était inexacte.

CXXVI

LETTRE DE FRANCIS COTTINGTON A SALISBURY

(Extrait)

Les Espagnols ont pris Larache sans coup férir. — Manifestations de la joie populaire.

Madrid, 20 [n. st. 30] novembre 1610.

Au dos, alia manu: 20 November 1610, *stilo veteri.* — Mr Cottington to my Lord, from Madrid.
En marge : Alaracha.

My most honourable good Lord,

This King hath now at length gotten Alaracha, with which all thes people are soe contented, as in theyr churches, howses and streets they make demonstration of extraordinary joye.

The town and fort was peaceably delyvered unto them without any kind of resistance[1]. With how much money yt hath cost them, my next may peradventure tell your Lordship very punctually.

. . . .

Your Lordship faythfull and obedient servant,

Signé : Fra. Cottington.

Madrid, 20° 9{bris} 1610, *stilo veteri.*

Public Record Office. — State Papers, Foreign, Spain, vol. XVII, ff. 217-218. — Original.

---

[1]. Sur la prise de Larache, qui eut lieu le 20 novembre 1610, V. 1re Série, Espagne, année 1610; Rojas, ff. 79-83; Guadalajara, ff. 120-123; Galindo y de Vera, pp. 228-229; Fernandez Duro, *Armada española*, t. III, pp. 328-329.

CXXVII

LETTRE DE FRANCIS COTTINGTON A SALISBURY

(Extrait)

Les Espagnols ont versé, pour la remise de Larache, 500 000 ducats à Moulay ech-Cheikh. — Ils se sont engagés à maintenir l'ordre dans la région. — Leur joie est à peine croyable.

Madrid, 4 [n. st. 14] décembre 1610.

Au dos, alia manu : 4 December 1610. — Mʳ Cottington to my Lord. — Received 17 January.

My most honourable good Lord,

My last lettre unto your Lordship was dated the 20ᵗʰ of the last month, and conveyed by the way of Paris, in which I advertysed that this King had gotten possession of Alaracha in Barbary; for which they have given unto the Morisco King who was lately in thes parts and his sonne the some of 500 000 duckettes in money, besides what theyr many journeys and armadas hath cost them. This King ys allso oblyged by artycles to keepe that cuntry, for many leagues compass, in peace and quyett to the use of the Moores, and in such sort as they may enjoye the fruytes of the earth without any kind of molestation. Here enclosed I send your Lordship a modell of the place. You can hardly beleeve the joye that possessed the people for having had so good success.....

Signé : Fra. Cottington.

Madrid, 4° decembris 1610, *stilo veteri.*

Public Record Office. — State Papers, Foreign, Spain, vol. XVII, f. 234. — Original.

CXXVIII

LETTRE DE RALPH WINWOOD A SALISBURY

(Extrait)

L'ambassadeur de Moulay Zidân a pris congé des États. — Il a conclu un traité établissant la liberté du commerce. — Une offre d'un million et demi de ducats faite par lui aux États-Généraux n'a pas été suivie d'effet. — Un Espagnol, nommé de Aguila, a proposé aux États ses services auprès de Moulay Zidân; mais la prise de Larache a changé ses intentions.

La Haye, 29 décembre 1610 [n. st. 8 janvier 1611].

Au dos, alia manu : 29 December 1610. Sir Raphe Winwood to my Lord, from the Haghe. Received 11 January.

Right Honorable, my very good Lord,

This dead season affordeth little, and nothing worth your Lordship's trowble. Here hath bin an ambassadour many monethes from the King of Morocco[1], who now is dispatched, and this weeke departed from this towne, towards Amsterdam, to make his returne. He hath treated with the States for liberty of entercourse, and of trade and commerce, between that countrey and these Provinces; the treaty I send herewith translated out of the Duche[2]. At the first beginning of this treaty, which was commenced the laste yeare, offer was made to lende the States a million of ducattes, or, if they would, a million and a halfe; but sence it was not followed, and, if

---

1. Cet ambassadeur, nommé Ahmed ben Abdallah el-Merouni, était arrivé à Rotterdam le 18 juin 1610. V. *1re Série, Pays-Bas*, t. I, p. 516 et *passim*.

2. Voir le texte de ce traité, *ibidem*, pp. 577-585 et 613-621.

it had, the States of Holland and Zeland would not have accepted it, out of feare that the remboursement of that somme would have fallen solely uppon their charge, whose marchantes onely doe trade in those partes.

Here is a Spaniard maried in Guelderland, who calleth himself d'Agula[1]. He presented his service to the States, to be employed to the King of Morocco, in exchange of the dowble ambassage[2] which hath come from him; but the late newes of the surprise of Larache hath advised him to change his mynde; dowbting of the surety of his passage, and of his treatment (being banished out of Spayne), if his ill fortune should be to be taken.

. . . .

Your Lordship's in all duety humbly to be commanded,

Signé : Raphe Winwood.

Haghe, this 29th of December 1610.

Public Record Office. — *State Papers, Foreign, Holland, vol. LXVII, f. 230.* — *Original.*

1. Francisco de Gamboa, dit Enrique de Aguila. V. 1re *Série*, Pays-Bas, t. I, p. 531, note 2.

2. Il y avait en effet deux ambassadeurs, Ahmed ben Abdallah el-Merouni et Samuel Pallache, tous deux accrédités par Moulay Zidân et qui signèrent l'un et l'autre le traité. V. *ibidem*, pp. 500 et 585.

CXXIX

LETTRE DE HUGH LEE A THOMAS WILSON

(EXTRAIT)

Les Maures se repentent d'avoir livré Larache aux Espagnols. — Moulay ech-Cheikh se fortifierait à La Mamora.

Lisbonne, 15 mai 1611.

Suscription : To the right worshipfull Thomas Wilson, secretary to the right honourable the Earle of Salisbury, Lord High Thresorer of England, at Salisbury Howse, in the Strand, London.

Right Worshippfull, my very good friend,

..... The newes from Barbary ys that the Moores repent theym much of the yeldinge upp of Alarach unto the Spanyards, but knowe nott howe to helpe theymselves. Mully Sheck lyeth at Mammora, with all his power, and theare fortifyeth[1]. He hath bought 4 great Hollandes shipps and hyred other 4[2]. The sayde Mammora ys the harbour where the pirates uzed to make sayle of theire stolen goodes.....

Signé : Hugh Lee.

Lixboa, the 15 of Maye 1611, *stilo novo*.

Public Record Office. — State Papers, Foreign, Portugal, vol. III. — Original.

1. Cette nouvelle était erronée, et Hugh Lee la rectifia dans sa dépêche suivante. V. *infra*, p. 460.

2. Il s'agit de la flotte de l'amiral Martin van Rysbergen mise à la disposition de Moulay Zidân par les États-Généraux des Pays-Bas. V. *1re Série*, Pays-Bas, t. I, p. 545, et *infra*, p. 461 et note 1.

CXXX

LETTRE DE HUGH LEE A THOMAS WILSON

(Extrait)

Tranquillité au Maroc; Moulay Zidân à Merrakech; Moulay Abdallah à Fez. — Impopularité de Moulay ech-Cheikh. — Navires de guerre hollandais au service de Moulay Zidân. — L'armement de la flotte espagnole ne vise ni les Turcs ni les Hollandais.

Lisbonne, 29 mai 1611.

Suscription : To the right worshippfull Thomas Wilson, secretary to the right honourable the Earle of Salisbury, Lord High Treasorer of England, geve these at Salisbury Howse, at London. *Au dos, alia manu :* From Lisbone, 29 May 1611.

Right Worshippfull,

My last to you was 14 dayes past, under cover to Mʳ Bothby.
. . . .
Here ys this day one Englishman come from Barbary, who sayeth that there the Moores are at quiett within theymselves, and that Mully Sedan ys in Marrocus, and Mully Abdela in Fess. And Mully Shecke, whose strenght ys nott above 4000 men, he kepeth at an olde towne of his owne, which lyeth betwen Alarach and Tanger[1], relyinge uppon the succoure of the Spanyerds; for the cuntry ys much bent against hym for the yelding upp of Alarach.

And where, in my laste, I sayd that Mully Shecke was fortifiinge at Mamora, yt ys otherwise; and that he had bought and hyred

1. El-Ksar el-Kebir. V. El-Oufrâni, p. 320.

serteyne Flemish shippinge; for then was the report such here. But the thruth ys that Mully Sedan hath there three Hollands shippes[1], which are newely trymmed and putt to the sea, and have in theeym 300 Hollanders and Flemynges; and these Flemynges begann to fortefy in Mamora; they serve Mully Sedan, who expecteth sixe shippes more from Holland to come to serve hym, as yt ys reported, against the Spaniard. The three shipps that are already in service, the one ys sayde to be of 400 tonns, the second of 250 tons, and the third of 150 tonns.

Here ys no more speach of the comynge downe of the Turke[2], and, to subpresse the Hollanders preparinge to serve Mully Sedan, a less army[3] by much were sufficient thereunto; so that the lykelyhodd ys that they shall eyther be devided and ymployed in severall services; otherwise ys there some greate pretence in hand. Of eyther, as tyme shall discover, I will in my best maner geve notice, for that I thinke this wilbe the place of theyre principall rende-vou.

. . . .

Leavinge you herewith to the protection of the Allmighty, who graunte you all your good desyres, I rest,

Your Worship's ever at comaunde to my power,

Signé : Hugh Lee.

Lixboa, the 29 of Maye 1611, new stile.

Public Record Office. — *State Papers, Foreign, Portugal, vol. III.* — Original.

1. Sur le sort de cette flotte, V. *1re Série*, Pays-Bas, t. I, pp. 672-674; Espagne, année 1612; FERNANDEZ DURO, *Armada española*, t. III, p. 330.

2. On supposait que les Turcs méditaient une attaque contre Oran et que les Espagnols armaient contre eux. V. lettre de Hugh Lee du 23 avril [n. st.] 1611, State Papers, Foreign, Portugal, vol. III.

3. La flotte espagnole en armement était destinée à aller obstruer le port d'El-Mamora. L'opération fut exécutée le 29 juillet 1611, sous les ordres de D. Pedro de Toledo, mais elle ne donna aucun résultat. Cf. *1re Série*, Pays-Bas, t. I, pp. 624-626; France, t. II, p. 531.

CXXXI

DÉPOSITION DE MARINS ANGLAIS

Renseignements sur l'association de pirates anglais établis à El-Mamora. — Ils sont 2 000 hommes et arment en course 40 navires. — Leur ravitaillement est surtout assuré par des marchands de Livourne.

Plymouth, 4 [n. st. 14] juillet 1611.

Suscription : For his Maties service. — To the Right Honourable, my verie good Lord the Earle of Salisbury, Lord Heigh Tresorer of England, give theise att the Court. — *Signé* : Ferd. Gorges[1].

Au dos, alia manu : 5 July 1611. Sir Ferdinando Gorges to my Lord.

The examination of John Collever, John Ffisher, Humphry Corser, Robert Spenser and John Dose, taken at Plymouth the 4th of July 1611.

Who saith that, being in a shipp called the « Concord » of London, of the burden of 240 tonne, bound for the Straites, in whose company there was one other shipp of Dover called the « Philipp Boniventure », they mett, some 16 leages to the southwards of Scyllie, the xxvith of June last past, with six sayle of pyratts. In the one was captaine Peter Easton[2], in a shippe of 200 tonne and 24 peces of ordinance; another was called William Hewes[3], in a

---

1. Sir Ferdinando Gorges (1566?-1647), gouverneur des forts et îles de Plymouth en 1595. Il devint, en 1639, lord-propriétaire du Maine et gouverneur de la Nouvelle-Angleterre.

2. CORBETT, *England in the Mediterranean*, t. I, p. 57, lit : Peter Croston or Easton. V. *supra*, p. 278.

3. Ce capitaine de pirates a déjà été mentionné, *ibidem*.

shipp of 160 tonne, wherein was 16 peces; the others weere called William Bough¹, William Wolmer and William Harry, in like shippes of 160 tonne and 18 pece in everie shippe, saving Harry, who was in a pinke of 60 tonne with 8 peces. These fellowes had in them some 600 men, all English, who take the said « Concord » and her consort. But, the « Concord » being a tall shippe and verie well fitted with ordinance and munition, they caryed away with them, dismissing the shippe of Dover (after they had kept them one whole weeke), taking on of her such things as they thought fitt, given out the ment to come into Causen Bay², to take in men and such other things as they thought they should be provided withall in those partes.

In the tyme they weere aboard the said Easton and his partners, they mett, of Ushing³, with another consortshippe of their crewe, being three sayle, wherein was for captaine one Steavens, in a shippe of 300 tonne and 24 peces of ordinance; in another of 200 tonne there was one Ffrank, and in the third there was one Arthur Greye, in a shippe of 200 tonne, the which it seemed they had taken not long befor, being a Holander. These men, this furnished, threaten the world, and give yt out they expect to be called in verie shortlie by his Majesties pardon for 40 000 powndes, of whome notwithstanding they speak verie aprobrouslie ; but withall they say, yf they bee not, they will take and spoyle all they meete with.

Of the South Cape⁴ there lyes one Sir John Fferne⁵, late of London, with ten sayle of shippes, who likewise is of the same company, but he hath bound himselfe to keepe that parte.

They say farder that there is in all, of these kind of wermen to the nomber of 40 sayle and 2 000 men, all English. Their common randevoe is at Mamora⁶ in Barbarie, where they have marchants

---

1. V. *supra*, p. 273.
2. *Causen Bay*, la baie de Cawsand, à l'entrée de la rade de Plymouth.
3. *Ushing*, Ouessant.
4. *South Cape*, le cap de Ceuta, c'est-à-dire la pointe Elmina.
5. Sir John Fern ou Fearn obtint son pardon, et, en 1620-1621, il commanda le « Marygold », un des vaisseaux de l'escadre de Sir Robert Mansell, qui fut envoyée contre Alger. V. *infra*, p. 522 et note 2. Sur ce personnage, V. CORBETT, *op. cit.*, t. I, pp. 41, 57, 114, 131 note, 152.
6. Sur le repaire de pirates anglais établi à El-Mamora, V. *supra*, p. 438 et note 2, pp. 442, 450 et *infra*, p. 503.

of all sorts, that trades with them for all kind of commodities, especiallie those of Leagehorne[1]. This it the effect of what they can say[2].

Signé : Ferd. Gorges.

Public Record Office. — State Papers, Domestic, James I, vol. LXV, n° 16, 1. — Original.

[1]. Sur les rapports des pirates anglais d'El-Mamora avec Livourne et la Toscane, V. 1re Série, Dépôts divers, Florence, années 1610-1613, *passim.*

[2]. Cette déposition fut envoyée par Sir Ferdinando Gorges à Salisbury par lettre du 5 [n. st. 15] juillet 1611. *State Papers, Domestic, James I, vol. LXV, n° 16.*

CXXXII

RELATION DE LA RÉVOLTE D'ABOU MAHALLI[1]

Titre : Late Newes out of Barbary, in a Letter written of late from a Merchant there to a Gentleman[2] not long sence impolyed into that countrie from his Majestie.

Containing some strange particulars of this new Saintish Kings proceedings, as they have been very credibly related from such as were eye-witnesses.

Imprinted at London for Arthur Jonson. 1613.

Première lettre.

Bataille du 20 mai 1612 entre le rebelle Abou Mahalli et Moulay Zidân aux environs de Merrakech. — L'armée de Moulay Zidân a été battue, bien qu'elle fût la plus forte et eût seule de l'artillerie. — Moulay Abdallah ez-Zobda, frère de Moulay Zidân, le caïd Ahmed ben Zoubir et plusieurs autres caïds ont été tués. — Abou Mahalli occupe Merrakech et Moulay Zidân s'est réfugié à Safi. — Il y a affrété un navire des Pays-Bas pour gagner Sainte-Croix, d'où il s'est rendu à Taroudant. — Abou Mahalli s'est rapproché de Safi. — Il annonce qu'il veut restaurer la religion musulmane et conquérir l'Espagne, la France et

---

1. Ce « gentleman » auquel sont adressées les deux lettres est vraisemblablement J. Harrison, envoyé en mission au Maroc en 1610-1611. V. *supra*, p. 441.

2. Cette relation est composée de deux lettres, l'une, en date du 19 septembre 1612, est signée R. S. ; la seconde, en date du 20 septembre, porte la signature G. B. On ne peut faire, au sujet des personnages désignés par ces initiales, aucune identification certaine. Signalons seulement que deux Anglais, Ralph Sidderon et George Blowe, résidaient à Safi vers cette époque.

V. 1re Série, Pays-Bas, t. III, p. 533, et *infra*, p. 501. — La révolte d'Abou Mahalli a fait l'objet d'une autre relation, qui a été publiée dans 1re Série, Pays-Bas, t. II, pp. 117-125, et dont l'auteur est vraisemblablement le marchand Paul van Lippeloo. On constate une grande similitude entre les deux relations, qui se présentent toutes deux sous la forme de lettres écrites de Safi à des dates très rapprochées. Les deux plaquettes ont paru en 1613 ; on ne peut dire laquelle a précédé l'autre.

l'Italie, mais il veut avoir de bonnes relations avec l'Angleterre, les Pays-Bas et les autres États. — L'auteur de la lettre est allé le voir dans sa mahalla. — Portrait d'Abou Mahalli ; ses partisans, son gouvernement. — Son pouvoir semble éphémère : les Chebana sont contre lui et les Arabes le quittent pour rentrer chez eux. — Origines du santon ; prédictions et légendes à son sujet. — Sa première victoire sur les troupes de Moulay Zidân, alors commandées par le caïd El-Hadj el-Mir. — Elles sont défaites une seconde fois à la bataille de Tidsi. — Les succès d'Abou Mahalli seraient dus à des pratiques de sorcellerie.

Safi, 9 [n. st. 19] septembre 1612.

Laus Deo! In Saphia, the 9 of September 1612.

Good Sir,

In most hearty manner I commend mee unto you, with desire of your good health, and all other content to your hearts desire, which the Lord grant you. Amen.

Since my last unto you, here is great alteration in this government, as I account you have understood before now. And because Master N. and Master F. have beene here, and heard and seene what hath passed, I doe referre the discourse to conference. For I assure myselfe they will visit you. Yet I will make bold to trouble you, to advise of some perticulers as followeth.

The tenth day of May[1], was the battaile betweene Mulley Sidan and our new King Mulley Om Hamet ben Abdela[2], not farre from Morocus, betwixt the mountaines and the city. Both sides very strong: yet, in mans judgement, Mulley Sidan of most force in horse and foote, and three and thirty peeces of good field ord-

1. Le 20 mai n. st. V. 1re Série. Espagne, à la date du 20 juillet 1612. Cf. infra, p. 467, note 5.
2. Ahmed ben Abdallah Abou Mahalli (1560-1613) était né à Sidjilmassa, mais s'était fixé depuis l'année 1592 dans la région saharienne de l'oued es-Saoura. — Sur la vie de ce personnage avant sa révolte, V. El-Oufrâni, pp. 325-335 et 1re Série, Pays-Bas, t. II, p. 20, note 6 et pp. 117-130. — La syllabe Om placée devant le nom Hamet forme peut-être avec ce dernier mot une transcription de Mohammed, ou plutôt de Mhammed, qui est écrit parfois au Maroc المحمد.

nance; the other no ordnance, and a few peece men; his chiefest force Larbies[1] of Sahara, a place distant hence twenty daies journey, these armed with launces, demy-launces and azagies[2]; and many Larbies that came into him, by the way as he came, some hee forced, some voluntary.

And at the day of battaile, his people beganne to be dismaied, perceiving Mulley Sidan was very strong. But hee encouraged them, saying, as they had found that come to passe which formerly he told them, so now they should see the like; and bid them not feare his ordnance, for onely three peeces should goe off and doe no harme; the rest should take fire, but not shoote a bullet, and hee would bee foremost, and goe in the face of the ordnance; and, finding his wordes true then at his commaund, to fall uppon his enemies.

So having satisfied his people with these perswasions, sent spies to know where Mulley Sidans lay, and so came right before it, with all his troopes. And comming within daunger, at Mulley Sidan's commaund, they gave fire, having both Moores and Christians that knew how to manage his ordnance. So three peeces went off, and did no hurt. But the bullets hard sing in the ayre a great height, and the rest of the ordnance tooke fire, and burnt out the powder, but shot no bullet, that remained in. So comming nearer, the musketiers placed upon them, with foure thousand shot, yet hurt no man.

So then they came on, and Mulley Sidan's people gave way and fled. They pursued them, and slue Mulley Abdela ben Hammet[3], alkaide Hammet ben Zebeare[4], and many moe alkaides[5], and betweene foure and five thousand people. So put his people into Marocus, and lay himself in the field.

---

1. On lit en marge : « Larbies are the country people dwelling in tents, Brebers those that inhabit the mountaines. »

2. On lit en marge : « Azagies are a kind of darts. »

3. Moulay Abdallah *ez-Zobda*. V. *supra*, p. 433 et note 3, et p. 450.

4. Mohammed ben Zoubir, gouverneur de Sainte-Croix. V. 1re Série, Pays-Bas, t. I, p. 671 et note 3 ; t. II, p. 55, et note 4, 173.

5. Les noms des principaux caïds tués dans cette bataille sont donnés par Moulay ech-Cheikh dans une lettre du 22 juin 1612. On y voit figurer « Baba Abdallah, hermano de Zidan » et le caïd Mohammed ben Zoubir. V. 1re Série, Espagne, à la date indiquée.

Hee hath not entered into Marocus, neither purposeth till he have destroied his enemies and put peace in his country. So Mulley Sidan fled and came downe to Saphia with his hackam[1], Abdela Kather[2], Abdela Sadocke[3] and the Jew Ben Wash[4], and a few others, besides his mother and women and luggedge. Heare made account to gather a head againe, and to give a new battaile, but in vain. The Larbies made a faire shew and came into him, and received some money, cloth and linnens from him, and so would have betraied him.

Whereupon he having some of his brother Mulley Sheck's children with him, to make friendship with his brother, sent him his children and wrote to him very kindly[5]. So betweene them I account is peace. So staied heere so long as he durst, for that Mulley Om Hammet pursued him. Whereby hee was forced to fraight a ship of Marselleis heere in port, with a French Ambassador[6], who came to him upon bussinesse out of France, and a Fleming that was in the roade ; and tooke his treasure and luggage, some women and children, some alcaids and servants, and Ben Wash and his followers, and went for Santa-Cruz, and there landed[7] in Sus and from thence to Tarradante; and there since remained. What force he hath or of his proceeding, wee here know not the certaintie.

1. On lit en marge : « Hackam is a chiefe officer in a City. » V. supra, p. 400.
2. Abd el-Kader ben Yazza. Cf. 1re Série, Espagne, à la date du 22 juin 1612.
3. Abd es-Saddok bou Dobeïra. V. ibid.
4. Brahim ben Ways. V. supra, p. 253, note 7.
5. On trouvera confirmation de cette mise en liberté des fils de Moulay ech-Cheikh dans 1re Série, Espagne, loc. cit.
6. Il s'agit du consul Castelane. V. 1re Série, France, t. II. p. 541, Sommaire, et t. III, pp. XXXIII-XXXVIII.
7. D'après Purchas (His Pilgrimage, édition 1625, p. 699), qui tenait ce renseignement d'un certain « Master Joseph Koble », alors à Safi et qui n'est connu que par lui, Moulay Zidân aurait embarqué ses deux cents femmes sur un navire des Pays-Bas et chargé sa bibliothèque, composée de cinquante paquets de livres arabes, sur un navire marseillais. Ce dernier fut capturé par l'amiral espagnol Luis Fajardo. V. supra, p. 443. Quant au navire des Pays-Bas, il se rendit à Santa-Cruz, où il retrouva Moulay Zidân et débarqua son sérail. Il y a contradiction entre ce récit et la présente Relation, qui nous montre Moulay Zidân se rendant de Safi à Santa-Cruz à bord du vaisseau des Pays-Bas, assertion confirmée par la déposition d'un Français capturé à bord du navire marseillais. V. 1re Série, Espagne, à la date du 20 juillet 1612. Le récit de Purchas, fait sur le rapport d'un témoin oculaire, nous paraît plus près de la vérité, et nous admettons que Moulay Zidân s'est rendu de Safi à Santa-Cruz par la voie de terre.

Some fewe dayes after his departure, came our new King into these parts, half a dayes journey from Saphia, and all the Larbies came into him and submitted themselves, and he receiveth all into favor, pardoning what passed. For, hee sayth, hee comes to make peace, and is sent from God, because of thee evill government of Mulley Hammet's sonnes the Xeriffes[1]; and to stablish their Prophet's religion, that was decaied; and to fight against the Christians, and recover those parts of Christendome the King of Spaine holds from them, as Granada, Andaluzia, etc., and tels his people they shall yet see greater wonders come to passe, where they shall acknowledge he is sent of God. He promiseth them Spaine, Italy and France; and, having put peace in these countries, there must now appeare a bridge in the mouth of the Straights, which hath been in former time (and so recorded in their writings) and sunk in the sea; now in his time it must appeare to carrie over the Moores. And having gayned these countries, he must raigne forty yeeres and then must com Christ, whom they call Sidie Nicer[2]; and he must surrender all to him; for he must judge the world, and then all must end. But, for England, Flanders or other parts, they have not to doe; they will have friendship with us, and desire trade and traffique with us in love and friendship, and would have his myracles and acts made knowne abroade the world.

I was in his almahalla[3] at first[4] fowre dayes, and spake with him, and saw his behaviour, and found him very humble and courteous, with many good speeches; and pittying the injuries all the Christians have by the ill government of his predecessors or usurpers, as he counted them. A man of some thirty-six[5] yeers, very civill, very plaine in habit, a course tucke[6] upon his head of

---

1. On lit en marge : « Kindred of Mahomet, which they challenge. »
2. *Sidi Nicer*, Sidna Aïssa.
3. On lit en marge : « Or camp ».
4. *At first*. Ces deux mots doivent être une glose de l'éditeur, car l'auteur de la lettre ne fit qu'une seule visite à Abou Mahalli. Elle eut lieu le 12 juillet 1612;

plusieurs marchands chrétiens y assistèrent, entre autres Paul van Lippeloo, l'auteur présumé de la relation néerlandaise sur ces mêmes événements. V. *supra*, p. 465, note 2.
5. Abou Mahalli avait, en réalité, 52 ans en 1612. V. *supra*, p. 466, note 2.
6. On lit en marge : « Or turban. »

died callico, a holland shirt, an alheick[1] of lile grogram, a plain sword by his side, hanged with a plaine leather thong; a man of great wisdome and learning, as none like amongst them, and a good astrologer, a great polititian. And hath drawne unto him alkaide Azus[2], of whom you have heard, the principall councellor of the land, Shecke Zimbie[3], Shecke Glowie[4], and many other Saints and principall men. And, since his comming, maried the widow of Mulley Bu Fferis[5]. And now divers libels in Larby verse against Mulley Sidan and his proceedings, and of further misery must come unto him, till he and his race be consumed.

And, for his government at Morocus, placed his Hackam, to see every one have peace, and a very honest man for justice. So Morocus is in peace and quietnes. And amongst the Larbies, he demands his due, either corne, horse, cattell or money; and tels them he coms to put peace amongst them; neither to rob them, nor yet to lose his right; not to give them pay, but force them to serve him, as need requireth. If they yeelded not to such conditions, his sword should force them. He came amongst them as a guest, and was to be entertained by them, and not to give them to gaine their favour. By which speeches, myracles past and policy, hee hath made them all to tremble: so he puts all to silence. Some content themselves, of the greatest in former time, to heare and see, shew obedience and say nothing; others change with the time, and have great imploiements, and professe loialty to him, and renounce their old master. What the event may be, I know not: for, we have learned, « the hearts of Kings are in the hands of the Lord, he turned them as rivers of waters which way hee pleaseth[6] ».

But having been in his almahalla, seeing the manner of it,

---

1. Haïk. On lit en note: « A long loose garment, much like an Irish mantle. »

2. Sur le caïd Azzouz, V. supra, p. 48 et note 2, et passim; il fut tué le 30 novembre 1613 aux côtés d'Abou Maballi. El-Kadiri, Trad., t. I, p. 273.

3. Probablement le caïd des Aït Zineb, qu'on appelait communément le Zaïnbi, comme on dénomme plus bas Guelaoui le caïd des Guelaoua. — Ce cheikh Zimbie est mentionné dans la relation attribuée à Paul Van Lippeloo. 1re Série. Pays-Bas, t. II, p. 119. Cf. 2e Série, France, t. II, p. 64 et note 4, et pp. 120-121.

4. Glowie, Guelaoui. V. note ci-dessus.

5. Moulay Abou Farès avait été tué en août 1609, par ordre et en présence de son neveu Moulay Abdallah. V. supra, p. 379, et note 1.

6. Proverbes, XXI, 1.

his plainnesse and policy, mixt with a shew of mercy and a kind of saintish government, I feare mee it will come to passe according to the fable in Æsop, when the frogs desired a king : a blocke was throwne downe into the water, which dash at the first made them feare him, but, lying still, they grew familiar, and sunned themselves upon him, and grew in dislike; so had the storke. But it were to be wished they would now content themselves, when peace and justice is offered.

If he do continue, it is like to be with trouble and bloud-shed; for already the people begin to disobey, and the Shabenites[1], Mulley Sidan's cast[2], are got to the mountaines neare Marocus, and have procured some of those Brebers[3] (as we tearme them) to joine with them and one Mulley Om Hammet Bolassad[4]; and these have robbed to the gate of Marocus. Wherupon this King sent forces to expell them, but found them so strong that they durst not meddle with them; whereupon was forced to rehale his almahalla[5], some fifteen daies since, and is gone towards the mountaines, where at this present hee is neere Frugo[6]. And, what hath passed since, we know not, only expect every howre to heare some good newes that he may prevaile; but here it is greatly feared, because many of his own people be departed from him, and those Larbies he caried along with out of these parts run away and returned. So, if he lose, the other bee the friends of Mulley Sidan, and he is expected againe.

But the beginning and rising of this King and his proceedings are very strange. He is a great saint and learned in the law, and was sought unto by many of the principallest of the land for his blessings and favour, according to their superstition. He findes it in ancient books writ of him by way of prophecy, that such a man of that place named Messa[7], whence he is, by name Mulley Om Hamet ben Adela, should bee sent at this time, to put peace in the

---

1. Les Chebâna. V. supra. pp. 350-351.
2. On lit en note : « Or kindred. »
3. On lit en note : « Mountainers. »
4. Nom qui n'a pu être identifié.
5. Cette expression, qui est à rapprocher de celle dont se sert Harrison (V. supra,
p. 453 et note 3), signifie : « décamper ».
6. Frugo, Frouga.
7. Massa, à 40 kilomètres au sud de l'embouchure de l'oued Sous. — Abou Mahalli était de Sidjilmassa et non de Massa. V. supra, p. 466, note 2.

country and to revive their law, and put out the race of Mulley
Sidan and name of Xeriffes, and so to raigne forty yeers till Christ
come to judgement. His beginning must be, hee must strike up a
drum hee should finde in that zowie[1] at Missa[2], and then should
repaire unto him people, to make him King. The manner of his
proceedings, and what encounters hee should have, and what he
found written, all the talbies and learned men now do confesse to
find the same written in their bookes. At his beginning, he put
forth only one tent and a kitchen. So resorted to him the Shrokies[3],
a saintish people in their lawe, but otherwise in behaviour very
savages. These without pay came to him, to the number of 150 or
200, at most; and with their helpe hee brake Alhadge Lemiere[4]
and his forces, servants of Mulley Sidan, being 5 000 strong. So
more of the sayd Shrokies came to him to the number of 5 000
and with them and such people as joined with him in the way, he
overthrew Mulley Sidan's forces thrise before the battell.

And so came to some strong places in the mountaines, never
brought to subjection in the time of Mulley Sidan nor his father.
Those withstood him, but hee overcame them and made them pay
him what he demanded, serve and obey him; so forced the principallest Shecks in the countrie to come to him. After this, marched
towards Morocus, and by the way was to pass a river; and the daie
before, he warned his people, in passing such a river no man to
take up water in their hands to drinke : if he did, he would die.
After comming to the river weary and hot, many not remembred
or not regarded his words, but tooke up water in their hands,
drunk, and anon after dyed; the rest all escaped. Which strooke
a feare into them to breake his command, and a perswasion that hee
is more then a man : for they say he is their Fatamie, that is a Saviour[5].

---

1. On lit en marge : « Or Saint's house. »
2. Entendez : Sidjilmassa. V. p. 471, n. 1.
3. On désignait sous le nom de Cheraga
une tribu formée de familles venues de
l'Est, et plus spécialement de la région de
la basse Moulouïa. V. p. 370. On les avait
établies aux environs de Fez. Les Cheraga
faisaient partie du *guich*, c'est-à-dire des
tribus astreintes au service militaire.

4. *Lemiere*, le caïd El-Hadj el-Mir. Il
commandait à Sidjilmassa pour Moulay
Zidân. Au commencement de mars 1611,
il sortit à la rencontre d'Abou Mahalli et
fut complètement battu. EL-OUFRÂNI, pp.
332, 336, 337 et 341 ; EL-KADIRI, Trad.
t. I, pp. 264-265 ; et *1re Série*, Pays-Bas ;
t. II, p. 118, notes 2 et 4.
5. Explication inexacte. Le surnom de

Next in comming to Marocus, divers great Saints and Sheckes resorted together, and would goe to visit him, that they might see what hee was, and understand whether that which passed was true or not. So comming, after salutations, hee told them they came to enquire and see what newes and what wonders he did, and so meant to depart. Now therefore, beeing men of account and talbies, hee would satisfie them, that they might satisfie others. So appointed them a time to come againe, and to bring such bookes hee nominated with them. So they did. Then he willed them to turne to such places and reade what they found written of him. So they did. To wit, both his name, his beginning and course he was to take, and withall found written seaven speciall markes or signes hee must have uppon his bodie, a wart above his right eye, a blacke tooth before, a bunch of hayre growing betweene his shoulders, a signe of a ring in the palme of his right hand, the signe of a spurre upon the outside of his right legge; the rest I remember not, but these and the rest hee shewed them. Which seeing, they did honor him and swore to him to serve him, and to live and die with him or in his cause.

Next, comming to a place named Dets[1] in the mountains very strong, where much people were gathered together against him, so that some of his owne people began to faint and be afraied, hee bad them feere nothing; for that before to-morrow they should see that there was more with him then against him. So that night, he commanded to take up his almahalla and march towards that place Dets. So they did, and all night long, to the thinking of al his people, there marched another almahalla greater then theirs, and went before them; and, comming to the place Dets, vannished away. And, at sight of it, his enemies fled, leaft the place and goods, also the spoile; so comming thither, had the spoile of all without fighting. This our countryman M. W. affermeth, with divers others, upon solemne oth to have seene.

At his being in these parts, myselfe with others went to welcome

---

el-Fatimi signifie descendant de Fatma, fille du Prophète. C'est un des noms que doit porter le Madhi. V. 1re Série, Pays-Bas, t. II, p. 122 et note 1.

1. Tidsi, sur l'oued Draâ, dans le district de Ternata, et non Tidsi dans le Sous.

him[1]. He entertained us very kindly, and told us he would shew the English what favour he could, and permit them free trade; willing us to take knowledge that he was sent by God's appointment to releeve the oppressed, as wel Moores and strangers as Christians and al sorts, and what we had seene and heard to advertise; saying we should see yet more strange matters come to passe then what had passed. His meaning, as we gather, is the conquering of Spaine, France and Italy; with which oppinion hee possesseth the foolish and credulous Moores.

Now, having bin tedious to trouble you with such news as the time affoords (not al, but part as it comes into my memory), I pray you take it in good part; the censure hereof I leave to your wisdome and consideration. For my owne part, I am perswaded they bee delusions of the Divell done by witchcraft, and permitted by the Lord, to seduce them to further error: God deliver us Christians well from among them, and grant us the use and true knowledge of his holy word preached in Christian countries, which heere wee want, and the use and comfort of his holy Sacraments, to the sealing up of our faith in Christ Jesus. Amen.

I am sorry I have nothing for remembrance to present unto you, but, God willing, when the time betters, I will not bee forgetfull; in the meanetime, I pray you accept of these few lines in good part. So resting ever at your service, I commit you to God's holy tuition, who blesse you in this world with health and content, and in the world to come with eternal joy. Amen.

Your loving friend to command,

R. S.

Seconde lettre.

On s'attend au succès prochain de Moulay Zidân. — Abou Mahalli prétendait n'en vouloir qu'à Mazagan, Ceuta et Tanger et non aux Maures. — Ses accusations contre Moulay Zidân. — Les 2 500 Cheraga qu'il

---

1. Il semble que ce soit une redite. L'auteur a déjà relaté son entrevue avec Abou Mahalli, le 12 juillet 1612. V. *supra* p. 469 et note 4.

avait avec lui l'ont abandonné. — *Ses cavaliers arabes désertent chaque jour.* — *On attend le retour prochain de Moulay Zidân.*

[Safi,] 10 [n. st. 20] septembre 1612.

Another Letter received from another Friend at the same time, dated the tenth of September.

  Good Sir,

Pardon me in that, at my going away, I came not to take my leave of you[1]; the ship went downe two daies sooner than I made account off. But for all your courtesies alwaies towards mee, I heartily thanke you and remaine your debtor, etc.

For the state of this country and of the wars of this new King, I know Master S. hath enlarged you more than I can a great deale. But, for all this and the troubles Mulley Sidan hath had, it is thought he will be King again, and that in short time; staying but for a new moone to give battaile.

This Saint or King told his Shrokies which came with him at first, his comming was to take Mazagant, Sute and Tanger, not to fight against the Moores, unlesse they would resist and not let him take the Christian townes. Hee said againe that Mulley Sidan and his followers were Christians, one who robbed all men without reason, killed and slue many men upon no occasions, but in his angry minde. And withall said he dranke wine and eate oppium; therefore said it could not bee but that hee was an Unsrony[2], which amongst them they hold to bee an unjust or ungodly man, as they say wee Christians are.

His Shrokies two thousand five hundreth, almost all footmen, with no peeces, but halfe launces, that was their weapons, bare-headed men. Never in their lives they weare shert or cloth to their backes, but an alheik. Which Shrokies have left this King, and are all gonne for their country. This King's forces are of Larbies, which are horsemen; every day they flee from

1. John Harrison. V. *supra*, p. 465 et note 1.

2. *Unsrony*, Nassarani, c'est-à-dire Chrétien.

him more and more; as alkaid Syde[1], whom you knew alkaid of this place, is come from him with sixe hundreth horse. So that very shortly Mulley Sidan is expected to come heare againe[2].

And thus, with my commendations to your good selfe and all our good friends, I commit you to the Almighty[3].

Yours assured to command.

G. B.

FINIS.

British Museum. — Printed Books, Press Mark : 1046. D. 26. — Late News out of Barbary[4]... — Londres, 1613. in-8°.

1. *Sydé*, Saïd.
2. Malgré ces prévisions, Abou Mahalli se maintint à Merrakech plus de 14 mois après la date de la présente lettre. Ce ne fut que le 30 novembre 1613 qu'il fut battu et tué à la bataille du Djebel Guiliz, près de Merrakech, par Yahia ben Abdallah, marabout du Sous, que Moulay Zidân avait réussi à intéresser à sa cause. EL-OUFRÂNI, pp. 339-341; 1re Série, Pays-Bas, t. II, p. 443. — PURCHAS (*op. cit.*, pp. 699 et ss.) donne un récit intéressant du recours de Moulay Zidân à Sidi Yahia et de la rupture qui se produisit ensuite entre le Chérif et ce marabout. Le récit de Purchas, qui va jusqu'en 1616, s'appuie principalement sur le rapport de « master Joseph Keble ». Cf. *supra*, p. 468 et note 7.

3. PURCHAS, *op. cit.*, p. 699, donne un résumé de la présente relation.

4. V. le titre complet de cette plaquette, *supra*, p. 465.

CXXXIII

LETTRE DE JOHN CHAMBERLAIN A DUDLEY CARLETON

(Extrait)

Il y a à Londres un pirate juif, qui a été arrêté, sur la plainte de l'ambassadeur d'Espagne, pour avoir fait des prises sur les Espagnols. — Il était au service du roi de Maroc; ses vaisseaux et leurs équipages avaient été fournis par les Pays-Bas.

Londres, 4 [n. st. 14] novembre 1614.

Suscription : To the right honorable Sir Dudley Carleton, K^t, L. Ambassador for his Matie at Venice.

Au dos, alia manu : Mr Chamberlain, 4th of November 1614.

My very good Lorde,

Meeting yesterday with Mr Rookes, I delivered the ring which I have caried about me.

Here is a Jew pirat[1] arrested, that brought three prises of Span-

---

1. Ce Juif pirate était Samuel Pallache. Après avoir rempli plusieurs missions pour Moulay Zidân auprès des États-Généraux des Pays-Bas (V. *supra*, pp. 427 et n. 2, 442, 458, n. 2), il avait obtenu de ceux-ci qu'ils missent à la disposition du Chérif un vaisseau de guerre et son yacht, équipés à leurs frais ; ces deux navires étaient destinés à protéger les sujets du Chérif et ne devaient servir que contre les puissances en état de guerre avec le Maroc. V. *1re Série*, Pays-Bas, t. II, p. 209. Parti pour le Maroc en avril 1614, Samuel Pallache tomba en disgrâce ; il résolut alors de faire à son profit la course contre les Espagnols, en profitant d'une commission qu'il s'était fait délivrer par Moulay Zidân. Il quitta Safi dans les premiers jours de juillet, resta près de quatre mois en mer et fit deux prises espagnoles qu'il envoya aux Pays-Bas. Son yacht l'avait abandonné ; quant au vaisseau, il échoua devant Plymouth. Sur la plainte de l'ambassadeur d'Espagne, Diego de Cuña, Samuel Pallache fut arrêté à Dart-

iardes into Plimmouth[1]. He was set out by the King of Maroco, and useth Hollanders ships and for the most part theyre mariners. But yt is like he shall passe yt over well enough, for he pretendeth to have leave and licence[2] under the King's hand for his free egresse and regresse, which was not beleved till he made proofe of yt.

So, with all due remembrance to my Lady, I commend you to the protection of the Almighty.

From London, this 4th of November 1614.

Your Lordships to commaund,

Signé : John Chamberlain.

Public Record Office. — State Papers, Domestic, James I, vol. LXXVIII, n° 61. — Original.

mouth et amené à Londres sous l'accusation de piraterie. V. *ibidem*, pp. 425-428 et *passim*.

1. Renseignement erroné. Samuel Pallache n'avait fait que deux prises, envoyées aux Pays-Bas.

2. Ce sauf-conduit avait été obtenu de Jacques 1er par l'intermédiaire de John Harrison. V. *1re Série*, Pays-Bas, t. 1, p. 326, et *supra*, p. 442.

CXXXIV

LETTRE DE MOULAY ZIDÂN A JACQUES Ier [1]

John Harrison est arrivé au Maroc, porteur de la lettre écrite par Jacques Ier, pendant l'insurrection du rebelle Abou Mahalli. — Cette révolte a été heureusement réprimée. — Le Chérif a accueilli l'envoyé anglais favorablement. — Les troubles sont un motif pour les souverains de resserrer les liens qui les unissent. — Les réclamations présentées par Harrison ont été écoutées avec bienveillance. — Celui-ci est chargé d'un message verbal.

Camp de l'oued Tensift, 3ᵉ décade de Choual 1023 [24 novembre-2 décembre 1614] [2].

En tête : هُوَ

SIGNE DE VALIDATION.

صدر هذا المكتوب العلى الامامى الكريم المظهرى الناصرى الزيدانى الحسنى الفاطمى الهاشمى السلطانى عن الامر العلى النبوى الشريف العلوى الذى دانت بطاعته الكريمة الممالك الاسلامية وانفادت لدعوته الشريفة سائر الاقطار المغربية وخضعت لأوامره جبابرة الملوك السودانية واقطارها الفاصية والدانية الى السلطان الذى له بين سلاطين الملل النصرانية والامم المسيحية القدر

---

1. V. un fac-similé de cette lettre, p. 482, Pl. VI.
2. Dans l'exemplaire espagnol de cette lettre, la date est précisée : 25 Choual 1023, mais elle est accompagnée d'une équivalence inexacte. V. *infra*, p. 485 et note 1.

الشامخ والملك الذي له في وراثة ملك آبائه واسلافه القدم الراسخ والعز الباذخ السلطان يعقوب صاحب مملكة لنكلاطرّة

اما بعد حمد الله الذي جعل بين ملوك الارض وان اختلفت في الأديان وصلة تعتبرها باعتبار احكام السياسة وقوانين الرياسة الملوك والامراء والأعيان وتوجب لها الحق في كل ما يدور بينها من المخاطبة والمراسلة في الامور التي لها البال والشان

فكتابنا هذا اليكم والاحوال والحمد لله في جميع ممالكنا الشريفة السلطانية الزيدانية وسائر اقطار بلادنا المغربية والسودانية على ما يسر والحمد لله من كمال الطاعة والتمهيد وقطع دابر كل جاحد وعنيد واجتماع كلمة المسلمين على السمع والطاعة لاوامرنا العلية المطاعة في كل قطر من ممالكنا الشريفة قريب وبعيد لله الحمد وله الشكر هذا

وانه ورد علي مقامنا مقامكم خديمكم الاثير المرضي النبيل جوان هرشون ومعه كتابكم الذي كنتم خاطبتم به مقامنا الكريم في مدة الفتن البارطة مع المخذول المحل الذي ادار الله عليه سوء الدائرة وقطع والمنة لله بسيوفنا الظاهرة دايره فلم يقدر الله بوصول هذا الكتاب الا بعد ان اراح الله من تلك الفتن واطمأنّ الحال بنا في دار ملكنا ولله الحمد وله الشكر على ما اسدى من جزيل المنن واقبلنا على رسولكم غاية الاقبال والقيناه من انعامنا بجزيل الاحسان والإفضال رعيا لما لجانبكم عندنا من جميل الاعتبار في كل حال وقد اطلعنا من كتابكم الواصل

LETTRE DE MOULAY ZIDÂN A JACQUES Iᵉʳ

على ما كان قد تحرّك منكم حينئذ من شديد الامتعاض والتنفس الذي تشتد به من الملوك الغيرة والنعرة على بعضهم لبعض بى كل فطر وارض لاسيما من يكون معه مثلكم قديم الصداقة والمحبة الموروثة من عهد الاسلاف فشكرنا لمكانكم المكين ذلك شكرًا جميلا و اعتبرناه لكم اعتيارًا جليلا واستنتجنا منه على صدف ودكم والوفاء بعهدكم برهانًا واضحًا ودليلا

وحضر بين يدينا خديمكم المذكور انجده الله بالفى الى مسامعنا الكريمة كلامًا تلفيناه منه و فرره بى مجلسنا فوجد منّا لذلك صاغية واودعه منّا اذنا واعية وفد الفينا اليه ما يبثه من الكلام لديكم وينهيه مشابهة اليكم والمراد ان تعطوا له منكم مجلسا وفسحة حتى يفرر عليكم ذلك مستوبى ويبثه عندكم مستـ..... ان شاء الله وبه كتب بى تاريخ اواخر شوال عام ثلاثة وعشرين

والب

British Museum. — Cotton Mss., Nero B. XI, f. 318. — Original.

CXXXIV^{bis}

LETTRE DE MOULAY ZIDÂN A JACQUES Ier

(Traduction française)

Camp de l'oued Tensift, 3e décade de Choual 1023 [24 novembre-2 décembre 1614].

En tête : Lui !

Signe de validation.

Émane cette lettre auguste, imamienne, illustre, triomphante, victorieuse, zidanienne, hassénienne, fatimienne, hachémienne, sultanienne, de l'autorité haute et prophétique du Chérif Alaoui, celui qui a rallié les empires de l'Islam à sa domination bienfaisante, dont les pays du Maghreb acceptent la noble juridiction et sous les ordres duquel se courbent les puissants souverains du Soudan et des contrées qui en dépendent, tant proches que lointaines.

Au Roi qui, parmi les souverains des sectes et des peuples chrétiens, possède une haute considération, qui, parmi les héritiers du trône de ses pères et de ses ancêtres, occupe un rang élevé et jouit d'une grande puissance, le prince Jacques, roi d'Angleterre.

Louons d'abord Dieu qui a établi entre les souverains de ce monde, malgré la diversité de leurs croyances, une solidarité dont rois, princes et notables doivent tenir compte dans ce qui regarde la politique et les principes de la souveraineté, et qu'ils doivent observer dans leurs relations, comme dans leurs négociations et leur correspondance relative à des affaires d'importance.

Nous vous écrivons cette lettre dans un moment où, grâce à Dieu, nos États chérifiens, impériaux, zidaniens, nos territoires maghrébins et soudaniens se trouvent dans une situation satisfai-

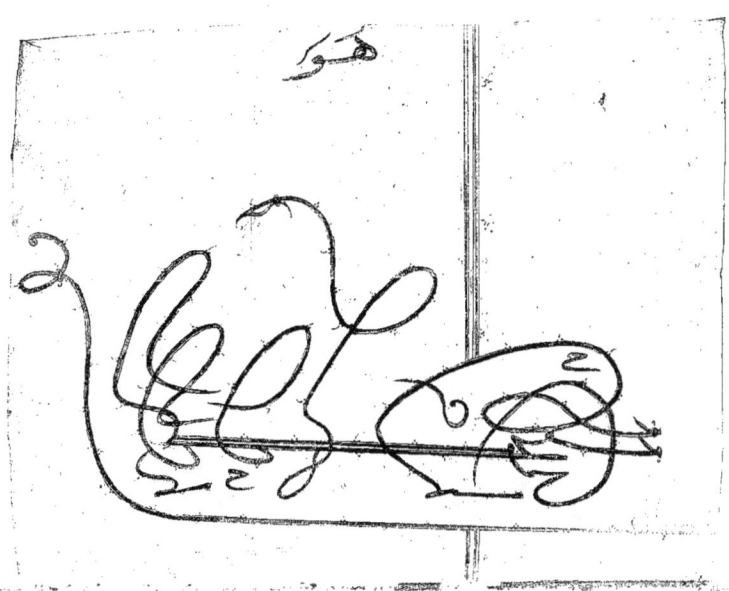

LETTRE DE MOULAY ZIDAN AU ROI JACQUES Ier
3e DÉCADE DE CHOUAL 1023 (24 Novembre-2 Décembre 1614).
D'après l'original conservé au British Museum.

sante. La soumission y est complète et la sécurité y est assurée ; les rebelles ont été exterminés, les Musulmans sont unanimes à obéir à nos ordres sublimes, qui, d'ailleurs, sont respectés partout dans nos Etats chérifiens, tant proches que lointains. Louange et grâce à Dieu !

Votre serviteur distingué et agréable, le noble John Harrison, nous a apporté la lettre que vous aviez adressée à notre haute seigneurie, au moment des troubles suscités par le méprisable Abou Mahalli, auquel Dieu destinait un triste revirement du sort en faisant détruire [ses partisans] jusqu'au dernier par nos épées victorieuses. Grâce à Dieu ! Il a voulu que cette lettre ne nous fût transmise qu'après nous avoir délivré de ces troubles et avoir ramené la paix dans notre pays[1]. Louange et grâce à Dieu pour les bienfaits qu'Il nous a octroyés !

C'est alors que nous avons fait à votre ambassadeur l'accueil le plus bienveillant ; nous l'avons comblé des meilleurs de nos bienfaits et de nos faveurs, le tout en considération de la haute estime dont Votre Majesté jouit auprès de nous en toutes circonstances.

Votre lettre nous a fait connaître les fortes émotions que Votre Majesté avait éprouvées en nous sachant dans de pareilles vicissitudes. C'est ainsi que se raffermit la solidarité qui unit les rois de tous les pays, et tout particulièrement les rois qui, comme vous, sont liés à nous par une ancienne amitié héritée des ancêtres. Nous remercions bien votre éminente Majesté de ses sentiments et nous en sommes profondément touché ; ils sont une preuve éclatante de la sincérité de son amitié et de sa fidélité à tenir ses engagements.

Votre serviteur susnommé — Dieu l'assiste ! — s'est présenté devant nous et a transmis à notre auguste audience vos communications. Nous les avons reçues et nous y avons prêté toute notre attention. C'est à une oreille bienveillante qu'il les a confiées. Nous l'avons de même chargé pour vous d'un message verbal. Nous désirons que vous lui accordiez une audience, afin qu'il puisse s'acquitter pleinement de sa mission, s'il plaît à Dieu.

Écrit dans la troisième décade de Choual de l'année mil vingt-trois.

1. Sur la deuxième mission de John Harrison auprès de Moulay Zidân, V. *supra*, p. 442.

CXXXIV^{ter}

LETTRE DE MOULAY ZIDÂN A JACQUES Ier

(Traduction espagnole[1])

Camp de l'oued Tensift, 25 Choual 1023 [28 novembre 1614].

Au dos, alia manu : Spanish translation of the King of Morocco's letter to his Ma^{ty}. 1614.

Escriviose esta carta y ordenamiento real por el mandamiento supremo, enaltezido del rey Zeyden el victorioso, favorezedor, descendiente de la casa mahometana, a cuya obedencia estan subjetos los reynos de los Moros, y siguen sus rreales mandamientos y ordenanças en todas las partes y provincias del Poniente, y se humillaron a su potestad los tiranos reyes de los reynos del Zeuden y sus rejiones cercanas y desviadas.

Al muy poderoso y muy exelente Rey, aquel que tiene, entre los reyes de la ley christiana y sus naciones, el poder enaltecido, y el que tiene, en la herencia de sus padres y antepasados, el bastante firmeza y el ensalzamiento sublime y poderoso, Jacobo, rey de la Gran Bretaña.

Y despues de las alabanças a Dios, aquel que a puesto y ordenado que aya entre las naciones, aunque sus leyes sean diferentes, ajuntamiento considerado por el buen govierno y preceptos del rejimiento de los reyes y governadores y gente principal, y se le afirma y aclara la verdad en todo lo que se tratare de palabra y por escripto y embaxadas, en los casos de estima y consideracion.

Y lo que escrivimos a V. Mag^d que, por la bondad de Dios, la disposicion de nuestros reynos y provincias y tierras de este Poniente y Zeuden estan de la manera que dan contento ¡ sea Dios loado! pues dan obedencia cumplida, y estan sosegados y quietos,

---

1. Cette traduction faite à la chancellerie chérifienne constitue un original. V. p. 68.

y consumidose de todo punto todo enemigo y contrario malo, y se an conformado los Moros nuestros subditos de oyr y obedecer nuestros reales mandamientos en todas las partes de nuestros reynos, ansi las que estan cerca como las que estan desviadas ¡a Dios sean dadas gracias y alabanzas!

Y es que ante nuestra alta presencia a venido el criado aventajado y leal y prudente, Juan Harison, con carta de Su real Mag^d, la qual se nos avia escrito en el tiempo de las guerras y disenciones acabadas con el vencido Bomhaly, aquel que fue cercado y rodeado de la yra de Dios, y le corto y consumio por su infinita bondad con nuestra espada victoriosa. Y ansi no permitio Dios que la carta real nos allegase, asta que las disenciones y rebueltas fuesen acabadas y nos descansados en nuestros palacios reales. Por lo qual, y por lo que nos da de sus bienes, le damos gracias y alabanças.

Y recevimos su criado con grande voluntad, y entendimos verdaderamente de la real carta que V. Mag^d fue movido, en aquel tiempo, de tales cosas como se movieron, como los reyes suelen, en favor unos de otros, en todas partes y rejiones, los que son leales y verdaderos como V. Mag^d, tienen perfecta amistad eredada de los antepasados. Por lo qual damos muchas gracias a V. Mag^d, y lo tenemos en grande consideracion, y conocimos y entendimos con bastante prueva y satisfacion el aver cumplido.

Y parecio ante nuestra alta presencia el dicho criado, que Dios guarde, y nos dixo razones, las quales recevimos, despues de aver las declarado en nuestros asientos reales, y las tenemos en la memoria. Y nos comunicamos con el lo que el declarara y hara saber vocalmente, y deseamos se le de lugar a ello y audiencia particular a solas, hasta que declare lo que tiene a cargo, sin dexar cosa alguna, con el favor de Dios, el qual guarde a V. Mag^d.

Fecha en el campo de Tensifte, cerca de Marruecos, a los veynte y cinco de Seguel de mil y veinte y tres; concuerda con los diez y siete de Noviembre de 1614[1].

Public Record Office. — State Papers, Foreign, Royal Letters, vol. II, n° 35. — Traduction.

1. La supputation est erronée; l'équivalence exacte est le 28 novembre.

CXXXV

LETTRE DE MAURICE DE NASSAU A JACQUES Ier

Il demande la mise en liberté de Samuel Pallache, arrêté à Londres sur les dénonciations calomnieuses de l'ambassadeur d'Espagne.

La Haye, 11 décembre 1614.

Adresse: Au roy de la Grande Bretaigne, etc.
Au dos, alia manu: Count Maurice lettre touching Samuell Palachy. 11 December 1614.

Sire,

Le sieur Samuel Palache, agent du roy de Barbarie, m'a donné à cognoistre que, pour quelques sinistres accusations que l'ambassadeur du roy d'Espagne auroit fait à Votre Majesté, icelle l'auroit fait constituer prisonnier à Londres[1], avec quelques matelotz qu'il avoit prins en service en ces pais, avec consentiment et sceu de Messieurs les Estatz Generaulx, me priant de vouloir interceder pour luy, affin qu'il pleut à Votre Majesté le faire remettre en liberté avec lesditz matelotz, et luy faire restituer les biens que luy appertiennent. Et d'aultant que Vostre Majesté aura entendu à la longue, par les lettres que lesdits Seigneurs luy ont escript sur ce subject[2], que ledit Palache n'a riens fait sinon que par commandement du roy de Barbarie son maistre, avec lequel lesdits seigneurs Estatz ont traicté amitié et alliance, je n'ay peu laisser de

---

1. V. *supra*, p. 477 et note 1.
2. La minute de cette lettre, datée de La Haye, 29 novembre 1614, a été publiée dans 1re *Série*, Pays-Bas, t. II, p. 425.

supplier Vostre Majesté très-humblement qu'il luy plaise de prendre regard aulx raisons deduictes ès lettres desditz Seigneurs Estatz, et de donner ordre que ledit sieur Palache soit remis en liberté avec les matelotz et biens que luy appertiennent.

Et ne servant ceste à aultre fin, je prie Dieu, Sire, de maintenir Vostre Majesté en sa saincte protection.

A La Haye, le xie de decembre 1614.

De Vostre Majesté très-humble et très-obéissant serviteur,

Signé : Maurice de Nassau.

Public Record Office. — *State Papers, Foreign, Holland, vol. LXX, f. 124.* — *Original.*

CXXXVI

LETTRE DE NOËL DE CARON[1] A RALPH WINWOOD[2]

La solution de l'affaire Pallache est retardée par l'absence du Chief Justice. — Les États-Généraux des Provinces-Unies et le prince Maurice ne cessent d'écrire à Noël de Caron à ce sujet. — Celui-ci prie Winwood d'intervenir auprès du Roi.

South-Lambeth, 3 [n. st. 13] mars 1615.

Au dos : A monsieur Winwood, Chevalier, Conseiller et Secretaire d'Estat de Sa Majesté.
Alia manu : From Sir Noell Caron, about Palache.

Monsieur,

J'ay faict solliciter Milord Chieff Justice[3] pour pouvoir avoir une fin de l'affaire du sieur Palache, veu qu'il a dessa sept ou huict jours passez qu'il avoit delivré son opinion sur ledit affaire. Mais ledit Chieff Justice m'a mandé ce jour d'hy qu'il ne le pouvoit pas faire sinon qu'après qu'il seroit retourné de son voiage qu'il doibt aller faire au quartier du Nort pour les Cheises[4], qui durera pour le moins ung mois ou davantage. Cependant je reçois lettres sur lettres de Messieurs les Estatz et de Monsieur le prince Maurice

---

1. Noël de Caron, ambassadeur des Pays-Bas en Angleterre. Sur ce personnage, V. 1re Série, Pays-Bas, t. I, p. 249, note 1.
2. Noël de Caron avait écrit aux États-Généraux, les 8 et 17 janvier, leur rendant compte de ses démarches pour obtenir la mise en liberté de Samuel Pallache. Le 7 mars, il leur faisait savoir qu'il considérait la chose comme faite (V. 1re Série. Pays-Bas, t. II, pp. 446, 466 et 494). Devant un nouvel ajournement, il écrivit la présente lettre.
3. Sir Edward Coke (1549-1634), Chief Justice en 1613.
4. *Cheises*, assises.

que je voudroi mouvoir Sa Majesté pour sa deliverance ; car, à ce que je puis appercevoir, ilz ont en mains quelque service d'importance qui doibt estre conduit par ledit Palace, à ce printemps, pour le bien commun et dont l'occasion se perdera, si ne le pouvons avoir ascetheure en liberté ; oultre ce que ledit sieur Palache ne cesse de me solliciter à toutes heures, veu sa longue detention et des six povres mariniers de notre nation qui sont detenus en la prison fort miserablement et à très-grands despens ; tellement que je suis meu vous prier fort affectueusement d'en vouloir parler de ma part à Sa Majesté, afin que, de sa faveur et grace, nous pouvons par son authorité estre assistez pour pouvoir tirer une fin de cest affaire, comme j'ay mesmes parfois entendu par sa bouche roiale que telle estoit sa volonté[1].

Et ne servant ceste à nulle autre fin, je prie Dieu qu'il vous veuille, Monsieur, garder heureusement en santé et toute felicité.

Votre bien humble serviteur,

Signé : Noël de Caron.

A Surdt-Lambeth, le iij^e jour de mars 1614-5.

Public Record Office. — *State Papers, Foreign, Holland, vol. LXXI, f. 54.* — *Original.*

---

[1]. Sir Ralph Winwood répondit à la présente lettre le 6 [n. st. 16] mars 1615. V. 1re *Série. Pays-Bas*, t. II, p. 503. — Le 20 [n. st. 30] mars 1615, sur le rapport du Chief Justice, le Conseil Privé décida que Samuel Pallache n'était passible d'aucune peine, attendu que l'état de guerre existait réellement entre l'Espagne et le Maroc. *Hist. Mss. Commission. Reports on the Mss. of Captain Loder-Symonds, pp. 382-383.*

CXXXVII

LETTRE DE CRÉANCE DE YAMIN BEN REMMOKH [1]

Moulay Zidân recommande à la bienveillance des souverains chrétiens son serviteur, Yamin ben Remmokh, qu'il envoie vendre en Europe 235 caisses de sucre.

Du camp, 20 Redjeb 1024 [15 août 1615].

Au dos : The Kinge of Morocco's letter, 1615.

Wee send our royall letter, the most powerfull conqueringe and high Kinge Mully Sydon, Emperor of Moroccos, Kinge of Fesse and Suss, of Gynnye and all the west partes of Affrica, to whom is subject all the power and forces of that part by sea and land, with our servant Yeamyn ben Remoghe, one of those which serveth in our royall howse, in our port of Saphia. We doe send him with two hundred thirty and five chestes of sugars, of our owne proper goodes, to sell them in any part of Christendome, that by the proceed of them he may bringe unto us such marchandize and goodes for our service. We doe therefore commend him to all the Christian Lordes, Kinges and Princes, to everye one in his kingedome, that they would receive him under ther protection and favour, and that they do not consent or suffer any disturbance or wronge, either by sea or lande, to be donne unto him, untill he be dispatched towards our Court. And I shall be ready to doe the like with any such marchandize or passingers of their kingedomes.

Given in our royall campe, the 20th day of the moone Rachab of the year 1024, which is, in the Christian accompt, August, the yere 1615.

British Museum. — Cotton Mss., Nero B. XI, f. 306. — Traduction.

1. Yamin ben Remmokh, juif employé par Moulay Zidân dans ses négociations avec les Provinces-Unies. Sa mission en Angleterre est signalée par Albert Ruyl. V. Pays-Bas, t. III, p. 532. Il est aux Pays-Bas en 1624-1628. *Ibid.*, t. IV, *passim*.

CXXXVIII

RELATION DE WILLIAM LITHGOW[1]

(Extrait)

Lithgow quitte Alger, pour se rendre à Fez, en compagnie d'un joaillier français nommé Chatteline. — Il traverse, pendant trois jours, une région très peuplée et très riche. — Il entre ensuite dans une contrée montagneuse, où abondent des moutons énormes et des chèvres. — Il arrive, le septième jour, à Fez et s'installe avec Chatteline dans une grande auberge. — Emplacement de la ville sur deux collines. — Son centre dans la vallée. — Ses soixante-sept ponts. — Ses marchés, places, mosquées, collèges, hôpitaux; une centaine d'auberges luxueuses. — Ses rues couvertes; marchandises de toutes sortes. — Le costume. — Maisons de prostitution; sodomie. — Tribunaux. — Les maisons et les jardins, les mosquées et les tours sur les pentes des deux collines. — Moulins à vent. — Les deux grands collèges. — Fez, qui eut jadis trois remparts, n'en a plus qu'un, ruiné par endroits. — La mosquée principale: ses minarets et ses tours, ses portes, ses innombrables colonnes, ses chœurs, ses neuf cents

---

[1]. William Lithgow (1582-1645?) naquit à Lanark en Écosse. Esprit aventureux, il accomplit de nombreux voyages, mais son manque absolu de sincérité empêche de lui accorder confiance. En septembre 1615, il se trouve à Tunis et c'est de cette ville qu'il prétend s'être rendu à Alger et à Fez. De retour à Londres le 9 septembre 1617, il repart en 1620 pour l'Espagne; à Malaga, il est arrêté comme espion et mis à la torture; on le relâche en 1621. En avril 1622, il a une altercation dans les appartements du Roi avec l'ambassadeur d'Espagne, comte de Gondomar; on l'emprisonne et il ne recouvre sa liberté que le 21 janvier 1624. Son nom n'est plus mentionné après 1645. — En 1614, William Lithgow avait fait paraître un résumé de ses premiers voyages; il le réédita en le complétant en 1632 et en 1640. C'est de cette dernière édition qu'est tiré le présent extrait. Il contient de telles invraisemblances qu'on peut se demander si l'auteur est réellement allé au Maroc et si l'on n'est pas en présence d'une œuvre faite d'imagination et de plagiat. La description de la ville de Fez, qui forme la presque totalité de ce récit, est un démarquage de Léon l'Africain (ff. 34-48, édition de 1550). Dans ces conditions, il a paru inutile d'accompagner d'un appareil critique complet le présent extrait, qui n'est publié ici qu'en raison de la notoriété dont l'auteur jouit bien à tort. Toutefois, comme cette relation a été malheureusement utilisée parfois comme une source originale, nous croyons devoir en signaler les principales invraisemblances et les erreurs les plus grossières.

lampes allumées la nuit, ses prédicateurs, ses revenus. — Fez compte plus de quatre cent soixante autres mosquées, dont cinquante richement décorées. — Lithgow et Chatteline obtiennent de visiter la mosquée principale. — Abondance des vivres à Fez. — Un million d'habitants. — Les fêtes : combats de taureaux, mascarades, chants, processions de prêtres. — Ancienne réputation des Maures pour la médecine et la philosophie. — Nombreux poètes à Fez. — Concours annuel de poésie sur la place du Marché. — Comment se passait ce concours sous les Mérinides. — Chatteline et Lithgow quittent Fez, au bout de dix-sept jours, pour se rendre à Araouan. — Chatteline est arrêté par la maladie à Ahetzo. — Lithgow continue seul le voyage.

1615-1616.

. . . .

And now it was my fortune here in Algier[1], after 12 days abode, to meete with a French lapidator, monsieur Chatteline[2], borne in Aise du Provance, who, intending to visit Fez, joyned company with me, and we with certaine merchants of Algier that were going thither, being in all 30 passengers, with two janizaries and a dragoman.

Whence advancing our way, some on mules and some on foot, with asses carrying our baggage and provision, we left the marine townes of Saly and Tituana far to the west on our right hand, and facing the inland, wee marched for three dayes through a fruitfull and populous soyle. And also the people barbarous and disdainefull countenances were awfull, yet we two went still free of tributes, as not being a thing with them accustomary to execute exaction on Francks, as the Turkes and Moores do in Asia. Neither understood they what wee were, being clad with company and after their fashion; save only that nature had set a fairer stamp on my face than theirs, which oft I wished had beene as blacke as their uglines. In this misculat journeying of paine and pleasure, we found everywhere strong wines[3], abundance of excellent bread,

1. Lithgow avait obtenu à Tunis, par l'intermédiaire du capitaine Ward, renégat anglais (V. *supra*, p. 272 et note 3), un sauf-conduit pour Alger.

2. Personnage inconnu par ailleurs.
3. Le fait de rencontrer partout (*everywhere*) des vins forts est impossible à admettre. D'ailleurs, Lithgow, voyageant en

and the best and greatest hens bred on the earth, with plenty of figs, fruits, olives and delicious oile, yea, and innumerable villages, the houses whereof are all builded with mud and plateformed on their tops, and so are they in Asia and all Affrick over.

Upon the fourth day, having past the plains, we entred in a hilly countrey, yet pastorable; where I beheld here and there clouds of tents, filled with maritime people, that were fled hither from the sea-coast for the fresh and cooling aire.

And upon these pleasant and umbragious heights, I saw the fields overclad with flocks of sheep and goats; which sheep are wondrous great, having from their rumps and hips broad and thick tayls growing, and hanging to the ground; some wherof, when sold, will weigh 16, 18 or 20 pounds weight, and upwards. Here among the mountains, our company, knowing well the countrey, tooke a great advantage of the way; and, on the seventh day in the morning, wee arrived at the great towne of Fez, where the Frenchman and I were conducted by some of our company to a great Moorish inne or tavern; and, there received, we were as kindly and respectively used as ever I was in any part of the Turks dominions, being now out of them, and in the empire of Morocco.

This city of Fez is situate upon the bodies and twice double devalling faces of two hils, like to Grenada in Andelosia in Spain; the intervale or low valley betweene both, through which the torrid river of Marrabeba[1] runneth southward, being the centre and chiefest place, is the most beautifull and populous part of the city; the situation of which, and of the whole, is just set under the tropick of Cancer.

Over which river, and in this bottome, there are three score and seaven bridges of stone and timber, each of them being a passage for open streetes on both sides. The intervaile consisteth of two miles in length, and half a mile broad; wherein, besides five Che-

---

habits musulmans, pour ne pas éveiller les soupçons, devait, pour le même motif, éviter toute boisson alcoolique. On cite quelques rares tribus riffaines ou djebala faisant clandestinement du vin. C'est peut-être ce fait qu'aura exagéré le voyageur.

1. *Marraheba*, faute d'impression pour : Marrabeha. Il s'agit de l'oued Oumm er-Rbia, placé à tort dans la ville de Fez, alors qu'il en est éloigné de 200 kilomètres environ. Les cours d'eau qui traversent la ville sont des affluents de l'oued Sebou,

reaffs or market places, there are great places, magnificke mosquees, colledges, hospitalls and a hundred palatial taverns, the worst whereof may lodge a monarchicke trayne; most part of all which buildings are three and foure stories high, adorned with large and open windowes, long galleries, spacious chambers and flat textures and square platformes.

The streetes being covered above[1], twixt the plaineset fabricks, have large lights cut through the textur'd tops everywhere; in whose lower shops or roomes, are infinite merchandize and ware of all sorts to bee sold.

The people of both kinds are cloathed in long breeches and bare ancles, with red or yellow shooes shod with iron on the heeles, and on the toes with white horne[2]; and wear on their bodies long robes of linning or rimmery, and silken wastcoates of divers colours; the behaviour of the vulgars being far more civill toward strangers then at Constantinople or elsewhere in all Turkey.

The women here go unmasked abroad, wearing on their heads broad and round capes, made of straw or small reedes[3], to shade their faces from the sunne; and damnable libidinous, being prepared both wayes to satisfie the lust of their luxurious villaines[4]; neither are they so strictly kept as the Turkish women, marching where they please.

There are some twelve thousand allowed brothel-houses in this town, the curtezans, being neatly kept, and weekely well looked to by physicians; but, worst of all, in the summer time, they openly lycenciate three thousand common stewes of sodomiticall boyes. Nay, I have seene at mitday, in the very market places, the Moores buggering these filthy carrions, and without shame or punishment go freely away.

There are severall seates of justice heere (though none to vindi-

---

1. « Plusieurs rues sont voûtées et certaines promenades semblent être parfois des excursions souterraines. » Henri Gaillard, *Une ville de l'Islam*, p. 113.

2. Cette description de la chaussure indigène est tout à fait fantaisiste.

3. Ces grands chapeaux de paille ou de jonc sont encore la coiffure des femmes arabes de la campagne. Elles en portent peu dans la ville.

4. Malgré la mauvaise réputation de la ville de Fez, tout ce que raconte Lithgow des mœurs de ses habitants est empreint d'exagération.

cate beastlinesse), occupied by Cedeis[1] and Sanzackes[2], which twice a week heare all differences and complaints; their chiefe Seriff, or Viceregent, being sent from Morocco, is returned hither againe every third yeare.

The two hills on both sides the planur'd citty, east and west, are overclad with streetes and houses of two stories high, being beautified also with delicate gardens, and, on their extreame devalling parts, with numbers of mosquees and watchtowers; on which heights, and round about the towne, there stand some three hundred windmils[3], most part whereof pertain to the mosquees and the two magnifick colledges erected for education of children in the Mahometanicall law. One of which accademies cost the king Haba Hennor[4], in building of it, foure hundred and three score thousand duckats.

Jacob, sonne to Abdulach[5], the first King of the families of Meennons[6], divided Fez in three parts, and with three severall walles, though now invironed with onely one, and that broken down in sundry parts.

The chiefest mosque in it is called Mammo-Currarad[7], signifying « the glory of Mahomet », being an Italian mile in compasse, and beautified with seventeene high ground steeples, besides turrets and towers; having thirty-four entring doores; being supported within and by the length with forty-eight pillars, and some twenty-

---

1. *Cedeis*, cadis.

2. *Sanzackes*. Mot mal transcrit, ou plutôt erreur, car le mot sandjak, qui est évidemment celui qu'on a voulu reproduire, signifie : drapeau, étendard.

3. Les nombreuses monographies de Fez écrites du xive au xvie siècle par des auteurs arabes ou chrétiens signalent toutes l'existence dans la ville de nombreux moulins hydrauliques, dont beaucoup sont encore conservés (V. MASSIGNON, p. 223); mais aucune de ces descriptions ne mentionne un moulin à vent, et, là encore, Lithgow est coupable d'inexactitude. Les moulins sont d'ailleurs, comme il le dit, propriété habous (biens de mosquée).

4. *Haba Hennor*, Abou Eïnan, souverain mérinide, qui régna de 1348 à 1358. Tout ce passage est tiré de Léon, f. 35 v°, qui nomme ce souverain Habu Henon.

5. Yacoub, fils d'Abd el-Hakk. Ce dernier, comme l'écrit Lithgow, fut le premier souverain de la dynastie des Beni Merin; il régna de 1213 à 1217. Son fils Yacoub, qui ne lui succéda pas directement, occupa le pouvoir de 1258 à 1286. Ce fut lui qui, le 21 mars 1276 (3 Choual 674 Hég.), jeta les fondements de la nouvelle ville de Fez, Fez-el-Djedid.

6. *Macnnons*, faute d'impression, pour Merinin.

7. La principale mosquée de Fez est celle d'El-Karaouin, nom difficile à reconnaître dans *Mammo-Currarad*.

three rangers of pillars in breadth, besides many iles¹, quires and circulary rotundoes; every pillar having a lampe of oile burning thereat; where there, and through the whole mosque, there are every night nine hundred lamps lighted². And, to maintaine them, and a hundred totsecks and preaching talsumans, the rent of it extendeth to two hundred duccats a day.

Neverthelesse, there are in the city, besides it, more than foure hundred and threescore mosques³. Fifty whereof are well benefited and superbiously decored within and without, with glorious and extraordinary workmanship; whose roofes within are all mosaicke worke, and curiously indented with gold, and the walles and pillars being of grey marble, interlarded with white alablaster. And so is the chiefe mosque too, in which Monsieur Chatelline and I had three sundry recourses, accompanied with our Moorish hoste, who from their priests had procured that licence for us⁴.

This city aboundeth in all manner of provision fit for man or beast, and is the goodliest place of all North Affrick, contayning a hundred and twenty thousand fire-houses, and in them a million of soules⁵. Truely this is a world for a city, and may rather second Grand Caire than subjoyne itselfe to Constantinople, being farre superior in greatnesse with Aleppo: for these are the foure greatest cities that ever I saw in the world, either at home or abroad.

The citizens here are very modest and zealous at their divine service, but great dancers and revellers on their solemne festivall dayes, wherein they have bul-baiting⁶, maskerats, singing of rimes and processions of priests.

The Moores, in times past, of Fez and Morocco, had divers

---

1. *Iles*, ailes, nefs latérales, bas-côtés.

2. Lithgow donne ici, p. 368, une vue de Fez, avec la légende : « The modell of the great City of Fez. »

3. Sous le règne de l'almohade El-Mansour, on comptait à Fez 785 mosquées, d'après l'auteur du *Roudh el-Qartas*, dont la monographie est d'ailleurs empreinte d'exagération.

4. Il est plus vraisemblable d'admettre que Lithgow et son compagnon français visitèrent la grande mosquée de Fez à la faveur de leur costume musulman, sans demander une autorisation qui eût été certainement refusée à des voyageurs chrétiens.

5. Sur la population de Fez au milieu du xvi⁰ siècle, V. Massignon, p. 224. Le chiffre de 100000 habitants, qui est donné par Tonnès (cap. 70), semble près de la vérité. Fez était sans conteste la plus grande ville du Maghreb. V. Gaillard, p. 62.

6. Lithgow est le seul voyageur avec Edmond Hogan (V. t. I, p. 246 et note 4) à signaler ces combats de taureaux.

excellent personages well learned and very civill; for, amongst the Kings Mahometan, on cannot praise too much the Kings Almansor, Maunon and Hucceph[1], being most excellent men in their superstition. In whose times flourished the most famous medicines and philosophers that were among the Pagans, as Avicenne, Rasis, Albumazar, Averrues, etc., with other great numbers maintained by the Kings of Morocco, that then were masters of all Barbary and Spaine; as in Spaine may be seene yet, though now fallen in decay, a great number of their colledges, shewing they were great lovers of their religion and doctrine. And are so to this day, save only in their drinking of wine, forbidden by their Alcoran. They were great devisers too of gallant sportings, exercices, turnaments and bulbaiting, which Spaine retaineth to this time; yea and the Romans did learne and follow many of them.

Here in Fez there bee a great number of poets, that make songs on divers subjects, especially on love and lovers, who they openly name in their rimes, without rebuke or shame; all which poets, once every yeare, against Mahomets birthday, make rimes to his praise. Meanewhile in the afternoone of that festivall day, the whole poets assembling in the market place, there is a decked chayre prepared for them, whereon they mount, one after another, to recite their verses in audience of all the people; and who by them is judged to be best, is esteemed all the yeare above the rest; having this epithite « the Prince of Poets », and is by the Vicegerent and towne rewarded. But in the time of the Maennon[2] Kings, the prince on that day in his owne pallace did conveine the whole citizens, in whose presence hee made a solemne feast to all the best poets, causing every one of them to recite the praise of Mahomet before his face, standing on a high scaffold; and to him that was thought to excell the rest, the King gave him 100 sultans of gold[3], a horse, a woman slave and the longue robe that was about him

---

1. Il faut probablement rétablir les trois souverains almohades Yacoub el-Mansour = Almansor, Abd el-Moumen = Maunon et Youssef = Hucceph; mais leurs noms ne sont pas cités dans l'ordre chronologique.

2. *Maennon*, Merinin. V. *supra*, p. 495.

3. Le sultani d'or était une monnaie d'Alger dont le taux a varié, suivant les époques, entre 6 francs et 12 francs. BEAUSSIER, *Dictionnaire*, au mot سلطاني.

for the time. And to each one of the rest he caused give fifty sultans, so that every one should have some recompense for their paines. Indeede a worthy observation; and would to God it were now the custome of our Europian princes to doe the like, and especially of this Isle; then would bravest wits and quickest braines studdy and strive to show the exquisite ingeniosity of their best stiles and pregnant invention, which now is eclipsed and smothered downe, because, nowadayes, their is neither regard nor reward for such excellent pen-men.

Fez was aunciently named Sylda; whose kingdome hath Atlas to the south; the river of Burdraga[1] to the east, and Tremizen; Morocco to the west, and the confines of Guargula[2]; and a part of the sea to the north.

Having spent in Fez 17 dayes, in all which time we daily conversed with some Christian Abasines[3], Heragenes[4] or Æthiopian Nigroes, some whereof were merchants, and some religious; and Monsieur Chattelines businesse not effected, seeking diamonds and precious stones to buy, was seriously advised by them to goe for Arracon[5], a great towne on the frontiers of the Northern Æthiopia, where he would find abundance of such at an easie rate, giving him a perfect direction for his passage hither, being 30 daies journey. He concluded with their counsell his resolution, and perswading me to the same intention, I yeeld, being overmastred with the greedy desire of more sights.

Meanwhile, for our conduct, we hire a dragoman Moore, that spoke Italian, to be our interpreter, and with him a tent and two Moorish drudges to guide, guard and serve us by the way, for fifty-eight sultans of gold, eighteene pounds foure shillings English; having sixe of their kinsmen fast bound to a Sansak[6] or Justice, for our lives, liberties and moneyes.

Hereupon, having provided for ourselves with all necessary things and a mule to carry our victuals, water and baggage, we discharged our conscionable hostage at 20 aspers[7] a day the man.

1. *Burdraga*, Bou Regrag.
2. *Guargula*, Ouargla. Cf. Léon l'Africain, f. 41 v°.
3. *Abasines*, Abyssins.
4. *Heragenes*, harathin, mulâtres.
5. *Arracon*, Araouan.
6. Sur ce mot, V. supra, p. 495, note 2.
7. *Aspers*. L'aspre est une petite mon-

being thirty-four shillings to each of us, and were brought on our way by the aforesaid Christian Heragenes some foure leagues. Where having left them with dutifull thankes, wee set forward in our journey; and for seven dayes together wee were not violently molested by anything, save intolerable heat, finding tented people and scattered villages all the way.

The eight day, the way being fastidious and rockey, and Chatteline on foote being weary, and could not subsist, not being used to pedestriall travaile; and for our better speed and his reliefe, we mounted him aloft on the top of our baggage. At last, arriving at Ahetzo[1] (where wee reposed), being the furthest and southmost towne of the kingdome of Fez, composed of a thousand fire-houses well fortified with walles, and a garrison of Moores in it, subject to the emperour of Marocco, the Frenchman, long ere day, fell sick of a burning feaver. Whereupon wee stayed five daye, expecting his health; which growing worse and worse, and hee mindfull to returne, which I would not, I left him in safe custodie, and one of our drudges to attend him. And bearing the charges of the other two, according to the former condition, I set forward for my purpose, which ere long turned to sad repentance.

Leaving Ahetzo behind us, and entring the country of the Agaroes, wee found the best inhabitants halfe clad, the vulgars naked, the country void of villages, rivers or cultivage, but the soil rich in bestiall, abounding in sheep, goats, camels, dromidores and passing good horses[2].

. . . .

William Lithgow. — The Totall Discourse of the rare Adventures... — Londres, 1640, in-4°, pp. 364-373[3].

naie d'argent chez les Turcs.

1. Ahetzo, localité non identifiée.
2. Lithgow raconte ensuite qu'il se perdit dans le désert, où lui et son drogman durent se nourrir de tabac pendant sept jours; ils rencontrèrent des sauvages et l'un d'eux les conduisit à Tunis.
3. Le titre complet de l'ouvrage est : *The Totall Discourse of the rare Adventures and painefulle Peregrinations of long nineteen yeares Travailes from Scotland to the most famous Kingdomes in Europa, Asia and Africa......* Imprimé à Londres, 1640, par I. Okes, in-4°, 514 pp. La 1re édition est de 1632 (V. *supra*, p. 491, note 1), sous le même titre, 507 pp. La douzième édition a paru à Leith en 1814, un vol. 8°, 412 pp.

CXXXIX

LETTRE DE FRANCIS COTTINGTON A RALPH WINWOOD

(EXTRAIT)

Capture de deux navires anglais par les Turcs et vente de leurs cargaisons à Salé.

Madrid, 30 novembre [n. st. 10 décembre] 1616.

Au dos, alia manu : 30 November 1616. — From Mr Cotington.

May it please your Honour,

My last unto you was of the 8th of this month, by the ordinary conveyance.

. . . .

I understand of two English shippes, whos masters were one Whary and one Lingwood, loaden lately with wynes and other commodities in Malaga, that were taken by the Turkes men of warr about the South Cape[1], and caried for Sali[2] in Barbary, wher sale was made of all theyr loading. The shippes are carryed to Argier and the two masters are come to Cadiz. Whary had, besides his loading, 1000£ of Barbary gould put aboard him, in the roade of Malaga, from a shipp caled the « Dragon », who had been trading in Barbary; and doubtless it wyll fall very heavy uppon some marchantes in London.....

Your Honour's to be commaunded,

Signé : Fra. Cottington.

Madrid, the last of November 1616, *stilo Angliæ*.
Mr Secretarie Wynwood.

Public Record Office. — *State Papers, Foreign, Spain, vol. XXII.* — Original.

1. *South Cape*, le cap de Ceuta. V. *supra*, p. 463 et note 4.
2. Sur la piraterie à Salé, V. *infra*, p. 558 et note 1.

CXL

CONTRAT D'AFFRÉTEMENT DU NAVIRE L' « ELIZABETH »[1]

Safi, 31 mars 1617.

Au dos, alia manu: Contract of the « Elisabeth » of London and the factors of Barbarie.

Witnesseth by these presentes that we, Jode Levey[2], Izraell ben Sroall[3], Mussy Levey[4] and Benjamin Coheine[5], Jewes resident in Barbarey, factors being servantes unto Mulley Sidan, Emperrador of Marrocus and Kinge of Barberey, have by his order fraighted the good ship named the « Elizabeth » of London (master, under God, for this present voyage is George Blowe) by consort made with Phillip Bull[6] and Edward Carter, marchantes of the said ship, for a voyage from this port of Saphea, in Barbarey, unto the port of Middlebrought, in Zealland, to carrey hides, shugars, Campeachia wood, or what else we have to lade, unto their full ladeinge; and for fraight are to pay unto the said marchantes or their assignes, after safe arrivall of ship and goodes in Zealland, soe neare unto the port of Middlebrought as the good ship may well and conveniently come, as the bills of ladeinge may appeare, the some of five hundreth and sixtey Barbarey dokits (rateinge the dokit att

---

1. Ce navire était chargé de diverses marchandises appartenant à Moulay Zidân et confiées par celui-ci aux Juifs Israël ben Chelouha et Moïse Lévy pour être vendues à Middelbourg. V. *1re Série*, Pays-Bas, t. III, p. 14 et note 1.

2. *Jode Levey*, Judas Lévy, frère de Moïse. Sur ce personnage, V. *1re Série*, Pays-Bas, t. VI, à l'Index.

3. *Izraell ben Sroall*, Israël ben Chelouha. V. *ibidem*.

4. *Mussy Levey*, Moïse Lévy. V. *ibidem*.

5. *Benjamin Coheine*, Benjamin Cohen. V. *ibidem*.

6. Il certifie conforme, le 12 mars 1617, la traduction de la lettre de Moulay Zidân aux États, en date du 21 février 1617. V. *ibidem*, t. III, p. 15.

20 s. 6 d. starlinge the dokit, amountes to starlinge monney the some of two hundreth nyntey and foure poundes, which, after the rate of 33 s. 4 d. the pound Flemish, is, Flemish monney, the some of foure hundreth and fiftey poundes), which we are to pay in good and corrant monney amongst marchantes, with prymage, average and all dueties as acostomed, within xv dayes after the arrivall of the said ship and goodes in Zealland, without fraud, deseit or delay.

And for performance and securety, as aforesaid, we, the foresaid Jewes, servantes unto Mulley Sidan, doe, by vertue of his power and authorrety given unto us his servantes, binde, transport and set over whom, and particularly, all such hides, shugars, woodes, or any other comoditie, is by us laden aboard the good ship, as aforesaid; and by these presentes doe give and graunte full authoretey and absolute power unto Phillip Bull and Edward Carter aforesaid, of all the said goodes in what nature soever, and that by vertue of this our transport, if fault of good payment of the fraight aforesaid and in manner as above said, to sell, barter, or to pawne the said goodes, all or parte, and out of the presedent to pay themselves all fraight, prymage and averages abovesaid, with all charges and damages whatsoever shall arrise in seeckinge of content, by desposeinge of the said goodes. And for good performance of the premisses we doe by these presentes binde all the goodes aforesaid, our persons, and all other goodes whatsoever. In witness of a trueth, we have heareunto subscribed our names and set our firmes, in presence of these witnesses whose names are heareunder subscribed.

Written and datted aboard the foresaid ship, named the « Elizabeth » of London, in the road of Saphea, in Barbarey, this 31st day of March, *anno Domini* 1617.

In wittnes of these persons, *scilicet*:

George Blowe. — William Brouse. — Heugh Leucombe.

We came with our ship soe neare as we could conveniently come, the 7th day of June, *stillo novo*, 1617.

Public Record Office. — *State Papers, Foreign, Barbary States.* vol. XII. — Traduction[1].

---

[1]. L'original devait vraisemblablement être rédigé en espagnol.

CXLI

MÉMOIRE DE HENRY MAINWARING[1]

(Extrait)

Mainwaring n'est devenu pirate que contraint par les circonstances. — Énumération des services qu'il a rendus à l'Angleterre et à ses compatriotes : grâce à son intervention, les pirates d'El-Mamora n'ont pas attaqué de navires anglais ; capture de trois vaisseaux turcs, dont il a libéré les prisonniers anglais ; il a respecté les navires anglais, manquant les occasions de s'enrichir ; il a refusé l'argent et le pardon que lui offrait le duc de Medina-Sidonia, à condition de remettre El-Mamora à l'Espagne ; le duc de Savoie et le grand-duc de Toscane lui ont promis son pardon ; le bey de Tunis lui a fait des avances ; le comte de Portalegre lui a proposé, avec son pardon, le commandement d'une escadre ; il a procuré un sauf-conduit à Saint-Mandrier ; ouvertures faites par l'ambassadeur d'Espagne à Londres. — Mainwaring a tout refusé, préférant servir son pays et son Roi en sujet respectueux. — Renseignements sur les ports marocains et sur leur commerce.

[1618[2].]

To my most gratious soveraigne, that represents the Kinge of Heaven, whose mercy is above all his works.

---

1. On sait peu de choses sur les débuts du capitaine Mainwaring, originaire du comté de Chester, ainsi que sur les circonstances qui l'amenèrent à faire la course maritime. En 1614, il exerçait une certaine influence sur la bande de pirates qui avait El-Mamora pour repaire (V. *supra*, p. 438 et note 2, et pp. 442, 450 et 462), mais qui en fut bientôt délogée, le 7 août 1614, par les Espagnols. En 1615, il croise avec trois vaisseaux au large de Larache, cherchant à surprendre les bâtiments espagnols et portugais, car « il ne faisait pas, disait-il, la guerre aux autres nations ». V. 1re *Série*, Espagne, à la date du 9 août 1615. Il obtint sa grâce en juin 1616. *State Papers, Domestic, James I, vol. XC, no 24.* En 1618, Mainwaring passa au service de Venise, mais il s'en lassa vite et, en 1619 et 1620, il est lieutenant du château de Douvres. V. Corbett, *op. cit.*, pp. 56-59, 86, 93 et 99-100.

2. Sur la manière dont est établie cette date, V. *infra*, p. 508 et note 2.

Give leave, I humblie beseech your Grace, to mee your owne creature (being newly recreated and restored by your gracious pardon to that life which was forfeited to the lawe) humbly to offer, with a faithfull, loyall, obedient, and a thankfull harte, to your Majesties favor this, as some oblacion for my offences, and a perfect signe of the true and harty acknowledgment I make of your Highnes grace unto mee. I am so far from justifying my owne errors that I can scarce affoord them those reasonable excuses which might be perhaps allowable in another man, as that I fell not purposely, but by mischaunce, into those courses; being in them, ever strove to do all the service I could to this State and the marchaunts.

As that, where there were 30 saile of piratts in Mamora, I suffered none to goe in or out but with condicion not to disturbe any your Maties subjects. I made peace with Sally, which tooke many small shipps, and bought out the prisoners. Have cutt of three Turkes men of warre, the one of them had bene as high in Theames as Lee, sett free the slaves and captives, and taken Englishmen's shipps and goods from the Turkes, and redelivered them to the true owners. Have wafted them from other men of warr.

Made peace with Tunis for all your Highnes subjects. And at the same time bought as many English slaves as cost mee neere 5000 ducketts. Dishartened the Flemings from venturing to Newfoundeland, by which they would quickly have overthrowne the west of England. Bene the occasion that all English shipps throughout all Christendome have bene better fraighted then before.

Lastly I have abstayned from doing hurte to any your Majestie's subjects, where by it I might have enriched myself more then 100 000^{li}, being that most of the best shipps that trade for the Straights and the coast of Spaine and Barbary, as also divers others have come through my fingers.

All theis things the marchaunts of London had justified under their hands, with purpose to have shewne it to your Highnes in favor of mee; but I feared I should rather have bene troublesome then accepted.

Theis truthes, though they cannot expiate, yet they might extenuate the offence in another man and may be called *pulchrum scelus*, but in mee so little, that, did not the lawes of Christianity and Nature interdict mee, I could easily be evidence, jury, judge and execucioner to myself.

I trust your Majestie will not undervalue, but rather esteeme mee the more, for having refused the free and voluntary pardons with proffers of good entertainement from other princes, as namely the Duke of Medina sent to mee that, if I would deliver upp Mamora to the King of Spaine, that I should have a greate somme of money for me and my company, with a free pardon to enjoy all our shipps and goods, and good entertainement if I would commaund in the Kings shipps.

The Duke of Savoye sent me my pardon. The Duke of Florence sent me my pardon and gave leave to the shipp to waite on mee till I was willing to come in, which did so for a greate while. The Dey of Tunis eate bread and salt and swore by his heade (which is the greatest asseveracion they use) that, if I would stay with him, he would devide his estate equally with mee, and never urge mee to turne Turke, but give mee leave to departe, whensoever it should please your Majestie to be soe gratious as to pardon mee.

Theis I knowe of myne owne knowledge and so do many more; and, since my comming home, I have heard that the Condy of Portolegro[1], after I had putt off 5 saile of the King of Spaine's men of warre (being in fight with them all Midsommer day last[2]), myselfe having but 2, he offered that, if any would goe oute and advertise mee, he would gette mee my pardon and give mee 20 000 duckatts a yeare to goe generall of that squadron.

Mounsire Mantei[3] was mett in the Straights with my protection from the Duke of Guyse[4].

1. Diogo de Silva, comte de Portalegre.
2. Le jour de la Saint-Jean, 24 juin.
3. Antoines de Salletles, sieur de Saint-Mandrier. Il avait été envoyé à El-Mamora avec un vaisseau par le duc de Savoie, en 1614; sa mission était de persuader aux pirates de reconnaître l'autorité du duc. Saint-Mandrier arriva le 7 juin à El-Mamora. Ses négociations avec les pirates furent bientôt sans objet, car, le 7 août suivant, la place était occupée par les Espagnols. Saint-Mandrier s'enfuit vers l'intérieur; il fut fait prisonnier par les Maures et entra, comme ingénieur, au service de Moulay Zidàn; il tenta vainement de s'évader et finalement fut décapité le 14 avril 1626. V. 1re Série, France, t. III, pp. XXXIX-XLVII.
4. Charles de Lorraine (1571-1640),

I forbeare to speake how willing the Spanish Embassador[1] seemed to my brother to have mee serve his maister at that time, when he mov'd him for his concente to my pardon. By theis it may appeare to your Majestie that I did not labour my pardon as one being banished from all Christian princes, but as a dutifull subject, preferring the service of my country and my perticuler obedience to your roiall person before my owne ends.

In this respect, I doubt not but your Majestie hath had many malicious informacions of mee from other States who, being themselves refused, would, by disgracing mee in your Majestie's favor, make me incapable of it. But lett mee humbly beseech your Majestie that, since life and honor are *individui comites* in every honestly resolved spiritt, and that your gracious favor hath restored the one, so likewise to doe the other by your favorable acceptance of me, and that they may either live or dye togeather by your Majestie's commaund. Though my course, I confesse, were not honorable, yet, since it was ordained to be unfortunate, I am glad t' was in a way which hath somewhat enabled mee to doe your Majestie service, if occasion were given.

This small discourse of a boisterous argument, and as roughly handled as also so unworthy your Maties eye, of myselfe I durst not have presented, but at the commaundement of one of your Majesties most worthy servants.

Your Maties new creature,

Henry Maynnaringe.

OF THE BEGINNINGS, PRACTISES AND SUPPRESSION OF PIRATS.

Cap. 4.

Those [pirates] of Argeere doe for the most parte come without

---

4ᵉ duc de Guise, gouverneur de Provence depuis 1595. Il recherchait Saint-Mandrier, en raison d'un meurtre que celui-ci avait commis à Toulon en 1611, à la suite duquel il s'était réfugié en Savoie.

1. D. Diego Sarmiento de Acuña, comte de Gondomar, ambassadeur d'Espagne à Londres.

the Straights, or, if they stay in the Straights, they lye either of Capp Gatt, Cape Paule or Cape Martine[1], and seldome goe lower towards the bottome-going in of the Straights; they keepe close aboord the Barbary shoare, but going out on the Christian.

At **Tituan**, the first towne on the Barbary side going in, a pirat may water well, have good refreshing by, store of powder, which is for the most part brought in by English and Flemish marchants, and sell their goods well, which is quickly landed and dispatched by reason of the boates of the towne. But heere is no commaund but to ride upon their guarde; they ride also in foule ground, and must perforce put to sea if the Levant come. Heere the people are very just and trusty.

. . . .

At **Arzeele**, betwixt Cape Spratt[2] and Allaroch, being on the coast of Barbary, they may sell goods well and have fresh victualls.

At **Sally**, if it be faire weather, they may ride before the barr, and have victualls and water, and sell goods well; but for the most part the sea breakes so on the barr that they can hardly water.

At **Fidally**, they may sell goods very well, have store of victuals, good ballast, and ground a ship that drawes nyne foot; but heere is no water. Besids, if the winde comes to the north-west, it is a most dangerous roade; yet heere they use much.

At **Taffny**[3], a smale man that dares ride neere the shore may water well.

At **Saphie**, a man may sell goods well, have fresh water and victuals; but the road is dangerous if the winde comes to the south-warde of the south-east, soe that then they must put out; yet the sea will give them warninge of any foule wether. Besids, the castle cannot defend them, in which respects they seldome stay, though they stoppe there; and heere ships may chance to take good purchase in the roade of English, Dutch and French.

At **Maggador**, they sell goods well and have fresh victuals, but no water. On the ilands, at the tyme of yeare, there is great store

---

1. Cap de Gata, cap de Palos et cap San-Martin.
2. Cap Spartel.
3. *Taffny*, Teftana.

of yong hawkes and pigeons, which they use to eate, and heere they use much.

At Santa Cruce, they may water, wood, ballast, have fresh victualls, sell their goods and ride safe under the castle. The road is very good also, so that there they stay long and use much.

At Missa, 5 leagues to the southward of Santa Cruce, they sell goods very well, and have fresh victualls and water; but they ride farre of, and the roade dangerous, so that they must be beholding to the Moores for their nossaveries[1], els they can do nothing. And this is the farthest southward that they use on the Barbary coast, unlesse very rarely some goe to Rio d'Ore, where they can have nothing but water.

. . . .

Cap. 5.

. . . .

My humble sewte now unto your Highnes is that, if there be any thing remembred heere that may serve to informe your Matie in the course of theis affaires, as they may not be taken as a perticuler informacion against any; for I protest on my allegeance I ayme at no perticuler ends, but meerely to serve your Highnes and freely to tell the truth; which I humbly desire may serve to advise your Highnes hereafter, and not as an occasion to calle any thing past in question.

British Museum. — Bibl. Reg., 17, A, XLVII. — Original[2].

1. *Their nossaveries*, their no-savories, eur trafic peu honorable, c'est-à-dire, la vente des marchandises provenant de la piraterie.

2. Une copie de ce document se trouve dans les mss. de Sir P. T. Mainwaring, à Peover. Elle porte le titre suivant : « *A Discourse written by Sir Henry Manwaringe and by him presented to the Kinges Majestie, anno Domini 1618*. » 53 pp. *Historical Mss. Commission, X, IV, 202*. Sir Henry Mainwaringe était capitaine dans la marine royale et fut membre du Parlement pour Douvres de 1620 à 1623. *Ibidem.* D'après Corbett, *op. cit.*, p. 59, le doc. que nous avons reproduit est le Mémoire original.

CXLII

LETTRE DE FRANCIS COTTINGTON A JOHN COKE

(EXTRAIT)

Harrison, envoyé par Jacques Ier au Maroc, n'a obtenu aucune réponse du Sultan et n'a pu délivrer aucun prisonnier.

Madrid, 31 mars [n. st. 9 avril] 1618.

Au dos, alia manu : 31 March 1618. — Mr Cottington.
Au bas : Mr Secretarie Coke[1].

May it please your Honour.

. . . .

At Alicant, I understand, is arryved one Mr Harris[2], who sayes he was employed to the King of Barbary with his Ma^{tie's} letters. Butt withall I understand that he hath gotten no aunsweare at all, nor any kind of release for his Ma^{tie's} subjectes ther prysonars. He reportes that he durst not goe on shore, butt remayned a shipp-board, and sent the letters to the King, from whom he hath gotten no aunswere.

With the remembrance of my dewtie, I rest
Your Honour's to be commaunded,

Signé : Fra. Cottington.

Madrid, 31 Martii 1618, *stilo veteri.*

Public Record Office. — *State Papers, Foreign, Spain, vol. XXIII.* — *Original.*

---

1. Sir John Coke (1563-1644). Il fut premier secrétaire d'État de 1625 à 1639.

2. John Harrison. Il revenait de son quatrième voyage. V. *supra,* p. 443.

CXLIII

LETTRE DE FRANCIS COTTINGTON A ROBERT NAUNTON[1]

(Extrait)

Moulay Zidân, battu par Yahia ben Abdallah, négocie le secours de l'Espagne. — Des troupes de Mazagan ont récemment délivré ce chérif assiégé dans Safi.

Madrid, 21 février 1618 [n. st. 3 mars 1619].

Au dos, alia manu: 21° Febr[ii] 1618. — Mr Cottington to me.
Au bas: Mr Secretarie Naunton.

May it please your Honour.

..... Mulley Sedan, being beaten out of Moruecos by a certayn rebell, whom the Moores call a saint[2], is lyke to receave some assistance, at least in money, from hence for the reestablishing him in his kingdom, it being treated by certayn mynisters of his with the Vicerey at Lisbone; but they suffer them nott to come to this Court. Certayn forces sent from Maszagan, by order of his Matie here, lately releeved Mulley Sedan in Safia from a dangerous seege which that rebell had layd, having followed him from Moruecos thither[3].....

Signé: Fra. Cottington.

Madrid, 21° Feb. 1618, *stilo Angliæ*.

Public Record Office. — State Papers, Foreign, Spain, vol. XXIII. — Original.

1. Sir Robert Naunton (1563-1635), secrétaire d'État de 1618 à 1623.
2. Yahia ben Abdallah. Sur ce personnage, V. *supra*, p. 476, note 2, et *1re Série*, France, t. III, p. 18, note 3.
3. Le gouverneur de Mazagan n'eût pas à intervenir. La discorde se mit dans l'armée de Yahia ben Abdallah, qui leva le siège de Safi. V. *ibid.*, p. 20 et ss., et Do Couto de Albuquerque, *Memorias...*, p. 62.

CXLIV

LETTRE DE JOHN DIGBY[1] A BUCKINGHAM[2]

(Extrait)

Il ne conseille pas une expédition contre les pirates. — Les Anglais en souffrent peu maintenant. — Les Espagnols en sont au contraire fort incommodés, à cause des Moriscos expulsés, qui, chaque année, guident les Turcs et les Maures sur leurs côtes.

5 [n. st. 15] avril 1619.

Au dos, alia manu : My Lord Digbie, concerning preparations against the pyrats and the King of Spain.

My singular good Lord,

. . . .

And therfore it may be not unworthy consideration, whether it will not be fitter to reserve this to augment our preparations the next yeare, then to expend it now on uncerteyn enterprese; espetially for these two reasons :

First, for that his Ma$^{tie's}$ subjects are now nothing so much anoyed by the pirats as they were three yeares since, when they made their complaynt; for they have now built strong and warrlike ships, and are in their trade litle endamaged; and hereof I intreat your Lordship to ask Mr Secretary Calvert[3], who was pres-

---

1. John Digby, baron de Sherbourne, plus tard comte de Bristol (1580-1654). Ambassadeur extraordinaire en Espagne (1611-1620 et 1622-1624).

2. George Villiers, comte, puis duc de Buckingham (1592-1628), était alors Lord Grand Amiral.

3. George Calvert (1580 ?-1632) secrétaire d'État de 1619 à 1625, premier Lord Baltimore.

ent when the marchants themselves affirmed at the Councell Table that they of late receaved litle or no hurt from the pirats.

Secondly, it is certeyn that there is no nation so much anoyed and infested with the pirats as the dominions of the King of Spaine, very many of them being of the Moriscos, which were expelled thence, and every yeare are guides to the Turkes and Mores to do mischeifes upon the coast towns of Spaine; so that it may be considerable whether we should make so much hast to pull this thorne out of the King of Spaines foote or not.

. . . .

And so, with the remembrance of my service, I rest
Your Lordship's humble servant,

Signé : **J. Digbye.**

April the 5th, 1619.

British Museum. — Harleian Mss, 1580, ff. 106-109. — Original.

CXLV

LETTRE DE DUDLEY CARLETON AU CONSEIL PRIVÉ

Il a poursuivi auprès des États la restitution du navire l'« African », pris dans la rade de Safi. — Il a réfuté l'accusation portée contre ledit navire de favoriser les pirates et les ennemis de Moulay Zidân. — Ordre a été donné de rendre le navire et sa cargaison.

La Haye, 14 [n. st. 24] avril 1619.

Au dos: To the right honorable, my most singular good Lordes, the Lordes of His Majestie's Privy Consayle.

Alia manu: 14 Aprill 1619. — A letter from Sir Dudley Carelton, Knight, Ambassador with the States, concerninge his proceedings in procureinge restitution of a shipp called the « Affrican », taken in the roade of Saphia.

May it please your Lordships.

In conformitie to your Lordshipps' lettres of the 23th of February concerning the « Affrican[1] » of London, lately taken in the roade of Saphia uppon the coste of Barbarie by two men of warre of this province of Holland and, since the receit of your Lordshipps' lettres, conducted by one of the said shipps to Roterdam, I have used my best indeavours, both by publique audience and memorials in the assembly of the States General, and likewise by divers conferences with the Prince of Orange and those of the Admiralty[2], to procure the interested parties a speedie restitution of their ship and goods and satisfaction for their dommages. Wherin I found those of the

---

1. Sur la capture de l'« African » et les démarches accomplies par Dudley Carleton auprès des États à son sujet. V. 1re Série, Pays-Bas, t. III, pp. 83 et 94.
2. *The Admiralty*, l'amirauté de Rotterdam.

Admiralty willing to admit such accusations, for excuse of their captaines, as they alleadged for the lawfulnes of the prise: as first that they found it furnished with amunition for assistance of the pyrates; and then that it gave ayde to the ennemyes of the King of Morocco[1]. In both which I made it appeare unto the States that there was neyther ground of truth nor reason.

Wherupon they ordayned, by their expresse lettres to the Admiralty of the 9th of this present, restitution of the ship with the goods and marchandise in state as it was taken, and such reparation of dommages as might give the interessed parties contentment. The execution of which command the Admiralty doth in part suspend, forasmuch as concernes dommages, untill the other Captaine[2], by whose commandement as Admiral the prise was taken, doth come in: he being yet at sea, but expected within few dayes. Meanewhile restitution is made of the ship to the owners, though with some detriment in the goods, which goeth in the account of dommages; in which likewise, when time shall serve, I will not fayle of my best indeavours to procure full satisfaction.

Thus I most humbly take leave.

From the Hagh, this 14th of Aprill 1619.

Your Lordshipps' most humbly to be commaunded,

Signé : Dudley Carleton.

Public Record Office. — State Papers, Foreign, Holland, vol. LXXXIX, f. 186. — Original.

1. Le navire l' « African » avait été saisi à l'instigation de Moulay Zidân, qui croyait que son capitaine, John Cravyn, était en relation avec le marabout Yahia ben Abdallah. V. *1re Série*, Pays-Bas, t. III, *loc. cit.*

2. Le capitaine Adriaen van Crimpen, qui fit sa déposition à Amsterdam le 30 mai 1619. V. *ibidem.* p. 94.

CXLVI

LETTRE DE FRANCIS COTTINGTON A ROBERT NAUNTON

(Extrait)

Le gouverneur de Mazagan a péri en mer dans une rencontre avec des pirates turcs.

Madrid, 11 [n. st. 21] novembre 1619.

Au dos, alia manu : 11 9^{ber} 1619. — Mr Cottington to me.
Au bas : Mr Secretarie Naunton.

My it please Your Honour.

..... The governor of Massagan[1], in Barbery, comming lately from thence (leaving another in his roome) with thre shipps of warr which were sent for him, mett with the Turkish pirates and, fighting with them, had by a misfortune his shipp fired and in it perished himselfe, his wyfe and many children[2]. He was a gentleman of very good qualitie and is here much lamented.....

Signé : Fra. Cottington.

Madrid, 11° Novembris 1619, *stilo veteri.*

Public Record Office. — *State Papers. Foreign. Spain, vol. XXIII.* — *Original.*

1. D. Jorge Mascarenhas, plus tard comte de Castello-Novo (V. *1re Série*, France, t. III, p. 20, note 3). Gouverneur de Mazagan depuis 1615, il venait de remettre, en septembre 1619, son commandement à Braz Telles de Menezes.

2. La nouvelle n'était pas exacte. Seul un des fils de Mascarenhas périt dans le combat et un autre fut blessé. Lui-même fut amené à Alger et se racheta au prix de 32000 cruzades, avec l'aide de Philippe III et des Pères de la Rédemption. Mascarenhas fut ensuite gouverneur de Tanger de 1622 à 1624 (Menezes, *Hist. de Tangere*, pp. 133-134).

CXLVII

LETTRE DE WALTER ASTON[1] A FRANCIS NETHERSOLE[2]

(Extrait)

L'escadre de Sir Robert Mansell a capturé un navire turc en rade de Tétouan.

Madrid, 12 [n. st. 22] mars 1620 [n. st. 1621].

Au dos, alia manu : 12 March 1620. — From Sir Walter Ashton and Sir Francis Cottington.

Sir,

..... Sir Robert Mansell[3] with that fleete is now in Gibraltar, where it seemes he intends to trim his shipps. A squadron of the fleete tooke latelie a smale barke of the Turk's ; but for that some of the Stats men of warre assisted in the chace, the prize was shared betweene them. And I am now againe newlie advertised of another of good importance which some of the English have taken in the shipp road of Tituan. Soe, as I hope, Sir Robert Mansell will everie waye answere the expectation had of him.....

Signé : Wa. Aston.

Madrid, 12 March 1620, *stilo veteri.*

Sir Francis Nethersoll.

Public Record Office. — State Papers, Foreign, Spain, vol. XXIV. — Original.

1. Sir Walter Aston (1584-1639) ambassadeur ordinaire en Espagne de 1620 à 1625 et de 1635 à 1638.
2. Sir Francis Nethersole (1589-1659), agent de l'Angleterre auprès des princes de l'Union protestante et secrétaire de l'Électeur Palatin de 1619 à 1623.
3. V. *infra*, p. 522 et note 2.

CXLVIII

LETTRE DE WALTER ASTON A BUCKINGHAM

(Extrait)

Siège d'El-Mamora par les Maures.

Madrid, 1er juin 1621.

Au dos, alia manu: Sir Walter Aston, the 1 of June 1621, *stilo novo*.

My very good Lord,

..... This King's armada is now ready to putt to sea, and, as I am informed, some of them are already gone out to succour Mamora[1], which is beseiged[2] by a great army of Moores by land, and by certaine shyping by sea, of which I have receaved severall advise, some reporting them to be Hollanders, others of Argiers.

From Lisbone they also arme divers ships of war, and doe reinforce other armadas, with much confidence that they shalbe able to defend themselves from such invasions as shalbe attempted upon this coast by the fleetes of those partes.....

Signé: Wa. Aston.

Madrid, 1 of June 1621, *stilo veteri*[3].

Public Record Office. — *State Papers, Foreign, Spain, vol. XXIV.* — *Original.*

1. En mai 1621, El-Mamora, défendue par son gouverneur D. Cristobal de Lechuga, fut assiégée par terre par Sidi Ahmed el-Ayachi et par mer par les Moriscos de Salé. El-Oufrâni, p. 438; Cespedes, p. 138.

2. Le 23 mai [n. st. 2 juin], Walter Aston, dans une lettre à Calvert, annonçait également le siège d'El-Mamora, dans des termes identiques. *State Papers, Foreign, Spain, vol. XXIV.*

3. La mention *stilo veteri* est sans doute un lapsus et la date de la lettre est bien en nouveau style comme il est indiqué au dos.

CXLIX

LETTRE DE WALTER ASTON A GEORGE CALVERT

(Extrait)

Les Espagnols ont fait lever le siège d'El-Mamora et renforcé la place.

Madrid, 13 [n. st. 23] juin 1621.

Au dos, alia manu : 13 June 1631. — Sir Walter Aston to Mr Secretary Calvert. — Received 22 June. — For Mr Secretarey Calvert.

Right Honourable,

My last unto you was of the 23 of the last month, by the ordinary conveyance

. . . .

In my last, I advertised your Honour of the beseeging of Mamora. This therefor shall tell you that 12 gallions sett out from Cales, came seasonably to the succor of itt, so that the Turkes by sea and the Moores by land instantly left the seege; and the gallions are retourned, having left the fort strengthened both with men and munition [1].

. . . .

Soe, with the remembrance of my dutye, I rest
Your Honour's to command,

Signé : Wa. Aston.

Madrid, 13 June 1621, *stilo veteri.*

Public Record Office. — *State Papers, Foreign, Spain, vol. XXIV.* — *Original.*

---

1. Le 23 juin [n. st. 3 juillet], Aston écrivait de nouveau à Calvert et lui confirmait la levée du siège d'El-Mamora. *State Papers, Foreign, Spain, vol. XXIV.*

CL

LETTRE DE WALTER ASTON A GEORGE CALVERT

(Extrait)

Sir Robert Mansell a envoyé des vaisseaux pour surprendre des pirates turcs dans la rivière de Tétouan.

Madrid, 5 [n. st. 15] septembre 1621.

Au dos, alia manu : 7[1] September 1621. — Sir Walter Aston to Mr Secretary Calvert. — For your Honour.

Right Honourabl,

My last was on the 25 of August, by a post dispatched from hence unto the Conde of Gondomar.

. . . .

Since the passing by of thos two posts which you dispatched unto Sir Robert Manssell, by whom I alsoe wrote unto him, I have not hard anything from him, nor have I yet any notice that thos messengers have found him, though I presume the first of them, who went Giberaltar, hath ther delivered him the letters, having understood by divers letters from marchants that he atended therabowte the comming of his provisions out of England.

From Malaga, I am adverticed that Sir Robert, having notice of certain barks of Turks richly loden in the river of Tituan, ready to sett sayle for Argirrs, sent 250 of his best men, joyned with so many more soldiers which the governor of Ceuta[2] gave him[3], with boates

---

1. Mention erronée. La date originale est : 5 September 1621. V. à la fin du doc.

2. *The governor*, D. Luiz de Noronha e Menezes, comte et marquis de Villa Real, gouverneur de Ceuta de 1606 à 1622.

3. Un accord conclu à Madrid pour trois ans, le 29 avril 1619, stipulait la coopération de l'Angleterre et de l'Espagne contre les pirates. Fernandez Duro, *Armada española*, t. III, pp. 360-361.

fitting for the attempt, with hope to surprise them. So as, if this adverticement be trew, we shall shortly understand of their succese; for my adverticement says that these forces departed from the fleet on the 26 of August[1]. Your Honour may be pleased to aquaint my Lord Admirall with these perticulars, for that I doe not now trowble his Lordship with any letters.

. . . .

Therefore, with the remembrance of my service, I rest
Your Honour's to command,

Signé : Wm. Aston.

Madrid, 5 september 1621, *stilo veteri*.

Public Record Office. — State Papers, Foreign, Spain, vol. XXIV. — Original.

1. On ignore la suite de cette tentative.

CLI

LETTRE D'AHMED EN-NEKSIS[1] A WALTER ASTON

John Duppa est arrivé à Tétouan, chargé par l'amiral Robert Mansell de traiter l'échange des Andalous capturés par la flotte anglaise. — Antérieurement, une négociation avait été entamée par Robert Mansell, venu à Tétouan avec son escadre. — L'amiral anglais avait présenté au Mokaddem une réclamation au sujet du capitaine George Friswell, réduit en captivité. — Le Mokaddem avait répondu que c'était en représailles de la capture par le capitaine Touching d'une saétie appartenant à ses fils. — Quant à l'échange des captifs andalous que Robert Mansell avait à son bord contre des prisonniers anglais, le Mokaddem avait élevé des prétentions inacceptables et l'amiral était parti pour Alicante où il avait vendu quelques-uns des captifs. — Il avait ensuite fait voile vers l'Angleterre, laissant les autres à Cadix aux soins de John Duppa. — Entre temps, le Mokaddem avait racheté de leurs propriétaires huit esclaves anglais ; il proposait de les échanger contre les seize Andalous laissés à Cadix et demandait que l'opération ait lieu à Ceuta. — Il remettrait en même temps un projet de traité aux conditions suivantes : 1° L'achat et la vente des sujets anglais sera interdite à Tétouan ; 2° Ceux qui y viendront munis d'un sauf-conduit pourront y commercer librement ; 3° La cargaison de tout navire échoué appartiendra au Sultan, mais l'équipage sera libre ; 4° Les marchandises débarquées à Tétouan pourront y être vendues, en acquittant la dîme ; 5° Toute flotte anglaise venant à Tétouan pourra y faire aiguade et s'y ravitailler. — Walter Aston est prié de donner des instructions à John Duppa pour la conclusion de ce traité. — Il demande que le capitaine Touching soit recherché et puni.

[Tétouan], 21 décembre 1621

Au dos, alia manu : The Governors lettre of Tetuan of the 21 December 1621, sent me by Mr Duppa[2].

1. Ahmed en-Neksis, mokaddem de Tétouan. Sur ce personnage, V. *supra*, p. 438, note 1.

2. John Duppa, interprète de la flotte

Excellentisimo Señor,

Aqui llego Juan Duppa, cavallero ynglez, a tratar el rescate de los Andaluses cautibados por la armada del rey de la Gran Bretaña; y, por orden que tiene de su general, no puede darlos en otra manera que cabeza por cabeza.

Assi que aviso a V. Ex° que esta gente, como passajeros, salian del rio de esta ciudad en una saetia de Turcos[1], confiados en la amistad que ha abido, y que yban a sus casas sin yr a cosso, sino como mercaderes, que lo eran, y que, aunque la armada del dicho rey topassen con ellos, no harian daño a nadie dellos. Assi que el dicho navio, poniendose a la mar, encontro con el general Don Roberto Mansel, que los cautibaron a todos.

Y despues llego a este puerto con toda la armada[2], y embio de su gente a tierra a tratar el rescate de la dicha gente que cautibo. Y, en este estado, me preguntaron porque se cautibo a George Frisuel[3]. Y respondi que de antes, aviendo llegado a este puerto un mercader llamado Touching[4], aviendo intervenido mi siguro, tomo del propio puerto una saetia de mis hijos con su gente, y fue a Malaga, donde bendio Moros y saetia. Luego, quando llego Jorje Frisuel, sin tomar mi siguro, abaxo a tierra. Y, siendo esto, clamaron las mugeres de los Moros que se vendieron en Malaga y, pidiendo justicia, pidieron que se detubiesse hasta que hiziere bueno Moros y saetias. Y, en quanto a esta ultima disgracia destos Andaluses, me pidio el general tomasse los Andaluses y passajeros por los Yngleses que ay en esta ciudad vassallos del rey de la Gran Bretaña; pero no quisieron los Andaluses y demas Moros aceptar aquella partida sin la hazienda que se las tomo aquella pobre gente sin raçon.

Y, en efeto, no queriendo concluyr en esta conformidad, se partio

---

de Sir Robert Mansell; il s'était rendu à Tétouan pour accomplir sa mission à bord d'un navire marchand.

1. Cette saétie était française, mais elle avait été capturée par les Turcs. V. supra, p. 519.

2. V. le Journal du voyage de Robert Mansell intitulé : *Algiers Voyage... under the command of Sir Robert Mansell, Knight. Vice Admirall of England*, plaquette imprimée, 1621, *State Papers, Domestic, James I, vol. CXXII, n° 106*.

3. Ce capitaine est nommé Friswell, *infra*, p. 528.

4. Le fait s'était passé en 1619. V. *infra*, p. 528 et note 1.

la armada y vendio algunos de los esclavos y pobre gente en Alicante ; y despues, partiendo la armada a Ynglaterra, dexo en Cadiz con el dicho Juan Duppa los que quedaron de aquella pobre gente, los quales estan fuera de raçon, porque son muy pobres porque no tienen ningun pariente ni hazienda en Tetuan ni en otra parte. Y yo, movido a piedad, he dado orden de juntar entre los Andaluses la limosna que montaren ocho Yngleses, por diez y seis Andaluses que ay en Cadiz en poder de Juan Duppa y Edmundo Cason[1], yngleses.

Y, trayendolos a Ceupta, entregandolos al general de aquella fuerça[2], reciviere los ocho Yngleses y una escritura firmada de mi mano y nombre, y de mis hijos y del caidi y ciudadanos desta ciudad que ningun Yngles, Escoces o Yrlandes vassallos de Su Mag.d el rey de la Gran Bretaña que no seran comprados ni vendidos en Tetuan, excepto los que aora estan captivos ; y que qualquiera mercader vassallo del dicho rey que llegare a este puerto puede con mi siguro abajar a la ciudad a tratar y contratar con todos los mercaderes, assi desta ciudad como de Fes y otras partes de Berveria, trayendo buenas mercadurias y haziendo trato llano sin engaño. Mas, si algun navio por fortuna diera en tierra, se a de entender que la hazienda es del Rey[3] y la gente libre. Y si, por miedo de cossarios destas naciones, quisiere disembarcar alguna hazienda, la puede sacar libremente y venderla, pagando el diezmo como es custumbre, sin hazer esclavo a ninguno. Y si alguna armada del dicho rey llegare a este puerto, pueden tomar agua por sus ordenes y qualquiera bastimentos ; y, mientras no se hizieren agravio a ninguno de la tierra, recibiran toda la cortesia possible.

Y esto es lo que se ofrece escribir a V. Ex.ª, porque de la orden al dicho Juan Duppa que concluya esta buena obra, que en efeto lo es, y que assentemos nuestras amistades. Y V. Ex.ª responda, a quien guarde Nuestro Señor.

De Tetuan y Diziembre 21 de 1621.

1. Edmund Carson, consul d'Angleterre à Gibraltar.
2. D. Luiz de Noronha. V. *supra*, p. 519, note 2.
3. Il s'agit ici du Sultan, en fait de Moulay Abdallah, roi de Fez, dont le mokaddem Ahmed en-Neksis reconnaissait la suzeraineté nominale. V. *infra*, p. 536.

Y quiero de V. Ex* que se busque (que esto he acordado despues de aver escrito las capitulaciones de arriba, para que tenga todo buen efeto) y pido que se castigue al que llevo la saetia, estando debajo de siguro, y que sea castigado y buscado en España o en Ynglaterra.

Signé : El almocaden Ahmet Anecasis, gobernador de Tetuan[1].

Public Record Office. — State Papers, Foreign, Spain, vol. XXIV. — Original.
British Museum. — Additional Mss., 36445, f. 333. — Copie.

---

1. Ce fut sans doute la réponse de Walter Aston à cette lettre qui fut interceptée par D. Jorge Mascarenhas, en même temps qu'une autre d'un marchand anglais. V. 1re Série, France, t. III, p. 83 et note 1, et Portugal, aux dates des 8 juin et 11 juillet 1622.

CLII

LETTRE DE JOHN DUPPA A WALTER ASTON

Il rend compte de sa mission et de son voyage à Tétouan. — Mansell avait chargé Carson et Duppa d'échanger les Andalous faits prisonniers par sa flotte, tête pour tête, contre les Anglais captifs à Tétouan, sinon de racheter ceux-ci avec l'argent de la rançon de ceux-là. — L'échange tête pour tête est impossible en raison de la pauvreté des Andalous, qui ont été capturés avec tous leurs biens, et qui, étant tous de la même famille, ne peuvent attendre aucune aide de parents restés au Maroc. — Duppa a profité du passage à Cadix du marchand Thomas Aston qui se rendait à Tétouan, pour accompagner celui-ci. — Le mokaddem de Tétouan lui envoie un sauf-conduit et l'invite à conférer avec lui. — Duppa fait monter un otage à bord et se rend le lendemain dans la ville. — Il trouve autour d'En-Neksis ses fils et les principaux Andalous de la ville. — Il leur expose l'objet de sa mission. — Les Andalous refusent de donner pour leurs compatriotes une rançon supérieure à celle de huit Anglais. — Duppa a protesté; En-Neksis lui a répondu longuement. — Duppa demande à Walter Aston qu'il lui soit délivré des pleins pouvoirs pour mener à bien cette négociation et qu'on lui rembourse le montant de ses dépenses.

28 décembre 1621 [n. st. 7 janvier 1622].

My honourable and very good Lord,

I, knowing your Lordship's zealous affection and readiness to further anything which may tend to our countryes good and of his Maties subjects, am bould at this present to acquaint your Lordship with my proceedings and with the treaty which I have lately had with the Muccaden of Tetuan; wherein, if in anything I have exceeded the limits of my commission, I hope it will be imputed to my small experience, and not to any bould presumption in perticuler of myself, who wholly relieth on your Lordships favourable censure.

I have formerly acquainted your Lordship with the commission which Sir Robert Mansel left with Mr Carson and myselfe, about the Andalusaes taken by our fleet and now captives in Cadiz: first that I should redeem them head for head by his Majesties subjects captives in Tettuan; and, in case they could not be so redeemed, that, then, we should ransom them for mony, and, with the mony raised by that meanes, we should redeem, as far as the mony would goe, those of our nation captives as before sayd.

For the first, they have denyed, and as it appeareth impossible by reason of theire poverty and that the English are bought by divers, who with their monies have bought them. Secondly, the sayd slaves have bin kept at 20 reales *per diem* for the space of fower months and cannot procure from Tettuan any meanes to ransom them. The cause whereof is they were all people who lived up in the mountaines neere Tettuan, untill a brother of theires cayme from Argir and sought out thease people, who are most of one family and of his kindred, perswading them to sell theire houses, cattle and other revenues and to transport theire money, or what goods they had left, to Argir; whose advise these poore people followed, and by chaunce there cayme into Tettuan roade a prise taken by the Turks, bound for Argir, wherein they putt themselves as passengers; and so, being at sea, they were taken by our English fleet, who presently pillaged them of all the goods and mony they had, not leaving behind them in Tettuan goods or any one of theire kindred which can or is able to releeve them or give them any comfort.

Whereupon, considering their poverty, the misery of our English captives, and no autority expressed in our commission to sell them, there being in Cales one Mr Thomas Aston, a marchant of London, bound for Tettuan, I resolved to go with him, hoping that, being in the roade to treat with them, I might make som good conclusion about the liberty of these people.

When being arrived there, the muccaden of Tettuan haveing heard of my being aboard, sent mee his siguro and write me a letter, wherein hee tould mee he would conferre with mee about the conclusion of the redeeming the sayd captives and concerning the benefitt of his owne country and the espetiall good of our English marchants. Which haveing well considered, demanded a pledg to be sent aboard till my returne ; the which they performed. And, the next day, I went up to the towne, when, being com before the Muccaden, he sent for the principall of the Andalusaes of the citty, whom, in the presence of his sonnes, were demanded what answer they would give me concerning the busines I cayme about, which was the liberty of people of theire nation, Andalusaes made slaves by the English armado. They answered that for those people, they were nothing to them, nor had eyther frends or kindred amongst them, yett out of alms they had procured soe much money as would buy out eight English captives and that was all they would give. I answered them, if I had known theire resolutions to be such, I had spared my paynes to com thither, and of myselfe had no power to doe otherwise then my commission left with mee would permitt. After which, the Muccaden, by his interpretor, sayd unto mee as followeth :

Déclaration d'Ahmed en-Neksis.

Le capitaine anglais Touching est venu à terre avec un sauf-conduit d'En-Neksis. — Moulay Abdallah étant venu assiéger Tétouan, Touching a pris le large et s'est emparé près de Ceuta d'une saétie d'En-Neksis. — En représailles, le navire anglais de George Friswell, se présentant au port de Tétouan, a été capturé. — Postérieurement, l'amiral Mansell a capturé des Andalous. — Duppa n'ayant pas de pouvoirs suffisants pour négocier cette affaire, En-Neksis en référera à Walter Aston. — Il lui proposera un traité sur les bases suivantes : Si un navire anglais fuyant des pirates échoue sur la côte, l'épave sera laissée aux propriétaires du navire. — Si le naufrage est le fait du mauvais temps ou de l'impéritie du capitaine, l'épave ne sera pas restituée, mais l'équipage et les passagers seront laissés en liberté. — Les navires anglais trouveront toutes facilités à Tétouan pour faire des vivres et pour écouler leurs marchandises, en acquittant les droits de douane. — En-Neksis propose à Duppa d'attendre à Tétouan la réponse de Walter Aston.

« In all the time of Queen Elizabeths rayne, and many yeeres before, and likewise since his Majesties coming to the crowne, our country of Barbary hath held peace and good correspondency with the English nation, and have endeavored to continue yt so. Until there cayme into this roade an English ship whose captaine or master was called Touching, who, as the custom is of all marchants, demanded my seguro for to trade with us; but, one a suddain, there coming downe our King[1], with an army of Alarbes, they beseeged our citty, whereby he was not able to utter any of his goods, and therefore weyghed ankor and sett sayle for som other port. When, descrying a satty coming from Ceuta Point, took hyr and carred hir to Malaga, where he sould both the men and vessel. This satty was a satty of my sons, which somtimes they manned forth to defend our coast from the boats of Ceuta and Tanger, as likewise to make prise of them if wee could, but never did any wrong to English or any other nation, but to our sayd enimyes with whome we dayly fought.

« This wrong being don us, and haveing lost our best deffence at sea, besides the continuall exclamations of theire wives for the losse and slavery of theire husbands, my sonnes, with the cheefe of this towne, did resolve to make slaves of any of the King of Englands subjects which were brought to bee sould, and to lay hands on the first English marchant which should com into this roade. As afterward fell out with one George Friswell, a Scotich man, who cayme heather with a ship, and, presuming upon the former liberty he had receaved in this place, he cayme ashoare without my seguro, and, being in the towne, was made prisoner untill sattisffaction should be made to my sonnes for the satty and the men in hir, or otherwise, to have a promis from his Majesty of Great Brittaynne of punishing the sayd Touching, who hath don the wrong, and who first brake the peace betweene us and the English nation.

« Now wee are to consider wee have receaved two wrongs, the one in what the sayd marchant hath don us, the other in that the English armado hath sould som and made slaves of the rest of poore passengers, who went from this roade for Argir. For the last perticuler, you say you dare nott alter the order left with you by the English general,

---

1. Moulay Abdallah ben ech-Cheikh. Le siège de Tétouan par ce prince eut lieu dans les premiers jours de 1619. V. El-Oufrâni, p. 392.

unless his Majesty, out of England, or the Ambassador for his Majesty at Madrid, doth give you especiall order. Wherefore, out of the desire I have to renew our former frendship with your nation, I will write unto his Majesty's Ambassador at Madrid to give you power and autority to deliver freely and without charge the Andalusaes which you have left in captivity, in the citty of Ceuta, where in exchange you shall receave eight English; likewise that the sayd ambassador shall give mee promis that justice shall be don on the said Touching.

« And then, eyther in Ceuta or if you will com overland to Tettuan, you shall receive a writing subscribed with my owne hand, my sonnes and the cady of the citty of Tettuan, that, whereas at this present every one hath freedom to buy and make slaves of any of the King of England's subjects, from the day of signing of the sayd writing, wee shall command, upon pain of their lives, that none doe buy or sell or make slaves any of the sayd Majesty's subjects, but all those of the sayd nations which are brought hither, excepted those that are now slaves, shall have theire liberty to Ceuta or Tanger.

« Moreover, if by chance there be any of the King of Great-Brittaine's subjects shipps which by pirats should be chast into this roade, or any other part of our coast within our dominion, and so should be enforced to runne ashoare, theire shipp and goods which they can save, they may freely dispose of as they please; and, for theire persons, they should bee free from slavery or imprisonment.

« But, if a ship suffer shipwrack by foule weather or carelesnes, that in such a case both ship and goods are forfaited, but theire persons free.

« Besides, if there cometh into our roade the King of Great-Brittain's armado, they shall be treated with all cortesy and shall have free liberty to buy for theire mony any provision of victuales or any other wants which our country may afford them, unles they offer treachery or wrong unto our people.

« Lastly, that any of his Majesty's marchants may freely trade in any port or roade within our dominion; and likewise, if they cannot make a sudden dispatch of theire goods according to their desires, then what goods they will unlade and bring up to our citty of Tettuan, paying the custom, they may there sell them or send them up into the country, to Fez or what other place they shall like of.

« Now, you, having heard thease my propositions, you may assure yourselfe that the Ambassador, haveing considered these things, will willingly condesend to the delivery of those poore people upon such honourable and good conditions. Wherefore, if you will remayne heere till you have an answeare from the Ambassador, you may, that soe you may be a witnes at the concluding of this busines, which, I greatly desire, may be effected for the good of both nations. »

Thus, haveing given unto your Lordship a full accompt of my proceedings with the Muccaden about the Andalusaes left in my charge, I now beseech your Lordship to give me authority to dispose of them, even as in your wisdom you shall think best, which I will effect with all care and dilligence. And likewise, if soe your Lordship pleaseth, I will give you an accompt of my charges, which Mr Carson hath been at, both with these people and the Jewes[1]; of whome, if you shall think fitt, we will receave 500 pieces of eight[2], and the rest uppon security of som person dwelling in Cales, able and sufficient to discharge the rest of 1 000 pieces of eight within the time of six monthes. And soe wee may be free of any farther charge and have monies to pay what allreaddy hath bin disbursed; and, when your Lordship shall please, I shall give you a perticuler accompt of all.

Soe, humbly craving pardon for troubling your Lordship's serious busineses with these occasions, I rest

Your Lordship's humble servant,

Signé : John Duppa.

December the 28th 1621 — 8 [January] *stilo novo*[3].

Public Record Office. — *State Papers, Foreign, Spain, vol. XXIV, ff. 333-334.* — *Original*[4].

---

1. Sur ces Juifs, V. le document suivant.
2. *Pieces of eight*, piezas de a ocho, monnaie espagnole de la valeur de huit réaux.
3. Concordance inexacte. Le 28 décembre 1621 répond au 7 janvier 1622.
4. Une autre lettre de John Duppa, racontant son voyage et exposant les propositions d'En-Neksis, figure au *British Museum, Additional Mss., 36445, f. 335.*

CLIII

LETTRE DE JOHN DUPPA A WALTER ASTON

Les cinq Juifs détenus à Gibraltar n'ont personne à Tétouan qui veuille payer la rançon demandée. — John Duppa propose qu'on les échange contre cinq captifs anglais de cette ville. — Rançon de cinq autres Juifs qui se trouvent à Cadix. — Il sollicite le poste de consul à Tétouan. — Il enverra plus tard la lettre du Mokaddem.

Gibraltar, 10 janvier 1622.

Au dos : My second letter to your Lordship.

My honourable good Lord,

Since my comming to Gibraltar, I have bin much importuned by the consull of Gibraltar[1] to write unto your Lordship to be pleased to give him and I autority to give the five Jewes (left with him, and now are in prison) theire liberty. They were heere putt in prison by Sir Robert Mansells order, untill they had payed the summe of 200^{li}, which by a writing they promised to performe within a month; the which monny was assigned to a marchant called Giles Pen, he haveing lent unto the fleet (which releeved theire wants) the summe of 550^{li}. Which mony part of it, to the summe aforesayd, he was to receave of the Jewes, and some in Malaga, and the rest in England; but none are payed. And concerning the Jewes, they have no frends in Tettuan that once would treat of them; wherefore I consider, rather then they would have endured five monthes imprisonment, with yrons on theire leggs, they would, if they could, have sought theire remedy. But they say, by reason of the Generalls threats, they cutt themselves at 200^{li}; but they are not able to performe it; so that, if it shall like your Lordship that they bee redeemed for five English slaves, who are

---

1. Edmund Carson. V. *supra*, pp. 523, 526 et 530.

in Tettuan, there [are] there som Jewes who have som of the nation, and they are assu[red] to be redeemed for them. But I leave it to your Lordship's pleasure, which I am readdy to obey.

Your Lordship was pleased to write unto mee to Cadiz concerning the five Jewes I have there. They offer to give mee five hundred peeces of eight of the 1 000 they are cutt at, which they will pay presently, and for the rest they will give the security of one John Brabo de Laguna, a marchant in Cadiz, to be payed within the tyme of six monthes. So that, to avoyde any further charge with them, if your Lordship shall think fytt, I shall accept of this proffer.

Lastly, I would beseech your Lordship that Mr. Carson may be accomptable to your Lordship for what he hath layed out, and what mony he hath made of things committed to his charge by the General. And that you would please to consider the paynes I have taken about thease people, and a 12 months tyme I spent as linguist for the fleet, writing all Spanish letters, and being sent ashoare when any occasion was offered for the fleets service.

In recompence of all which service, all my desire is that I may bee made consull for his Maties subjects which should trade at Tettuan; the which by a letter of favor from your Lordship I should hope to procure that. The gayne I should gett thereby is litle; but the hopes I have to keepe many of my contrimen out of slavery by my living there is the cheefe thing I ayme at; which humble request I hope to obtayne.

For the Muccadens letter[1], which I should have sent with my letter, I have not sent till I com to Cales, which will be the surest; and I intend by the next ordinary from Cadiz to send yt to your Lordship.

So humbly craveing pardon for troubling your Lordship with these things, I rest

Your Lordship's humble servant,

Signé: John Duppa.

From Gibraltar, January the 10th 1622.

Public Record Office. — State Papers, Foreign, Spain, vol. XXVI. — Original.

1. V. *supra*, Doc. CLI, p. 521.

CLIV

LETTRE DE JOHN DUPPA A WALTER ASTON

Il lui envoie une lettre de Thomas Aston, exposant les avantages qu'une paix solide avec Tétouan procurerait au commerce anglais, ainsi que la lettre du Mokaddem.

Gibraltar, 13 [janvier] 1622.

Au dos : My third letter unto your Lordship.

My honourable good Lord,

Craving pardon for my bouldness with troubling your Lordship with my occasions, but being much importuned by Mr Thomas Aston[1], marchant of London (who was with mee at Tettuan), to send his letter to your Lordship, I could not refuse to send yt by this propio. By which letter you shall understand, by a marchant who trades there, the benifyt a setled peace might be unto those that trade there, and that it is more proffitable unto our kingdom then the selling of six slaves. Howsoever, I leave it unto your Lordship's consideration.

I thought to have gon to Cales two dayes since, and from thence to have sent your Lordship the governor of Tettuans letter[2]; but, being uncertayne when the weather will suffer mee, I have likewise sent now his letter, and doe beseech your Lordship to favor mee with your answer to Cales, whether I doubt not but within thease few dayes to have passage, and I hope to morrow.

1. Sur ce marchand, V. *supra*, p. 526. C'est sans doute lui qui écrivit au mokaddem Ahmed en-Neksis une lettre qui fut interceptée en avril 1622 par D. Jorge Mascarenhas, gouverneur de Tanger, en même temps que celle de Sir Walter Aston. V. *supra*, p. 524 et note 1.

2. V. *supra*, Doc. CLI, p. 521.

Soe humbly beseeching your Lordship for to pardon this my continuall troubling you, I rest
Your Lordship's assured and affectionate servant,
Signé : John Duppa.
Gibraltar, the 13th 1622.

Post-scriptum : I have sent back unto your Lordship the Jewes' letter you sent mee, and cannot deny anything they object for themselves ; and what makes most for them is that the Generall[2] gave liberty to 4 English, the master and other marriners, Itallyens, and hath left these Jewes as slaves to be sould, or els to pay 1 200 peeces of eight, if I can gett yt, but, rather then to be troubled with them, to take a 1 000 peeces.

Public Record Office. — *State Papers, Foreign, Spain, vol. XXV.* — *Original.*

1. Sur ces Juifs, V. *supra*, pp. 530-532.   2. **The Generall**, Sir Robert Mansell.

CLV

LETTRE DE JOHN DUPPA A WALTER ASTON

Il a conclu avec le mokaddem de Tétouan l'échange des Moriscos pris par Sir Robert Mansell contre huit Anglais captifs, qu'il a amenés à Cadix. — Ahmed en-Neksis a interdit le commerce des esclaves anglais à Tétouan; il en a avisé le roi de Fez, Moulay Abdallah, pour l'engager à prendre semblable mesure. — Il suggère l'envoi d'un agent anglais à Tétouan et à Fez. — J. Duppa demande à être chargé de cette mission. — Situation politique du Maroc: Moulay Zidân est roi de Merrakech et Moulay Abdallah, roi de Fez; Moulay Mohammed Zeghouda s'est emparé depuis trois ans d'El-Ksar el-Kebir; il a fait périr tous les Maures ayant quelque valeur, ce qui a dégagé les Portugais à Tanger. — Moulay Abdallah est auprès d'El-Ksar el-Kebir et se propose de chasser ou de mettre à mort Moulay Mohammed Zeghouda. — La mort de ce dernier rendrait la paix à la contrée et la sécurité au commerce

Cadix, 10 juillet 1622.

Au dos, alia manu : Mr. John Duppa unto my Lord, at his return from Barbary.

Right honourable, my very good Lord,

My humble service remembered unto your Lordship, — I, being returned from Tangier[1], have thought fit to give an account unto your Lordship of my proceeding with the Moriscoes left in my charge, and likewise of the present estate of the country from Tangier to Fez; wherein if I shall, in your Lordships opinion, have

---

1. John Duppa, dans un second voyage pour l'échange des captifs, s'était rendu à Tanger, d'où il traita par lettres avec le mokaddem de Tétouan. V. ci-après.

carefully performed the commands of the General who employed me, I shall then be assured that, whensoever I shall be called to account, my proceeding therein shall be pleasing to all.

I formerly informed[1] your Lordship that Sir Robert Mansell left the Moriscoes with me, to redeem so many of our nation out of slavery from Tetuan as they were in number, or else that they should be ransomed; which not being possible to be accomplished, I writ unto Sir Robert Mansell both by sea and by land, to know what course I should take with them, but never received answer from him, or any one else out of England. Besides, Sir Robert Mansell, before his departure for England, sent for the said Moriscoes to come aboard his ship, and assured them before me that they should not be sold; the which I having considered, and not being able to perform his order so punctually as I was commanded, I at length resolved to carry them over to Tangier; and from thence by letters of treaty with the Muccaden of Tetuan we came to an agreement that the Moriscoes should pay the charges of diet, which we had disbursed for them, and to give eight English (not being able to procure more[2]); whom I have brought with me to Cadiz.

Moreover, the said Muccaden hath by proclamation commanded that no English, Scottish or Irish subjects unto his Majesty of Great Britain (more than those who remain there at the present, which are sixteen) shall be suffered to be bought or sold in the city, or under his command; and, as appeareth by his letter here enclosed[3], which I send unto your Lordship, he intendeth to give account of what he hath done in this particular unto Muley Abdala, the King of Fez, whom he acknowledgeth for his King, that so the said King would in the like manner make proclamation in all parts of Barbary under his command, that none of our Kings subjects be suffered to be bought or sold, and that in all his ports the merchants of our country may have good trade and justice done them.

But, for the final conclusion of the good which hereby our

---

1. Le 7 janvier 1622. V. supra, Doc. CLII, p. 525.

2. Entendez que le Mokaddem n'avait pu en racheter davantage; car on voit, quelques lignes plus loin, qu'il resta 16 esclaves anglais à Tétouan.

3. Cette lettre du mokaddem Ahmed en-Neksis n'a pas été retrouvée.

merchants may receive, as likewise the freedom of those of our nation, which may be brought into Barbary to be sold, the said Muccaden doth request that his Majesty, by letter of credit, would send some person to Tetuan, and from thence to the King of Fez, that so, by his Majestys letter, the Moors or Moriscoes who shall trade with our nation might not be wronged, but receive justice either in the place where the wrong is offered, or else in England, according to the nature of the cause.

In which particular, if your Lordship shall think it fit to acquaint his Majesty, and that the Kings Majesty shall be pleased to employ any one herein, I shall be much bound unto your Lordship to be a means that I may be employed upon such an occasion; which [if] I may obtain, though as yet I have received no recompense or little hope of any for my labour and two years time which I have spent in this employment and in his Majestys fleets service[1], I shall herein esteem myself much honoured and very well recompensed, my hopes not being to enrich myself by the employment, but am assured I shall be a comfort to those who in that country are in misery, of his Majestys subjects, and may prevent the like which might happen to many a poor seaman.

Concerning the present affairs of Barbary, Muley Sedan commandeth from Fez to Maroccos. In Fez is King Muley Abdala, and entitleth himself King from Fez and all the country and seacoast of Barbary nearest Christendom. But Muley Mahomet[2] by usurpation hath, for the space of three years, possessed the command of Alcasser, which was a city of strength and very fair buildings till this Muley Mahomet, who, to gain the possession thereof, hath much destroyed it; and afterwards, not only in the city and where he was obeyed, when he understood of any Moor who was esteemed for his valour and beloved of the people, for fear he should dispossess him, he would privately send for him, as for some occasion of business, and to cut his throat. So that, whereas some few years past the Portuguese of Tangier, who then durst not go forth

---

1. V. *supra*, p. 521, note 2.
2. Moulay Mohammed *Zeghouda*, frère de Moulay Abdallah. Il se révolta contre son frère et occupa Fez au mois de Chabân 1028, mais il en fut chassé le 1ᵉʳ Ramadan suivant (12 août 1619). EL-OUFRÂNI, p. 393.

of their gates, by reason of continual assaults given by Moors of great fame and valour, now, by reason that the said Muley Mahomet hath by treachery cut the throats of many of them, the Portuguese are at more ease, and sally forth sometimes ten leagues.

Now, by reason of the many complaints which have been made unto the King of Fez of the oppression and tyranny of Muley Mahomet, the said King of Fez is not far off Alcasser with purpose to drive that tyrant out of the country, or to cut his throat; which [is] likely to happen unto him, by reason the people of the country hate him. And the Portuguese have already sent him word that they will not protect him nor receive him into their town[1]. So that by his death the said Muley Abdala will cause much quietness in the country, and the cafaloes[2] will go more securely from the ports of the seacoast, to the great good of merchandise.

Thus have I given your Lordship this unperfect relation of what I have understood of the present estate of Barbary; and so, humbly craving pardon for my tediousness herein, I rest

Your Lordships humble servant to command,

Signé : John Duppa.

From Cadiz, the 10th of July 1622.

Post-scriptum : I beseech your Lordship by the next ordinary to send me back the Muccadens letter[3], unless you shall think it fit to dispose otherwise of it.

State Papers collected by Edward, Earl of Clarendon, t. I, Oxford, 1767, pp. 1-2.

1. Il était question à cette époque de recevoir Moulay Mohammed *Zeghouda* en Espagne. V. *infra*, p. 540.

2. *Cafaloes*, cafila (caravanes).

3. La lettre du Mokaddem envoyée par Duppa avec la présente. V. *supra*, p. 536.

CLVI

ORDRE DE PHILIPPE IV

On parlera à l'ambassadeur d'Angleterre des agissements des Anglais au Maroc et de leur commerce dans les fronteiras. — En ce qui concerne les trêves sollicitées par divers cheikhs, ainsi que les différends entre Moulay Abdallah et Moulay Mohammed Zeghouda, Mascarenhas donnera à chacun de bonnes paroles, en évitant de s'engager avec qui que ce soit. — Tenter l'incendie de la flotte algérienne n'est pas opportun présentement.

25 août 1622.

En tête : Portugal, 25 de Agosto 1622.

Sobre lo que avia escrito D. Jorge Mascareñas, general de Tanger, en diversas materias.

Sobre el trato que Ingleses tienen en los puertos de Berberia, se hablara aqui al Embaxador de Inglaterra y escribira alla a mi Embaxador en la forma que parece, y que tambien den a entender lo del comercio en mis plaças.

Y, en quanto a las pazes que pidieron algunos Jeques y diferencias que tienen entre si Muley Xeque y Muley Hamet[1], se responda a D. Jorge que a todos entretenga con buenas palabras, sin prendarse con ninguno, dexandolos correr con sus inquietudes. Y no es agora sazon para lo que ofrece de quemar los navios de Argel.

Idem. Otra consulta con avisos de Berberia. Esta bien.

British Museum. — Egerton Mss., 323, f. 42. — Minute.

1. Il faut entendre Moulay Abdallah ben ech-Cheikh et Moulay Mohammed *Zeghouda*.

CLVII

CONSULTE DU CONSEIL DE PORTUGAL

D. Luiz de Noronha, gouverneur de Ceuta, écrit que Moulay Mohammed Zeghouda, à Ksar el-Kebir, se préoccupe de la marche de son frère Moulay Abdallah, qui s'avance contre lui. — Dans le cas où Moulay Mohammed Zeghouda demanderait à passer en Espagne, il y aurait lieu d'envisager les bonnes relations que Moulay Abdallah a entretenues avec les fronteiras, et la sécurité qui résulterait de l'éloignement de Zeghouda. — D. Antonio Pereira, s'appuyant sur le précédent de l'autorisation accordée à Moulay ech-Cheikh en 1612, est d'avis d'agir de même à l'égard de Moulay Mohammed Zeghouda. — Mendo da Motta et D. Francisco de Bragance estiment qu'il faut apporter en l'occurrence beaucoup de circonspection, parce que, d'une part, Moulay Abdallah est ami de l'Espagne et parce que, d'autre part, le séjour de Moulay Mohammed Zeghouda en Espagne entraînerait à de grandes dépenses. — Le duc de Villahermosa opine pour qu'on en réfère au Roi, si la demande de Moulay Mohammed Zeghouda se produit à la suite d'événements graves; si, au contraire, les circonstances ne sont pas pressantes, on usera d'atermoiements.

Madrid, 20 septembre 1622.

Señor,

Dom Luis de Noronha[1], governador e capitão geral de Ceita, escreve a V. Mag.^{de} que se diz que Muley Hamet[2] esta em Alcacere, muy temeroso da vezinhança de seu irmão, o qual tras tambem intento de o castigar, por se lhe haver levantado com aquella cidade e outros povos[3]. E, para que lhe não possa fugir, tem Muley Abdala mandado

---

1. V. *supra*, p. 519, nota 2.
2. Moulay Mohammed *Zeghouda*. Sur ce prince, V. *supra*, p. 537, nota 2.
3. Moulay Mohammed *Zeghouda* venait d'être complètement battu par les Beni Gourfet (V. *1re Série*, Espagne, à la date du 26 juillet 1622), mais la nouvelle de cet évènement n'était pas parvenue à

por outro caminho muita gente de pe e de cavallo sobre Alcacere.

E que, em caso que Muley Hamet peça a V. Mag^de seguro para se passar a Espanha (como se affirma) lhe pareceo lembrar a V. Mag^de que tem o darse-lhe por materia de estado, porque a quietação do reyno de Muley Abdala he de muyta importancia para aquellas fronteiras de V. Mag^de, com quem aquelle rey mostrou querer toda boa correspondencia, e tal a conservou com elle Dom Luis nas pazes que se offereceo em Tangere, de que deu conta a S. Mag^de que haja gloria. E, ficando em Berberia Muley Hamet, he contingente escapar a seu irmão. E, como os Mouros são tão amigos de novidades por qualquer causa leve, o tornarão a admittir e receber, para inquietar a Muley Abdala, o que não pode ser, se huma vez se vier para Espanha, quanto mais que pode ser tambem a sua mudança meo para a fazer de ley e tomar Deos esta occasião para instrumento de sua conversão.

Quando, no anno de 612, Muley Xeque, rey de Fez, pay de Muley Abdala e Muley Hamet, que agora contendem sobre o reyno, esteve alojado perto de Tangere no sitio em que o mattarão[1], havia ordenado el Rey, que haja gloria, que, se elle se viesse a amparar de alguma das fronteyras, fosse admittido com pouca gente, tendosse esta ordem em segredo, para que se não retirasse, se não obrigado da necessidade[2].

E, vendosse agora o que Dom Luis de Noronha escreve, pareceo a Dom Antonio Pereira[3] que V. Mag^de, por seu officio real e por sua grandeza, tem obrigação de favorecer aos que, oprimidos de seus enemigos, se vem valer do amparo de V. Mag^de, posto que estranhos e que o não hajão merecido. E por esta parte foy o costume das fronteyras, donde sempre forão abrigados os Mouros que accudirão a guarecerse nellas. Por lo que se deve ordenar aos capitães que, fazendo-o Muley Hamet, o recolhão com pouca gente e procedão com elle com a cautela e cuidado que comvem, avisando a V. Mag^de, para mandar o que for servido.

D. Luiz de Noronha, lorsqu'il écrivit au Roi la lettre soumise au Conseil de Portugal.

1. Moulay Mohammed ech-Cheikh fut assassiné le 21 août 1613, à Feddj el-Feras. EL-OUFRÂNI, p. 323; EL-KADIRI, Trad., t. I, p. 273.

2. Sur cette affaire, V. 1re Série, Espagne, aux dates des 14 mai et 15 juin 1612.

3. Antonio Pereira avait été gouverneur de Tanger. V. supra, p. 240 et note 1.

Mendo da Motta e Dom Francisco de Bragança lembrão a V. Mag.^de que, havendo Muley Abdala, que de presente possue a Fez, tido sempre boa correspondencia com as fronteiras, e importante ao bem dellas tello obrigado e satisfeito; deve V. Mag.^de mandar que se considere com particular attenção o que se fara com Muley Hamete, seu irmão, em quem passa tudo pello contrario, para que se não falte a amizade de Abdala, tendosse tambem respeto a que, se Hamet se recolhesse e passasse a Hespanha, se haveria de fazer com elle despeza de importancia, sem esperança de tirar delle frutto algum.

Ao duque de Vilhahermosa[1], presidente, parece que se deve dar ordem em segredo aos capitães das fronteiras para que, se, em alguma rota e caso repentino, Muley Hamet vir demandar aquellas praças e ampararse dellas, o recolhão com pouca gente, e trattando da segurança do lugar com o recato e vigia que a assistencia de tais vezinhos requere, avisem a V. Mag.^de, para mandar o que for servido; porem que se elle, por resolução de suas comodidades, e sem o obregar necessidade precisa, se quizer recolher, lhe respondão que não tem ordem de V. Mag.^de para o receber e que a pedirão.

Em Madrid, a 20 de Setembro de 1622.

(Quatre paraphes.)

British Museum. — Egerton Mss., 1131, f. 57. — Original.

1. D. Carlos de Borja, duc de Villahermosa.

CLVIII

MÉMOIRE D'ANTHONY SHERLEY[1]

(Extrait)

Dissensions qui se produisent, à la mort de Moulay Ahmed el-Mansour, entre ses trois fils Moulay ech-Cheikh, Moulay Abou Farès et Moulay Zidân. — Les agents de la France et des Pays-Bas s'emploient à rétablir la concorde entre ces princes. — Sherley, au contraire, pour servir les intérêts de l'Espagne, excite la discorde. — Avec l'aide du caïd Azzouz, il décide Moulay Abou Farès et Moulay Zidân à marcher contre Moulay ech-Cheikh. — Ce dernier se réfugie en Espagne, avec son conseiller Gianettino Mortara. — Sherley, qui les y avait précédés, avait soumis aux ministres un plan pour occuper Larache avec 200 hommes au plus. — Gianettino Mortara exagère l'importance de l'entreprise, dont l'exécution a coûté à l'Espagne des sommes considérables. — Néanmoins ce dernier en recueille l'honneur et le profit. — Sherley critique l'occupation qui a été faite d'El-Mamora. — Les pirates européens qui y avaient leur abri se sont réfugiés à Alger et ont appris aux Turcs à se servir des vaisseaux ronds. — Généralités sur la population du Maroc et sur les frontieras. — Inutilité de Mazagan et d'El-Mamora. — Importance de Ceuta et de Tanger. — Renseignements sur le commerce d'importation et d'exportation. — Les sucreries sont détruites. — Mogador et Santa-Cruz rendraient de grands services comme points d'appui pour la flotte des Indes.

Grenade, 2 novembre 1622.

Pesso polytico de todo el Mundo, por el conde D. Anttonio

---

[1]. Il y a peu à retenir de ce Mémoire, écrit rétrospectivement par Anthony Sherley (V. *supra*, p. 283), seize ans après son équipée au Maroc. On sait combien cet aventurier plein d'imagination avait peu le sens politique. Retiré en Espagne, sans moyens d'existence, cherchant à intéresser la Cour à des projets plus ou moins chimériques, il a rédigé un mémoire, dans lequel il s'attribue un rôle au Maroc qu'il n'a nullement joué. On n'a pas cru devoir relever ses forfanteries et les inexactitudes du récit; le lecteur les reconnaîtra facilement et en fera justice.

Xerley. Al excelentissimo señor conde-duque de Olivares[1], del Conssejo de Su Mag[d], su sumiller de corps y su cavallerizo mayor.

. . . .

BARBERIA.

La Barberia[2] siempre a sido mal vecino a estos reynos; y, dexados aparte los tiempos antiguos, conmença de haver podido serlo mas de lo ordinario en el reynado de Muley Hamet, el qual presto muy grandes fuerzas al Reyno con conbidar a el basta contrataciones de diversas naciones, de las quales todo el Reyno an menester. Y procuro de poblarlo con reducirlos a mas cibil vida, y con poner mas assiento en el govierno, y con la conquista que hizo de los reynos de Tanbotu y de Gagoa tan ricos en oro, y con aver sugetado a los moradores de la Zahara para tener el passo a los referidos reynos dissembaraçado y seguro. En fin, para rey moro era muy entendido, muy sagaz, grande hombre de govierno y gran rey. Duro muchos años en el reynado.

Pero, muerto, sin haver podido antes de la muerte componer las cosas de su subcession, los tres hijos que tubo, que eran Muley Xeque, Muley Bu Fares y Muley Zidam, cada uno, apoyado de sus parciales, se allo con el pedaço de reyno que tuvo en su govierno. Muley Bu Fares con Marruecos, Muley Xeque con Fez, y Muley Zidam con Tarudante y Sus.

Pero Zidam, entre todos los hermanos, era de mayor valor y tubo mexor derecho, por ser los otros dos hixos de concubina y Zidam hijo de legitima muger[3], aunque tuvo menores fuerzas para adquirir su derecho que los otros dos para defender y conservar lo que tenian ussurpado de el. Pero, ni el que tenia justicia, ni los otros que reynavan sin ella, se aquietaron, aspirando cada uno a todo el reyno. Con que binieron a rompimiento de armas; en el qual hubieron diversos acontecimientos, mudanzas y variaciones en los subcessos de las partes, hasta que todos, de puro cansados, abrieron practica de concierto y unidad por medios que se inter-

---

1. D. Gaspar de Guzman, comte d'Olivares et duc de San Lucar de Barrameda (1587-1645), premier ministre d'Espagne de 1621 à 1643.
2. *La Barberia.* Entendez le Maroc
3. V. *supra*, p. 331 et note 2.

pussieron. Y esto fue en el tiempo que yo estuve en Marruecos, embaxador del señor emperador Rudolfo.

Para concertarles, travaxaron mucho Monsieur de [1]......, embaxador del rey Enrique quarto de Francia, y Pedro Martinez[2], el agente de los Reveldes[3], y Juan Esquero[4], el principal de los mercaderes ingleses. Pero yo, que supe quanto convenia a estos reynos la desunion de aquel y quanto regalo tendria en calentar su lado a la lumbre atizada en el, usse todos los medios possibles para encenderla ; y, con hallar que el alcayde Azus, que era el todo del govierno de la parte de Muley Bu Fares, se inclinava a faborecer a Zidam, y como enemigo capital de Xeque, en razon de la muerte que dio a un hixo suyo, se desconformava en todas las propossiciones que se anteponian para qualquier concierto de su parte, concertado el negocio con el baxa Mustafa, que era el govierno de Zidam y estava de assiento en Marruecos para negociar en aquellos tratados y assistir en ellos, hallamos que convenia de concertar a Bu Fares con Zidam, y que Zidam, como general de Bu Fares, fuesse con sus proprias fuerzas juntas contra Muley Xeque. Negocio que, aunque en vos se dezia concierto, era el mayor desconcierto que se podia hazer ; en razon de que las discordias quedaron vivas y en pie, y la ynquietud natural y altiveza de Zidam no prometian menos. Y, para efectuar este negocio, me costo mis dineros, en el unto de los quales ablande al alcayde Azus, para que se abreviasse y se cerrasse el negocio.

Muley Xeque, espantado de esta junta de las armas de ambos a dos sus hermanos contra el, con ser muy cobarde de su natural, ressolvio de huyrse a Hespaña ; y hizo su trujeman para ello a un cierto Janetin Mortara[5], mercader ginoves, retirado de Marruecos a Fez para no acarrearse con gruesas deudas que tenia en Marruecos. Antes de esta ressolucion de Xeque, yo havia buelto de Berberia a

---

1. En blanc dans le manuscrit. Il faut rétablir Arnoult de Lisle. Sur ce personnage, V. *supra*, pp. 277, 295 et note 4.

2. Pieter Maertensz. Coy. V. *supra*, pp. 277 et 319 et note 1.

3. *Reveldes*, les Rebelles, nom sous lequel sont désignés les habitants des Provinces-Unies.

4. *Juan Esquero*, Juan Skerone, marchand ; il signa, le 7 juillet 1609, à Merrakech une attestation en faveur de P. Maertensz. Coy. V. *1re Série*, Pays-Bas, t. I, p. 348.

5. V. *supra*, p. 381 et note 1.

Hespaña[1] y propusse a los ministros de aquel tiempo la importancia y facilidad de la empressa[2], en la qual no se devia haver ocupado mas que 200 hombres; y no solo bastavan para ello, sino sobravan.

Pero, dada licenzia a Muley Xeque que viniesse a Hespaña y venido que fue, ensancho la opinion y precio de la mercaduria, de manera que el corredor que anduvo en el negocio, que era Janetin Mortara, subio el concierto[3] a 300 ℧ u 400 ℧ ducados en armas y dineros a Xeque, no incluyendo en el el entrego de la plaça, pero solo por su derecho, y 30 ℧ ducados de renta por dos vidas situados en el estado de Milan por su corretage; y esto en recompenssa de la hazienda que el havia perdido confiscada en Marruecos en razon de esse servicio, donde yo se que no tubo 4 ℧ ducados y muy escassos, y estos puestos en carega de Diego de Cosgaya[4], mercader hespañol nacido en Francia, para que no fuessen enbargados.

Y, como los designios de los que podian y valian[5] con Su Mag.d (que Dios tiene en gloria) eran de mantener el estado remendado, sin darlo ni a Su Mag.d ni a sus subcessores, y corromper enteramente el estado, y con tener menester para los discurssos que tubieron de los millones, para que el reyno no viesse que no eran menesterosos en tanta paz, aunque es verdad que en aquel tiempo se recelava y no poco de las armas del rey Henrique 4° de Francia y de sus movimientos, hizieron creyente al Rey, y el reyno como obedientissimo se dio por creyente, que esta empressa era muy grandiosa y que se hazia en ella mucha conquista, pero en verdad era mal comprada en mucho mas precio que no valia; y tubo demas un rabo muy largo, que era, sobre la compra del derecho de Muley Xeque para tomar el processo, por estar dispuestos los Moros con el ruydo, eran menester las armas de Su Mag.d para tomar la possession.

Excelentissimo Señor, buelvo muy alto; pero con la seguridad que tengo que, si cayere, con caer a los pies de V. Ex.ª,

---

1. Sherley arriva à Madrid en novembre 1606; Moulay ech-Cheikh s'embarqua pour l'Espagne le 4 mars 1609. V. supra, p. 410 et note 1.
2. La empressa, l'expédition sur Larache.
3. Sur ce traité, V. supra, p. 417, n. 5.
4. Diego de Cosgaya, marchand florentin, qui mourut à Morrakech en décembre 1607. V. 1ʳᵉ Série, Pays-Bas, t. I, pp. 298, 336 et 338.
5. Le duc de Lerme. V. supra, p. 245 et note 2.

escapare de molimiento, me atrevo. Y mas me atrevo, con saver quanto importa que V. Ex^a sepa las verdades y quan pocos ay que puedan o quieran dezirlas; y yo, que tengo el pellexo tan viexo y tan passado de heridas que no vale para remiendos de zapatos viejos, y no temo de perderlo, ni tengo ambicion mayor que de servir a Su Mag^d y a V. Exª. Y, en fin, yo pusse a Muley Xeque en desesperacion y abrir la empressa de Larache, y declare la facilidad y poca costa que podia tener. Pero, como mi propossicion fue estrecha y ajustada al cuerpo con verdad, parecio vestido de poco paño; y otro, con dar mas anchurosa medida, con la qual cupo algo para los que quissieron, tuvo la honrra y provecho del negocio.

Y mas adelante, para dar entender a Su Mag^d que su monarquia andava ensanchandose siempre, aunque realmente andava perdiendo en ella, y de ella se hizo aquella empressa de la Mamora[1], en todos sus puntos pestilencial a estos reynos y sin possibilidad por lo que es ser de yntereses, provecho o beneficio. De la qual an salido todos los malos que estos reynos tienen o pueden tener de Argel, y toda la Christiandad con ellos, pues que los cossarios que acudian a estos puertos son sin cuerpo en manera de gotas, mojavan a pocos y aquellos Ingleses, Franceses y Reveldes; y en alguna manera no eran muy contrarios del discursso de estado, o, a lo menos, de buen disconto, de los haver dexado exercitar en este puerto su oficio, y cerrados los oxos a la ocasion, pues que lo hazian a los que eran enemigos ciertos de estos reynos o tenian mal affecto a ellos, y en ninguna manera prejudicavan a los vassalos de estos reynos. Y el haverse recogido halli era para no estar sugetos a los de Argel y para poder exercitar su oficio con mas livertad y sin agravio de pension en este puerto hiermo, en el qual eran señores y vendian sus pressas a los Moros a bordo de sus vageles y tomavan sus defrescos, sin los passados lances que tenian con los Turcos en puertos poblados y havitados, como son Susa, Tunez y Argel. Pero, hechados que fueron de este puerto, fueron forçados de acudir a Argel, como hombres de oficio que no podian vivir sin el; adonde los Turcos, cevados con las ganacias que ellos trayan,

1. El-Mamora fut occupé le 7 août 1614. V. 1re Série, France, t. II, pp. 566-572.

se aficionaron a navigar en vageles redondos[1]; y, acompañandolos con Turcos, con la gente de un vagel armaron 20. Y, con esta sola arte y industria tan facil, an echo el cuerpo grande que tienen y an tenido cada dia.

Y este puerto es de barra, en ninguna manera provechoso para faborecer o para abrigar a los vageles de las armadas de Su Mag^d, los quales, como son mayores, pescan mas agua. Solo sirve para despeñadero de muchas almas; las quales, por no ser encarceladas en aquel matadero, huyen a los Moros y reniegan, y muchos mueren por las incomodidades que passan. Y se tomo y se conserva y se sustenta con mucho gasto de hombres, de dineros, de mantenimientos y de municiones, sin beneficio ninguno. Aunque aora es verdad que, con haverse armado el Turco como se ha armado, no se puede dexar, por poder ser de servicio harto importante para el abrigo de los vageles menores de los cossarios turquescos, los quales nunca huvieran venido, si este puerto no huviesse sido quitado a unos pocos de ladroncillos de poco o de ningun momento.

Pero con estos combites de duendes se satisfizo Su Mag^d (que Dios tiene en gloria), aunque el reyno arto murmuraria de ellos, por ser muy costosas apariencias y de ninguna substancia.

La Barberia esta poblada de 5 generaciones de gentes: de Araves, los quales se estiman por cavalleros y se señalan por parentela o cassa, obedecen su alcayde que es el principal de la misma casta; y de Ciudadanos, que son gente de trato y oficiales; y de los Barbaros, que [son] les montañeses; y de Andaluzes, que son la mayor parte de la milicia, aunque toda su milicia es ynhabil y inperfecta; y de Judios, que viven debaxo de su seque, pero muy avassallados.

Son los de Barberia muy perberssamente opuestos a estos reynos, por ser Moros fronteros y ofendidos de las fuerzas que Su Mag^d tiene en su costa y muy sospechosos de ellas. Algunas de las quales son de ningun servicio, como es Mazagante y esta Mamora; Zeuta y Tanger importan, por caer en los Estrechos, como lo hacen Oran, Melilla y Peñon y Mazalquivir, los quales, en el repartimiento

---

1. Sur cette transformation des navires pirates et sur ses conséquences, V. 1re Série, Pays-Bas, t. V, Introduction, p. XIII et notes 5 et 6.

que aora tienen los reyes de Barberia, non caen en ellos, pero, si se toma a Tremesen por dependiente del reyno de Fez, como era antes de los Jarifes, son del distrito y termino de la Barberia.

Y ojala que Su Mag.d huviesse gastado no mas de diez mill ducados o a lo mas andar la 6ª parte de lo que gasto en la Mamora, por haversse enseñoreado de la isla de Magador y del puerto de Santa Cruz en Tarudante, grandes puertos ambos a dos, de consideracion y aprovechamiento, y con los quales Su Mag.d se hazia absoluto señor de la Barberia, con tener en su poder las llaves de todas sus contrataciones. Las quales tienen muy grandes con Ingleses, Reveldes y Franceses, los quales sirven de paños, cariseas[1], perpetuanes[2], serguetas[3], cambrayes[4], creas[5], ruanes[6], sedas labradas, municiones, armas y muchos jeneros de mercaderias y cosas necessarias. Y, en trueque de ellas, sacavan grandissima cantidad de azucares, en tiempo que los havia, añil, cera, cordobanes[7] y plumas de avestruz, datiles y oro en grandissima cantidad, en especie y en polvo. Y algunos Portugueses, en trueque de las mismas mercaderias, que benian por mayor de sus correspondientes en Sevilla y Cadiz, les servian con aljofar[8] mayor y menor, bonetes colorados de lana[9], algunos damascos de color, de Granada y de Toledo, rubies y esmeraldas. Pero, con estas guerras, ya el trato es mas moderado y por lo menos del todo acavado, por ser los ingenios de azucar todos consumidos, de manera que no ay azucar en estas partes del mundo, sino la que se haze en los reynos de Su Mag.d. Y lo digo a V. Ex.a por avisso y que aquellos dos puertos de Magador y de Santa Cruz serian de grandissima consideracion para

---

1. *Cariseas*, en français carsayes, carisels, créseaux, en anglais kersoys, étoffe de laine croisée à deux envers, qui se fabriquait en Angleterre, spécialement dans le comté de Kent.
2. *Perpetuanes* ou sempitornes, étoffe de laine croisée fabriquée en Angleterre, à Colchester et à Exeter, où elle était appelée « lasting ».
3. *Serguetas*, sarguetas, sergettes, étoffes de laine croisée, étroites, minces et légères.
4. *Cambrayes*, toiles de Cambrai.
5. *Creas*, crès, crées, toiles de lin fabriquées à Morlaix. Elles étaient très en faveur au Maroc avant le blocus continental, qui favorisa l'introduction des toiles de coton de provenance anglaise. On les appelle aussi bretagnes.
6. *Ruanes*, toiles de Rouen.
7. *Cordobanes*, des cordouans (maroquins).
8. *Aljofar*, el-djouher, la perle.
9. Sur le commerce des « bonetes colorados de lana » ou chachias et sur les pays d'Europe où cet article se fabriquait, V. *supra*, p. 91 et note 2.

la seguridad de las flotas de las Indias y para su refresco, conservacion en sus bueltas, si por casso fuessen echadas al mediodia con los nortes o mudassen de rumbo para huyr el cuerpo de los enemigos, si por casso los aguardassen en las Terceras[1]. Este reyno no tiene substancia natural suya en lo mas necessario y es desunido.

Y lo que suplico a V. Ex.ª es, pues que, devajo del seguro que me da esta confianza que tengo en V. Ex.ª, he tenido ossadia de descubrir muchos secretos de mucha calidad y consideracion, que este papel sea solo de V. Ex.ª y con V. Ex.ª. Cuya excelentissima perssona Dios guarde por muchissimos y felicissimos años, con el augmento que yo el verdadero y humilde servidor de V. Ex.ª y siempre desseare.

Granada, y Noviembre 2 de 1622 años.

Finis coronat opus.

British Museum. — Egerton Mss., *1824, ff. 77-82.* — *Original.*

1. *Las Terceras*, los Açores.

CLIX

CONSULTE DU CONSEIL DE PORTUGAL

Le gouverneur de Ceuta a rendu compte de la mort de Moulay Mohammed Zeghouda et a proposé d'appuyer Moulay Abdallah. — Il n'en devra rien faire et laissera libre cours aux compétitions.

7 novembre 1622.

En tête : Portugal, 7 de Noviembre 1622.

Con aviso de que el governador de Ceuta[1] escrive que es muerto Muley Hamet[2], y que combernia ayudar a Muley...[3], para que sea obedezido en Tetuan.

Al Consejo parece que no conviene sino dejarlos correr.

British Museum. — Egerton Mss., 323, f. 124. — Minute.

1. D. Luiz de Noronha.
2. Moulay Mohammed *Zeghouda*. V. *supra*, p. 537 et note 2. — La nouvelle de sa mort était fausse, mais en novembre 1622, il fut chassé d'El-Ksar par le caïd Ben Guedor, partisan de Moulay Abdallah. V. *1re Série*, Portugal, 16 novembre et 7 décembre 1622. Moulay Mohammed *Zeghouda* reparut en 1628 ; il occupa la kasba de Fez et fut mis à mort en juin de cette année. El-Oufrâni, p. 404 ; El-Kadiri, Trad., t. I, p. 336.
3. Lacune dans la minute. Il faut suppléer Moulay Abdallah. Ce prince mourut le 22 juin 1623. *Ibidem*, p. 324 et *1re Série*, Portugal, à la date du 26 juin 1623.

CLX.

CONSULTE DU CONSEIL DE PORTUGAL

Approbation de la trêve conclue par D. Jorge Mascarenhas avec les cheikhs des environs de Tanger.

19 novembre 1622.

En tête : Portugal, 19 de Noviembre 1622.

Sobre la tregua que D. Jorge Mascareñas, governador de Tanger, asento por un año con los Xeques vezinos de alli[1], se pidio parecer a los governadores[2] y al Consejo de Estado.

Y todos dizen que la tregua esta bien hecha y se le embien a D. Jorge 1 U 500 cruzados que pidio para repartir prestados entre los Moros labradores.

Al Consejo parece lo mismo, y advierte que no se le ha de embiar a D. Jorge otra vez, por no yntroducir el haver trigo de los Moros por comutacion de mercaderias.

Como parece al Consejo.

British Museum. — Egerton Ms., 323, f. 138. — Minute.

---

1. Un traité de paix pour une année avait été conclu à Larache, le 15 mai 1622, par ordre de D. Jorge Mascarenhas, avec Moulay Mohammed *Zeghouda*. V. *1re Série, Portugal*, à cette date. Le projet de traité, dont il est ici question, était négocié avec les cheikhs des Maures voisins de Tanger, ennemis du même Moulay Mohammed Zeghouda. D. Jorge Mascarenhas n'avait pas voulu le conclure avant d'y être autorisé par Philippe IV. V. *ibidem*, à la date du 26 juillet 1622. Le 17 décembre 1622, Philippe IV écrivit à D. Jorge Mascarenhas approuvant cette trêve ; elle ne paraît pas avoir été conclue, et, dès le 5 février 1623, les tribus attaquèrent Tanger. *Ibidem* et FERNANDO DE MENEZES, *Historia de Tangere*, pp. 135-136.

2. *Los governadores*, les gouverneurs du Portugal.

CLXI

LETTRE DE PHILIPPE IV A JUAN DE CIRIÇA[1]

Un ingénieur français, M. de Saint-Mandrier, au service de Moulay Zidân, se rend en Angleterre et dans les Pays-Bas. — Il emmène avec lui, à titre de présent, tous les captifs anglais et néerlandais. — Il a mission de conclure des conventions commerciales relatives aux usines à sucre, ainsi qu'au trafic du Soudan et de la Guinée. — Écrire au marquis de Mirabel et à D. Carlos Coloma de se renseigner à ce sujet.

Madrid, 1er mai 1623.

En Madrid, el 1° de Mayo 1623. — Juan de Ciriça.

Por aviso que se ha dado, se ha entendido que Monsieur de San Manrrique[2], ingeniero frances, que sirve a Muley Cidan, va a Ingalaterra y a Olanda, con un pressente de todos los cautivos ingleses y olandeses que ay en Berberia, y para hacer nuevo assiento de contratacion, no solo de los açucares, cuyos ingenios ya trabajan, sino de abrirla tambien en Gagoa, en el cabo de las Palmas, en Guinea, distante de las minas del oro veinte leguas. Sera bien se le escriva al marques de Miravel[3] y a D. Carlos Coloma[4], para que se informen si ha ydo a aquellas provincias, y esten con cuydado de apurar a que va y que genero de hombre es, y que avisen lo que huviere.

British Museum. — *Egerton Mss., 335, f. 372.* — *Copie.*

1. Secrétaire d'État.
2. San Maurricque, Saint-Mandrier. V. supra, p. 505 et note 3.
3. Le marquis de Mirabel, ambassadeur d'Espagne en France.
4. D. Carlos Coloma, marquis d'Espinar (1573-1637), ambassadeur d'Espagne en Angleterre.

CLXII

LETTRE DU CONSEIL DE PORTUGAL A PHILIPPE IV

Le gouverneur de Mazagan, Bras Tellez de Meneses, a fait deux sorties victorieuses contre les Maures, le 30 mars et le 6 avril 1623. — Ceux-ci l'ont attaqué, le 29 avril, en rase campagne, comme il était occupé à fourrager. — Bras Tellez s'est replié sur les ouvrages avancés de la place, dont sa femme avait fait fermer les portes. — Les Maures ont été repoussés avec de grosses pertes; les Portugais n'ont eu qu'un seul mort. — Bras Tellez demande des armes, des munitions et des vivres. — L'affaire a été remise au Conseil de la Guerre, qui est d'avis qu'on écrive aux gouverneurs de Portugal de satisfaire à cette demande, les frais de ce ravitaillement devant être supportés par le Portugal.

3 juin et 4 juillet 1623.

En tête: Portugal, 3 de Junio 1623.

Señor,

Bras Tellez de Meneses, governador de Mazagan[1], avisa que, aviendo tenido, el domingo de Lazaro[2] y el de Ramos[3], dos vitorias de Moros, apellidaron mucha gente, y, en 29 de Abril, le vinieron a sitiar mas de 10 ℧ Moros, que, por no tener aviso, los cogio en el campo, cogiendo yerba, que se recogieron en buena ordenança al primer rebelin, de donde pelearon y ayudo la artilleria de la fortaleza; que su muger, viendo el peligro, cerro las puertas de la dicha fortaleza, para que no se perdiesse, y hizo sacar el Santisimo Sacramento, con que los Moros se retiraron con mucha perdida de gente, y entre ella dos alcaydes; que fue cosa muy a proposito, no

---

1. Il fut gouverneur de 1619 à 1624.
2. Le cinquième dimanche de Carême, soit le 2 avril 1623.
3. Le 9 avril 1623.

aviendo mas de 400 soldados, y juzgar-se-ya los Moros por hombres bien armados con lo que Olandeses[1] les han enseñado; que, de nuestra parte, solo murio uno, y no hubo ningun herido; que, en esa ocasion, rebentaron dos pieças de artilleria grandes, y desencabalgaron quatro, y rebentaron tanbien ciento y tantos mosquetes, y se quebraron muchas lanzas. Pide se le provean armas, municiones y bastimentos, de que se halla falto y con miedo de que los Moros se querian vengar[2].

El Consejo dize que se ha acordado a los Governadores el socorro desta plaça y las demas de Berberia. A Thomas de Ibio Calderon se ha escrito tambien para que anda, y que en Lisboa se le satisfara. Y propone el Consejo a V. Mag.d mande escrivir al duque de Medina Sidonia que haga luego embiar a Mazagan la mayor cantidad de armas, municiones y bastimentos que fuere posible, y la gente que huvieren menester, y que las letras de lo que esto costare se pagaran puntualmente en Lisboa[3].

4 de Julio.
Remitiose al Consejo de Guera y dize que se puede responder a los gobernadores de Portugal que de alla tengan cuydado de proveer esta plaça, porque de aca no se puede, y, quando mucho, le daran armas y pagando luego el precio dellas, y que, entregando las dos pieças que dizen han rebentado, se fundiran para hazer otros dos; y quanto a bastimentos, que ni el duque de Medina ni Thomas de Ibio los tienen, y que, embiando el dinero, se podrian recojer.

British Museum. — *Egerton Mss., 1131, f. 157.* — *Original.*

1. V. 1re Série, Pays-Bas, t. III, pp. 201, 240 et note 1, 415 et note 1 et 412.
2. En marge, de la main de Philippe IV : « Respondase a los Governadores que me da muchissimo cuydado esta plaza, y no serme posible probearla luego de aca, y que assi les encargo mucho procuren todos los medios que huviere para socorrerla, assi de bastimentos como de todo lo demas, por no tenerlos el duque de Medina Sidonia ni Tomas de Ibio ; y que, entregando las piezas rebentadas, se fundiran otras ; y en las armas se hara lo que se pide. »
3. En marge de la main de Philippe IV : « Hazer la respuesta de esta consulta. »

CLXIII

PÉTITION DE SAMUEL CADE[1]

Venu en Angleterre afin d'acheter des marchandises pour le compte du marabout Sidi Ali, il a passé en 1621 un contrat avec John Ball, marchand de Londres. — Celui-ci lui refuse la rémunération promise. — Samuel Cade demande justice.

24 juillet [n. st. 3 août] 1623.

To the right honourable the Lords and others of his Majesties most honourable Privy Counsill.

The humble peticion of Samuel Cade of London, gentleman.

Sheweth : that your poore suppliant, having heertofore lived in the courte of a certaine prince of Barbary called Sidey Alley[2], where never any Christian lived before, did there obtaine the love of the said Prince and people, so farre as that they became suitors to your suppliant to come for England and retourne thether againe with a shipp laden with such goods as they then gave directions for, in leiw whereof, your suppliant was to have Barbary gould and other commodities to his content. Whereupon your suppliant came for England accordingly, and, being heere in London, one Mr John Ball, marchant of this cittie, fell in with your suppliant and promised a roiall content if he would undertake the same. And thereupon, in August 1621, did sett fourth a shipp for the said place, furnished with such commodities, as by the said Prince was formerly requested, ymploying your suppliant as marchant therein ; who, accordingly, brought the said shipp to the said place and went on shoare and rode to the courte and brought downe the

---

1. Le 1er [n. st. 11] juin 1610, ce personnage était en prison comme pirate et cité à Southwark pour avoir pris la « Suzan » de Bristol et pillé sa cargaison de sucre dans la rade de Safi (*Br. Mus., Lansdowne Mss.*, 145, f. 52 v°).

2. Sidi Ali ben Moussa, marabout d'Iligh. V. 1re Série, France, t. III, p. 573 et note 3.

Prince with divers marchants of Moores and Jewes to the number of 500, who in a very short space did joyfully truck with us to the value of 5 000 lb. worthe of commodities, for gold and amber greece. And would so have continewed, had not the master of the shipp dealt injuriously with them.

Now, so it may please your Lordships, your suppliant having beene there and made a good voiage for the said Mr Ball, though to the greate charge of your poor suppliant, amounting to the some of 78 lb. 17 s., 6 d., partly in riding to and from the Princes court, as also by taking up of divers commodities from the company of the shipp and giving them as presents to the Prince and people, which commodities your suppliant hath paid out of his owne purse, amounting to a valluable some, and having been almost drowned by being cast away in adventuring only for the good of the voiage, yet notwithstanding hath the said Mr Ball not given any satisfaction to your poore suppliant; and, for what cause your suppliant knoweth not, doth still refuse so to doe, contrary to his contracte and promise. All which is true, as the cape marchant of the said shipp and others can justify.

In tender commiseracion whereof, and for that your suppliant is damnified by the said voiage to the vallue of 500 lb., beside the chargs by him disbursed, as may plainly appeare unto your good Lordships, that your Honours would bee pleased to take the same into your honourable deliberacion and commannd the said Ball to shewe cause before your Honours, or any others whome your Lordships shall please to appointe, why hee should not satisfy your poore suppliant according to his contract and promise.

For which as by duty bound.

Alia manu : The Lord President, the Lord Brooke, Mr Controler, the Master of the Roles, or any 3 of them, are desyred to call this party Ball and the petitioner before them, and to make send end betwixt the parties or to certyfye there opinion to there Lordships.

24 july 1623.

Signé : B. Mandeville.

Public Record Office. — *State Papers, Domestic, James I, vol. CXLIX,* n° 32. — *Original.*

CLXIV

LETTRE DE THOMAS CEELY AU CONSEIL PRIVE

La présence de pirates salétins sur les côtes anglaises est attestée par deux témoins, dont Thomas Ceely envoie les dépositions au Conseil. — Une lettre écrite par un captif anglais de Salé annonce que 30 navires pirates se préparent à faire voile vers l'Angleterre.

Plymouth, 18 [n. st. 28] avril 1625.

Adresse : To the right honorable Lordes of his Maties most honorable Privie Councell. Hast, hast, post hast. — Plymouth, the eightenth of Aprill, eight in the evening. — Thomas Ceely, Maior.

Au dos, alia manu : For his Maties service. — 18 Aprill 1625. — From the Mayor of Plymouth.

Right Honorable,

My dutie in all humblenes remembred, — May itt please your Honours to bee advertised that this day I hard of certen Turkes, Moores and Dutchmen of Sally in Barbary[1], which lye on our coastes spoyling dyvers such as they are able to master, as by the examinacion of one William Knight (which your Honours shall heere inclosed receive) may appeare ; whose reporte I am induced the rather to beleeve, because two fisher-boates, mencioned in his examinacion, were verie lately found flotinge on the seas, havinge neither man nor any tackle in them, as also because, by the examinacion of one William Draper, of Plymouth, some parte of the said

1 Sur l'origine de la piraterie à Salé, V. Pays-Bas, t. IV, pp. VII-XVIII.

Knights examinacion is confirmed (which examinacion is alsoe heere inclosed sent your Honours).

And may your Honours bee pleased farther to bee advertised that I am crediblie informed that one Pethericke Honicombe, an English captive in Sally, hath lately writen a lettere, dated the fift of March last, to his wife, dwellinge in Stonehouse neere Plymouth, wherein, among other thinges, hee advises her that there were thirtie saile of shipps att Sally now preparinge to come for the coastes of Englande in the begynninge of the summer, and, if there were not speedy course taken to prevent itt, they would doe much mischeife. The lettere ittselfe I cannot by any meanes gett, but have received theise instructions from an honest understanding neighbour, which read the lettere. Heereof I thought itt my dutie to informe your Honours.

And soe I rest

Your Honours in all dutie bounden,

Signé : Thomas Ceely, Maior.

Plymouth, the xviiith of Aprill 1625.

Déposition de William Knight

Il a rencontré en mer un marin qui a été capturé par des Salétins. — Les pirates, 9 Hollandais, 6 Turcs et 3 Maures, à bord d'un navire d'une trentaine de tonneaux, ont pris un navire de Salcombe en route pour Terre-Neuve et deux bateaux de pêche de Looe. — Un navire, probablement un autre pirate, croise devant Looe. — Un des pêcheurs de Looe capturés a réussi à s'échapper. — Onze hommes et des marchandises valant 100 livres ont été pris sur le navire de Salcombe.

Plymouth, 18 [n. st. 28] avril 1625.

The examinacion of William Knight, of St. Butockes[1], taken before Thomas Ceely, marchant, Maior of the borroughe of Plymouth, the xviiith day of Aprell, anno Domini 1625.

1. St *Butockes,* Saint-Budeaux, à 6 km. N.-O. de Plymouth.

This examinate saith that, the fifteenth day of this instant moneth of Aprell, hee this examinate, cominge out of the river of Yalme[1] neere Plymouth, in a barge loaden with sande, he mett with a fisher-boate of Yalme, which then came from a shipp of Salcum[2] bounde for Newfoundlande, which was, as they of the said boate told hym, taken the twelveth of this instant Aprell by a shipp of Sally of thirtie tunes or thereabouts, wherein were nyne Dutchmen, six Turkes and three Moores, and one of them a blacke Moore[3]. And also said that there was one other pinke in company with the said shipp of Sally, that bore towardes Looe in Cornewall, which he thought was in consorte with the said shipp of Sally.

And this examinate farther saith that one which was in the said fisher-boate, whose name he remembreth not, told this examinate that hee, being in a boate of Looe aforesaid, in company with one other boate a fishing, were both taken the xi[th] of this moneth, neere Eddystone, in sight of the harbour of Plymouth, by the said shipp of Sally. And they did take all the men out of the said two boates of Looe, being in number xii[ve], and cutt of the tackle of the said boates, and after left them fleetinge on the streame.

And this examinate alsoe saith that the said partie told hym hee escaped out of the said shipp of Sally, after hee was taken, in this manner, to weete : beinge bounde in the said shipp of Sally with the others which were taken with hym, a blacke Moore of the said barke of Sally unlosed his bandes, and, after he was unbounde, hee crept out through a portholl of the said shipp of Salcum, lyinge neere the said barke of Sally.

And lastly saith that the said partie which so hardly escaped from the said barke of Sally told this examinate that there were eleven persons taken out of the said shipp of Salcum, and soe much provision as was worth a c^{li}, and so cast of the said shipp. And the said examinate saith that hee tooke the said partie out of the said boat of Yalme into his barge, and landed hym att Crymmell Passage, neere Plymouth, the day of this his examinacion.

1. Estuaire et port à 10 km. S.-E. de Plymouth.
2. *Salcum*, Salcombe, port du comté de Devon, à 30 km. S.-E. de Plymouth.
3. Ce pirate était parti pour la Manche en compagnie de cinq autres navires de Salé. V. le récit de leur course dans le document suivant, p. 562.

Déposition de William Draper

Il a vu, dix-huit jours auparavant, à Flessingue, un navire en partance pour Salé, d'environ 35 tonneaux. — Il croit que c'est ce corsaire qui a fait les prises dans les eaux anglaises.

Plymouth, 18 [n. st. 28] avril 1625.

The examinacion of William Draper, of Plymouth, taken before Thomas Ceely, marchant, Mayor of the borroughe of Plymouth aforesaid, the xviii[th] day of Aprill 1625.

Hee saith that, eighteene dayes sithence, hee was at Flushinge, and there did see a barke of French built of 35 tonnes or thereaboutes, with nyne Turkes, and dyvers other Dutch, and one blacke Moore in her; and, as they of Flushing reported, they were bounde for Sally, hald out their barke and began theire voyage about xviii dayes sithence; but, what is become of her sithence, hee knoweth not, but verely beleeveth that this was the barke that robbed the shipp of Salcum and fisherboates of Looe [1].

Signé : William Draper.

Public Record Office. — *State Papers, Domestic, Charles I, vol. I,* n[os] *68, 68*[I] *et 68*[II]. — *Originaux.*

---

1. La déposition de William Draper était erronée : les bâtiments en question avaient été capturés par un pirate venu de Salé. V. le document suivant.

CLXV

DÉPOSITION DE WILLIAM COURT[1]

Des pirates salétins l'ont capturé, l'année précédente, avec quatre autres matelots anglais, à bord d'un navire d'Amsterdam. — Emmené à Salé, il a été embarqué sur un navire faisant partie d'un groupe de six pirates; il a assisté ainsi à la capture au large des côtes anglaises d'un navire anglais et de six barques françaises. — Le vaisseau sur lequel il se trouvait s'est emparé près des îles Scilly d'un terre-neuvier de Plymouth; l'équipage a été fait prisonnier, à l'exception de six hommes, auxquels a été ajouté le déposant, qui ont été laissés sur le terre-neuvier, lequel est arrivé à Saint-Ives.

Plymouth, 7 [n. st. 17] mai 1625.

Au dos, alia manu : The examinacion of William Court, of Plimouth, ship-wright, 7° Maii 1625. — Received 23" Maii.

The examinacion of William Court, of Plymouth, ship-wright, aged twentie-three yeares, taken before Thomas Ceely, merchant, Maior of Plymouth aforesaid, the vii[th] of May 1625.

The said examinate saith that, about a yeare sithence, he went from the porte of Plymouth, in a shipp of Amsterdam called the « Fortune »[2], of the burden of two hundred tuns, in a merchant voyage for Portugall, of which shipp one William Thomas was master; and that, within six dayes after theire departure from Plymouth, they were surprized by a Turkish pirate of Sally, and that the said pirate tooke out of the said shipp the « Fortune », this examinate and fower other Englishemen; and the rest of the company, being Flemminges, they did not meddle with, but suffred them

---

1. Cette déposition fut envoyée au Conseil Privé par Th. Ceely, le 7 [n. st. 17] mai 1625. *Dom., Charles I, vol. II,* n° 36.

2. Par suite d'un lapsus, on lit sur l'original « Thomas » à la place de « Fortune » et vice-versa quelques lignes plus bas.

to proceede with theire said shipp the « Fortune » in theire intended voiage, but carried away this examinate and the other fower Englishe to Sally, where this examinate ever sithence hath remained as a slave.

And farther saith that, about eight weekes sithence, hee came out of Sally in a Turkishe shipp of Sally, in company with five other Turkishe shipps of the same place, who did bend theire corrse for the coastes of England ; and by the way, to weete about a moneth sithence, one of the said six Turkishe shipps tooke a shipp of London of three score tuns or thereabouts, in the Norther Cape, and tooke out of her cleaven men and theire ordinánce, and after sunke the said shipp. And, about six dayes after, they did take six French barkes, a little of from Sylly, and six score men which were in the said barkes, all which men the said pirates tooke into their shipps, and chayned them, and left the barkes fleeting on the streame.

And farther saith that, about twelve dayes sithence, the Turkishe pirate wherein this examinate was did, a little of from Sylly, take a shipp of Plymouth of the burden of threescore tuns, bound for the Newfoundlande in a fishinge voyage, wherein one William Legg was master, and did take out of her the said master and seaventeen others of her choisest men, all which alsoe they chayned, leaving in the said shipp of Plymouth six of her worst men, and put this examinate alsoe therein, and soe cast of the said shipp of Plymouth, which, about five dayes sithence, came into St Ives, in Cornewall.

And this examinate verilie beleeveth that the said five other Turkishe shipps have don great spoile, sithence the taking of the said six French barkes, but what spoile they have don he certenlie knoweth not.

And lastly saith that one Cooper was captaine of the said Turkishe shipp wherein this examinate was, and fower other Englishe, and five Flemishe runnegadoes, besides thirtie Turkes and Moores, and that he hath heard the Englishe and Flemmishe runnegadoes often saie that they would fetch the Christians from the shore.

Signé : Tho. Ceely, Maior.

Public Record Office. — *State Papers, Domestic, Charles I, vol. II,* n° 36[1]. — *Original.*

CLXVI

LETTRE DE HENRY ATYE A WALTER ASTON

(EXTRAIT)

Deux avisos espagnols ont été pris par les pirates de Salé.

Madrid, 11 [n. st. 21] mai 1625.

Au dos, alia manu : May 11, 1625. — Mr Atie to Sir Walter Aston. *De la main de Sir Walter Aston :* My Secretarie's lettere.

My very good Lord,

May it please your Lordship, — In my last of the 16th of Aprill, I advised that, uppon the dolefull newes of our gracious King's decease[1], the Conde de Gondomar was commanded not to proceed in his journy for England till he had further order.

. . . .

I wrytt your Lordship that the aviso of Nueva España was taken by the Moores of Sally. Now ther is certaine newes lately come that the second aviso from thence is lykwise taken and sunke uppon the barre going in, which doth not a little trouble them here.

. . . .

Your Lordship's most bounden servant to be commanded,

Signé : Henry Atye.

Madrid, 11 May 1625, *stilo veteri*.

Public Record Office. — *State Papers, Foreign, Spain, vol. XXXIII.* — *Original.*

1. Jacques Ier était mort le 27 mars 1625.

CLXVII

LETTRE DE CHARLES Ier A MOULAY ZIDÂN

Il rappelle les lettres écrites par Jacques Ier et par le roi de France en faveur des nombreux captifs anglais et français détenus au Maroc. — Il désire continuer les anciennes relations d'amitié entre le Maroc et l'Angleterre et prie Moulay Zidân d'accorder créance à son envoyé John Harrison, qu'il a chargé d'une mission spéciale.

[Entre le 27 mars et le 1er juin 1625.][1]

Au dos, alia manu : Copie of the Kings letters to the King of Morocco.

Charles, by the grace of God, Kinge of Great Brittaine, France and Ireland, Defendor of the Faith, etc., to the high and mighty Prince Mulli Sidan, Emporor of Morocus, Kinge of Fesse and Susse, sendeth greetinge.

Wee are informed there bee many poore Christians made captives in your contry, both Engelishe and Frenche, in whose behalfe letters have bin writ formerly, both from the Kinge our father, of blessed memory, and our brother of France, with whome now wee have contracted a more nearer leaage of frendeshipp, both

---

1. La restitution de cette date est fondée sur les données suivantes : 1° la lettre est postérieure à la mort de Jacques Ier, qui eut lieu le 27 mars 1625 ; 2° elle a pour but d'accréditer auprès de Moulay Zidân John Harrison, déjà employé au Maroc « quatre fois différentes ». Or la cinquième mission de Harrison eut lieu en 1625-1626 ; il dut partir d'Angleterre vers le 1er juin et arriver à Tétouan le 13. La lettre qu'il écrivit de cette ville le 30 juillet et à laquelle est emprunté ce détail (V. Doc. CLXXI, p. 573) fait, d'ailleurs, allusion (p. 574) au présent document.

alike senceable of each others grevances¹. There hath bin alsoe in tymes past, as wee are informed, greate amyty and corespondacy betwene your father, Mully Hamet, and the late Queene Elizabeth, of famus memory ; which the Kinge our father, for his part, hath bin very desirous to continewe, as may appeare by sundary letters written to yow by this our servant, John Harrison, fower severall tymes² imployed. Which wee alsoe wishe may continewe for the good of the subjects of both our dominions, and other reasons hee can more at large informe yow³ ; wherein we desire yow to give him creditt, as one in whome wee repose a very speatiall trust, as wee for our parts shall bee ready to make good that former frendeshipp punctually, as farther occation shalbe offered.

And soe wee comend yow to Gods blessed protection, etc.

Public Record Office. — *State Papers, Foreign, Royal Letters, vol. II, n° 73.* — *Copie.*

1. Charles Ier épousa Henriette de France à Paris, le 11 mai 1625.
2. Sur les voyages antérieurs de John Harrison au Maroc, V. *supra*, pp. 441-443.
3. Harrison devait proposer au Chérif de coopérer avec l'Angleterre à l'entreprise contre l'Espagne qui aboutit à la tentative sur Cadix. V. *supra*, p. 444.

CLXVIII

LETTRE DE JOHN HARRISON AUX MAURES

Il demande aux Maures de rendre la liberté aux captifs tant anglais que protestants ou juifs. — Ils pourraient être employés dans les guerres contre l'Espagne.

Tétouan, 27 juin [n. st. 7 juillet] 1625.

En tête : A generall letter to the Moores[1].

In the name of God[2].

Honorable Signiors,

Having bin foure severall tymes imployed from the King of Great Britagne, my maister, who is with God, into these partes, in the behalfe of his subjectes made captives here, and other occasions ; and now againe from the King, my maister, who now raigneth (whom God preserve !), concerning those occasions and other businesses of importance, as by his letters[3] may appeare, who is very willing to renew the former freindship begun and continued in the daies of his predecessors of famous memorie ; I thought it my dutie both out of the love I bear to my owne native countrie, and lykewise this your countrie, where I have bin so often imployed, to publish to all to whom his Maties letters cannot be communicated, nor myselfe torne in person by reason of the troublesomnese of

---

1. Sur les conditions dans lesquelles fut écrite cette lettre, V. *infra*, pp. 578-579.
2. On lit en marge le mot « Bismilla » qui est la traduction arabe de cette invocation.
3. V. le document précédent.

the country, this his princely intendment and disposition, the rather in respect of the present tymes and occasions, for the benefite and behoofe of both nations. Wishing it may accordingly take effect, and that Englishmen may no more be made captives as enemies, contrarie to those ancient priviledges in tymes past, but be released and set free with other Christians lykewise of the Religion[1], to serve in the warres against the enemies[2] of both nations, yea of all nations, and all lykewise enemies to them (lyke Ismael, Genesis 16, 12 : « his hand against everie man, and everie man's hand against him »); even as in England, the Low Countries (the States I meane) and all other partes who professe the Reformed Religion and not Romane, both Moores, Turkes, Jewes and all others are free and none captives.

And the lyke favour do I also desire, on God's behalfe, of the Kinge and the other governours of the Moores, yea, of the Kings and governours of all nations, for the Jews, God's auntient people, for the lyke reasons to them directed ; which I wish also and pray to God, in whose handes are the heartes of Kings, may take effect to His glorie and the finall confusion of Babylon, that is to say Rome and all her adherentes. Amen.

Your servant in one God omnipotent,

Signé : John Harrison.

At Tituan, 27 of June 1625.

Public Record Office. — State Papers, Foreign, Barbary States, vol. XII. — Traduction[3].

1. *The Religion*, le Protestantisme.
2. *The enemies*, les Espagnols, comparés plus loin à Ismaël.
3. Le document n'est pas un original, mais la traduction d'un original écrit en espagnol. V. *infra*, p. 578.

CLXIX

DÉPOSITION DE DAVID COCKBURNE

Pirateries des Salétins.

Plymouth, 5 [n. st. 15] juillet 1625.

Au dos : Cockebornes examinacion.

The examinacion of David Cockburne, of Leeth, in the kingdome of Scotland, marryner and master of the « Hopewell », of Leeth[1], taken before James Bagge, Esquire, Vice Admyrall of the South of Cornewall, the 5th of July 1625.

The examinate sayeth that, about the first of June, he came out of the ryver of Burdiox, and was then taken by Mounsiour Sabesa[2], and by him was kept twenty daies, untill he had paid him sixtie five pounds in money, beinge after the rate of twenty shillings for each ton of wyne he had abord.

Soe beinge freed from Sabesa, houldinge his corse for England, the 27th of June, 6 leagues to the eastward of the Start upon the coast of Devon, he was, with twelve men more, taken by a Turkish man of warr of Salley, of the burthen of 250 tons, which had in him one hundred Turkes and Moores, and for pylate one Arthur Drake of Plymouth, that lyves amongest the Turkes a freeman.

And further sayeth that, before he was taken, the said Turkes had taken a barke of Lyme, with certaine packes of cloth and eight men ; the men were tooke with the packes into there shipp,

---

1. Leith, ville près d'Edimbourg.
2. *Sabesa.* Benjamin de Rohan, seigneur de Soubise (1583-1642). Il commanda la flottille protestante, pendant les guerres de religion, de 1621 à 1628. Il se retira en Angleterre, où il mourut.

and suncke the barke. And also that, offe of the Start, they tooke three English fisher-boates, out of which they tooke twenty-two men and boyes, and suncke there boates. And further sayeth that they tooke a Briton, and from out of that shipp tooke sixe men and the goods, and suncke the shipp.

And lastlye, upon the last of June, they took a Norman returninge from the Banke, out of which they tooke fifteene men, and sent that Normans shipp to Salley, with the master of the Lyme barke, two English more and twelve Turkes. And likewise they sent this examinates shipp the « Hopewell », with three of his companye, for Salley, under the command of twelve Turkes more.

And further sayeth that, upon the second of Julye, at night, the Turke, offe of the Rame Head, nere Plymouth, gave chace unto three shipps, which comminge near, he found to be States men of warr, who hayled the Turkes; who refusinge to strike, they fell into fight, and, after sixe howers fight, was taken by the Duch, who tooke out all the English, Scotts and French, to the number of eightie-fyve; of which nomber there were some of the English that were formerlye taken by the Salley men of warr in the « Sampson » of Plymouth, in which was lost forty-fower men, and in the « Globe » of Plymouth, in which was lost twenty-two men, some two monethes sithence; insomuch as this examinate was informed that in Salley there are now six hundred English slaves.

The Duch captaines have taken out the Christians, lefte the Turkes in there shipp, about the Lizard, takinge nothinge from them. And this examinate, with other of the 85 Christians, upon the 4th of this July, was landed at Plymouth by the said Captaine Cornelius Loncke of Flushinge.

In witnes of truth he hath here unto sett his hand.

Public Record Office. — State Papers, Domestic, Charles I, vol. IV, n° 9. — Copie.

CLXX

LETTRE DE JOHN HARRISON A MOULAY ZIDÂN

Il regrette l'insuccès des missions dont l'avait chargé le feu roi auprès de Moulay Zidân. — Charles Ier *lui en a confié une nouvelle. — Il voulait gagner Salé par terre et de là Safi par mer, pour se rendre auprès de Moulay Zidân, mais le mokaddem de Tétouan lui a représenté les dangers du voyage par terre. — Dans le cas où quelques Anglais envoyés de la flotte à sa recherche viendraient à Safi ou à Salé, Harrison prie le Chérif d'écrire aux caïds de les accueillir et de conférer avec eux. — Le moment est venu pour Moulay Zidân de donner suite à sa promesse de se joindre à l'Angleterre contre l'Espagne.*

[Tétouan, entre le 13 juin et le 30 juillet 1625[1]].

Au dos, alia manu: Copie of the letteres of John Harrison to the King of Morocco. — No date. Tempore Caroli I.

To omitte all former disgustos, sorry my former imployements[2] and travells tendinge to peace and unity betwixt your Mag^{ti} and the Kinge my master, a prince of peace, who is now with God, hath taken so littell effect heatherto, and that occasion hath ben offered wherein I have any way offended your Mag^{ti}, as proceedinge cheefly out of patience, havinge lyen soe longe a shipp aboard, att that tyme, in the roade of Saphia, a whole yeare tossed upp and downe, without any order att all from your Mag^{ti} or ansers to the Kinge my master his letteres: which I tooke for a great affront to soe great prince from whome I came[3].

I am now come againe with letteres from the Kinge[4] my master

---

1. Cette date est restituée d'après les données suivantes : la lettre est écrite de Tétouan, comme il apparaît par le texte ; elle est postérieure au 13 juin, date de l'arrivée de Harrison dans cette ville et antérieure au 30 juillet, date où il en annonce l'envoi. V. *infra*, pp. 574 et 581-582.

2. V. *supra*, pp. 441-443.

3. Pendant son quatrième voyage au Maroc (1616-1618), Harrison resta seize mois devant Safi, sans recevoir aucune réponse de Moulay Zidân, V. *supra*, p. 443.

4. V. la lettre de Charles Ier à Moulay Zidân, *supra*, Doc. CLXVII, p. 565.

that now raingeth, Kinge Charles, who, upon my information, willenge to renewe the former frendeshipp begun betweene both your predesesors, hath put me in trust with a busines of importance to move to your Mag^ti, as may apeare by his letteres. But landinge here att Tittuan, in a shipp bounde for the Straights, and thinking from hence to have gone for Sally, and from thence by sea to Saphia, the Mocadene tould mee the wayes were soe dangerous, that itt was imposable for me to travelle by land, neather woulde they suffer mee, saiinge I was nowe under there horma[1], and, yf I shoulde miscary, cominge from so great a prince, an imputation might lye upon them.

And therefore I thought itt my duty to advertise your Mag^ti that, if perhaps in the meanetyme any of the fleet[2] touch att Saphia or Sally to inquire of mee, itt may please your Mag^ti to write to your alcayds there to confer with them, who, itt may bee, have the same comision I have from the Kinge my master or his Generall[3], in case I shoulde miscary, who is wise to forecast all such events.

Howsoever that much in generall, I must nedes intimate unto your Mag^ti beforehand, and thereby your Mag^ti may conceave more, that once[4], when I was with yow, as itt may please your Mag^ti to remember, yow intreated mee that, if there were any lykelyhood of wars, to advertise your Mag^ti, and yow woulde give your assistance; now is the tyme or neaver, both for the Engelishe and Moores, to right themselves against theire enimies. I say noe more.

And soe, expectinge to know your Mag^ties further pleasure, cravinge pardon for this my rude writinge, or any other errour, I comend your Mag^ti to Gods holy protection, high and mighty Prince.

Your Mag^ties humble servant,

Signé : Jn. Harison.

Public Record Office. — *State Papers, Foreign, Royal Letters, vol. II, n° 72.* — *Copie.*

1. *Horma*, protection, sauvegarde.
2. Quelque officier de la flotte britannique, qu'on attendait dans le Détroit. V. *supra*, p. 444 et note 8.
3. Le général, c'est-à-dire le commandant en chef de la flotte. V. la note précédente, et *infra*, p. 574 et note 3.
4. Lors du deuxième voyage de John Harrison en 1614-1615, V. *supra*, p. 442. Cf. la lettre de Moulay Zidân à Jacques Ier, 23 novembre-2 décembre 1614, p. 483 et note 1.

CLXXI

LETTRE DE JOHN HARRISON
AU COMMANDANT DE LA FLOTTE BRITANNIQUE[1]

Arrivée de Harrison à Tétouan. — Mort récente de l'ancien mokaddem et gouvernement collectif de ses quatre fils. — Ils reçoivent Harrison en audience secrète. — Joie causée à Tétouan par le bruit des préparatifs de l'Angleterre contre l'Espagne. — Les mokaddem déclarent que l'état anarchique du pays ne permet pas à Harrison de se rendre par terre auprès de Moulay Zidân. — Ils revendiquent l'indépendance absolue de leur État. — Royauté purement titulaire des souverains actuels au Maroc ; cohésion des Moriscos. — Les mokaddem protestent de leur dévouement au roi d'Angleterre et lui offrent leur aide contre l'Espagne. — Ils conviennent avec Harrison du langage à tenir en public pour garder secret l'objet de sa mission. — Vains efforts d'un Portugais pour le découvrir. — Harrison constate dans ses entretiens avec les Moriscos leur goût pour le protestantisme et leur haine de l'Espagne. — Il a rédigé trois lettres de propagande, aux Maures, aux Juifs et aux Espagnols. — Il reste à Tétouan, pour y attendre les ordres du commandant de la flotte britannique. — Avantages qu'offrirait la prise de Ceuta pour le commerce et la propagation de la religion protestante. — Ces avantages seraient accrus par la prise de Gibraltar. — Services que rendrait également la possession d'El-Mamora. — Les esclaves anglais à Salé. — Politique conseillée par Harrison au Maroc : bonnes relations avec les villes commerçantes, entretien des discordes intérieures, conquête des places espagnoles. — Cédant aux représentations des mokaddem, Harrison a renoncé à se rendre par terre auprès de Moulay Zidân. — Il a écrit à ce prince.

Tétouan, 20 [n. st. 30] juillet 1625.

Au dos, alia manu : Mʳ John Harrison.

---

1. Au moment où il écrivait la présente lettre, John Harrison ignorait le nom du commandant de la flotte, ainsi qu'il le dit lui-même. V. *infra*, p. 574 et note 3.

30 JUILLET 1625

En marge[1] : Jer[emias] 51, 6 ; Rev[elation] 18, 4 ; Rev[elation] 17, 17.

Right Honorable,

I was commanded by Mr Secretarie Morton[2] that, soe soone as I did heare of the fleetes arrivall on this coast, I should dispatch my letters away with all speed. Not knowinge, when I came out of England, who was to come chieffe commander in this service, and therefore must entreat pardon if I erre in matter of stile or such other curcumstances[3]. But to come to matter of substance, as touchinge my present imployment from his Ma[tie], whereof I am to give account, it pleased God to send us so faire and prosperous a wind from England, that in nyne daies wee were almost at the Straits mouth, but there met with a levant for a few daies[4].

The third of June arrived here, in this road of Tittuan. The same night, I sent ashore and writ to the Mocadens of my arrivall with his Ma[ties] letters. The next morning hee sent mee a letter of safe conduct for my coming ashore, where I understood that the old Moccaden[5] was lately dead, who was livinge when I was here, the other time[6], and writ leters by me to Muley Sidan, willinge mee to certify him that hee acknowledged no other King but him (as I have his letter yet to shew[7]). But now his sonnes, foure in number, equallie governe, and absolutely. Three of them weere sallied out, both with

---

1. Ces références sont comme l'épigraphe d'une lettre dans laquelle Harrison fait de nombreuses citations bibliques.

2. Sir Albertus Morton, né vers 1584, secrétaire d'État en 1625, mort en novembre de la même année.

3. Il résulte de ce passage que la présente lettre est écrite au commandant de la flotte britannique, dont John Harrison ignore le nom. A la date du 13 novembre n. st., il écrit à Buckingham qu'il vient d'apprendre que c'est lui qui commande la flotte et s'excuse de l'avoir ignoré. V. *infra*, p. 590 et note 1. Le commandement, en effet, avait d'abord été destiné au duc de Buckingham, mais il fut attribué à Lord Edward Cecil, vicomte de Wimbledon. La flotte, du reste, n'arriva devant Cadix que le 1er novembre n. st. 1625. V. *supra*, p. 444 et note 8.

4. Sur le cinquième voyage de John Harrison au Maroc (1625-1626), V. *supra*, pp. 444-445.

5. Ahmed en-Neksis. Sur ce personnage, V. *supra*, p. 438 et note 1.

6. En 1618, à la fin de son quatrième voyage, Harrison avait relâché à Tétouan, comme il le dit plus loin.

7. Harrison, en quittant Tétouan en 1618, n'était pas revenu à Safi, et la lettre du mokaddem Ahmed en-Neksis à Moulay Zidân était encore entre ses mains.

horse and foote (as they usually doe), in service against the Spaniardes of Ceauta and Tanger, one alwaies remayninge to keepe the towne; to whom I went and delivered his Maties letter[1], wherof hee was verie glad. After two or three daies, the rest retourned, and they all met togeather, and sent for mee, permittinge none to bee present, Moore nor Jew, but only their secretarie, on of the Moriscoes, their interpreter for the Spanish, by whom they all signified unto mee how welcome I was, comminge from so great a Prince, whose favour and frendship they did soe highly esteme. So did I lykewise understand that both Moores and Jewes did generally rejoyce, especiallie the Andaluzes or Moriscoes, banished out of Spaine, whereof in these partes and in Fez are verie manie, having some ynckling alreadie that his Matie had a great armada prepared; and my comminge made them presume it was for these partes and against Spaine.

I told them I had lykewise a letter from the King, my master, to Muley Sidan, concerninge the English captives and other occasiones, which I desired to goe to deliver with all speed, and the rather tooke my course this way, for that, when I was heer last, their father writt unto mee (which letter I showed them) that hee acknowledged Muley Sidan for Kinge, and no other.

They tould mee it was impossible for mee to travell by land, the countrye so troublesome, and the waies so dangerous, one Kinge in Fez, Mulay Abdela Meleck[2], verie young, an other King of Alcazar, Muley Mehamet[3], and Muley Sidan at Marroco; whom at this present Siddie Haya[4] and Sidda Allie[5], the great saintes of Suz, seeke to depose and to sett up an other King there; and that Muley Sidan hath of late sent for 1000 Moriscoes from Sallie, upon that occasion, which are accounted the best souldiers[6].

---

1. Harrison, qui avait pu constater l'indépendance dont jouissait Ahmed en-Neksis, s'était fait remettre pour ce dernier une lettre de Charles Ier. Cette lettre n'a pas été retrouvée.

2. Moulay Abd el-Malek, fils de Moulay Mohammed ech-Cheikh, succéda à son frère Moulay Abdallah et régna de 1623 à 1627. V. 1re Série, Angleterre, t. I, Pl. III, Tableau généalogique, note 33.

3. Moulay Mohammed *Zeghouda*. V. *ibid.*, note 32. Cf. *supra*, p. 537 et note 2; p. 540 et note 3; p. 551 et note 2.

4. Yahia ben Abdallah. V. *supra*, p. 476 et note 2; p. 510 et note 2.

5. Sidi Ali ben Moussa. Sur ce personnage, V. *supra*, p. 556 et note 2.

6. Les Salétins refusèrent de fournir ces

For themselves, they professed unto mee they acknowledged none of these Kings, nor no other Kinge but God; and that both their father and themselves had formerly donne service to Muley Sidan; but hee had soe ill requited them, and besides shewed himselfe so cruell and tyrannous in his government, that they had reason to stand upon their guard, and meant to maintayne themselves as a free state, as Venice and the Low Countryes, alledging that president in respect of the crueltie of the Spaniard; and so, it seemeth, doth the rest of the whole country: the name of a Kinge as odious amongst them as it was, in tymes past, among the Romanes. Neither have these Kings, any of them, at this present, as it seemeth, any great command, but only titular kings: Fez divided, the Andaluzes and the Moores at continuall bickeringes[1], for the Andaluzes hold fast togither in all places, and, as I said before, they are the best souldiours. Could they bee gathered togither under one head, they were able to do verie great service.

The Mocadens offered mee freelie, and of their owne accord, that if it pleased his Matie, or those who have commission under him, to attempt Ceauta, or any other place neare, they would aide him with above 10000, by land, the English only by sea and to land some small forces and ordinances for batterie: they should see that they would dye before their faces, to doe the King of England service against the Spaniard; and that both themselfes, the towne, which is verie populous, and the countrye all aboute, so far as they could commande, was at the King of Englands service, as his owne subjectes, desirous to put themselfes under his protection. Only they desired two thinges of me: that I would bee a meanes to helpe them to some powder, to doe his Matie service and defend themselfes against their enemies, and some peeces of ordinance they have heare, broken and unservicable, to bee carried for England

---

soldats; précédemment Moulay Zidân avait envoyé dans le Draâ 400 Moriscos de Salé. EL-OUFRÂNI, p. 439.

1. Sur les luttes qui éclatèrent alors à Fez entre les deux quartiers rivaux, celui des Lemthiens et celui des Andalous, V. EL-KADIRI, Trad., t. I, pp. 322, 324, 328 et 329. « Il y eut tant de troubles, écrit EL-OUFRÂNI, que l'atmosphère de Fez en fut obscurcie et que ses émanations parfumées devinrent fétides. La plus grande partie de la ville devint déserte, se couvrit de ruines, et les hostilités persistantes entre les habitants des deux Quartiers faillirent amener la destruction complète de la cité. » Traduction, p. 395.

to bee new cast and sent backe; offeringe all manner of supplies or necessaries this place can affoord, either for his Maties shipes, or otherwise, as was partly desired in his Maties letter.

And thereby also, havinge commission to move further matter, as I should see occasion, and seeinge their forwarding (with a caution beforehand of secrecie, which they promised most faithfully, and enjoyned their secretarie lykewise), I asked them, if there were such occasion as perhaps there might bee verie quicklie (but the particular designes I did not know myselfe), whether they would give assistance, as by land they had promised alreadie, that Moriscoes, or others, might bee transported into some other partes, where they should be verie well entreated.

They tould mee they could not force any to goe nor leave their towne unmanned and naked, for feare of there enemies, but they would give free leave to all both Moriscoes, Jewes or others, that would goe voluntary; but, if it were by land (as before) against Ceauta, or any other place neere, they would goe themselfes in person, with all the countrie hereaboutes, and forces they could make; assuringe me they would stand by their wordes, and not promise more than they meant to performe.

And with this good satisfacion I departed, but concludinge beforehand, amongst ourselves, accordinge to that caution I gave at the first for secrecie (Ceauta beinge so neare at hand, and a fryer and some cavalleroes sent from thence hither to redeeme captives), that whosoever inquired any thinge concerninge my busines, wee agreed, amongst ourselfes, to answere (and it was the Mocadens owne motion that wee might all agree in one tale, as the secretarie delivered) that I came lykewise to redeeme captives, and to make peace, and settle trade for marchantes, and to that end, and so blind the eyes of the Spaniard.

Within a few daies after, caused a pregon or proclamation to bee made that noe Englihsman heareafter should bee bought or sould, as hearetofore, by the Turkes, or made captives, but freelie trade, as in times past; and that under a great penaltie. Notwithstandinge, a Portuguez, one of those cavalleroes, came divers tymes to visite me, but indeed, as I perceived, to sift me; whom I answered accordingly.

But these Moriscoes, continuallie one or other is with mee, desirous to heare of nothinge so much as wares against the Spaniard, and to confer with me, and reade in the Spanish Bible I have ; havinge alsoe one of their owne amongst themselfes, in pravate, and desirous of moe, as also of Calvin and other bookes of our religion, so many as they can get in Spanish, which I have promised. Yea, both, Moores, Jewes and all, listeninge after nothinge but wares against Spaine, and peace and freindship with England, with generall disposicion and inclination both towardes our nation, and even to Christian religion, havinge observed, and no doubt God hath a finger in it, who ruleth in the heartes of all men and can turne them which way soever he pleaseth, even the heartes of Kings, as Solomon saith, I thought it my dutie, both to God and his Maj^{tie}, not to spend this tyme of my imployment idlie, all Christendome now up in armes, but to blow the fire alreadie kindled; hopinge, if it please God to second these proceding with that expedition hee hath begune, it may in tyme growe to a great flame, and finallie consume the enemie. Nay, I dare presume upon it, for the mouth of the Lord hath spoken it : Babylon shall fall, as it is in the Revelation. *Macte virtute,* o noble English ! march valiantlie, as in tymes past. It is fallen, it is fallen, etc[1].

And to this end, it came into my minde, and I hope it is from God lykewise, to write two generall letters, in Spanish, the one to the Moores, the other to the Jewes, which, so sone as I heard the fleete was upon the coast[2], I gave to the Andaluzes to disperse, and one generall letter or admonition, lykewise, to the Spaniardes themselves and Portugales, all three written in that manner as neither Moore, Jew, nor Spaniard, can take just exception. For the first, I am sure they will not, for they have alreadie accepted and given way to it ; for the other, if they will not be admonished, they are altogither without excuse. Their blood bee upon their owne heads ! Gods decree and sentence must bee executed, and that with all severitie, as therein may appeare. The copie of which letters I

---

1. « Elle est tombée, elle est tombée, cette grande Babylone. » *Apocalypse,* XIV, 8. — C'est de Rome et de toute la Catholicité, que veut parler Harrison, comme il le dit lui-même, V. *supra,* p. 568.

2. La flotte anglaise n'arriva devant Cadix que le 1er novembre. V. *supra,* p. 574 et note 3.

have sent by this bearer[1], who can further informe your Lordshipp in other particulars too tedious here to write.

But thus much, for the present, of the state of the countrie I thought it my dutie to informe your Lordshipp, and to stay here, till I know your Lordship's further pleasure; not knowinge how much this place may import the present service, or how it is further intended, from whence the fleete may bee better and soner supplied than from any other parte of Barberie, or whether perhaps your Lordshipp may consider further of the Mocadens offer.

Concerning the taking of Ceauta, it standeth verie conveniently for all our marchantes ships bound for the Straightes to touch there, and to be supplied with all necessaries, from tyme to tyme, from England; and, havinge this towne of Tittuan to freind, and all the countrie round aboute, who have promised all assistance, a small garison would mayntaine it. And there might our marchantes land their goodes saffelie and make it a magazine of all commodities, both for the kingdome of Fez, and other partes, which stand in great wante thereof, and cry out for trade. But, which is cheifly and first of all to bee respected, the glorie of God, and plantation of religion in these partes, and of the Christian faith, whereof his Matie is cheife defender, beinge put in the ballance, will weigh downe all; whereof there is a great probabilitie, as may be, both for the Jewes and Moriscoes, alreadie Christians in heart, most of them. Who would all flocke thither, yea, and the Moores themselves; so that his Matie could not want supply, both of men and all other provisions this countrie could affoord, from tyme to tyme. And if his Matie had also Gibraltar, might command the Straightes; and the rest of the townes upon the coast of Barberie, which the Spaniard houldeth, could not longe subsi[s]t, for want of corne and other provision, whereof, at this present, they say they stand in verie great neede, yea, in Spaine itselfe; but here, in Barbarie, great store.

But Mamora could I wish also in his Maties handes, for the reasones before mentioned, that river going up to Fez; from whence his Matie might much annoy the Spaniard by sea; and would bee

1. V. *supra*, Doc. CLXVIII, p. 567, la lettre de John Harrison aux Maures.

a refuge for our ships, upon all occasiones. Sallie Muley Sidan holdeth, but 15 myles from Mamora ; but what command hee hath there, at this present, among the Larbies, whose cheife strength consisteth in horse, I know not.

I moved, when I first undertooke this imp[l]oyment, that I might have had the command of some small ship, or other, and first to have touched at Sallie, there to have understood the state of the countrie, knowinge it to bee so variable and subject to alterations ; and, longe before this tyme, could I have dispatched with Muley Sidan. But, not knowinge (as before) how much this place may import the present service, I hope God hath done all for the best.

And some captives come latly from Sallie heere to be sould, and telling mee how hardly both they and other English captives there have bine used, taken by those ships of Sallie under Muley Sidans command (presuminge to come even to the English Channell, and not far off Silley), there, I say, taken, almost threescore[1], bound for Newfoundland; and now, these Mocadens lykewise standinge upon such tearmes with Muley Sidan, and havinge so great a command heere, bothe overe the towne and the countrie round about, I thought it my dutie to acquaint your Lordshipp with all these passages, humblie refferinge all to your Lordshipp with your honorable Counsell, to advise further what is to be donne, both in respect of his Ma[ties] honour, the furtherance of the present service, which God prosper, and the good of his Ma[ties] subjectes, both the captives before mentioned and the marchantes who trade both here and elswhere. Which, in my opinion, and under correction, is to hold correspondence with all, so neere as may bee, where there is trade (which is a good excuse and policie for Christian princes) ; to nowrishe these civill wars of Infidels, by Gods speciall providence sent amongst them (otherwise they would grow too stronge, now especiallie the whole Christian world so distracted) ; and to drawe strength from all partes, especiallie those two before mentioned, Ceauta and Mamora, easie to be atchieved (and by the way, as it were), lyinge so conven-

---

1. Sur cette expédition de corsaires salétins dans la Manche en avril-juin 1625. V. *supra*, Doc. CLXIV, CLXV et CLXIX, pp. 558, 562 et 569.

iently, the one within, the other without the Straightes; yea, even from the Spaniards themselves.

Had his Matie also Gibraltar, or any other porte neare on that side, one to second another, I doubt not but many, even in Spaine and Portugale, as well as in Barbarie, groaning under that antichristian tyrannie, would fall awaie, or rather flee away (as God commandeth) out of Babylon[1]; to whom therefore my generall letter[2], or admonition, is directed, and, I hope, upon good warrant, as also the other two[3], and, as I said before, without all exception to be taken against any of them, any just exception. And I doubt not but God hath alreadie put into his Maties heart, who is defender of the faith, and other Christian princes, to make good; and for this lykewise I have sufficient warrant that the resolution hold.

For my goinge to Muley Sidan, with his Maties letters, it must bee by sea, and not by land, as the state of the countrie now standeth. Neither will the Mocadens, by their goodwils, permitte me; for they say, if I should miscarie, comminge here under their horma[4] or sanctuarie, and from so great a prince, an imputation might be upon them. But, so fare as I could gather, both by their owne speeches and others lykewise, they had no mind at all of my going to Muley Sidan, saying he would promise much, but performe little; but, for themselves, they would be better than their promises, when tyme came.

So that I have remayned hitherto (and do still) in suspence, not knowing (as before) how his Maties service may be farther intended. For, had I gone to Muley Sidan, these Mocadens would have bin verie jealous, and perhaps, for feare of him, have cleaved to the Spaniard. And so we should have had no relieve from this place, the governour of Suta (as a few told me) having alreadie sent unto them for a seguro or a protection, if hee should be put to extremitie, and two cavalleroes lying here only for spyes, and to advertise upon all occasions. But, in the meanetyme, I have

---

1. C'est à ce passage que s'appliqueraient les références placées en marge au début de cette lettre de Harrison, V. p. 574. Babylone figure Rome. V. p. 578, n. 1.

2. La lettre générale aux Espagnols et aux Portugais. V. supra, p. 578.

3. Les lettres aux Maures et aux Juifs. V. ibidem.

4. Sur ce mot arabe, V. supra, p. 572 et note 1.

written to Muley Sidan[1] of my arrivall here, with his Maties letters, and, upon some generall tearmes formerly passed betwixt him and me, putting him in mind of his former promises, and to know his further pleasure. Yf it be your Lordship's pleasure I goe there, I must first come fairely off from hence, and goe by sea, with the first levant, in any small vessell I shall be readie, God willing.

And so expecting to know your Lordship's further pleasure, praying God to prosper all your honourable enterprizes to his glorie, and the honour of his Ma[ty] and our nation, I rest
  Your Lordshipp's humble servant,
    Signé : John Harrison.
From Tituan, this 20th of July 1625.

Post-scriptum. — The Andaluzes here have written to their frends to Sallie and other parts, to prepare them. And one of these Moriscoes left these lynes with me, here inclosed, whereby your Lordshipp may conceive the generall inclination of all, having also some old prophecies of their owne, tending to that effect; which I thought good to seacond, by informing them truly in ours, out of Gods word.

Sur une feuille séparée : Con el favor de Dios, los Moros y los Ynglezes tomaran a España y con los santos y cruces guisaran las comidas y destruyran a España; y seran todos ermanos y ayudara Dios a los que sus mandamientos segieren. Y Dios sobre todo.

This is the copie of those lynes inclosed in the other letter[2].

British Museum. — *Harleian Mss., 1581, ff. 320-328.* — *Original.*

1. V. cette lettre *supra*, Doc. CLXX, p. 571.
2. Harrison avait joint à la présente lettre l'original de la note qui lui avait été remise au nom des Moriscos. Il faut admettre que, pour une raison quelconque, on aura fait une copie de cette note, qui aura seule été conservée.

CLXXII

LETTRE DE JAMES BAGG[1] A BUCKINGHAM

(Extrait)

Pirateries commises par les Salétins et les Turcs sur la côte anglaise. — Il serait à propos de la faire surveiller par de bons navires. — Les Hollandais favorisent ces corsaires, à qui ils envoient des munitions et achètent des marchandises. — Le pirate Compaen a vendu une prise à Salé.

Plymouth, 2 [n. st. 12] août 1625.

Au dos, alia manu : 2ᵈ August 1625. — Mʳ Bag to my Lord...

Sir,

My last was the 27ᵗʰ, which humbly presented my answere to the complaint put up to your Grace against me, which I hope I have soe done as to live and dye in your favour, and so your servant for present.

. . . .

But I finde from these partes divers townes have written to there burgisses[2] of the daily oppression they are subject to by the Salley and Turkie pyrattes, that are even nowe to the nomber of twentye sayle upon this coast; within these sixe daies have taken a Scott and two English ofe the Lizard, one beinge of this Flarburrowe and worth five thousand pounds; which will invite those of the Parlament to capitulate in passing that bill. Of which I have thought

---

1. James Bagg, vice-amiral du sud de Cornouailles. V. *supra*, p. 569.

2. *There burgisses*, leurs représentants au Parlement.

it fitt to advertise your Grace, hopinge that some shipps in speciall, and that of the best burden which is most fitted, wilbe provided, that yt appeare unto the House your Grace hath ordred a remedye ere the complaint be presented.

. . . .

The increase of these pirates is the Duch, that both bringe them munytion and buy there commodities. As now, for instance, there is a shippe of Mr Peter Curten's[1] of Middleborrough past by this place; I hope will meete with the fleete, full of Sally commodities, worth fifteene or twenty thousand poundes. I should have bine happie in doinge the service to your Grace to have stayed this shipp, yf shee had putt into my vice admiralty; but she is past by, and unles the fleete meete her, Curten growes by unlawfull waies rich.

Campane[2] the pyrate, the 23rd of June, was at Salley; hath there made sale of the commodityes taken from the « Goulden Phenix » of London. Yf either hostilitye or pardon could bringe him in, the sea were well disburdned of him.

. . . .

Sir Francis Steward[3] desires me, that would rather come under his cover, to convey his incloses. I disclose my bouldnes and my weakenes unto your Excellence by my rude lynes. Your favor will, I hope, pardon there faultes; and beleeve they proceed from an honest part of your Grace's most humble faithfull bounde servant.

Plymouth, 2^d of August 1625.

Public Record Office. — State Papers, Domestic, Charles I, vol. V, n° 6. — Copie.

1. Pieter Curten, négociant et armateur de Middelbourg en Zélande On le trouve en relations commerciales avec le Maroc en 1612, 1624 et 1627. V. *1re Série*, Pays-Bas, t. II, pp. 12, 92 et note 2; t. IV, pp. 1 et 172.

2. Claes Gerritsz. Compaen. Sur ce personnage, V. *ibidem*, t. III, p. 513 et note 2.

3. Sir Francis Steuart, avec quelques vaisseaux, était chargé de protéger les côtes anglaises de la Manche contre les pirates salétins. V. *infra*, p. 587.

CLXXIII

LETTRE DE THOMAS CEELY A EDWARD CONWAY[1]

Il le prie de transmettre au Conseil une pétition relative aux captifs retenus à Salé et aux pirates qui menacent la côte anglaise.

Plymonth, 3 [n. st. 13] août 1625.

Adresse : For his Maties speciall service. — To the right honorable the Lord Conway, Principall Secretary to his Matie.

Plymouth, the 3rd of August 1625, at one of the clocke in the afternoone. These hast, hast, post hast, hast, post hast.

Our honorable good Lord,

May it please you to be advertised that the lamentable complayntes which lately we have received from the poore captives nowe in Sally under the barbarous cruelty of the Moores, being to the number of 800 at the least, and the danger which the shipps are nowe in, that are comming from Newe-England and Newefoundland, by reason of divers shipps of Sally which nowe lye here on our coastes, hath enforced us to tender our humble supplications unto the Lordes of his Ma[ties] most honorable Privy Counsell, which we here inclosed send your Lordshippe, earnestly craving that you would be pleased to farther our requestes, soe as we may have some speedy redresse therein; otherwise the whole country will have just cause to rue it. We have soe farre imboldened ourselves on your Lordships favour, as to inclose a letter directed to Sir William Strode in this packet.

Soe, in humble manner remembring our duties, we rest
Your Honnours to be commaunded,

Signé : Thomas Ceely, Maior, and his Brethern.

Plymouth, this 3d of August 1625.

Public Record Office. — *State Papers, Domestic, Charles I, vol. V, n° 8.* — *Original.*

1. Edward, vicomte Conway. Secrétaire d'État de 1623 à sa mort en 1631.

CLXXIV

LETTRE DE FRANCIS STEUART[1] A BUCKINGHAM

(Extrait)

Il réfute les marchands anglais qui l'ont accusé auprès de Buckingham de n'avoir pas protégé leurs côtes. — Les Salétins ne cesseront d'infester ces côtes tant que les flibustiers des Provinces-Unies les approvisionneront et que les pêcheurs de Terre-Neuve ne s'uniront pas pour se défendre.

A bord du « Lion », 16 [n. st. 26] août 1625.

Adresse : For my most honorable Lord the Duke of Buckingham his Grace, Lord High Admirall of England.

My most honorable Lord,

I am much greived that theis westerne gents and merchantes should informe your Grace that I have given them no helpe, since my coming hither for securing theis coastes. If their complaintes were just, and that I should so abuze the truste your Grace hath committed unto mee, I should judge myself as fitter for Wapping[2] than to command the meanest shipp in the Fleete. After I hadd run upp the Channell with such shipps as accompanied mee from the Downes, and mett with many homewards-bound, some from the Southwards, some from the Frenche coaste, some from Irrland, and some from out the Severne, who assured us the coaste was cleere of Sally men and other piratts, the weather being thick and hawsey, the winde highe and in our teethe, we were forced backe into Plymouth, where wee tooke in victualls, I being then

[1]. V. *supra*, p. 584 et note 3.   [2]. V. *supra*, p. 273 et note 2.

come to our iron-bound coaste, the last refuge in a long voiage.

. . . .

The « Raynebowe », who hath been also leake, will be shortly ready ; but, beeing a shipp of so greate importance, I would willingly knowe your Graces pleasure, whether you would have her putt to sea or not against theis picaroones of Sallye; who, as long as they are supplyed by the Flemishe freebooters[1] with men, munition, victualls, and all manner of sea-stores (most wherof they have from our shoares, and therewithall barter with those Infidelles for the Englishe and other Christians goodes), and that our Newfoundland fleete, consisting of 300 saile or nere upon, as I am informed, will not arme themselves for their défence, choose out some few of their best shipps, and fitting them accordingly to attend and wafte them, nor appointe a certaine tyme and rendez-vous when and where to meete, and so procced securely on their voiage as other nations doe, but goe sattering both outwards and homewards, bound by twoes and threes, and single, to make the best of their markett, as they terme it, theis picaroones, I say, will ever lye hankering upon our coastes, and the State will find it both chargeable and difficult to cleere it, or secure the Newfoundland fishermen from them ; unless it bee directly resolved to sacke Salley, sure waye, if easy to bee performed, as some report it is, that are lately come from thence.

. . . .

So, with the best thanckes an honest heart can returne for your Graces many and great favours, and with my earnest preyers to the Almighty for your healthe and happiness, I kisse your hands.
Your vowed servant,
Signé : Franc. Steuart.

My most honorable Lord, theis come from on board the « Lion », 16 August 1625.

Public Record Office. — *State Papers, Domestic, Charles I, vol. V, n° 49.* — *Original.*

---

1. Sur les munitions et les approvisionnements fournis par les Provinces-Unies aux Salétins, V. *1re Série,* Pays-Bas, t. V. Introduction, p. xiv et note 5.

CLXXV

LETTRE DE FRANCIS STEUART A BUCKINGHAM

(Extrait)

Il a pris un certain Bennet, marchand de Londres, qui était muni d'un sauf-conduit du pirate Compoen.

A bord du « Lion », 5 [n. st. 15] septembre 1625.

Adresse: For the Duke of Buckingham his Grace, Lord Highe Admirall of England, and Lord Generall of his Maties forces both by sea and land.

My verie good Lord,

. . . .

There is one Bennett, a merchant of London, fallen also lately into our hands with a protection from the piratt Campaigne to all the picaroones of Salley, laden with bagges of aniseeds and almonds. Aniseeds, as I am informed, is now worthe 7^{li} per cente in England, and, were it worth 7000 there, shall not bee a pennie's worthe embezelled either of that or any other goods coming into my hands, or disposed off but as your Grace shall command.

. . . .

Your Graces faithfull servant,

Signé: Franc. Steuart.

On board the « Lion », 5° September 1625.

Public Record Office. — *State Papers, Domestic, Charles I, vol. VI, n° 19.* — *Original.*

CLXXVI

LETTRE DE JOHN HARRISON A BUCKINGHAM

Il a envoyé précédemment un messager par voie de terre à Salé pour avoir des nouvelles de la flotte. — Postérieurement, il a appris l'arrivée de celle-ci à Cadix. — Lorsqu'il a écrit au commandant de la flotte, il ignorait que celui-ci était Buckingham; il le prie donc d'excuser les termes dont il s'est servi. — Il reste à Tétouan, en attendant ses ordres. — Il aurait voulu se rendre lui-même auprès de Buckingham, mais les mokaddem de Tétouan s'y sont opposés.

Tétouan, 3 [n. st. 13] novembre 1625.

Adresse: To the right honorable my verie good Lord, the Duke of Buckingham his Grace, Lord Generall of his Ma$^{tie's}$ fleete.

Au dos, alia manu: Received 20° april 1626. — Mr Harrison. — A letter of credditt for busynes in Barbary. — Dated att Tituan.

Right Honourabl,

I did latelie send a messenger by land to Sallie, not hearing here any certaine newes of the fleete, the gates, both of Ceuta and Tanger, having bin this long tyme kept shutte, neither Moore nor Jew suffered to enter, nor any to come out. At last, an English ship, having escaped from Mallaga, brought the newes hither of the seacond happie arrivall of the English fleete before Cadiz, and that it is taken; for which God be thanked.

I hope my other letters, by the waie of Sallie[1], are before this tyme with your Grace, and my former[2] lykewise, sent long since by another messenger, upon a false rumer that the fleete was then seene uppon the coastes, whom I sent in a Dutch ship, not know-

---

1. Ces lettres n'ont pas été retrouvées. 2. V. *supra*, Doc. CLXXI, p. 573.

ing as then that your Grace came in person in this service, till now by this ship. And therefore, I hope your Grace will pardon me if I have erred any waie in those my letters[1]; whereupon I depend, and rest here still to knowe your Grace his further pleasure.

And for feare my former letters might miscarrie, I have lykewise sent a third messenger, who can relate to your Grace all occurrents here, willing to have come myself, but the Moccadens would not suffer me, till more certayne newes came.

And so, praynig God to blesse all your honourabl enterprises, as he hath begun, I humblie rest

Your Graces servant,

Signé: John Harison.

Tituan, 3 of November 1625.

Public Record Office. — State Papers, Foreign, Barbary States, vol. XII. — Original.

1. Harrison était mal renseigné sur la personnalité du commandant de la flotte, qui n'était pas Buckingham. V. *supra,* p. 574 et note 3.

CLXXVII

LETTRE DE ROBERT ADAMS AU CAPITAINE ROBERT ADAMS

Il décrit son existence de captif. — Son maître, ayant entendu dire que sa famille était riche, l'a contraint, par un redoublement de torture, à convenir d'une somme pour sa rançon. — Il supplie son père de trouver cette rançon.

Salé, 4 [n. st. 14] novembre 1625.

Adresse: To his most lovinge father Captain Robert Adams, at his house, in Ratclif, give this. — I pray you pay the post. — From a poore captive in Salley.

Au dos, alia manu: 4 November 1625. — From Robert Adams, a poore captive at Salley, to his father. — For the King.

En marge: I pray lett mee hear an answer from you, [as] soone as possible you cann.

From Salley, this 4th of November, anno 1625.

Lovinge and kind Father and Mother, my humble duty remembred unto you, both prayinge to God continually for your health as my owne.

You may please to understand that I am hear in Salley, in most miserable captivitye, under the hands of most cruell tyrants. For, after I was sould, my patroone made mee worke at a mill like a horse, from morninge untill night, with chaines uppon my leggs, of 36 pounds waights a peece, my meat nothinge but a llittell course bread and water, my lodginge in a dungion under ground, wher some 150 or 200 of us lay altogether, havinge noe comforte of the light but a littell hole, and beeinge soe full of vermine for want of shift and not beeing alowed tyme for to pick myselfe, that I am allmost eaten up with them, and every day beaten to make me either turne Turke, or come to my ransome. For our master's boy had tould my patroons that I was the owner's sonn of the shipp and you ware able to ransome home 40 such as I was; which was no sooner knowne but they forced me to come to my ransome and agree to them, though I allwayes pleaded povertye. For then they made me grind moor then I did formerly, and continually beat me, and almost starved me. Soe, though unwillinge, I agreed at 730 duckats of Barbery; for I was forced to it, beeinge brought soe low for want of sustenance that I could not goe without a staff.

Soe I have 6 months tyme for my ransome to come, wherof 3 months are gone; and if it com not, then I must arme myselfe to indure the most miserye of any creature in the world. Therfore I humbly desire you one my bended knees, and with sighs from the bottam of my hart, to commiserat my poor destressed estate, and seek some meanes for my delivery out of this miserable slavery. For hear are some 1 500 Englishmen hear in as bad case as myselfe, though somthing better used; for they misuse none but such as are abl to pay their ransome. And, dear father, I humbly beseech you, for Christ Jesus sake, to take som course for my deliverance; for, if neither the Kinge take noe course, nor my ransome come, I am out of all hope ever to behould my cuntry againe.

Thus ceasing to troble you, I rest
Your most dutifull and obedient sonn till death,

Signé: Robert Adams.

Mʳ Legg[1] is hear at ransome for 730 Barbery duketts likewise. I have sent 3 or 4 letters before this by severall men and never heard from you.

Public Record Office. — State Papers, Foreign, Barbary States, vol. XII. — Original.

1. William Legg. V. *supra*. p. 563.

CLXXVIII

LETTRE DE THOMAS CEELY AU CONSEIL PRIVÉ

(Extrait)

Il envoie au Conseil les dépositions de deux captifs récemment arrivés de Salé. — D'après l'un d'eux, Nicholas Godfrey, Salé renferme 1500 captifs anglais, écossais et irlandais. — Les pirates ont plus de quarante navires et amènent, à chaque printemps, des captifs. — Ils viendraient de capturer, près de Lisbonne, tout l'équipage d'un vaisseau du Roi. — L'autre captif, Edward Perry, fut pris, au mois d'avril dernier, avec trente et un compagnons, sur un navire à destination de Terre-Neuve, et emmené à Salé, d'où il s'est évadé.

Plymouth, 2 [n. st. 12] décembre 1625.

Au dos: December 2, 1625. — Mayor of Plimouth to the Lords. — Abstract.
En tête: Mayor of Plimouth, 1625.

He desires that the Lordes would be pleased to give order to the Deputie Lieutenantes and Justices of Peace of Devon and Cornewall for receiving and disposing of the sicke men which are to returne from the fleete in the 15 shipps expected, or any others that may hereafter come.

. . . .

He advertiseth of 1500 English, Scottish and Irish men, women and children, now prisoners at Sally, and send the examinations of two captives lately discharged from thence.

. . . .

The examinations of Nicollas Godfrey and Edward Perry, sailors.

The first saith he was taken in the « Anne » of Portsmouth, of the burden of 70 tunne, being upon a marchant voyage, by a man of warre of Sally, about two yeares since; and, with 12 others in that shipp was carried to Sally, where he continued untill within these 9 weekes. Att his comming from thence, there were 1500 captives English, Scottish and Irish men, women and children. And they had 40 shipps and upwardes, some of 300 tunne, some lesse, which they sett forth upon the Christian coast. And that att every springtide they bring into Sally Christians which they make captives; and that att his comming forth, five good shipps of warre came out from thence for the coast of England. And he had heard that, about 5 weekes since, they met att sea a catch[1] of his Ma[ties] fleete neare Lisbon, and, taking forth all the men, had left her floating on the sea.

Perry saith he was taken in Aprill last, in the « Anne » of Yarmouth, bound to Newfoundland, of the burden of ninety tunne, and with 31 others in the said shipp was carried to Sally, whence he escaped 7 weekes since, by running into a Flemish man of warre then in the harbor. And for the rest reports as Godfrey hath done.

Public Record Office. — State Papers, Domestic, Charles I, vol. XI, n° 5. — Extrait officiel.

1. *Catch,* écrit plus souvent aujourd'hui ketch, en français caiche, petit bâtiment, qui a un pont et deux mâts, du port de 100 à 250 tonnes.

CLXXIX

REQUÊTE DE JOHN HARRISON A CHARLES Ier

Il demande que le Roi lui fournisse les moyens de rentrer en Angleterre pour rendre compte de sa mission. — Il recommande les captifs anglais qui sont à Tétouan.

[Tétouan, fin de 1625[1].]

En marge, alia manu : Mr Harrisons petition. — Barbarie.

To the Kings most excellent Ma[ty].

The humble peticion of John Harrison, heirtofore servand to prince Hendrie[2], and late governour of the Sommer Ylands[3], and now sent into Barbary by your Maties appointment.

Whereas your peticioner hath been four severall tymes imployd by your Ma[ties] royall predicessors of famous memorie into Barbarie, and now lately imployd by your Ma[tie] for the dispatching of some bussines for the good of your Ma[ties] royall fleet, and to take some order for your Ma[ties] subjects that are kept heere in captivitie. And for the better performance of the bussines wherin I was imployd, I did send my servandis, as soone as ever I hard any newes of your Maties fleet, both in frigatts and in shipis, to my great chairges, but could not heare any newes.

And last of all, when your Maties fleet was at Cails[4], I sent this

---

1. La date approximative résulte du fait que la présente requête est postérieure à la lettre de John Harrison du 13 novembre [n. st.]. V. *supra*, p. 589. Cet agent, d'autre part, quitta Tétouan pour Salé au commencement de 1626. V. *supra*, p. 445.

2. Henry, prince de Galles, dont Harrison avait été gentilhomme de la Chambre. V. *supra*, p. 441.

3. Nom donné aux îles Bermudes. Cf. *supra*, p. 444 et note 4.

4. *Cails*, Cadix.

my servand with letters of information[1], I being given to understand that my Lord Deuck of Buckinghame was generall. But, my servand being carried to Italy by a master of London, contrarie to his promise, I could heare no newes.

Therefore, I humblie beseech your Ma[tie] to consider both of the paines that I have taken in your Ma[ties] service here, and the chairges that I have been at, in sending too and againe. And that your Ma[tie] would be gratiouslie pleased to send me meanes, that I may come home and give your Ma[tie] acompt of all passages and kynd offers here[2]. And that your Ma[tie] would be gratiouslie pleased to send some releife for those poore men that are in captivitie here, being in nomber 34.

And, as in duty bound, I shall rest ever praying for your Maties prosperus and hapie reigne here on earth, and lyf everlasting in the world to come.

Public Record Office. — State Papers, Foreign, Barbary States, vol. XII. — Original.

1. Ce serviteur était porteur de la lettre du 13 novembre [n. st.] 1625. V. *supra*, p. 590.

2. Les offres que les mokaddem de Tétouan avaient faites à Harrison en juin précédent. V. *supra*, pp. 576-577.

TABLE CHRONOLOGIQUE

NUMÉROS des pièces	DATES	TITRES	PAGES
I	1590, février	Lettre d'Élisabeth à Moulay Ahmed *el-Mansour*..	1
II	» 3 mars	Lettre de Beauvoir-La Nocle et de Fresne à Henri IV.	3
III	» » »	Lettre de Fresne à Revol.	5
IV	» 25 mai	Lettre de D. Christophe à Burghley.	9
V	» 30 »	Lettre d'Edward Prynne à Walsingham.	10
VI	» 22 juin	Lettre d'Edward Prynne à John Stanhope	15
VII	» 23 »	Lettre de Moulay Ahmed *el-Mansour* à Élisabeth (*Texte arabe*).	18
VII bis	» » »	Lettre de Moulay Ahmed *el-Mansour* à Élisabeth (*Traduction*)..	21
VII ter	» » »	Lettre de Moulay Ahmed *el-Mansour* à Élisabeth (*Traduction espagnole*).	24
VIII	» 4 juillet	Lettre d'Edward Barton à Robert Cecil.	26
IX	» av. le 28 août	Mémoire sur les affaires de Portugal.	30
X	» 30 août	Lettre d'Élisabeth à Moulay Ahmed *el-Mansour*..	34
XI	» 3 septembre	Lettre d'Élisabeth au Grand Seigneur	40
XII	» 23 décembre	Lettre envoyée d'Andalousie à Burghley.	43
XIII	1591, 20 janvier	Lettre de Melchior Petoney à Miguel de Moura..	44
XIV	» 18 avril	Lettre de Mathias Becudo à D. Antonio.	46
XV	» 1-7 mai	Affaire Abraham Reynolds contre William Resould.	56
XVI	» 28 juin	Requête de O. Style, N. Style et S. Lawrence.	62
XVII	» juillet	Requête des marchands trafiquant dans le Levant.	63
XVIII	1591	Note de Richard Tomson.	65
XIX	1592, 22 mars	Lettre de Moulay Ahmed *el-Mansour* à Élisabeth.	68
XX	1593, 13 juillet	Requête de Robert Zinzan à Élisabeth..	71
XXI	» 22 »	Mémoire de Richard Carmerden..	74
XXII	1593-1594	Relation du naufrage du « Tobie »..	77

NUMÉROS des PIÈCES	DATES	TITRES	PAGES
XXIII	1594, 11 août	Lettre de Lawrence Madoc à Anthony Dassel..	83
XXIV	» 9 septembre	Lettre de Lawrence Madoc à Anthony Dassel..	86
XXV	1595, ap. le 8 mai	Extrait d'une lettre d'Edward Holmden.	89
XXVI	1595	Mémoire sur le Commerce.	91
XXVII	1596, 1ᵉʳ juillet	Relation de Roger Marbeck.	93
XXVIII	» 11 septembre	Lettre d'Edmund Wedall à Robert Cecil.	95
XXIX	» 14-23 »	Lettre de Moulay Ahmed *el-Mansour* à D. Christophe.	96
XXX	» » »	Lettre de Moulay Ahmed *el-Mansour* à Élisabeth.	99
XXXI	» av. le 24 sept.	Requête de marchands de la Barbary Company.	101
XXXII	» 24 septembre	Lettre de Billingsley, Harvye et Carmerden à Burghley.	104
XXXIII	» 13 décembre	Lettre de William Lilly à Essex..	106
XXXIV	1597, 5 janvier	Lettre d'Alonso Nuñez de Herrera à Essex.	107
XXXV	» 30 »	Mémoire de Pedro Ferreira pour Essex.	109
XXXVI	» 7 mars	Instructions pour Matthew Bredgate.	112
XXXVII	» 7 juillet	Lettre de Joseph Maye à Robert Cecil.	115
XXXVIII	» 11 »	Lettre de Christopher Parkins à Robert Cecil..	117
XXXIX	» 11 »	Lettre d'Élisabeth à Moulay Ahmed *el-Mansour*.	119
XL	1597	Mémoire anonyme adressé à Robert Cecil.	121
XLI	1598, 25 mars	Acte du Conseil Privé.	122
XLII	» 30 mai	Lettre de Joseph Maye à Robert Cecil.	124
XLIII	» 20 juin	Avis du Maroc.	126
XLIV	» 19 août	Lettre de George Tomson à Robert Cecil.	128
XLV	1598	Lettre d'Élisabeth à Moulay Ahmed *el-Mansour*.	132
XLVI	»	Requête de J. Newton et Th. Owen à Robert Cecil.	134
XLVII	1599, 20 mai	Lettre d'Élisabeth à Moulay Ahmed *el-Mansour*.	137
XLVIII	» 24 juin	Lettre d'Élisabeth à Moulay Ahmed *el-Mansour*.	139
XLIX	» 4 juillet	Lettre de Jasper Tomson à Richard Tomson.	142
L	1600, 6 mars	Lettre d'Élisabeth à Moulay Ahmed *el-Mansour*.	147
LI	» 27 »	Lettre de Moulay Ahmed *el-Mansour* à Élisabeth (*Texte arabe*).	149
LIᵇⁱˢ	» » »	Lettre de Moulay Ahmed *el-Mansour* à Élisabeth (*Traduction*)..	152
LII	» 10 avril	Lettre d'Élisabeth à Moulay Ahmed *el-Mansour*.	154
LIII	» » »	Lettre d'Élisabeth à Moulay Ahmed *el-Mansour*.	155
LIV	» 20 »	Requête de D. Philippe d'Afrique à Philippe III.	156
LV	» 15 juin	Lettre de Moulay Ahmed *el-Mansour* à Élisabeth (*Texte arabe*).	157

TABLE CHRONOLOGIQUE

NUMÉROS des pièces	DATES	TITRES	PAGES
LVbis	1600, 15 juin	Lettre de Moulay Ahmed *el-Mansour* à Élisabeth (*Traduction*).	159
LVI	» 20 »	Lettre de John Waring à Robert Cecil..	161
LVII	» 1er juillet	Note de George Tomson pour Richard Tomson.	164
LVIII	» 4 »	Lettre de Thomas Bernhere à Edward Wright.	168
LIX	» 30 »	Acte du Conseil Privé.	171
LX	» 31 août	Lettre de George Tomson à Robert Cecil.	173
LXI	» 23 septembre	Mémorandum d'Abd el-Ouahed.	177
LXII	» ap. le 25 sept.	Mémorandum d'Abd el-Ouahed.	180
LXIII	» 2 octobre	Ordonnance du Conseil Privé.	181
LXIV	» » »	Acte du Conseil Privé.	184
LXV	» 6 »	Lettre de George Tomson à Robert Cecil.	186
LXVI	» 8 »	Acte du Conseil Privé.	189
LXVII	» 9 »	Acte du Conseil Privé.	190
LXVIII	» 18 »	Acte du Conseil Privé.	191
LXIX	» 25 »	Lettre de John Chamberlain à Dudley Carleton..	192
LXX	» 30 »	Lettre d'Élisabeth à Moulay Ahmed *el-Mansour*.	193
LXXI	» » »	Lettre d'Élisabeth à Moulay Ahmed *el-Mansour*.	196
LXXII	» » »	Lettre d'Élisabeth à Moulay Ahmed *el-Mansour*.	198
LXXIII	» 31 »	Lettre de John Chamberlain à Dudley Carleton..	199
LXXIV	» octobre	Mémoire de Philipp Honyman.	200
LXXV	» 11 novembre	Lettre de Nicholas Mosley à Robert Cecil.	201
LXXVI	1601, ap. janvier	Note sur l'ambassade marocaine..	202
LXXVII	» 27 février	Lettre de Moulay Ahmed *el-Mansour* à Élisabeth.	204
LXXVIII	» » »	Mémoire de Moulay Ahmed *el-Mansour* pour Élisabeth..	206
LXXIX	1602, 3 juillet	Lettre de Moulay Ahmed *el-Mansour* à Élisabeth (*Texte arabe*).	210
LXXIXbis	» » »	Lettre de Moulay Ahmed *el-Mansour* à Élisabeth (*Trad. franç.*).	212
LXXIX[Ier]	» » »	Lettre de Moulay Ahmed *el-Mansour* à Élisabeth (*Trad. angl.*).	214
LXXX	» 16 août	Avis d'Espagne.	216
LXXXI	» 30 septembre	Lettre de Thomas Wilson à Robert Cecil.	218
LXXXII	1603, av. le 3 avril	Lettre d'Élisabeth à Moulay Ahmed *el-Mansour*.	220
LXXXIII	» ap. le 3 avril	Mémoire de Henry Roberts à Jacques Ier.	222
LXXXIV	» 9 novembre	Lettre de George Tomson à Robert Cecil.	229
LXXXV	Fin de 1603	Requête de Thomas Pate à Jacques Ier..	236
LXXXVI	1604, 23 février	Lettre d'Antonio Pereira à Philippe III.	240

TABLE CHRONOLOGIQUE

NUMÉROS des PIÈCES	DATES	TITRES	PAGES
LXXXVII	1604, 23 février	Lettre d'Affonso de Noronha à Philippe III.	244
LXXXVIII	» 4 mars	Lettre de Juan de Borja au duc de Lerme.	245
LXXXIX	1604	Lettre de Moulay Abou Farès à Jacques Ier.	247
XC	»	Relation de George Wilkins.	248
XCI	»	Relation de John Smith.	266
		Anthony Sherley et le Maroc (1605-1606).	274
XCII	1605, 23 octobre	Lettre de Moulay Abou Farès à Anthony Sherley.	284
XCIII	» 28 »	Lettre de Charles Cornwallis à Salisbury.	286
XCIV	» 10 décembre	Lettre d'Anthony Sherley à Barvitius.	287
XCV	1606, 8 septembre	Lettre de Hugh Lee à Salisbury.	290
XCVI	» 16 »	Lettre de Charles Cornwallis au Conseil Privé.	292
XCVII	» 17 »	Lettre d'Anthony Sherley à Salisbury.	294
XCVIII	» 8 octobre	Lettre de Hugh Lee à Thomas Wilson.	297
XCIX	» octobre	Lettre de Charles Cornwallis à Salisbury.	299
C	1607, ap. le 4 janv.	Relation des guerres civiles du Maroc.	301
CI	» 4-5 février	Lettre de Hugh Lee à Salisbury.	306
CII	» 31 mars	Lettre de R. Cocks à Thomas Wilson.	308
CIII	» 12-13 juillet	Lettre de Hugh Lee à Salisbury.	310
CIV	1608, 20 avril	Lettre de Hugh Lee à Thomas Wilson.	312
CV	» 4 septembre	Lettre de Hugh Lee à Thomas Wilson.	314
CVI	» 27 »	Lettre de Charles Cornwallis à Thomas Edmondes.	316
		La Relation de Ro. C. — *Note bibliographique*.	318
CVII	1609	Relation de Ro. C.	322
CVIII	1609, 26 mars	Lettre de Hugh Lee à Thomas Wilson.	409
CIX	» 4 avril	Lettre de Hugh Lee à Thomas Wilson.	410
CX	» 7 »	Lettre de Charles Cornwallis à Thomas Edmondes.	412
CXI	» mai	Lettre de Hugh Lee à Thomas Wilson.	414
CXII	» 11 juillet	Lettre de Charles Cornwallis au Conseil Privé.	416
CXIII	» 18 »	Lettre de Moulay Zidân à Jacques Ier.	418
CXIV	» 18 septembre	Lettre de Hugh Lee à Thomas Wilson.	422
CXV	» 8 octobre	Lettre de Francis Cottington à Charles Cornwallis.	423
CXVI	» 17 »	Lettre de Ralph Winwood à Salisbury.	426
CXVII	» 21 »	Lettre de Hugh Lee à Thomas Wilson.	428
CXVIII	» 27 novembre	Lettre de Ralph Winwood à Salisbury.	430

TABLE CHRONOLOGIQUE

NUMÉROS des PIÈCES	DATES	TITRES	PAGES
CXIX	1610, 31 mars	Lettre de Francis Cottington à Salisbury.	431
CXX	» 6 juin	Lettre de Francis Cottington à Salisbury.	432
CXXI	» 9 »	Lettre de Hugh Lee à Thomas Wilson.	433
CXXII	» 16 »	Relation de l'expédition de Larache.	435
		Les huit voyages au Maroc de John Harrison (1610-1632).	441
CXXIII	» 20 »	Lettre de John Harrison à Salisbury.	449
CXXIV	» 25 »	Lettre de Francis Cottington à Salisbury.	451
CXXV	» 24 octobre	Lettre de John Harrison à Salisbury.	452
CXXVI	» 30 novembre	Lettre de Francis Cottington à Salisbury.	455
CXXVII	» 14 décembre	Lettre de Francis Cottington à Salisbury.	456
CXXVIII	1611, 8 janvier	Lettre de Ralph Winwood à Salisbury.	457
CXXIX	» 15 mai	Lettre de Hugh Lee à Thomas Wilson.	459
CXXX	» 29 »	Lettre de Hugh Lee à Thomas Wilson.	460
CXXXI	» 14 juillet	Déposition de marins anglais.	462
CXXXII	1612, 19-20 sept.	Relation de la révolte d'Abou Mahalli.	465
CXXXIII	1614, 14 novembre	Lettre de John Chamberlain à Dudley Carleton.	477
CXXXIV	» 24 nov.-2 déc.	Lettre de Moulay Zidân à Jacques Ier (*Texte arabe*).	479
CXXXIVbis	» » »	Lettre de Moulay Zidân à Jacques Ier (*Traduction française*).	482
CXXXIVter	» 28 novembre	Lettre de Moulay Zidân à Jacques Ier (*Traduction espagnole*).	484
CXXXV	» 11 décembre	Lettre de Maurice de Nassau à Jacques Ier.	486
CXXXVI	1615, 13 mars	Lettre de Noël de Caron à Ralph Winwood.	488
CXXXVII	» 15 août	Lettre de créance de Yamin ben Remmokh.	490
CXXXVIII	1615-1616	Relation de William Lithgow.	491
CXXXIX	1616, 10 décembre	Lettre de Francis Cottington à Ralph Winwood.	500
CXL	1617, 31 mars	Contrat d'affrètement du navire l' « Elizabeth ».	501
CXLI	1618	Mémoire de Henry Mainwaring.	503
CXLII	1618, 9 avril	Lettre de Francis Cottington à John Coke.	509
CXLIII	1619, 3 mars	Lettre de Francis Cottington à Robert Naunton.	510
CXLIV	» 15 avril	Lettre de John Digby à Buckingham.	511
CXLV	» 24 »	Lettre de Dudley Carleton au Conseil Privé.	513
CXLVI	» 21 novembre	Lettre de Francis Cottington à Robert Naunton.	515
CXLVII	1621, 22 mars	Lettre de Walter Aston à Francis Nethersole.	516
CXLVIII	» 1er juin	Lettre de Walter Aston à Buckingham.	517
CXLIX	» 23 »	Lettre de Walter Aston à George Calvert.	518

TABLE CHRONOLOGIQUE

NUMÉROS des pièces	DATES	TITRES	PAGES
CL	1621, 15 septembre	Lettre de Walter Aston à George Calvert.	519
CLI	» 21 décembre	Lettre d'Ahmed en-Neksis à Walter Aston.	521
CLII	1622, 7 janvier	Lettre de John Duppa à Walter Aston.	525
CLIII	» 10 »	Lettre de John Duppa à Walter Aston.	531
CLIV	» 13 »	Lettre de John Duppa à Walter Aston.	533
CLV	» 10 juillet	Lettre de John Duppa à Walter Aston.	535
CLVI	» 25 août	Ordre de Philippe IV.	539
CLVII	» 20 septembre	Consulte du Conseil de Portugal.	540
CLVIII	» 2 novembre	Mémoire d'Anthony Sherley.	543
CLIX	» 7 »	Consulte du Conseil de Portugal.	551
CLX	» 19 »	Consulte du Conseil de Portugal.	552
CLXI	1623, 1er mai	Lettre de Philippe IV à Juan de Ciriça.	553
CLXII	» 3 juin-4 juillet	Lettre du Conseil de Portugal à Philippe IV.	554
CLXIII	» 3 août	Pétition de Samuel Cade.	556
CLXIV	1625, 28 avril	Lettre de Thomas Ceely au Conseil Privé.	558
CLXV	» 17 mai	Déposition de William Court.	562
CLXVI	» 21 »	Lettre de Henry Atye à Walter Aston.	564
CLXVII	» entre 27 mars-1er juin	Lettre de Charles Ier à Moulay Zidân.	565
CLXVIII	» 7 juillet	Lettre de John Harrison aux Maures.	567
CLXIX	» 15 »	Déposition de David Cockburne.	569
CLXX	» entre 13 juin-30 juillet	Lettre de John Harrison à Moulay Zidân.	571
CLXXI	» 30 juillet	Lettre de J. Harrison au commandant de la flotte britannique.	573
CLXXII	» 12 août	Lettre de James Bagg à Buckingham.	583
CLXXIII	» 13 »	Lettre de Thomas Ceely à Edward Conway.	585
CLXXIV	» 26 »	Lettre de Francis Steuart à Buckingham.	586
CLXXV	» 15 septembre	Lettre de Francis Steuart à Buckingham.	588
CLXXVI	» 13 novembre	Lettre de John Harrison à Buckingham.	589
CLXXVII	» 14 »	Lettre de Robert Adams au capitaine Robert Adams.	591
CLXXVIII	» 12 décembre	Lettre de Thomas Ceely au Conseil Privé.	593
CLXXIX	Fin de 1625	Requête de John Harrison à Charles Ier.	595

TABLE DES PLANCHES

	Pages
Anthony Sherley, ambassadeur au Maroc. . . . . Frontispice	
I. — Lettre de Moulay Ahmed *el-Mansour* à Élisabeth (23 juin 1590) (Texte arabe).	18
II. — Invocation et signe de validation de la lettre précédente. . .	20
III. — Lettre de Moulay Ahmed *el-Mansour* à Élisabeth (23 juin 1590) (Traduction espagnole).	26
IV. — Lettre de Moulay Ahmed *el-Mansour* à Élisabeth (3 juillet 1602).	212
V. — Titre de la Relation de Ro. C.	318
VI. — Lettre de Moulay Zidân à Jacques Ier (24 nov.-2 déc. 1614). . .	482

CHARTRES. — IMPRIMERIE DURAND, RUE FULBERT.

LES SOURCES INÉDITES
DE
L'HISTOIRE DU MAROC

Première Série. — **Dynastie Saadienne (1530-1660).**

SOUS-SÉRIES

I. Archives et Bibliothèques de France. — Trois volumes parus *(complet)*.
II. Archives et Bibliothèques des Pays-Bas. — Six volumes parus *(complet)*.
III. Archives et Bibliothèques d'Angleterre. — Deux volumes parus ; le troisième et dernier en préparation.
IV. Archives et Bibliothèques d'Espagne. — Premier volume paru ; second en préparation.
V. Archives et Bibliothèques de Portugal. — En préparation.
VI. Dépôts divers (Italie, Autriche, Belgique, Allemagne, Russie, Suisse). — En préparation.

Deuxième Série. — **Dynastie Filalienne (1661-1757).**

I. Archives et Bibliothèques de France. — Deux volumes parus ; un troisième sous presse.

Troisième Série. — **Dynastie Filalienne (1757-1845).**

CHARTRES. — IMPRIMERIE DURAND, RUE FULBERT.

www.ingramcontent.com/pod-product-compliance
Lightning Source LLC
Chambersburg PA
CBHW051320230426
43668CB00010B/1091